W9-CBJ-323

The New York Times

THE TIMES OF THE SIXTIES

The New York Times

THE TIMES OF THE SIXTIES

The Culture, Politics, and Personalities that Shaped the Decade

Edited with commentary by John Rockwell

Black Dog & Leventhal Publishers
New York

Published by
Black Dog & Leventhal Publishers, Inc.
151 West 19th Street
New York, NY 10011

Distributed by
Workman Publishing Company
225 Varick Street
New York, NY 10014

Manufactured in China

Cover design by Evan Gaffney Design

Interior design by Pauline Neuwirth, Neuwirth & Associates, Inc.

Cover and interior images courtesy of Getty Images

ISBN-13: 978-1-57912-964-4

h g f e d c b a

Library of Congress Cataloging-in-Publication Data available in file.

Contents

Introduction vii

National 1

International 43

Business 79

New York 91

Science, Technology & Health 111

Life & Style 145

Sports 185

Arts & Entertainment 209

Index 319

Introduction

Sex! Drugs! Rock 'n' Roll! Plus the Vietnam War and protests, race riots and civil rights legislation, the Great Society and assassinations, the space race and men walking on the moon (or on a Hollywood soundstage, if you bought into the swirling conspiracy theories of the day)! It was a decade of exclamation points.

Most of us who were there remember it well. For nostalgists, or those blitzed beyond recall, or you young'uns who didn't have the good fortune to live through that thrilling, turbulent decade: Here's this book. It's a record of the times by The Times—and, hence, a record of those recording that time. For us 1960's survivors who worked at The New York Times (I arrived in 1972, which was still part of the 60's if you accept the narrative that the decade leaked well into the next one), the stories condensed here are also part of the history of this particular newspaper. How it has since changed, its many strengths and occasional biases (East Coast versus West; sometimes a little slow to register the arts and lifestyles upheavals happening under its very nose)—all that is of interest to an examination of the decade, and of newspapers.

For us Times veterans, this book is a chance to revisit the bylines of writers we knew, or at least worked with, and to savor such endearing Times quirks as Mr. and Mrs. and fancy words that would not be tolerated today, like catenary and malefic. The Times is very different now—hipper, trendier, more international and populist, online. It is no less serious but also less wedded to the Upper East and West sides of Manhattan. Still, it was the newspaper of record in the 60's, as it is today, and this book is a distilled account of that noble mission.

As has been asserted over and over ever since, the 1960's was the key decade of the 20th century—the most dramatic, the most controversial, the most thrilling. Only the 20's might be able to challenge it; but for transformative impact, nothing tops the 60's. Its resonance echoes to this day, positively and negatively. Of course, depending on where you stand along the political spectrum, what seems positive to you could seem negative to someone else, and vice versa. Our own daughter, 25, buys into most of the values of the 60's but professes herself sick of hippies. Forget not: The 60's were when the reaction against the 60's began—the right-wing populist uprising led by Barry Goldwater, the election of Ronald Reagan as governor of California, the onset of the Republicans' "Southern strategy" that flipped the Southeast into nearly solid red-state territory.

Controversy starts with where you measure the decade. Not only did it maybe not end on December 31, 1969 (although it does in this book), it also didn't maybe begin until 1964, with the student protests in Berkeley. And while values and lifestyle of the 60's persisted into the 70's, as good an ending as any, certainly for this book, was the Altamont Festival just north of Berkeley—a pairing of idealistic protest and biker brutality that attests to the role of the West Coast as the epicenter of lifestyle innovation.

Another way of looking at the decade is as not exactly a war but a tension between the political and the nonpolitical, which is yet another way of looking at coastal differences. Crudely considered, nonpolitical issues—the hippies, drugs, exotic religions, murderous maniacs—defined the American West Coast. The Times, not yet the national (and international) newspaper it was to become, paid heed to what was going on out there but from afar (even in a failed West Coast edition, published from 1962 to 1964). Despite East Village hippies and their attendant tribal customs, politics ruled in the east. Protests against the Vietnam War and, underlying it, the draft somehow seemed more intense in New York. Angrier, too.

This book is divided into sections that are roughly comparable to sections of The Times. We begin with National news, which was amazingly rich, intense and scary. The struggles and triumphs of the civil rights movement claim pride of place—the lunch counter sit-ins, the Freedom Riders, the landmark court cases, the rise of the black power movement, and the stain of assassinations cutting down black leaders as well as white. The Times may have slighted the west, but it was rock-solid in its coverage of the south.

Those murderous assaults that snuffed out the optimism of John F. Kennedy's Camelot, blighting the country's image and self-image, extending to Robert Kennedy and Dr. Martin Luther King Jr. and Malcolm X and even the actress Sharon Tate, at the hands of the crazed Manson cult, were a terrifying reminder of the instability of both public and private life.

The Vietnam War brought down Lyndon B. Johnson, who, with a solid economy and Democratic majorities in Congress after 1964, achieved a string of legislative domestic victories that are the envy of our stalemated present day. The war also fueled youth protests of the decade, in turn linked to the momentous changes in lifestyle and culture that recur throughout the decade and these pages.

The war dominated internationally, at least from the American perspective, but so did the larger cold war, which triggered the space race—a source of building excitement and tragedy, potential and actual, throughout the decade (covered here in the Science section). That culminated with Neil Armstrong and his fellow astronauts walking on the moon (which I, for one, choose to believe actually happened). The cold war inspired terror (fallout shelters), but it also galvanized our society and federal government into grand projects (men on the moon) that have shrunk in recent decades as the costs of other wars pile up and large segments of the population—glued to Fox News and recoiling from the New Deal and the Great Society—seek to diminish the role of national government in the execution of such grand national, international and extraterrestrial achievements.

But the world beyond the United States was full of other dramas, too, and The Times was there for most of them. The Berlin Wall. The failed Bay of Pigs invasion and the Cuban missile crisis, which arguably counts as the scariest confrontation of the cold war. Israel's Six-Day War and the rise of the Palestine Liberation Organization. Seemingly uncountable African nations taking shape in the wake of colonialism. Reforms within the Catholic Church. China's hydrogen bomb and brutal Cultural Revolution. Student protests abroad, in Paris and Berlin and Mexico City and beyond. The Prague Spring and its stark repression by Soviet tanks.

Economically, the 60's seem in retrospect to have been relatively stable. Growth was steady and solid, unemployment tolerable, inflation of concern but not excessive. The income of the average American, and hence the lifestyle that income permitted, blossomed during the decade. That economy, in turn, made Kennedy's and Johnson's federal programs more affordable, however controversial they were at the time. The huge corporate mergers that have persisted down to our own time gained momentum, and today's commonplaces like credit cards and certificates of deposit got under way.

The Times understandably paid considerable attention to its home city. Even more than now, New York dominated the country in finance, media, culture and, at least when it came to the Yankees, sports. Given its national prominence, some news that transpired in New York has been rightly apportioned to other sections in this book. Other local stories—like the rescue of Carnegie Hall from demolition and Robert Moses's reshaping of the city, or Mayor John V. Lindsay's triumphs and troubles, or crippling labor strikes and power blackouts and disasters, or even the opening of the Lincoln Center complex—were municipal and national all at once.

Similarly, the space race wasn't just a political story emblematic of the cold war. It was a saga of scientific achievement, and thus properly dominates the Science section. But there was much more: DNA and quarks and cloning, not to speak of Masters and Johnson. We found out about lasers as weapons and healers, and holograms and videocassettes and eight-track tapes, along with the first stirrings of the Internet. Japan built its first bullet trains, and America the first jumbo jet. The birth control pill had an enormous impact on the sex part of sex, drugs and rock 'n' roll. Republicans, implacable in their opposition to "socialized medicine," defeated Medicare before the Democrats regained control of Congress and passed it.

Youth fashions and habits shaped the coverage of Life and Style—the hippies, in short. But there was more here, too: style icons Audrey Hepburn and Jackie Kennedy and Twiggy, Ken joining Barbie in platonic intimacy, muscle cars in an era of cheap gasoline, groovy fashions and interior design. Micro-minis and Nehru suits and Mary Quant epitomized swinging London. Feminism roiled the patriarchy, and the matriarchy, too.

Julia Child elevated American eating habits. The Immigration Act of 1965 allowed an influx of Asians and South Americans, who in turn transformed our restaurants. And there was the rise of high-end restaurants and nouvelle cuisine.

The Times focused on sports in New York more than in the nation, and in the nation more than in the rest of the world. In baseball, the Yankees dominated early in the 60's, but Sandy Koufax was the pitcher of the decade. The Dodgers and the Giants had fled to California, but the scrappy new Mets won the World Series in 1969. Professional football had its Ice Bowl and, with the merger of the American Football League and the National Football League, its first Super Bowls, won twice by the Green Bay Packers and then, improbably, by the upstart New York Jets. The Boston Celtics were the team of the decade in pro basketball, UCLA in college basketball. Cassius Clay won the heavyweight championship, became Muhammad Ali, refused induction into the draft and was stripped of his title. Records fell in the Olympics, but the 1968 installment was marked by the assertion of "black power" on the medal stand.

Last but by no means least, the arts and entertainment were transformed by new waves in pop music and films, and American popular culture was revolutionized by a British invasion and world music.

In the visual arts, the 60's was the decade of major shows and major museum acquisitions and loans. But there was also the rise of downtown Manhattan as a newfound neighborhood for style-setting artists, with minimalism and pop art. There were major buildings by major architects, which The Times covered with new sophistication when Ada Louise Huxtable joined its ranks in 1963. (She won the first Pulitzer Prize for distinguished criticism in 1970 honoring her work in the 60's).

Books saw the rise of remarkable new American novelists, and also a fading of parochialism with the advent of a wave of extraordinary Latin American writers led by Gabriel García Márquez.

Rudolf Nureyev defected and American Ballet Theater visited Moscow. Downtown New York experimental dance, from Merce Cunningham to the Judson Church coterie, revitalized modern dance, although the Ford Foundation's support for George Balanchine and ballet tipped the balance back in that direction.

Broadway saw big musicals, Jerome Robbins in his prime, and the young Neil Simon and Stephen Sondheim, but also serious plays from Tennessee Williams, Edward Albee and Tom Stoppard. Joe Papp built the summertime Delacorte Theater in Central Park and the regular-season Public Theater downtown.

A new wave of French and Italian film directors were not always perceptively considered by The Times's film criticism of the early- to mid-60's. Hollywood blockbusters were more congenially received, if not always loved. Television, full of cheery sitcoms and variety shows and the very occasional serious drama, became the medium through which most Americans formed their political opinions, starting with the first Kennedy–Nixon presidential debate in 1960.

Finally, there was music, which meant classical landmarks: concerts at Carnegie Hall, Leonard Bernstein and his New York Philharmonic's move to the acoustically problematic Philharmonic (now Avery Fisher) Hall at Lincoln Center, the Rudolf Bing years at the Metropolitan Opera.

But national attention was gripped by popular music—overwhelmingly, by the British invasion, an onslaught led by the Beatles, who changed music, fashion and lifestyles forever. But there was far more to 60's pop music: Bob Dylan, rhythm and blues and Motown, world music and newly respected country (no longer "hillbilly") music, the club rock scene in Los Angeles. And there were the first great rock festivals that culminated in Woodstock and Altamont in 1969. If Woodstock was the apex of the peace-and-love Age of Aquarius, Altamont came to be regarded as its dark underside, a symbol as good as any for the end of a miraculous decade.

National

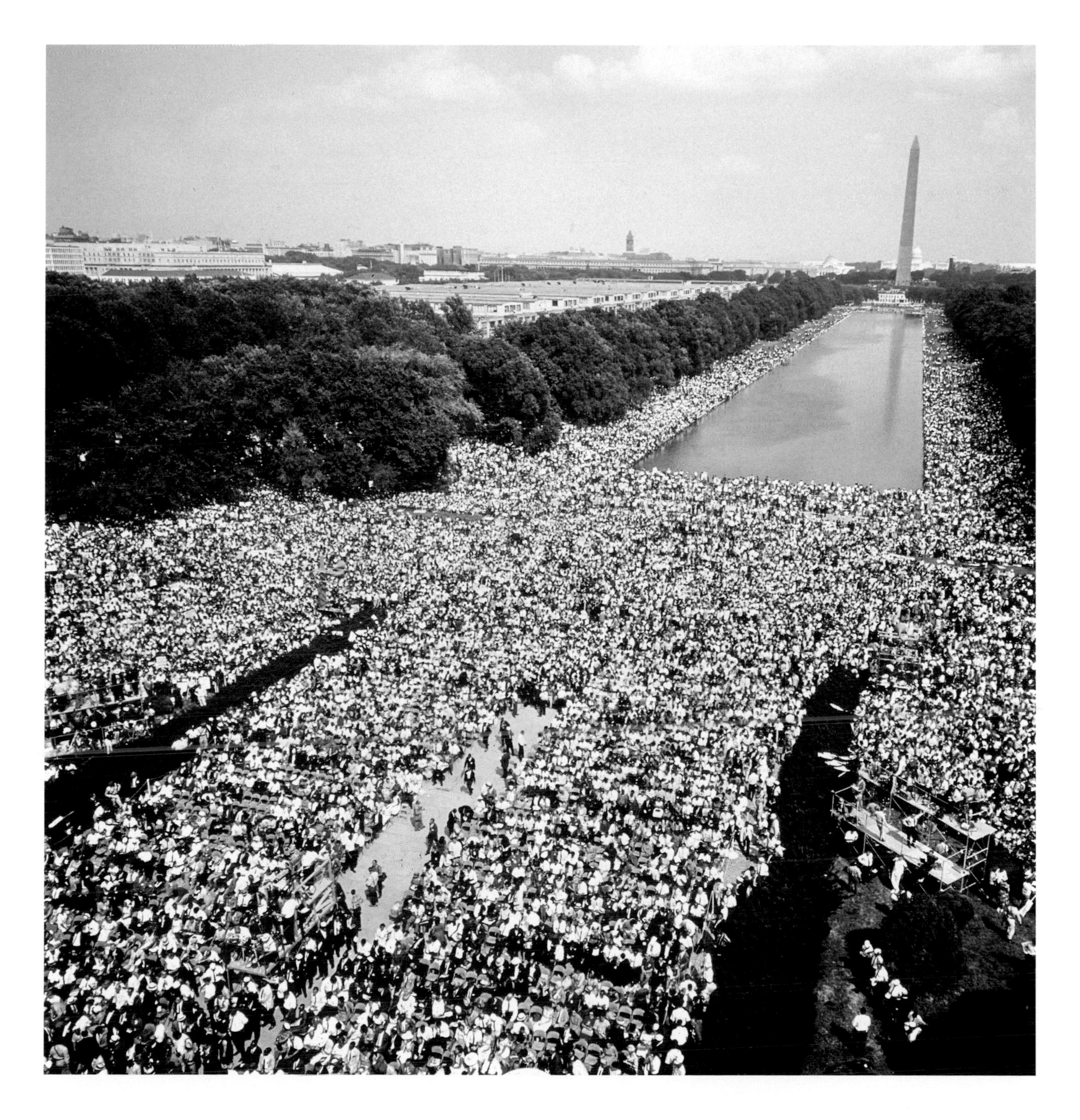

The times were most definitely a-changin'—for some a beacon of hope; for others an existential threat; for those in the middle, a cause for alternating excitement and unease—as the deaths among leaders at home and G.I.'s in the rice paddies of faraway Southeast Asia began piling up.

John F. Kennedy's inauguration gave the nation a brief burst of optimism and hope. Grand plans were announced, the Vietnam War was still on the distant horizon and Fidel Castro's presence in nearby Cuba was more an irritant than a threat—at least until the Cuban missile crisis. Youth, energy and style radiated from the White House, this before our more recent era, in which every politician's peccadilloes have become a potential cause of humiliation or impeachment.

JFK's assassination ended all that, and the rest of the decade—even with the drama and heady triumphs of the civil rights movement—seemed an endless parade of protests and confrontations in the South, speeches and rights legislation up north, race riots in the inner cities and, yes, assassinations of assassins and of black leaders from Medgar Evers to Malcolm X to Martin Luther King Jr. Lyndon Johnson, buoyed by a prosperous economy and Democratic majorities in Congress along with his own formidable legislative skills, was able to realize much of what JFK had envisaged domestically. But faced with the increasingly unpopular Vietnam War, he shocked the nation by announcing he would not seek reelection. Student protests, begun in Berkeley, convulsed the nation's campuses, largely in opposition to the war and the draft. Robert Kennedy was gunned down, too, and Chappaquiddick compromised Teddy Kennedy (and cost Mary Jo Kopechne her life). Richard Speck led a parade of mass murderers, and the Manson family's slaughters blighted Southern California. Things seemed to be unraveling at the seams.

Yet there was more to the nation's news than gloom and turmoil. For some, the hippie groundswell promised a new beginning. Feminism took root, along with the early stirrings of the gay rights movement. Environmental consciousness became a rallying cry in late-60's protests. César Chávez led a farm workers' union. It was a time of memorable oratory: "Ask not what your country . . . ", "I have a dream."

To the horror of conservatives, an activist Supreme Court pushed through a series of landmark decisions. But after Barry Goldwater's sweeping defeat in 1964, the conservative counter-revolution gained traction. Ronald Reagan became governor in California and cracked down on the dreaded University of California, until then the pride of the nation's state higher-education system. In 1968 Eugene McCarthy and the left wing of the Democratic party's animus against the Vietnam War drew enough votes from Hubert Humphrey to allow Richard Nixon a narrow victory in the race for the White House.

Much of what made the 60's a fond memory for some is covered elsewhere in this book—in Lifestyle and Music, especially. The stories in the National section offer hope—for a bridging of the racial divide, for progress in so many of the other issues that have divided this country. But the parade of disappointments and deaths cast a sad pall.

FEBRUARY 15, 1960

NEGRO SITDOWNS STIR FEAR OF WIDER UNREST IN THE SOUTH

Claude Sitton

CHARLOTTE, N.C., Feb. 14—Negro student demonstrations against segregated eating facilities have raised grave questions in the South over the future of the region's race relations. A sounding of opinion in the affected areas showed that much more might be involved than the matter of the Negro's right to sit at a lunch counter for a coffee break.

The demonstrations were generally dismissed at first as another college fad of the "panty-raid" variety. This opinion lost adherents, however, as the movement spread from North Carolina to Virginia, Florida, South Carolina and Tennessee and involved fifteen cities.

Students of race relations in the area contended that the movement reflected growing dissatisfaction over the slow pace of desegregation in schools and other public facilities.

Moreover, these persons saw a shift of leadership to younger, more militant Negroes. This, they said, is likely to bring increasing use of passive resistance. The technique was conceived by Mohandas K. Gandhi of India and popularized among Southern Negroes by the Rev. Dr. Martin Luther King Jr.

The spark that touched off the protests was provided by four freshmen at North Carolina Agricultural and Technical College in Greensboro. "Segregation makes me feel that I'm unwanted," said McNeil A. Joseph. "I don't want my children exposed to it."

The 17-year-old student from Wilmington, N.C., said that he approached three of his classmates the next morning and found them enthusiastic over a proposal that they demand service at the lunch counter of a downtown variety store.

Young blacks stage a sitdown at a Woolworth store's lunch counter in Greensboro, N.C., 1960.

About 4:45 P.M. they entered the F. W. Woolworth Company store on North Elm Street in the heart of Greensboro. Mr. Joseph said he bought a tube of toothpaste and the others made similar purchases. Then they sat down at the lunch counter.

A Negro woman kitchen helper walked up, according to the students, and told them, "You know you're not supposed to be in here." She later called them "ignorant" and a "disgrace" to their race.

The students then asked a white waitress for coffee.

"I'm sorry but we don't serve colored here," they quoted her.

"I beg your pardon," said Franklin McCain, 18, of Washington, "you just served me at a counter two feet away. Why is it that you serve me at one counter and deny me at another. Why not stop serving me at all the counters?"

The four students sat, coffeeless, until the store closed at 5:30 P.M. Then, hearing that they might be prosecuted, they went to the executive committee of the Greensboro N.A.A.C.P. to ask advice.

The protests generally followed similar patterns. Young men and women and, in one case, high school boys and girls, walked into the stores and requested food service. Met with refusals in all cases, they remained at the lunch counters in silent protest.

The reaction of store managers in those instances was to close down the lunch counters and, when trouble developed or bomb threats were received, the entire store.

The demonstrations attracted crowds of whites. At first the hecklers were youths with duck-tailed haircuts. Some carried small Confederate battle flags. Later they were joined by older men in faded khakis and overalls.

North Carolina's Attorney General, Malcolm B. Seawell, asserted that the students were causing "irreparable harm" to relations between whites and Negroes.

Mayor William G. Enloe of Raleigh termed it "regrettable that some of our young Negro students would risk endangering these relations by seeking to change a long standing custom in a manner that is all but destined to fail." ■

NOVEMBER 10, 1960

KENNEDY VICTORY WON BY CLOSE MARGIN

Election Doubts Finally Cleared

Stanley Levey

President-elect John F. Kennedy makes his victory speech in the Hyannis Armory on November 9, 1960.

For hours after the polls closed Tuesday a wild electoral numbers game went on. It confused newspapers, networks and voters alike.

Even the two Presidential candidates did not quite know what to make of the figures that came streaming over the airwaves, out of newspaper columns and from the recesses of computer machines.

The result was that a clear picture of the election outcome did not appear until after midday yesterday. Only a few hours before that it seemed as if concessions and claims of a victory for Senator John F. Kennedy might have to be withdrawn.

In its second Late City Edition, which began to come off the presses shortly after 2 A.M., The New York Times carried a headline reading: "Kennedy Elected President." The article on which the headline was based said that with 53 percent of the popular vote in, Senator Kennedy had 19,912,917 votes to 17,801,568 for Vice President Nixon.

For some hours the television and radio networks had been reporting a substantial Kennedy plurality. For example, at 11:44 P.M., the National Broadcasting Company gave the Massachusetts Senator a lead of 1,800,000. By 1:02 A.M. it had dropped to 1,500,000.

Meanwhile the key states of California and Illinois were floating into and out of the Kennedy column in the electoral vote total. At 1 A.M. Illinois seemed certain for Mr. Kennedy. But two hours later the state was in the doubtful list. The reports from Illinois grew increasingly conflicting.

The networks, The Times and Chicago newspapers at first counted the state's twenty-seven electoral votes for Mr. Kennedy, but by about 2:45 it began to appear that Mr. Kennedy's electoral total included states that were leaning to the candidate but that had not been won.

At 3:20 A.M. Vice President Nixon gave the Kennedy backers an apparent lift, despite the Senator's dropping plurality, when he suggested that Mr. Kennedy would be elected if the trend prevailing at that time continued. He said he was going to bed, but he didn't, and he made no concession. The Democratic candidate sat tight and silent at Hyannis Port, Mass.

Beginning about 4 A.M. Mr. Nixon began to cut deeply into Senator Kennedy's lead in California and Illinois. By 5 A.M. in California, with half the districts uncounted, the Kennedy margin had been slashed from 300,000 to 100,000. Officials in many key voting districts stopped counting, thus putting the state's thirty-two electoral votes in doubt.

At 7 A.M. The Times modified the headline it had been carrying since 2:30 A.M. Now instead of calling Senator Kennedy "elected," The Times declared: "Kennedy Is Apparent Victor."

By this time Mr. Kennedy's prospects had improved slightly. He needed only eleven electoral votes to win, and he could get these by holding California or Illinois or by winning Minnesota. Mr. Nixon had to win all three states and some others besides.

Mr. Kennedy took Minnesota by about noon. The numbers game was over. ■

NOVEMBER 10, 1960

KENNEDY IS YOUNGEST PRESIDENT

The election of John Fitzgerald Kennedy as thirty-fifth President of the United States breaks precedents right and left.

At 43, Mr. Kennedy is the youngest man ever elected to the White House.

A Roman Catholic, he is the first member of his faith to win the American Presidency.

As a millionaire he is not unique in the White House. But he is probably the first President who had a million to his account while still in his teens.

As a well-groomed Senator not the least of his distinctions was the fact he once addressed the Senate with his shirttail hanging out.

The facts of his life are fairly well known. His father is Joseph P. Kennedy, one-time

EISENHOWER'S FAREWELL URGES VIGILANCE

Felix Belair Jr.

WASHINGTON, Jan. 17—President Eisenhower cautioned the nation in a farewell address from the White House tonight to be vigilant against dangers to its liberties implicit in a vast military establishment and a permanent armaments industry unparalleled in peacetime.

In his speech, which brought down the curtain on fifty years of public service, the President also warned of a second threat—"the prospect of domination of the nation's scholars by Federal employment, project allocations and the power of money." He said this danger was "ever present and is gravely to be regarded."

President Eisenhower also spoke as an old soldier preparing to turn over the burdens of the Presidency to his much younger successor, President-elect John F. Kennedy. The two men will hold their second and final discussion of problems confronting the nation Thursday morning.

Foremost among these problems, the President listed the continuing Communist threat to the West and the need to combat it while striving for universal disarmament. It was "with a definite sense of disappointment" that he contemplated the failure to make greater progress toward a lasting peace.

The President stressed the need to guard against "the acquisition of unwarranted influence, whether sought or unsought, by the military-industrial complex."

This warning against the political potential of the huge military-arms production apparatus by the President came as a surprise to many in the capital. A more sentimental leave taking had been expected from the old soldier. The address was an assessment of the nation's condition today and a frank effort to penetrate the uncertainties of the future.

The President said America today was "the strongest, the most influential and the most productive nation in the world" even though it has been involved in three major wars during the first sixty years of this century.

There will always be crises ahead, foreign and domestic, he said, but the real dangers lie not in the exigencies themselves but in the means chosen for meeting them.

Finally, President Eisenhower saw as the nation's "continuing imperative" the ultimate goal of disarmament with mutual honor and confidence.

"As one who has witnessed the horror and the lingering sadness of war—as one who knows that another war could utterly destroy this civilization which has been so slowly and painfully built over thousands of years—I wish I could say tonight that a lasting peace is in sight," the President said.

He noted that war had been averted and steady progress had been made toward the ultimate goal, but said that much remained to be done. ■

New Dealer of the early Roosevelt days, Ambassador to the Court of St. James, a millionaire at 30 and a multi-millionaire today. His mother is Rose Fitzgerald, a daughter of John J. Fitzgerald, who successfully campaigned for Mayor of Boston by singing "Sweet Adeline" in a faultless Irish tenor.

Jack attempted to enlist in the Army when this country became involved in the war, but he was turned down because of a back weakness caused by a football injury. He did special exercises for several months and finally received a Navy commission.

Assigned first to a desk in Washington, he finally was able to win a transfer to motor torpedo boats, one of the most dangerous assignments, and in 1943 found himself in the Solomon Islands fighting night actions against Japanese vessels.

In one such encounter, his torpedo boat was rammed and cut in two and two of the crewmen were killed. The incredible story of how Lieutenant Kennedy helped save the others and led them to a near-by island where they finally were rescued was told by John Hersey in a small wartime book titled "Survival."

Lieutenant Kennedy's back was injured in the mishap and the malaria he contracted finally combined to bring his discharge from the Navy in the spring of 1945.

With the Kennedy family backing him, ringing doorbells, holding teas and buttonholing voters, he finished first in a nine-man primary and went on to win the election in November 1946 from the Democratic Eleventh District of Massachusetts.

Mr. Kennedy did not distinguish himself in his three terms in the House of Representatives, but he was a hard-working young legislator who did his homework well and had a better record of attendance than most.

Then came his startling Senate victory in 1952 over Henry Cabot Lodge, whose grandfather had defeated Mr. Kennedy's grandfather for the same post almost half a century before, his fast run for the Vice Presidential nomination in 1956 at Chicago, and his Presidential campaign since for the Democratic nomination and the election.

Mr. Kennedy's close friends admit that he does not have the warm personality of many of his predecessors. But they emphatically deny that he has no feeling at all and does everything on the basis of its effect, not because of a basic belief in its rightness.

After many years of carefree bachelorhood in Washington, New York, Hyannis Port and Palm Beach, Mr. Kennedy in 1953 married Jacqueline Lee Bouvier, the 24-year-old daughter of Mr. and Mrs. John V. Bouvier 3rd. She was a true cosmopolitan having attended Vassar, the Sorbonne and George Washington University before becoming an inquiring photographer for The Washington Times-Herald.

Their wedding in St. Mary's Roman Catholic Church in Newport on Sept. 12, 1953, was a major social event. Newport was Jacqueline's summer home after her mother divorced her father and was married to Hugh D. Auchincloss.

The Kennedys have one daughter, Caroline, 2, and are expecting another child soon. ■

JANUARY 21, 1961

KENNEDY'S INAUGURAL: 'PAY ANY PRICE' TO KEEP FREEDOM

W. H. Lawrence

John F. Kennedy delivering his inaugural speech on January 20, 1961.

WASHINGTON, Jan. 20—John Fitzgerald Kennedy assumed the Presidency today with a call for "a grand and global alliance" to combat tyranny, poverty, disease and war.

In his Inaugural Address, he served notice on the world that the United States was ready to "pay any price, bear any burden, meet any hardship, support any friend, oppose any foe to assure the survival and the success of liberty."

But the nation is also ready, he said, to resume negotiations with the Soviet Union to ease and, if possible, remove world tensions.

"Let us begin anew," Mr. Kennedy declared. "Let us never negotiate out of fear. But let us never fear to negotiate."

He called on his fellow citizens to join his Administration's endeavor:

"Ask not what your country can do for you—ask what you can do for your country."

Warning that civility should not be mistaken for weakness and that sincerity was always subject to proof, Mr. Kennedy asked "both sides" to explore what problems "unite us instead of belaboring those problems which divide us."

"Let both sides seek to invoke the wonders of science instead of its terrors," he went on. "Together let us explore the stars, conquer the deserts, eradicate disease, tap the ocean depths and encourage the arts and commerce."

In an apparent allusion to the regime of Premier Fidel Castro of Cuba, with which the Eisenhower Administration broke diplomatic relations earlier this month, the new President sounded a warning to the Russians not to interfere in the Western Hemisphere.

"Let all our neighbors know that we shall join with them to oppose aggression or subversion anywhere in the Americas," he said. "And let every other power know that this hemisphere intends to remain the master of its own house."

Robert Frost, the New England poet, read his poem, "The Gift Outright," which President Kennedy had especially requested in inviting Mr. Frost to the Inaugural.

In his day of triumph President Kennedy seemed unaffected and unfrightened as he approached the responsibilities of leadership. Recalling that President Eisenhower had broken with tradition eight years ago by decreeing black homburgs instead of tall silk top hats for inaugural wear, Mr. Kennedy was mockingly severe when he spotted a newsman in a homburg today.

"Didn't you get the word?" he asked. "Top hats are the rule this year."

Mr. Kennedy, who is usually hatless, seemed self-consciously uncomfortable in his topper. He wore it as briefly as possible in the trips back and forth from the White House to Capitol Hill. He also shed his coat frequently in the long day outdoors. Bronzed by the Florida sun during his pre-inauguration holiday, with his brown hair neatly brushed, he looked the picture of health as he tackled the White House job.

MARCH 2, 1961

KENNEDY SETS UP U.S. PEACE CORPS

Peter Braestrup

WASHINGTON, March 1—President Kennedy issued an executive order today creating a Peace Corps. It will enlist American men and women for voluntary, unpaid service in the developing countries of the world.

Announcing the move at his news conference, the President described the Peace Corps as a "pool of trained American men and women sent overseas by the United States Government or through private organizations and institutions to help foreign governments meet their urgent needs for skilled manpower."

The President's expressed hope was to have 500 to 1,000 Peace Corps workers "in the field by the end of this year."

Life in the Peace Corps, the President stressed, "will not be easy." Members will work without pay but they will be given living allowances. They will live at the same level as the inhabitants of the countries to which they are sent.

The President emphasized that "we will send Americans abroad who are qualified to do a job," particularly those with technical skills in teaching, agriculture and health. "There is little doubt," the President said in his subsequent message to Congress, "that the number of those who wish to serve will be far greater than our capacity to absorb them."

President Kennedy first broached his version of the Peace Corps idea in a campaign speech at San Francisco last Nov. 2. Previously, Senator Hubert H. Humphrey, Democrat of Minnesota, and Representative Henry S. Reuss, Democrat of Wisconsin, among others, had advocated such a plan.

White House spokesmen outlined the Peace Corps operation as follows: The initial cost for the fiscal year ending June 30 will be paid out of foreign aid funds that have already been appropriated. For the following years, a special appropriation will be required from Congress. The cost for a worker a year is estimated at $5,000 to $12,000—including training, transportation, living allowances, medical care and administrative overhead. The State Department will be in charge of the program. ■

MAY 23, 1961

MONTGOMERY TENSION HIGH AFTER THREATS OF BOMBING

Claude Sitton

Freedom Riders escorted by Mississippi National Guardsmen on their way from Montgomery, Alabama, to Jackson, Mississippi.

MONTGOMERY, Ala., Tuesday, May 23—National Guardsmen are enforcing an uneasy truce here under martial law following renewed racial violence. Bomb threats, two attempted house-burnings and minor incidents kept tension high in this first capital of the Old Confederacy in the wake of efforts to end segregation on interstate buses and in waiting rooms.

Some 1,800 pupils were evacuated from two junior high schools after telephoned bomb threats. Similar threats were received at the Greyhound bus station and Radio Station WAPX.

The police and firemen found no explosives.

Flaming "Molotov cocktails," bottles of gasoline stoppered with rags, were tossed at two homes yesterday but neither was damaged. One house was occupied by Negroes and the other by a white restaurant operator who was acquitted recently in the shotgun slaying of a member of the Ku Klux Klan.

White-helmeted troops in green fatigues rolled through the streets in jeeps. Others with slung rifles stood watch at bus, train and airport terminals.

One hundred additional National Guardsmen were called to the Greyhound Bus Terminal late last night. It was feared there might be trouble, with several buses scheduled to arrive close together. There was no incident, and the men were ordered to return to their posts.

The local police and the state highway patrol were also on the alert. Concern was expressed over reports that Negro and white "Freedom Riders" would renew their efforts to carry the anti-segregation drive across Alabama and into Mississippi and Louisiana.

Judge Walter B. Jones has ordered the demonstrators to show cause today in Montgomery's Circuit Court why they should not be found in contempt. He had earlier issued an injunction against them forbidding a continuation of their activities.

State officials have contended that the demonstrators violated Alabama's segregation laws. Whites and Negroes among them

(cont'd. on next page)

(cont'd. from previous page)

have shared seats on buses and have sought service in terminal restaurants restricted to either white or Negro passengers.

The Supreme Court has ruled that a state cannot enforce segregation in transportation. This is so whether bus, plane or train is used or whether the journey crosses a state border. The court has also found that interstate waiting rooms in terminals may not be segregated. In a ruling this term, it decided also that a private restaurant in an interstate terminal designed to serve interstate passengers could not be segregated.

Gov. John Patterson, who imposed martial law here last night, is expected to address a joint session of the Legislature at noon today on the controversy.

In a statement yesterday, he reiterated his contention that "the Federal Government has no business or legal authority to interfere in our internal problems."

The demonstration on wheels began in Washington under the sponsorship of the Congress of Racial Equality. Angry whites attacked one group last week in Anniston, Ala., and then put a torch to a bus on which another group was riding.

When the riders reached Birmingham, a bloody riot ensued. The demonstrators discontinued their efforts and left the state by plane.

But other demonstrators from the Nashville, Tenn., Student Nonviolent Coordinating Committee boarded a bus in Birmingham last Saturday and reached Montgomery.

A second riot broke out here upon their arrival and a third came Sunday when they gathered at a Negro mass meeting in the First Baptist Church.

Federal marshals, and, later, the city police and highway patrolmen, held a mob of whites at bay with tear gas and night sticks. An automobile was overturned and burned and a number of persons were injured.

The Rev. Dr. Martin Luther King Jr. of Atlanta, president of the Southern Christian Leadership Conference, and other Negro leaders met here late yesterday to plan other anti-segregation activities.

Meanwhile, interstate buses entering the state were stopped for Alabama highway patrolmen to read the state court order barring more persons seeking to end segregation. Officials said this was done to put riders "on notice" so that violators of the injunction could receive contempt citations. ■

SEPTEMBER 21, 1962

NEGRO REJECTED AT MISSISSIPPI U.

Claude Sitton

James Meredith accompanied by U.S. Marshals after registering for entry at the University of Mississippi, 1962.

OXFORD, Miss., Sept. 20—Gov. Ross R. Barnett denied James H. Meredith, a 29-year-old Negro, admission to the University of Mississippi today. In so doing, the Governor defied orders of the Federal courts.

In rejecting the application of Mr. Meredith, an Air Force veteran, Mr. Barnett set the stage for one of the most critical conflicts between state and Federal authority yet seen in the South. The controversy poses grave problems of international significance for the Kennedy Administration.

Shortly before flying here from Jackson, the state capital, Governor Barnett persuaded the Board of Trustees of Institutions of Higher Learning to appoint him as special registrar to deal with the "registration or non-registration" of the Negro student.

Governor Barnett, who has asserted his willingness to go to jail to prevent the desegregation of the university, confronted Mr. Meredith today in a dramatic 20-minute meeting.

Approximately 100 uniformed State Highway patrolmen and scores of sheriffs, deputies, plainclothesmen and policemen held back a crowd of 2,000 jeering students.

As the automobile carrying Mr. Meredith and Federal officials pulled away toward Memphis, the students swarmed across a grassy, tree-shaded mall in a futile attempt to stop them.

Following their departure, Governor Barnett emerged and told newsmen:

"The only statement I have to make is this: The application of James Meredith was refused."

There are no immediate indications as to the outcome of the dispute, which comes during the week of the 100th anniversary of the Emancipation Proclamation under which President Lincoln declared slaves in the Confederate States free.

Governor Barnett threw down the gauntlet of defiance in a television address a week ago tonight. He invoked the legally discredited doctrine of interposition.

By this act, he contended, he "interposed" the power of the state between the Federal Government and the university and thus nullified the desegregation order.

If the Governor's present strategy fails, his only apparent recourse is to close the university. ■

OBITUARY

NOVEMBER 8, 1962

MRS. ROOSEVELT DIES AT 78 AFTER ILLNESS OF SIX WEEKS

Mrs. Franklin D. Roosevelt died last night.

The former First Lady, famous as the wife and widow of the 32nd President of the United States and an international figure in her own right, died at 6:15 P.M. in her home at 55 East 74th Street. She was 78 years old.

Reaction to Mrs. Roosevelt's death was quick and deep.

The woman who was a noted humanitarian, author and columnist, delegate to the United Nations and active force in the Democratic party was mourned by people over the world.

President Kennedy called her "one of the great ladies in the history of this country." The President and former President Harry S. Truman announced they planned to attend Mrs. Roosevelt's funeral.

Mrs. Roosevelt succumbed four weeks after her birthday, which was Oct. 11, and six weeks after she entered a hospital with anemia and a lung infection.

Her family announced that a private funeral service would be held at St. James's Protestant Episcopal Church in Hyde Park, N.Y., at 2 P.M. Saturday.

Mrs. Roosevelt will be buried next to her husband, who died on April 12, 1945. There is a tombstone over his grave, in the rose garden of the Hyde Park home, which contains his name, the year of his birth and the year of his death. Also carved into the stone are the name Anna Eleanor Roosevelt and the year of her birth.

Shortly after the first signs of illness, she went to the Columbia-Presbyterian Medical Center, on Sept. 26. She marked her 78th birthday in the hospital and, it was learned last night, began pressing to be released so that she could convalesce at home.

Three of Mrs. Roosevelt's children were at the apartment last night. In addition to her daughter Anna Roosevelt Halsted, wife of Dr. James A. Halsted, there were Franklin D. Roosevelt Jr. and John. The two other sons took planes to come here. Elliott was flying from Miami and James arrived early today by plane from California, where he won re-election to the House of Representatives in Tuesday's elections.

Mrs. Roosevelt's body was taken last night from the five-story building where she had occupied the second and third floors, placed in an unmarked hearse at 8:25 and taken to the Columbia-Presbyterian Medical Center for an autopsy.

During her illness, Mrs. Roosevelt had only one visitor who was not a member of the family—Adlai E. Stevenson, the United States representative at the United Nations. Mrs. Roosevelt had worked closely with Mr. Stevenson in the United Nations for many years, and she had asked him to talk with her about the Cuban crisis.

The family announced shortly after Mrs. Roosevelt's death that no one would be permitted inside the house here, but an exception was quickly made for Mr. Stevenson. He stayed five minutes.

Besides her five children, Mrs. Roosevelt is survived by 19 grandchildren and 15 great-grandchildren.

APRIL 13, 1963

Dr. KING ARRESTED IN BIRMINGHAM

Foster Hailey

BIRMINGHAM, Ala., April 12—The Rev. Dr. Martin Luther King Jr. was arrested this afternoon when he defied a court injunction and led a march of Negroes toward the downtown section.

The marchers were halted after four and a half blocks—but not before more than a thousand shouting, singing Negroes had joined in the demonstration.

In addition to Dr. King, the Rev. Dr. Ralph D. Abernathy, secretary of the Southern Christian Leadership Conference, and more than 60 others were taken into custody. There was no violence.

The march was the most spectacular of many demonstrations held since a direct action assault on Birmingham racial barriers was begun 10 days ago under the leadership of the local affiliate of the Southern Christian Leadership Conference.

There has been much opposition in the Negro community here of more than 100,000 to pressing the campaign just as a new and moderate city administration is taking office and to the participation of Dr. King, even though he has said he was invited to come. There also has been some reported grumbling that Dr. King was letting local people get arrested and staying safely behind the lines himself.

Today's march was the most widely advertised demonstration yet held and was viewed by larger groups of Negroes than any of the others. It was originally scheduled to start at noon from the Sixth Avenue Zion Hill Baptist Church, a small church at 14th Street and Sixth Avenue North, three blocks inside the main Negro section of the city.

It was 2:40 P.M., however, before Dr. King and the others emerged from the church doors and started east up Sixth Avenue. Dr. King and Dr. Abernathy were at the head of a procession of 40 or 50 marchers. They were dressed in blue jeans and blue cotton shirts to dramatize the efforts they have been making to bring about a Negro boycott of Easter buying at downtown white stores.

As the head of the march passed behind some trucks at the entrance to a garage, T. Eugene Connor, Birmingham's Commissioner of Public Safety, told his forces "stop them there."

Two motorcycle patrolmen and two detectives grabbed Dr. King and Dr. Abernathy and hustled them into a police van a few steps away. The order of the marchers, which had started out two abreast, had been disrupted as eager onlookers joined in behind them and on either side. Thus police had difficulty trying to sort the marchers from spectators.

Dr. King and the local leaders say that no matter who is arrested others will step forward to take their place. They say that the campaign will be continued until there is at least a beginning made in easing discrimination. ■

MAY 13, 1963

U. S. SENDS TROOPS INTO ALABAMA AFTER RIOTS SWEEP BIRMINGHAM; Kennedy Alerts State's Guard

Anthony Lewis

Protesters being hit by a high-pressure water jets from a firehoses by police in Birmingham, Alabama, 1963.

WASHINGTON, May 12—President Kennedy tonight dispatched Federal troops to bases near Birmingham, Ala., for use if racial violence breaks out again.

His action followed three hours of rioting early this morning in which 50 persons were injured. The rioting erupted after two buildings were bombed.

The President also ordered all "necessary preliminary steps" be taken to call the Alabama National Guard into Federal service. The actual call can then be accomplished in minutes if the President decides it is needed.

The President made known these emergency moves at the White House tonight. He appeared before the press and television cameras at 8:48 P. M, to read a grave statement on the Birmingham crisis,

The President declared:

"This Government will do whatever must be done to preserve order, to protect the lives of its citizens and to uphold the law of the land. I am certain that the vast majority of the citizens of Birmingham, both white and Negro—particularly those who labored so hard to achieve the peaceful, constructive settlement of last week—can feel nothing but dismay at the efforts of those who would replace conciliation and good will with violence and hate."

The Defense Department would not identify the troop units or indicate their size, except to say that all came from outside Alabama.

Mr. Kennedy acted after conferring for three hours with Secretary of Defense Robert S.

McNamara, Attorney General Robert F. Kennedy, Secretary of the Army Cyrus Vance and other officials.

The President's statement made clear the deep concern of the Administration over last night's bombings of Negro residences in Birmingham and the resulting riots and police action.

Government sources said the events of the night gave an entirely new cast to the Birmingham racial crisis. From a protest demonstration, they said, it had become an ugly, violent struggle.

In addition to concern over the bombings and the rioting, officials were disturbed by the police reaction. It was reported that the Birmingham police, behaving efficiently and fairly, had the situation under control when state troopers came in and revived tensions.

The eruption of violence threatened the agreement reached last week, with the help of Federal mediation, to end the Negro protest demonstrations. White business leaders had agreed to gradual desegregation of their facilities. ■

protest

ALABAMA ADMITS NEGRO STUDENTS; WALLACE BOWS TO FEDERAL FORCE

Claude Sitton

Gov. George Wallace is confronted by Deputy U.S. Attorney Nicholas Katzenbach, right, at the University of Alabama in Tuscaloosa on June 11, 1963.

TUSCALOOSA, Ala., June 11—Gov. George C. Wallace stepped aside today when confronted by federalized National Guard troops and permitted two Negroes to enroll in the University of Alabama. There was no violence.

The Governor, flanked by state troopers, had staged a carefully planned show of defying a Federal Court desegregation order.

Mr. Wallace refused four requests this morning from a Justice Department official that he allow Miss Vivian Malone and James A. Hood, both 20 years old, to enter Foster Auditorium and register.

This was in keeping with a campaign pledge that he would "stand in the schoolhouse door" to prevent a resumption of desegregation in Alabama's educational system.

The official, Nicholas deB. Katzenbach, Deputy Attorney General, did not press the issue by bringing the students from a waiting car to face the Governor. Instead, they were taken to their dormitories.

However, the outcome was foreshadowed even then. Mr. Katzenbach told Mr. Wallace during the confrontation:

"From the outset, Governor, all of us have known that the final chapter of this history will be the admission of these students."

Units of the 31st (Dixie) Division, federalized on orders from President Kennedy, arrived on the campus four and a half hours later under the command of Brig. Gen. Henry V. Graham.

A Birmingham real estate executive in civilian life, General Graham is the former State Adjutant General who enforced modified martial law in Montgomery, the state capital, following the Freedom Rider riots in 1961.

In a voice that was scarcely audible, General Graham said that it was his "sad duty" to order the Governor to step aside.

Mr. Wallace then read the second of two statements challenging the constitutionality of court-ordered desegregation and left the auditorium with his aides for Montgomery.

This sequence of events, which took place in a circus atmosphere, appeared to have given the Governor the face-saving exit he apparently wanted.

Whether the courts find that he actually defied the order issued last Wednesday by District Judge Seybourn H. Lynne in Birmingham remained to be seen. Significantly, Edwin O. Guthman, special assistant for information to Attorney General Robert F. Kennedy, noted that the students had not presented themselves for admission until Mr. Wallace had left the campus.

It thus appeared that the Kennedy Administration had saved itself the political embarrassment of bringing a contempt-of-court action against a second Southern Governor.

Gov. Ross R. Barnett of Mississippi now faces a trial for contempt as a result of his repeated defiance of orders directing the admission of James H. Meredith, a Negro, to the University of Mississippi last fall.

Tonight Mr. Guthman, in a news conference, said that it would be up to the courts to determine if Mr. Wallace should be prosecuted. He declined repeatedly to say whether the Justice Department would bring charges.

Governor Wallace gave no indication whether he still planned a show of defiance Thursday, when another Negro is scheduled to register at the university's Huntsville branch.

He is Dave M. McGlathery, 27, a mathematician for the National Aeronautics and Space Administration at the George C. Marshall Space Flight Center in that northern Alabama city.

However, there was speculation among Wallace aides that the Governor would not seek to interfere with Mr. McGlathery's registration.

(cont'd. on next page)

(cont'd. from previous page)

Mr. Guthman told newsmen that Federal officials did not now plan to send troops to Huntsville. "The situation will be handled by state and university officials," he said.

There were indications that the 500 to 600 Guardsmen dispatched to Tuscaloosa might not be needed for a lengthy period.

Judge Lynne's preliminary injunction against Governor Wallace followed a finding by District Judge H. H. Grooms that the university must admit the three students under a permanent injunction issued by Judge Grooms in 1955.

That order brought the registration of Miss Autherine Lucy, the first Negro to attend a formerly white public education institution in this state.

Miss Lucy, now Mrs. H. L. Foster, went to classes for three days in 1956. She withdrew and was later expelled after her lawyers had accused university officials of conspiring with the rioters who opposed her presence.

The long-awaited confrontation between Governor Wallace and the Federal officials came shortly after 11 o'clock [1 P.M., New York time] on the sunbaked north steps of Foster Auditorium, a three-story building of red brick with six limestone columns.

Governor Wallace stood waiting behind a lectern placed in the doorway by a state trooper. He wore a microphone around his neck that was connected to a public address system.

Mr. Katzenbach said he had a proclamation from President Kennedy directing Governor Wallace to end his defiant stand. He asked the Governor to give way, but Mr. Wallace interrupted him and began reading a lengthy statement.

Mr. Wallace cited the provision of the 10th Amendment that provides that powers not delegated to the Federal Government are retained by the states.

"I stand here today, as Governor of this sovereign state, and refuse to willingly submit to illegal usurpation of power by the Central Government," he said.

"I take it from that statement that you are going to stand in the door and that you are not going to carry out the orders of the court," said Mr. Katzenbach, "and that you are going to resist us from doing so. Is that correct?"

"I stand according to my statement," replied Mr. Wallace.

After several pleas in a similar vein, including the one in which he forecast the students' admission, Mr. Katzenbach waited for the Governor to reply. Mr. Wallace stood defiantly in the door, his head thrown back, his lips pressed tightly.

At 3:16 P.M., three National Guard troop carriers escorted by Tuscaloosa motorcycle patrolmen and followed by a jeep roared up to Mary Burke Hall. Infantrymen, dressed in green fatigues and armed with M-1 rifles, jumped down and formed beside the auditorium.

Another convoy arrived on a street northwest of the auditorium. General Graham pulled up beside it in a green, unmarked command car.

General Graham walked to within four feet of the Governor. Standing at attention and leaning forward, he began to speak in a grim voice.

"It is my sad duty - " and his voice sank so low that bystanders could barely hear it.

Governor Wallace pulled a crumpled piece of paper from his pocket and read a brief statement. He said that had the Guardsmen not been federalized, "I would at this point be your commander. I know that this [duty] is a bitter pill for you to swallow."

He then reiterated earlier requests that white Alabamians refrain from violence.

The Governor denounced what he termed a trend toward "military dictatorship" in the nation. "We shall now return to Montgomery to continue this constitutional fight," he said.

General Graham saluted the Governor smartly. After returning the salute, Mr. Wallace and his aides walked swiftly to waiting cars and were driven away, to the cheers of students.

Three minutes after their departure, Mr. Hood walked into the auditorium with Federal officials to register. Miss Malone followed a minute later. ■

OBITUARY

AUGUST 28, 1963

W. E. B. DUBOIS DIES IN GHANA; LEADER AND AUTHOR, 95

ACCRA, Ghana, Wednesday, Aug. 28— W. E. B. DuBois, the American Negro philosopher and writer, who settled in Ghana a few years ago, died last night, the Government announced. He was 95 years old.

Dr. DuBois, who had come here as a special guest of President Kwame Nkrumah, was director of the Encyclopedia Africana, which is sponsored by the Government. He became a citizen of Ghana this year.

As a sociologist, educator and writer, he frequently disagreed not only with whites but with members of his own race. Early in his career, he challenged the philosophy of Booker T. Washington. Dr. DuBois was one of the founders of the National Association for the Advancement of Colored People, but later broke with the organization under conditions of bitterness.

During his later years, he was active in many left-wing and Communist activities. In the fall of 1961—at the age of 93—he joined the Communist party. At about the same time, he went to Ghana as head of the secretariat planning the new Negro encyclopedia.

Among Dr. DuBois' major writings were "Souls of Black Folk," published in 1903; "Darkwater," 1920; "Dark Princess," 1924; "The Encyclopedia of the Negro," 1931-1946; "The Gift of the Black Folk" and "In Battle for Peace," 1952.

For the next 20 years, he said, he attacked the Democrats, Republicans and Socialists. He said that he had "praised the attitudes of the Communists but opposed their tactics in the case of the Scottsboro boys and their advocacy of a Negro state."

In recent years, Dr. DuBois traveled extensively in Communist China and the Soviet Union. On his 91st birthday, he was honored in Peking by a celebration attended by Premier Chou En-lai.

JUNE 13, 1963

N.A.A.C.P. LEADER SLAIN IN JACKSON; Protests Mount

Claude Sitton

JACKSON, Miss., June 12—A sniper lying in ambush shot and fatally wounded a Negro civil rights leader early today.

The slaying touched off mass protests by Negroes in which 158 were arrested. It also aroused widespread fear of further racial violence in this state capital.

The victim of the shooting was Medgar W. Evers, 37-year-old Mississippi field secretary of the National Association for the Advancement of Colored People. Struck in the back by a bullet from a high-powered rifle as he walked from his automobile to his home, he died less than an hour later—at 1:14 A.M. (3:14 A.M., New York Time)—in University Hospital.

Agents of the Federal Bureau of Investigation joined Jackson, Hinds County and state authorities in the search for the killer.

A 51-year-old white man was picked up, questioned for several hours and released. Investigators discovered a .30-06-caliber rifle with a newly attached telescopic sight in a vacant lot near the honeysuckle thicket from which they believed the fatal shot had been fired.

The first demonstration today occurred at 11:25 A.M., when 13 ministers left the Pearl Street African Methodist Episcopal Church and walked silently toward the City Hall.

Mrs. Evers spoke tonight to some 500 persons at a mass meeting in the Pearl Street church. Dressed in a pale green dress, she appeared tired but composed. Many women in the audience wept openly.

Referring to her husband's death, she said, "It was his wish that this [Jackson] movement would be one of the most successful that this nation has ever known."

Mr. Evers, a native of Decatur, Miss., and an Army veteran of World War II, had been one of the key leaders in the Negroes' drive here to win a promise from the city to hire some Negro policemen and to appoint a biracial committee.

He left a mass meeting at a church last night, stopped at the residence of a Negro lawyer and then drove to his home on the city's northern edge. Before leaving the church, he remarked to a newsman that "tomorrow will be a big day."

He arrived at his neat, green-paneled and buff-brick ranch-style home on Guynes Street shortly after midnight. The accounts of the authorities, his wife and neighbors showed that the following series of events had taken place:

He parked his 1962 light blue sedan in the driveway, behind his wife's station wagon.

As he turned to walk into a side entrance opening into a carport, the sniper's bullet struck him just below the right shoulder blade.

Mr. Evers staggered to the doorway, his keys in his hand, and collapsed near the steps. His wife, Myrlie, and three children rushed to the door.

The screaming of the children, "Daddy! Daddy! Daddy!" awoke a neighbor, Thomas A. Young. Another neighbor, Houston Wells, said he had heard the shot and the screams of Mrs. Evers.

Mr. Wells, according to the police, said he had looked out a bedroom window, saw Mr. Evers' crumpled body in the carport and had rushed out into his yard. He said he had crouched behind a clump of shrubbery, fired a shot into the air and shouted for help.

The police, who arrived a short time later, helped neighbors place Mr. Evers in Mr. Wells' station wagon.

As the station wagon sped to University Hospital, those who accompanied the dying man said he had murmured weakly, "Sit me up," and later, "Turn me loose."

Dr. A. B. Britton, Mr. Evers's physician, a member of the Mississippi Advisory Committee to the Federal Civil Rights Commission, rushed to the hospital. He indicated that the victim had died from loss of blood and internal injuries.

Mr. Evers expressed a premonition several weeks ago that he might be shot, according to Dr. Britton. The physician said he and other friends believed that they should have taken steps then to protect him.

Myrlie Evers (right) with her son Darryl Kenyatta during the funeral of her husband, civil rights activist Medgar Evers, Jackson, Mississippi, June 18, 1963.

AUGUST 29, 1963

200,000 MARCH FOR CIVIL RIGHTS

Dr. Martin Luther King Jr. who delivered his "I Have a Dream" speech during the March on Washington, August 1963.

E.W. Kenworthy

WASHINGTON, Aug. 28—More than 200,000 Americans, most of them black but many of them white, demonstrated here today for a full and speedy program of civil rights and equal job opportunities. It was the greatest assembly for a redress of grievances that this capital has ever seen.

One hundred years and 240 days after Abraham Lincoln enjoined the emancipated slaves to "abstain from all violence" and "labor faithfully for reasonable wages," this vast throng proclaimed in march and song and through the speeches of their leaders that they were still waiting for the freedom and the jobs.

The march leaders went from the shadows of the Lincoln Memorial to the White House to meet with the President for 75 minutes. Afterward, Mr. Kennedy issued a 400-word statement praising the marchers for the "deep fervor and the quiet dignity" that had characterized the demonstration.

At the Lincoln Memorial early in the afternoon, in the midst of a songfest before the addresses, Josephine Baker, the singer, who had flown from her home in Paris, said to the thousands stretching down both sides of the Reflecting Pool: "You are on the eve of a complete victory. You can't go wrong. The world is behind you." Miss Baker said, as if she saw a dream coming true before her eyes, that "this is the happiest day of my life."

But paradoxically it was Dr. King—who had suffered perhaps most of all—who ignited the crowd with words that might have been written by the sad, brooding man enshrined within.

As he arose, a great roar welled up from the crowd. When he started to speak, a hush fell.

"Even though we face the difficulties of today and tomorrow, I still have a dream," he said.

"It is a dream chiefly rooted in the American dream," he went on.

"I have a dream that one day this nation will rise up and live out the true meaning of its creed: 'We hold these truths to be self-evident, that all men are created equal.'

"I have a dream..." The vast throng listening intently to him roared.

"...that one day on the red hills of Georgia, the sons of former slaves and the sons of former slave-owners will be able to sit together at the table of brotherhood.

"I have a dream..." The crowd roared.

"...that one day even the State of Mississippi, a state sweltering with the heat of injustice, sweltering with the heat of oppression, will be transformed into an oasis of freedom and justice.

"I have a dream..." The crowd roared.

"...that my four little children will one day live in a nation where they will not be judged by the color of their skin but by the content of their character.

As Dr. King concluded with a quotation from a Negro hymn—"Free at last, free at last, thank God almighty"—the crowd, recognizing that he was finishing, roared once again and waved their signs and pennants.

The day dawned clear and cool. At 7 A.M. the town had a Sunday appearance, except for the shuttle buses drawn up in front of Union Station, waiting.

By 10 A.M. there were 40,000 on the slopes around the Washington Monument. An hour later the police estimated the crowd at 90,000. And still they poured in.

There was no violence to mark the demonstration. In fact, at times there was an air of hootenanny about it as groups of schoolchildren clapped hands and swung into the familiar freedom songs.

But if the crowd was good-natured, the underlying tone was one of dead seriousness. The emphasis was on "freedom" and "now." At the same time the leaders emphasized, paradoxically but realistically, that the struggle was just beginning. ■

SEPTEMBER 11, 1963

WALLACE ENDS RESISTANCE AS GUARD IS FEDERALIZED

Claude Sitton

BIRMINGHAM, Ala—Sept, 10— Twenty Negroes attended previously white schools in three Alabama cities today after President Kennedy's federalization of the state's, National Guardsmen ended the defiance of Gov. George C. Wallace.

The police here arrested 12 whites in a "rowdy, two-hour demonstration over the admission of two Negro girls to West End High School under a Federal court order. This coupled with already existing racial tension, raised a threat of further disorder.

No major incidents the desegregation of to other schools here, four in Huntsville—where classes began yesterday and one each in Tuskegee and Mobile. The 425 Guardsmen ordered to active duty by Federal officials remained in their armories.

Combined school attendance here at West End and Graymont elementary school, where two Negroes enrolled, dropped by almost 90 percent. But Ramsay High School, which accepted one Negro, showed a slight increase.

Only some 165 of an expected total of 550 students appeared for classes at the Tuskegee public school, which 13 Negroes are attending. Attendance figures at four Huntsville schools that have one Negro pupil each and at Murphy High School in Mobile, which has two, were near normal.

Governor Wallace conceded at a news conference in the state Capitol in Montgomery that for the second time in three months he had been forced to retreat from a posture of massive resistance to desegregation in education. "I can't fight bayonets with my bare hands," he said.

The Kennedy Administration had given every indication that it would avoid, if possible, any confrontation with the Governor that might result in his arrest. This was the policy in the dispute over desegregation at the University of Alabama last June. Mr. Wallace staged a show of defiance there by blocking two Negro students, but he retreated in the face of National Guardsmen called out by the President. ■

SEPTEMBER 15, 1963

Birmingham Bomb Kills 4 Negro Girls In Church

Claude Sitton

Birmingham, Ala., Sept. 15—A bomb severely damaged a Negro church today during Sunday school services, killing four Negro girls and setting off racial rioting and other violence in which two Negro boys were shot to death.

Fourteen Negroes were injured in the explosion. One Negro and five whites were hurt in the disorders that followed.

Some 500 National Guardsmen in battle dress stood by at armories here tonight, on orders of Gov. George C. Wallace. And 300 state troopers joined the Birmingham police, Jefferson County sheriff's deputies and other law-enforcement units in efforts to restore peace.

Sporadic gunfire sounded in Negro neighborhoods tonight, and small bands of residents roamed the streets. Aside from the patrols that cruised the city armed with riot guns, carbines and shotguns, few whites were seen.

At one point, three fires burned simultaneously in Negro sections, one at a broom and mop factory, one at a roofing company and a third in another building. An incendiary bomb was tossed into a supermarket, but the flames were extinguished swiftly. Fire marshals investigated blazes at two vacant houses to see if arson was involved.

The explosion at the 16th Street Baptist Church this morning brought hundreds of angry Negroes pouring into the streets. Some attacked the police with stones. The police dispersed them by firing shotguns over their heads.

Governor Wallace, at the request of city officials, offered a $5,000 reward for the arrest and conviction of the bombers.

None of the 50 bombings of Negro property here since World War II have been solved.

The bombing came five days after the desegregation of three previously all white schools in Birmingham. The way had been cleared for the desegregation when President Kennedy federalized the Alabama National Guard and the Federal courts issued a sweeping order against Governor Wallace, thus ending his defiance toward the integration step.

The four girls killed in the blast had just heard Mrs. Ella C. Demand, their teacher, complete the Sunday school lesson for the day. The subject was "The Love That Forgives."

During the period between the class and an assembly in the main auditorium, they went to the women's lounge in the basement, at the northeast corner of the church.

The blast occurred at about 10:25 A.M. (12:25 P.M. New York time).

Church members said they found the girls huddled together beneath a pile of masonry debris.

Both parents of each of three of the victims teach in the city's schools. The dead were identified by University Hospital officials as:

Cynthia Wesley, 14, the only child of Claude A. Wesley, principal of the Lewis Elementary School, and Mrs. Wesley, a teacher there.

Denise McNair, 11, also an only child, whose parents are teachers.

Carol Robertson, 14, whose parents are teachers and whose grandmother, Mrs. Sallie Anderson, is one of the Negro members of a biracial committee established by Mayor Boutwell to deal with racial problems.

Addie Mae Collins, 14, about whom no information was immediately available.

The blast blew gaping holes through walls in the church basement. Floors of offices in the rear of the sanctuary appeared near collapse. Stairways were blocked by splintered window frames, glass and timbers.

Chief Police Inspector W. J. Haley said the impact of the blast indicated that at least 15 sticks of dynamite might have caused it. He said the police had talked to two witnesses who reported having seen a car drive by the church, slow down and then speed away before the blast.

KENNEDY KILLED BY SNIPER AS HE RIDES IN CAR IN DALLAS; JOHNSON SWORN IN ON PLANE

Tom Wicker

DALLAS, Nov. 22—President John Fitzgerald Kennedy was shot and killed by an assassin today.

He died of a wound in the brain caused by a rifle bullet that was fired at him as he was riding through downtown Dallas in a motorcade. Vice President Lyndon Baines Johnson, who was riding in the third car behind Mr. Kennedy's, was sworn in as the 36th President of the United States 99 minutes after Mr. Kennedy's death.

Shortly after the assassination, Lee H. Oswald, who once defected to the Soviet Union and who has been active in the Fair Play for Cuba Committee, was arrested by the Dallas police. Tonight he was accused of the killing.

Mr. Johnson, who was uninjured in the shooting, took his oath in the Presidential jet plane as it stood on the runway at Love Field. The body of Mr. Kennedy was aboard. Immediately after the oath-taking, the plane took off for Washington.

Standing beside the new President as Mr. Johnson took the oath of office was Mrs. John F. Kennedy. Her stockings were spattered with her husband's blood.

Gov. John B. Connally Jr. of Texas, who was riding in the same car with Mr. Kennedy, was severely wounded in the chest, ribs and arm. His condition was serious, but not critical.

The killer fired the rifle from a building just off the motorcade route. Mr. Kennedy, Governor Connally and Mr. Johnson had just received an enthusiastic welcome from a large crowd in downtown Dallas.

Mr. Kennedy apparently was hit by the first of what witnesses believed were three shots. He was driven at high speed to Dallas's Parkland Hospital. There, in an emergency operating room, with only physicians and nurses in attendance, he died without regaining consciousness.

Mrs. Kennedy was in the hospital near her husband when he died, but not in the operating room. When the body was taken from the hospital in a bronze coffin about 2 P.M., Mrs. Kennedy walked beside it.

Malcolm Kilduff, the assistant White House press secretary, announced the President's death, with choked voice and red-rimmed eyes, at about 1:36 P.M.

The details of what happened when shots first rang out, as the President's car moved along at about 25 miles an hour, were sketchy. Secret Service agents, who might have given more details, were unavailable to the press at first, and then returned to Washington with President Johnson.

No witnesses reported seeing or hearing any of the Secret Service agents or policemen fire back. One agent was seen to brandish a machine gun as the cars sped away. But the events had occurred so quickly that there was apparently nothing for the men to shoot at.

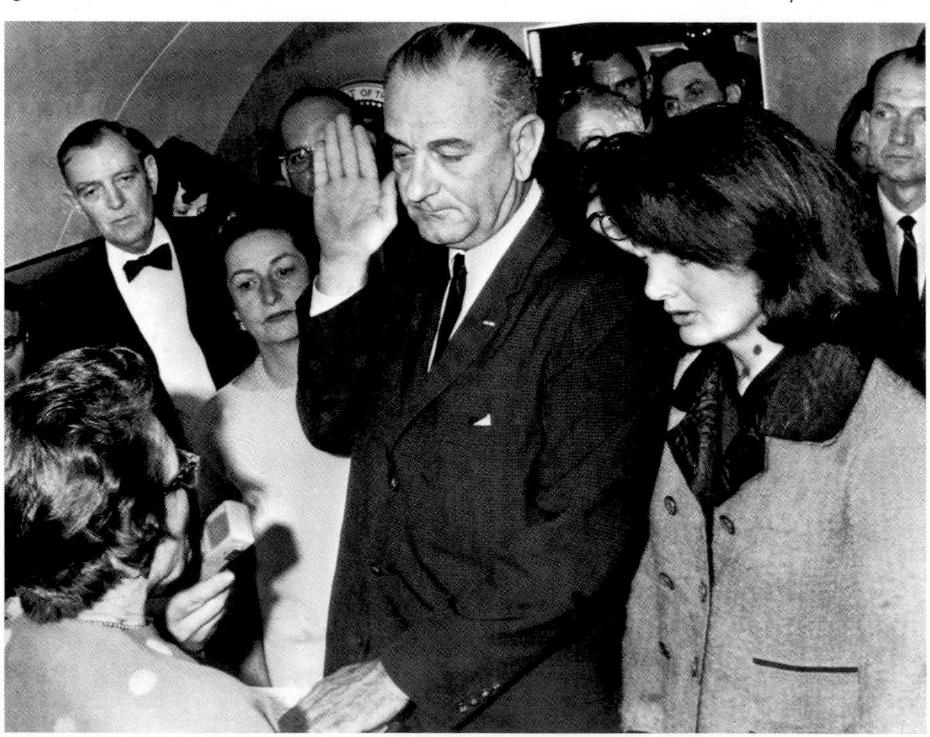

Lyndon B. Johnson being sworn in as president aboard Air Force One with Lady Bird Johnson and Jacqueline Kennedy.

NOVEMBER 25, 1963

NIGHT-CLUB MAN IS OSWALD'S SLAYER

Gladwin Hill

Lee Harvey Oswald being taken into custody by police after allegedly shooting President Kennedy, November 22, 1963.

DALLAS, Nov. 24—President Kennedy's assassin, Lee Harvey Oswald, was fatally shot by a Dallas night-club operator today as the police started to move him from the city jail to the county jail.

The assailant, Jack Rubenstein, known as Jack Ruby, lunged from a cluster of newsmen observing the transfer of Oswald from the jail to an armored truck.

Millions of viewers saw the shooting on television.

As the shot rang out, a police detective suddenly recognized Ruby and exclaimed: "Jack, you son of a bitch!"

A murder charge was filed against Ruby by Assistant District Attorney William F. Alexander. Justice of the Peace Pierce McBride ordered him held without bail.

Oswald was arrested Friday after Mr. Kennedy was shot dead while riding through Dallas in an open car. He was charged with murdering the President and a policeman who was shot a short time later while trying to question Oswald.

As the 24-year-old prisoner, flanked by two detectives, stepped onto a basement garage ramp, Ruby thrust a .38-caliber, snub-nose revolver into Oswald's left side and fired a single shot.

The 52-year-old night-club operator, an ardent admirer of President Kennedy and his family, was described as having been distraught.

District Attorney Henry Wade said he understood that the police were looking into the possibility that Oswald had been slain to prevent him from talking, The Associated Press reported. Mr. Wade said that so far no connection between Oswald and Ruby had been established.

Oswald slumped to the concrete paving, wordlessly clutching his side and writhing with pain.

Oswald apparently lost consciousness very quickly after the shooting. Whether he was at any point able to speak, if he wanted to, was not known.

The politically eccentric warehouse clerk was taken in a police ambulance to the Parkland Hospital, where President Kennedy died Friday. He died in surgery at 1:07 P.M., less than two hours after the shooting. The exact time Oswald was shot was not definitely established.

Four plainclothes men, from a detail of about 50 police officers carrying out the transfer, pounced on Ruby as he fired the shot and overpowered him.

Ruby, who came to Dallas from Chicago 15 years ago, had a police record here listing six allegations of minor offenses. The disposition of five was not noted. A charge of liquor law violation was dismissed. Two of the entries, in July 1953, and May 1954, involved carrying concealed weapons.

Back at the jail, Ruby was taken to the same fourth-floor cellblock where his victim had been the focus of attention the last two days. Reports that filtered out about his preliminary remarks said that he had been impelled to kill President Kennedy's assassin by sympathy for Mrs. Kennedy. It was reported he did not want her to go through the ordeal of returning to Dallas for the trial of Oswald. ■

MARCH 17, 1964

PRESIDENT URGES A $1 BILLION DRIVE AGAINST POVERTY

Marjorie Hunter

WASHINGTON, March 16—President Johnson placed his controversial billion-dollar war on poverty on the Congressional firing line today and declared, "Our objective: total victory."

His long-delayed program, embracing both new proposals and some similar to ones pending in Congress, would focus primarily on two areas:

- Helping 380,000 underprivileged young people—in the first year alone—to break the cycle of poverty through job training and education in camps, centers, communities and campuses. This would cost $412.5 million.

(cont'd. on next page)

(cont'd. from previous page)

- Stimulating local communities throughout the nation into waging antipoverty wars of their own with Federal assistance. This would cost $315 million.

One startling new proposal would authorize Federal loans to nonprofit corporations to acquire rural land and develop it into family-size farms for sale to low-income families.

There are other proposals to create new jobs for the unemployed, to reduce welfare rolls by providing job training for breadwinners and to create a sort of domestic peace corps.

"The war on poverty," Mr. Johnson said in his special message on poverty to Congress, "is not a struggle simply to support people, to make them dependent on the generosity of others. It is a struggle to give people a chance."

Already under attack in some quarters as an election-year bid for votes, the President's program faces an uncertain fate in Congress. Its success could rest largely on the President himself and on the persuasiveness of the man he has named as his "personal chief of staff" for the war against poverty: Sargent Shriver, director of the Peace Corps.

Many parts of the President's program echo proposals made by President Kennedy and already before Congress: a domestic peace corps, work-study for college students, work-training for young people, work-relief for parents of children on welfare rolls and civilian work-training camps for youths.

But Mr. Johnson proposed new programs, too, principally ones to induce community action and to assist rural families. By wrapping all these programs—new and old—into one package, the President hopes to convince Congress that a concerted drive could go far in wiping out poverty in America.

Mr. Johnson declared that his plan "charts a new course." He said it "strikes at the causes, not just the consequences, of poverty."

The program would cost $962.5 million the first year—about 1 per cent of the national budget. The cost in subsequent years has not been determined. ■

OBITUARY

APRIL 6, 1964

MACARTHUR IS DEAD;

LED ALLIED FORCE IN JAPAN'S DEFEAT

Jack Raymond

WASHINGTON, April 5—General of the Army Douglas MacArthur died today after a determined fight for life. He was 84 years old.

The general, who led the Allied victory over Japan in World War II and commanded the United Nations forces in the Korean War, died at 2:39 P.M. at the Walter Reed Army Medical Center, where he had been a patient since March 2. Death was attributed to acute kidney and liver failure.

The general's wife, Jean; their only child, Arthur, 26; and his wartime aide and principal assistant, Maj. Gen. Courtney Whitney, were at the hospital at the end.

President Johnson, leading the nation in mourning, said:

"One of America's greatest heroes is dead. General of the Army Douglas MacArthur fought his last fight with all the valor that distinguished him in war and peace."

Tributes to the general poured in from around the globe.

Mr. Johnson ordered that American flags be flown at half-staff around the world until after the burial next Saturday in the General Douglas MacArthur Memorial in Norfolk, Va.

The body of General MacArthur was taken to New York City, where it will lie in repose Tuesday. On Wednesday, it will be returned to Washington, to lie in state in the Capitol Rotunda until Thursday at noon.

Nineteen-gun salutes will be fired at noon tomorrow and on Saturday at military installations in the United States and in the Pacific area.

General MacArthur, one of the most decorated as well as one of the most controversial American military leaders, was the senior five-star officer at the time of his death.

Born on an Army frontier post in Indian territory, near Little Rock, Ark., on Jan. 26, 1880, General MacArthur had an active military service that spanned nearly half a century before his forced retirement in 1951.

Since his retirement, General MacArthur had served first as chairman of the board of Remington Rand, Inc., and then of the Sperry Rand Corporation.

He had won the Medal of Honor in World War I, served as Chief of Staff of the Army, commanded Allied forces in the Pacific in World War II and the Korean War and headed the occupation forces in Japan.

In the Korean War, however, President Harry S. Truman removed General MacArthur for publicly disputing the war strategy approved by the Joint Chiefs of Staff.

The general, who was at times considered an active candidate for the Republican Presidential nomination, left active service April 12, 1951. In a farewell speech to a joint session of Congress, he observed that "old soldiers never die—they just fade away."

His final battle with death appeared to bear out this self-characterization.

Once before he fooled those who thought he would die when he was operated on in March 1959, for a prostate gland condition at the Lenox Hill Hospital in New York. After a series of grim daily hospital bulletins, he recovered.

This time he entered the Army hospital here on March 2 for observation of abdominal complaints, subsequently diagnosed as obstructive jaundice.

AUGUST 5, 1964

F.B.I. FINDS 3 BODIES BELIEVED TO BE RIGHTS WORKERS

Claude Sitton

JACKSON, Miss., Aug. 4— Bodies believed to be those of three civil rights workers missing since June 21 were found early tonight near Philadelphia, Miss.

Federal Bureau of Investigation agents recovered the bodies from a. newly erected earthen dam in a thickly wooded area about six miles southwest of Philadelphia, in, east-central Mississippi.

The dam is several hundred yards off State Highway 21, near the Neshoba County fairgrounds.

Roy K. Moore, special agent in charge of the Jackson F.B.I. office, said physicians and fingerprint experts would seek to make positive identification and establish the cause of death.

Gov. Paul B. Johnson Jr. of Mississippi said in a statement:

"If these are the bodies of the three civil rights workers who have been missing several weeks, the investigative forces of the State of Mississippi will exert every effort to apprehend those who may have been responsible."

The missing men were Michael H. Schwerner, 24 years old, and Andrew Goodman, 20, both white and both from New York City, and James E. Chaney, 21, a Negro of Meridian, Miss.

All three had been taking part in the Mississippi Summer Project, a state-wide civil rights drive, which began on the weekend of their disappearance. The drive is sponsored by the Council of Federated Organizations, a coalition of civil rights groups.

Mr. Schwerner and Mr. Chaney were members of the Congress of Racial Equality. Mr. Goodman was one of more than 400 student volunteers in the campaign, which is seeking to get Negroes registered to vote.

The three men had left Meridian, their headquarters, on Sunday, June 21, to drive to the site of a burned Negro church in the Longdale community, about 12 miles east of Philadelphia.

After talking with Negroes there, they left to return to Meridian.

Cecil Price, the Neshoba County deputy sheriff, said he had arrested Mr. Chaney late that afternoon for driving 65 miles an hour in a 35-mile-anhour zone and that he had held the two whites "for investigation."

The three were imprisoned at the Neshoba County Jail in Philadelphia until late Sunday night, according to Mr. Price, and were released after Mr. Chaney had posted a $20 bond.

County authorities at first denied that they had any knowledge of the whereabouts of the three, according to civil rights leaders who called them late that Sunday night.

However, Mr. Price said later that he had escorted the late-model Ford station wagon in which the three were riding to the Meridian highway, a short distance from the jail, and had not seen them since. The burned-out station wagon was found the following Tuesday in the Bogue Chitto Swamp, some 30 feet off a highway, 10 miles north of Philadelphia. ■

JULY 3, 1964

PRESIDENT SIGNS CIVIL RIGHTS BILL

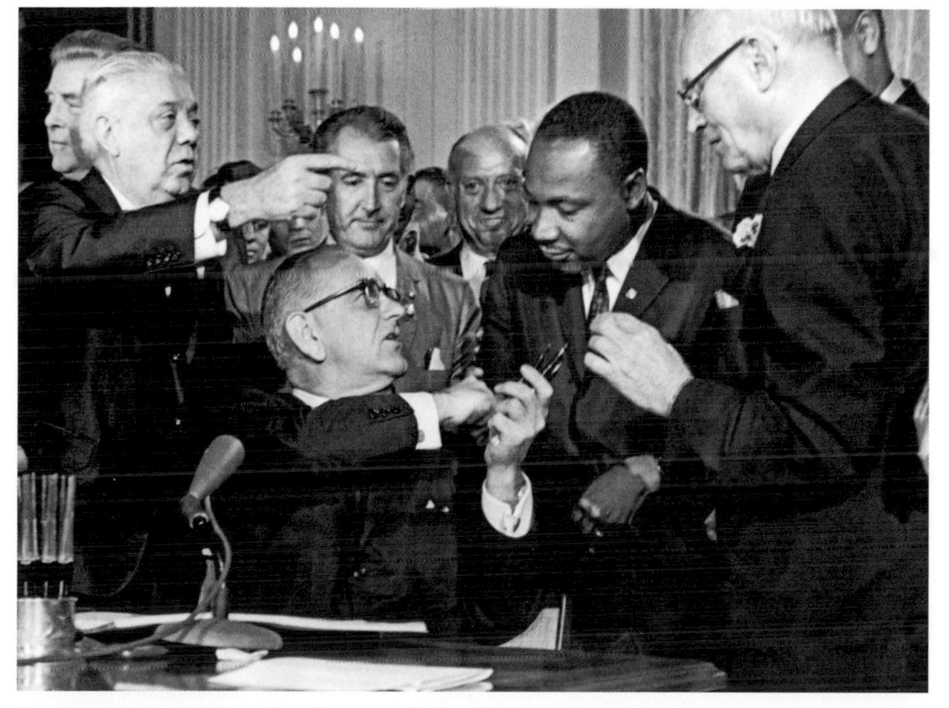

President Lyndon B. Johnson hands a pen to the Rev. Martin Luther King Jr. after signing the historic Civil Rights Bill, July 1964.

E.W. Kenworthy

WASHINGTON, July 2—President Johnson signed the Civil Rights Act of 1964 tonight.

It is the most far-reaching civil rights law since Reconstruction days. The President announced steps to implement it and called on all Americans to help "eliminate the last vestiges of injustice in America."

"Let us close the springs of racial poison," he said in a short television address.

The President signed the bill in the East Room of the White House before television cameras shortly before 7 o'clock. That was about five hours after the House of Representatives had completed Congressional action on the sweeping bill.

Among other things, it prohibits discrimination in places of public accommodation, publicly owned facilities, employment and union membership and Federally aided programs.

The House approved, by a vote of 289 to 126, the changes that the Senate had made.

(cont'd. on next page)

SEPTEMBER 28, 1964

Warren Commission Finds Oswald Guilty and Says Assassin and Ruby Acted Alone

Anthony Lewis

Washington, Sept. 27—The assassination of President Kennedy was the work of one man, Lee Harvey Oswald. There was no conspiracy, foreign or domestic.

That was the central finding in the Warren Commission report, made public this evening. Chief Justice Earl Warren and the six other members of the President's Commission on the Assassination of President John F. Kennedy were unanimous on this and all questions.

The commission found that Jack Ruby was on his own in killing Oswald. It rejected all theories that the two men were in some way connected. It said that neither rightists nor Communists bore responsibility for the murder of the President in Dallas last Nov. 22.

Why did Oswald to it? To this most important and most mysterious question the commission had no certain answer. It suggested that Oswald had no rational purpose, no motive adequate if "judged by the standards of reasonable men."

Rather, the commission saw Oswald's terrible act as the product of his entire life—a life "characterized by isolation, frustration and failure." He was just 24 years old at the time of the assassination.

"Oswald was profoundly alienated from the world in which he lived," the report said. "He had very few, if any, close relationships with other people and he appeared to have had great difficulty in finding a meaningful place in the world.

The commission analyzed every issue in exhaustive, almost archeological detail. Experts traced the path of the bullets. Every critical event was re-enacted. Witnesses here and abroad testified to the most obscure points.

The report often achieves a genuine literary style. The very detail of the narrative is fascinating, and there are many moving passages.

Few who loved John Kennedy, or this country, will be able to read it without emotion.

As the President's motorcade drove through Dallas on Nov. 22, large crowds cheered. Gov. John Connally's wife, who was in the car, said to Mr. Kennedy, "Mr. President, you can't say Dallas doesn't love you." He answered, "That is very obvious."

A moment later the shots were fired.

Mrs. Kennedy, according to the report, "saw the President's skull torn open" by the second bullet that hit him. She testified that she cried out, "Oh, my God! They've shot my husband. I love you, Jack."

The commission found that in all probability three bullets were fired. One of the bullets missed, the report said. It was not certain whether this came before, between or after the two that hit.

The first of the two shots that did not miss hit the President in the lower back of the neck and emerged at the lower front. Mr. Kennedy grabbed at his throat and said, "My God, I'm hit."

"President Kennedy could have survived the neck injury," the commission found. But between 4.8 and 5.6 seconds later—the time was calculated from an amateur movie film—the fatal bullet hit the back of the President's head.

(cont'd. from previous page)

All provisions of the measure became effective with President Johnson's signature except the one prohibiting the discrimination in employment and union membership. This one goes into effect a year from now.

In announcing his implementation program, the President said he was, as had been previously indicated by White House sources, appointing former Gov. LeRoy Collins of Florida as director of the new Community Relations Service. Mr. Collins is now president of the National Association of Broadcasters.

Among other implementation steps, the President said he would name an advisory commission to help Mr. Collins resolve disputes arising under the bill. He will also ask Congress, Mr. Johnson said, for a supplemental appropriation to finance initial operations under the new law.

Surrounded by the leaders of both parties in both houses, who had labored to frame and pass the bill, President Johnson began his address to the nation by recalling that 188 years ago this week, "a small band of valiant men began a struggle for freedom" with the writing of the Declaration of Independence.

That struggle, he said, was a "turning point in history," and the ideals proclaimed in the Declaration of Independence still shape the struggles "of men who hunger for freedom."

Nevertheless, he declared, though Americans believe all men are created equal and have inalienable rights, many in America are denied equal treatment and do not enjoy those rights, or the blessings of liberty, "not because of their own failures, but because of the color of their skins."

The reasons, the President said, can be understood "without rancor or hatred" because they are deeply embedded in history, tradition and the nature of man.

"But it cannot continue," the President said with great earnestness.

The new law—the most sweeping civil rights legislation ever enacted in this country—goes beyond the proscribing of various forms of discrimination.

It gives the Attorney General authority to initiate suits to end discrimination in jobs and public accommodations when he finds such discrimination is part of a practice or pattern. It also gives him new powers to speed school desegregation and enforce the Negro's right to vote.

While the bill provides for the final enforcement of its sanctions by Federal court orders, it also gives state and local agencies primary jurisdiction to deal with complaints for a limited time. ■

OBITUARY

OCTOBER 21, 1964

HERBERT HOOVER IS DEAD; EX-PRESIDENT, 90, SERVED COUNTRY IN VARIED FIELDS

McCandlish Phillips

Herbert Clark Hoover, former President of the United States, died here yesterday at the age of 90.

Death came at 11:35 A.M. in his suite on the 31st floor of the Waldorf Towers, following massive internal bleeding that began Saturday. His two sons were with him as he slipped into a deep coma that kept his final hours free of pain.

Mr. Hoover, born in an Iowa village, the son of a Quaker blacksmith, was an exponent of a credo of personal initiative that he summed up as "rugged individualism," and his life exemplified it.

His parents were poor and he was orphaned at 9, but he amassed a fortune as a mine engineer and owner.

With the start of World War I, he directed the evacuation of 200,000 Americans from Europe. It was the first of a series of massive economic, evacuation and food relief activities that spanned half a century. He was Secretary of Commerce in the Administrations of Harding and Coolidge and was elected President on the Republican ticket in 1928.

The crash of the stock market on Oct. 29, 1929, plunged the nation into its worst economic crisis in history. His policies were attacked as insufficient to spur economic revival. He was voted out of office in 1932 under the cloud of the Great Depression, called the "Hoover Depression" by his opponents.

Some later judgments, however, have suggested that he was the victim of events that coincided with his tenure. And 30 years of public service, including tasks for two Presidents after he left the White House, restored him in the affections of millions.

At news of Mr. Hoover's death, President Johnson proclaimed a 30-day mourning period and ordered the flags lowered to half-staff at the White House and on all Federal buildings and grounds in the nation, on Navy vessels at sea and at embassies and military stations abroad.

NOVEMBER 4, 1964

JOHNSON SWAMPS GOLDWATER AND KENNEDY BEATS KEATING

Tom Wicker

Lyndon Baines Johnson of Texas compiled one of the greatest landslide victories in American history yesterday to win a four-year term of his own as the 36th President of the United States.

Senator Hubert H. Humphrey of Minnesota, Mr. Johnson's running mate on the Democratic ticket, was carried into office as Vice President.

Mr. Johnson's triumph, giving him the "loud and clear" national mandate he had said he wanted, brought 44 states and the district of Columbia, with 486 electoral votes, into the Democratic column.

Senator Barry Goldwater, the Republican candidate, who sought to offer the people "a choice, not an echo" with a strongly conservative campaign, won only five states in the Deep South and gained a narrow victory in his home state of Arizona. Carrying it gave him a total of 52 electoral votes.

A heavy voter turnout favored the more numerous Democrats.

In Austin, Tex., Mr. Johnson appeared in the Municipal Auditorium to say that his victory was "a tribute to men and women of all parties."

The election meant, he said, that "our nation should forget our petty differences and stand united before all the world."

But the totals were not the only marks of the massive Democratic victory. Traditionally Republican states were bowled over like tenpins—Vermont, Indiana, Kansas, Nebraska, Wyoming, among others.

In New York, both houses of the Legislature were headed for Democratic control for the first time in years. Heralded Republicans like Charles H. Percy, the gubernatorial candidate in Illinois, went down to defeat.

Former Attorney General Robert F. Kennedy, riding Mr. Johnson's long coattails, overwhelmed Senator Kenneth B. Keating in New York.

Senator Goldwater had proposed a sharp curtailment of Federal Government activities, particularly in the welfare field and in matters affecting the economy. He had called for a foreign policy of "brinkmanship," in which the nation's military might would be used as a threat against the Communist-bloc nations.

And he had raised doubts whether he would continue to lend Federal influence and authority to the drive for Negro equality in the United States.

Mr. Johnson, in head-on conflict with Mr. Goldwater on almost every campaign issue, thus received decisive endorsement from the nation for the general line of policy pursued by the nation for more than a quarter-century, through Administrations of both parties.

For himself, he won the distinction of being the first candidate from a Southern state to be elected to the White House in more than a hundred years.

And he won a massive vote of approval for the manner in which he had conducted its business since taking over the Presidency when John F. Kennedy was assassinated last Nov. 22. ■

DECEMBER 3, 1964

BERKELEY STUDENTS STAGE SIT-IN TO PROTEST CURB ON FREE SPEECH

Wallace Turner

BERKELEY, Calif., Dec. 2—Demonstrating students took possession of the University of California administration building today.

About 1,000 supporters of the Free Speech Movement moved into the corridors of Sproul Hall at about noon.

Some were still there late tonight. Many slept and others read while still others sang. There was no attempt by the campus police to remove them.

The doors to Sproul Hall were locked at 7 P.M., Pacific standard time (10 P.M., Eastern standard time), as is customary, with many of the demonstrators still inside. Guards at the doors permitted those who wanted to to leave, and a steady stream of departures joined a crowd of about 1,000 outside.

"The time has come for us to put our bodies on the machine and stop it," said Mario Savio, a student leader, in a speech on the steps of the building as the demonstration began. "We will stay until the police remove us."

Mr. Savio, a philosophy major and a frequent speaker in the several months of demonstrations, rejected the plea of the student body's president, Charles Powell, not to demonstrate further.

Mr. Powell had pleaded with a crowd of several thousand gathered in the plaza by the modernistic Students Union Building, "do not do this thing."

The sit-in was one of several that have come about here on this 27,500-student campus since classes began in late September.

There was a near-riot on Oct. 1 when police were prevented for 32 hours from taking away a nonstudent they had arrested.

The issue originally was a plea for the right to recruit and solicit money for off-campus activities. After early demonstrations eight students were suspended, but they were ordered reinstated by the university regents two weeks ago.

The regents also ordered the university administration to enforce discipline on the campus here.

The regents said that students should be able to organize political activities on the campus. They also should be held accountable for their off-campus political activities that had campus beginnings, the regents said. This was a change in the direction sought by the student group.

In the two weeks since then, an uneasy truce has existed.

Last week, letters were mailed by the university administration to Mr. Savio, Arthur Goldberg, his sister Jackie Goldberg and Brian Turner.

They were advised that charges had been made against them in connection with their campaign against the university administration.

The charges included one that they had incited students to resist the police on Oct. 1 when a police car was immobilized. Mr. Savio was also accused of biting a policeman.

Yesterday the Free Speech Movement demanded that the charges against the four be withdrawn, that the university promise that no more charges of similar nature would be made, and that no new rules inhibiting freedom of political activity be made.

Mario Savio, the political activist and key member of the Berkeley Free Speech Movement, addresses a rally at the University of California at Berkeley, 1964.

FEBRUARY 22, 1965

MALCOLM X SHOT TO DEATH AT RALLY

Peter Kihss

Malcolm X, the 39-year-old leader of a militant black nationalist movement, was shot to death yesterday afternoon at a rally of his followers in a ballroom in the Washington Heights area of New York City.

Shortly before midnight, a 22-year-old Negro, Thomas Hagan, was charged with the killing. The police rescued him from the ballroom crowd after he had been shot and beaten.

Malcolm, a bearded extremist, had said only a few words of greeting when a fusillade rang out. The bullets knocked him over backward.

Pandemonium broke out among the 400 Negroes in the Audubon Ballroom at 166th Street and Broadway. As men, women and children ducked under tables and flattened themselves on the floor, more shots were fired. Some witnesses said 30 shots had been fired.

About two hours later the police said the shooting had apparently been a result of a feud between followers of Malcolm and members of the extremist group he broke with last year, the Black Muslims. However, the police declined to say whether Hagan is a Muslim.

Malcolm, a slim, reddish-haired six-footer with a gift for bitter eloquence against what he considered white exploitation of Negroes, broke in March 1964 with the Black Muslim movement called the Nation of Islam, headed by Elijah Muhammad.

Assemblyman Percy Sutton, Malcolm's lawyer, said the murdered leader had planned to disclose at yesterday's rally, "the names of those who were trying to kill him." Mr. Sutton added that Malcolm had taken to carrying a pistol "because he feared for his life" and had notified the police by telephone that he was doing so even though he did not have a permit. Assistant Chief Inspector Taylor, however, said Malcolm was unarmed when he was shot.

While the Nation of Islam searches for weapons on anyone attending its meetings, Malcolm's new movement emphasized self-defense even with weapons. And so there was no search of anyone at yesterday's rally, a regular Sunday affair of Malcolm's Organization of Afro-American Unity. White persons were barred.

Former Nation of Islam leader and civil rights activist El-Hajj Malik El-Shabazz (aka Malcolm X) in February 1965.

A woman who was wearing a green scarf and a black felt hat with little floral buds, and who would identify herself only as a registered nurse, said she had seen "two men rushing toward the stage and firing from underneath their coats."

"I rushed to the stage even while the firing was going on," she said. "I don't know how I got on the stage, but I threw myself down on who I thought was Malcolm—but it wasn't. I was willing to die for the man. I would have taken the bullets myself. Then I saw Malcolm, and the firing had stopped, and I tried to give him artificial respiration.

"I think he was dead then."

Malcolm was placed on a stretcher and wheeled one block up Broadway to the Vanderbilt Clinic emergency entrance at 167th Street. A team of doctors cut through his chest to massage his heart. But Malcolm was "either dead or in a death-appearing state," the spokesman said. The effort was given up at 3:30 P.M. ■

AUGUST 8, 1965

U.S. ACTS TO ENFORCE NEW VOTING RIGHTS ACT

John Herbers

WASHINGTON, Aug. 7—The Government began today to enforce the Voting Rights Act of 1965, which was signed into law by President Johnson yesterday. Enforcement began in two phases.

First, literacy tests as a prerequisite to voting were suspended in seven states—Alabama, Alaska, Georgia, Louisiana, Mississippi, South Carolina and Virginia—and in 26 counties of North Carolina and one county in Arizona.

Second, the Justice Department filed suit in the United States District Court in Jackson, Miss., to abolish the Mississippi poll tax as a requirement for voting in state and local elections. The department will file similar suits Tuesday in the other poll tax states—Texas, Alabama and Virginia.

About 45 Federal voting examiners, all employees of the Civil Service Commission, were standing by in the Deep South, waiting to move into 15 to 20 counties that have a history of resistance to Negro voting. These counties are to be designated Monday by the Justice Department, and the examiners will begin registering eligible Negroes on Tuesday.

The new act, a landmark in civil rights legislation, is expected to result in the addition of several hundred thousand Negroes to the voter registration rolls of the Deep South in the next year or so.

In signing the bill yesterday in a ceremony at the Capitol, President Johnson said: "Congress acted swiftly in passing this act. I intend to act with equal dispatch in order to enforce it."

Suits testing the constitutionality of the law can be filed in the United States District Court in the District of Columbia. But there is no provision for delaying the effect of the law while such a suit is being adjudicated.

The Civil Service Commission published today regulations that will govern the action of examiners in registering voters. The regulations made it clear that an applicant could not be rejected because he could not sign his name.

(cont'd. on next page)

(cont'd. from previous page)

Registration of illiterates is expected to be the main point of opposition to the act in the South. Literacy tests will continue to be in use in about a dozen other states outside the South that are not covered by the act.

The Justice Department, however, has contended that white illiterates have been registered in all of the states and counties covered by the law.

"This just extends to the Negro the same opportunities that have been in existence for whites," a Justice Department spokesman said.

The Justice Department, which has wide discretion under the act, will give other counties covered by the act a period of time to achieve voluntary compliance before examiners are sent in.

"We don't want to build up an unnecessary bureaucracy," a department spokesman said. ■

AUGUST 14, 1965

TROOPS ENTER L.A. ON THIRD DAY OF RIOTING

Peter Bart

Armed National Guardsmen during the street fires of the Watts riots, Los Angeles, California, August 1965.

LOS ANGELES, Saturday, Aug. 14—Two thousand heavily armed National Guardsmen moved into Los Angeles last night to battle rioters in the burning and looted Negro area. The Guardsmen were under orders to use rifles, machine guns, tear gas and bayonets in support of a battered contingent of 900 policemen and deputy sheriffs.

Four persons were killed in the rioting yesterday, including three Negroes and a police officer. Thirty-three police officers had been injured, 75 civilians seriously injured, and 249 rioters had been arrested. This morning violence spread to white areas.

The National Guardsmen were being brought into the riot zone early this morning in small convoys led by jeeps with machine guns mounted on them. The convoys contained one or two troop carriers. One Guard unit opened machine-gun fire for 10 minutes on a gang of Negroes who then fled down the street. One Guardsman said the rioters fired with pistols and at least one rifle. No one was apparently hit. The Guardsmen continued to penetrate the riot area.

"They've got weapons and ammo," one Guard spokesman said. "It's going to be like Vietnam."

Throughout the Negro section, crowds numbering in the thousands were chanting, "White devils what are you doing here?"

Officials reported that they had abandoned efforts to halt a fire sweeping a three-block section after Negroes hurled fire bombs and rocks at the fire fighters. Negro youths later took complete control of another two-block area and set 15 fires to homes and stores.

As many as 14 fires were raging on one street alone—103rd Street in Watts—and it was believed that not a single business in that commercial center would remain intact. Most of the stores are believed owned by whites.

The rattle of gunfire was heard increasingly in the Negro section during the hot, smoggy evening as the police confronted roving bands of rampaging Negroes. The Negroes, in three days and nights, have looted uncounted stores, overturned and burned more than 150 automobiles and set over 100 fires.

The 150-block section of Los Angeles last night took on the appearance of a war zone with men crouching in the shadows, streets littered with debris or completely torn up, store windows broken and scorched and a pall of smoke hanging over the area.

The rioting started Wednesday night after a routine drunken-driving arrest near the predominantly Negro Watts section of Los Angeles. It was resumed Thursday night when some 7,000 Negroes took to the streets.

Sociologists were divided on the causes of the riots. Some blamed Negro resentment over civil rights strife in the South, while others cited a lack of communication between the whites and Negroes.

"It's guerrilla warfare," said Chief of Police William H. Parker. As the night wore on the warfare seemed to be shifting steadily north toward downtown Los Angeles.

Helicopters operated by the police and by radio and television stations covering the riots were repeatedly fired upon by Negroes on the ground.

Mayor Samuel Yorty tonight said it might be several days before the situation is in complete control. The riots were being spearheaded by "the criminal element," he said.

Witnesses described the scene inside the riot zone as "terrifying" and "hysterical." One Negro merchant said a pack of shrieking Negro teenagers suddenly hurtled into his store. Within minutes he said they had looted the store and set it afire.

Witnesses at the riot scene described a bizarre atmosphere.

"Everything seems calm for a moment, then suddenly there's a pack coming down on you," a Negro minister said. ■

OCTOBER 1, 1965

CONGRESS APPROVES IMMIGRATION REFORM BILL

Cabell Phillips

WASHINGTON, Sept. 30—Congress approved and sent to the White House today a historic and far-reaching reform of the nation's immigration law. President Johnson promptly announced he would sign the bill Sunday at the Statue of Liberty in New York Harbor.

The main purpose of the bill is to strike from the law the national origins quota system. Under this arrangement, first incorporated in the law in 1924, immigrant quotas are allotted to countries on the basis of the representation of their nations in this country under the 1920 census.

This system greatly favored Britain and the countries of northern Europe at the expense of southern Europe and the countries of Asia and Africa.

In place of the country quotas, the new bill assigns an overall quota of 170,000 annually to all countries of the world excluding those in the Western Hemisphere. This quota is available on a first-come, first-served basis but with the stipulation that not more than 20,000 immigrants may be admitted from any one country in a given year.

Another principal feature of the bill is that it establishes, for the first time, a ceiling on immigration from the countries of the Western Hemisphere. This limitation which was opposed by the Administration, is set at 120,000 immigrants annually, exclusive of the husbands, wives, unmarried children and parents of persons who already are citizens of or resident aliens in the United States.

The bill passed today supplants most existing legislation on the admission of refugees by setting up an annual quota of 10,200 for this purpose exclusively.

Mr. Johnson, who will remain in New York overnight to meet with Pope Paul VI on Monday, will be the first President to visit the statue since Franklin D. Roosevelt went there on Oct. 28, 1936, to mark the 50th anniversary of its dedication. ■

JULY 3, 1966

WHY THE CRY FOR 'BLACK POWER'

Gene Roberts

ATLANTA, Ga., July 2—The Student Nonviolent Coordinating Committee's "black consciousness" philosophy and its "black power" chant were formally unveiled on the recent civil rights march through Mississippi, but they grew out of six years of cumulative anger on the part of student committee members.

This anger has been given fuel by incident after incident, disappointment after disappointment, in the drive for civil rights. In the minds of the student committee members, the most damning indictment of white society is the fact that there have been more than 30 civil rights killings in the last decade and only three convictions—none for more than 10 years.

The black power movement is not "black nationalism" in the sense that the term is normally used. It is not paramilitary or dedicated to all-black states or to the transport of Negroes back to Africa. And, unlike the Black Muslims, it does not exclude whites—providing that they are willing to join on the student committee's terms.

All in all, the philosophy tells Negroes that white society has failed them, that American democracy is a collection of impressive catchwords that command only lip service from the white man, that the Negro is as good if not better than the white man, and that his only salvation lies in seizing political power wherever he possesses the numerical strength to outvote the white man.

After six years of being the cutting edge of the civil rights movement, of being frightened and jailed more times than they care to remember, many student committee members are not too weary to listen to the argument against their new philosophy—that civil rights murders and nonviolent reaction have led to legislation while riots and retaliation have produced reaction and inaction.

Perhaps Stokely Carmichael, the student committee chairman, who at 24 has been jailed 27 times and has seen friends die in the civil rights cause, summed up the new mood of the student committee best just ten days ago. It was after 2,500 Negroes and white supporters had been routed by tear gas from a public school for Negroes in Canton, Miss., where they had been trying to pitch tents for the civil rights march.

Two student committee members held up Mr. Carmichael, who had been immobilized by tear gas fumes, anger and emotional exhaustion. "I'm so tired, so weary, so tired," Mr. Carmichael said again and again before disappearing with his friends into the darkness. ■

OCTOBER 2, 1966

MIRANDA V. ARIZONA

The Miranda decision of the Supreme Court takes its name from one of four cases in which the Court last June 13 reversed convictions of men who had confessed to crimes of rape, robbery and murder. In the best-known case, Ernesto A. Miranda, a 25-year-old mentally retarded Arizonian, was convicted of kidnapping and raping an 18-year-old girl and received concurrent 20-to-30-year sentences. After having been identified in the police lineup by the girl, he had admitted the crime but he was not effectively warned of his right to counsel or that his statements could be used against him.

The principals in the three other cases were:

Michael Vignera, sentenced in Kings County Court, N.Y., to 30-to-60 years' imprisonment for robbing a Brooklyn dress shop. He had been detained 24 hours before the police brought him before a judge, and he had been held for about 12 hours before he had confessed. He was not advised of his right to counsel or other rights.

Carl Calvin Westover, sentenced in San Francisco to 15 years' imprisonment for the armed robbery of a bank and two savings and loan associations in Sacramento. He had been informed of his right to counsel but was held incommunicado and had no opportunity to obtain a lawyer during his 17 hours of interrogation.

Roy Allen Stewart, sentenced to death in Los Angeles after being convicted of robbery and murder in a purse-snatching in which the victim died of injuries. He had been held for five days during which, except for one confrontation by an accuser, he had seen no one but the police. He was questioned nine different times and confessed during the ninth interrogation; there was no indication that he had at any time been advised of his rights.

In the 5-to-4 decision reversing Miranda's conviction, Chief Justice Earl Warren delivered the majority opinion, declaring: "We hold that when an individual is taken into custody or otherwise deprived of his freedom by the authorities and is subjected to questioning, the privilege against self-incrimination is jeopardized. Procedural safeguards must be employed to protect the privilege..."

Bitter dissents were filed by Justices Tom C. Clark, John M. Harlan, Potter Stewart and Byron R. White. In his opinion, Justice White observed: "More than the human dignity of the accused is involved; the human personality of others in the society must also be preserved. Thus the values reflected by the privilege are not the sole desideratum; society's interest in the general security is of equal weight."

NOVEMBER 9, 1966

REAGAN ELECTED GOVERNOR BY WIDE MARGIN

Lawrence E. Davies

LOS ANGELES, Nov. 8—Republican Ronald Reagan was elected Governor of California tonight, defeating Gov. Edmund G. Brown, a two-term Democrat.

The Republican nominee, a movie and television actor seeking office for the first time, took an early lead, which grew to commanding proportions as the vote was counted.

A smiling Governor Brown, with his wife at his side, stood before massed supporters at the Ambassador Hotel late tonight and conceded the election to Mr. Reagan. Groans and shouts of protest greeted his words. While Governor Brown spoke at the Ambassador, the loudspeakers were turned up in the Biltmore Bowl so that the crushing crowd of Reagan admirers could hear the Governor's acknowledgement of defeat.

A full minute of pandemonium followed. The band played, a surging throng knocked over two policemen and an enormous "Reagan for President" banner was promptly unfurled.

Mr. Reagan, emerging from his hotel room to go to his victory celebration, was asked what he considered the significance of the outcome. "It seems to be all over the country," he said. "The people seem to have shown that maybe we have moved too fast, and want to pause and reconsider the course we've been following."

Ronald Reagan campaigning during the 1966 California gubernatorial race.

"Republican" cloudy skies that dripped rain over parts of conservative Southern California failed to hold down the vote. Traditionally a light vote is interpreted in this state as a vote of the "dedicated" core of the electorate, usually applied to Republicans. But "Democratic sunshine" prevailed in many areas and gave that party fresh hope.

Returns put a crowd at Reagan election night headquarters at the Biltmore Hotel in a festive mood. Predominantly middle-aged, well-dressed, well-behaved supporters of the actor-rancher overflowed the ballroom and prepared for a victory celebration that they sensed was in the offing.

A huge cake with the inscription, "Congratulations Governor Reagan" occupied the center of a long buffet table in the Biltmore Bowl.

The ruggedly handsome, 55-year-old Mr. Reagan and his wife, Nancy, voted at 9:15 A.M. at nearby Pacific Palisades, where the candidate said the race would be close despite the pollsters. Asking reporters, "How do you vote with your fingers crossed?" he added with a smile that had become a campaign trademark: "This is the beginning of the longest day in the world."

The election, with its bearing on the 1968 national campaign, ended a long and arduous campaign in which ideology, and during the last several weeks, charges of racism, had supplanted usually accepted issues in the public's mind. Each side accused the other of "smears" and each candidate denied responsibility for any scurrility attributed to his supporters.

More than a year and a half ago Mr. Reagan had considered the gubernatorial race at the urging of conservative Republicans. They had been impressed with his speaking and money-raising ability as co-chairman of Barry Goldwater's unsuccessful 1964 California contest against President Johnson.

The movie and television actor, who had once been a liberal Democrat, then a Goldwater conservative, sought in his 1966 campaign to unify California's Republican party, divided by the bitter 1964 Presidential primary between Senator Goldwater and Governor Rockefeller of New York. Meanwhile, his newly hired public relations concern, Spencer Roberts & Associates, set out to change his public image to that of a middle-of-the-road Republican. ■

NOVEMBER 19, 1966

MEATLESS FRIDAYS WILL END FOR U.S. CATHOLICS

George Dugan

WASHINGTON, Nov. 18—American Roman Catholics will no longer be required to abstain from meat on Fridays.

A pastoral statement by the National Conference of American Bishops, meeting in annual session at Catholic University, said that the abstinence requirement would end Dec. 2.

Exceptions to the dispensation are the Fridays during the 40-day Lenten period and Ash Wednesday, the first day of Lent.

The lifting of the meatless Friday law is in accord with reforms advocated by the Second Vatican Council to bring the practices of the church in line with modern conditions.

Catholic leaders agree that in the world of the 20th century, dietary habits have become irrelevant as a means of penance. It is their feeling that penance would be more meaningful if works of charity and other forms of personal penance were substituted for abstinence and fasting.

The sin of eating meat on Friday can be abrogated by the American hierarchy because it pertains to church law or discipline and not Divine law.

National episcopal conferences have been granted the authority to determine their own forms of penance by Rome. The more than 200 bishops who attended the meeting here are the spiritual leaders of some 46 million Catholics.

The abolishment of meatless Fridays, in effect, will start next Friday as most American Catholics are traditionally dispensed from Friday abstinence on the day after Thanksgiving. The Archdiocese of New York has already declared this dispensation.

The pastoral statement issued today reflected these concepts.

"For all other week days of Lent," the statement said, "we strongly recommend participation in daily mass and a self-imposed observance of fasting. In the light of grave human needs which weigh on the Christian conscience in all seasons, we urge particularly during Lent, generosity to local, national and world programs of sharing of all things needed to translate our duty to penance into a means of implementing the right of the poor to their part in our abundance."

It would bring great glory to God and good to souls if Fridays found our people doing volunteer work in hospitals, visiting the sick, serving the needs of the aged and the lonely, instructing the young in the faith, participating as Christians in community affairs, and meeting our obligations to our families, our friends, our neighbors and our community, including our parishes, with a special zeal born of the desire to add the merit of penance to the other virtues exercised in good works born of living faith."

A statement issued by Archbishop John F. Dearden of Detroit, president of the National Conference of Catholic Bishops, said in part:

"I believe that I express the sentiments of the bishops of the United States when I state that we have resolved this week to carry out the spirit of the Second Vatican Council by inaugurating the implementation of its directives in this country. With further study, reflection, prayer and God's grace, we will revitalize the church in our nation for the years ahead." ■

NOVEMBER 22, 1966

WOMEN MEET TO DEMAND 'TRUE EQUALITY'

Lisa Hammel

Although no one in the dim ruby and sapphire Victorian parlor actually got up and cried: "Women of the world, unite! You have nothing to lose but your chains," that was the prevailing sentiment yesterday morning at the crowded press conference held by the newly formed National Organization for Women.

NOW, which is the organization's urgent acronym, was formed three weeks ago in Washington to press for "true equality for all women in America...as part of the world-wide revolution of human rights now taking place."

The organization has been informally styled by several of its directors the "N.A.A.C.P. of women's rights."

The board of directors asked President Johnson, in the text of a letter released yesterday, to give "top priority among legislative proposals for the next Congress to legislation which would give effective enforcement powers to the Equal Employment Opportunity Commission," which, the letter stated, "is hampered...by a reluctance among some of its male members to combat sex discrimination as vigorously as they seek to combat racial discrimination."

"As part of the Great Society program," the letter to the President read, "your administration is currently engaged in a massive effort to bring underprivileged groups—victims of discrimination because of poverty, race or lack of education—into the mainstream of American life. However, no comprehensive effort has yet been made to include women in your Great Society program for the underprivileged and excluded."

The press conference was held amid the dark Victorian curlicues and oriental carpeting in the apartment of the organization's president, Betty Friedan. Mrs. Friedan, who became a household word when she gave "the problem that has no name" the name of "The Feminine Mystique" in a bestseller

(cont'd. on next page)

(cont'd. from previous page)
published three years ago, explained in her book to disgruntled housewives across the country that they had been sold a bill of goods by society.

Speaking in a gravelly alto from the depths of the large fur collar that trimmed her neat black suit, the ebullient author suggested that women today were "in relatively little position to influence or control major decisions."

"But," she added, leaning forward in the lilac velvet Victorian chair and punching the air as if it were something palpable, "what women do have is the vote.

"We will take strong steps in the next election," Mrs. Friedan continued, "to see that candidates who do not take seriously the question of equal rights for women are defeated."

"This is not a feminist movement," said Sister Mary Joel Read, chairman of the department of history at Alverno College in Milwaukee. "It is not a question of getting male privileges. In the past the possibility of realizing one's humanity was limited to an elite group at the top. Women are not equal in our society. This movement centers around the possibility of being human." ■

Betty Friedman, feminist and founding member of the National Organization of Women (NOW), in 1969.

JUNE 6, 1967

SPECK IS SENTENCED TO CHAIR FOR SERIAL MURDERS

Donald Janson

PEORIA, Ill., June 5—Richard F. Speck was sentenced to death in the electric chair today for the murders last summer in Chicago of eight young nurses.

The 25-year-old drifter stood mute and expressionless a foot in front of the bench as Circuit Court Judge Herbert C. Paschen ordered the execution for Sept. 1.

Before sentence was passed, the public defender, Gerald W. Getty, told the judge that the lanky, itinerant seaman had nothing to say in his own behalf.

A jury of seven men and five women found Speck guilty of each of the murders last April 15 after a two-week trial. It recommended the death penalty.

Judge Paschen could have imposed a prison term of not less than 14 years instead of following the jury's recommendation.

Judge Paschen stayed Speck's death order pending an appeal to the Illinois Supreme Court. Review by the Supreme Court is mandatory in Illinois in death sentences.

The court session lasted nine minutes. Speck, in a black cardigan sweater and open-necked white shirt, entered the sparkling new walnut and marble courtroom of the Peoria County Courthouse with a grin on his pock-marked face.

While the white-haired judge was passing sentence, Speck glanced back over his shoulder at the crowded gallery. Four of the fathers of the victims were among the spectators.

The drifter, a native of nearby Monmouth, Ill., stood with his hands clenched behind him as Judge Paschen ordered that he be executed "by causing to pass through the body...a current of electricity of sufficient intensity to cause death."

Speck shrugged as officers led him from the courtroom. He was manacled and driven immediately to the Illinois State Penitentiary at Joliet.

Judge Paschen assigned Mr. Getty to make the automatic appeal for the indigent defendant. He ordered, however, that if any books or articles are written that produce income for Speck, the funds must be applied to the costs of the trial.

Dr. Marvin Ziporyn, former Cook County jail psychiatrist who spent 100 hours interviewing Speck while he was being held for trial, has said that Speck suffered brain damage from multiple head injuries during his childhood. After the trial ended, Dr. Ziporyn said that this brain damage, in combination with the drugs and liquor Speck took before the murders, had left the killer "not responsible for his actions."

The jury, hearing the case in Peoria on a change of venue because of "prejudicial" publicity in Chicago last summer, deliberated only 49 minutes in finding Speck guilty.

The state based its case on fingerprints identified as Speck's that were found in the dormitory townhouse where the girls were knifed and strangled July 14, and on identification of Speck as the killer by the sole survivor.

Miss Corazon Amurao, a 24-year-old Filipino, survived the night of terror by rolling, although bound by the wrists and ankles, under a double-decked bunk bed in the townhouse near South Chicago Community Hospital.

The victims of the slaughter were Gloria Jean Davy, 22; Patricia Ann Matusek, 20; Nine Jo Schmale, 24; Suzanne Farris, 21; Mary Ann Jordan, 20; Pamela Wilkening, 20; Merlita Gargullo, 23; and Valentina Pasion, 23.

The first six were student nurses at the hospital. The other two were registered exchange nurses from the Philippines.

In court today, as they had been frequently during the trial and hearings since the crime was committed, were Joseph Matusek, Charles Davy, John Farris and John Wilkening, fathers of four of the murdered girls. ■

JUNE 13, 1967

JUSTICES UPSET ALL BANS ON INTERRACIAL MARRIAGE

WASHINGTON, June 12—The Supreme Court ruled unanimously today that states cannot outlaw marriages between whites and nonwhites.

The opinion by Chief Justice Earl Warren was directed specifically at the antimiscegenation laws of Virginia, which had been challenged by Richard P. Loving, a white man, and his part-Negro, part-Indian wife, Mildred. However, the wording was sufficiently broad and disapproving to leave no doubt that the antimiscegenation laws of 15 other states are also now void.

"We have consistently denied the constitutionality of measures which restrict the rights of citizens on account of race," Chief Justice Warren said. "There can be no doubt that restricting the freedom to marry solely because of racial classifications violates the central meaning of the [Constitution's] equal protection clause."

In writing the opinion that struck down the last group of segregation laws to remain standing—those requiring separation of the races in marriage—Chief Justice Warren completed the process that he set in motion with his opinion in 1954 that declared segregation in public schools to be unconstitutional.

He rejected the argument by Virginia that the framers of the 14th Amendment had not intended to invalidate the many antimiscegenation laws in effect at that time. While history casts some light on the proper interpretation of the amendment, it is not conclusive, he said.

Chief Justice Warren rejected the reasoning that had prompted the Supreme Court to uphold antimiscegenation legislation once before, when it considered the Alabama statute in 1883. The Court held then that the law did not discriminate against Negroes, since whites could be equally punished for violating it.

In today's opinion the Court followed the theory of the earlier desegregation cases that racial classifications in state laws are constitutionally odious, even if the punishments are even-handed.

Virginia's "racial integrity law" was unusual in that it forbade whites to marry "colored persons," but did not prohibit the union of Negroes and members of other races.

A "white person" was defined as one who "has no trace whatsoever of any blood other than Caucasian," with the exception of a special saving clause for certain Indians, designed to protect the descendants of Pocahontas and John Rolfe.

In a footnote, Chief Justice Warren said that this quirk in the Virginia law does not save other antimiscegenation laws from being affected by today's ruling.

The other states that have these laws are Alabama, Arkansas, Delaware, Florida, Kentucky, Louisiana, Mississippi, Missouri, North Carolina, Oklahoma, South Carolina, Tennessee, Texas and West Virginia.

The Lovings are natives of Caroline County, near Richmond. They were married in the District of Columbia in 1958. When they returned to Virginia they were prosecuted under the antimiscegenation law, which allows a sentence of up to five years in prison. ■

Supreme Court Chief Justice Earl Warren, 1965.

JUNE 14, 1967

MARSHALL FIRST NEGRO FOR HIGH COURT

Roy Reed

Thurgood Marshall (left) with President Lyndon Johnson, following Marshall's appointment as a member of the Supreme Court in 1967, making him the first African American to hold the post.

WASHINGTON, June 13—President Johnson named Solicitor General Thurgood Marshall to the Supreme Court today. Mr. Marshall, the great-grandson of a slave, will be the first Negro to serve on the Court if the Senate confirms him.

He is the best-known Negro lawyer of the century because of his battles against segregation. Southerners in the Senate once delayed his appointment to the Federal judiciary for several months. But judging from initial reaction in the Senate today, his confirmation to the Court seems likely.

Non-Southern Senators applauded the appointment and Southerners accepted it, at least for the moment, in silence.

It had been expected for years that Mr. Marshall would eventually become the first Negro justice, but recent speculation had given him no special edge over other prospective nominees at this time.

The President, as is his custom, gave no advance hint of his selection. Reporters were unexpectedly called into the White House Rose Garden outside his office shortly before noon.

Blinking in the sun, Mr. Johnson stepped in front of the microphones and matter-of-factly announced what may be the most dramatic appointment of his Presidency.

Mr. Marshall stood by with his hands in his pockets, his usually mobile face solemn, as the President told of his nomination. "I believe he has already earned his place in history," Mr. Johnson said. "But I think it will be greatly enhanced by his service on the Court."

Mr. Johnson declared that Mr. Marshall had earned the appointment by his "distinguished record" in the law. He added: "He is best qualified by training and by very valuable service to the country. I believe it is the right thing to do, the right time to do it, the right man and the right place."

Mr. Marshall was the towering figure of the legal phase of the Negro's fight for equality in this century. He tried and won dozens of lawsuits striking down discriminatory laws, including the suit that led to the Supreme Court's 1954 decision outlawing school segregation.

That case and other school suits—he was involved in such notable battles as the desegregation of the schools of Little Rock and New Orleans—once cast considerable doubt on his chances of sitting on the Supreme Court. Powerful Southerners in the Senate saw him as one of the nation's baleful influences.

But in recent years he has become identified with a more moderate element of Negro leadership, in large part because younger men have emerged as more militant. And he has now proved his acceptability to the Senate twice, winning its confirmation first as a Federal judge and then as Solicitor General.

The appointment was hailed by Negro leaders, including the Rev. Dr. Martin Luther King Jr., president of the Southern Christian Leadership Conference; Roy Wilkins, executive director of the National Association for the Advancement of Colored People; and Whitney M. Young Jr., executive director of the National Urban League.

Chief Justice Earl Warren said he was "very happy" about the appointment. As the President did, Mr. Warren pointed to Mr. Marshall's long legal experience.

One Southerner who made his opposition clear was Senator Strom Thurmond, Republican of South Carolina. He said that Mr. Marshall had many qualifications "from the standpoint of both training and experience," but would add another liberal voice to the Court. He said he had opposed Court nominations for that reason. ■

justice

U.S. TROOPS SENT INTO DETROIT; 19 DEAD; JOHNSON DECRIES RIOTS

Gene Roberts

Wreckage after fires during the riots in Detroit, late July 1967.

DETROIT, Tuesday, July 25—President Johnson rushed 4,700 Army paratroopers into Detroit at midnight last night as Negro snipers besieged two police stations in rioting that brought near-paralysis to the nation's fifth largest city.

The death toll stood at 19, and damage from fire and looting—estimated by police at $150 million—was worse than in any riot in the country's history.

Tanks rumbled into the city's East Side to rescue more than 100 policemen and National Guardsmen who were trapped inside the precinct houses. Negro snipers fired into windows and doors, and policemen and Guardsmen fought back with machine guns, shotguns and high-velocity rifles.

"It looks like Berlin in 1945," said Mayor Jerome P. Cavanagh, who along with Gov. George Romney had met with resistance from the White House in trying to have the Federal troops put into action here immediately.

Mayor Cavanagh and Gov. George Romney had pleaded with Cyrus H. Vance, the President's personal representative here, until just before midnight when a reluctant White House finally agreed to send the paratroopers into action.

Hundreds of new fires were reported, bringing the total in two days of violence to more than 731. Large areas of the city were blanketed in smoke.

Thousands of workers stayed away from their jobs, scores of downtown restaurants and businesses shut down and two airlines—Tag and Commuter—canceled their night flights for fear of sniper fire.

Meanwhile, the arrest total climbed to nearly 2,000. More than 800 were injured, including 20 policemen and 15 firemen.

Late at night, the police and National Guardsmen were battling with snipers entrenched in apartment buildings. They are also spreading to the south.

Variety stores and shops of every description were put to the torch over a 14-square-mile-area of the city. Windows were smashed at Saks Fifth Avenue in the shadow of the General Motors headquarters.

Property damage in the city was already three times greater than that in the Watts area of Los Angeles in 1965, when rioting destroyed $40 million to $50 million in property and claimed 35 lives.

Death tolls higher than Detroit's also occurred in interracial rioting in East St. Louis and Houston, Tex., in 1917; Chicago in 1919, Detroit in 1943 and in Newark this month. But property damage in all of these riots was only a fraction of that in Detroit this week.

The rioting started at 3 A.M. on Sunday with a police raid on a Negro speakeasy. The police tried to contain the violence, but fired only at snipers under what they said were orders from City Hall.

But with the rioting spreading, the police and National Guardsmen began firing

(cont'd. on next page)

(cont'd. from previous page)
at looters, and within three hours five Negroes died of gunshot wounds.

Many of Detroit's leaders had hoped that the city would escape racial violence. Under Mr. Cavanagh, Detroit had fashioned one of the nation's most aggressive urban renewal and antipoverty programs. Spending totaled more than $250 million in recent years and was still climbing when the riot flared.

But despite all the efforts, Negro unemployment ranged from 6 to 8 percent a year, about double the national average for all races, and pockets of substandard housing still remain.

Anti-white feeling ran high on 12th Street in the heart of the city's major Negro ghetto, but elsewhere—and especially in integrated neighborhoods—Negro looters smiled and waved at white policemen and newsmen.

Along one section of Grand River Avenue, where Negroes and Southern whites live in adjoining neighborhoods, stores were raided by integrated bands of looters. At Packer's, a block-long food and clothing center, a Negro looter boosted a white looter through a window. Scores of other Negroes and whites looted and chatted side by side in the store, loading shopping carts, boxes and bags with booty. When a busload of policemen arrived at the scene, the white and Negro looters scampered away, shouting to one another to "run fast." ■

AUGUST 13, 1967

BLACK MILITANT RAP BROWN 'SCARES THEM A LITTLE'

Earl Caldwell

To some in Congress and others searching for simple answers for the nation's hottest summer, H. Rap Brown, virtually unknown until he became chairman of the Student Nonviolent Coordinating Committee late last spring, is the man who causes Negroes to riot. To the black power militants, he is a champion of heroic proportions. To others, both black and white, he is a shadowy figure, a confused young agitator with no clear idea of just what end he is trying to reach.

It was late last Sunday afternoon and the ballroom in St. Albans, Queens, was hot, stuffy and overcrowded with dark faces. Rap Brown was more than an hour late, but that seemed to make no difference to those waiting. They stood in the aisle and grabbed at his hands, whistled, stomped and shouted as he made his way toward the speaker's platform.

Most of the audience was young and when he called for violent action, it was on its feet in frantic applause. The audience understood. It was from the ghetto and he talked its language, he said what it had come to hear, his style was off the streets.

Mr. Brown emerged full-blown on the American scene back in May with his election as chairman of the student committee. Until then, the 23-year-old native of Baton Rouge, La., had been a figure of importance only within the increasingly closed confines of the student committee, which he had joined in 1963 as a field worker in Mississippi after three years as a sociology student at Southern University in Louisiana.

It is certain that the bulk of his influence is with the militant young activists. The so-called Negro middle class, while it has not moved to censure him, has not blessed him with an endorsement either.

But when accused of inciting Negroes to riot, Mr. Brown answers: "I don't start riots, conditions do."

"It doesn't matter how big you get, you're still just a nigger to the white man." There was no flash of anger, no tantrum or anything else. It was a cold hard fact with him.

MARCH 11, 1968

CESAR CHAVEZ: Farm-Bred Unionist

The deep hunger that Cesar Chavez felt yesterday as he came off his 25-day fast in California was not entirely new for the Mexican-American labor leader. He has experienced hunger before.

The unionist was born on March 31, 1927, on a small Arizona farm near Yuma, where his family scratched out a precarious living. His father went broke when Cesar was 10 years old, and the family began to trail the harvest as migrant workers.

The young labor leader remembers the winter of 1938, when he stopped on the way home from school to fish and cut mustard greens to keep the family from starving. Even today, as director of the United Farm Workers Organizing Committee of the A.F.L.-C.I.O., Mr. Chavez, his wife Helen and eight children live in a faded two-bedroom frame house in Delano, Calif., and scrape along on about $300 a month.

Cesar Estrada Chavez's almost complete lack of interest in material comforts tells a great deal about the short (5 feet 6 inches) and once stocky labor leader with the shock of jet black hair. He is soft-spoken and unassuming, but he burns with a consuming desire to lift the lot of his people.

Why does a talented and energetic young man make such a sacrifice? "For many years I was a farm worker," he once explained, "a migratory worker, and, well, personally, and I'm being very frank, maybe it's just a matter of trying to even the score, you know."

Mr. Chavez first came to wide public attention in 1965, when he called a strike of grape pickers in the hot and fertile San Joaquin Valley around Delano. Since then, his fledgling union has won about a dozen contracts with major wine processors.

The struggle, Mr. Chavez himself admits, is far from over. But he has succeeded, where others failed for 30 years, in building the foundation for the nation's first viable farm workers union.

One reason for his success is that Mr. Chavez is a charismatic leader who has capitalized on the ethnic bonds among the Mexican-Americans, and invested his cause with religious and civil rights overtones. The growers fighting him accuse him of being an outside agitator, socialist—or worse.

Another reason for his success is that Mr. Chavez is a patient and diligent man who began his strike only after three years of laying groundwork. Even before that, he had honed his organizing talents for 10 years with Saul Alinsky's Community Service Organization in California, rising to national director in 1958.

Fred Ross, an Alinsky associate who now is the union's organizing director, "found" the young Mexican-American while trying to get a program going in San Jose in 1952. "He looked to me like potentially the best grass roots leader I'd ever run into," said Mr. Ross, who had been dealing with farm workers since the 1930's. After the meeting, Mr. Chavez accompanied Mr. Ross to another event and, before the night was out, "he just burst into flame about the thing."

"There is a large and increasing demand for organization from many places around the country," Mr. Chavez said in a recent interview. "Almost everywhere I go to speak, somewhere in the vicinity there are farm workers. So a network is being built."

"A big job has to be done and we know it," he said. "It will take many years. But," he added with quiet conviction, "we know that a union of farm workers is going to be built somehow because the workers are on the move, and they want a union." ■

rebel

APRIL 1, 1968

JOHNSON SAYS HE WON'T RUN

President Johnson waiting to make his nationally televised speech announcing his decision not to seek re-election of the presidency in 1968.

Tom Wicker

WASHINGTON, March 31—Lyndon Baines Johnson announced tonight: "I shall not seek and I will not accept the nomination of my party as your President."

Later, at a White House news conference, he said his decision was "completely irrevocable."

The President told his nationwide television audience:

"What we have won when all our people were united must not be lost in partisanship. I have concluded that I should not permit the Presidency to become involved in partisan decisions."

Mr. Johnson, acknowledging that there was "division in the American house," withdrew in the name of national unity, which he said was "the ultimate strength of our country."

"With American sons in the field far away," he said, "with the American future under challenge right here at home, with our hopes and the world's hopes for peace in the balance every day, I do not believe that I should devote an hour or a day of my time to any personal partisan causes or to any duties other than the awesome duties of this office, the Presidency of your country."

Mr. Johnson's announcement tonight came as a stunning surprise even to close associates. They were informed of what was coming just before Mr. Johnson went on national television at 9 P.M. with a prepared speech on the war in Vietnam.

Mr. Johnson ended his prepared speech and then launched into a peroration that had not been included in the printed text and that White House sources said he had written himself.

In his 37 years of public service, he said, he had put national unity ahead of everything because it was as true now as it had ever been that "a house divided against itself by the spirit of faction, of party, of region, of religion, of race, is a house that cannot stand."

Mr. Johnson spoke proudly of what he had accomplished in the "52 months and 10 days" since he took over the Presidency, after the assassination of John F. Kennedy in Dallas, Tex., on Nov. 22, 1963.

But these gains, Mr. Johnson said, "must not now be lost in suspicion and distrust and selfishness and politics. . . . . I have concluded that I should not permit the Presidency to become involved in the partisan divisions that are developing."

The war was unquestionably the major factor in Mr. Johnson's slump in public esteem. He began a major escalation in February 1965, by ordering the bombing of North Vietnam, just a few months after waging a Presidential campaign in which he had convinced most voters that he would not expand what was then a conflict involving only about 16,000 noncombatant American troops.

Over the years since then, the war has required a commitment of more than half a million combat troops, an expenditure of about $30 billion a year and heavy American casualties. ■

APRIL 5, 1968

MARTIN LUTHER KING JR. FATALLY SHOT IN MEMPHIS

Earl Caldwell

MEMPHIS, Friday, April 5—The Rev. Dr. Martin Luther King Jr., who preached nonviolence and racial brotherhood, was fatally shot here last night by a distant gunman who then raced away and escaped.

Four thousand National Guard troops were ordered into Memphis by Gov. Buford Ellington after the 39-year-old Nobel Prize-winning civil rights leader died.

A curfew was imposed on the shocked city of 550,000 inhabitants, 40 percent of whom are Negro.

But the police said the tragedy had been followed by incidents that included sporadic shooting, fires, bricks and bottles thrown at policemen, and looting that started in Negro districts and then spread over the city.

Dr. King's mourning associates sought to calm the people they met by recalling his messages of peace, but there was widespread concern by law enforcement officers here and elsewhere over potential reactions.

In a television broadcast after the curfew was ordered here, Police Director Frank Holloman said, "rioting has broken out in parts of the city" and "looting is rampant."

Yesterday Dr. King had been in his second-floor room—Number 306—throughout the day. Just about 6 P.M. he emerged, wearing a silkish-looking black suit and white shirt.

Dr. King was shot while he leaned over a second-floor railing outside his room at the Lorraine Motel. He was chatting with two friends just before starting for dinner.

Dr. Martin Luther King Jr. lies dying on the balcony of the Lorraine Motel in Memphis, where the Civil Rights leader was supporting the city's striking garbage collectors. His assassination set off racial riots in a number of cities, including Washington, Baltimore and Chicago. James Earl Ray was later arrested and convicted in the killing.

The Rev. Ralph W. Abernathy, perhaps Dr. King's closest friend, was just about to come out of the motel room when the sudden loud noise burst out.

Dr. King toppled to the concrete second-floor walkway. Blood gushed from the right jaw and neck area. His necktie had been ripped off by the blast.

Someone rushed up with a towel to stem the flow of Dr. King's blood. Rev. Samuel Kyles said he put a blanket over Dr. King, but "I knew he was gone." He ran down the stairs and tried to telephone from the motel office for an ambulance.

Policemen were pouring into the motel area, carrying rifles and shotguns and wearing riot helmets.

Dr. King was apparently still living when he reached the St. Joseph's Hospital operating room for emergency surgery. He was borne in on a stretcher, the bloody towel over his head.

"He was pronounced dead at 7:05 P.M. Central standard time by staff doctors," said Paul Hess, assistant administrator at St. Joseph's. "They did everything humanly possible."

The Rev. Andrew Young, executive director of Dr. King's Southern Christian Leadership Conference, recalled there had been some talk Wednesday night about possible harm to Dr. King in Memphis.

Mr. Young recalled: "He said he had reached the pinnacle of fulfillment with his nonviolent movement, and these reports did not bother him." ■

JUNE 6, 1968

SENATOR KENNEDY IS DEAD, VICTIM OF ASSASSIN

Gladwin Hill

New York Senator Robert F. Kennedy celebrating his victory in the Democratic California Primary at the Ambassador Hotel on June 5, 1968, in Los Angeles, California, shortly before he was assassinated.

LOS ANGELES, Thursday, June 6—Senator Robert F. Kennedy, the brother of a murdered President, died at 1:44 A.M. today of an assassin's shots.

The New York Senator was wounded more than 20 hours earlier, moments after he had made his victory statement in the California primary.

At his side when he died today in Good Samaritan Hospital were his wife, Ethel; his sisters, Mrs. Stephen Smith and Mrs. Patricia Lawford; his brother-in-law, Stephen Smith; and his sister-in-law, Mrs. John F. Kennedy, whose husband was assassinated 4 1/2 years ago in Dallas.

In Washington, President Johnson issued a statement calling the death a tragedy. He proclaimed next Sunday a national day of mourning.

The man accused of shooting Mr. Kennedy early yesterday in a pantry of the Ambassador Hotel was identified as Sirhan Bishara Sirhan, 24 years old, who was born in Palestinian Jerusalem of Arab parentage and had lived in the Los Angeles area since 1957. Sirhan had been a clerk.

Yesterday, he was hurried through an early-morning court arraignment and held in lieu of $250,000 bail.

Five other persons in addition to the 42-year-old Senator were wounded by the eight bullets from a .22-caliber revolver fired at almost point-blank range into a throng of Democratic rally celebrants surging between ballrooms in the hotel. The shots came moments after Senator Kennedy had made a speech celebrating his victory in yesterday's Democratic Presidential primary in California.

The defendant, seized moments after the shooting, refused to give the police any information about himself. He was arraigned as "John Doe."

Mayor Samuel W. Yorty said the defendant's identification had come through a brother, Adel Sirhan, after the police had traced the ownership of the .22-caliber revolver involved in the shooting to a third brother, Munir Bishari Salameh Sirhan, also known as Joe Sirhan.

Senator Kennedy, accompanied by his wife, Ethel, was wheeled into the Good Samaritan Hospital shortly after 1 A.M. yesterday after a brief stop at the Central Receiving Hospital. A score of the Senator's campaign aides swarmed around the scene.

Less than five years back many of them had experienced the similar tragedy that ended the life of President John F. Kennedy.

Hopes had risen slightly when more than eight hours went by without a new medical bulletin on the stricken Senator, but the grimness of the final announcement was signaled when Frank Mankiewicz, Mr. Kennedy's press secretary, walked slowly down the street in front of the hospital toward the littered gymnasium that served as press headquarters.

He stepped to a lectern in front of a green-tinted chalkboard and bowed his head for a moment while the television lights snapped on.

Then, at one minute before 2 A.M., he told of the death of Mr. Kennedy. ■

AUGUST 29, 1968

HUMPHREY NOMINATED ON FIRST BALLOT; POLICE BATTLE DEMONSTRATORS IN STREETS

178 Are Arrested as Guardsmen Join in Using Tear Gas

J. Anthony Lukas

Police knock down a anti-Vietnam War demonstrator during an anti-war demonstration outside the Democratic Convention Hall, August 28, 1968.

CHICAGO, Thursday, Aug. 29—The police and National Guardsmen battled young protestors in downtown Chicago last night as the week-long demonstrations against the Democratic National Convention reached a violent and tumultuous climax.

About 100 persons, including 25 policemen, were injured and at least 178 were arrested as the security forces chased down the demonstrators. The protesting young people had broken out of Grant Park on the shore of Lake Michigan in an attempt to reach the International Amphitheatre where the Democrats were meeting, four miles away.

The police and Guardsmen used clubs, rifle butts, tear gas and chemical mace on virtually anything moving along Michigan Avenue and the narrow streets of the Loop area.

Shortly after midnight, an uneasy calm ruled the city. However, 1,000 National Guardsmen were moved back in front of the Conrad Hilton Hotel to guard it against more than 5,000 demonstrators who had drifted back into Grant Park.

The crowd in front of the hotel was growing, booing vociferously every time new votes for Vice President Humphrey, who won his party's nomination for president, were broadcast from the convention hall.

The events in the streets stirred anger among some delegates at the convention. In a nominating speech Senator Abraham A. Ribicoff of Connecticut told the delegates that if Senator George S. McGovern were President, "we would not have these Gestapo tactics in the streets of Chicago."

Even elderly bystanders were caught in the police onslaught. At one point, the police turned on several dozen persons standing quietly behind police barriers in front of the Conrad Hilton Hotel watching the demonstrators across the street.

For no reason that could be immediately determined, the blue-helmeted policemen charged the barriers, crushing the spectators against the windows of the Haymarket Inn, a restaurant in the hotel. Finally the window gave way, sending screaming middle-aged women and children backward through the broken shards of glass.

The police then ran into the restaurant and beat some of the victims who had fallen through the windows and arrested them.

At the same time, other policemen outside on the broad, tree-lined avenue were clubbing the young demonstrators repeatedly under television lights and in full view of delegates' wives looking out the hotel's windows.

Afterward, newsmen saw 30 shoes, women's purses and torn pieces of clothing lying with shattered glass on the sidewalk and street outside the hotel and for two blocks in each direction.

It was difficult for newsmen to estimate how many demonstrators were in the streets of midtown Chicago last night. Although 10,000 to 15,000 young people gathered in Grant Park for a rally in the afternoon, some of them had apparently drifted home before the violence broke out in the evening.

Estimates of those involved in the action in the night ranged between 2,000 and 5,000.

Although some youths threw bottles, rocks, stones and even loaves of bread at the police, most of them simply marched and countermarched, trying to avoid the flying police squads.

Some of them carried flags—the black anarchist flag, the red flag, the Vietcong flag and the red and blue flags with a yellow peace symbol.

As in previous nights of unrest here, newsmen found themselves special targets of the police action. At Michigan Avenue and Van Buren Street, a young photographer ran into the street, terrified, his hands clasped over his head and shrieking "Press, press."

As the police arrested him, he shouted, "What did I do? What did I do?"

The policeman said, "If you don't know you shouldn't be a photographer."

Barton Silverman, a photographer for the New York Times, was briefly arrested near the Hilton Hotel. ■

NOVEMBER 7, 1968

NIXON NARROWLY ELECTED

Max Frankel

President-elect Richard Nixon, celebrating his election victory over Democratic candidate Hubert Humphrey, November 1968.

Richard Milhous Nixon emerged the victor yesterday in one of the closest and most tumultuous Presidential campaigns in history and set himself the task of reuniting the nation.

Elected over Hubert H. Humphrey by the barest of margins—only four one-hundredths of a percentage point in the popular vote—and confronted by a Congress in control of the Democrats, the President-elect said it "will be the great objective of this Administration at the outset to bring the American people together."

He pledged, as the 37th President, to form "an open Administration, open to new ideas, open to men and women of both parties, open to critics as well as those who support us" so as to bridge the gap between the generations and the races.

The verdict of an electorate that appeared to number 73 million could not be discerned until mid-morning because Mr. Nixon and Mr. Humphrey finished in a virtual tie in the popular vote, just as Mr. Nixon and John F. Kennedy did in 1960.

With 94 percent of the nation's election precincts reporting, Mr. Nixon's total stood last evening at 29,726,409 votes to Mr. Humphrey's 29,677,152. The margin of 49,257 was even smaller than Mr. Kennedy's margin of 112,803.

After receiving Mr. Humphrey's concession, congratulations and offer of cooperation at noon yesterday, Mr. Nixon replied before television cameras with a statement that implicitly recognized this possible obstacle to his rule. Of all the signs, friendly and hostile, thrust at him on the campaign trail, he said, the one that touched him the most appeared in the hands of a teenager one evening in Ohio, reading "Bring Us Together."

Above all, the campaign demonstrated that the American political system as a whole could still adjust itself to the most violent strains. The bitter conflict over the war, the unexpected abdication of President Johnson in March, the shooting of the Rev. Dr. Martin Luther King Jr. and of Senator Kennedy in April and June, the riots in the Negro ghettos and the turbulence, inside and out, at the Democratic National Convention, had spread disgust and disaffection through political ranks.

The widespread fear that neither Mr. Nixon nor Mr. Humphrey would win a clean victory and that weeks of bizarre maneuvering would result both in the Electoral College and in the House of Representatives persisted through the long night of return watching and analysis. The close escape at the end may now encourage the forces of reform who wish to alter or abandon the elector system, Mr. Humphrey among them.

But harrowing as the campaign proved to be and narrow as Mr. Nixon's margin unexpectedly came to be, the system held and turned, under the leadership of the retiring President and the defeated Vice President, to the swift and orderly passage of power. ■

DECEMBER 7, 1968

BLACK PANTHERS GROWING, BUT THEIR TROUBLES RISE

Earl Caldwell

SAN FRANCISCO, Dec. 6—It was late afternoon and outside the cluttered storefront that the Black Panther movement occupies on Fillmore Street noisy teenaged youths raced along the block hustling newspapers.

On the sidewalk, they stopped passersby. They ducked in and out of shops, and in the street, they stopped every car. "Buy a black newspaper," they urged. "Get the Black Panther news. Support your community paper." As they worked their way up the block, they enjoyed remarkable success.

"You're damn right they sell a lot of those papers," a Negro who stood at the corner said. "A lot of people are afraid not to buy it. They don't want any arguments or anything so they just buy the paper.

"It's a funny thing," he said. "Everyone gets excited because the Panthers scare white people but what they don't know is that they scare some of these blacks around here too."

Even after 26 months of heavy publicity and great growth, the influence of the Black Panthers is difficult to assess.

While whites fear that the ultimate aim is to make war on the white community, many Negroes fear that a Panther-led revolution could produce a pogrom of innocent, peaceful blacks. Many Negroes are also concerned over any move toward black separatism and are critical of Panther attacks on moderate, black politicians, ministers and other community figures.

However, such doubts have not kept the organization from growing.

Its membership has swelled from a few hundred to several thousand with chapters in major cities. The movement's leaders have also acquired influence in black communities and among white radicals and students across the country.

At the same time, the Panthers are losing strong and effective leaders because of trouble with legal authorities. Internal problems are budding. The organization's base in the Negro communities needs widening.

(cont'd. on next page)

The Black Panthers marching to protest at the trial of one of their members, Huey Newton, in July 1968.

(cont'd. from previous page)

The Panthers suffered a serious jolt when they lost Eldridge Cleaver, their minister of information. Rather than return to prison as a parole violator, Cleaver went into hiding. Cleaver was the organization's hottest property. He was an articulate spokesman for the revolution that they espouse and his fiery oratory moved both white and black audiences. He ran for the United States Presidency as the Peace and Freedom party's candidate.

His book, "Soul on Ice," is a best seller. He was also a senior editor of Ramparts magazine, a publication of great influence among white radicals.

While the Panthers have been successful in increasing their numbers in the slums, they have not been able to pull in the community movers.

"They can get the kids off the block," one observer said. "But they haven't shown yet that they can draw the black intellectuals and the professionals who have the expertise that they need."

In a recent article in the Panther newspaper, The Black Panther, members of the organization were told that too much emphasis was being put on the military aspects of the Panther program and not enough on the political approach.

"We should not confine ourselves merely to fighting," the article said, "but we must also shoulder important tasks such as doing propaganda among the people, organizing the people, arming the people, and helping them to establish revolutionary political power for black people."

The article concluded:

"Without these objectives, fighting loses its meaning and the Black Panther party loses the reason for its existence." ■

OBITUARY

MARCH 29, 1969

EISENHOWER DEAD AT 78 AS AILING HEART FAILS

Felix Belair Jr.

WASHINGTON, March 28—Dwight David Eisenhower, 34th President of the United States, died peacefully at 12:25 P.M. today at Walter Reed General Hospital after a long fight against coronary heart disease. He was 78 years old.

Death came to the five-star General of the Army and hero of World War II as members of his immediate family stood at his bedside.

The end had been foreshadowed in a midmorning medical bulletin that said the general's condition "continues almost imperceptibly downhill." It added that Mrs. Eisenhower was at his side.

The former President's doctors gave no immediate cause of death, presumably because they considered this unnecessary. His damaged heart—scarred by seven attacks and weakened by recent episodes of congestive heart failure—finally gave out despite the best efforts of medical science to prolong his life.

In all corners of the earth where the name Eisenhower was associated with victory in war and a tireless crusade for peace, great men and small were moved by the passing of the man whose rise from a farm boy in Kansas to supreme Allied commander and conqueror of the Axis powers and President of the United States was a story of devotion to duty.

Trained to command, he welded together the greatest military coalition in history by the tactic of conciliation. After he became President in 1952 he ended the war in Korea, and he refused to give fighter planes to the French forces in Vietnam because he was fearful the United States might become directly involved as a result.

As President he governed effectively through the sheer force of his popularity among average Americans of both major parties, and it was the average American who was the real source of his power.

His critics at home accused him of playing too much golf and of garbling syntax at his news conferences. But the voters loved him and twice elected him President by the largest pluralities ever recorded at the time.

In his infectious grin and his highly expressive face, most Americans thought they saw in "Ike" a dim reflection of themselves.

In Paris, it was announced today that President de Gaulle, leader of the Free French forces when General Eisenhower was supreme Allied commander in Europe during World War II, would come to Washington for the funeral ceremonies on Monday.

JULY 20, 1969

WOMAN PASSENGER KILLED, KENNEDY ESCAPES IN CRASH

EDGARTOWN, Mass., July 19—A 28-year-old woman passenger drowned today when a car driven by Senator Edward M. Kennedy plunged 10 feet off a bridge into a pond on Chappaquiddick Island near this community on Martha's Vineyard.

The woman was Mary Jo Kopechne of Berkeley Heights, N.J., a former secretary to the Massachusetts Democrat's brother, the late Senator Robert F. Kennedy.

The police here said that Edward Kennedy had told them he wandered around in apparent shock after the accident and did not report it to them for about eight hours.

"I remember walking around for a period of time and then going back to my hotel room," Senator Kennedy was quoted by the police as saying. "When I fully realized what had happened this morning, I immediately contacted the police."

In a telephone interview tonight, Police Chief Dominick J. Arena said there was "apparently no criminal negligence involved in the accident itself."

But the Edgartown police said late tonight that a formal charge of leaving the scene of an accident, a misdemeanor, would be filed against Senator Kennedy Monday morning in the Dukes County Courthouse in Edgartown.

"On July 18, at approximately 11:15 P.M.," the police quoted Senator Kennedy as saying, "I went over to Chappaquiddick. Later, I was driving my car on Main Street, Chappaquiddick, to get the ferry back to Edgartown. I was unfamiliar with the road and turned right onto Dyke Road instead of bearing hard left on Main Street.

"After proceeding for approximately half a mile on Dyke Road, I descended a hill and came upon a narrow bridge. The car went off the side of the bridge. There was one passenger with me, one Miss Mary (the Senator did not give the name at this point), a former secretary of my brother, Senator Robert Kennedy.

"The car turned over and sank into the water, and landed with roof resting on the bottom. I attempted to open the door and the window of the car, but had no recollection of how I got out of the car.

"I came to the surface and repeatedly dove down to the car in an attempt to see if the passenger was still in the car. I was unsuccessful in the attempt."

The police in Edgartown said that Senator Kennedy appeared at the police station to report the accident about 9 A.M.

Police Chief Arena said he was convinced that "the accident is strictly accidental."

"As far as the circumstances surrounding it," he said, "there doesn't appear from the principal evidence to be any excessive speed there."

Senator Kennedy, who is 38 years old, was elected to the United States Senate in 1962 and is currently the majority whip. He is regarded as a possible contender for the Democratic Presidential nomination in 1972.

OCTOBER 30, 1969

SCHOOL INTEGRATION ORDERED BY SUPREME COURT

Warren Weaver Jr.

WASHINGTON, Oct. 29—The Supreme Court ruled unanimously today that school districts must end segregation "at once" and operate integrated systems "now and hereafter."

The decision will unquestionably apply to Southern states where dual educational systems exist. The initial reaction of most legal authorities in the civil rights area was that it would not affect de facto segregation in Northern cities.

The Court replaced its 14-year-old decision that school desegregation should proceed with "all deliberate speed" with a new and much more rigorous standard: immediate compliance.

The effect of today's decision is to write a legal end to the period during which courts have entertained various excuses for failure to integrate Southern schools. Its basic message was integrate now, litigate later.

The decision was a stinging setback for the Nixon Administration. The Justice Department had argued less than a week ago that delays were permissible in requiring integration in some districts and that providing a continuing education should take precedence over enforcing social justice.

It was the first major decision handed down by the Court with Warren E. Burger sitting as Chief Justice. He is President Nixon's first appointee to the Court, a man chosen to help restore a measure of conservative balance to the tribunal.

The ruling specifically affected 33 school districts in Mississippi, but its broad language will be a precedent for all pending Court cases involving school segregation and in all future suits that may be filed.

In the Mississippi cases, the Supreme Court held, all requests for additional time to present desegregation plans should have been denied "because continued operation of segregated schools under a standard of allowing 'all deliberate speed' for desegregation is no longer constitutionally permissible."

(cont'd. on next page)

(cont'd. from previous page)

"Under explicit holdings of this Court," the opinion continued, "the obligation of every school district is to terminate dual school systems at once and to operate now and hereafter only unitary schools."

The Supreme Court ordered an end to school segregation in 1954 in Brown v. Board, a case involving challenges in several states. Its establishment of the "all deliberate speed" standard came in an implementing decision a year later.

The decision was applauded by the organization that had brought the Mississippi suits on behalf of 14 Negro children, the N.A.A.C.P. Legal Defense and Educational Fund, Inc.

"Now that the Court has accepted the principle which we urged of no further delays and that integration should exist during litigation, we are going to press for such relief in all pending school cases," Jack Greenberg, director of the fund, said.

desegregation is no longer constitutionally permissible

At his last general news conference on Sept. 26 the President replied to a question about delaying school segregation with this statement:

"It seems to me that there are two extreme groups. There are those who want instant integration and those who want segregation forever. I believe that we need to have a middle course between these two extremes. That is the course on which we are embarked. I think it is correct."

The Nixon Administration's decision to permit the Mississippi school districts to delay filing their integration plans had been regarded by critics of the President as further evidence that he had adopted a political strategy of favoring the South, to encourage Republican gains there in the elections of 1970 and 1972. ■

250,000 WAR PROTESTERS STAGE PEACEFUL RALLY IN WASHINGTON;

Young Marchers Ask Rapid Withdrawal From Vietnam

John Herbers

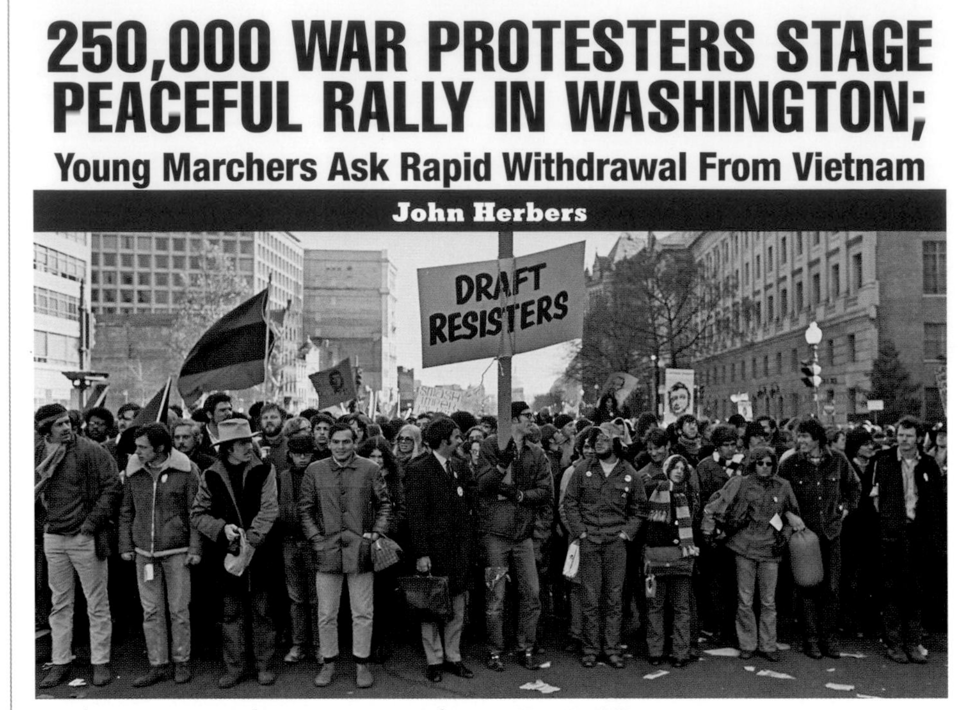

Marchers at an antiwar demonstration in Washington, Nov. 15, 1969.

WASHINGTON, Nov. 15—A vast throng of Americans, predominantly youthful and constituting the largest mass march in the nation's capital, demonstrated peacefully in the heart of the city today, demanding a rapid withdrawal of United States troops from Vietnam.

The District of Columbia Police Chief, Jerry Wilson, said a "moderate" estimate was that 250,000 had paraded on Pennsylvania Avenue and had attended an antiwar rally at the Washington Monument. Other city officials said aerial photographs would later show that the crowd had exceeded 300,000.

Until today, the largest outpouring of demonstrators was the gentle civil rights march of 1963, which attracted 200,000. Observers of both marches said the throng that appeared today was clearly greater than the outpouring of 1963.

At dusk, after the mass demonstration had ended, a small segment of the crowd, members of radical splinter groups, moved across Constitution Avenue to the Labor and Justice Department buildings, where they burned United States flags, threw paint bombs and other missiles and were repelled by tear gas released by the police.

There were a number of arrests and minor injuries, mostly the result of the tear gas.

The crowds brought to Washington a sense of urgency about a Vietnam peace and impatience with President Nixon's policy of gradual withdrawal. This theme, which was repeated throughout the day in various forms, was expressed at the beginning of the march by Senator Eugene J. McCarthy, Democrat of Minnesota, who ran for President last year on an antiwar platform.

"The record of history, I think, is clear," Senator McCarthy told the demonstrators as they gathered on the Mall for the march early this morning, "the cases in which political leaders out of misjudgment or ambition in ancient time and in modern times basing their action on the loyalty of their people have done great harm to their own countries and to the world.

"The great loyalty of the Roman citizens moved the Caesars to war," he went on. "The great loyalty of the French moved Napoleon to actions which should never have been taken. Let us in the United States take warning from that experience."

Except for clusters of middle-aged marchers and a few in their latter years, the crowd in appearance could have been a merging of the college campuses across the nation. There was a small percentage of blacks.

Among the black leaders marching here

today were Mrs. Coretta Scott King, widow of Dr. King; Phil Hutchings, a former officer of the Student Nonviolent Coordinating Committee, who is a columnist for The Guardian; George Wiley, head of the National Welfare Rights Organization; and Dick Gregory, the comedian-turned-activist.

Among the performing artists: Mary Travers, of the Peter, Paul and Mary singing group; the actor-playwright Adolph Green; and Leonard Bernstein, the composer and former conductor of the New York Philharmonic, who looked out at the crowd around the Monument this afternoon and said, "I'm with you. You're beautiful." ■

DECEMBER 3, 1969

TATE CASE TIES TO GURU AND 'FAMILY'

Steven V. Roberts

CHATSWORTH, Calif., Dec. 2—Here in the barren, boulder-strewn Santa Susanna Mountains, the persons accused of killing Sharon Tate, the actress, and at least seven other victims lived a life of indolence, free sex, midnight motorcycle races and apparently blind obedience to a mysterious guru.

It was here that Charles Manson and his "family" of about 18 young people lived for a number of months before the murder of Miss Tate and four others in a lonely hillside home on Aug. 9. They left about a week after the killings when policemen raided their camp looking for stolen automobiles and made several arrests.

Manson, 34 years old, has not been charged in the murder case but three other members of the "family" have. Manson is being held in Independence, Calif., on charges of suspicion of arson and receiving stolen goods.

The third suspect in the murder case was arrested in Concord, N.H., today. She is Linda Louise Kasabian, 19, cited on five counts of murder. Two other suspects in custody are Charles D. Watson, 23, held in McKinney, Tex., and Patricia Kernwinkel, 21, held in Mobile, Ala.

Six other persons are believed held in Los Angeles in connection with the murders, but the police would not discuss their relationship with the case.

Today, persons who knew Manson were afraid to talk about him publicly. "He's got his zombies out," said one employee of the Spahn ranch. "There's more than one family that's been conditioned to believe that Charlie Manson is always right."

Manson and the "family" were allowed to stay on the Spahn ranch simply because people were afraid of him.

The next home for the nomadic band was a ranch near Death Valley, where they

(cont'd. on next page)

Charles Manson, who would be convicted, along with seven members of his cult, of killing the actress Sharon Tate and four others.

(cont'd. from previous page)

set up a fortress-like camp guarded by sentries and reportedly continued their car-stealing activities. They remained there until mid October when policemen moved in and arrested Manson and several others on charges of receiving stolen property.

The "family"—about 6 men and 12 women—arrived in a broken-down school bus after a slow trip from San Francisco's Haight-Ashbury district. During cold spells they slept in the abandoned buildings of the movie set but during the summer they camped out in the fields and woods.

"They lived very carelessly," said one man who knew them. "It was a real monotonous life but they kept telling themselves they were happy."

The center of this life was Manson, who has a five-page police record stretching back 18 years. Little is known of his early life, but several years ago he started collecting young girls with a powerful magnetic attraction.

The lawyer for one of his followers, Susan Denise Atkins, said today that his client was under "hypnotic spells" from Manson. Another girl, Sandra Pugh, told a reporter:

"He was magnetic. His motions were like magic, it seemed like. The first time I saw him he was petting a cat. I don't know why that struck me, but he seemed so kind." ■

DECEMBER 8, 1969

DRAFT LOTTERY LEADS SOME TO SHELVE PLANS

The new draft lottery has set into motion a complex set of crosscurrents among young people that range from sharp changes in career plans to assertions from moderates and radicals that draft protests will continue unabated.

Interviews with draft-eligible young men, counselors, student activists and draft board workers in 20 cities since last week's draft lottery show the following things:

- Many draft-age men appear to be relieved that they can now see their futures more clearly because they have a better idea of their chances of being drafted.
- Both moderate and radical young people say that they will continue to protest the draft until the entire Selective Service System is eliminated, although some concede that the lottery has caused a division on the draft among the young.
- Some of those who are now least vulnerable to the draft have dropped plans to pursue deferred careers such as teaching and are seeking to get out of military reserve commitments they had made before they were "safe."
- There is some evidence that those who are now most vulnerable to the draft have been "radicalized" against the war in Vietnam, while those with the lowest risk have lost some of their antagonism.
- College and occupational deferments continue as the most popular means of avoiding the draft, while a minority still says it prefers jail or exile to military service.

Military experts say the draft pool for the coming year will include about 850,000 men between the ages of 19 and 26, about 250,000 of whom will be drafted. Thus, young men whose birthdays were picked in the lowest numerical third of the lottery are virtually assured of being drafted, while those in the highest third are relatively safe. Those in the middle third fall into the "uncertain" group.

Generally, those who were awarded the "safe" numbers were jubilant. "You know, I was born a month late," said Peter Steinberg, a junior at Columbia College, who drew 366, the "safest" number. "I would just like to thank my mother."

But for others, the jubilation was tempered. The comment of Harold Kletnick, a 21-year-old University of Chicago senior, who also ranked 366th, was typical.

"I definitely didn't want to go to the Army," he said, "but I don't feel good at all about beating the system."

Others who drew high numbers said they still opposed the draft because of the "immorality of the war," the inequities that remain and the basic concept of forced military service.

For many, the cold reality of a low draft number seemed to crystallize their resentment. William Tortu, a 19-year-old student at the University of Pennsylvania, who holds No. 18, said: "The lottery jolted me out of my complacency and made me realize the threat of the Army and dying in Vietnam.

"To call the lottery fair in comparison with the previous system is to call hanging fair compared to drawing and quartering."

David Sable, a counselor, said that more young men seemed to be gaining sophistication in avoiding the draft. In the last year, he said, "we have had more people apply for conscientious objector status than we have in the last two combined."

International

International and national news coverage has long been a special pride of The New York Times, and that tradition goes back to well before the 60's. Hence extensive and sophisticated coverage of hard news at home and around the world, albeit from a securely mainstream position, lasted throughout the decade.

If one rubric defines the international news of the 60's, it is the cold war. Starting with the shooting down of Francis Gary Powers's U-2 spy plane over Russia, the cold war subsumed most everything—from the space race to the Cuban missile crisis to the Vietnam War to Soviet muscle-flexing in Berlin and Prague. The escalation of military arsenals and nuclear warheads put a strain on the United States' economy and ultimately bankrupted the Soviets. Even if, as some might argue, the mutual fear of nuclear annihilation and the dominance of two (or three, counting China) nuclear superpowers helped suppress the national, tribal and religious conflicts of later decades.

In Vietnam (and, eventually, in Cambodia and Laos), the United States' escalation proceeded, seemingly unstoppable, with Washington mesmerized by the "domino theory" of inexorable world Communist conquest. Thousands died in a failed (for the U.S.) war, and the draft galvanized the youth of America into protest. Ho Chi Minh's death at the end of the decade impeded the ultimate victory of the North Vietnamese not at all. China, slowed by its disruptive Cultural Revolution and disturbed by the Orwellian (in the sense of the three mega-powers' constantly shifting alliances) break with Russia, was only at the beginning of its eventual rise to become a true world power. In Moscow, Khrushchev fell and was replaced by Brezhnev.

In the Middle East, the Israelis triumphed in the Six-Day War, but that only helped inspire the Palestine Liberation Organization into a more militant posture. Golda Meir became Israeli prime minister in 1969 and Yasir Arafat took over the PLO. India fought Pakistan over Kashmir; Nehru died and was succeeded by Indira Gandhi. Ferdinand Marcos won power in the Philippines, and Muammar el-Qaddafi seized the reins in Libya. The Irish sectarian conflict and attendant terrorism grew ever more brutal. New nations arose in sub-Saharan Africa, and Nelson Mandela was sentenced to life imprisonment for challenging apartheid in South Africa.

Closer to home, Castro tightened his hold on Cuba, even with Che Guevara's assassination in Bolivia. Cuba's ties with the Soviet Union strengthened after its isolation by the United States and the botched Bay of Pigs invasion, although the Cuban missile crisis brought the world dangerously close to war.

On a lighter note, the British enjoyed a salacious sex scandal involving politicians, party girls and shadowy spies. In his deliriously received speech in Berlin, which bolstered the shaken West Berliners at the foot of the newly constructed Berlin Wall, John Kennedy said he was a jelly donut: "Ich bin ein Berliner." His German audience knew what he meant, but this was still a linguistic faux pas, explained only later: If he'd wanted to identify himself with Berlin's citizens, as he clearly hoped to, he should have said "Ich bin Berliner." Oh, well: lost in translation.

MAY 9, 1965

AMERICAN PILOT FRANCIS G. POWERS CAPTURED BY RUSSIANS

Hanson W. Baldwin

American pilot Francis Gary Powers's U-2 spy plane was shot down over the Soviet Union in May 1960, igniting a cold war crisis.

One young American faced his "moment of truth" about 65,000 feet over the Soviet Union a week ago yesterday. He apparently decided that life was better than death and his instinctive reaction produced an international incident of unpredictable consequences. The capture of Francis G. Powers, pilot of a United States reconnaissance aircraft, gave Premier Khrushchev an important political and psychological advantage just prior to the East-West summit conference. It was an advantage the Soviet leader was quick to exploit.

The United States Government, many members of Congress and much of the press had been mouse-trapped into premature denials. Mr. Khrushchev was able to show—with the capture of the pilot—that these were, as he bluntly put it, "complete lies." The United States had been caught red-handed in a major espionage operation, with all the embarrassment that such a coup causes.

Two deductions are possible from this successful firing of an anti-aircraft missile against the U-2. The shot could have been "lucky"—that is, the pilot might have blundered within firing range of a missile battery that reconnaissance planes normally would try to avoid.

At the same time, the Soviet Union may at last have corrected some of the faults in its antiaircraft missiles and may now have in operation weapons comparable in effectiveness to the United States' earlier Nike-Ajax, or perhaps approximating the Nike-Hercules.

Both deductions are probably correct. A broader evaluation of the U-2's career gives reason to conclude that it probably has been one of the most successful reconnaissance planes ever built.

Was the flight authorized by Washington?

Saturday's somewhat equivocal United States statement, probably deliberately cloudy on this point, declared that "in so far as the authorities are concerned, there was no authorization for any such flights as described by Mr. Khrushchev."

But it would be stretching a very long bow to infer from this, as Harold E. Stassen, former disarmament advisor to President Eisenhower, did, that some United States military commander had gone off "half-cocked" on his own initiative. The whole history of the U-2 project, as revealed piecemeal in Washington and through Mr. Khrushchev's revelations, shows clearly that the activities were managed and probably closely directed by Washington.

Why did the pilot survive?

This is a question that only Mr. Powers can answer, and he may spend the rest of his life trying to answer it satisfactorily.

The instinct of self-preservation is strong in every human and it is contrary to the Judean Christian and the American ethic to destroy one's own life.

Yet an unwritten law of every secret intelligence organization postulates the suicide of an agent rather than capture, possible torture and revelations of importance to an enemy.

The plane apparently was hit by a fragment of the rocket's explosive warhead and was disabled. Apparently Mr. Powers rode it down for some distance and then parachuted. The U-2 almost certainly had a self-destructive charge, which apparently was not set off.

Films Aid Khrushchev

Mr. Powers' alleged confession, the plane's wreckage and even films from its camera thus have aided Mr. Khrushchev's dramatic psychological coup. It is safe to guess that all that Mr. Powers knew about the U-2 operations is now known to the Russians.

MAY 25, 1960

SECRET AGENTS SEIZED KILLER NAZI ADOLF EICHMANN, TOOK HIM TO ISRAEL

Lawrence Fellows

JERUSALEM (Israeli Sector), May 24—Adolf Eichmann, captured S. S. colonel who headed the section for Jewish affairs in Hitler's Secret State Police, was spirited from his home in an undisclosed country by Israeli security agents.

Israel charges Eichmann with having played a leading role in planning and carrying out the killing of 6,000,000 Jews. Premier David Ben-Gurion announced yesterday that Eichmann had been captured and would stand trial for his life.

This afternoon the head of Israel's Security Service called a news conference to state that Eichmann had been traced and captured through the efforts of his agents alone. He added that no foreign officials had been bribed into cooperating with the Israeli agents nor would any money be passed to them in the future. However, it is suspected here that one or more foreign countries were deeply involved in the case, if only in permitting Israeli agents to work freely in their search for people they consider their enemies. Speculation in the Israeli press is narrowing to South America.

Eichmann is accused of having committed his crimes against Jews in his dual capacity as an important official in the Gestapo (Geheime Staats-polizei) or secret police and the S. S. (Schützstaffel), the black uniformed military and political élite of the Nazi movement, led by Heinrich Himmler.

Evidence is being assembled in preparation for the trial of Eichmann. One highly placed legal authority suggested today that the trial might not come until next year. The authority explained that Eichmann would find it difficult to find witnesses to testify on his behalf.

Joseph Nahmias, Inspector General of the police, said tonight the 54-year-old Eichmann was being well cared for in an Israeli jail. He promised the same treatment for Nazis who were thinking about testifying for Eichmann, but he left the impression that he did not expect many Nazis to risk a trip to Israel.

A Polish Jew who escaped the gas chambers in a Nazi concentration camp was identified here yesterday as the key figure in the capture of Adolf Eichmann.

Eichmann's capture was credited here by Benjamin R. Epstein, national director of the Anti-Defamation League of the B'nai B'rith, to 37-year-old Tuvia Friedmann, whose long campaign of personal retribution against Nazi war criminals has brought him to his current post as the director of Israel's war crimes documentary center in Haifa. ■

Adolph Eichmann during his trial in Jerusalem, 1961. He was executed the following year.

OCTOBER 13, 1960

Khrushchev Bangs His Shoe on Desk

Benjamin Welles

UNITED NATIONS, N. Y., Oct. 12—Premier Khrushchev waved his shoe today and banged it on his desk, adding to the lengthening list of antics with which he has been nettling the General Assembly.

This time Mr. Khrushchev was apparently infuriated by a statement by Lorenzo Sumulong, a member of the Philippine delegation. Mr. Sumulong said in debate that the peoples of Eastern Europe had been "deprived of political and civil rights" and that they had been "swallowed up by the Soviet Union." Mr. Khrushchev thereupon pulled off his right shoe, stood up and brandished the shoe at the Philippine delegate on the other side of the hall: He then banged the shoe on his desk.

Later, during the debate on colonialism in which tempers flared among several delegations Mr. Khrushchev alternately shouted, waved a brawny right arm, shook his finger and removed his shoe a second time. The second shoe incident occurred during a speech by Francis O. Wilcox, an Assistant United States Secretary of State. Mr. Khrushchev and Foreign Minister Andrei A. Gromyko exchanged smiles and winks and Mr. Khrushchev then reached down and slipped his shoe back on.

Mr. Khrushchev's first break with decorum came Sept. 26, a week after he had arrived, when he began pounding the top of his desk in open disapproval of a speech being made by Secretary General Dag Hammarskjold. Mr. Gromyko, after a moment's hesitation, followed suit, as did Valerian A. Zorin and other members of the Soviet delegation. Then Communist delegations throughout the Assembly pounded in unison as Western delegates looked on in silent disapproval.

Three days later, during a temperate address by Prime Minister Macmillan, Mr. Khrushchev interrupted the Prime Minister with shouts in Russian.

Serious observers here believe Mr. Khrushchev has a deadly serious purpose in his histrionic excesses. They noted that a standard Communist practice, whenever the Communists believe they cannot win in a court of law, is to destroy the prestige and sanctity of the court. "That may well be what Khrushchev is up to now," one delegate said. "He can't get the votes and win here fairly, so he'll turn the place upside down if he can. I think that the new nations are too smart to fall for that technique, though."

Premier Khrushchev's behavior outside the United Nations has also been unorthodox. Two days after the Premier landed here on Sept. 19 he turned the balcony of the headquarters of the Soviet delegation to the United Nations at 680 Park Avenue into an impromptu Soviet forum. He appeared on it twice within a few hours to give a running stream of opinions on a wide range of questions fired at him by newsmen standing on the sidewalk below.

A few days later the Soviet leader held a roadside news conference outside the gate of the Soviet estate at Glen Cove, L. I. The conference blocked traffic and the police asked Mr. Khrushchev to cut his remarks short.

The unpredictable Premier has also accepted an Indian Peace pipe from Mr. and Mrs. Watson Pierce, dealers in antiques, and led a sidewalk rendition of "The Star-Spangled Banner." ■

MAY 14, 1961

U.S. Will Give More Arms and Money to Vietnamese

Robert Trumbull

MANILA, May 13—South Vietnam and the United States have agreed on an eight-point program for increased American military and economic assistance. Long-range measures to meet the Communist guerilla threat and to improve social conditions in South Vietnam were announced in a communiqué issued following Vice President Johnson's visit to Saigon.

The agreement was made public after Mr. Johnson had arrived in Manila today from Saigon on the second leg of his Southeast Asian tour on behalf of President Kennedy.

President Ngo Dinh Diem of South Vietnam and Mr. Johnson, on behalf of their Governments, declared that assistance from other free nations in South Vietnam's fight against Communist guerilla forces "would be welcome," the communiqué said.

"It was agreed by the two Governments to extend and build upon existing programs of military and economic aid and to infuse into their joint actions a high sense of urgency and dedication," it added.

It was agreed that South Vietnam's armed forces should be increased and that the United States would extent its military assistance programs to support the extra troops, the document continued.

This was understood to envisage the addition of 20,000 men to South Vietnam's army of 150,000. The Communist guerrilla force, the Viet Cong, is believed to number 12,000, while an army of about 300,000 exists in the Communist-held northern part of Vietnam.

The communiqué said the United States had agreed to provide support for the Vietnamese civil guard force. The civil guard, equivalent to the National Guard in the United States, now numbers about 40,000. About 32,000 more men are in training.

The two Governments agreed to "collaborate in the use of military specialists to assist and work with the Vietnamese armed force in health, welfare and public works activities."

The expected cost of the plan to the United States has been estimated at $40,000,000.

The steps agreed upon for immediate implementation may be followed by more far-reaching measures if necessary, the communiqué stated. It was assumed that such measures could include direct military participation by the United States and its allies in the Vietnam fighting. ■

AUGUST 16, 1961

REDS TIGHTEN SQUEEZE ON BERLIN

The Brandenburg Gate, August, 1961.

Sydney Gruson

BERLIN, Tuesday, Aug. 15—The East German Communists, apparently emboldened by success, tightened their squeeze on West Berlin early today.

Shortly after 1 A. M., with an uneasy quiet prevailing on the intra-city border, the East German Interior Ministry announced that all West Berlin cars and other vehicles must have special permits to cross into East Berlin. The announcement said the freedom of movement permitted the West Berliners after the border was closed early Sunday had been abused for espionage purposes. However, pedestrian traffic by West Berliners is still permitted at the twelve border crossings unclosed to them.

Aware of the danger of clashes on the border, the authorities on both sides acted separately but similarly yesterday to reduce the risks. They created a three-quarter-mile No Man's Land for civilians on both sides of the wide road running through the Brandenburg Gate, the most sensitive border point. The Communists closed the Brandenburg Gate, a huge multi-column monument standing just inside their territory. The gate was one of thirteen crossing points between the two Berlins left open by the Saturday midnight decrees barring East Berliners and East Germans from going into West Berlin "without special permits."

Bit by bit the East Germans were isolating their people from both West Berlin and West Germany. They cut telephone communications from East Germany and East Berlin early yesterday. In Bonn, Richard Stuecklen, West German Minister of Posts, said postal and telegraph service between the two parts of Germany had also been interrupted.

The purpose of all this was not yet entirely clear. It also was not known how long the interruptions were to last. It was presumed that the communications would remain cut until the situation brought about by the closing of the border had been stabilized to the Communists' satisfaction.

Since last September, West Germans, as distinct from West Berliners, have had to get special permits to enter East Berlin or East Germany. A West Berlin official commented on the lack of a prohibition on West Berliners' crossing to the east by foot or on the elevated railway.

"It's another slice of the salami," he said, clearly reflecting the belief of the majority of West Berliners that one pretext or another would be found for further Communist restrictions.

At the Brandenburg Gate, about 100 armed men of a factory fighting brigade, neat and tough-looking in gray uniforms, lined the front of the monument, tommy guns and rifles at the ready. Behind them were six water-gun trucks, which the Communists have been using to disperse unruly crowds, and six armored cars.

The Communists announced that the gate had to be closed because of "continuing provocations" instigated by Western officials among the West Berliners. At the time the latter were massed 5,000 strong behind rope barriers about 100 feet from the border.

The East Berliners, now barred from crossing to the West, went about their business with no apparent joy but also with no apparent will to test the overwhelming military strength brought in by the Communists. A few East Berliners swam the canals that form the border at some points, but the bulk of the 1,500 people registered at the West Berlin camp yesterday were in the city since Saturday, before the border was closed.

The bitterness of the West Berliners over the lack of Allied reaction was becoming more apparent. The feeling among ordinary people was that the Communists were "getting away with it," as one man put it, "without our lifting a finger." ■

APRIL 18, 1961

ANTI-CASTRO UNITS LAND IN CUBA

Tad Szulc

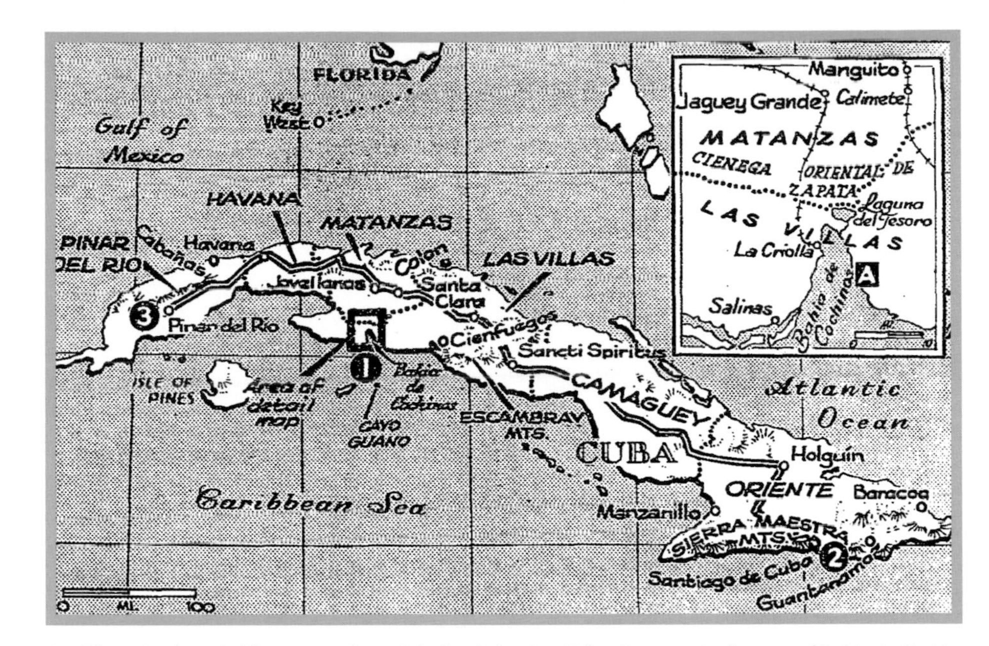

Caribbean Strife: Rebel forces attacking Cuba landed in Las Villas Province in the area of Bahia de Cochinos (1, and A on the inset map). Other anti-Castro landings were said to have taken place in the area of Santiago de Cuba (2) and Pinar del Rio (3).

MIAMI, Tuesday, April 18—Rebel troops opposed to Premier Fidel Castro landed before dawn yesterday on the swampy southern coast of Cuba in Las Villas Province. The attack, which was supported from the air, was announced by the rebels and confirmed by the Cuban Government.

The invaders, in undetermined numbers, are under the orders of the Revolutionary Council. In the words of its declaration, the Council seeks the overthrow of the Castro regime and the freeing of Cuba from "international communism's cruel oppression."

Premier Castro declared shortly before noon a state of national alert and called all his militia forces to their posts. The Cuban official radio devoted most of its time yesterday to broadcasts of Dr. Castro's three proclamations and to vituperation against United States "imperialists."

It was believed that the rebels landed near Playa Larga, on the eastern bank of the Cochinos Bay, which means the Bay of Pigs. This bay is wedged into the vast swamp of the Cienega de Zapata.

The Revolutionary Council members were standing by, ready to move into Cuba and proclaim a "government in arms" as soon as the beachhead is firmly secured.

The total strength of forces available to the rebels is estimated at somewhat over 5,000 men. Opposed to them is a military establishment of 400,000 of the regular army and the militia armed with the most modern Soviet bloc weapons.

The rebel command is known to believe that one or more major landings would set off internal uprisings and many desertions by soldiers and the militia. Today it was too early to tell whether this optimism was justified.

The use by the rebels yesterday of planes and gunboats covering the landing indicated that it was an operation of major scope and not just another guerrilla foray of the type that has been occurring in the past.

It was believed here that the attacking forces came from the camps in Guatemala, where they have been trained for the last nine months. Some of the units may have come from a rebel camp in Louisiana.

Radio messages on the Government microwave network monitored here—which gave a dramatic minute-by-minute account of the first hours of the landing—included appeals for reinforcements from additional militia battalions and a request for ambulances for the "many wounded."

The climate for the invasion—anticipated and promised by the Cuban rebels for many weeks—was created to a large extent by events of last week. Final preparations for the move against the Castro regime started in earnest about three weeks ago after the Revolutionary Council was formed and a secret mobilization order went out to rebel volunteers. For the last three weeks hundreds of volunteers had been leaving the Miami and New York areas for the camps in the training grounds in Guatemala.

In his proclamations, Dr. Castro appealed repeatedly for support by Latin-American nations. The Havana radio broadcast reports of Latin-American solidarity for the Cuban cause.

The Revolutionary Council also addressed itself to Latin America. Its dawn declaration stated that the rebels were convinced that "the freedom-loving people of this hemisphere will make common cause with them and support them." ■

APRIL 20, 1961

CASTRO SAYS ATTACK IS CRUSHED; CUBA REBELS GIVE UP BEACHHEAD

Tad Szulc

MIAMI, Thursday, April 20—The Government of Premier Fidel Castro claimed today that it had "completely defeated" the invasion force that landed Monday.

The announcement came amid insistent reports that two new rebel landings might be in progress on the northern coast of the island.

The rebel forces abandoned their beachhead on the southern coast and apparently

(cont'd. on next page)

Cuban Communist leader Fidel Castro in the 1960s.

(cont'd. from previous page)
"merged with guerrillas operating in" the nearby Escambray Mountains.

Premier Castro's claim of "a victory came in a Government radio broadcast monitored here. The announcement said both sides had suffered heavy losses.

The Castro communique said that the last strongholds of the "mercenary troops" of the invasion force had been overrun at 5:30 P.M. yesterday. The attackers were said to have been on Cuban soil less than seventy-two hours.

Quantities of military equipment of North-American make were seized, including Sherman tanks, the broadcast said.

The Cuban radio said that part of the invasion force had attempted to evacuate their positions by boat, but that many boats had been sunk. The communique, which was signed by Premier Castro, said that the remnant of the liberation force had been trapped in a swampy area, apparently near their landing ground at Las Villas Province.

Early today, Radio Swan, an anti-Castro station on Swan Island off the coast of Honduras, reported that a rebel force had landed at, or near, "Moron, a sugar port on the northern coast of Camaguey Province. The broadcast, which did not mention the scope of the operation, said that Capt. Nino Diaz, a one-time Castro lieutenant in the Sierra Maestra, had led the landing.

Yesterday a "terrific explosion" was reported in Moron by the Cuban Government internal communications network.

A broadcast heard at the United States Naval Base at Guantanamo Bay in Cuba reported that Captain Diaz was in command of a force that had landed in Oriente Province not far from Holguin. It was noted here that since Holguin and Moron are about 200 miles apart Captain Diaz could be in charge of forces in the two areas.

A communique of the Cuban Revolutionary Council declared last night that "the major portion" of the original landing party had reached the Escambray hills, despite "tragic losses" among a small holding force.

The reported link-up with the Escambray guerillas which earlier bad been represented as a success seemed to have been a defensive action under the impact of what the rebels described as an offensive by the government's heavy tanks, MIG jet fighters and artillery.

As the military picture in strife-torn Cuba continued to present considerable confusion, indications appeared of a lack of coordination in the top rebel leadership.

These difficulties led to some doubts as to the future of joint operations involving the rebels. The force from the beach was reported to have broken through militia lines to move fifty miles to the Escambray area to join what is left of the guerilla units there.

The area surrounding the Escambray Mountains is known to be heavily garrisoned by the troops of Premier Fidel Castro.

Yesterday Havana had announced that nine rebel aircraft bad been shot down since Monday. Four of the planes had been downed early yesterday, the regime asserted. One of the planes was alleged to have been flown by a United States pilot.

Tuesday night a rebel plane bombed an air base near Havana. The Cuban radio also announced last night that Maj. Raul Castro, the Premier's brother and Minister of Revolutionary Armed Forces, was in Santiago, capital of Oriente Province.

This was the first indication since Monday of the whereabouts of any of the high leaders of the regime.

The Havana radio announced that "militias" from Ecuador were ready to travel to Cuba to fight "Yankee aggressors" and that a Soviet woman deputy now in Cuba, who is a doctor, had offered her services.

The communique of the Cuban Revolutionary Council announced that the landing Monday on the Bahia de Cocilinos on the swampy coast of Las Villas Province had been "inaccurately" described as an invasion.

It was, the Council said, merely an operation designed to provide supplies for the underground in Cuba. In its initial communique at dawn Monday, the Council had termed the landing as the beginning of "the battle to liberate our homeland." Virtually the entire world took the landing to be a major military enterprise with equivalent political repercussions.

Last night, the Council said: "We did not expect to topple Castro immediately or without setbacks, It certainly is true that we did not expect to face unscathed Soviet armaments directed by Communist advisers,"

The anti-Castro rebels are reported to have about 5,000 more men at training camps outside Cuba. ■

SEPTEMBER 25, 1961

THRONGS MOURN HAMMARSKJOLD

John Wicklein

Envoys from many nations and many faiths attended a memorial service for Dag Hammarskjold yesterday in the Protestant Epsicopal Cathedral Church of St. John the Divine. Four thousand persons were in the congregation and thousands attended other services here and elsewhere mourning the death of the United Nations Secretary General.

The large attendances and the comments of speakers at the services indicated that there had been a widespread deep emotional attachment for Mr. Hammarskjold. Gen. Clark M. Eichelberger, president of the American Association for the United Nations, reported that it had received letters expressing grief from people all over the country. Some of the writers said they had wept when they heard the news last Monday that Mr. Hammarskjold had been killed in a plane crash in Northern Rhodesia.

Every delegation to the United Nations had been invited to attend the cathedral service. Thirty-nine were officially represented, none of them from the Soviet bloc. They heard Henry Cabot Lodge, former United States representative at the United Nations, praise the late Secretary General as a fighter for whom "nonresistance to evil was not a part of his creed."

The Right Rev. Horace W. B. Donegan, Protestant Episcopal Bishop of New York, delivered a sermon of eulogy. In his address. Mr. Lodge said this of Mr. Hammarskjold: "While much of his work in the United Nations was to harmonize the actions of nations— and for this he had a brilliant talent—he did not hesitate to take a stand within the United Nations, and, once the United Nations had acted, to be its gallant defender before the world."

Bishop Donegan, in a brief sermon, said: "The debt we owe this man with his discipline and dedication is incalculable. He had a vocation as a blessed peacemaker. He lived up to it. Indeed he lived out his calling right to the end. We are also met here today to thank God for the United Nations and to pray a merciful Providence that He would prosper it as our present best hope for a world where men and women dwell together as children of a common Father."

General Eichelberger described Mr. Hammarskjold as a man of "great physical courage, great moral courage," who "stood for the development of a society of free nations based on law and equality for all."

OCTOBER 24, 1961

Premier Chou Quits Talks with Red Leaders

Seymour Topping

MOSCOW, Oct. 23—Premier Chou En-lai of Communist China left Moscow unexpectedly tonight for Peiping after an apparent worsening of his quarrel with Premier Khrushchev over Soviet denunciations of Albania. The Chinese leader, who had been attending the twenty-second congress of the Soviet Communist party, turned over the leadership of his delegation to his deputy, Peng Chen, a Politburo member.

Tass, the official Soviet press agency, announced that Premier Chou had flown home "in connection with the forthcoming session of the National People's Congress." It did not say whether he would return here for the latter part of the party congress. Premier Chou was believed to have returned to Peiping to consult with Mao Tse-tung, chairman of the Chinese Communist party, and Liu Shao-chi, chairman of the Chinese People's Republic, on the public ideological dispute with Mr. Khrushchev over Albania, a close political ally of Communist China.

The Chinese leader may then return to Moscow for the foreign policy and ideological discussions of the Communist bloc leaders scheduled to be held in private at the end of this month or in early November. If Premier Chou does not fly back to the Soviet capital, his abrupt departure from the congress would be interpreted here as a protest demonstration and confirmation of the widening of the breach between Peiping and Moscow.

Premier Chou left after another day during which Soviet leaders ignored his appeal that they abstain from further public criticism of Albania. Mr. Chou said Thursday that any one-sided public denunciation of any member of the bloc before the eyes of the West "could not be regarded as a serious Marxist-Leninist approach." Mr. Chou implicitly rebuked Mr. Khrushchev, who on Tuesday had denounced the Albanian leadership for adhering to the Stalinist "cult of personality" and deviation from the agreed foreign policy line of the bloc.

Among the Soviet leaders who continued to castigate Albanian Communist leaders was Nikolai G. Ignatov, a member of the Presidium. At one point he appeared to make a veiled criticism of Premier Chou. According to Communist observers in the Kremlin's palace of Congresses, Mr. Ignatov accused the Albanians of a lack of sincerity. He then went on to say: "They spoke lies to the leaders of the Central Committee of the Soviet Communist party and we cannot hide this even if we see somebody does not like it."

Among the delegates who spoke today and backed the Soviet position were Elizabeth Gurley Flynn of the United States Communist party and representatives of the parties of Spain, Chile, Finland, Algeria and West Germany. ■

NOVEMBER 26, 1961

BERLIN WALL BECOMES A 'LIVING, GROWING THING'

David Binder

BERLIN, Nov. 25—The Communist wall that cuts jaggedly through Berlin is a living, growing thing. It is composed of inanimate parts—concrete posts, blocks and slabs, barbed wire, wooden barricades, glass chips, bricks, fiberboard screens, steel stakes, copper trip wires and earthen breastworks.

The twenty-eight-mile wall lives in the minds of the Germans and it grows day by day at the hands of East German soldiers and civilian work crews commandeered under a new emergency defense law. It is made wider in some places, higher in others, and ever more impenetrable.

A month ago twenty or more East Germans managed to make their way across the barriers each night. Now the nightly number of successful escapes reported by West Berlin police averages three or four.

There is a liquid measure for the wall, too—the blood of a dozen escapers shot down by Communist border guards and the tears of the Germans on both sides who are divided from loved ones.

This week the Communists made spectacular additions to the barriers when they raised steel and concrete tank obstacles at seven strategic points in the heart of the city. The operation, involving more than a thousand men, was finished in forty-eight chilly hours.

East German propagandists boasted that the tank trap job would have taken 11,000 workers seven days under "normal" circumstances.

Neues Deutschland, organ of the ruling Socialist Unity (Communist) party, said afterward the new barriers were designed to prevent a Western Allied tank thrust into East Berlin.

"Our peace wall is insurmountable," it added.

There is constant activity on the Communist side of the wall. Trucks come and go with loads of concrete posts, barbed wire rolls, searchlights and other barrier supplies. Guards are changed frequently to prevent them from laying escape plans. They stand watch at intervals of fifty to seventy-five yards—with new Czechoslovak submachine guns.

On the Western side only a few policemen armed with wartime Sten guns go on patrol, occasionally with an unarmed customs guard in green uniform. Their main job now is to keep crowds of West Berliners away from the wall.

Last Monday night a thousand youths, fired up by a torchlight rally protesting against the wall, marched five miles to the barriers at Wilhelmstrasse to hurl burning torches and burning words into East Berlin. Some tried to storm the wall and West Berlin riot policemen had a difficult time driving them back.

Policemen on both sides threw tear gas grenades and a heavy white cloud hung over the scene. East German workmen who were putting the finishing touches on the "dragons teeth" steel tank traps had to flee the acrid fumes, eyes streaming.

There are tear gas duels nearly every night along the wall. West Berlin police have orders to answer every Communist grenade with a Western grenade. The exchanges are always begun by the East Germans, the cause most often being the arrival of a loudspeaker truck operated by the West Berlin city government.

There are six Western loudspeaker trucks that go to the wall to broadcast news and music. The Communists have 189 loudspeakers mounted along the wall that answer with propaganda slogans, march music and jazz.

Sometimes they blare at each other when no one else is about and only the big earlike megaphones appear to be listening to the cacophony.

"This wall is built to last 1,000 years," said Franz Amrehn, Deputy Mayor of the West Berlin, after viewing the latest barriers.

For East Germans the wall is an obsession. The desperate ones think only of escape: swimming across icy waters, running in the face of gunfire across open fields under the glare of searchlights, slithering between strands of barbed wire, leaping three and four stories, crawling through sewers. Some succeed; many fail; their bodies riddled with machine gun bullets.

This week one man reached the Western bank of the Spree River with nine bullets in his body.

The wall enters ghost-like into every conversation in East Berlin, where virtually everyone has relatives in the West.

"I stayed here because my parents are here," said a young man. "Now I would go in spite of them. It's odd, I don't even care about my family anymore, I just want to be free."

The middle-aged secretary adds, "we didn't even know how free we were before August 13. Now they can do anything with us." ■

Soldiers building the Berlin Wall, a 28-mile barrier that sealed off East Berlin from the western sector of the city.

OCTOBER 11, 1962

Vatican II Opens

The Second Vatican Council opening in Rome today will be the largest gathering of Roman Catholic prelates in history. It may also turn out to be the most important. Pope John XXIII has set an impressive goal for the council "fathers." In essence he has asked for a reform or renewal of the church that will bring it into closer accord with the needs and conditions of the modern world.

Translated into specifics the list of items is overwhelming. High among these will be re-evaluation of the role of the episcopacy, liturgical reform that may permit fuller use of the vernacular, more equitable apportionment of dioceses, dewesternization of the missions, a new look at religious tolerance and the fuller participation of laymen in the life of the church. Implicit in the papal plea for "aggiornamento" or reform is the hope that a rejuvenated church can more effectively cope with its greatest enemy, Communism, with a positive approach rather than with what seems at times to be mere negativism.

Also implicit in the council's deliberations is a tendency toward eventual reunion of all Christendom. Most leaders of the Roman Catholic, Protestant and Eastern Orthodox churches deplore the existence of the great divisions within the church in the 20th century. The obstacles appear insurmountable. Yet with perhaps prophetic vision Pope John has gone about the business of first setting his own house in order. At the same time he has invited non-Roman Catholic observers to sit in on the council sessions and has obviously endeavored to create a friendlier ecclesiastical climate.

Protestantism is no less concerned with Christian unity. In the last half century it has made great progress in bringing together many of its own divided churches.

The results of Vatican II may not be fully apparent in this generation. It is clear, however, that if all branches of Christendom can forget old hates and instead re-emphasize old truths, the miracle of a united Christianity may yet come to pass. ■

OCTOBER 23, 1962

U.S. IMPOSES ARMS BLOCK ON CUBA

Anthony Lewis

President John F. Kennedy's television announcement of the Cuban blockade being played in a department store, October 1962.

WASHINGTON, Oct. 22—President Kennedy imposed a naval and air "quarantine" tonight on the shipment of offensive military equipment to Cuba.

In a speech of extraordinary gravity, he told the American people that the Soviet Union, contrary to promises, was building offensive missile and bomber bases in Cuba. He said the bases could handle missiles carrying nuclear warheads up to 2,000 miles.

Thus a critical moment in the cold war was at hand tonight. The President had decided on a direct confrontation with—and challenge to—the power of the Soviet Union.

Two aspects of the speech were notable. One was its direct thrust at the Soviet Union as the party responsible for the crisis. Mr. Kennedy treated Cuba and the Government of Premier Fidel Castro as a mere pawn in Moscow's hands and drew the issue as one with the Soviet Government.

The President, in language of unusual bluntness, accused the Soviet leaders of deliberately "false statements about their intentions in Cuba."

The other aspect of the speech particularly noted by observers here was its flat commitment by the United States to act alone against the missile threat in Cuba.

The President made it clear that this country would not stop short of military action to end what he called a "clandestine, reckless and provocative threat to world peace."

Mr. Kennedy said the United States was asking for an emergency meeting of the United Nations Security Council to consider a resolution for "dismantling and withdrawal of all offensive weapons in Cuba."

He said the launching of a nuclear missile from Cuba against any nation in the Western Hemisphere would be regarded as an attack by the Soviet Union against the United States. It would be met, he said, by retaliation against the Soviet Union.

He called on Premier Khrushchev to withdraw the missiles from Cuba and so "move the world back from the abyss of destruction."

All this the President recited in an 18-minute radio and television address of a grimness unparalleled in recent times. He read the words rapidly, with little emotion, until he came to the peroration—a warning to Americans of the dangers ahead.

"Let no one doubt that this is a difficult and dangerous effort on which we have set out," the President said. "No one can foresee precisely what course it will take or what costs or casualties will be incurred."

The President's speech did not actually start the naval blockade tonight. To meet the requirements of international law, the State Department will issue a formal proclamation late tomorrow, and that may delay the effectiveness of the action as long as another 24 hours.

Congressional leaders of both parties, who were summoned to Washington today to be advised by the President of the crisis and his decision, gave him unanimous backing.

Mr. Kennedy went into considerable detail in his speech in outlining the nature of the military threat in Cuba, and this country's response.

He said:

"This urgent transformation of Cuba into an important strategic base by the presence of these large, long-range and clearly offensive weapons of sudden mass destruction constitutes an explicit threat to the peace and security of all the Americas."

He said the Soviet Union's action was "in flagrant and deliberate defiance" of the Rio (Inter-American) Pact of 1947, the United Nations Charter, Congressional resolution and his own public warnings to the Soviet Union. ■

OCTOBER 29, 1962

U.S. AND SOVIET REACH ACCORD ON CUBA

E.W. Kenworthy

Washington, Oct. 28—President Kennedy and Premier Khrushchev reached apparent agreement today on a formula to end the crisis over Cuba and to begin talks on easing tensions in other areas.

Premier Khrushchev pledged the Soviet Union to stop work on its missile sites in Cuba, to dismantle the weapons and to crate them and take them home. All this would be done under verification of United Nations representatives.

President Kennedy, for his part, pledged the lifting of the Cuban arms blockade when the United Nations had taken the "necessary measures," and that the United States would not invade Cuba.

Essentially this formula meets the conditions that President Kennedy set for the beginning of talks. If it is carried out, it would achieve the objective of the President in establishing the blockade last week: the removal of Soviet missile bases in Cuba.

While officials were gratified at the agreement reached on United States terms, there was no sense either of triumph or jubilation. The agreement, they realized, was only the beginning. The terms of it were not nailed down and Soviet negotiators were expected to arrive at the United Nations with a "bag full of fine print."

Although Mr. Khrushchev mentioned verification of the dismantling by United Nations observers in today's note, sources here do not consider it unlikely that the Russians may suggest that the observers be under the procedures of the Security Council.

This would make their findings subject to a veto by the Soviet Union as one of the 11 members of the Council.

United States officials did not expect a Cuban settlement, if it materialized, to lead to any great breakthroughs on such problems as inspection for a nuclear test ban and disarmament.

On the other hand, it was thought possible that a Cuban settlement might set a precedent for limited reciprocal concessions in some areas.

The break in the crisis came dramatically early this morning after a night of steadily mounting fears that events were running ahead of diplomatic efforts to control them.

The break came with the arrival of a letter from Premier Khrushchev in which the Soviet leader again changed his course.

Friday night, Mr. Khrushchev had sent a lengthy private letter to the President. Deep in it was the suggestion that the Soviet Union would remove its missiles from Cuba under supervision and not replace them if the United States and other Western Hemisphere nations would not invade Cuba.

The President found this proposal generally acceptable and yesterday morning his aides were preparing a private reply when the Moscow radio broadcast the text of another letter that was on its way.

The second letter proposed that the Soviet Union remove its missiles from Cuba in return for the dismantling of United States missiles in Turkey. This was advanced as an equitable exchange.

Fearing that it would be viewed in this light by many neutral nations, the White House immediately postponed a reply to the first letter and issued a statement on the second.

The White House said that the "first imperative" was the removal of the threat of Soviet missiles. The United States would not consider "any proposals" until work was stopped on the Cuban bases, the weapons were "rendered inoperable," and further shipments of them were halted.

The President accepted the first Khrushchev proposal as the basis for beginning talks.

The President said that he welcomed Mr. Khrushchev's message because "developments were approaching a point where events could have become unmanageable."

Mr. Kennedy said:

"I think that you and I, with our heavy responsibilities for the maintenance of peace, were aware that developments were approaching a point where events could have become unmanageable. So I welcome this message and consider it an important contribution to peace."

The President hopes that the "necessary measures" could be taken "at once" through the United Nations so that the quarantine could be removed on shipping. ■

MAY 26, 1963

30 Africa States Form Loose Union

Jay Walz

ADDIS ABABA, Ethiopia, May 25—The leaders of 30 independent African states formed today an Organization of African Unity. They adopted an all-Africa charter calling not only for unity in a loose federation but for far-reaching cooperation in politics, economics, education and defense.

Before adjourning their four-day conference, the heads of state or government also pledged to join in an effort to eradicate colonialism from the continent. They agreed to set up a fund to help freedom fighters in territories remaining under foreign control.

The charter was drafted by the foreign ministers of Ethiopia, Nigeria, Cameroon, Senegal, Ghana and the United Arab Republic. The signing took place at a public ceremony tonight.

The African leaders adopted a series of resolutions. One expressed the "deep concern" of the African people over racial discrimination throughout the world, saying they were particularly distressed about the situation in the United States. The resolution voiced "appreciation for the efforts of the Federal Government of the United States to put an end to these intolerable malpractices." It was plain that the Africans had in mind the incidents in Birmingham, Ala., though these were not specifically mentioned.

Addis Ababa was chosen as the site of temporary headquarters of the Organization of African Unity. The secretariat will be established in Africa Hall, where the conference was held.

The new charter is the first instrument bringing together free African states on a continental basis. The countries of the new organization occupy most of Africa from the Mediterranean to the boundaries of the still colonized territories in the south of the continent. South Africa, although independent, is excluded from the organization because of its racial segregation policy.

The countries that took part in the conference are Algeria, Burundi, Cameroon, the Central African Republic, Chad, the Congo Republic (Brazzaville), the Congo (Leopoldville), Dahomey, Ethiopia, Gabon, Ghana, Guinea, Ivory Coast, Liberia, Libya, Madagascar, Mali, Mauritania, Niger, Nigeria, Rwanda, Senegal, Sierra Leone, Somalia, Sudan, Tanganyika, Tunisia, Uganda, Upper Volta and the United Arab Republic. Morocco sent an observer.

The heads of state and government worked in closed session this morning on a final draft of the charter prepared by their foreign ministers. The session followed two and a half days of speeches in which the leaders all favored unity but differed sharply on how to approach that goal.

President Kwame Nkrumah of Ghana was the sole advocate of a union of African states that would unify the nations under a strong central government. Other state leaders favored a loose association in which the various states would preserve their sovereignty while agreeing to cooperate in economics, culture, education, transport and communication.

The charter says all free African states shall be "dedicated" to liberation of all African territories still under foreign rule. There are 14 major territories so ruled, including Portuguese Angola and Mozambique and the British colony of Kenya, which is now in the process of achieving independence. Unity is to be promoted through understanding and collaboration, and the states affirm their adherence to the United Nations.

In form and machinery, the African organization follows the pattern of the Organization of American States. The charter provides for a permanent headquarters, at a place yet to be chosen, and for a permanent Secretariat.

The ceremonies of the conference culminated last night in a state banquet given for 2,000 guests by Emperor Haile Selassie in the brilliantly illuminated great hall of King Menelik II, Ethiopia's monarch half a century ago. A fireworks display was held outside, and the orchestra of the imperial guard played. Miriam Makeba, the South African singer, also performed. ■

JUNE 4, 1963

POPE JOHN XXIII IS DEAD AT 81;

Reign of 4½ Years Devoted to Peace and Christian Unity

Pope John XXIII during Ecumenical Council in Rome, Italy, 1962.

Arnaldo Cortesi

ROME, June 3—Pope John XXIII, champion of world peace and a tireless fighter for the union of all Christian churches, died in the Vatican tonight while Cardinals and other prelates and several of his relatives prayed around his sickbed. He was 81 years old.

John XXIII was the 261st Pope to sit on the throne that was first occupied by the Apostle Peter. In the four years, seven months and six days of his reign he conquered the hearts of people throughout the world.

Few other Popes before him were so universally admired.

The Pope's death came at 7:49 P.M. After a long struggle the Pope developed peritonitis, brought on by a stomach tumor.

The Pope had dedicated much of his pontificate to promoting Christian unity and the unity of all men as brothers with a common God.

In his last words, addressed to the assembled Cardinals and prelates around his sickbed, the Pope said:

"Ut unum sint." They are Latin words meaning "That they may be one."

The words were originally spoken by Jesus after the Last Supper.

John XXIII was elected Pope Oct. 28, 1958. He was born in the village of Sotto il Monte in northern Italy on Nov. 25, 1881. He was 81 years, six months and nine days old at his death.

Pope John passed his last days in his bedroom on the top floor of the Vatican Palace. A small crowd of ecclesiastics and laymen had congregated there when they were told that the Pope was near death.

At 2:30 P.M. the Vatican radio said that prayer was the only comfort that could be offered to the Pope. Fifteen minutes later the radio said that opportunities for papal doctors to help the Pope were diminishing.

At 6:15 P.M. an announcer said that "the disease continues its inexorable work of demolishing the remaining strength of what was formerly the robust organism of John XXIII."

PRESIDENT HAILED BY OVER A MILLION IN VISIT TO BERLIN

Arthur J. Olsen

President John F. Kennedy delivers his 'Ich bin ein Berliner' speech to a massive crowd in Berlin, June 26, 1963.

Berlin, June 26—President Kennedy, inspired by a tumultuous welcome from more than a million of the inhabitants of this isolated and divided city, declared today he was proud to be "a Berliner."

He said his claim to being a Berliner was based on the fact that "all free men, wherever they may live, are citizens of Berlin."

In a rousing speech to 150,000 West Berliners crowded before the City Hall, the President said anyone who thought "we can work with the Communists" should come to Berlin.

However, three hours later, in a less emotional setting, he reaffirmed his belief that the great powers that must work together "to preserve the human race."

His earlier rejection of dealing with the Communists was a warning against trying to "ride the tiger" of popular fronts that unite democratic and Communist forces, Mr. Kennedy explained in an interpolation in a prepared speech.

The President's City Hall speech was the emotional high point of a spectacular welcome accorded the President by West Berlin. He saluted the city as the front line and shining example of humanity's struggle for freedom.

Those who profess not to understand the great issues between the free world and the Communist world or who think Communism is the wave of the future should come to Berlin, he said.

In his later speech, at the Free University of Berlin, President Kennedy returned firmly to the theme of his address at American University in Washington June 10 in which he called for an attempt to end the cold war.

"When the possibilities of reconciliation appear, we in the West will make it clear that we are not hostile to any people or system, provided that they choose their own destiny without interfering with the free choice of others," he said.

Then the President introduced an extemporaneous paragraph into his prepared text.

"As I said this morning, I am not impressed by the opportunities open to popular fronts throughout the world," he said. "I do not believe that any democrat can successfully ride that tiger. But I do believe in the necessity of great powers working together to preserve the human race."

Nuances of policy, however, were not the center of attention today in this city of at least 2,200,000 alert people. For them the only matter of importance was to give a heartfelt and spectacular welcome to the United States President and to see a youthful-looking smiling man obviously respond to their warmth.

Pierre Salinger, the President's press secretary, said the reception here was "the greatest he has had anywhere."

Along the route from Tegel airport to the United States mission headquarters in the southwest corner of Berlin, waving, cheering crowds lined every foot of the way.

The crowds must have nearly equaled the population of the city, but many persons waved once and then sped ahead to greet Mr. Kennedy again.

Only once in a jammed eight hours, during which he was almost uninterruptedly on a television screen, did Mr. Kennedy fail to dominate the scene.

Shortly before noon he approached Brandenburg Gate where he caught his first view of the Communist-built wall that partitions Berlin.

The President had been scheduled to gaze over the wall through the gate onto Unter den Linden, once the main avenue of the German capital. However, the five arches of the gate were covered by huge red banners, blocking his view there of East Berlin.

The cloth barrier was put up by East Berlin officials last night.

At Checkpoint Charlie, the United States-controlled crossing point to East Berlin on the Friedrichstrasse, Mr. Kennedy had an unobstructed view several hundred yards into the eastern sector.

About 300 yards away, well beyond the 100-yard forbidden zone decreed by the Communists last week, he glimpsed a small group of East Berliners attracted by his presence. Though he could not hear them, they cheered. ■

JUNE 16, 1963

TORY CHIEFS HEAL RIFT AFTER SCANDAL

James Feron

LONDON, June 15—Conservative party leaders lined up behind Prime Minister Macmillan today as the party prepared for a crucial debate in the House of Commons Monday over the Profumo scandal. John Profumo, 48-year-old former Secretary of State for War, touched off the political crisis that has shaken the Government by admitting a week and a half ago that he had lied to Parliament in denying improper relations with Christine Keeler, a 21-year-old party girl.

Labor party leaders have charged that Mr. Macmillan was either negligent or naive in not recognizing the seriousness of the situation, especially one involving a girl who was having a simultaneous affair with a Soviet deputy naval attaché stationed in London.

This aspect was highlighted yesterday when Michael H. B. Eddowes, a London lawyer, said that the Soviet attaché, Capt. Yevgeni E. Ivanov, who was recalled last December, had asked Miss Keeler to get military information from Mr. Profumo. Miss Keeler's lawyers issued a statement in her behalf denying Mr. Eddowes' allegations. He had previously submitted his information to the Government.

Miss Keeler said in her memoirs, being published by The News of the World, that it was "a friend," not Captain Ivanov, who "asked me directly to find out from Jack [Profumo] when Germany was going to be armed with atomic weapons."

"I refused," she said. "I felt instinctively and deep down that this was spying."

Mr. Eddowes is a former patient of Dr. Stephen Ward, a London osteopath who brought the parties together and is now in custody charged with living off the earnings from prostitution.

A formal inquiry into the entire security aspect of the case, going back to Mr. Profumo's first meeting with Miss Keeler, was not initiated by the Government until a few weeks ago, when the Opposition began to apply pressure. The inquiry, conducted by Lord Dilhorne, the Lord Chancellor, apparently found no indication of a security breach.

Labor party leaders will want to know why the Government waited so long to begin a detailed inquiry. They will also ask whether the first investigation, in February, failed to disclose what is now known about Miss Keeler's friends, or whether, having uncovered a suspicious situation, the Government decided to ignore, suppress or disbelieve it.

There were reports that the party whips were going to great lengths to insure loyalty. The debate has been designated a "three-line whip," an infrequently used summons to attend debates that are underlined three times and carry the greatest urgency. A Conservative who fails to show up without being, as one official put it, "dead or well out of the country," can lose party support.

It was also reported that party unity had been assured by an understanding that, once the Profumo issue had been settled in the party's favor, Mr. Macmillan would give way for a younger man who could lead the Conservatives into the next general election. The party's mandate will expire in October 1961. ■

SEPTEMBER 26, 1963

SOVIET RATIFIES TEST BAN TREATY

Henry Tanner

MOSCOW, Sept. 25—The Soviet Union ratified today the treaty for a limited nuclear test ban. The action, which came a day after a similar move by the United States Senate, was taken unanimously by the Presidium of the Supreme Soviet.

About 25 members of the 33-member Presidium were present at the meeting under the chairmanship of President Leonid I. Brezhnev.

The Presidium is the highest legislative body of the Soviet Union between the brief sessions of the Supreme Soviet (Parliament), which are held once or twice a year.

The ratification vote took place without prior announcement. Only Soviet newsmen were present. Izvestia, the Government newspaper, devoted almost its entire front page tonight to the meeting.

Vasily V. Kuznetsov, a First Deputy Foreign Minister, submitted the Government report for ratification.

Tass, the official press agency, said he emphasized that the treaty, though permitting a continuation of underground nuclear tests, did not give "any unilateral advantage to the United States."

The test ban treaty obligates signers not to explode nuclear devices in the air, in space or under water.

Mr. Kuznetsov was quoted by Tass as having said: "The measures recently taken by the Soviet Government to strengthen its defenses included tests of the most powerful nuclear weapons existing in the world."

This, he said, gives the Soviet Union every possible assurance that the treaty is in its interests and in the interests of other Socialist countries.

The Foreign Affairs Committee of the Supreme Soviet recommended ratification almost a month ago. The delay in Presidium action was viewed by observers here as a possible gesture designed to show the Chinese Communists and others in the Communist bloc that the Soviet Union took no chances and accepted the treaty as binding only after the United States had done so.

Pravda, the newspaper of the Communist party, wrote that it amounted to a "victory of common sense over recklessness." ■

NOVEMBER 3, 1963

DIEM AND NHU REPORTED SLAIN

David Halberstam

SAIGON, South Vietnam, Nov. 2—President Ngo Dinh Diem and his brother, Ngo Dinh Nhu, are dead in the wake of the military uprising that ended their regime.

While the Saigon radio announced that they had committed suicide, reliable private military sources said that they had been assassinated.

With Saigon under military rule, crowds of jubilant youths set fire to the homes of government security officials, offices of government-controlled newspapers and police stations.

The military sources that reported that the brothers had been killed said they had escaped from the palace by a tunnel shortly before U.S. Marines overran it.

Later, Ngo Dinh Diem was seen in a small Roman Catholic church in Cholon, a suburb of Saigon, it was reported. The military leaders sent troops and armored cars and both men were taken prisoner.

The military, denouncing what it termed the Diem Government's despotism and corruption, suspended the Constitution and ended the presidential system. Imprisoned Buddhist monks were freed.

The military coup d'état ended nine years of Ngo Dinh Diem's rule shortly before 7 A.M. when the palace was stormed by marines. Moments before this, both Ngo Dinh Diem and Ngo Dinh Nhu had told the military they were surrendering. But, according to reliable sources, they then escaped.

The new military revolution committee immediately pledged itself to continue the war against the Communist insurgents.

Though Nguyen Ngoc Tho served under Ngo Dinh Diem he is considered acceptable to varying elements in country and was considered by many sources a dissident within the Cabinet who was disturbed by the Government's treatment of the Buddhists.

Buddhist leaders who led the religious political protest movement against the Government and had been imprisoned since Aug. 21 when the Government raided pagodas were freed today by the army. They were acclaimed by a huge, emotional crowd at Xa Loi Pagoda as they returned from prison.

Seven Buddhists monks had burned themselves to death as part of the protest.

Throughout the city, the population acclaimed the troops and food was given to the soldiers by many people. Though the city was under martial law, there was an air of jubilation. ■

OCTOBER 17, 1964

FALL OF KHRUSHCHEV

Harrison E. Salisbury

Soviet Premier Nikita S. Khrushchev in 1960.

Evidence of what went on in the Soviet Union in the last 72 hours suggests that Nikita S. Khrushchev was removed from office in a virtual coup d'état by a group of close associates with the aid and support of the Soviet armed forces.

Specialists in Soviet affairs, after a close study of the available evidence, think that the deposed Communist leader is almost surely under the strictest guard. It is entirely possible, they suggested, that Mr. Khrushchev was prevented forcibly from participating in the key proceedings that led to his removal, which was made nominally on the ground of age and health.

The instant housecleaning launched to rid high Government and party offices of men personally associated with him, it was said, emphasized that a genuine shift of power had occurred.

In the power shift, it was stressed, the role of the Soviet military was vital if not conclusive. The precise factors that caused the military to back the Khrushchev opposition are not yet entirely clear.

However, it was believed that the emergence of Communist China as a nuclear power, the increasing security threat along the Soviet-Chinese frontier, the deterioration of the Soviet security situation in East Europe, including East Germany, as a result of intra-Communist differences formed the major argument in winning the backing of Soviet marshals for the power shift.

The dramatic circumstances of the Khrushchev displacement and the forces mobilized to accomplish it, in the opinion of the same quarters, almost certainly portend dramatic new power confrontations in the Kremlin.

As to the mechanism by which Mr. Khrushchev was deposed, abundant clues were available.

Mr. Khrushchev had been at Gagra, on the Black Sea, relaxing at his villa there. With him as late as Monday was President Anastas I. Mikoyan, his closest political associate, longtime friend and ally in many a political campaign. On Monday, Mr. Khrushchev and Mr. Mikoyan spoke by radio to the three Soviet astronauts in orbit in the Voskhod. The conversation was brief but warm. At one point Mr. Khrushchev said he was forced to stop speaking because Mr. Mikoyan was "literally tearing the phone" from his hand.

On Tuesday, Mr. Khrushchev had an appointment to meet with the French Minister of Atomic Research, Gaston Palewski. Mr. Palewski arrived at the villa, expecting an afternoon and possibly an evening of talks with Mr. Khrushchev. The meeting turned out to be brief. After half an hour Mr. Krushchev suddenly rose, excused himself and said he had to leave.

Was the meeting interrupted because Mr. Khrushchev had just received word that he must return to Moscow?

Did he at that moment receive word that he had been deposed by the Presidium of the Central Committee of the Communist party?

The answer is not clear. Some Moscow reports say that Mr. Khrushchev returned to the capital Tuesday. If so, the key action to oust him—the vote by the party's Presidium—had almost certainly been taken before he arrived.

But sometime between midnight Tuesday and early Wednesday, the Presidium did meet and vote Mr. Khrushchev out. This is certain because by Wednesday evening the party's Central Committee had been summoned to Moscow where it confirmed the removal of Mr. Khrushchev as First Secretary of the party and as a member of the party's Presidium.

The Central Committee members must be summoned from all over the country. The meeting must have been hastily called and probably could not have included the full membership on such short notice.

Where was Mr. Khrushchev? Possibly in Moscow but almost certainly not permitted full freedom to argue his case before the Central Committee.

On Thursday, the Presidium of the Supreme Soviet (Parliament) met and deprived Mr. Khrushchev of his post as Chairman (Premier) of the Council of Ministers, his last office. By this time, certainly, Mr. Khrushchev was under the closest kind of surveillance, immobilized behind a thick wall of security guards and prevented from any possibility of maneuver. ■

MAY 31, 1964

Palestinians Set 'Liberation' Goal

BEIRUT, Lebanon, May 30—Three hundred fifty delegates claiming to represent one and a half million Arab refugees from Palestine vowed this week to "sacrifice our blood for the liberation of Palestine."

They were pledging allegiance to the Palestine Liberation Organization, established at the National Palestine Congress now meeting in Jerusalem's Jordanian sector. They rejected plans to resettle refugees in host Arab countries and declared: "Palestine is ours, ours, ours. We shall accept no substitute homeland."

A large emblem of the organization adorned the assembly hall in Jerusalem's new Intercontinental Hotel, where the congress convened. The emblem carried a map of Palestine, including the "occupied" area that is now Israel. Inscribed across the map were the words, "We shall return."

Ahmed Shukairy, a lawyer from Haifa, is the leader of the new organization. He was chosen last January at a conference of Arab leaders in Cairo to establish what is now referred to as the "Palestine entity." One plan suggested by him to accomplish this, called the Palestine National Charter, laid down general rights and obligations for Palestinians. It defined Palestine as the area that existed under the British mandate that ended in 1948. A second plan proposed the liberation organization, which is to have an executive committee and an army of Palestinians.

Mr. Shukairy declared that the organization was based on "faith in the inevitability of the liberation of Palestine and the determination of Palestinians to mobilize all their material, military and spiritual energies toward this end."

The Palestine National Congress and the liberation organization are regarded as the first serious effort since the Palestine war 16 years ago to mold refugees into an effective force. Although Arab governments agree in principle on the need for a Palestinian "entity," they are divided over the methods through which this should be achieved. Mr. Shukairy's plan falls short of some Arab and Palestinian expectations. ■

JUNE 12, 1964

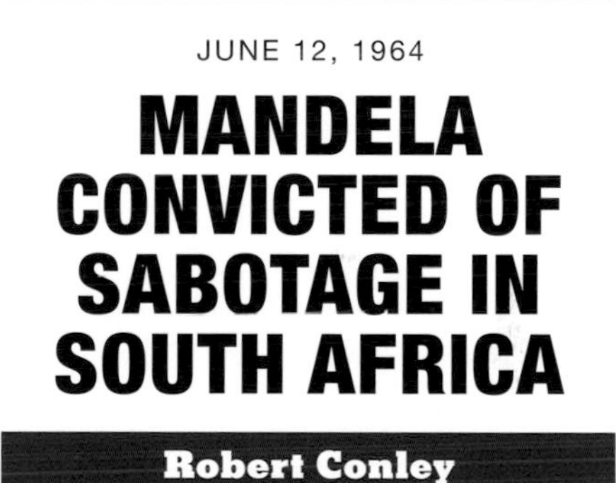

MANDELA CONVICTED OF SABOTAGE IN SOUTH AFRICA

Robert Conley

PRETORIA, South Africa, June 11—Nelson R. Mandela, Walter M. E. Sisulu and six other men were convicted today of having planned a "violent revolution" against South Africa's racial policies.

Mandela and Sisulu are two of the most prominent black nationalist leaders in South Africa.

A ninth defendant in the sabotage trial, Lionel G. Bernstein, was acquitted. But he was arrested immediately by the Security Police on a new charge, that he had furthered the aims of communism. He is white.

The eight convicted—six black Africans, a white and an Indian—were found guilty by the Supreme Court of having recruited persons for military training in South Africa and abroad for a sabotage organization

(cont'd. on next page)

Eight men sentenced to life imprisonment in the Rivonia trial, among them anti-apartheid leader Nelson R. Mandela, leave the Palace of Justice in Pretoria, South Africa, June 1964.

(cont'd. from previous page)
known as Umkonto we Sizwe (Spear of the Nation). All could receive the death penalty in the sentencing tomorrow.

They were said to have conspired to have the recruits trained in the preparation, manufacture and use of explosives for acts of "violence and destruction" against the white government of Prime Minister Hendrik F. Verwoerd. The court also found that the training covered conventional warfare and guerrilla warfare.

Nearly 150 Africans waiting on the street outside the court building greeted the news of the verdict with shouts of "Amandla nga wethu" (Strength is ours). As the police moved up, those in the crowd thrust their arms into the air in the clenched fist and upright thumb sign of the African Nationalist Congress party, South Africa's oldest black political movement. The party was banned by the Government for its opposition to the country's policy of apartheid, or racial separation.

Mandela, a 45-year-old lawyer and tribal prince who won the nickname "Black Pimpernel" for his ability to elude the police, had been the party's deputy national president. Sisulu, 52, had been its secretary general. Both Mandela and Sisulu admitted having organized a sabotage campaign, as had four other defendants. The presiding Justice, Quar-tas de Wet, termed Mandela the "prime mover" in establishing the Spear of the Nation.

This sabotage organization was founded in 1961, with the approval of the Congress party leadership, to attack targets seemed to be "symbols of apartheid" or held likely to damage South Africa's economy. Those targets included government African Affairs offices, steel pylons carrying high-tension electricity wires, telephone lines and railroad signal boxes.

The court found that Chief Albert J. Luthuli, winner of a Nobel Peace Prize, had been aware of the organization's operations. Justice de Wet ruled that Chief Luthuli, former national president of the Congress party, had been "informed about activities of Umkonto and consulted from time to time."

Justice de Wet dismissed charges that Umkonto had conspired to commit guerrilla warfare and to open the country to invasion by unidentified outside military forces. Those convicted, in addition to Mandela and Sisulu, were the following: Dennis T. Goldberg, 33, white civil engineer from Capetown; Govan A. Mbeki, 53, a black African journalist and member of the Congress party's national executive; and Ahmed M. Kathrada, 34, an Indian who is the former secretary general of the Transvaal Indian Congress party. Also, Elias Motsoaledi, 39, and Andrew Mlangeni, 38, both Congress party members, and Raymond Mahlaba, a party organizer. The last three named are black Africans. ■

JANUARY 9, 1964

POPE'S PILGRIMAGE FOR UNITY

Dana Adams Schmidt

BEIRUT, Lebanon, Jan. 8—Roman Catholic and Orthodox churchmen who attended the meetings between Pope Paul VI and the Ecumenical Patriarch of Constantinople, Athenagoras I, are agreed that the way for reconciliation of their churches has been eased. But there is also a feeling among some in the Orthodox Church that what happened in Jerusalem was the easiest of the giant steps that will have to be taken before a complete reconciliation can be effected.

The Pope's pilgrimage to the Holy Land and his meetings with the Patriarch, the most eminent representative of the Eastern Orthodox Church, created an emotional basis for progress toward the ultimate reunification of the two main Western and Eastern segments of the Christian religion. The Pope's visit to the places where Christianity originated symbolized the search for the fundamental truths of Christianity.

Years of detailed examination of liturgical and doctrinal differences lie ahead of the church leaders. The Orthodox conference at Rhodes last September took the first step by proposing a "dialogue on the basis of equality" with the Catholic Church.

It was left to Patriarch Athenagoras to consult with the heads of all the Orthodox churches on the drafting of the Orthodox invitation to Rome. He has not yet finished these consultations, and it may yet be many months before a formal invitation is sent.

The two churches are seeking to repair a breach that developed in 1054 and that became fixed in 1472. Before 1054, Orthodox Christians recognized the Pope as Patriarch of the West and Bishop of Christendom's primatial see.

Some Orthodox officials have been thinking about the cultural systems and philosophical thought in the light of which East and West interpreted Jesus and out of which theological differences grew. The Western mind, as Orthodox churchmen see it, insists on defining everything. Catholic doctrines, such as those of the Immaculate

Conception and Purgatory, deal with areas that the Orthodox Church is prepared to leave unclear.

On the whole, the Orthodox Church feels it is more liberal and democratic in its approach to Christianity. For that reason, Orthodox churchmen usually feel closer to Anglicans and Protestants than to Catholics.

Orthodox misgivings about the Roman Catholic approach to reunification were aroused by a passage in the Pope's speech at Bethlehem, in which he said that unity was not to be "at the expense of faith." "We cannot be false to Christ's heritage," the Pope said, "the door of the fold is open." This sounded to some more like a call for a return of those who had strayed from the truth than a call for a meeting on a basis of equality.

MAY 28, 1964

India Mourning Nehru, 74, Dead of a Heart Attack

NEW DELHI, May 27—Jawaharlal Nehru, maker of modern India and her Prime Minister for the 17 years since independence, died today at the age of 74.

Twelve days of mourning have been ordered throughout the country. Late today thousands of Indians of all levels, including peasants on foot from distant areas, were arriving for the funeral tomorrow.

Mr. Nehru suffered a paralytic stroke in January when he went to a Congress party meeting. This caused a weakening of his left limbs.

Although Mr. Nehru resumed his full responsibilities as Prime Minister in recent weeks, he was not the same. In Parliament he rose with an effort to answer questions. When he walked he dragged his left foot.

As soon as Parliament assembled this morning to begin a 10-day special session to vote a land bill, the members were told that Mr. Nehru had been "suddenly taken seriously ill" and that his condition was "causing anxiety." At 2 P.M., Steel Minister Coimbatore Subramaniam walked into Parliament to announce Mr. Nehru's death. He said:

"The light is out."

Several members wept.

As news of Mr. Nehru's death spread, several thousand people gathered at the gates of his residence. Men, women and children stood in mile-long queues in the hot sun, through the late evening and then a drizzle to see their dead leader, whom they had affectionately called "Chacha (Uncle) Nehru."

The body will lie in state until tomorrow afternoon. The funeral procession is scheduled to begin at 1 P.M. After four hours of winding through the main streets, the body will be cremated in Rajghat on the banks of the Jamuna River.

Traditional Hindu rites will take place 300 yards north of the spot where Gandhi was cremated.

AUGUST 6, 1964

PRESIDENT REQUESTS SUPPORT OF CONGRESS ON VIETNAM

E. W. Kenworthy

WASHINGTON, Aug. 5—President Johnson asked Congress today to pass a joint resolution assuring him of full support "for all necessary action" he might have to take to protect the armed forces of the United States in Southeast Asia. The President also asked that the resolution give prior sanction for any necessary steps, including the use of armed force, to assist nations covered by the Southeast Asia Treaty Organization that requested help in defense of their freedom.

As soon as the clerk had finished reading the special message from the White House, identical resolutions were offered by Senator J. W. Fulbright of Arkansas, chairman of the Senate Foreign Relations Committee, and Representative Thomas E. Morgan of Pennsylvania, chairman of the House Foreign Affairs Committee. Hearings on the proposed resolution will begin tomorrow.

The President made his request for Congressional support a day after he told the nation over television of a second attack within three days on United States destroyers by North Vietnamese PT boats. In his message the President emphasized, as he did in his broadcast, that "the United States intends no rashness and seeks no wider war." He went on to make clear that the United States would not tolerate such attacks as have taken place this week. Then he said:

"We must make it clear to all that the United States is united in its determination to bring about the end of Communist subversion and aggression in the area."

There was general support on Capitol Hill for the retaliatory action ordered by the President and for the resolution. The principal discordant note—and it was extremely bitter—was sounded by Senator Wayne L. Morse, Democrat of Oregon, who over the last five months has directed almost daily attacks on what he calls "McNamara's war."

As soon as the reading of the President's message and proposed resolution was completed, Mr. Morse rose and said the resolution was tantamount to a "declaration of war" and "war should not be declared by resolution." The incident inspiring the resolution, Mr. Morse said, "is as much the doing of the United States as it is the doing of North Vietnam." He charged that "the role of the United States in South Vietnam" over the last 10 years "has been that of a provocateur, every bit as much as North Vietnam has been a provocateur."

There has been mounting evidence for months, he said, that the Pentagon and State Department "were preparing to escalate the war into North Vietnam." He charged that before the attacks on the United States destroyers, "South Vietnamese naval vessels bombarded two North Vietnamese islands within three to five or six miles of the main coast of North Vietnam."

According to newspaper reports, the Senator went on, United States naval vessels were patrolling the Gulf of Tonkin, "presumably some six to 11 miles off the shore of North Vietnam," during the attack by the South Vietnamese vessels. "Was the United States Navy standing guard while vessels of South Vietnam shelled North Vietnam?" he asked. "That is the clear implication of the incident."

The Pentagon has said that during the first attack by the North Vietnamese boats, the United States destroyer was 20 to 30 miles off shore, and during the second attack the two destroyers were 50 to 60 miles offshore. ■

JANUARY 21, 1965

CHURCHILL IS DEAD AT 90; WORLD MOURNS HIM

Anthony Lewis

LONDON, Jan. 21—Winston Churchill's struggle for life ended this morning and the people he had cherished and inspired and led through darkness mourned him as they have no other in this age.

Sir Winston died just after 8 o'clock, in the 10th day of public anxiety over his condition after a stroke. He was in his 91st year.

Britons small and great—village curate, Prime Minister and Queen—paid him tribute through the day and this evening. Statesmen around the world joined in homage to the statesman they acknowledge as the greatest of the age.

The radio today carried the Churchill voice—recordings of speeches that aroused a people to deeds of valor in a grim time.

"We shall never surrender." It was such Churchillian words as these—and the conviction with which he spoke—that many believe saved Britain and her allies from defeat and subjection to Hitler.

The weekly journal The Spectator said:

"We are a free people because a man called Winston Churchill lived."

It is as the great wartime Prime Minister that he will above all be recorded. But those who mourned him today were moved by more than that. He was a great personality, not just a statesman. He was human with emotions and desires and faults, some on an Olympian scale.

He drank wine for breakfast when it pleased him to do so and champagne and brandy and whisky in quantities through the rest of the day. He smoked cigars continuously. He never exercized. And his health was amazing.

He lived on controversy. The adjectives often applied to him were pugnacious and combative. He was famous for ridicule and invective debate, for witticisms such as the one he applied to the Puritan figure of Sir Stafford Cripps: "There, but for the grace of God, goes God."

He was this age's nearest equivalent to a Renaissance man.

The procession at the state funeral of Sir Winston Churchill, January 30, 1965.

He was a soldier, escaped war prisoner, historian, novelist, orator, journalist and politician.

He spent 60 years in the House of Commons but found time to write more than two dozen books.

In the midst of war and grand strategy, as he himself recorded in his history of World War II, he took time to note the pleasures of the flesh in Marrakesh in Morocco, and the plumbing in Yalta. He had passion for detail.

It was his zeal for life that Londoners are remembering above all.

FEBRUARY 25, 1965

U. S. Admits Shift in Vietnam Stand

Max Frankel

WASHINGTON, Feb. 24—The Administration tacitly acknowledged today that it had changed the rules of United States involvement in the war in South Vietnam. It cited Congressional authority for the move.

The use of American planes and crews on combat missions against the Vietcong guerrillas supplants an earlier policy of having Americans "advise and assist" the South Vietnamese, and fight only in self-defense. The acknowledgment of the change had the effect of stiffening Washington's position in the face of continuing appeals abroad for negotiations. The White House summarized official responses to these appeals by stating that it had received "no meaningful proposals" for negotiation. By implication, the statement made little of the mediation efforts of U Thant, Secretary General of the United Nations, and of British and French diplomats who have been sounding out the Soviet Union.

"There are no authorized negotiations under way with Mr. Thant or any other government," George E. Reedy, the White House press secretary, said. "I am not going into any diplomatic chitchat that may be going forth, or way-out feelers," he added. "But authorized or meaningful negotiations—no."

His statement also implied that no encouraging offer of a settlement developed at the regularly scheduled meeting in Warsaw today between the Ambassadors of the United States and Communist China. Officials here have repeatedly said that they cannot envision negotiations until Communist China and North Vietnam indicate a willingness to "leave South Vietnam alone." They say they have seen no such indication and doubt that Moscow can speak for its Communist allies.

This view is also being endorsed more vigorously on Capitol Hill. A growing number of members of both houses of Congress are speaking out in defense of the Administration's reluctance to define the limits of possible military action in both North and South Vietnam and its refusal to consider negotiations now.

A small village bursts into flames under a spread of phosphorus explosives dropped during an American air strike against Viet Cong positions, 1966.

The "advise and assist" definition of the role of American troops in Vietnam was abandoned by the State Department today in its assessment of the disclosure that B-57 bombers and F-100 fighter-bombers with American crews were now being used to attack Vietcong troops in support of ground action. The jets were sent into action at the request of the Government of South Vietnam, a spokesman said, adding: "Such action was carried out because of the concentration of Vietcong in this area [Binhdinh Province] as a result of increased infiltration of men and equipment in recent months.

"This is consistent with the Congressional resolution approving and supporting the determination of the President as Commander in Chief to prevent any further aggression and is in accordance with the Government's stated policy of continuous action that is appropriate, fitting and measured."

The reference was to a joint Congressional resolution on Southeast Asia adopted with only two dissenting votes in the Senate and unanimously by the House last Aug. 7. That was after North Vietnamese PT boats had attacked United States warships in the Gulf of Tonkin, leading to retaliatory air strikes against the boats' bases in North Vietnam.

The resolution defined peace and security in Southeast Asia as "vital" to the national interest and said the United States was "prepared, as the President determines, to take all necessary steps, including the use of armed force" to assist any nation that belongs to or is covered by—as South Vietnam is—the Southeast Asia collective defense treaty.

The rules of American combat engagement in Vietnam have developed gradually since the first large contingents of troops were assigned there in 1961. At first, they were described as only advisers. Later they were authorized to shoot when shot at. Gradually, Americans assumed more prominent roles in leading South Vietnamese troops into action. Helicopters at first carried Vietnamese guides and had authority only to fire in self-defense. Then, on appeal to the Joint Chiefs of Staff, the helicopter pilots were permitted to define the danger and to fire protectively at and around landing sites. Ground action had hitherto been supported by T-28 propeller-driven trainer planes with a Vietnamese co-pilot beside the American pilot-gunner. ■

SEPTEMBER 3, 1965

WAR IN KASHMIR

Kashmir has suddenly and frighteningly become the most explosive spot in the world. India and Pakistan, for all practical purposes, are at war; the whole South Asian complex of nations will be affected; the icy blast of the cold war is blowing on India's northeastern flank from Communist China. Add the possibility of communal strife between Moslems and Hindus in both countries and the extent of the peril becomes only too clear.

It is a peril that ripples outward from Kashmir like lava from a volcano. The world is the victim, and the world should try to do something quickly in the only forum available to every country—the United Nations. Secretary General Thant has been trying his best by personal appeals to Indian and Pakistani leaders, but so far without avail. The Security Council, which is in permanent session, could and should now throw its weight into the peace efforts.

The observer team that the council has kept on the Kashmir cease-fire line can only watch and report. It has no peacekeeping authority, as have the U.N. forces in Cyprus and the Gaza Strip. Since diplomacy has failed, and since the great powers are in no position to intervene in any other way, the only visible hope is for the Security Council to use its authority to set up some peacekeeping machinery for Kashmir.Whether the U.N. can respond effectively to the crisis in Kashmir will be an important indicator of whether it has come out of its own internal crisis as something more than a debating society.

The seriousness of the Kashmiri conflict, among other things, lies in its deliberate character. India made plain her determination to hold on to her two-thirds of Kashmir, and Pakistan obviously concluded that the issue could only be settled by force.

Both sides now seem determined to fight it out. This is what must be blocked if the danger of a world conflagration is to be averted. The United States, Great Britain and Russia have a special responsibility when it is considered that the Kashmiri war is being fought with their arms, tanks and planes. The Security Council would respond if all three powers unite on a common course of action. Secretary of State Rusk already has informed both belligerents of this country's deep concern over their conflict.

So far as India and Pakistan are concerned, they must be made to realize that, while Kashmir is a great prize, war is too high a price to pay for it.

NOVEMBER 14, 1965

MARCOS—NEW MAN IN MANILA

Seymour Topping

MANILA, Nov. 13—Senator Ferdinand E. Marcos, a tough dynamic politician who has been groomed all his life to lead his nation, was elected this week the sixth President of the Republic of the Philippines. Thirty million Filipinos knew he would give them strong leadership, but they were uncertain just where he would steer them. Nevertheless, Senator Marcos won a smashing victory, defeating President Diosdado P. Macapagal.

The election campaign, which featured mud slinging, 47 political murders and less dramatic voting irregularities that strained the democratic process, was fought out in terms of personalities rather than on concrete issues of Government.

In foreign policy Senator Marcos is considered pretty much of a blank who has neither discovered the Far East nor been discovered by it. As for his relations with the United States, before the week was history and before President Macapagal could assemble his dignity to concede the election, the Senator summoned a news conference and reassured Washington that the old friendship between the two countries would be respected. Senator Marcos said he would stand by the long-term agreement for the maintenance of the United States naval and air bases in the Philippines which are now being employed to support operations in Vietnam. He implied that he might dispatch combat troops to Vietnam to help persuade the Communists that they should negotiate.

On domestic affairs, he said that when he assumes office at the end of December and Congress assembles, he intended to seek a reduction of the budget, clean up the notoriously corrupt customs service so as to "set a new moral tone'" for his administration. It was a characteristically forceful gambit of the country's most decorated war hero and most ambitious politician.

Nevertheless, a cynical nation, bedeviled by endless economic disorders and official corruption, is waiting to see if the new President would truly rectify the sins of omission and commission of the outgoing and unmourned Macapagal Administration.

As his first Presidential chore, the Senator must cope with the problems of a country exhausted by a year-long election campaign. The administration of the country lapsed while the politicians went vote hunting. A depleted treasury might also compel the Senator to turn to Washington for economic help.

When Senator Marcos was asked if he would visit the United States, he replied that if he was invited he would go immediately to visit President Johnson. ■

'RED GUARD' RALLIES IN PEKING

Ian Stewart

Chinese leader Mao Tsetung during a rally in Tiananmen Square, Peking (Beijing), 1966.

HONG KONG, Sept. 3—The Chinese Communist hierarchy was acting this week like a man with a tiger by the tail. It was showing considerable uneasiness over the fury of the young "Red Guards" it had let loose to eradicate Western influences and enforce puritanical austerity throughout China.

Half a million "revolutionary teachers and students" representing Red Guard units from all over China were summoned to Peking for a meeting with the "great teacher, great leader, great supreme commander and great helmsman of the Chinese people," Mao Tsetung, at a rally on Tiananmen Square.

It was at a rally on the same square earlier last month that the Red Guards had made their first appearance. Since then, acting in the name of Mr. Mao's new "cultural revolution," they had launched a fierce attack on "old ideas, old culture, old customs and old habits." Virtually seizing control of many cities, they had subjected "bourgeois" victims to public humiliation and even physical assault. There were some bloody street fights in Peking and elsewhere as a result.

At the new rally, Chairman Mao and Defense Minister Lin Piao again held center stage, and Mr. Mao again appeared in army uniform to symbolize his close relationship with Mr. Lin—his new choice as heir apparent. Mr. Lin again spoke on Mr. Mao's behalf. He had some words of praise for the Red Guards, declaring that they had done many good things and put forward many good proposals. But the main purpose of the meeting was clearly to bring the rampaging Red Guards to heel.

"Don't hit people," Marshal Lin said, calling on the youngsters to use reasoning and not coercion or force in their campaign. His speech echoed Peking newspaper editorials asking for an end to violence and asserting that the Red Guards should emulate the "iron discipline" of the army. It also reflected a published report by a "control committee of the Red Guards" on the mistakes committed—molesting Government officials, searching their homes and offices, and shaving the heads of persons with "bourgeois" haircuts. There were some brawls in Peking and other cities as a result; in Canton two Red Guards were reported to have been killed.

The 72-year-old Mr. Mao and his aging comrades appear to have been rather surprised at the ferocity of the Red Guards. Perhaps this is due to the disparity in years between the leaders and the militant youth. Most of the guards are teenagers. Many of them are not yet in their teens.

When eight elderly European nuns expelled from China crossed into Hong Kong this week, a group of about 200 Red Guards was standing some distance back from the border, chanting slogans and shaking their fists. From the Hong Kong side of the border they looked like a formidable mob. A British police inspector picked up a pair of binoculars for a closer look and said, "Why, it's a bunch of kids!"

The nuns themselves said of the Red Guards who had invaded their Peking convent, 'They were just children, just children. We must not judge them." Children they may be, but by virtue of their energy, exuberance and sheer numbers, they represent a force which could prove a significant factor in future political developments in China.

Direct responsibility for setting the Red Guard movement in motion is believed to rest with the Peking municipal committee of the Chinese Communist party, which was reorganized after Peng Chen, Mayor of Peking, was purged. The first members were "activists" chosen in various schools to lead the "cultural revolution" against "bourgeois" teachers and students. But with the subsequent development of the Red Guard campaign as a mass movement, its members constitute a cross-section of China's youth, ranging in age from 12 to 20, with some teachers acting as their directors.

Neither Mr. Mao nor Mr. Lin nor their ally, Premier Chou En-lai, appear too happy about the excessive zeal of the Red Guards. But they clearly hope to shape the movement into a disciplined paramilitary organization. Speaking at the Peking rally, Mr. Chou said the Red Guards must be built into a "highly organized and disciplined militant army, with high political consciousness." ■

INDIRA GANDHI ELECTED PRIME MINISTER

J. Anthony Lukas

NEW DELHI, Jan. 19—Mrs. Indira Gandhi became India's third Prime Minister today. Her father, Jawaharlal Nehru, was the country's first, and held the job for 17 years. In the first direct contest ever held for the post, Mrs. Gandhi was elected by legislators of the Congress party gathered in the great teak and green plush central hall of Parliament. She became the second woman in modern history to head a government. The other is Mrs. Sirimavo Bandaranaike, who recently was deposed as Ceylon's Prime Minister.

Mrs. Ghandi received 355 votes to 169 for her only rival, Morarji Desai, a former Finance Minister and bitter opponent of the party leadership. She succeeds Prime Minister Lal Bahadur Shastri, who died Jan. 11 in Tashkent, in Soviet Central Asia, shortly after signing a troop-withdrawal agreement with Pakistan. Mr. Shastri succeeded Mr. Nehru in June 1964.

Mrs. Ghandi is the 48-year-old widow of Feroze Gandhi, who was not related to Mohandas K. Gandhi, leader of India's fight for independence from Britain. Technically, the election was only for the leadership of the Congress parliamentary party. However, the party has overwhelming majorities in both houses and its leader automatically becomes Prime Minister.

At a news conference in the garden of her white bungalow residence at 1 Safdarjang Road, Mrs. Gandhi said she expected to announce her Cabinet "within a few days." Dressed in a sparkling white sari, with a brown wool shawl draped over her shoulders, she stood at a cluster of microphones, answering questions from more than 200 reporters who trampled her flower beds and hedges.

Although she carefully avoided committing herself to any specific policy, she handled a bristling array of pointed questions with considerable skill. She turned away others with a quip and a smile.

The first question was: "How does it feel to be the first woman Prime Minister of India?" Mrs. Gandhi, with a slight edge in her voice, replied: "In the Indian Constitution, all citizens are equal regardless of sex, religion, language, state or any other division. I am just an Indian citizen and the first servant of my country." The fact that Mrs. Gandhi is a woman played virtually no role in the maneuvers of the last week. More than 50 women sit in the Indian Parliament and several women hold important jobs in ministries and the civil service.

Mrs. Gandhi was asked what message she had for the nation. She said she would recall her father's message: "Create a climate of peace."

"We shall work for peace at home and abroad," she declared. Mrs. Gandhi said India would honor the Tashkent declaration in which Mr. Shastri and President Mohammad Ayub Khan of Pakistan agreed not only on troop withdrawals but on the restoration of full diplomatic relations, repatriation of prisoners and other steps to restore friendly ties. "We have to honor the pledge made by our Prime Minister," she said. "The Tashkent declaration is the first step. Any step toward peace is a good step."

Mrs. Gandhi said she would also favor peace talks with Communist China "if conditions are created in which we can talk." However, she said, "The Chinese threat to our frontier still remains; certain things will have to happen before any talks."

Asked about American peace moves in Vietnam, she said: "I am in favor of any peace move. Of course it has to be accepted by both sides, but any first step taken for peace is always a step in the right direction."

On domestic policy, Mrs. Gandhi was vague. She said she would carry out the policies set by her father and continued by Mr. Shastri. "It must be our aim to get results rather than talking about them," said Mrs. Gandhi, who was Minister of Information and Broadcasting in Mr. Shastri's Cabinet.

After the results were announced, the legislators almost smothered Mrs. Gandhi with garlands of marigolds, bouquets and congratulations. Early this morning Mrs. Gandhi visited the monuments to Gandhi and Nehru on the bank of the Jumna river. She also went to the former Nehru residence, now a museum, where she stood in silence before a portrait of her father. ■

Indira Gandhi with acting Prime Minister Gulzarilal Nanda, left, and President of the Congress Party Kumarasami Kamaraj, making a gesture of peace after her election as leader of the Congress Party in 1966.

MAY 3, 1966

ADENAUER BEGINS 8-DAY VISIT TO ISRAEL

James Feron

LYDDA, Israel, May 2—Dr. Konrad Adenauer arrived in Israel tonight for an eight-day private visit. He was met by Israeli officials and political figures and by several dozen chanting demonstrators.

The 90-year-old former West German Chancellor said at Lydda Airport that today was "one of the most beautiful and most serious days in my life of political service." Addressing Foreign Minister Abba Eban, who welcomed him in an airport lounge jammed with German and Israeli officials, policemen, photographers and newsmen, the German statesman said:

"It is one of the most beautiful days because I can see what this people who have suffered so much injustice have been able to achieve. I have the greatest respect for your people. For your daring and your energy. The best that history and humanity have done is to resurrect this people who have been dispersed for 2,000 years into a state."

Sitting next to Dr. Adenauer as he spoke into the din was David Ben-Gurion, who, like Dr. Adenauer, is now retired from governmental leadership but is a potent political factor in his country.

As Dr. Adenauer spoke of his "eagerness" to see the country, about 50 demonstrators outside waved banners and chanted, "Adenauer Raus!" [Out!] The banners accused the former Chancellor of having revived German militarism and of having freed Nazi war criminals from prison. ■

"It is one of the most beautiful days . . ."

MAY 3, 1967

Nazi Restitution Talks Go On

BONN, May 2—A talk that Dr. Konrad Adenauer had in New York in 1960 with Mr. David Ben-Gurion, who was then Israel's Premier, has been making headlines here. Dr. Adenauer was reported to have promised Mr. Ben-Gurion $500 million in economic aid when the restitution payments to Israel and to Nazi victims expire this year.

The Israelis, now engaged in economic negotiations with the West German Government, are insisting that Bonn is still bound by Dr. Adenauer's promise. Bonn rejects this position. The talks between the two Governments continued today with little progress. The discussions were abbreviated because Israel's Ambassador to Bonn, Asher Ben-Natan, accompanied Dr. Adenauer to the airport.

According to informed sources, the sum of economic aid proposed by West German negotiators at previous meetings has been rejected as insufficient. Reports that the offer was for a loan of about $40 million have not been confirmed or denied.

JUNE 8, 1967

ISRAELIS JUBILANT AT CAPTURED EGYPTIAN BASE

EL ARISH, Sinai, June 7—Israeli troops on the road to Suez were flushed with victory today, but the fighting was by no means over. Grinning Israeli soldiers drove captured Soviet-built trucks northward today, elatedly fingering the V-sign to oncoming traffic. But pockets of Egyptian troops in Sinai and Palestinian commandos in the Gaza Strip continued desperate resistance.

This oasis and communications center, 35 miles inside Sinai, was seized yesterday afternoon by a force that earlier took Rafah, a small town on the old Palestine-Egypt border. The army base here was also in Israeli hands yesterday evening after a three-hour battle. Heavy casualties were inflicted, more than 1,000 prisoners surrendered and some Egyptian soldiers fled into the desert.

At dawn today an Egyptian commando company struck back. An officer told reporters that the enemy had stormed the camp at daybreak with submachine guns blazing. They inflected casualties, but were shot down.

Later this morning, when a battalion commander went toward the home of the governor to arrange for a formal surrender, fire was opened from several houses in the town. The Israelis withdrew and orders were given to subdue the enemy by shelling.

Brief and sporadic bursts of machine-gun fire were heard between mortar blasts. Reporters were told that Egyptians were being flushed out of stone-lined trenches around the town. A medical officer said wounded prisoners had also put up desperate resistance. He said one gravely injured Egyptian had exploded a grenade in an ambulance, killing himself, an Israeli nurse and medical personnel.

About 50 Soviet tanks, some of them dug in, and more than 100 trucks were scattered in the yellow sands on either side of the black asphalt highway. Tank treadmarks and craters testified that the Egyptian force had been overcome by aerial bombardment and armor. Many of the tanks apparently had not been hit. Some of the trucks appeared to be in good condition. Anti-aircraft positions, including one that was fully loaded, were also abandoned without having been hit. Army boots were scattered in the sands. Apparently Egyptian peasants found them cumbersome in flight.

Prisoners were also being moved northward in Tel Aviv delivery trucks that had been mobilized. Egyptians squatted dejectedly on the floors of the trucks, their hands on their heads and fingers entwined. A

(cont'd. on next page)

(cont'd. from previous page)

soldier with a submachine gun sat on the roof of the cabin of each truck.

Some of the prisoners were in their underwear.

An Israeli soldier said they had discarded their uniforms and put on bedouin robes in an attempt to pass as civilians. The Israeli soldiers were unshaven and their dress was assorted. Some wore civilian trousers and army shirts, some army trousers and civilian shirts. They appeared to be reservists called up last week.

However, the battlefield suggested that on the whole Egyptian resistance was not so determined.

Wrecked railway trains between Rafah and El Arish and burned-out tanks testified to the accuracy of the Israeli bombardment. Vehicles dug into the sand and covered with tarpaulins that matched the color of the desert were not hit. Apparently the camouflage was effective. The bodies of Egyptians were strewn on both sides of the road, but few were near fortified positions or manned emplacements. ■

Israeli soldiers celebrating their victory in the Six Day War, June 1967.

JULY 25, 1967

'Vive Quebec Libre!' De Gaulle Cries Out To Montreal Crowd

Jay Walz

MONTREAL, July 24—President de Gaulle shouted a call for a "free Quebec" tonight before a cheering, chanting crowd dominated by French-Canadian extremists. Speaking from a balcony at City Hall on his arrival in the city, the general told the crowd of about 10,000 that he sensed "liberation" in the air. In the context of his remarks, his only allusion could be to the separation of French-speaking Quebec from English-speaking Canada.

"Vive le Quebec!" the 76-year-old French leader called out at the climax of the headiest reception he has received since arriving in Canada yesterday for a five-day visit. Then he added: "Vive Quebec libre! Vive le Canada Français! Vive la France!"

The general is here officially to honor the centennial of the confederation that brought French and English Canada together.

A half-hour before General de Gaulle arrived at City Hall after an all-day motor trip from Quebec, groups of young people waving separatist banners took up positions at either side of the entrance. Their ranks swelled as the time for the general's appearance approached.

Mounting the City Hall steps, he joined the crowd in the lusty singing of the "Marseilles." When the band struck up "O Canada," the Canadian national anthem, the crowd booed.

During the trip from Quebec, General de Gaulle made a half-dozen speaking stops at which he told mildly applauding villagers and townsmen that he saw French Canada "emerging" into an era of freedom and self-development. To the delight of each group he referred frequently to Quebec as "New France." The President spoke of recent cultural and educational agreements between France and Quebec. He said there would be more, and added: "We must work together for a fine achievement."

Prime Minister Lester B. Pearson watched a live television broadcast of the City Hall reception for General de Gaulle tonight. Concerned at what he had heard, the Prime Minister asked the French Embassy in Ottawa for a text of the remarks. It is considered an act of discourtesy for any head of state to take a side in domestic issues in a country he is visiting.

So far President de Gaulle has not suggested how far he thinks French Canada should go to "emancipate" itself from English Canada or to protect its "independence" from the United States. He has not proposed separation of Quebec from the rest of Canada, but he has made frequent use of a favorite phrase of the Quebec separatists: "to become masters in our own house."

"Quebec, alive, is on its way to becoming master of itself," the general told 1,000 people who waited an hour in the rain to greet him at Donnacona this morning. General de Gaulle told another audience that Quebec "must depend on no one but itself." He gave assurance that France stood ready "as ever to bring New France its brotherly love." ■

JUN 18, 1967

CHINA TESTS HYDROGEN BOMB

HONG KONG, June 17—Communist China announced today that it had successfully exploded a hydrogen bomb less than three years after becoming a nuclear power. Reporting this major breakthrough, Hsinhua, the Chinese Communist press agency, gave no details of the yield from the explosion or the manner in which the test was carried out.

The Hsinhua announcement declared: "Today, on June 17, 1967, after the five nuclear tests in two years and eight months, China successfully exploded her first hydrogen bomb, over the western region of the country."

The latest test coincides with the visit to the United Nations of Premier Aleksei N. Kosygin. The timing of previous Chinese tests had been arranged to give them the greatest possible impact on world opinion, and analysts said the explosion announced today was no exception.

A Hsinhua report earlier today condemned Premier Kosygin's visit to the United Nations, declaring that it was aimed at promoting "worldwide American-Soviet collaboration" and predicted that the talks between Premier Kosygin and President Johnson would result in a "deal on a nuclear non-proliferation treaty."

The test announcement will provide much-needed enhancement of the prestige of Chairman Mao Tse-tung and his followers after a year of turbulence in which they appeared to have made little progress in efforts to crush opposition elements and enforce Mr. Mao's policies.

China exploded its first hydrogen bomb on June 17, 1967.

Internally the announcement is expected to strengthen the hand of the Maoists and, as a national achievement, the tests probably will have a unifying effect on the country's quarreling factions. The announcement also indicates that despite continuing reports of anti-Maoist activity in Sinkiang, Communist China's nuclear progress does not appear to have been affected by the Cultural Revolution.

The worldwide effect of the hydrogen bomb test will be to underline the military threat posed by Communist China, which has become more unpredictable and belligerent during the course of its internal convulsions.

Although Mr. Mao's ideological pronouncements have derided the nuclear weapon as a "paper tiger," the explosion of a hydrogen bomb reflects the high priority that China has given to the development of a nuclear arsenal and takes the nation a step further toward operational nuclear capability.

"Amidst the song of decisive victory of the great proletarian Cultural Revolution of our country, we solemnly announce to the people of China and the whole world that this brilliant prediction, this great call of Chairman Mao's, has been realized," the Hsinhua announcement said. Hsinhua said the Chinese people were proud of this, and revolutionary people the world over would also take it as a matter of pride.

The agency said the success of China's hydrogen bomb tests had "further broken the nuclear monopoly of United States imperialism and Soviet revisionism and dealt a telling blow at their policy of nuclear blackmail. It is a very great encouragement and support to the Vietnamese people in their heroic war against United States aggression and for national salvation, and to the Arab people in their resistance to aggression by the United States and British imperialists and their tool, Israel, and to the revolutionary people of the whole world."

The communique added: "We solemnly declare once again that at no time and in no circumstances will China be the first to use nuclear weapons."

The Chinese have opposed the treaty for a partial nuclear test ban and declined a United Nations invitation to take part in a world disarmament conference. ■

BOLIVIA CONFIRMS GUEVARA'S DEATH

Ernesto (Che) Guevara when he was Minister of Industries in Cuba, January 1965.

VALLE GRANDE, Bolivia, Oct. 10—The army high command officially confirmed today that Ernesto (Che) Guevara, the Latin revolutionary leader, was killed in a clash between guerrillas and Bolivian troops in southeastern Bolivia last Sunday.

The armed forces commander, Gen. Alfredo Ovando Candia, said Mr. Guevara had admitted his identity before dying of his wounds. General Ovando said at a news conference that the guerrilla leader had also admitted that he failed in the seven-month guerrilla campaign he organized in Bolivia.

The body was flown here yesterday, lashed to the landing runners of a helicopter that brought it from the mountain scene of the clash. The army said yesterday that it had received a report that Mr. Guevara had been killed near Higueras, but it declined to make immediate positive identification at the time.

After the body, dressed in bloody clothes, arrived here, it was fingerprinted and embalmed. The Guevara fingerprints are on file with the Argentine federal police. As an Argentine citizen, Mr. Guevara was required to be fingerprinted to obtain a passport when he left his homeland in 1952. These official records have provided the basis for comparison with the fingerprints taken by the Bolivians from the body said to be that of Mr. Guevara. The scanty beard, shoulder-length hair and shape of the head resembled the features of Mr. Guevara as shown in earlier photographs. He was 39 years old.

An Englishman in the crowd, which except for the press was kept away at bayonet point, said that he had seen Mr. Guevara in Cuba and that he was "absolutely convinced" it was the long-sought revolutionary leader.

The body appeared to bear wounds in places—two in the neck and one in the throat. It was dressed in a green jacket with a zippered front, patched and faded green denim pants, green woolen socks and a pair of homemade moccasins.

A nun assisted doctors and intelligence men in preparing the body for display. After the work was finished, the body was raised on a stretcher for the crowd, which appeared jubilant.

General Ovando arrived from La Paz and immediately went to the officers' mess to pay his respect to the four soldiers killed in the clash.

Mr. Guevara was a familiar bearded figure in olive green fatigues in Havana, where he was Minister of Industries before he dropped out of sight in March 1965. His whereabouts since have remained a mystery, leading to rumors that he had been killed in a dispute with Premier Fidel Castro and later that he was leading guerrillas in various parts of Latin America. His name was linked with guerrilla activity in Venezuela, Colombia, Brazil, Argentina, Peru and Bolivia.

On Sept. 10, the Bolivian President, Rene Barrientos Ortuno, described reports that Mr. Guevara was active in Bolivia as a myth. The next day he announced a $5,000 reward for his capture dead or alive.

Reports published in the press here today said that a diary believed to have belonged to Mr. Guevara was in Army hands. These reports said that the diary had been found in a knapsack owned by the guerrilla leader. ■

ISRAEL'S RESOLUTE NEW LEADER: GOLDA MEIR

JERUSALEM, March 7—On June 29, 1946, following the dynamiting of frontier bridges by Haganah, the Jewish underground army, the British interned most leaders of the Jewish community in the Palestine mandate. When it was noticed by imprisoned members of the Jewish Agency, the predecessor of the Israeli Government, that Mrs. Golda Meir was not among them at Latrun, presumably because she was a woman, one of them is said to have remarked: "Oh, we're all right, because she was the only real man in the agency anyway."

Today, almost 23 years later, she has emerged from retirement to take over as Premier of the country she helped to form.

Mrs. Meir's legendary resolve—toughness, some call it—has placed her in the front rank of Israel's leaders since they began to come here in large numbers early in the century. She was, in fact, one of the signers of the Declaration of Independence. Now, nearly 71, she has been called out of formal retirement to do what many feel she has often done anyway, run the country.

Through the years Mrs. Meir has served as an Ambassador (in Moscow), as a Cabinet minister (of Labor and of Foreign Affairs), and as leader of the nation's most powerful party, Mapai. She has emerged as the most influential political leader in the nation. Although her appointment to replace Mr. Eshkol has annoyed some Israelis, who feel it is time for the next generation to take over, it has surprised no one.

She was born May 3, 1898, in Kiev, the Ukraine. Of eight children, only three survived—Shana, the oldest; Golda; and a younger sister, Ziphorah. Her father, Moshe Mabovitch, went to America and the family waited for him to send for them. They moved to Pinsk, the mother's town, in Belorussia. In 1906 the Mabovitches were summoned by the father and moved to Milwaukee.

Golda met Morris Myerson, a young sign painter, and became interested in politics, particularly Zionism. She said she would not marry Morris unless he promised to go to Palestine. They were married in 1917. Although he accompanied her to Palestine, he was never enthusiastic about the country. They tried life on a kibbutz, or communal settlement, but finally abandoned it.

Two children, Menachem and Sarah, were born in 1924 and 1926. The family lived in a two-room apartment in Jerusalem, Golda working as a washerwoman, Morris as a carpenter.

Mrs. Meir—the Myerson name Hebraicized—has said that this was the most wretched period of her life.

Mrs. Meir's early political experience was in the Histadrut, the joint labor federation. Critics of her approach would say that she viewed the Histadrut not as an organization for workers but as a political instrument. She began to work with the activists of the movement and of the prestate organizations, men such as David Ben-Gurion, Moshe Sharett and Levi Eshkol, all of whom were to hold the post of Premier before her.

Mrs. Meir was separated from her husband more than 20 years ago. He has since died. Their children remain in Israel; the son in Tel Aviv and the daughter on a Negev kibbutz, Reyiyim.

Israeli Prime Minister Golda Meir in 1969.

MARCH 23, 1968

Westmoreland to Leave Vietnam, Head the Army

Max Frankel

WASHINGTON, March 22—President Johnson announced today at a news conference his intention to appoint Gen. William C. Westmoreland as Army Chief of Staff, replacing him as commander of American forces in Vietnam sometime before July 2.

No successor for the Vietnam command was announced.

The shift of General Westmoreland, whose tactics in the war have been heatedly debated here in recent weeks, was recommended to the President, he said, by both Robert S. McNamara, the former Secretary of Defense, and his successor, Clark Clifford.

The first suggestion from Mr. McNamara, the President said at the news conference in his office, came on Jan. 19—eight days before the start of the enemy's Lunar New Year offensive against the South Vietnamese cities. The offensive seriously set back General Westmoreland's campaign.

Mr. Johnson held up a handwritten note from Mr. McNamara and went on to praise General Westmoreland as a "very talented and very able officer." Mr. Johnson said no changes in strategy or tactics were implied by the change of personnel as such. But he left open the possibility that the new commander might make some new strategic or tactical recommendations.

General Westmoreland has been criticized particularly for his "search and destroy" concept of chasing enemy forces even into uninhabited terrain so as to inflict high casualties and wear them down by attrition. Questions have also been raised concerning his willingness to stand in static defense posts, as part of this strategy, far from the major population centers that have been shown vulnerable to enemy assault.

But these tactics have had the approval of the President and the Joint Chiefs of Staff, after careful and constant scrutiny. Recommendations for their revision would still pass through General Westmoreland's hands after he becomes chief of staff and the hands of his superior, Gen. Earle G. Wheeler, the chairman of the Joint Chiefs of Staff.

Mr. Johnson's brief praise of General Westmoreland today was merely an echo of the strong expressions of confidence the President has offered him on many occasions.

Neither those remarks nor those added by the President today, however, foreclosed a change of approach to the war with General Westmoreland's departure. Asked if such a change was implied in the promotion, Mr. Johnson said that strategy and tactical operations "have nothing to do with the appointments as such," but he added that he could not speak for the plans of the next commander.

There is thought to be considerable pressure in the Administration to halt the almost steady increases in manpower that General Westmoreland's strategy has required over the last three years.

Ironically, General Westmoreland first went to Vietnam at a time when his predecessor, Gen. Paul D. Harkins, was being similarly criticized for over-optimism, wrong tactics and failure to grasp the political realities of the war against the Vietcong. That was in early 1964 and in June of that year General Westmoreland succeeded to the top command post. Since then he has presided over the vast increase in American forces, from more than 20,000 in 1964 to 510,000 at present. ■

MAY 19, 1968

STUDENT UNREST IN FRANCE

Henry Tanner

PARIS—What started modestly as little more than a student "happening" three weeks ago has become a country-wide tide of discontent and revolutionary fever that threatens the basic institutions of France and may yet bring the downfall of the Government. So serious has the situation become that President de Gaulle rushed back yesterday from a visit to Rumania, a day ahead of his scheduled return.

How did so small an event become so big and potent?

The movement started with a mere handful—a few dozen—student extremists of vaguely Trotskyite persuasions at the Nanterre branch of the University of Paris. The Government closed the Nanterre College, and the handful of Enrages moved to Paris and the Sorbonne. The police occupied the courtyard of the venerable old university to prevent the Nanterre leftists from clashing with Paris rightists. The occupation brought out a few thousand other students who clashed with the police.

The police clubbed, gassed and kicked the students with unbelievable brutality and this, in turn, touched off a general uprising of students throughout the country. From then on it was a movement of hundreds of thousands of youngsters. It was at this point that the revolt, by its spontaneous, totally uncontrolled and uncontrollable nature, had become a truly revolutionary event.

Last Tuesday, the workers moved in for the first time. Strikers at an aircraft plant in Nantes, on the Atlantic coast, took a leaf from the students' book, and occupied their factory, keeping the manager and his executives prisoners. They are still being held this weekend. The men at Nantes acted without instructions from their Communist and other labor unions and without consulting the opposition parties. This meant that the traditional opposition parties as well as the Gaullist regime were in jeopardy.

Two counter-offensives waged for different reasons and with different means by the Gaullist Government and the traditional opposition parties have the same goal: To stop the spread of the popular uprising that had been touched off by the freelance revolutionaries among the students and the workers.

The Government, in the person of Premier Pompidou, announced Thursday night that the "agitators" were out "to destroy the nation" and that the Government would fight to protect the country's institutions and the national heritage. The opposition parties and the labor unions have a more complicated and more ambitious task. They want to harness the movement of revolt and to bend it to their own purposes—against the Government.

The Communist party and the Communist C.G.T., the largest union federation, both disavowed the students in a striking rebuff—perhaps in reaction to student disavowal of Communist ties since, they said, Communism was just another facet of the Establishment—and announced that their own "militants" would forthwith lead the revolt. Striking workers in all parts of the country were warned against fraternizing with the students.

Student and worker demonstrators marched in Paris in May 1968 demanding changes ranging from government policy to job security. Demonstrations led to riots and general strikes throughout the country.

This was the situation yesterday: The students had relinquished the center of the stage to the workers. But the occupation of practically every university in the country continued. Hundreds of thousands of students and high school children were still defying the Government. The strike movement of the workers was still spreading.

But it was too early to tell whether the nature of the revolt had changed. Were the new strikes, which were announced from all parts of the country, the result of spontaneous action by local men caught in the contagious fever of revolt? Or were they organized and controlled by the unions and Communists?

The answer, when it becomes apparent, will be all-important. If the movement is an uncontrolled revolutionary upsurge, the country may be plunged into anarchy.

If the Communist party has managed to take over the movement, then, ironically, the institutions are safe and the political contest is likely to move back into the National Assembly, with votes of confidence and votes of censure and traditional speeches—and sooner or later a new election. ■

JULY 4, 1968

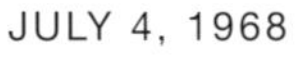

EDITORIAL

Food for Starving Biafra

The awful dimensions of starvation in what is left of the Nigerian secessionist state of Biafra are now starkly evident. An International Red Cross official says that more than a million Biafrans will die of hunger within a month unless at least 200 tons of food can be sent daily into the area.

Biafran propaganda fixes sole responsibility for this catastrophe on Nigeria's Federal Military Government for its unwillingness to grant an unconditional ceasefire in the civil war and permit the mounting of a mammoth airlift rescue operation. Lagos is not without blame for the frustrations encountered by the Red Cross and the United Nations Children's Fund, but the situation is not so simple as the Biafrans contend.

The fact is that Col. C. Odumegwu Ojukwu, head of the Biafran regime, still refuses to accept Red Cross and UNICEF supplies shipped overland from Federal territory. Lagos agreed a month ago to permit such shipments under truce in Red Cross trucks.

Biafra says it fears food coming from Lagos would be poisoned, but the real reason is political. Even in this situation Colonel Ojukwu is unwilling to concede Biafra's dependence on Lagos to avert mass starvation. He insists on an unconditional cease-fire and an airlift of food from outside Nigeria because these would enforce Biafra's claim to sovereignty.

It is probable, however, that only overland food shipments can cope with Biafra's needs. Biafra now has only one or two makeshift airfields, which could not handle the necessary food traffic. Federal officials say Port Harcourt cannot be opened for normal shipping for months because the channel from Bonny has not been entirely cleared of obstacles left by the retreating Biafrans, and in any case must be dredged.

Lagos has recently proposed a simultaneous ceasefire and renunciation of secession by Biafra. It has agreed to an international observer force to police the cease-fire and to guarantee the safety of Biafra's Ibo majority. Lagos has also indicated it will not send the Federal armies into the Ibo heartland unless forced to do so by Biafran guerrilla activity.

AUGUST 12, 1968

For Those Under 30, Prague Seems The Right Place to Be

Paul Hofmann

PRAGUE, Aug. 11—If you are under 30, Prague seems the place to be in this summer. This ancient city, capital of a Communist state that has just weathered a dramatic confrontation with its more conservative allies and may be in for more pressure, is thronged these days with young sympathizers from the West.

"The Czechs are the good guys this year," said Robert Engle, a New York-born graduate of Harvard Law School. "I hope I get a few ideas in Prague." Mr. Engle, who sports a blond mustache, has been touring Europe on a skimpy budget since last fall, after deciding that practicing law in California, where he had passed the bar examination, was not for him. He does not care for the more radical American left, and hopes Europe will help him find out what kind of society he wants to live in and what role he wants to play in it.

"To give a human face to socialism," a humanities student from the Sorbonne, Monique Chaillot, said dreamily, quoting one of the catch phrases recurring today in Czechoslovakia. "How beautiful this is. To give a human face to modern society. That is exactly what we wanted to do in Paris this spring." Miss Chaillot, who lives with her parents in Vanves, near Paris, asserted that she played a part in the French student rebellion, but would not say exactly what part.

The motivations for this summer's youth pilgrimage to Prague are diverse, and politics is only one facet. Helmut Krone, a serious, bespectacled literature student from Hamburg, explained:

"The new situation in Czechoslovakia made me wish more strongly than ever to visit the city where Kafka lived. You can not understand Kafka without Prague, and you cannot understand modern literature without Kafka."

The German student, too, reported that he had found Czechoslovak student friends and had had long conversations with them, not only about Kafka, but "about everything." Czech is not an easy language, but there seems to be no communications problem between the young Western visitors and local students. Many Prague residents speak at least some German, French or English.

Before they open their mouths, it is not easy at times to tell whether the young people clustering on the medieval Charles Bridge and in other places are Czechoslovaks or foreigners. With their long hair, beards, turtleneck sweaters, Levis and their relaxed bearing they all look alike. To them, the atmosphere is electrifying this summer in a city that rather sedately goes about its affairs beneath its brooding old castle.

Young Czechoslovaks and young foreigners drink beer together in the taverns, they go together to the movies and discuss them afterward, they hold joint dance and folksong sessions, they eat greasy sausages together late at night at outdoor stands in Wenceslaus Square.

Young foreigners contribute to the graffiti that cover Prague's walls and monuments these days. "Viva Dubcek and his boys!" proclaims an English-Spanish inscription on the Gothic Prasna Brana tower. And another epigraph on a trade school near the Old Ghetto reads in English: "Kennedy Everywhere! — Johnson Never!"

Many older people are not insensitive to the excitement of the young in Prague today and identify with them. When President Tito of Yugoslavia arrived here Friday, television showed the cheering crowds outside Hradcany Castle. The camera focused on an unidentified tall girl in the midst of the throng, who was chewing gum. There were chuckles from a group of Czechoslovaks who were watching TV sets from outside an appliance store.

"Americanska," one of them said tolerantly.

AUGUST 22, 1968

RUSSIANS SEIZE DUBCEK AND 6 COLLEAGUES; MACHINE-GUN FIRE IS EXCHANGED IN PRAGUE; CZECHS BALK AT FORMATION OF NEW REGIME

Tad Szulc

PRAGUE, Thursday, Aug. 22—Soviet troops were reported early today to have seized seven liberal Czechoslovak Communist leaders, including the party's First Secretary, Alexander Dubcek, and to have taken them to an undisclosed destination.

In the wake of the invasion of Czechoslovakia by forces of the Soviet Union and four of its allies, as many as 23 persons were reported killed in clashes in Prague and in two provincial cities.

Exchanges of machine-gun fire with red tracer bullets soared over Hradcany Castle overlooking Prague, near the United States Embassy, and heavy small-arms fire was heard on the opposite right bank of the Vlatava River. A white artillery flare rose over the castle.

At midnight an announcement was made over the radio that a curfew was in effect until 5 A.M. and that anyone in the streets would be shot on sight.

It was presumed that the order emanated from Soviet authorities following an evening of sniper fire against the occupation troops throughout the city and counteraction by Soviet tanks and machine-gunners.

Despite the disappearance of the leaders of Czechoslovakia's democratization and the presence of Warsaw Pact troops estimated at close to 200,000 men, the military intervention has not so far been able to produce a new Czechoslovak leadership.

A combination of deeply rooted Czechoslovak allegiance to the nine-month-old Dubcek-led democratic evolution and widespread revulsion against the invasion carried out by Soviet, East German, Polish,

Hungarian and Bulgarian troops seemed to have produced a deadlock in the efforts to create a leadership more to Moscow's liking.

For nearly 30 hours now—since Warsaw Pact land and airborne troops entered the country—Czechoslovakia has been without a government or a party leadership.

In a confusing situation, in which the Soviet-led forces clearly had no readily available candidates to replace the Dubcek group, the supreme authority loomed in the person of the commander of the invading forces—believed to be Marshal Ivan I. Yakubovsky, the commander in chief of the Warsaw Pact forces, and of Ambassador Stepan V. Chervonenko of the Soviet Union.

Driven away with the First Secretary were the chairman of the National Assembly, Josef Smrkovsky; Josef Spacek and Frantisek Kriegel.

Since the occupation of Prague, these four leaders have been kept under guard of Soviet tanks and paratroopers in the Central Committee building on the river bank of the Vlatava River.

In a brief radio address, President Ludvik Svoboda said, "The situation must be solved rapidly and the troops must depart."

President Svoboda added that free democracy and socialism must be preserved in Czechoslovakia and "now there is no way back."

Despite pleas of pro-Dubcek radio stations not to resist, the Czechoslovaks fought their invaders with Molotov cocktails, stones and sticks and bare hands as well as with an extraordinary display of passive resistance that seemed to rally much of the nation around Mr. Dubcek.

Seven persons were believed to have been killed in Prague in two battles, one at dawn and one at noon, for the control of the Prague radio station in the city's center. Soviet tanks firing machine guns killed four youths while Bulgarian units killed three others. ■

OCTOBER 8, 1968

Rioting Reopens Old Wounds in Northern Ireland

John M. Lee

Riots in Londonderry, 1968.

LONDONDERRY, Northern Ireland, Oct 7— Old antagonisms between Northern Ireland's Protestants and Roman Catholics have erupted in the worst violence seen since the nineteen-twenties in Londenderry, Northern Ireland's second largest city.

The riots on Saturday afternoon and Sunday night are acknowledged by all sides as a setback for the moderate program of Prime Minister Terence M. O'Neill. Mr. O'Neill has sought Protestant-Catholic cooperation to erase the ancient religious scars that still blemish the life of the country.

The 1920 act that divided Protestant Northern Ireland from the Catholic south gave each country its own prime minister and its own parliament with responsibility and authority for local affairs, including law and order.

About 100 people, including Gerard Fitt, a Catholic Republican member of the British Parliament, were treated at hospitals for injuries after the Londonderry skirmishes between police and a Catholic civil rights group. Twenty-nine persons were arrested.

(cont'd. on next page)

dissent

(cont'd. from previous page)

In the weekend battles, the Royal Ulster constabulary used batons and water cannons against the demonstrators. The marchers accused the police of brutality.

The demonstrators threw gasoline bombs, stoned police and burned two constabulary huts. They smashed shop windows in the center of Londonderry and looted a few stores.

Late tonight three gasoline fire bombs were thrown at two police Land-Rovers as they crashed through a barricade of oil drums and timber erected by the demonstrators in the center of the old city. The vehicles, undamaged by the explosions, were stoned by the demonstrators and left the scene. Earlier, policemen had dispersed crowds of young men from the area.

William Craig, Northern Ireland's strong-minded Minister of Home Affairs, said that Communist elements, acting through the Irish Republican Army, had exploited the discontent of Londonderry Catholics to turn a civil rights demonstration into a riot.

Policemen wielding clubs subdued Roman Catholic demonstrators Sunday in Londonderry after Mr. Craig had refused permission for the Irish Civil Rights Association to parade through Protestant areas to protest against discrimination in housing and voting. Mr. Craig said that such a route would incite violence. The marchers defied the ban and skirmished with policemen who sought to block off restricted areas.

About 300 demonstrators were involved Saturday in an area known as the Waterside Ward across the Foyle River from the city center. Last night, about 800 young men, angered by police tactics on Saturday, assembled in the center of the city in a square known as the Diamond. They fought with the policemen all along the old city walls.

These walls protected Protestant Londonderry from a siege by King James II, a Catholic, in the late seventeenth century. Today, Londonderry is two-thirds Catholic in a country that is two-thirds Protestant. However, the Catholics, through the Nationalist party, hold only eight seats on the City Council compared with 12 for the Protestant Unionist party. ■

FEBRUARY 5, 1969

FATAH WINS CONTROL OF PALESTINE GROUP

BEIRUT, Lebanon, Feb. 4—Al Fatah, the commando organization headed by Yasir Arafat, has taken control, politically and militarily, of the Palestinian national movement. This was the effect of the election in Cairo yesterday of a new 11-man executive committee of the Palestine Liberation Organization, which today elected Mr. Arafat as its chairman. The results of the election, held in secret session, were announced by the Cairo radio.

The new chairman and executive committee, in contrast to the organization's first leadership headed by Ahmed Shukairy, introduce a style of leadership emphasizing action. Speaking briefly after his election, Mr. Arafat promised to intensify the "armed revolution in all parts of our Palestinian territory to make of it a war of liberation."

"Armed struggle," he said, "is the only way. We reject all political settlements."

Mr. Arafat, the soft-voiced leader and spokesman of Al Fatah, is generally known by his old pseudonym Abu Amar. ■

MAY 9, 1969

RAIDS IN CAMBODIA BY U.S. UNPROTESTED

William Beecher

WASHINGTON, May 8—American B-52 bombers in recent weeks have raided several Vietcong and North Vietnamese supply dumps and base camps in Cambodia for the first time, according to Nixon Administration sources, but Cambodia has not made any protest.

In fact, Cambodian authorities have increasingly been cooperating with American and South Vietnamese military men at the border, often giving them information on Vietcong and North Vietnamese movements into South Vietnam.

Officials say that there is no Administration interest at this time in extending the ground war into Cambodia, or Laos either.

Discussing the on-again, off-again statements of Prince Sihanouk on the re-establishment of relations with the United States, one official said: "Although the Prince has made various statements in recent speeches questioning the sincerity of our recognition of his frontiers, he has made none of these protestations to us. It may be that he's simply demonstrating to his people that any new deal he makes will be on his own terms."

Some American ground commanders have long urged that battalion-size forces occasionally be allowed to sweep into sanctuaries in Laos and Cambodia to follow up air strikes. This plea has been rejected by President Nixon as it was by President Johnson.

But sources here say that to assure that accurate information can be obtained to provide "lucrative" targets for the bombers, small teams of men are permitted to slip across both the Cambodian and Laotian borders to locate enemy concentrations of men and matériel.

The raids into Cambodia, the sources say, coincided with heavy B-52 raids on the Vietnamese side of the border 50 to 75 miles northwest of Saigon.

Over the last two weeks more than 5,000 tons of bombs have been dropped by B-52's in this area, according to one estimate.

There are reported to be three enemy divisions operating back and forth across the border in this area: the First and Seventh North Vietnamese Divisions and the Ninth Vietcong Division. Another division, the Fifth Vietcong, is now operating south and southeast of Saigon.

The decision to demonstrate to Hanoi that the Nixon Administration is different and "tougher" than the previous Administration was reached in January, well-placed sources say, as part of a strategy for ending the war. ■

A shopping center in Cambodia destroyed by bombing, 1969.

SEPTEMBER 2, 1969

Junta in Libya Ousts Monarchy, Sets Up Republic

BEIRUT, Lebanon, Tuesday, Sept. 2—A revolutionary council took control of Libya yesterday after overthrowing the conservative regime of the 79-year-old King Idris I, according to reports from Tripoli. Libya was proclaimed a socialist republic with the new name of the Libyan Arab Republic.

The coup—the fourth in the Arab world in little more than a year—was reported to have been bloodless. Crown Prince Hassan al-Rida, 40-year-old nephew of the King, announced by radio that he was relinquishing all his powers in support of the revolution. King Idris has been in Turkey for several weeks undergoing medical treatment.

In its first policy statement, which was broadcast over the Tripoli radio, the new regime announced that it would follow an Arab nationalist policy and would seek to cooperate with nonaligned nations. However, it emphasized that the coup was not aimed against any foreign power and was a purely domestic movement.

The Libyan junta has adopted the Arab nationalist and Baathist slogan of "Socialism, Unity and Freedom." It emphasized that one of the aims of the revolution was to concentrate on solving the country's problems of underdevelopment.

Observers believe that the new leaders may have difficulty finding grounds on which to accuse the monarchy. King Idris and other members of the royal family have been living relatively modestly and are known to have avoided corruption.

Libya has grown into a major oil exporting country in the last few years. Income from oil this year is expected to total about $700 million, but it is thought that this may grow to as much as $1.5 billion in the next 10 years. King Idris, who is regarded as a hero of the Libyan struggle for independence against the former Italian rule, has used most of the oil revenues of recent years to develop his backward country socially and economically. He has ruled since 1951. Libya became a member of the Arab League in 1953.

The Libyan coup appears to have tipped the scales in favor of the Arab Leftists in the balance of power among the 14 member states of the Arab League. Eight of the fourteen now have leftist governments: the United Arab Republic, the Sudan. Iraq, Syria, Yemen, South Yemen, Algeria and Libya. The countries still with conservative or semi-conservative governments are Saudi Arabia, Kuwait, Jordan, Lebanon, Tunisia and Morocco. Only three Arab kings are still in power: Faisal of Saudi Arabia, Hussein of Jordan and Hassan of Morocco.

For the Arab radical cause, Libya has special importance because of her huge oil wealth. The country already contributes one-fourth of the annual subsidy of about $390 million paid annually to the United Arab Republic and Jordan since the Middle East War. The other contributors are Saudi Arabia and Kuwait.

Diplomatic quarters here believed it likely that the new Libyan regime might turn against the West in general and the United States in particular. This, they point out, could cast doubt on the future of the U.S.'s Wheelus Air Force Base in Tripoli.

These quarters observed that the base now is important for the United States not only because most of the oil companies operating in Libya are American-owned but also because of Libya's strategic position on the Eastern Mediterranean. Since Libya began to export oil in large commercial quantities, she has become a main source for Europe. ■

SEPTEMBER 4, 1969

HO CHI MINH DEAD AT 79

North Vietnam Expected to Hold to War Policies

Tillman Durdin

HONG KONG, Thursday, Sept. 4—President Ho Chi Minh of North Vietnam died yesterday morning in Hanoi at the age of 79.

A Hanoi radio report at 7 A.M. this morning announced that he succumbed at 9:47 A.M. Hanoi time yesterday "after a very sudden, serious heart attack."

The radio disclosed only at 4 A.M. yesterday that President Ho had been gravely ill for several weeks and was under emergency treatment day and night by "a collective of professors and medical doctors." There was no explanation for the delay of almost 24 hours in announcing the President's death.

Under the North Vietnamese Constitution, the Vice President takes over if the President dies or is incapacitated, pending a new election. The Vice President is an obscure figure, Ton Duc Thang, 81.

The Hanoi announcement said: "We feel boundless grief in informing the entire party and the entire Vietnamese people that Comrade Ho Chi Minh, President of the Central Committee of the Vietnam Workers party and President of the Democratic Republic of Vietnam, passed away at 9:47, Sept. 3, 1969, after a very sudden, serious heart attack at the age of 79."

A further special communiqué recapitulated the account of the death and described Mr. Ho as "the great, beloved leader of our Vietnamese working class and nation who all his life devotedly served the revolution, the people and the fatherland."

A thin, gaunt and stooped bachelor with a mustache and wispy beard, Mr. Ho was the prime mover of revolution in Vietnam for almost half a century and enjoyed enormous prestige even among anti-Communist Vietnamese.

He was titular Head of the North Vietnamese Government and President as well of the Central Committee of the party, and though ill health in recent years impaired his functioning, he was the symbol of unity and continued struggle over South Vietnam.

Business

In 1966, the Dow Jones industrial average broke through the "magic" 1,000-point barrier for the first time to giddy excitement on the floor of the New York Stock Exchange. One of the amusing sidelines of this book is the contrast between numbers that seemed gargantuan then (stock indices, Broadway ticket prices) and comparable numbers today. Those from the 60's seem minuscule now: In early 2014 the Dow was above 16,000.

Still, the excitement about the Dow's rise 50 years ago indicates that life was good then, economically speaking. There were no crippling or prolonged recessions after 1961, and the average American's real income increased by 50 percent in the course of the decade.

Part of the growth could be attributed to the stimulus of President Johnson's War on Poverty and Great Society programs, along with the Vietnam War defense budget, all of which pumped federal money into the economy. But business was good in the private sector as well. Corporate mergers were on the rise, signaled by the alliance between two huge railroads, the Pennsylvania and the New York Central, and in 1969 oil companies bid avidly for the rights to drill on Alaska's North Slope.

The "income inequality" so lamented today was mitigated by a rise in the minimum wage in 1961 (all the way up to $1.15, from $1) and a measure passed in Congress for equal pay for women. For better (to encourage spending) or worse (to saddle Americans with debt), the proliferation of nationwide credit cards gained momentum. In 1962 the steel industry capitulated to John F. Kennedy's campaign and rolled back their proposed price increases, and in 1967 world economic leaders agreed in Geneva on a wide-ranging tariff-reduction treaty in the so-called "Kennedy round" of trade negotiations.

As for The Times's business coverage, it seems over the decades to have grown far more extensive than in the 60's, due in part to the division of the daily paper into sections, one devoted entirely to business (with Sports as a back-of-the-book addendum most days). The paper now ranges around the world in its search for economic news and stresses entertainment business stories as a major aspect of is coverage—reflecting perhaps not just the paper's increased attention to popular culture but also, with the decline of department-store advertising, the importance of film ads, in particular, to the paper's bottom line.

MAY 4, 1961

CONGRESS PASSES MINIMUM PAY BILL; PRESIDENT WINS

Tom Wicker

WASHINGTON, May 3—President Kennedy's minimum wage bill received final Congressional approval today. It assures raises for 2,500,000 workers.

In addition to those directly benefited by the minimum wage increase and the extension of a Federal minimum to about 3,624,000 workers not now protected, millions more could get additional wages from a so-called "balloon effect."

That is, employers forced to increase the pay of low-wage workers are expected to maintain wage differentials now in effect. That would mean subsequent raises for higher-paid workers.

Raises would vary for those workers, mostly in manufacturing, whose present $1-an-hour minimum would go to $1.15. About 1,900,000 will get raises up to 15 cents an hour.

Increases for newly covered workers, most of whom are in retail, service and construction industries, also would vary. About 663,000 earn less than $1 an hour now and in many cases their raises will be more than 15 cents an hour.

The wage bill, the second of the President's five top-priority legislative requests to be passed, moved through both houses with surprising ease.

Secretary of Labor Arthur J. Goldberg called the bill passed today "a great advance in our nation's social legislation." It affords, he said, "long overdue protection to a large group of underprivileged Americans who previously did not share fully in the benefits of our society."

The measure extends for the first time a $1-an-hour minimum to 3,624,000 workers, mainly by requiring the wage to be paid by retail establishments doing more than $1,000,000 in annual business and importing more than $250,000 in goods for resale across state lines. Large gasoline stations, construction companies and transit companies also must pay the minimum for the first time.

The newly covered would begin to earn overtime for more than a forty-four-hour week two years after the minimum took effect. One year after that their minimum would go to $1.15 and overtime would start at forty-two hours.

After four years from the effective date, their minimum would rise to $1.25 and they would earn overtime after forty hours, putting them on a par with those now covered.

Passage of the bill in the House was made possible when thirty-three Republicans crossed the party line to vote with 197 Democrats. There were 138 Republicans in opposition.

Democratic leaders also succeeded, as they had planned, in attracting substantial Southern Democratic support. Fifty-eight Democrats, mostly Southerners, opposed the bill but that was far below the potential of ninety-odd votes.

The main arguments against the bill were made by Senator Everett Dirksen of Illinois and Representative Charles A. Halleck of Indiana, the House Republican leader. Senator Dirksen contended that the exemptions left the measure "no philosophical unity."

"Shall the House of Representatives without firing a shot surrender its position?" Mr. Halleck asked. "I say no!" he declared.

But it did about an hour later, thus wiping out the only major defeat President Kennedy had suffered on Capitol Hill. ■

APRIL 14, 1962

STEEL GIVES IN; RESCINDS RISE UNDER PRESSURE BY PRESIDENT

Kennedy Is Victor; Uses His Full Powers for 72 Hours to Subdue Industry

Richard E. Mooney

President John F. Kennedy in the Oval Office during the steel crisis, 1961.

WASHINGTON, April 13—President Kennedy triumphed today over the titans of the steel industry. Almost precisely seventy-two hours after the United States Steel Corporation's abrupt announcement of a price increase, the corporation backed down and rescinded the increase late this afternoon.

The action by United States Steel, the nation's largest steel producer, followed announcements by the Inland Steel Company and the Kaiser Steel Corporation that they would not increase their prices, and a statement by Bethlehem Steel Corporation, the nation's second largest producer, that it was canceling its rises.

By early evening seven of the eight companies that had raised their prices in the last three days had canceled them. The eighth, Wheeling Steel Corporation, said it would announce its decision tomorrow.

For three days the great forces at the command of the President of the United States had been brought to bear on the steel industry.

Some of the effort was exerted in the open—the President's open denunciation of the companies, calculated to arouse public opinion against them; the opening of grand

(cont'd. on next page)

(cont'd. from previous page)
jury proceedings leading to possible anti-trust action, and the threat to divert orders to companies that had not raised prices.

But privately as well, the President and his advisers were bringing every form of persuasion to bear on the industry, trying to hold back the companies that had not yet raised prices and induce the others to roll back the price increase.

President Kennedy was informed of the actions by United States Steel and Bethlehem off Norfolk, Va., where he was aboard a cruiser observing naval maneuvers. He issued this statement:

"The people of the United States are most gratified by the announcements of Bethlehem and United States Steel Company that their proposed price increases are being rescinded.

"In taking the action at this time, they are serving the public interest and their actions will assist our common objective of strengthening our country and our economy."

Tonight it was evident that President Kennedy had scored a great success such as few Presidents had experienced in their relations with American industry.

He strengthened his position for dealing with the business community. He had regained stature in the eyes of labor leaders. He has aroused a resounding chorus of popular support that would do his party no harm in next fall's elections. ■

MAY 29, 1963

EQUAL-PAY-FOR-WOMEN MEASURE SENT TO WHITE HOUSE

C. P. Trussell

WASHINGTON, May 28—The Senate accepted today House amendments to a measure providing equal pay for women.

The bill was then sent to the White House. President Kennedy had supported the measure, so his approval was assured.

The question of equal pay for equal work, regardless of the sex of the worker, had been before Congress for years. Both the Senate and the House had in the past approved differing versions of the program but had not agreed on a final version.

Women would be the principal beneficiaries under the measure, written with a view to halting payroll discriminations against them on grounds of sex. The law amends the Fair Labor Standards Act of 1938 and will be administered and enforced by the Wage-Hours Division of the Department of Labor.

Under the amendments, no employer of persons working or producing in interstate commerce may pay more to one sex than to another, generally, for "equal work on jobs the performance of which requires equal skill, effort, and responsibility, and which are performed under similar working conditions."

Exceptions would be allowed where a seniority or merit system was in force, or where earnings were measured by the quality or quantity of production. Exemptions would also be made where a differential was based on a factor other than sex.

Employers would not be permitted to effect a payroll balance between the sexes by cutting the pay of men. Any wages owing to an employee that had been withheld in violation of the law would be considered "unpaid minimum wages" or "unpaid overtime compensation." Those sums would be collectible from the employer for payment to aggrieved workers.

The new statute is made effective one year after its final enactment, except where collective bargaining contracts are in force. In such cases, up to an extra year is allowed for adjustment.

Sponsors of the legislation, which has had strong backing from women's organizations, viewed the closing actions with great satisfaction. Apprehension was expressed in some quarters, though, that the new law might cause reductions in the employment of women where men were available for the same jobs.

DECEMBER 10, 1963

Studebaker Auto-Making Ends Except in Canada

Joseph C. Ingraham

The Studebaker Corporation, which says it is the oldest name in highway transportation in the world, announced yesterday that it was abandoning automobile production in the United States.

Byers A. Burlingame, Studebaker's president, said auto operations would be shifted to Canada "on a more restricted basis." The end of domestic production by Studebaker means the closing of its auto plants at South Bend, Ind., and the layoff of 6,000 workers there—a sharp blow to the economy of the city.

Mr. Burlingame said the company's United States dealer organization would be continued but that cars for this country and for export would be produced at its modern assembly plant at Hamilton, Ont., on the St. Lawrence Seaway near Buffalo.

Observers consider the move to Canada a last-ditch gamble to keep Studebaker in the automotive business. Speculation was divided as to the likelihood of success, mainly because no one ever has tried to sell Canadian-built cars in the United States before.

While the corporation will not die—its non-automotive divisions are making money—many of automotive industry leaders believe Studebaker faces an almost impossible task in trying to keep its cars on the road.

Auto executives say that one of Studebaker's major problems has been its inability to build a strong dealer organization. No matter how good the car, the industry has found that unless dealers push the product, sales slump.

Most Detroit executives also contend that a company as small as Studebaker cannot get by with what is called "a me too" car and must cut out a special niche, as American Motors did with its compact Rambler.

The sharply and admittedly well-restyled 1964 Studebaker lines, which were the first change from the stubby appearance that marked the Lark compact in

1958, were a year too late, market experts assert.

Moreover, just as Studebaker hoped to move into the thick of the compact ranks this year, most of the industry was moving to larger and higher horsepower cars.

While Studebaker's primary automotive base is being moved to Canada, Mr. Burlingame said he hoped some parts operations might be retained at South Bend. However, the auto unit has an 86-day supply of cars on hand so there seemed little likelihood of any resumption of production for some time.

He also made known that to keep costs down few major styling changes are planned. The decision to stick with their present line also strengthened industry belief that Studebaker's days in the car business were numbered. ■

Studebaker's Avantia sports car.

JANUARY 9, 1964

JOHNSON OFFERS PROGRAM TO FIGHT POVERTY

John D. Pomfret

WASHINGTON, Jan. 8—President Johnson presented today the broad outlines of his proposed attack on poverty.

In declaring war on poverty in his State of the Union Message to Congress, he indicated that he wanted to help "that one-fifth of all American families with incomes too small to even meet their basic needs."

The people he referred to are the 30 million who live in families with yearly incomes below $2,000. His program is also designed to help 3 million more unattached persons whose annual incomes are below $1,500.

Four-fifths of the poor are white. But the incidence of poverty is much higher among Negroes. Of all Negroes, nearly 45 percent are living in poverty, while less than 20 percent of all whites are.

The poor are likely to be uneducated and there is a 50-50 chance that they live in the South.

The chief weapons in the attack, Mr. Johnson said, will be "better schools and better health and better homes and better training and better job opportunities to help more Americans, especially young Americans, escape from squalor and misery and the unemployment rolls where other citizens help to carry them."

The President intends to make some new proposals for legislation. These will be along lines advanced by President Kennedy,

(cont'd. on next page)

President Lyndon Johnson with sharecropper William David Marlow (left) and his family at the Marlow home on Ervin Stone Farm in Nash County, North Carolina, 1964.

(cont'd. from previous page)

but not passed by Congress. Part of the attack will be waged through existing programs.

The Administration's present thought is to wage the attack on poverty through comprehensive plans worked out at the community level with Federal consultation, bringing into play all available Federal, state and local resources.

The Federal contribution to underwrite the community plans would be something over one billion dollars. This would be spending authority to be used over the next few years.

A major emphasis is expected to be on education. Another will be on a regional program to help the poverty-stricken Appalachian area running from eastern Pennsylvania to Alabama.

Part of the President's approach to the problem will include special school aid funds to improve the quality of teaching, training and counseling in the most impoverished areas.

Under such a program, which would be new, it would be possible for the Government to award project grants in an area where, for example, there were high numbers of high school dropouts obviously headed for unemployment and low incomes. Such funds might provide special teachers and counselors, and even special schools.

A major emphasis is expected to be on education.

In addition the President indicated he would press for a youth employment program, a proposal made by President Kennedy, to put unemployed youths back to work. The jobless rate among teenagers has been running at 15 per cent.

The President proposed several other ways to attack poverty, including a strengthened area-redevelopment program; a National Service Corps along the lines of the Peace Corps; Federal unemployment insurance standards; a broader food stamp program; extension of the minimum-wage coverage to 2 million more workers; construction of libraries and hospitals; and an accelerated housing plan. ■

JANUARY 14, 1966

PRESIDENT NAMES WEAVER: FIRST OF HIS RACE PICKED FOR CABINET

Robert B. Semple, Jr.

WASHINGTON, Jan. 13—Robert C. Weaver was named by President Johnson today to be the Secretary of the new Cabinet-level Department of Housing and Urban Development.

If confirmed by the Senate, Dr. Weaver will become the first Negro to serve in the Cabinet. There was little doubt here that he would be confirmed.

Dr. Weaver, who was 58 years old on Dec. 29, has been administrator of the Housing and Home Finance Agency since the beginning of the Kennedy Administration in 1961. The agency, a conglomeration of New Deal and Fair Deal housing agencies, is likely to form the core of the new department.

For Dr. Weaver, the appointment marks the end of a long journey. Twice he came close to becoming a member of the Cabinet, and twice he was denied the job because Congress refused to establish a Department of Urban Affairs.

When President Kennedy proposed the establishment of such a department in 1961, it seemed clear that Dr. Weaver, as one of the country's leading housing experts, would get the job. This apparently contributed to resistance to the bill, particularly among Southerners, and it failed to clear the House Rules Committee.

Mr. Kennedy then tried to create the department through his reorganization powers and said he would nominate Dr. Weaver but this, too, was defeated in Congress.

The plan was finally authorized by Congress last year, and the search for an able man to run the department began in the White House. In answering a question at a news conference last Nov. 8, Dr. Weaver openly declared that he would like the job.

Mr. Johnson, however, did not make up his mind until quite recently, and then only after an intensive canvass of potential nominees. The product of the search was Dr. Weaver, the man who, in effect, had been there all along. As the President put it:

"After looking over 300 outstanding potential candidates and talking to literally dozens of people about him, I have come to the conclusion that the man for the job is Robert Weaver. I talked to Mr. Weaver this afternoon and told him that I will send his nomination to the Senate tomorrow."

Mr. Johnson's public dreams for a better urban society have been generous. In his special message to Congress on cities last March he called for urban housing construction during the balance of this century that would equal "all that we have built since the first Colonists landed on these shores."

Even if his new responsibilities are not appreciably larger, Dr. Weaver's job will continue to be one of the most difficult and frustrating in the Federal bureaucracy. In addition to his own department, he must also establish some authority over a vast assemblage of special interest groups, all of them competing for special attention or funds. These include the Mayors, the home builders, the real estate agents, the bankers who lend money, the planners, the architects, and various minority groups.

The National Association for the Advancement of Colored People and the National Urban League joined yesterday in praising the appointment of Mr. Weaver as housing chief.

"He [Weaver] will be a loyal and effective member of your Administration's family and his services will benefit all the citizens of our country," said Roy Wilkins, N.A.A.C.P. executive director, in a telegram to President Johnson. ■

JANUARY 19, 1966

DOW'S INDUSTRIAL AVERAGE PIERCES 1,000-MARK

J. H. Carmical

Trading on the floor of the New York Stock Exchange in 1966.

The stock market climbed to record highs yesterday for the third successive session, but some profit taking in the afternoon erased part of the early gains.

Most major groups participated in the advance, with interest centered in the defense, television, steel and motor issues, and in a spate of special-situation stocks. Gains in some issues went beyond 5 points.

The Dow-Jones industrial average crossed the magic 1,000-mark during the day, when it reached an intra-day high of 1,000.50. Although this was at a historic peak, as far as statistics are concerned, Dow theorists did not accept it as such because they measure new records only on the closing level.

The Dow-Jones industrial average closed at 944.20, a gain of 1.15 for the session and a new closing peak.

There is some evidence that many of the institutional investors, especially the investment trusts, are again accumulating stocks. Monday's odd-lot figures show that the public may have returned to the market in force.

Economic news developments continued favorable. Personal income in December, as reported by the Department of Commerce, rose to a seasonally adjusted record rate of $550.5 billion a year. Earnings reports for 1965 are beginning to appear in steadily increasing numbers and for the most part show profits above those for 1964, with many reporting results at record levels. In addition, dividend increases and stock splits appear to be on the rise.

All divisions of Standard & Poor's index closed at record highs, with the exception of the utility group.

The defense stocks continued to reflect continued high military spending as result of the war in Vietnam.

OCTOBER 23, 1966

Certificate of Deposit Pool Shrinking Runoff Stirs Bankers

H. Erich Heinemann

The negotiable time certificate of deposit, which has revolutionized American banking in the nineteen-sixties, is facing its first test of fire.

Started by the First National City Bank of New York in 1961, outstanding CD's grew to a peak of more than $18.5 billion last August.

Funds drawn by this device have fueled a major part of the loan expansion at the nation's largest banks in the last few years.

Now, however, the CD money pool is starting to evaporate, and fast. From a peak of $18.56 billion on Aug. 17, the total of CD's on the books of major banks, which report weekly to the Federal Reserve System, skidded to $16.6 billion on Oct. 12—a drop of almost $2 billion.

The reason for the decline is simple: The Federal Reserve has been fighting to restrain inflationary pressures in the economy, and is trying to hold down business-loan expansion, thus dampening demands for goods and services financed by bank credit.

To help accomplish this, the Reserve has refused to let banks pay more than 5 1/2 percent for certificates of deposit—even though interest rates in the open market have risen to higher levels.

The CD money has simply moved out of the banks and into more profitable channels of investment elsewhere.

The Reserve's aim has been to pinch the supply of lendable funds at the nation's largest banks, which have been the prime source of the recent expansion of bank loans to business, and thus to force a slowdown in the rate of their credit extension.

From all appearances, the policy seems to be succeeding. The major New York City banks—which not only invented the CD, but also have been its chief beneficiary—have taken the brunt of the recent runoff.

Major banks here have issued about 38 percent of all outstanding CD's, but well over 50 percent of the recent CD runoff has come from their coffers.

The magnitude of the decline and the speed with which it has occurred is stirring a lot of soul searching in the banking community.

The certificate of deposit had long been known and used in the banking system. But for a corporation treasurer, the CD, as it existed before 1961, had one major drawback.

Once the funds had been deposited at the bank, they had to be left there until the deposit matured. A "time deposit," as its name implies, is a deposit that must be left at the bank for a fixed period of time.

Thus, if the treasurer should miscalculate his requirements for cash—and forecasting the flow of funds in a multibillion-dollar company is *not* the most precise of arts—he would be simply out of luck. The money could not be withdrawn until the deposit matured.

But National City introduced two major innovations—it made its certificates negotiable, and it arranged for the Discount Corporation of New York, an important dealer in United States Government bonds, to buy and sell certificates issued by First National City.

Now the treasurer who guessed wrong on his cash requirements could get his money anytime he needed it—not from National City but by selling the certificate to Discount Corporation.

Quickly thereafter, practically every other important bank in the country joined in offering CD's, and Government security dealers generally joined in buying and selling them.

Rising totals of interest paid have been the principal factor in the sharp narrowing of bank profit margins that has occurred in the last two or three years.

Despite the costs and problems, the CD has been an essential defensive device that big banks have had to use in order to maintain their share of the banking business.

But what now when the total of CD's is starting to run down? Some bankers, for example, Alfred H. Hauser of the Chemical Bank New York Trust Company, believe strongly that the rundown of CD balances has not had any important impact on the banking system.

"There is no money squeeze," Mr. Hauser flatly says.

Other bankers, however, are less confident than Mr. Hauser. They point out that at the present time banks in New York City are succeeding in rolling over only about 75 percent of the CD's that are coming due.

And, so long as interest rates in the open market stay above the 5 1/2 percent ceiling that the banks are allowed to pay on new CD's, the runoff is likely to continue.

MAY 10, 1967

Kennedy Round Negotiators Set Sunday Night Deadline on Pact

Clyde H. Farnsworth

GENEVA, May 9—The world's major trading nations today gave themselves until Sunday night to reach agreement in the Kennedy Round negotiations to lower world trade barriers.

It represents the first time the six countries of the European Economic Community, negotiating as a unit in Geneva, have committed themselves to a deadline.

The decision gives extra time to the Common Market and the United States, the big two in world trade, to resolve their differences in grains and chemicals, which are holding back over-all agreement by the 53 participating nations to the biggest round of trade liberalization in history.

The decision also removes somewhat the crisis atmosphere that had developed following failure of the big two to come to terms during a dramatic marathon negotiating session last night and this morning.

With all parties accepting the deadline now, the chances are seen as moderately good that agreement will be reached.

Both the Common Market and the United States took steps today that could make the negotiations easier.

The United States withdrew its demand that the Common Market guarantee access in its market for grains exporters.

The Common Market came closer to meeting an American demand in the chemical sector, by agreeing with certain alterations made by Eric Wyndham White, director general of the organization supervising the General Agreement on Tariffs and Trade, some weeks ago.

With the Americans under intense deadline pressure, the Common Market used a brinksmanship tactic of holding back on concessions hoping that the Americans would cave in on their demands to get an early settlement.

The United States had demanded that the Common Market commit itself to importing as much grain as it has in the last three years—that is about 13 per cent of its requirements—as part of an international grains agreement.

The Common Market was telling the exporters they would have less access than they already enjoy. This was totally unacceptable to the United States. A grains agreement is actually a treaty which the American Senate would have to ratify. There would be no chance of getting ratification with such a provision.

And if the Common Market came anywhere near meeting the American demand, then the United States would have to pay for it probably by agreeing to a fixed world price for feed grains. This, the United States refuses to do—so far in the negotiations—because it feels American farmers would lose competitive advantage. ■

JANUARY 16, 1968

PENNSY AND CENTRAL RAILROADS SEE MERGER AS OPPORTUNITY FOR PROFIT GROWTH

Robert E. Bedingfield

WASHINGTON, Jan. 15—The merger of the Pennsylvania and the New York Central railroads, which has just received the Supreme Court's blessing, started as a marriage of necessity but will be consummated as a union of convenience.

Back in November 1961, when the two roads' idea of getting together reached the formal proposal stage, both could state convincingly that they needed each other. The Pennsylvania had run a deficit of $7.8 million in 1960, the second loss in its 112 year history, and the Central was in the black by only $1 million.

Each railroad knew that a big part of its troubles was costly duplication of service and facilities with the other.

Today the duplication still exists. But now both carriers are making money, both are paying dividends and the stocks of both are selling close to their highest levels since 1929.

Why, then, do they want to merge? And why are the Interstate Commerce Commission and the United States Supreme Court allowing them to merge?

It is not just because the two giant carriers have known hard times before and their managements are not so sold on the new economics that they don't believe hard

(cont'd. on next page)

A Pennsylvania Central train at the Pittsburgh, Pennsylvania station in the late 1960s.

(cont'd. from previous page)
times can come again. Even if both roads could count on making money in a less buoyant economy—only a year ago Alfred E. Perlman, the Central's president, called the Central a depression-proof system—both Mr. Perlman and the Pennsylvania's chairman and chief executive officer, Stuart T. Saunders, share the normal businessman's receptivity to ideas that hold the prospect of greater profitability.

Mr. Saunders and Mr. Perlman confidently believe that the consolidated carrier (which will be known as the Pennsylvania-New York Central Transportation Company) will realize operating savings amounting to $81.2 million annually after eight years of unified operation. Almost every knowing observer of the railroad scene agrees that this is a most conservative estimate.

These savings are expected even though the entire present work force of the two railroads—the Central's 41,000 employees and the Pennsylvania's 54,800—is assured total job protection. The only offset to this obligation to keep everyone on the payroll for the rest of his working life is that the consolidated company may transfer employees throughout the system.

It is customary to charge much of the delay in the merger to the lengthy I.C.C. hearings and to actions in the courts. There also have been delaying maneuvers by other railroads, particularly the Norfolk & Western and the Erie-Lackawanna. Those railroads have insisted that they do not object in principle to a Pennsy-Central consolidation but have only wanted to see it deferred until completion of their own arrangements to compete with the new giant.

Despite the delays, for the last several years the Pennsylvania and the Central have had as many as 70 executives working on plans to expedite the merger and fit the two lines together. ■

JULY 28, 1968

CARDS WON'T REPLACE CURRENCY—YET

H. Erich Heinemann

Melvin J. Roberts, president of Colorado National Bank of Denver, with a representation of the card used in the BankAmericard system, 1967.

Karl Hinke, executive vice president of Marine Midland Banks, Inc., in Buffalo, calls them a "new medium of exchange."

Mr. Hinke is talking about bank credit cards, which have swept across the country in the last few years. Three or four years ago there were only a relative handful of bank credit card plans in operation. Today, however, according to American Bankers Association estimates, there are roughly 2,000.

By some estimates, more than $2 billion in retail sales will be charged with bank credit cards this year, in contrast to less than two-thirds of that amount in 1967.

According to figures published recently by the Federal Reserve Board, total credit outstanding under bank credit card plans totaled only $800-million at the end of last year—which was equal to only 2.4 percent of consumer installment debt held by banks on that date and only 1 percent of the total consumer installment debt of about $80 billion.

Similarly, for most banks, credit cards are far from profitable. It is true that the Bank of America, the nation's largest bank, gets about 5 per cent of its net income from its BankAmericard, which appropriately enough is the largest bank credit card operation.

But the vast majority of banks that have jumped into the credit card business in the last few years are still losing money, and expect to continue to do so for some years ahead.

Yet for all the problems, Mr. Hinke is essentially correct when he says that bank credit cards represent, potentially, at least a "new medium of exchange." They won't supplant money, but they will certainly supplement it.

Mr. Hinke's own company, Marine Midland, which is New York's only statewide bank holding company, was one of the first to get into credit cards in a major way, and Mr. Hinke, personally, has been one of the leaders in the formation of Interbank Card, Inc.

Indeed, the rapid growth of Interbank—and of its archrival, the BankAmericard, which is licensed on a nationwide basis to other banks—represents the wave of the future in bank credit cards.

Chase Manhattan Bank and the Bankers Trust Company in New York reject credit cards, for the present at least, and offer only check credit.

Ironically, Chase was a pioneer in credit cards in the late 1950's, but it had unfavorable experience and eventually sold its plan.

One feature that most bank-sponsored credit cards share—with the notable exception of the BankAmericard—is an almost exclusive orientation to retail shopping convenience.

For the most part, bank credit cards cannot be used to charge airline tickets, nightclub entertainment or hotel bills. These travel and entertainment expenditures are the specialty of the credit cards issued by American Express, Diners' Club and Carte Blanche.

Some banks have formed a new organization called the Eastern States Bankcard Association, and next spring—when they are due to start issuing cards to their customers—the cards will all carry the imprint "Master Charge," plus the name of the bank.

The Bank of America, for its part, has also been expanding rapidly. It has licensed almost 40 banks across the country to issue cards under the BankAmericard name, and another 580 banks are associated with these licensee banks in issuing cards. All told, some $300-million in sales were charged with BankAmericards in the first half of this year, up 60 per cent from the same period a year ago, and the cards were being honored by more than 211,000 merchants. ■

SEPTEMBER 11, 1969

$900-Million Bid for Oil Leases in Alaska

Lawrence E. Davies

North Slope oil rush, Alaska, 1969.

ANCHORAGE, Sept. 10—Alaska's state treasury was potentially richer by $900-million tonight as the greatest competitive sale of oil-land leases in the country's history ended after nine suspenseful hours.

The sum represented the total of apparently high bonus bids submitted by petroleum companies and combinations competing for drilling rights on the state's North Slope.

Record-breaking bids, drawing whistles and cheers, had convinced oil men and state officials by mid-afternoon that the total would reach $1 billion, as widely predicted in the industry and in banking circles.

But Thomas E. Kelly, Alaska's Commissioner of Natural Resources, gave the unofficial final figure as $900,220,590.21. He said amid applause: "This is the largest dollar

(cont'd. on next page)

(cont'd. from previous page)
value sum ever realized from a competitive oil lease sale, Federal or state, a fantastic thing for Alaska." Later he declared the total set a world record for competitive bidding.

Backed by huge sums in certified checks, more than 1,100 bids were received in what had been touted as the greatest competitive oil-land lease sale in history.

Bidders representing individual companies and petroleum combinations of this country and abroad agonized for hours while their bids for 450,858 acres of tundra on the North Slope were opened and read in the Sydney Laurence Auditorium in downtown Anchorage. They followed the bidding on a huge map at the back of the stage.

A combination consisting of the Gulf Oil Corporation, British Petroleum, Ltd., and B.P.'s Alaska subsidiary stole the show at the start with a clean sweep of the first six of the 179 tracts covered in the sale. Its apparent high bid for Tract 1 was $15,528,960, or $6,066 an acre.

Gulf and British Petroleum continued their joint success on the second and third tracts, in the same area as Tract 1. The high bid on Tract 2 was $20,705,218, or $8,088 an acre. On Tract 3 it shot up to $31,006,720, or $12,112 an acre.

After Gulf Oil and British Petroleum had swept the bidding on the first six tracts, the Standard Oil Company of California was high on Tract 7. Then Mobil-Phillips submitted the top bids for the next two tracts.

Each bid had to be accompanied by a check for 20 percent of the total amount, the remainder payable in 10 days.

Gov. Keith H. Miller told the audience of bidders, legislators, more than 125 representatives of the American and foreign press and about 250 persons from the general public that the event was "a milestone in Alaska history, with more eyes on us today than at any time since statehood."

He said, "Alaska will never again be the same," adding to a remark he made in a television address last night: "Tomorrow we will reach out to claim our birthright. We will rendezvous with our dreams."

Outside the auditorium, members of a little group calling itself Concerned Alaskan Native Citizens picketed the sale with signs reading: "Two billion dollars native land robbery" and "Eskimos own North Slope."

Alaskan natives—the term applied to Eskimos, Indians and Aleuts—were disappointed that leaders of the Federation of Alaskan Natives were not present to head the pickets protesting the sale. ■

New York

TIMED BY
BENRUS
4:47
DAYLIGHT SAVING TIME
Coca-Cola
SOUVENIRS
NOVELTIES

There are New York stories, and then there are stories about things that happened to have taken place in New York but speak to the nation and the world. Indeed, for the purposes of this book it has sometimes been difficult to decide whether a story—the 1964 World's Fair, the Jets upsetting the Baltimore Colts in the third Super Bowl (sorry: Super Bowl III), Judy Garland at Carnegie Hall—belonged to New York, or the nation, or the arts. Certainly the centricity of New York news in our national culture (Hollywood and rock excepted) merits its inclusion in all those sections.

That said, lots happened in this big, bustling city, and The Times covered it all in a Manhattan-centric way (the tabloids did and do a better job with the outer boroughs). Isaac Stern, seemingly single-handedly, put down his violin and saved Carnegie Hall from demolition (it was to be replaced by an ugly red skyscraper). Casey Stengel, a New York institution, was cold-bloodedly fired by the then-dominant Yankees when he turned 70. There were disasters, including two passenger jets that collided in fog, one crashing in Brooklyn and the other in Staten Island, and a fire that killed some 50 workers at an aircraft carrier under construction at the Brooklyn Navy Yard (back when the Navy Yard still constructed ships). The Twist may have been a nationwide dance and music sensation, but The Times perked up when Manhattan socialites danced it at the Peppermint Lounge.

There was indeed a World's Fair in 1964, buildings from which still stand in Queens. There were riots in Harlem and all manner of strikes, including a 114-day, citywide newspaper strike. The legend of New Yorkers' indifference to suffering grew when 27 neighbors failed to call the police as a young woman in Queens was being murdered. The Verrazano Bridge, another big construction project seemingly left over from the governmental activism of the 1930's, stretched from Staten Island to Brooklyn. There was a Northeastern blackout in which multiple babies were happily conceived, and the aesthetically barbaric decision to demolish the old Penn Station and replace it with a claustrophobic new underground station, a faceless office tower and a new Madison Square Garden. The three major theaters at Lincoln Center—Philharmonic (now Avery Fisher) Hall, the New York State (now David H. Koch) Theater and the Metropolitan Opera—opened, in a rolling sequence, from 1963 to 1966, with lots of parties, social display and—oh, yes—some performing arts, too.

Hippies and student protests happened in New York, as in everywhere else. A rundown former light-industrial neighborhood called SoHo (echoing London but here shorthand for "south of Houston Street") turned into a haven for artists, as seen in early, then-illegal loft conversions. Construction began on the twin towers of the World Trade Center, which now puts a chill through anyone who lived through 9/11.

Above all, for politically minded New Yorkers, was the sad saga of John V. Lindsay, the handsome, patrician mayor of the city. Lindsay arrived in 1965 as a star and left, by most accounts, a failure, weighed down by battles with the unions that he never seemed capable of resolving. If the national economy was in good shape, that of the city had faltered, with manufacturing jobs in decline and the middle classes decamped for the suburbs. Lindsay was accused of favoring Manhattan over the outer boroughs, and even though he eked out reelection in 1968, he had alienated important constituencies. It was hardly "Fun City" for him.

MAY 31, 1960

NEW UNIT FORMED TO SAVE CARNEGIE HALL

The move to save Carnegie Hall gained impetus at City Hall yesterday.

Thirty members of the Citizens Committee for Carnegie Hall called on Mayor Wagner and were assured of his "full cooperation" in the effort to preserve the venerable concert hall.

Also at City Hall, the committee announced the formation of the Carnegie Hall Society, a nonprofit, tax-exempt group to consist ultimately of twenty-nine members.

The society will be prepared—if the city acquires Carnegie Hall—to lease the building and undertake its renovation, management and operation.

Mayor Wagner assured the group that the city was pressing for passage at Albany of its bill to preserve Carnegie Hall. The bill would permit the city to acquire Carnegie Hall and lease it to the new nonprofit corporation set up for that purpose.

Isaac Stern, the violinist, as chairman of the citizens' committee, was the principal spokesman for the visiting group at City Hall. The speakers included Harold Riegalman, counsel to the newly formed society.

Mrs. Franklin D. Roosevelt is honorary chairman of the citizens' committee. Cochairmen with Mr. Stern are Jacob M. Kaplan and Frederick W. Richmond. Raymond S. Rubinow and Jack deSimone are executive vice chairmen.

The Mayor said Governor Rockefeller was sympathetic to the preservation project.

The present owners plan to sell Carnegie Hall to private investors who would replace the building with an office or apartment structure. ■

OCTOBER 19, 1960

STENGEL, 70, IS LET GO BY YANKEES

John Drebinger

Casey Stengel celebrating his 70th birthday in Yankee Stadium on July 30th, 1960.

Casey Stengel, who in the last twelve years brought ten American League pennants and seven world series championships to New York, was let go yesterday as manager of the Yankees.

Ostensibly his contract was not renewed because of an age-limit program which the co-owners of the Yankees, Dan Topping and Del Webb, have decided to put into effect. Stengel was 70 last July 30.

But Stengel, addressing a roomful of writers and photographers at the Savoy-Hilton Hotel, where announcement of his retirement was made, left no doubt that the owners gave him no chance to remain.

"I was told that my services no longer were desired," said a grim-faced Stengel, who appeared in a role totally unlike the one of flamboyant, wise-cracking half-clown and half-philosopher the baseball world has known these many years.

Stengel made it clear he would have stayed as manager had the owners agreed to certain demands. These, he said, would have continued to give him sole authority over player personnel, such as had been granted to him in the last twelve years.

But the chance to present these demands, Stengel said, was never given to him.

In his remarks he even eliminated his double-talk, which in the past has made him almost as famous as his managerial manipulations on the field. Stengel strove to keep bitterness out of his voice, but he gave the unmistakable impression that he did not like what had happened.

"Yes, sir," he said, "Mr. Topping and Mr. Webb paid me off in full and told me my services were no longer desired because they want to put in a youth program as an advance way of keeping the club going. That was their excuse—the best they've got.

"When I heard their demands, about this new program they said they were trying to build, I told them, 'If that's your program, gentlemen, don't worry about Mr. Stengel. He can take care of himself.'"

Stengel refused to discuss his plans, but left the impression that he had no intentions of permanently retiring from baseball.

Asked whether he thought a man of 70 was too old to manage, he replied:

"It depends on what you can instill into a ball club and how you run the club. The results—a pennant in 1960—prove it."

Stengel is under contract to manage the Yankees until Nov. 1 and cannot associate himself with another club until after that date. But he did say: "I never will return to the Yankees."

Not until someone asked him whether his wife, Edna, wanted him to step out of baseball, did Stengel's familiar impish grin emerge.

"Well, now," said Casey, who, even in this tense moment could not resist getting in a laugh, "naturally Mrs. Stengel is my wife and she'd like to see me make some money somewhere."

And so ends, as far as the Yankees are concerned, the career of a manager whose record is unparalleled in major league history. ■

DECEMBER 17, 1960

AIRLINERS COLLIDE IN FOG

Homer Bigart

The wreckage from United Airlines Flight 826 in Park Slope, Brooklyn, after it collided with TWA Flight 266 over the New York Harbor.

Two airliners collided over New York harbor yesterday in fog and sleet, killing 127 passengers and crewmen. One plane crashed in Brooklyn, killing five more persons on the ground, and the other fell on Staten Island.

A United Air Lines DC-8 jet from Chicago plunged into the crowded Park Slope section of Brooklyn shortly after 10:30 A.M. All but one of its seventy-seven passengers and the crew of seven were killed. The survivor was an 11-year-old boy.

The plane demolished a church and killed a Department of Sanitation worker who was shoveling snow. Burning debris caused a seven-alarm fire, destroying ten brownstone apartment buildings, several shops and a funeral home. Nine persons were injured on the ground.

Three persons were unaccounted for, including the 90-year-old custodian of the Pillar of Fire Church, 123 Sterling Place, a Gothic structure that was leveled by flames.

At almost the same instant as the Brooklyn disaster, a Trans World Airlines Lockheed Super-Constellation crashed near Miller Army Air Field, New Dorp, S. I., eleven miles to the southwest.

This plane, out of Dayton and Columbus, Ohio, apparently exploded in the air just before the crash. All thirty-nine passengers and the crew of five were killed or fatally injured.

Parts of the plane fell in the Lower Bay and parts on the northwest corner of Miller Field.

Federal agencies were investigating the crashes. The United jet was due at New York International Airport at 10:45 A.M. The TWA plane was due at LaGuardia at 10:40 A.M.

Approaching the city, the United jet was ordered by traffic controllers to fly a holding, or stacking, pattern 5,000 feet over Preston, N.J., until cleared to proceed to Idlewild. The TWA plane was directed to fly a holding pattern 6,000 feet over Linden, N.J., until cleared for LaGuardia. Their courses from the holding pattern to the airports would have been several miles apart.

Last night, under floodlights, policemen and firemen were still engaged in the grim task of searching for bodies in the debris at Seventh Avenue and Sterling Place, Brooklyn. Eighty-seven bodies had been taken to the Kings County Hospital morgue. The three missing persons were presumed to be among them.

The search centered on the ruins of the Pillar of Fire Church. The stone façade of the church, which had towered over the four story brownstones of Sterling Place, had collapsed, and it was feared that several bodies of passengers lay under tons of debris.

The only surviving passenger, Steven Baltz, 11, of Wilmette, Ill., who was flying here to meet his mother, was thrown clear of the blazing wreckage and landed in a snowbank.

For fifteen minutes after the disaster police and firemen did not know they were dealing with the wreckage of a giant jet airliner. They thought at first that a propeller plane had crashed and that no more than a dozen persons were aboard. Not until the arrival of aviation accident investigators was it indicated that scores of persons lay dead in the wreckage.

After the extent of the disaster was apparent, all auxiliary policemen in Brooklyn were ordered out. The seven-alarm blaze brought out 250 firemen and fifty pieces of apparatus. ■

DECEMBER 20, 1960

FUEL TANK IGNITES ON AIRCRAFT CARRIER

Charles Grutzner

At least forty-six workmen were killed, more than 150 were injured and at least seven others were missing yesterday in a fire that swept the nation's largest aircraft carrier, the Constellation, at her pier at the Naval Shipyard in Brooklyn.

The $275,000,000 carrier, still under construction, burned all day and into the night.

Workmen leaped from open decks into the icy river or raced down gangways and clambered down ropes as the fire spread rapidly through the ship's decks and into the lower areas of the hold. Acrid fumes billowed through the hold and cut off the escape of many.

Scores of trapped workmen sealed themselves in compartments, closing the watertight doors to keep the smoke out.

Many of these were rescued by Fire Department and Navy emergency crews that went into the burning interior with oxygen tanks on their backs. In some cases rescuers had to cut their way into the closed compartments with acetylene torches.

Fire Commissioner Edward F. Cavanagh Jr. announced at 10:46 P.M. that the blaze, which started at 10:30 A.M., had been brought under control on the still smoldering ship.

A high police official said seven persons still were unaccounted for late last night. Commissioner Cavanagh said there was "no hope left" of bringing anyone else out of the ship alive.

Rear Admiral Schuyler N. Pyne, commander of the Navy Yard, estimated damage to the carrier at $75,000,000. He said the fire would set back the completion of the vessel about a year.

All of the dead were part of a 4,000-man civilian work force putting finishing touches on the 1,047-foot-long vessel, which is almost as long as the Empire State Building is tall and which rises twenty-five stories from keel to masthead.

The blaze started when a lift truck on the hangar deck sheared off the main plug on a full 500-gallon tank of a kerosene-like fuel used to test generators.

Every available ambulance was used to transport the injured and the smoke victims. A Department of Hospitals supply truck took the first six bodies to a temporary morgue in a near-by supply building.

The dead were victims of suffocation, flames or smoke poisoning. Firemen and civilian workers, many of whom joined the rescue teams after making their own escapes, were overcome by smoke and fumes. All forty Navy members of the skeleton crew aboard the ship, which was to be commissioned in March, got off safely.

The scene of yesterday's tragedy was less than two miles from where a plane crashed in Brooklyn on Friday, bringing death to all eighty-three persons aboard and others on the ground. The Brooklyn plane crash was part of a double tragedy that killed forty-four persons aboard a second plane, which crashed in Staten Island, after the two aircraft had collided. ■

OCTOBER 19, 1961

Habitues of Meyer Davis Land DANCE THE TWIST

Arthur Gelb

Cafe society, having ignored rock 'n' roll for years, has suddenly, by an apparent process of mass hypnosis, embraced the teenage craze.

The elite of the social set and celebrities of show business have discovered a sensuous dance called the Twist, performed to rock 'n 'roll, and are wallowing in it like converts to a new brand of voodoo.

Although the Twist appeared earlier this week in such haunts as the Stork Club and the Barberry Room, the high temple of the new cult is an unprepossessing place called the Peppermint Lounge.

Adjoining the Knickerbocker Hotel on the south side of Forty-fifth Street east of Seventh Avenue, the Peppermint and its surroundings are the scene of a grotesque display every night from 10:30 to 3 o'clock.

Patrolmen are bedeviled by a stream of limousines and taxis. Passers-by are shoved off the curb or forced to elbow their way through gaping throngs. The strident sounds of rock 'n' roll pour into the street from a doorway reinforced by five bouncers.

The Twist, stemming from a dance called the Madison that erupted a number of years ago in Philadelphia, is a rhythmic, shoulder-shaking, hip-swiveling step in which the partners synchronize their movements but do not touch.

Hank Ballard, a singer, recorded a song called "The Twist" five years ago. Its fame was spread by Chubby Checker, a 19-year-old singer, who has been plugging the song and the dance across the country.

Early yesterday morning, the Peppermint looked and sounded like a surrealistic nightmare. In the hot, jammed, smoky room, which holds 200 persons, patrons were squeezed against the wall and bunched together at a mass of small tables.

On the dance floor, couples gyrated in a joyless frenzy. They scrupulously confined themselves to a few inches of space apiece, but everyone was being jostled nonetheless.

"There's nothing like this anywhere," said Earl Blackwell, publisher of Celebrity Register, with profound satisfaction yesterday morning. "It's different from anything I've ever seen. The rhythm is contagious. It makes you want to get up and dance. What's most important is that it's an easy dance to do. Everyone can do it." ■

Dancing the twist at the Peppermint Lounge, 1961.

APRIL 1, 1963

114-DAY NEWSPAPER STRIKE ENDS

Sheldon Binn

The 114-day-old New York newspaper strike came to an end shortly after noon yesterday.

Minutes after the striking photoengravers voted 213 to 104 to accept a revised contract proposed by Mayor Wagner, pickets departed from the eight affected newspapers and smiling employees began returning to work.

The photoengravers voted to ratify a two-year package of wage increases and fringe benefits totaling $12.63 a man a week. They thus accepted a pact that fell within the framework of a pace-setting contract approved last Sunday by the printers—the first union to strike.

The New York Printing Pressmen's Union 2 also ratified its contract yesterday by a vote of 626 to 150. It falls within the $12.63 package formula.

The economic losses from the longest and costliest newspaper blackout in New York's history were placed at between $190,000,000 and $250,000,000. The newspapers, which normally publish 5,700,000 papers daily, were estimated to have lost more than $108,000,000 in advertising and circulation revenues.

The 19,074 newspaper employes who were deprived of their normal livelihood lost $50,400,000 in wages and benefits.

Queues of customers waited at many newsstands last night, some for an hour and more, to buy the early editions of this morning's papers. Supplies were quickly sold out. Many readers bought two or more morning newspapers, reading one while waiting for stacks of another newspaper to be delivered to the stand.

The first papers began to roll off the presses of The New York Mirror at 6:55 P.M. The presses at The Daily News got under way at 7:18, The New York Times at 9:28 and The New York Herald Tribune at 10:41.

The strike against four newspapers and the initial voluntary suspension of publication by five others affected nearly every aspect of the city's life. It caused economic loss to large corporations and individuals, and dislocations to people in many walks of life. ■

JANUARY 19, 1964

BIGGEST BUILDINGS IN WORLD TO RISE AT TRADE CENTER

Bernard Stengren

Twin 1,350-foot towers, the world's tallest buildings, will be erected to house the World Trade Center planned downtown. The towers and a cluster of 70-foot-high satellite buildings will form a ring around the five-acre plaza containing reflecting pools.

Plans for the $350 million complex on the Lower West Side were disclosed yesterday at a preview in the New York Hilton Hotel.

The center will gather governmental and private activities in the export-import field now widely scattered in the metropolitan area. It will have exhibition halls, shops, restaurants and a 250-room hotel, for travelers whose business brings them to the center.

Each of the center's twin towers will be eight stories—and 100 feet—taller than the Empire State Building. Without its 222-foot television antenna mast, the Empire State is 1,250 feet high and has 102 stories.

The center is the latest of a number of self-contained "communities"' in the city. It follows the trend of the Lincoln Center for the Performing Arts, the projected Civic Center near City Hall and the Brooklyn Bridge Southwest development almost directly across Manhattan.

The center will occupy a 16-acre site bounded by Church, Vesey, Liberty and West Streets. It will have 10 million square feet of rentable space, direct access to major mass transportation systems and off-street parking for 1,600 vehicles.

Construction is to begin early next year and will be completed in stages by 1970. The architects are Minoru Yamasaki & Associates and Emery Roth & Sons. The Port Authority, which will build and operate the center, estimated that $200 million of the $350 million cost of construction would go for wages of construction workers.

Office rentals range from about $4.50 a square foot for older buildings to $7.50 a square foot in prime midtown Manhattan locations. The new Pan Am Building charges $6.50, the same as the center proposes. Some observers considered the price at World Trade Center somewhat high for the neighborhood.

However, only 4 million of the 10 million square feet will be occupied by private businesses. The balance will be taken by Federal, regional and state government units.

New Jersey Governor Richard Hughes stressed the employment potential of the center and of the industries in his state keyed to the export-import trade. He also noted that the reconstructed Hudson Tubes—now designated PATH for Port Authority Trans Hudson—would make the center only five minutes from Jersey City.

Among the major features of the center will be a completely rebuilt terminal for PATH.

There will be 230 passenger elevators in the center, including 11 express elevators going nonstop from the ground floor to the 41st floor and 12 express cars with the first stop at the 74th floor. At each of these two floors there will be "sky lobbies," where passengers will change to reach intermediate floors.

Seventy-two local elevators in each tower will make stops at floors on the lower, middle and upper zones of the buildings. All will be automatic elevators. It has not yet been decided whether aluminum or stainless steel will be used for the spandrels, or vertical facade, of the building. But the metal frame will provide the principal strength of the structures. Normally this is a function of the elevator shafts, but the arrangement of elevators precludes their use. ■

SALE OF TICKETS TO WORLD'S FAIR TOPS $35 MILLION

Joseph Lelyveld

Aerial view of World's Fair in Flushing, Queens, New York, 1964.

The World's Fair announced yesterday "the biggest box office in history": $35,219,602 on 28,034,987 tickets.

That was the state of its advance sale on Saturday, the day it stopped selling $2 tickets for $1.35. The sale, nearly three times what the fair had predicted, was also:

- Equal to the total paid admissions in the first year of the 1939-40 fair here.
- Three times the paid admissions at the Seattle Fair in 1962.
- More than last year's box-office receipts for all major league baseball games.
- And more than the total ticket sales for all Broadway shows last year.

Most of the sales were made in large blocks to corporations and institutions. Banks and investment houses, for instance, took 10 million tickets. The concerns will continue to sell these tickets at reduced rates to the public until they are sold out.

As an augury of financial success for the fair, the huge advance sale was a source of gratification for its president, Robert Moses—the man chosen to make sure that the fair more than paid its way. At a press conference yesterday he allowed himself a fleeting smile of satisfaction.

"We may have a success on our hands," he said with the kind of understatement that might be expected from a governor of the Bank of England. Pressed to say more, he replied that he was not Cassius Clay.

As a result of the huge advance sale, the fair corporation announced, it was repaying $3 million in 5 percent bank loans that it took last November. The loans were due in August.

Also, it predicted that before the end of the year it would pay off $30 million in 6 percent notes that are not due until August, 1966. ■

MARCH 27, 1964

37 WHO SAW MURDER DIDN'T CALL THE POLICE

Martin Gansberg

Catherine "Kitty" Genovese, 1964.

For more than half an hour 37 respectable, law-abiding citizens in Queens watched a killer stalk and stab a woman in three separate attacks in Kew Gardens.

Twice the sound of their voices and the sudden glow of their bedroom lights interrupted him and frightened him off. Each time he returned, sought her out and stabbed her again. Not one person telephoned the police during the assault; one witness called after the woman was dead.

That was two weeks ago today. But Assistant Chief Inspector Frederick M. Lussen, in charge of the borough's detectives and a veteran of 25 years of homicide investigations, is still shocked.

He can give a matter-of-fact recitation of many murders. But the Kew Gardens slaying baffles him—not because it is a murder, but because the "good people" failed to call the police.

"As we have reconstructed the crime," he said, "the assailant had three chances to kill this woman during a 35-minute period. He returned twice to complete the job. If we had been called when he first attacked, the woman might not be dead now."

Twenty-eight-year-old Catherine Genovese, who was called Kitty by almost everyone in the neighborhood, was returning home from her job as manager of a bar in Hollis. She turned off the lights of her car, locked the door and started to walk the 100 feet to the entrance of her apartment at 82-70 Austin Street, which is in a Tudor building, with stores on the first floor and apartments on the second.

She got as far as a street light in front of a bookstore before the man grabbed her. She screamed. Lights went on in the 10-story apartment house at 82-67 Austin Street, which faces the bookstore. Windows and open and voices punctured the early-morning stillness.

Miss Genovese screamed: "Oh, my God, he stabbed me! Please help me! Please help me!'

From one of the upper windows in the apartment house, a man called down: "Let that girl alone!"

The assailant looked up at him, shrugged and walked down Austin Street toward a white sedan parked a short distance away. Miss Genovese struggled to her feet.

Lights went out. The killer returned to Miss Genovese, now trying to make her way around the side of the building by the parking lot to get to her apartment. The assailant stabbed her again.

"I'm dying!" she shrieked. "I'm dying!"

Windows were opened again, and lights went on in many apartments. The assailant got into his car and drove away. Miss Genovese staggered to her feet.

The assailant returned. By then, Miss Genovese had crawled to the back of the building, where the freshly painted brown doors to the apartment house held out hope of safety. The killer tried the first door; she wasn't there. At the second door, 82-62 Austin Street, he saw her slumped on the floor at the foot of the stairs. He stabbed her a third time—fatally.

It was 3:50 by the time the police received their first call, from a man who was a neighbor of Miss Genovese. In two minutes they were at the scene. The neighbor, a 70-year-old woman and another woman were the only persons on the street. Nobody else came forward.

Six days later, the police arrested Winston Moseley, a 29-year-old business-machine operator, and charged him with the homicide. Moseley had no previous record. He is married, has two children and owns a home at 133-19 Sutter Avenue, South Ozone Park, Queens. On Wednesday, a court committed him to Kings County Hospital for psychiatric observation.

JULY 19, 1964

THOUSANDS RIOT IN HARLEM

Paul L. Montgomery and Francis X. Clines

Thousands of rioting Negroes raced through the center of Harlem last night and early today, shouting at policemen and white people, pulling fire alarms, breaking windows and looting stores.

At least thirty persons were arrested.

There was no estimate on the number injured. Scores of persons with bloodied heads were seen throughout the eight-block area between Eighth and Lenox Avenues and 123rd and 127th Streets, where most of the rioting occurred.

The riot grew out of a demonstration in front of the West 123rd Street police station protesting the slaying of a Negro youth by a white police lieutenant last Thursday. The demonstration followed a rally at 125th Street and Seventh Avenue, where speakers decried the shooting of the boy, 15-year-old James Powell, by Lieut. Thomas Gilligan in Yorkville.

When the police sealed off the block in front of the station house, between Seventh and Eighth Avenues, the shouting, keyed-up crowd spread out in angry groups in the surrounding neighborhood.

Shots fired into the air by policemen to disperse the milling crowds echoed through streets littered with overturned garbage cans and broken glass.

More than 500 policemen, including all members of the tactical patrol force on duty in Manhattan and Brooklyn, were called out to control the mobs. However, the crowds continued to grow as rumors of the rioting spread through the community.

By 3 A.M., five and a half hours after the riot started, the situation was not under control.

Police roamed the streets with revolvers drawn.

On Lenox Avenue, between 125th and 126th Streets, police fired at people who were throwing bottles and bricks down at them from roofs. Some people milling at the corner of 125th Street and Lenox Avenue ran as the policemen fired. Others stood their ground, laughing and applauding.

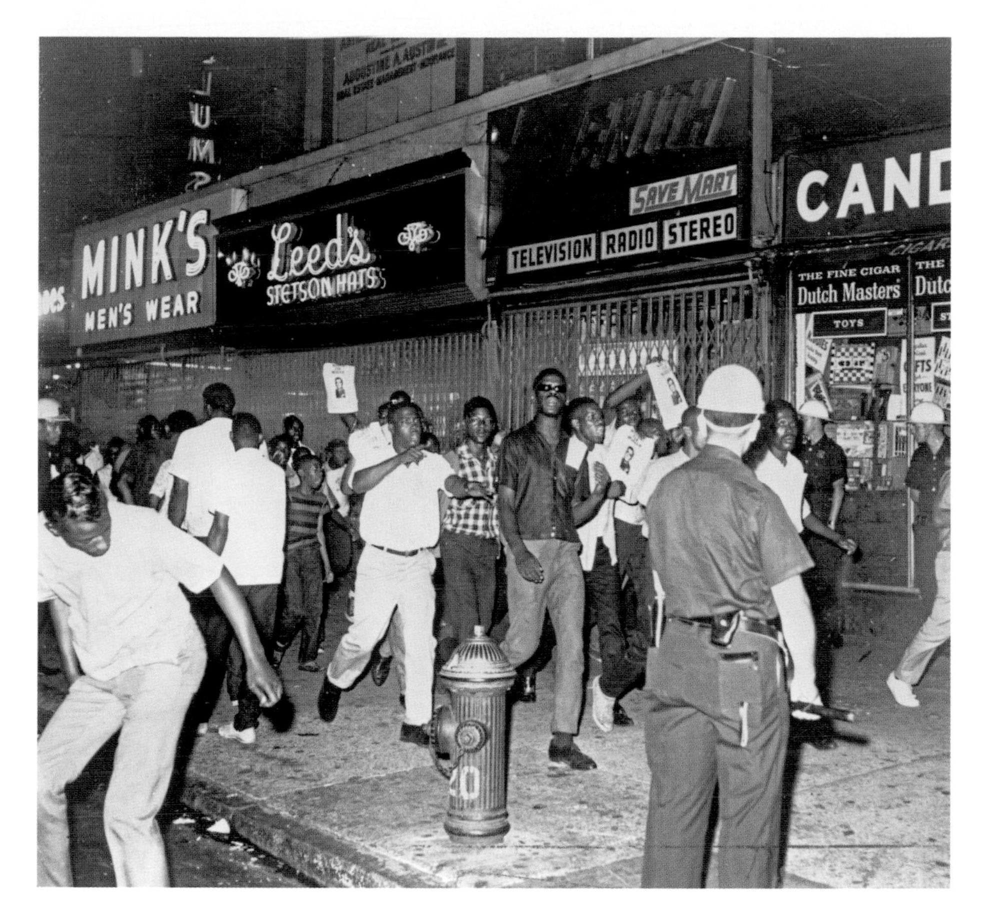

Riots in Harlem following the fatal shooting of 15-year-old black youth by a New York policeman.

Attempts to disperse the crowds by appealing to them through loud speakers failed.

"Why don't you go home," pleaded a policeman through a bull-horn on one block.

"We are home—this is our home," answered a person from a crowd.

Traffic was diverted because youths were stopping traffic to beat on cars and harangue drivers, particularly if they were white. Windows were broken in at least one auto.

People from the area ran up and down the streets from group to group. Refuse baskets were set afire and Molotov cocktail bombs, bottles filled with gasoline, were thrown into the streets. Windshields of at least two police cars were smashed by hurled objects. Policemen on foot moved gingerly along the streets to avoid objects thrown from roofs.

Crowds even yelled "Killers, killers" at policemen who went to the aid of a young Negro girl who apparently was struck by a hit and run driver on 125th Street.

Throughout the evening routine calls for aid in upper Manhattan were going unheeded as the police concentrated their strength in the trouble spot.

A march to the police station had been stirred by several speakers at the rally, held at Seventh Avenue and 125th Street by three chapters of the Congress of Racial Equality.

After persons representing CORE had spoken, the speakers platform, a kitchen chair, was turned over to speakers representing various other groups, including the United African Movement and the Harlem Progressive Labor Movement.

One of the last speakers, the Rev. Nelson C. Dukes of the Fountain Spring Baptist Church, 158 West 126th Street, called for the march on the station house to demand the arrest of Lieutenant Gilligan on a murder charge. After the rally broke up at 8:45 P.M., Mr. Dukes led the crowd down Seventh Avenue to the station house. There it attempted to push its way in through the front door, but was blocked by five policemen who locked their arms.

Mr. Dukes was shaken by the developments. Speaking to a police officer, he said:

"If I knew this was going to happen, I would not have said anything." ■

OCTOBER 31, 1964

STAR OF INDIA STOLEN FROM MUSEUM

Tania Long

A collection of rare and precious gems—among them the famed Star of India sapphire—has been stolen from the American Museum of Natural History in one of the most daring burglaries in recent history.

The 22 gems were removed from their glass display cases in the J. P. Morgan Hall of Gems and Minerals on the fourth floor after 9 P.M. Thursday.

A glass cutter and a metal window-washing squeegee taken from a porter's locker were used to break open the cases.

Entrance into the closely locked hall was believed to have been made through a window that was found open at 10 A.M. yesterday, when a museum attendant discovered the theft.

There was no insurance on the gems, as the premiums would have been too high, according to museum officials. A burglar-alarm system attached to the display cases was discontinued years ago, as was the practice of locking a man into the hall overnight.

Dr. James A. Oliver, director of the museum, said that security throughout the museum was not good. He said the museum had been pleading with City Hall for more than 10 years to increase the staff.

A museum official said the market value of the gems was about $380,000. Dr. Oliver said, however, that the gems were, in fact, priceless because they were irreplaceable.

The Star of India, donated by the late J. P. Morgan, weighs 563.35 carats and is the world's largest star sapphire. It is light blue, about two and a half inches in diameter and round like an oversized golfball. Its value was estimated at $100,000.

Taken from the same case were two other rare stones. They are the Edith Haggin DeLong Star Ruby, weighing 100.32 carats, considered the world's most perfect star ruby, and the purplish blue Midnight Sapphire, donated by Mr. Morgan.

The thieves broke into three cases, passing up one that contained $100,000 worth of regular sapphires. Both the police and museum officials believed the thieves were amateurs, taking the three big stones because they were prominently displayed and well marked and ignoring the case of costly clear sapphires in favor of a case containing a variety of less costly emeralds and diamonds.

Amateurs or not, Dr. Oliver said he believed the thieves were familiar with the conditions of the hall, which is 100 by 60 feet long with 20-foot ceilings. "I'm not a detective," he said, "but the fact they knew where to find the squeegee shows they knew their way around."

In addition to leaving the squeegee behind, the thieves left many fingerprints, some showing the whorls of thumb and index finger.

The hall was closed to the public as the police took fingerprints and photographs. A large yellow sign outside said: "Scene of Crime. Public Prohibited."

NOVEMBER 4, 1964

Kennedy Victor in Senate Race

R. W. Apple Jr.

Robert F. Kennedy was elected to the United States Senate from New York yesterday in his first bid for elective office, overwhelming Republican Senator Kenneth B. Keating.

With more than 50 percent of the vote counted, Mr. Kennedy held a 6-to-5 lead. Because most of the untallied vote was in heavily Democratic New York City, it appeared that the former Attorney General's plurality might reach 650,000.

Mr. Keating conceded defeat at 11:39 P.M. with the announcement at the Roosevelt Hotel that he had sent a congratulatory telegram to Mr. Kennedy.

Governor Rockefeller, standing beside the white-haired Rochester legislator, said Mr. Keating's defeat was "a tragedy for the state and nation."

> "Come, my friends, 'tis not too late to build a better world."

Mr. Kennedy ran well behind President Johnson, who seemed to be headed for a record margin of 2.5 million votes or more in the state. The President won all of the state's 62 counties.

Mr. Kennedy appeared at a victory rally in the Statler Hilton Hotel at about 1:30 A.M. He said he had won "an overwhelming mandate" to continue the policies of his older brother, John F. Kennedy.

Then, as he often did during the campaign, he offered a quotation for his audience: "Come, my friends, 'tis not too late to build a better world."

"This," Mr. Kennedy added, "is what I dedicate myself to in the next six years for the State of New York." ■

NOVEMBER 22, 1964

VERRAZANO BRIDGE OPENED TO TRAFFIC

Gay Talese

The sun shone, the sky was cloudless; bands played, cannons echoed up and down the harbor, flags waved, and thousands of motorists yesterday became part of the first—and perhaps only—blissful traffic jam on the Verrazano-Narrows Bridge.

The bridge, which took more than five years to build and which reaches like a rainbow over the Narrows between Brooklyn and Staten Island, was officially opened to traffic at 3 P.M.

"This latest addition to our city's great wealth of bridges represents a new summit of achievement," Mayor Wagner told the crowd assembled near the world's longest suspended span. "Surely we must see it not only as the biggest, but as the most beautiful of all, the most princely, and the most stately."

A young man in a rented tuxedo, driving a pale blue Cadillac convertible with flags flapping from the fenders, was the first man to cross the bridge and pay the 50-cent toll. He, together with his young companions (also in rented tuxedos), had parked all week behind the Staten Island toll gate to assure their official position as the first to cross.

When they crossed the 6,690-foot span, passing through the arches of the two steel towers that are as tall as 70-story skyscrapers, the youths were cheered by the crowds standing on the Brooklyn side of the bridge.

It was a perfect day for crossing a bridge. They could see, as they moved in the motorcade across the 4,260-foot center span—the longest in the world—the whole view of the harbor, the ships below, the fireboats shooting spray into the air, the cannon smoke, the helicopters hovering over the tall bridge towers that stood 693 feet in the air.

In one limousine in the motorcade—the 18th car behind Mr. Moses' limousine—sat the 85-year-old designer of the bridge, O. H. Ammann. A quiet and modest man, he was barely recognized by the politicians and other dignitaries at the ribbon-cutting ceremony. He stood in the crowd without saying a word, although occasionally, as inconspicuously as he could, he sneaked a look at the bridge looming in the distance, sharply outlined in the cloudless sky.

"How do you feel, Mr. Ammann?" somebody asked, almost startling the lean engineer who wore a blue coat and blue muffler around his neck.

"Oh," he said, slowly, a little self-consciously, "as I feel every day."

When the official motorcade arrived in Staten Island, Mr. Ammann got out of the car and slipped quietly up into the grandstand and did not say another word the rest of the day.

Throughout Brooklyn and Staten Island yesterday and last night, there were other parties—small informal ones, and some larger ones in public rooms—celebrating the bridge, which is expected to do so much to facilitate traffic, and build up business and population in the hitherto isolated borough of Staten Island.

In the first hour after the bridge opened to traffic, about 5,000 cars crossed the span, more than 70 percent of them from the Staten Island side. By 4:30 P.M. the stream of curious motorists had dwindled and traffic rolled freely in both directions. ■

The Verrazano-Narrows Bridge in 1965.

NOVEMBER 3, 1965

LINDSAY DEFEATS BEAME IN CLOSE MAYORAL RACE

Richard Witkin

New York Mayor John V. Lindsay campaigning on Broadway and 72nd Street in 1965.

John V. Lindsay was elected Mayor of New York yesterday on the Republican-Liberal ticket, a victory that deeply affected the national political picture.

In the closest mayoral election in at least a quarter century, Mr. Lindsay, a maverick Republican Representative, defeated Controller Abraham D. Beame, who had sought to rally bitterly feuding elements of the Democratic party around him. The indicated majority is more than 100,000.

William F. Buckley Jr., whose Conservative party campaign became a key issue because of its possible impact on the conservative-vs.-moderate struggle for control of the Republican party, appeared to have polled about 13 percent of the vote. This was less than most politicians had expected.

The 43-year-old Mr. Lindsay will succeed Mayor Wagner, who threw the mayoral contest wide open by declining to run for a fourth term. Mr. Lindsay will take over City Hall Jan. 1. He will be the first non-Democratic Mayor since Fiorello H. LaGuardia ended his third term in 1945.

Mr. Lindsay, in his victory statement said: "I plan to give New York the most hard-working, the most dedicated and—I hope—the most exciting and successful administration this city has ever seen."

Warning against dissension, he said that "if we join together in the rigorous, exacting struggles ahead, we assure the eventual conquest of the pending, recurrent and unforeseen crises afflicting our city."

The election was expected to have vast repercussions across the country, and the returns were closely monitored by politicians everywhere. The outcome gave moderates from coast to coast a tremendous boost in their struggle against the right wing of the Republican party since the Goldwater disaster in the Presidential race a year ago.

It catapulted Mr. Lindsay into a position of national leadership in the party. He is almost certain to be considered a Presidential or Vice-Presidential possibility in 1968 or 1972, although he promised during the campaign to serve out his four years at City Hall in the hope of running for re-election.

Mr. Buckley, whose talent for arch phrasemaking provided much of the sparkle of the campaign, said his campaign had served an excellent purpose—"to re-introduce the two-party system to New York City."

Although a precise analysis of the vote was not possible right away, there were clear indications that Mr. Lindsay had made deep gains in many normally Democratic ethnic groups, particularly in the Jewish community.

All day, there was a particular air of excitement in New York. It grew from the fact that, during the voting hours, most people, from citizens waiting in the long lines at polling places to political chieftains in the campaign headquarters, had the feeling that the mayoral race was a toss-up. ■

NOVEMBER 10, 1965

POWER BLACKOUT AFFECTS NINE STATES

Martin Gansberg

Millions of persons in at least nine Northeastern states and two Canadian provinces were affected by the electric-power failure yesterday.

As confusion took hold in the gathering dusk, National Guard units and the police in major cities were alerted to prevent looting and to assist travelers.

The biggest problem in most areas was transportation. Planes, trains, subways and buses were unable to maintain operations. Autos had difficulty as pedestrians clogged roads trying to find their way home in the dark.

Residents of Rhode Island reported they were unable to make telephone calls during the early hours of the blackout. Switchboards in Providence gave busy signals for a long period, but an operator said that her board was "lit up like a Christmas tree."

Shortly before 7 P.M. some persons in

The blackout of 1965 affected more than 25 million people from New York City northward.

Providence said they had seen a red ball with an extended white tail moving across the sky from north to south over Narragansett Bay. Observers declared that it could have been a meteorite.

About 40 minutes later, lights were restored in most of the state as the Narragansett Electric Company put three 50,000-kilowatt generators into service. A state of emergency had been declared by the Governor's office a few minutes before the lights went on.

Radio and police reports indicated that the power failure had affected Syracuse, Utica, Rochester, Albany and other sections of New York State. But in Buffalo, power supplies were said to be functioning about half an hour after the blackout was first reported.

From New York City through most of New England a major concern during the blackout was the problem of coping with commercial airline flights that were scheduled to arrive. None were permitted to take off, however.

In Boston, Logan International Airport was shut down early and planes circled overhead, waiting for landing instructions. About an hour and a half passed before the airport was able to bring the flights down with emergency lighting.

In Toronto, businessmen discarded their briefcases to help the police direct traffic during the evening rush hours. Fire stations worked feverishly to assist persons who had become trapped in elevator in of office buildings. The problem was eased somewhat as lights in part of the downtown are remained in service. ■

JANUARY 7, 1966

JOHNSON SENDS WIRTZ TO TRANSIT PARLEY AFTER LINDSAY ASKS AID IN ENDING STRIKE

Damon Stetson

President Johnson, acting at the request of Mayor Lindsay, sent Secretary of Labor W. Willard Wirtz here last night to assist in trying to settle the crippling transit strike.

The Mayor, who had conferred with Secretary Wirtz by telephone during the last few days, called the President at 6:15 P.M. and said that he thought that the Secretary might be able to help in the crisis, which has defied solution for six days.

President Johnson immediately directed Mr. Wirtz to come to the city. The Secretary left on a 7 P.M. shuttle plane and arrived at La Guardia Airport at 7:53 P.M. He went to City Hall and spent about four and a half hours in conferences with the Mayor, a group of labor leaders and the three mediators in the dispute.

Asked if there was any possibility of Federal financial aid, Mr. Wirtz replied: "I would say no." At a news conference shortly before 1 o'clock this morning, Mayor Lindsay, with Mr. Wirtz at his side, said there had been some movement yesterday in the negotiations. But the Mayor emphasized that he did not want to sound either an optimistic or a pessimistic note.

The Mayor hinted that the Transit Authority might be considering a move to free Michael J. Quill, president of the Transport Workers Union, and eight other union leaders who were jailed Tuesday for having violated an anti-strike injunction.

Mr. Quill collapsed in jail and is now in Bellevue Hospital. Mr. Lindsay noted that Harry Van Arsdale Jr., president of the New York City Central Labor Council, had conferred with him and had expressed the hope that he would help get the "first teams" of the two striking unions back to the negotiating table.

He said that he had relayed Mr. Van Arsdale's request to Joseph E. O'Grady, chairman of the Transit Authority. The Mayor said that an Inquiry about the authority's intentions, if directed to Mr. O'Grady, might produce "an interesting response."

It was Justice Geller who found the union leaders guilty of civil contempt, but it was the Transit Authority that asked for the execution of the judge's order and the arrest of the labor leaders.

Shortly before 10 P.M., Mr. Van Arsdale and the other labor officials left City Hall for the Americana hotel, where they were expected to meet with negotiators for the Transport Workers Union.

The three-man mediation panel—Dr. Nathan P. Feinsinger, Theodore W. Kheel and Sylvester Garrett—have been trying to resolve the dispute between the Transit Authority and the two striking unions—the Transport Workers Union, which represents 33,000 workers, and the Amalgamated Transit Union, which represents 1,800 workers.

Among the Transport Workers Union original major demands in the negotiations are a 4-day, 32-hour work week without any reduction in pay, a 30 percent pay increase and improvements in health and welfare conditions.

There has been increasing speculation that a costly settlement with the transit workers might eventually lead to an increase in the 15-cent fare. ■

PENN STATION FAÇADE YIELDS TO MODERNITY

Ada Louise Huxtable

The waiting room of the original Pennsylvania Station (Penn Station) in 1962. The station was demolished two years later.

Pennsylvania Station succumbed to progress this week at the age of 56, after a lingering decline. The building's one remaining façade was shorn of eagles and ornament yesterday, preparatory to leveling the last wall. It went not with a bang, or a whimper, but to the rustle of real estate stock shares. The passing of Penn Station is more than the end of a landmark. It makes the priority of real estate values over preservation conclusively clear. It confirms the demise of an age of opulent elegance, of conspicuous, magnificent spaces, rich and enduring materials, the monumental civic gesture, and extravagant expenditure for esthetic ends. Obsolescence is not limited to land use and building function in New York.

It was still the Gilded Age in 1910 when the building was completed by Charles Follen McKim of McKim, Mead & White, one of the turn-of-the-century's most gilt-edged architectural firms. There was plush in the Pullmans, crisp damask in the diners, silver bud vases on tables, and the New York-bound traveler debouched into a Roman tepidarium.

Modeled after the warm room of the Baths of Caracalla, the station's concourse was longer than the nave of St. Peter's in Rome. Its vaulted ceilings were 138 feet high, and its grand staircase was 40 feet wide.

The soot-stained travertine of the interiors, reputed to be the first used in this country, was from quarries in Tivoli employed in building the Eternal City. Its mellow, golden-cream was used in the Coliseum in the first century A.D. and St. Peter's 15 centuries later. New York could be called the Mortal Metropolis.

Today, there are new symbols for a new age. The modern traveler, fed on frozen flight dinners, enters the city, not in Roman splendor, but through the bowels of a streamlined concrete bird, as at Trans World Airlines' Kennedy International airport terminal. Classic columns are replaced by catenary curves.

The station's decline began long before demolition. As time passed and grime gathered, life and architecture became noticeably less grand.

With the return of prosperity, and the traveler, demolition by commercialization began. Colored ads appeared like blasphemous utterances in the marbled halls; automobiles revolved on turntables; shops and stands were added in jazzy cacophony.

Functionally, the station was considerably less than noble. The complexity and ambiguity of its train levels and entrances and exits were a constant frustration. Except for its great glass and iron waiting room, it was a better expression of ancient Rome than of 20th-century America.

But its great spaces and superb materials were genuinely noble, in a sense that architecture can no longer afford, in cubage costs alone. The new terminal will have 9- to 22-foot ceilings, against the original 138, all below grade. ■

AUGUST 16, 1966

THE HERALD TRIBUNE IS DISCONTINUED

Paul L. Montgomery

With the closing of The New York Herald Tribune yesterday, there also ended the remnant of two of the city's great journalistic enterprises—James Gordon Bennett's Herald and Horace Greeley's Tribune.

Bennett and his brawling Herald, and Greeley and his urbane, influential Tribune—which merged in 1924 after 80 halcyon years of independent existence—did much to create modern journalism, and not a little to shape the temper of the city that nurtured them.

Although shaken in the last 20 years by almost continued financial and editorial crises, The Herald Tribune help up to the end the tradition of being a newspaper that attracted some of the liveliest reporters and writers in the business. It's foreign and Washington coverage were widely respected.

Most observers date the long decline of the newspaper from the death of Ogden

Reid, its fourth editor, on Jan. 3, 1947. Mr. Reid, who became editor in 1912, took little active part in the day-to-day operations, but in his unostentatious way was the pillar that kept business and editorial concerns separated.

"When Ogden Reid died, they buried The Herald Tribune," the late Lucius Beebe wrote.

In the late nineteen forties, when The Times and The Daily News were expanding, the Herald Tribune was having to economize.

The debts mounted. In 1955 under pressure from creditors, Ogden R. Reid, Whitelaw's younger brother, became president and editor. A tempestuous period of editorial changes followed during which some of the newspaper's best reporters and editors resigned. Reid instituted puzzle contests and stories from Hollywood of the fan magazine type.

However, The Tribune's finances became no better, and in August, 1958, John Hay Whitney, who had lending the Reid's money, acquired working control of The Herald Tribune. Mr. Whitney brought in a succession of new editors and in 1961, hired John Denson of Newsweek magazine as the Herald Tribune's managing editor.

Mr. Denson instituted radical changes, particularly in the makeup of the paper. Photographs were cropped to blow up details, headlines frequently posed questions, and fewer stories were run on the first page.

Despite circulation gains in the last few years and a considerable excitement in newspaper circles about the "new" Herald Tribune, the paper continued to lose money. After the 114-day strike of 1962-1963, which caused severe losses, many felt the end of The Tribune was near. ■

AUGUST 29, 1966

No Date This Weekend? Try First Avenue and 64th

Paul L. Montgomery

The entrance to Maxwell's Plum, a popular nightclub in New York City, circa 1966.

The stretch of First Avenue between 63d and 65th Streets has emerged this summer as a swinging big-city version of the small-town drugstore.

For the residents of the high-rent neighborhood—stewardesses and models, young executives and Wall Street lawyers—the street has become a kind of community living room where a party always seems to be going on.

And for the flocks of suburban visitors, it is a place to meet educated, interesting people and pretty girls, get a taste of East Side life, and perhaps even make a date.

"It's just like the Hamptons," said 20-year-old Faye Copeland of Rockville Centre, L.I., the other evening, "only not as far away."

The focal point of the night's activity are four chic bars—Friday's at 63d Street, Maxwell's Plum at 64th, Mister Laffs between 64th and 65th, and Sullivan's between 65th and 66th. On Friday evening—the busiest night of the week—it is not unusual for customers to wait a half-hour on the sidewalk before even getting inside one of the bars.

But as much of the life of the area goes on outside the bars as inside. The atmosphere and the informal dress are those of a summer resort. There are a few of the cruder types, and a few overage swingers lurking hopefully at the fringes of youthful groups, but most of the First Avenue habitués are well-off, well-dressed, well-favored and well-spoken.

There is a certain freedom on the street. Behavior by young men that might draw stares, or even the police, in other parts of the city is common. If a young man sees a girl he likes, he is expected to go up for her telephone number and perhaps even ask for a date. The more ambitious can end the evening with a half-dozen numbers and a choice of girls for a Saturday night date.

SEPTEMBER 17, 1966

FIRST LADY ADDS TO GLITTER AT OPERA HOUSE OPENING

Charlotte Curtis

The premiere of Samuel Barber's "Antony and Cleopatra" was only one of the diversions at the super-gala opening of the new $45.7-million Metropolitan Opera House in Lincoln Center last night.

The great arched house, a brightly lighted architectural toy that is expected to dominate salon conversations for weeks, was under as much scrutiny as the new opera. But neither the opera nor the house could outshine Mrs. Lyndon B. Johnson and an audience that included virtually every member of New York's predictably elegant diamond brigade.

Hundreds of formally dressed tycoons, aristocrats, nabobs, bankers, moguls, diplomats, potentates, fashion plates, grande dames and other assorted Great Society over-achievers were among the 3,800 persons who produced a record $400,000 gross—more than 12 times what the Met usually gets for a sellout—and the kind of glamour the nation has come to associate with New York on a good day.

The best red-plush seats in the boxes and orchestra went for $250, and dinner and champagne were extra. For $16, and the sense to have made advance reservations, guests could have filet of beef in either the Canteen Corporation's Grand Tier Restaurant or the Top of the Met.

The same dinner was served to members of the exclusive Metropolitan Opera Club, and varied only slightly for Mrs. Johnson and her party in the board room. Across the plaza in Philharmonic Hall, Sherry's was offering a filet of beef dinner for $12. And all the restaurants and bars were well stocked with champagne—250 cases (3,000 bottles) in the new Met alone.

"We'll never run out," said James Rogers, vice president of the Canteen Corporation. "It would be unthinkable."

It was a great night for furs, haute couture and enormous jewels. Mrs. C. V. Whitney, who can be depended upon to come up with something significant for the occasion, wore a gold and diamond tiara that had belonged to the Empress Elizabeth of Austria.

For a while, it looked as if Mrs. Joseph Lauder, the cosmetics queen, was going to appear without a tiara. She didn't like the idea of wearing her ruby and diamond tiara with a turquoise crepe from Irene Galitzine. But in the end, she found something better—a gold and diamond crown suitable for Queen Elizabeth II.

"You know how it is," she said. "You have to wear something."

Cecil Beaton, the British photographer and designer, left the wearing of big jewels to the women. But his cufflinks were white rock crystal set with emeralds. "The audiences aren't as freakish these days," he said before joining Mrs. Joseph P. Kennedy for dinner. "They don't make such fools of themselves."

At 8:10, the orchestra, under the direction of Thomas Schippers, played "The Star-Spangled Banner." John D. Rockefeller 3d chairman of Lincoln Center's board, welcomed everyone from the stage and introduced Anthony A. Bliss, president of the Metropolitan Opera. And at 8:27, just before the opera began, 65 photographers came out from behind the curtain, lined up and shot pictures of the auditorium. They received a sitting ovation.

"I've never seen this in Europe—Vienna, Berlin—never," said Mrs. Fritz Reiner, widow of the Chicago Symphony conductor, who was not pleased by the photographers. "Did you ever hear of it in your life?"

MARCH 2, 1967

HOUSE EXCLUDES POWELL, 307 TO 116

Joseph A. Loftus

WASHINGTON, March 1—The House voted tonight to exclude Adam Clayton Powell from the 90th Congress and probably created ground for a historic test of its decision in the Supreme Court. Not in 46 years, and only three times in the nation's history, has the House of Representatives refused to accept a duly-elected candidate.

Obviously rebellious, the chamber overrode the appeals of leaders of both parties and its own select committee. Even though the deed was done with far less passion and fireworks than usually accompany a decision of such far-reaching significance, there were a number of angry comments.

Exclusion, rather than expulsion, applies to an unsworn member-elect. Foes of exclusion questioned the House's authority to act as it did on a majority vote in view of a committee finding that Mr. Powell had met the three requirements of the Constitution for membership in the House. The requirements are that the member be at least 25 years old, that he have been a citizen for seven years, and that he inhabit the state in which he was elected.

The grounds for exclusion were the use of public funds for certain unauthorized expenses such as travel and salaries for nonworking staff members. Another basis was Mr. Powell's defiance of the New York courts stemming from the $164,000 judgment against him obtained by Mrs. Esther James, 68-year-old Harlem widow, for defamation of character. Mr. Powell had been found guilty of calling her a "bag woman," a collector of graft for corrupt police.

Representative Emanuel Celler, Democrat of Brooklyn, and chairman of the select committee, said after the vote: "I think he's got a good case."

If the Supreme Court should find that the House has violated Mr. Powell's Constitutional rights, it could order him seated. That would put two branches of government in conflict at the highest level. The House would have to decide at that point whether to accept such a decision and also whether to start new proceedings against Mr. Powell or drop the case. ■

SEPTEMBER 3, 1967

POVERTY FOUND RISING IN BRONX; MANY BUSINESSES GO TO SUBURBS

Will Lissner

Abject poverty afflicts one-fifth of the families in the Bronx and it is growing, sapping the borough's economic strength, according to a survey by a team of experts at Fordham University.

The report, which was made public yesterday, showed that the borough's economic situation is aggravated by a lack of industrial sites and tax ratables, factors that have been driving to the suburbs hundreds of businesses that provide jobs for the unskilled poor.

The two-year study was financed with a $100,000 grant from the Federal Office of Economic Opportunity. The team was made up of 45 economists, researchers and field interviewers.

The research director of the group, Dr. Joseph R. Cammarosano, said in an interview that "since the end of World War II, a significant movement of middle- and lower-middle-income families out to the suburbs has occurred and in their place have come thousands of Negro and Puerto Rican families."

Chronic unemployment in the Bronx last year was substantial. Of all the unemployed in the borough, 38 percent had been out of work for more than 6 months. They generally were those with the least education and training.

Of the unemployed, 56 percent were Negroes or Puerto Rican. As the influx of these groups continued, the family income structure deteriorated.

Of the Puerto Rican families, 27 per cent had incomes below $3,000 last year and 68 percent had income below $5,000. Of the Negro families, 26 percent had incomes below $3,000 and 57 percent had incomes below $5,000.

Migrating companies said the lack of industrial land for plant expansion was the single most important factor in their decision to move. They also blamed the high cost of industrial land, saying that sizable parcels of land could be readily assembled in the suburbs for new one-story plants following the newer designs at lower cost.

Lack of parking and loading facilities was blamed by some. They said it offset the Bronx's otherwise superior transportation network. Some also said the borough's tax burden from municipal real estate and business taxes put it at a serious competitive disadvantage to the suburbs.

Vandalism also was a major concern. Deterioration of the labor force as a consequence of population change was a lesser but an important concern cited by some.

From the information gathered, the economists developed a program for dealing with the borough's problems.

Professor Cammarosano said he did not agree with Mayor Lindsay and Anthony J. Travia, president of the State Constitutional Convention, that the state should be required to pay the city's welfare costs.

"The technological revolution in American agriculture, which has driven these people off the land, is a national problem," he said, "and the primary responsibility for coping with it is the Federal Government's." ■

OCTOBER 11, 1967

The East Village: A Changing Scene for Hippies

John Kifner

"This scene is not the same anymore," said the tall, thin Negro called Gypsy, fingering a fang-shaped bone ring in his right ear. "There are some very bad vibrations."

Gypsy was standing on the northeast corner of Avenue A and East 10th Street in the East Village. Around him dozens of hippies lounged, wandered in and out of the Something luncheonette or sat on the sidewalk with their backs against the building.

In quiet, murmured conversations, they talked about how James L. Hutchinson, a tattooed, 21-year-old neighborhood figure, and Linda Rae Fitzpatrick, the 18-year-old daughter of a wealthy Connecticut family, were found naked in the filthy cellar of a tenement a block and a half away on Avenue B, their heads smashed in with a brick.

And the word that was repeated in the conversations was no longer the hippie trademark "love" but "paranoid."

The psychedelic art shops, coffeehouses and antiques stores began to shoulder their way in among the Hungarian and kosher groceries and Puerto Rican bodegas about three years ago, and have multiplied rapidly in the past year.

But the hippies are finding that their easygoing, drug-oriented culture is causing conflicts with their impoverished neighbors trapped in the area's tenements, and to an extent among themselves.

"This scene is getting increasingly violent," said a tall young man with wire-rimmed glasses. "The love thing is dead; the flower thing is dead."

There were several small clashes last summer in Tompkins Square Park between Negro and Puerto Rican youth and the hippies, who have made the park their green. The Negroes and Puerto Ricans won the park from Italian and Polish youths in a series of bloody gang fights in the early sixties.

The hippies say they have been increasingly "taken down"—stopped and beaten or robbed—by young Negroes and Puerto Ricans.

"I had my throat almost slit the other night," said a tousle-headed youth, displaying a bandage around his neck.

For neighborhood residents, the hippie influx has meant higher rents, an increase in panhandling derelicts and narcotic pushers, and, for some, a source of irritation.

"The hippies really bug us," said a young Negro on East 11th Street, "because we know they can come down here and play their games for awhile and then escape. And we can't, man."

"A lot of the hippies make their own stuff

(cont'd. on next page)

The student demonstration at Columbia University, New York City, April 24, 1968

(cont'd. from previous page)
[narcotics] and this has angered the gangsters, who are paying the thugs to beat them up," he said. "There is more bad blood between them and the Puerto Ricans."

For the Puerto Ricans, who have come to the area like other immigrants, there is little shared culture with the hippies. Many Puerto Rican youths, raised with strict Roman Catholic or Pentecostal mores and steeped in Hispanic "machismo," are taken aback by the free-wheeling behavior of hippie girls, which has resulted in young Puerto Rican boys insulting and pinching them.

The double-murder hit the hippies particularly hard because while Linda Fitzpatrick was only on the fringes of the East Village scene—one of a number of white, upper or middle-class girls who drift into the area in search of life—James Hutchinson, known as Groovy, was one of its integral parts.

"Groovy was just...groovy," hippies said over and over. "He was a beautiful person." ■

APRIL 24, 1968

COLUMBIA STUDENTS BARRICADE OFFICE OF DEAN

David Bird

Three-hundred chanting students barricaded the Dean of Columbia College in his office yesterday to protest the construction of a gymnasium in Morningside Park and a defense-oriented program participated in by Columbia University. The protest against the gymnasium extended at one time to the building site, where students tore down a section of fence before being driven off by 30 policemen. The students say that construction of the gymnasium would be "racist" because it would deprive Negroes in the area of recreational facilities. The charge against the defense program, the Institute for Defense Analysis, was that it supported the war effort in Vietnam. The protest, organized by the leftist Students for a Democratic Society, has the support of other Columbia campus groups.

The protest began shortly after noon when about 500 students gathered around the sundial in front of Low Memorial Library, Columbia University's main administrative building. From the sundial, the demonstrators surged up the steps toward the Low building to take their protest directly to the administration.

Mark Rudd, Columbia chairman of Students for a Democratic Society, again addressed the group at the sundial. "We're going to have to take a hostage to make them let go of I.D.A. and let go of the gym," he shouted. With that, Mr. Rudd led the group to Hamilton Hall, the administrative building for Columbia College, the undergraduate arm of the university.

Dean Coleman was not in his office at the time. He appeared a few minutes later, elbowing his way through the crowd, and stood next to Mr. Rudd at the door of his office. Mr. Rudd asked the crowd: "Is this a demonstration?" and the crowd boomed back, "Yes!"

The university recently instituted a rule banning demonstrations in buildings of the campus, and so the question and answer were obviously meant to point up the group defiance of the rule.

"Are we going to stay here until our demands are met?" Mr. Rudd asked, and again there was a booming "yes" from his followers. The demonstrators then chanted, for several minutes, "Hell no, we won't go."

Dean Coleman, who stood and listened to the chanting, finally said, "I have no control over the demands you are making, but I have no intention of meeting any demands under a situation such as this."

The group started singing "We shall not be moved." Leaders of the protest urged the demonstrators to remain in the hall outside Dean Coleman's office, and they promised that food and drink were on the way. Dean Coleman turned and entered his office.

Once the students had taken over Hamilton Hall, no campus security guards were in evidence and there were no city police anywhere on the campus. By the early morning, the number of demonstrators had grown to about 400.

The Student Nonviolent Coordinating Committee, one of the most militant black organizations in the country, urged "all people who understand the urgency of this struggle to support the students, community people and their allies."

Columbia's relations with its neighbors in Harlem have been strained for several years.

One of the problems has been Columbia's expansion, which has resulted in the university's acquisition of more than 100 buildings in the last few years and the eviction of many long-time residents of low-cost rent-controlled housing. ■

protest

SEPTEMBER 23, 1968

LINDSAY ENTERS 3 CITY DISPUTES

HE SEEKS POLICE, SANITATION AND FIRE UNION CONTRACTS

Emanuel Perlmutter

Mayor Lindsay devoted his entire day yesterday to an effort to break up the impasse in the city's contract negotiations with its 50,000 unionized policemen, firemen and sanitation workers.

He held separate meetings at Gracie Mansion with the heads of the Patrolmen's Benevolent Association, the Uniformed Firefighters Association and the Uniformed Sanitationmen's Association, but he did not announce any substantial progress.

The contracts with the three unions expire next Monday, and their leaders have accused the city of failing to make a counteroffer to their demands for higher wages, a shorter work week and improved pensions.

Shortly after 10 P.M. the union leaders agreed that the 10-hour meetings yesterday had been fruitful, although real negotiations were yet to come.

The Mayor said, "I have urged intensive negotiations during the coming week."

Mr. Lindsay was assisted in his talks by Herbert L. Haber, the city's Director of Labor Relations; Deputy Mayor Robert W. Sweet and Deputy Mayor Timothy V. Costello.

The seriousness of the situation was emphasized when Victor Borella, labor adviser to Governor Rockefeller; Ralph C. Gross, executive vice president of the Commerce and Industry Association of New York; Harry Van Arsdale Jr., president of the New York City Central Labor Council, and Peter J. Brennan, president of the Building and Construction Trades Council, arrived in late afternoon to help.

Although Mr. Lindsay would not disclose what issues were under discussion, sources close to the negotiations said that the possible appointment of a panel to try to resolve the dispute had been explored.

The panel would consist of Arthur J. Goldberg, former United States Representative at the United Nations; Theodore W. Kheel, lawyer and mediator, and Vincent J. McDonnell, chairman of the State Mediation Board.

Part of yesterday's discussions involved an effort to determine whether the panel should serve merely as mediators or be instructed to make recommendations for settlement.

Before going to Gracie Mansion, Michael J. Maye, president of the firemen's union, said on the WNBC "Searchlight" television program that he believed his men would authorize a strike this week.

Asked if he would lead such a strike, he replied: "Yes, by God, I would."

"Will you defy the Taylor Law, which bans strikes by public employees?" he was asked.

"If necessary, yes," he responded.

Mr. Maye said he would resign as a fireman from the Fire Department to lead a strike. ■

FEBRUARY 13, 1969

AREAS OF QUEENS STILL SNOWBOUND Lindsay Booed on Borough Tour

Sylvan Fox

Near normal conditions returned to most of the city and its suburbs yesterday three days after a 15-inch snowstorm—but large sections of Queens remained snow-clogged and crippled.

(cont'd. on next page)

The Van Wyck Expressway near Kennedy Airport after a 1969 snowstorm dumped 15-inches on New York City.

As the city continued to dig out, there was mounting criticism of Mayor Lindsay and his administration for their handling of the snow emergency.

The Mayor was assailed by crowds of jeering, booing Queens residents on a tour of that borough yesterday morning.

Later in the day he received a telegram from Dr. Ralph J. Bunche the Under Secretary

General of the United Nations and a Queens homeowner who asserted that the city's efforts to clear snow in his borough were "a shameful performance."

"We have never experienced such neglect in snow removal as now," Mr. Bunche said in his telegram.

Other Queens residents put it less elegantly than the United Nations official when the Mayor visited their borough yesterday.

"He can't even run a snowstorm and he wants to run the country," one man shouted.

Others called out: "Lindsay, you're a bum" and "What does he do for an encore, this guy?"

At Main Street in Kew Gardens, a woman shouted: "You should be ashamed of yourself.

It's disgusting."

During most of the harassment, the Mayor remained impassive and sought to ignore the remarks. At one point, however, he commented: "I didn't put the snow there—we're doing our best to get it out."

Mayor Lindsay's office confirmed that in its efforts to remove snow in Queens, it had approved the hiring of two contracting concerns that had been blacklisted by the city. No other companies with the required equipment were available, the Mayor's office said.

The police reported that 42 persons had died of storm-related causes in New York City. More than half of the deaths occurred in Queens. ■

Science, Technology & Health

Science news in the 60's was dominated by the space race—which, of course, was also very much a political story. First the Soviets, who had already terrified Americans with Sputnik in 1957, took a decisive lead in the race by putting Yuri Gagarin into orbit. America followed the next year with John Glenn, but the moon was the prize. JFK vowed to put men on the moon by the end of the decade. He didn't make it that long, but Neil Armstrong and "Buzz" Aldrin did. However, before they did, there was a steady stream of breathtaking headlines and never-before-seen photos, from the first pictures of Mars to a Soviet soft landing on the moon to tragedy on the launch pad at Cape Canaveral to men flying around the moon to Armstrong's famous botched quote ("man" instead of "a man"). I remember clustering around the television in July 1969, awed at what we were seeing.

Of course, there was more to science in the 60's than astronauts and cosmonauts. Work on heredity advanced with penetration into the secrets of DNA. Discoveries of subatomic particles revolutionized our insights into that micro-world. A frog was cloned. But all that paled beside the thrill and romance of rockets into space, a romance that leaked over into television with the advent of the "Star Trek" franchise.

In technology, there were home and office advances like the electric toothbrush, touch-tone telephones and the Selectric typewriter. Funny how the breakthrough innovations of yesteryear look like dinosaur fossils today. (Other examples: audio cassettes and eight-track tapes.) Satellites began to transform international communications and weather forecasting (as well as spying). Lasers and holograms made their debuts, as did bullet trains and the jumbo jet, with the rollout of the 747.

In health news, pacemakers and heart transplants offered new hope for sufferers from heart disease, vaccines conquered former scourges, and contact lenses were much improved by the introduction of soft plastic. Valium quieted us down while Weight Watchers slimmed us down. The birth control pill liberated women (and their partners) and fueled the decade's heady sexual freedom, a threat to some. Masters and Johnson were among the best-known researchers (along with nonfiction writers and novelists) who offered new insight into how humans and especially women enjoyed their sexual encounters. On the down side, cigarette smoking was officially linked to cancer and thalidomide was taken off the market only after thousands of babies in Europe and the United States were born with deformations. The American Medical Association and Republicans fought "socialized medicine" and delayed Medicare until Democrats regained control of Congress in 1964.

APRIL 4, 1960

PHOTOS OF SOVIET TAKEN BY WEATHER SATELLITE

The United States weather satellite Tiros I has photographed parts of the Soviet Union and Communist China.

A spokesman for the National Aeronautics and Space Administration said yesterday that the two television cameras in the satellite had photographed many parts of the earth, including the Communist areas, since it was launched from Cape Canaveral, Fla., at 6:40 A.M. Friday.

The pictures, recorded on tape, are not good enough for military reconnaissance, but show cloud formations indicating weather conditions. However, far more sophisticated "spy" satellites are expected to be ready for testing in a few weeks or months. One, called Midas, is designed to detect missile launchings by infrared rays almost instantaneously. The other, Samos, would be equipped with cameras and other devices that could gather data on ground installations and activities.

At a news conference in New York, Dr. Abe Silverstein, director of space flight programs for the space agency, said the pictures had been of even better quality than expected.

The Tiros I satellite gets its instructions by radio signal from the ground at the start of each orbit. The satellite orbits the earth on a path that takes it as far north and south as about 48 degrees latitude. In the Western Hemisphere this is considerably north of Montreal and as far south as Santa Cruz, Argentina.

At the news conference in New York yesterday Dr. Silverstein and Dr. Sidney Sternberg of the Radio Corporation of America noted that the present weather satellite was only the first in a program that was expected ultimately to be of great value to meteorologists.

The present experiment is making it quite clear that satellites will be able to determine the weather conditions over the path they cover, Dr. Silverstein said.

SEPTEMBER 25, 1960

U.S. Launches World's Biggest Ship, First Nuclear Aircraft Carrier

Joseph Carter

NEWPORT NEWS, Va., Sept. 24—The Enterprise, the first atomic-powered aircraft carrier, was launched today after an unusual countdown. The carrier, described by the Navy as the largest ship ever built, did not go down the ways. Instead, the waters of the James River came to her. Officials of the Newport News Shipbuilding and Dry Dock Company, her builder, estimated that 15,000 people witnessed the christening and launching. The Enterprise, which is 1,101 feet long and displaces 83,350 tons, is the Navy's eighth fighting ship to bear that name. Mrs. William B. Franke, wife of the Secretary of the Navy and sponsor of the ship, broke the traditional bottle of champagne on the bow.

Features of the launching ceremony were an address by Admiral Arleigh A. Burke, Chief of Naval Operations, and a flight over the new carrier by sixteen Navy jet fighters. The completion of the launching was saluted by the new fleet ballistic missile submarine Robert E. Lee, which fired two test shots from her Polaris tubes. The Lee was in the shipway next to the Enterprise. It marked the first time a nuclear powered underseas craft and a nuclear surface vessel had been tied up side by side.

"Her eight nuclear reactors would enable the Enterprise to cruise twenty times around the world without refueling," Admiral Burke said.

"This great ship will add much to our nation's ability to deter military aggressions of any nature."

The Enterprise, which is capable of speeds in excess of thirty knots, is equipped with a data processing and communications system that could evaluate an enemy threat and speedily recommend counter action to shipboard commanders. The information would be digested by memory cells in the computer, but the final decision would be left to human minds.

The carrier's eight reactors will supply the power to drive four massive propellers, each the height of a two-story house. The reactors were designed and developed by the Westinghouse Electric Corporation in cooperation with the Atomic Energy Commission's naval reactors branch, headed by Vice Admiral Hyman G. Rickover.

"The Enterprise can cruise twenty times around the world without refueling."

The prototype of the vessel's nuclear system was built and tested at the naval reactor facility in the Idaho desert in a replica of the ship's hull.

Tomorrow the Enterprise will be moved to another part of the vast Newport News yard for fitting. She is scheduled for delivery in the fall of 1961.

Newport News shipyard spokesmen were reluctant to estimate the cost of the new Enterprise. However, one indicated that when completed the vessel would have cost "around $375,000,000." ■

APRIL 12, 1961

SOVIET YURI GAGARIN FIRST TO ORBIT EARTH

MOSCOW, Wednesday, Apr. 12—The Soviet Union announced today it had won the race to put a man into space. The official press agency, Tass, said a man had orbited the earth in a spaceship and had been brought back alive and safe.

A Moscow radio announcer broke into a program and said in emotional tones:

"Russia has successfully launched a man into space. His name is Yuri Gagarin. He was launched in a sputnik named Vostok, which means 'East.'"

Tass said that, on landing, Major Gagarin said: "Please report to the party and Government, and personally to Nikita Sergeyevich Khrushchev, that the landing was normal. I feel well, have no injuries or bruises."

Major Gagarin, 27 years old, is an industrial technician and married. He was reported to have received pre-flight training similar to that of astronauts who will man the United States' first space ships.

The announcer said the Sputnik reached a minimum altitude of 175 kilometers (109 1/2 miles) and a maximum altitude of 302 kilometers (187 3/4 miles).

He also reported the following: The weight of the Sputnik was 10,395 pounds, or slightly over five tons; everything functioned normally during the flight; constant radio contact was maintained between earth and the sputnik; and the duration of each revolution around the earth was 89.1 minutes.

The title of the announcement was "The First Human Flight into the Cosmos."

As soon as the Moscow announcement was made, Russians began to telephone congratulations to each other.

The first astronaut is a major in the Soviet Air Force and is believed to be a test pilot.

Reports of the launching of a Soviet space man had been reported repeatedly in Moscow for the last twenty-four hours.

The London Daily Worker and other sources had said the Soviet Union had sent a man into space last Friday and had brought him back alive.

Many persons in Moscow were convinced after today's announcement that another flight into space was attempted on Friday and there was speculation that something might have gone wrong.

Major Gagarin, the announcement went on, withstood satisfactorily the placing of the satellite ship into orbit. ■

Russian cosmonaut Yuri Gagarin, the first man in space, in 1961.

MAY 6, 1961

U.S. HURLS MAN 115 MILES IN TO SPACE; SHEPARD WORKS CONTROLS IN CAPSULE

Richard Witkin

Cape Canaveral, Fla., May 5—A slim, cool Navy test pilot was rocketed 115 miles into space today.

Thirty-seven-year-old Commander Alan B. Shepard Jr. thus became the first American space explorer.

Commander Shepard landed safely 302 miles out at sea fifteen minutes after the launching. He was quickly lifted aboard a Marine Corps helicopter.

"Boy, what a ride!" he said, as he was flown to the aircraft carrier USS Lake Champlain four miles away.

Extensive physical examinations were begun immediately. Tonight doctors reported Commander Shepard in "excellent" condition, suffering no ill effects.

The near-perfect flight represented the United States' first major step in the race to explore space with manned spacecraft.

True, it was only a modest leap compared with the once around-the-earth orbital flight of Maj. Yuri Gagarin of the Soviet Union. The Russian's speed of more than 17,000 miles an hour was almost four times Commander Shepard's 4,500. The distance the Russian traveled was almost 100 times as great.

But Commander Shepard maneuvered his craft in space—something the Russians have not claimed for Major Gagarin.

All in all, the Shepard flight was welcomed almost rapturously here and in much of the non-Communist world as proof that the United States, though several years behind in the space race, had the potential to offer imposing competition.

Commander Shepard, a native of East

Derry, N.H., was a long time starting his journey.

He lay on his contoured Fiberglas couch atop the Redstone missile—"the least nervous man of the bunch," the flight surgeon reported—for three and a half hours while the launching crew delayed the countdown because of weather and a few technical troubles.

Finally, at 10:34 A.M. Eastern daylight time, the count reached zero. A jet of yellow flame lifted the slender rocket off its pad as thousands watched anxiously from the Cape and along the public beaches south of here.

Hundreds of missiles had been launched here, but never before with a human being aboard.

The rocket and the pilot in the Project Mercury capsule on top performed flawlessly.

Commander Shepard kept up a running commentary with the command center during the flight. He experienced six times the force of gravity during the rocket's climb, then there were five minutes during which gravity seemed to have vanished.

The abrupt re-entry into the atmosphere pressed him into his couch with a force of more than ten times gravity.

At 7,000 feet, his capsule descending by a red and white parachute, Commander Shepard radioed, as if returning from a routine flight by plane:

"Coming in for a landing." ■

FEBRUARY 21, 1962

GLENN ORBITS EARTH THREE TIMES SAFELY

Richard Witkin

Astronaut John Glenn prepares to enter the Mercury launch vehicle on February 20, 1962, at Cape Canaveral, Florida.

CAPE CANAVERAL, Fla., Feb. 20—John H. Glenn Jr. orbited three times around the earth today and landed safely to become the first American to make such a flight.

The 40-year-old Marine Corps lieutenant colonel traveled about 81,000 miles in 4 hours 56 minutes before splashing into the Atlantic at 2:43 P.M. Eastern Standard Time.

The astronaut's safe return was no less a relief than a thrill to the Project Mercury team, because there had been real concern that the Friendship 7 capsule might disintegrate as it rammed back into the atmosphere.

There had also been a serious question whether Colonel Glenn could complete three orbits as planned. But despite persistent control problems, he managed to complete the entire flight plan.

The astronaut's landing place was near Grand Turk Island in the Bahamas, about 700 miles southeast of here.

Still in his capsule, he was plucked from the water at 3:01 P.M. with a boom and block and tackle by the destroyer Noa. The capsule was deposited on deck at 3:04.

Colonel Glenn's first words as he stepped out onto the Noa's deck were: "It was hot in there."

He quickly obtained a glass of iced tea.

He was in fine condition except for two skinned knuckles hurt in the process of blowing out the side hatch of the capsule.

The colonel was transferred by helicopter to the carrier Randolph, whose recovery helicopters had raced the Noa for the honor of making the pickup. After a meal and extensive "debriefing" aboard the carrier, he was flown to Grand Turk by submarine patrol plane for two days of rest and interviews on technical, medical and other aspects of his flight.

A situation that seemed at the moment to pose the greatest danger developed near the end of the flight.

A signal radioed from the capsule indicated that the heat shield—the blunt forward end made of ceramic-like material that dispels the friction heat of re-entry and chars in the process—might be torn away before it could do its job.

(cont'd. on next page)

OCTOBER 19, 1962

PENETRATING HEREDITY'S SECRETS

The award of the 1962 Nobel Prize for medicine to Dr. James D. Watson, an American, and his two British colleagues, Drs. Francis H. C. Crick and Maurice H. F. Wilkins, is a deserved and long overdue tribute to the men responsible for one of mankind's great scientific achievements. If, as seems likely, we are today at the threshold of understanding—and perhaps even harnessing—the exquisitely complex and subtle mechanism by which each biological species reproduces itself generation after generation, it is in large part the result of the evidence uncovered by Dr. Wilkins' X-ray diffraction studies and the interpretation of that evidence by Drs. Watson and Crick.

The secret of heredity, as shown by the work of the new Nobel laureates, resides in the architecture of the enormous molecule of deoxyribonucleic acid (DNA). This coil of life, as it has been aptly described, is a sort of submicroscopic double-railed spiral staircase, composed of two chains whose key parts—the steps of the staircase—are the substances that the biochemist calls nucleotides. This Watson-Crick model—made possible largely by the regularities Dr. Wilkins' X-ray studies had found earlier—has proved a key that in the past decade has permitted fantastic progress in our understanding.

The picture of heredity we now have can be summarized in these terms: it is the pattern of nucleotides in this coil which determines what each creature will be, that pattern constituting a sort of code of life. Great progress has been made just this past year in unraveling that code. The actual process of replication at this molecular level appears to center about the separation of the two chains and of their nucleotides during the process of cell division. Each separate chain then directs the synthesis of a complementary chain duplicating the one that it lost.

If all goes well, two identical DNA molecules are thus created where there had been only one before. If a mistake is made, however—perhaps because of the impact of radiation or of certain chemicals—the synthesized chain is not identical with the original complement and the result is a mutation which makes the final creature different in some small or large way from the original. This is the wonderful mechanism that guides the orderly reproduction of life from generation to generation.

The exposure of that mechanism in work at Cambridge University, England, is one of the great peaks of human discovery. The men responsible fully merit all the honors being heaped upon them. ■

(cont'd. from previous page)

If it had, the flight would have had a tragic end.

Colonel Glenn was asked by radio to flip a switch to check whether the shield had, in fact, become unlatched. When the light did not go on, it appeared that the "unlatch" signal had been spurious.

But the Mercury team was taking no chances. It changed the sequence of re-entry events to try to insure that, even if unlatched, the heat shield would not fall away prematurely.

Jettisoning was delayed today so that, in case the heat shield had become unlatched, the rocket-packet straps would hold the shield in place until this function was taken over by the force of re-entry into the atmosphere.

The package burned on re-entry. The heat shield did not drop away until it was supposed to. This indicated that the signal that had caused so much anxiety had, in fact, been a false one.

Today's orbital flight had been scheduled for just before Christmas. There had been ten attempts to send Colonel Glenn on his trip, and ten frustrating postponements, either because of weather or technical problems.

Colonel Glenn apparently had a fine, exhilarating time, right from the start. He experienced some vibration along with acceleration force, as he climbed through the atmosphere.

Then it smoothed out; the rocket burning stopped; the acceleration switched abruptly to weightlessness; and the capsule automatically turned its blunt end forward for the almost five hours he was to be in orbit.

"Capsule is turning around," he radioed. "Oh, that view is tremendous."

Today's flight gave the United States, by any standards, its greatest day in space.

The achievement, however, could still not be considered quite up to what the Russians had done.

Colonel Glenn's flight was two orbits more than were flown by Maj. Yuri A. Gagarin, the Soviet space man, last April 12, but fourteen less than another Russian, Maj. Gherman S. TItov, flew on Aug. 6.

In addition, there were some technical respects in which both Soviet orbital flights appeared to observers here to have an advantage: the size of the capsule orbited (five tons as against a ton and a half); the reliability of automatic controls; and the cabin atmosphere in which the pilot had to work.

But Colonel Glenn's trip was considered by most observers here to have gone a long way toward erasing this nation's "second-best" look in space.

JULY 21, 1963

The Continents Are Still on the Move

George H. T. Kimble

Three Australian scientists recently announced that their continent is on the move—at the rate of about two inches a year. This would hardly appear to be earth-moving news, but it is arousing a great deal of interest, nonetheless, for two reasons.

The first is the new insight it gives us into the history of the Australian continent. This movement, according to Messrs. E. Irving, W. A. Robertson and P. M. Scott, the scientists in question, has been going on for a very long time, approximately 100 million years. When it began, Australia was situated in the vicinity of the South Magnetic Pole in the heart of the Antarctic. Today it lies between the Pacific and Indian Oceans some 3,400 miles away.

The second reason for the interest the news is arousing is the light it is thought to throw on the history of all the continents. Up to now, earth scientists have found it difficult to agree for more than a week on how the continents came into being and how they came to be where they are. Upstart facts have continually dethroned reigning theories. About all that has generally been conceded is that, to begin with—say four billion years ago—there was nothing but land formed by fire out of cosmic dust and gases; that a very long time passes—perhaps a billion years—before the low ground, formed in the earth's cooling surface by shrinkage and collapse, was filled with water to become the oceans; and that it was only then that the land began to bring forth grass, herb and tree, and its rivers and streams began their never-ending cycles of erosion.

As for the continents themselves, these are generally conceded to have existed since that time (though not in their present shape and climatic conditions) and to be alike in structure, each consisting of a "shield" of granitic rocks, some 22 miles thick on the average, surrounded by young mountains and shelves, and resting in a bed of heavier material. Which, as anybody can see, leaves a lot of questions unanswered.

Exactly what questions the Australians' discovery will settle nobody is yet prepared to say. But it has certainly given a new lease of life to the displacement theory or, more popularly, the theory of continental drift, put forward by the German meteorologist, Alfred Wegener, half a century ago.

Observing, as many had done before him, that the opposing shores of the North and South Atlantic have a complementary look about them when viewed on a globe, Dr. Wegener asked whether it could be more than coincidence, whether it could perhaps be evidence that the land masses of the Old and New Worlds were once locked together like pieces in a jigsaw puzzle, and that they later split up and drifted away from each other, as icebergs "calve off" from glaciers and drift away in the heavier water beneath them.

While Wegener's theory looked good to many meteorologists and biologists (who were becoming increasingly troubled by the evidences of what they supposed to be the parallel evolution of living things in widely separated parts of the world), it failed to get much support from geologists.

Now, 50 years later, the theory is making a comeback. As the Australians and others have shown, there is some evidence that drifting is still taking place. Moreover, there is now reason to suppose that the material below the continents is not a solid in the usual sense of the term; that it is less like concrete than pitch, which will flow if left long enough.

More substantial still, there is now evidence provided by the new geophysical science of paleomagnetism (the study of the magnetization of ancient rocks) to show that at least some of the continents were once closer together than they are today. Working from the knowledge that many rocks become magnetized when they are formed and that their magnetism is in the direction of the earth's magnetic field at that time, the geophysicists have been able to get "fixes" on the position of the North and South Poles relative to the continents in different geological periods. ■

FEBRUARY 20, 1964

Key Particle Found in the Atom, Ending Nuclear Physics 'Chaos'

John Hillaby

LONDON, Feb. 19—The discovery of a new sub-atomic particle was disclosed today by a prominent British nuclear theorist. The discovery of the particle, called the omega-minus, establishes a new fundamental law of physics, in his opinion.

The properties of the omega-minus are regarded as the long-sought link in the relationship between scores of the sub-atomic particles in the center of the atom.

Prof. Paul T. Matthews of Imperial College, London, a Fellow of the Royal Society describes the discovery in today's issue of the British science journal, The New Scientist, as "dramatic."

The particle was found with the aid of high-energy apparatus at the Brookhaven National Laboratory, Upton, L.I., and the Center for European Research (CERN) at Geneva, Switzerland.

Because the omega-minus exists only for a fraction of a second and, together with its associated particles, is packed into a space less than a millionth of a millionth of a centimeter, the significance of the discovery is comprehensible only to nuclear physicists trained to think in mathematical terms. Nevertheless, as The Scientist puts it:

"Order has at last been made out of nuclear chaos."

The discovery means that man, who has been able to put the atom to work by utilizing some of its ultrafragmentary components, has taken a step toward understanding how the components of the atom stick together.

Many physicists have contributed, individually and collectively, to the discovery.

Among the principal investigators in the last stages are Prof. Y. Ohnuki of Japan; Prof. Murray Gell-Mann and his associates in the United States; Yuval Ne'man of Israel; and Prof. Abdus Salam and Dr. J. C. Ward of London.

The theoretical breakthrough came from Professor Ohnuki in a paper given at a conference on high-energy particles at Rochester, N.Y. in 1960.

As early as 1932, it was known that in hydrogen, the simplest atom, the core or nucleus is the relatively heavy particle called the proton. All other atomic nuclei are made of protons and neutrons packed together in ultramicroscopic spheres.

It was soon realized that very powerful forces must operate between the particles to overcome their enormous electrical repulsion.

In 1935 it was suggested that protons and neutrons interact by the exchange of other particles—pi-mesons—in much the same way that football players interact by exchanging the ball.

By 1960 physicists had discovered between 30 and 100 sub-nuclear particles, depending on the way they classified them. Some of the particles could be related to each other by the laws of visible (macroscopic) matter: that is, they were balanced by opposed electrical charges; or their weights were mathematically related; or they spun round each other in a predictable and comprehensible way.

But physicists also began to discover properties among them that had no counterpart outside the infinitely small subnuclear world

(cont'd. on next page)

(cont'd. from previous page)
of baryons and mesons. Among these properties were the concept of the hyper charge and different kinds of multi-dimensional "spin" called "U-spin" and "Vspin" that could be expressed only in mathematical formulas.

Throughout these discoveries physicists strove unsuccessfully to place all the particles in one all-embracing table of relationships—just as the element can be placed in an atomic table starting with hydrogen, the lightest.

Because they could not discover any evident factors that linked the particles together the physicists looked for hypothetical bonds.

In 1960 Professor Ohnuki suggested that the correct aspect of the problem' to consider was not rotating but a mathematically related notion called "unitary transformationst," a concept confined to nuclear physics. It was, In fact, a formula for relationships.

Hardly anyone took any notice.

But the notion was picked up by Professor Salam, who worked on it in London with Dr. Ward and Mr. Ne'man. Professor Gell-Mann, who spent some time in London on leave of absence from the California Institute of Technology, also became interested.

By utilizing Professor Ohnuki's new type of nuclear "spin," it gradually became possible to place the particles first in a linear relationship as if they were in three layers, one above the other, and then in the form of hexagonal (six-sided) figure.

By dividing the hexagonal figure into six triangles (each containing ten particles), the complicated cross— relationship of the nuclear network became apparent.

One vital factor alone was missing. This was the particle, the omega-minus, the need for which had been predicted but the presence of which had not been detected.

The omega-minus would have to have quite extraordinary properties. It would have to be negatively charged and yet hyper-charged. It would have to be produced by collisions between certain kinds of mesons and protons and it would have to disappear (decay) before it: plunged more than one inch through the detecting apparatus called bubble chambers.

The particle located at Brookhaven and in Switzerland possesses all these properties andi its place in the sub-atomic network discloses the long-sought pattern of particles to which all matter can be reduced.

Professor Matthews concludes by saying that "high-energy physicists are walking around with a slightly hysterical look as though they are actually witnessing the apple landing on Newton's head." ■

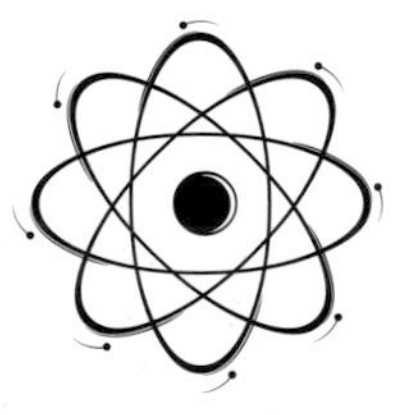

MAY 21, 1965

SIGNALS IMPLY A 'BIG BANG' UNIVERSE

Walter Sullivan

Scientists at the Bell Telephone Laboratories have observed what a group at Princeton University believes may be remnants of an explosion that gave birth to the universe.

These remnants are thought to have originated in the burst of light from that cataclysmic event.

Such a primordial explosion is embodied in the "big bang" theory of the universe. It seeks to explain the observation that virtually all distant galaxies are flying away from earth. Their motion implies that they all originated at a single point 10 or 15 billion years ago.

The Bell observations, made by Drs. Arno A. Penzias and Robert W. Wilson from a hilltop in Holmdel, N.J., were of radio waves that appear to be flying in all directions through the universe. Since radio waves and light waves are identical, except for their wavelength, these are thought to be remnants of light waves from the primordial flash.

The waves were stretched into radio waves by the vast expansion of the universe that has occurred since the explosion and release of the waves from the expanding gas cloud born of the fireball.

In what may prove to be one of the most remarkable coincidences in scientific history, the existence of such was predicted at Princeton University at the same time that scientists at the Bell Laboratories were puzzling over an observation of almost identical waves that they could not explain.

The Princeton group, led by Dr. Robert H. Dicke, Professor of Physics, was unaware of the Bell observation. Those at Bell had not heard of the Princeton prediction.

Like the recent discovery of objects, known as quasars, that lie near the fringes of the observable universe, the new observations may enable scientists to choose the correct picture of the universe: Is it eternal and unchanging? Was it born in a single "big bang" or is it oscillating?

It is clear that Dr. Dicke and others would like to see an oscillating universe come out triumphant. The idea of a universe born "from nothing" in a single explosion raises philosophical as well as scientific problems.

An oscillating universe gets around the problem of origin. The galaxies fly apart in the manner currently observed. Then, at a certain point, they begin to fall back together again.

Finally, the night sky becomes brilliant with the light of converging galaxies. In a frightful cataclysm they fall together into a mass of fragmented atoms, then burst forth as a new fireball. This scatters hydrogen in all directions, from which new elements and new galaxies are formed.

JULY 16, 1965

FIRST MARS PHOTO INDICATES PLANET LACKS A LIQUID CORE LIKE EARTH'S

Walter Sullivan

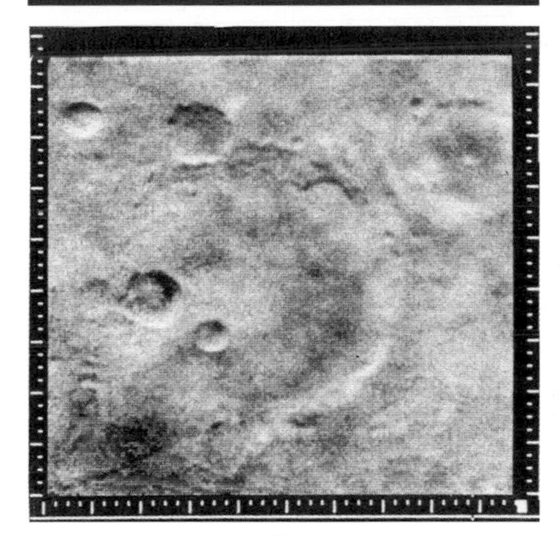

The Mariner crater in 1965.

PASADENA, July 15—Mariner 4 has sent to earth the first close-up photograph of Mars.

The picture, transmitted today in an eight-hour broadcast over a distance of 134 million miles, shows the "limb," or rounded edge of Mars, including a vast, desert-like region.

It does not show any of the controversial canals. But this is not necessarily significant, since the view is extremely oblique and covers a region under the noonday sun. Such lighting makes for little contrast.

Part of the second picture, which should overlap the first, has already been transmitted to earth and it is possible that as many as 22 pictures of the planet will be delivered in the next 10 days.

Officials here at the Jet Propulsion Laboratory, which is in charge of the project for the National Aeronautics and Space Administration, were jubilant.

Meanwhile, scientists associated with the project reported some of their initial findings. These include:

- Mars has virtually no magnetic field and hence, presumably, no liquid core. This means the planet may differ fundamentally from earth in terrain and the chemical composition of its surface. The radioactivity of its air must be comparatively high, as well as the exposure of its surface to space radiation.
- Mars has no significant radiation belt. This is good news for those planning the exploration of Mars. Vehicles will be able to orbit the planet for long periods without radiation hazard to their passengers or instruments.
- The atmosphere of Mars is extremely thin—probably too much so for the use of parachutes or other conventional devices in the gentle landing of instruments and, ultimately, astronauts on its surface.
- Mars, like the earth, has swept its orbit clear of much of the cosmic dust that would otherwise be adrift there. Since the orbit is elliptical, the distance of the planet from the sun varies from 128 to 155 million miles. It is this region that has been swept comparatively clean.

If Mars lacks a metallic core, it would appear that the planet has never gone through the churning internal processes that have given the earth its layered structure.

This would mean that Mars does not have continents formed of light-weight rocks, and oceanic basins underlain with basaltic rock, in the manner of the earth.

Mariner 4 was not designed to determine whether or not there is life on Mars. However, the planet's lack of a substantial magnetic field, plus the fact that its air is very thin, means that its surface is probably bombarded with radiation from space 50 times more intense than that striking the earth.

But Dr. William H. Pickering, director of the Jet Propulsion Laboratory, said, "I have always felt we will find some form of life on Mars," and added that he was not discouraged.

Dr. Pickering also pointed out that one explanation for the reddish hue of Mars may be the presence of limonite, an iron oxide. This suggests that iron is uniformly spread through the planet instead of being largely concentrated in the core, as on earth. ■

FEBRUARY 4, 1966

SOVIETS ACHIEVE A SOFT LANDING ON MOON

Peter Grose

Soviet moon probe, Luna 9, on display, 1966.

MOSCOW, Feb. 3—An unmanned Soviet spaceship made a successful soft landing on the moon tonight and immediately began transmitting telemetric signals, possibly including television pictures, back to the earth. The landing was the first of its kind.

(cont'd. on next page)

(cont'd. from previous page)

The spaceship, Luna 9, was launched from earth Monday. It followed four unsuccessful attempts by Soviet space scientists to bring down an experimental station intact on the moon.

In Britain, scientists said that two 15-minute transmissions of television signals from Luna 9 had been received at the Jodreil Bank radio telescope. The scientists said it would take considerable time to convert the signals into pictures, presumably of the lunar surface.

There was no confirmation from Soviet sources of a report from Britain that Luna 9 was sending back television pictures.

Measuring instruments on board Luna 9 are expected to supply data on the composition of the moon's surface, its temperature and heat-conducting characteristics and its strength for supporting heavy objects such as manned spaceships.

Soviet scientists also hoped to assemble data on the extent of meteorite bombardment of the moon and the frequency of moon quakes.

The soft landing is clearly a major turning point in space exploration, comparable to the successful launching of Russia's first Sputnik on Oct. 4, 1957, and the first Soviet space vehicle to hit the moon, on Sept. 13, 1959.

Space experts believe that it gives the Soviet Union a major lead over the United Sates in the program to land a man on the moon.

Luna 9 is believed to have achieved its gentle landing by an intricate coordination of retro-rockets that would have had to slow down the 3,000-pound spacecraft from the approach velocity of 6,000 miles an hour to 6 miles an hour.

Because the moon has no atmosphere, a parachute landing, requiring air resistance, would not be possible.

Luna 9 is believed to be equipped with special landing gear to maintain its position at rest suitable for radio transmission and the gathering of data on the surface adjacent to the landing point.

The spaceship is believed to have been launched from the Soviet cosmodrome at Baikonour, Kazakhstan, in the steppes of central Asia, a wide area closed to foreign travelers. ■

JANUARY 22, 1967

U.S. SCIENTISTS DECIPHER KEY ENZYME

Walter Sullivan

After 16 years of intensive work and an expenditure of $2 million, scientists have deciphered the extremely complex structure of an enzyme that plays a key role in all living cells.

The substance, known as ribonuclease, contains more than 1,000 atoms. These atoms are arranged as a chain of 124 amino acid units twisted, coiled and cross-linked in intricate ways.

The feat is the first of its kind in this country, according to those who performed it at the Roswell Park Memorial Institute, in Buffalo.

The molecular structure was explored with the techniques of the science known as X-ray crystallography. Two other proteins—myoglobin and lysozyme—have been similarly completely deciphered in Britain. Like all enzymes, ribonuclease is a protein.

These British and American achievements are regarded as being of momentous importance, for they demonstrate the feasibility of determining how enzymes are built and how they work. Without the help of enzymes most of the body's chemical reactions would proceed at an extremely slow pace—or not at all.

Discovery of the complex structure of an enzyme, and particularly of the points in its structure that perform the chemical mission of the substance, opens the way to a host of possible applications. Chemists, it is believed, may be able to alter the structure to modify the role of the enzyme. Such tinkering with molecules is a standard pathway toward new life-saving drugs.

Furthermore, knowledge of the active sites on a molecule has, in the past, made it possible to construct simpler man-produced versions that are just as effective—or even more so.

The role of ribonuclease is to break down another vital substance in the life process—ribonucleic acid, or RNA. The task of RNA is to carry, in its structure, the "blueprint" for manufacture of proteins by the cell. The RNA obtains this blueprint from another substance, DNA (for deoxyribonucleic acid), that serves as the archive of design. The DNA also passes the information on to future generations as the stuff of heredity.

There are stages in the life of a cell or an organism when it is important to deactivate RNA. This may be necessary to control cell growth or to dispose of the RNA when a cell dies. Such deactivation is the role performed by the newly deciphered enzyme.

Because this substance exerts control over cell growth, knowledge of its structure (and of ways in which it may become deformed) might help explain why cancer cells spread, unchecked, through the body. This, in turn, could provide clues for the development of ways to treat the disease. ■

JANUARY 29, 1967

SPACE TRAGEDY

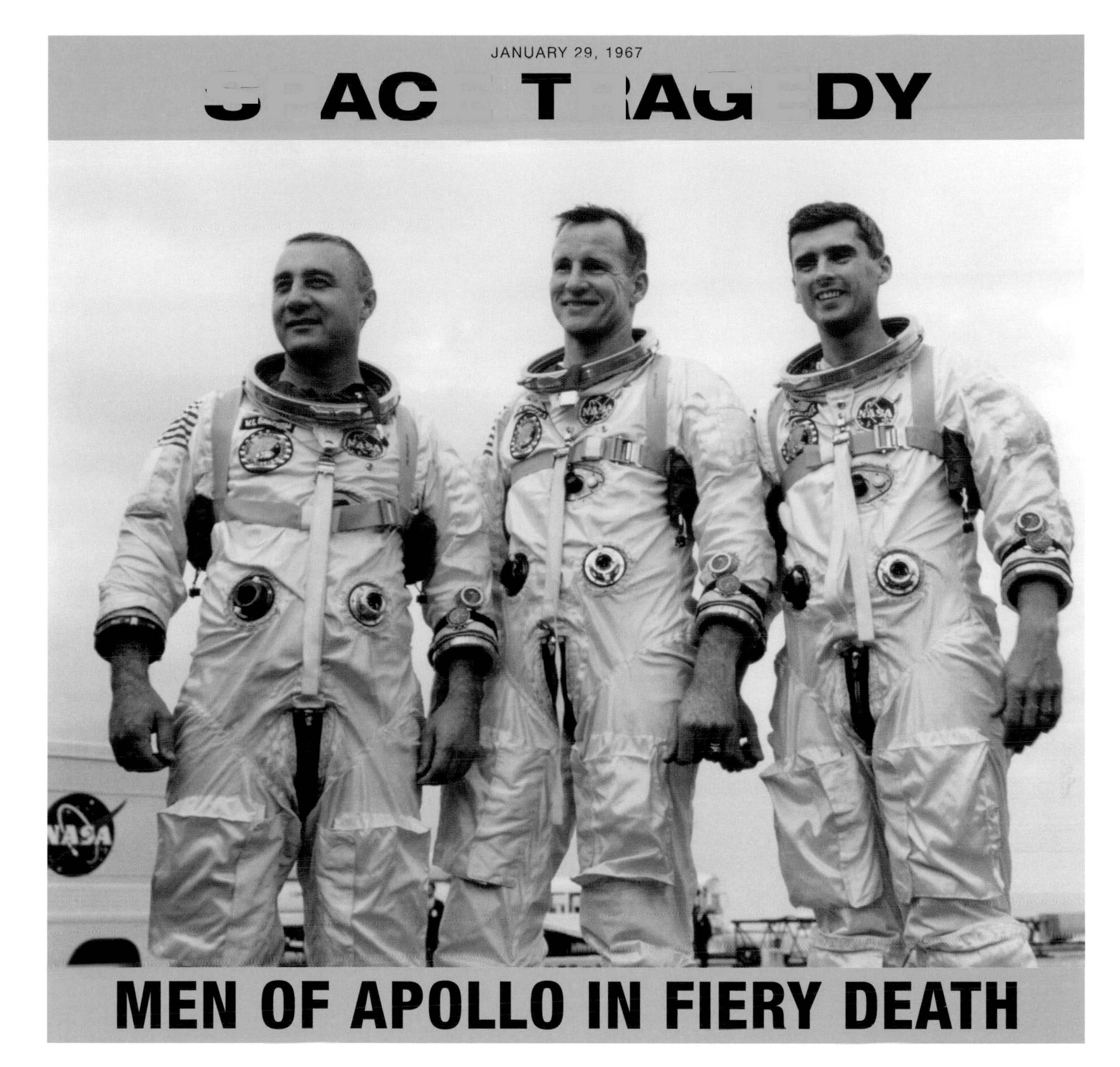

MEN OF APOLLO IN FIERY DEATH

The crew of the Apollo 1 space mission during training at Cape Canaveral, Florida, January 1967. From left, Command Pilot Virgil I. Grissom, Senior Pilot Edward Higgins White and Pilot Roger B. Chaffee.

Ironically, the deaths occurred on the ground.

Since the space age dawned nine years ago, American astronauts have accumulated about 1,900 man-hours in space. In six one-man Mercury missions and 10 two-man Gemini flights, the astronauts have flown more than 13 million miles, or the equivalent of 25 round trips to the moon. Throughout the massive undertaking, not one spaceman had been lost or even hurt prior to last week as the result of a flight mishap.

Then, last Friday, the space program suffered its first "on premises" fatalities in space equipment. Three astronauts were killed in a flash fire aboard the Apollo 1 spacecraft launch pad at Cape Kennedy.

The astronauts were the crew for the first of the three-man Apollo missions that are designed to culminate in the landing of men on the moon by 1970. They were taking part in a simulation of the Feb. 21

(cont'd. on next page)

(cont'd. from previous page)
launching that was to take them into 14 days of orbiting.

The victims, all married and with two children each, were:

VIRGIL I. GRISSOM, 40, Air Force lieutenant colonel, Commander of Apollo 1 and veteran of two space flights (one for Mercury, one for Gemini).

EDWARD H. WHITE 2nd, 36, Air Force lieutenant colonel, the first American to "walk" in space.

ROGER B. CHAFFEE, 31, Navy lieutenant commander; a rookie who had yet to fly his first space mission.

At 1 P.M. Friday, Colonel Grissom and his two colleagues, wearing their silvery space suits, wedged themselves into the three seats of the capsule atop a 200 foot Saturn 1-B launch vehicle. For the next five and a half hours they went through a full-scale simulation of a launching while space officials watched on closed-circuit television monitor.

"Suddenly there was a flash (on the TV monitor) and that was it. . ."

At 6:31 P.M., with only 10 minutes to go before the simulated liftoff that would have terminated the exercise, there came a chilling cry over the radio monitoring system from one of the astronauts: "Fire in the spacecraft!"

Workers at the pad rushed up the gantry to the capsule in a high speed elevator, but they were unable to reach the trapped astronauts in time to save them. The crewmen apparently died instantly in the blast of fire.

"Suddenly there was a flash (on the TV monitor) and that was it," a space official said.

The burned capsule, which is valued at about $35 million, was severely damaged. It was the only one at Cape Kennedy, and to bring another from California where they are built and to test it would require at least three months. NASA tentatively had had set six more Apollo flights before the actual moon mission.

As for the longer range effects on the space program, the nation's political leaders, who had responded to the urging of spacemen in 1961, to set a goal of reaching the moon by 1970, immediately expressed determination to go on with the plan despite the Apollo tragedy. Vice President Hubert Humphrey, who is chairman of the National Aeronautics and Space Council, said, "The United States will push ever forward in space and the memory of these men will be an inspiration to all future spacefarers." ■

OBITUARY

FEBRUARY 19, 1967

J. ROBERT OPPENHEIMER, ATOM BOMB PIONEER, DIES

PRINCETON, N.J., Feb. 18—Dr. J. Robert Oppenheimer, the nuclear physicist, died here tonight at the age of 62.

A spokesman for the family said Dr. Oppenheimer died at 8 o'clock in his home on the grounds of the Institute for Advanced Study. He had been ailing since early last year with cancer of the throat.

The physicist took part in the development of the first atomic bomb.

In 1954 he was stripped of security clearance by the Atomic Energy Commission because of alleged association with Communists.

The same agency nine years later awarded Dr. Oppenheimer the $50,000 Fermi award for "his outstanding contributions to theoretical physics and his scientific and administrative leadership."

Starting precisely at 5:30 A.M., Mountain War Time, July 16, 1945, J. (for nothing) Robert Oppenheimer lived the remainder of his life in the blinding light and the crepusculine shadow of the world's first manmade atomic explosion, an event for which he was largely responsible.

That sunlike flash illuminated him as a scientific genius, the technocrat of a new age for mankind. At the same time it led to his public disgrace when, in 1954, he was officially described as a security risk to his country and a man with "fundamental defects in his character." Publicly rehabilitated in 1963 by a singular Government honor, this bafflingly complex man nonetheless never fully succeeded in dispelling doubts about his conduct during a crucial period of his life.

The perplexities centered on a story of attempted atomic espionage that he told Army Counter-Intelligence officers in 1943 and that he later repudiated as a fabrication. His sole explanation for what he called "a cock-and-bull story" was that he had been "an idiot." Misgivings also sprang from the manner in which he implicated a close friend in his asserted concoction.

A brilliant nuclear physicist with a comprehensive grasp of his field, Dr. Oppenheimer was also a cultivated scholar, a humanist, a linguist of eight tongues and a brooding searcher for ultimate spiritual values. And from the moment that the test bomb exploded at Alamogordo, N.M., he was haunted by the implications for man in the unleashing of the basic forces of the universe.

As he clung to one of the uprights in the desert control room that July morning and saw the mushroom cloud rising in the explosion, a passage from the Bhagavad-Gita, the Hindu sacred epic, flashed through his mind. He related it later as:

"If the radiance of a thousand suns were to burst into the sky, that would be like the splendor of the Mighty One."

And as the black, then gray, atomic cloud pushed higher above Point Zero, another line—"I am become Death, the shatterer of words"—came to him from the same scripture.

Two years later, he was still beset by the moral consequences of the bomb, which, he told fellow physicists, had "dramatized so mercilessly the inhumanity and evil of modern war."

"In some sort of crude sense which no vulgarity, no humor, no overstatements can quite extinguish," he went on, "the physicists have known sin; and this is a knowledge which they cannot lose."

OCTOBER 7, 1968

FROGS MADE FROM SINGLE BODY CELLS

Walter Sullivan

OXFORD, England, Oct. 6—Experimenters at Oxford University believe they have removed any shadow of doubt as to the validity of a series of experiments in which frogs have been produced from single body cells extracted from another frog.

The experiments, in what is known as vegetative reproduction, bear on one of the most fundamental problems in biology—namely, what it is that turns on and turns off the genetic material buried within each cell of the body.

The frogs, according to the experimenters, have been produced from cells that line the intestine. This has demonstrated that even such highly specialized cells contain, within their nuclei, the information needed to construct an entire new individual. Normally such information lies dormant, but in the Oxford experiments it has been activated.

Until now, some scientists have believed that, in such specialized cells, the genetic information unrelated to that cell's function has been permanently erased. Those skeptical of the Oxford experiments, under way for several years, argued that the frogs raised here grew from nonspecialized cells that somehow made their way into the intestine.

In an interview, however, Dr. John Gurdon of Oxford, the zoologist in charge of the research, said it was now evident that this could not be so. With improved laboratory technique more than 30 percent of the intestinal cells can be made to grow at least to the tadpole stage.

This, he said, is compatible with the idea that these tadpoles have grown from rarely occurring nonspecialized cells. Only 1 or 2 percent of the cells used in the Oxford experiments have grown to fully mature and fertile frogs, but this in Dr. Gurdon's view is because of subtle damage to the cell nucleus during manipulation.

The experiments have created a sensation here because they imply that, in theory if not in practice, it should be possible to mass produce identical twins of people gifted with exceptional ability or beauty. However, Dr. Gurdon has struggled valiantly to dissociate himself from such speculation.

His goal, he explained during a visit to his laboratory last week, is to understand how the genetic information in a body cell is controlled. Thus, while the nucleus of a cell lining a man's intestine contains all the information needed to produce an identical twin, only one tiny bit of that information is active.

It says: "You are an intestinal liner; you must grow in a certain way and perform certain chemical functions."

What Dr. Gurdon and his co-workers have done is to take such a nucleus from the intestine of a tadpole and implant it inside a frog egg whose own nucleus had been destroyed by the researchers. Something in the cytoplasm, or non-nuclear material, of the egg tells that nucleus: "You are no longer an intestinal cell nucleus; you are an egg cell nucleus; go to work." The result, if all goes well, is a new frog.

Dr. Gurdon knows no one, to date, who has been able to carry out a comparable transfer of nuclei in mammals. The procedure, he said, is bound to be extremely difficult, if even possible.

Experiments in which plants have been derived from single cells (not seed cells) have been reported in the United States. It is also often possible to grow new plants from cuttings. This process, however, is more comparable to the regeneration of limbs in newts and salamanders, according to Dr. Gurdon.

While salamanders can grow a new leg, man cannot grow new limbs or replace damaged parts of his brain or heart. Those seeking to understand these differences have long hoped to know what it is that turns genes on and off. They suspect, as well, that cancer may occur when this control system runs amok.

For these reasons the Oxford experiments are attracting worldwide attention. ■

MARCH 25, 1968

PHOTOS HINT CLUE TO SPACE SIGNALS

Walter Sullivan

An examination of star photographs dating back to 1897 has indicated that the star British astronomers believe may be the source of recently discovered radio pulses is probably more than 100 light years away. This would mean that the radio emissions themselves take more than 100 years to reach the earth.

On other grounds the British had guessed the distance as close to 200 light years, one light year being the distance traveled by light at a speed of 186,000 miles per second.

The radio pulses, which occur with machine-like regularity, have created a sensation in the scientific world. Each is, in fact, a triplet, each of whose parts differs, in strength, from pulse to pulse, much as would be expected in a code.

However astronomers are holding at arm's length the idea that the signals are coming from a super civilization on some distant world. They argue, for example, that the power needed to generate the signals, particularly if they are radiated in all directions, must dwarf the total energy production of all power plants on earth.

The indication of a minimum distance of 100 light years derives from an absence of substantial motion by the star, relative to other stars, during the last 70 years. Such lack of motion is reported in Circular No. 2060 of the Central Bureau for Astronomical Telegrams. It was based on studies by Harvard College Observatory and David Dunlap Observatory in Toronto.

At Harvard, according to Dr. William Liller, from one to four photographs of the region were examined for every year from 1897 to 1962.

In a telephone interview he explained that the evidence for motion, relative to other stars, was so slight that it was not convincing. Nor did he find any marked change in brightness, as would be expected if the star had had an explosive history.

An early explanation for the pulses was that they originated in a "white dwarf" or else in a neutron star. A white dwarf is a

(cont'd. on next page)

DECEMBER 25, 1968

3 MEN FLY AROUND THE MOON ONLY 70 MILES FROM SURFACE

John Noble Wilford

Photo of Earth taken by astronauts on the Apollo 8.

HOUSTON, Wednesday, Dec. 25—The three astronauts of Apollo 8 yesterday became the first men to orbit the moon. Early today, after flying 10 times around that desolate realm of dream and scientific mystery, they started their return to earth.

They fired the spacecraft's main rocket engine at 1:10 A.M. to kick them out of lunar orbit and to carry them toward a splashdown in the Pacific Ocean on Friday.

Through the static of 231,000 miles, as Apollo 8 swung around from behind the moon and started for earth, one of the astronauts dispelled any doubts, saying, "Please be informed there is a Santa Claus."

It would be a 57-hour return trip from the most far-reaching voyage of the space age this far—or of any other previous age. The astronauts had seen, as no other men had, the ancient lunar craters, plains and rugged mountains from as close as 70 miles.

At 4:59 A.M. yesterday, about 20 hours before the return trip, Col. Frank Borman of the Air Force, Capt. James A. Lovell Jr. of the Navy and Maj. William A. Anders of the Air Force swept into an orbit of the moon by firing the spacecraft's main rocket. This occurred after they flew around the leading edge of the moon and were directly behind the earth's only natural satellite.

"We got it! We've got it!" exclaimed a mission commentator of the National Aeronautics and Space Administration as the spacecraft emerged from behind the moon 24 minutes later, and was clearly flying a safe and smooth orbit.

As they beamed their first live television from orbit on Christmas Eve morning, they described the surface of the moon as a colorless gray, "like dirty beach sand with lots of footprints on it" and said it "looks like plaster of Paris."

Colonel Borman described the moon as a "vast, lonely and forbidding sight," adding that it was "not a very inviting place to live or work."

Captain Lovell saw the earth as a "grand oasis in the big vastness of space."

Major Anders was more impressed by "the lunar sunrise and sunsets."

George M. Low, the spacecraft manager at the Manned Spacecraft Center, said he was "altogether happy" with the mission—the most ambitious and daring this far in the nation's $24 billion Apollo project to land men on the moon next year.

The astronauts' color movies and still pictures, expected to be the most spectacular and most valuable of all the pictures, will be brought back for processing and analysis by scientists. Many of the pictures were taken of a site in the Sea of Tranquility where American astronauts may land next year.

The lunar-orbiting mission, the second manned flight of the Apollo project, is expected to be followed by an earth-orbiting flight in February or March to test the lunar landing vehicle. The first landing on the moon could come as early as next June.

When night fell here and a bright quarter moon shone in the clear sky, mission control commented to Apollo 8 that "there is a beautiful moon out there."

Colonel Borman replied, "Now, we were just saying that there's a beautiful earth out there."

"It depends on your point of view," concluded the ground controller. ■

(cont'd. from previous page)

burned out star that has shrunk to the size of a planet and has extraordinary density. A neutron star is a hypothetical body of even greater density and smaller size.

Some believe that such stars, if they exist, are formed through an explosive process. A number of American astronomers are somewhat skeptical of the proposition that the signals are coming from the star in question. The star lies in a region of the Milky Way crowded with stars and dust clouds.

If the object can be seen at all, they say, it may be some time before it is identified.

The circular from the Central Bureau for Astronomical Telegrams identified the object producing the radio emissions as Pulsating Radio Source I, establishing it as a new form of celestial object many more of which may be found. The British have reported detecting three others.

Some American astronomers are calling them pulsars, for pulsating stars. Their British discoverers have facetiously called them LGN's, for "little green men." ■

MEN WALK ON MOON

John Noble Wilford

Astronaut Edwin E. Aldrin Jr. on the surface of the moon after the landing of Apollo 11. Astronaut Neil A. Armstrong took this photograph and can be seen reflected in Aldrin's visor, July 20, 1969.

Houston, Monday, July 21—Men have landed and walked on the moon.

Two Americans, astronauts of Apollo 11, steered their fragile four-legged lunar module safely and smoothly to the historic landing yesterday at 4:17:40 P.M., Eastern Daylight Time.

Neil A. Armstrong, the 38-year-old civilian commander, radioed to earth and the mission control room here:

"Houston, Tranquility Base here. The Eagle has landed."

The first men to reach the moon—Mr. Armstrong and his co-pilot, Col. Edwin E. Aldrin, Jr. of the Air Force—brought their ship to rest on a level, rock-strewn plain near the southwestern shore of the arid Sea of Tranquility.

About six and a half hours later, Mr. Armstrong opened the landing craft's hatch, stepped slowly down the ladder and declared as he planted the first human footprint on the lunar crust:

"That's one small step for man, one giant leap for mankind."

His first step on the moon came at 10:56:20 P.M., as a television camera outside the craft transmitted his every move to an awed and excited audience of hundreds of millions of people on earth.

Mr. Armstrong's initial steps were tentative tests of the lunar soil's firmness and of his ability to move about easily in his bulky white spacesuit and backpacks and under the influence of lunar gravity, which is one-sixth that of the earth.

"The surface is fine and powdery," the astronaut reported. "I can pick it up loosely

(cont'd. on next page)

(cont'd. from previous page)
with my toe. It does adhere in fine layers like powdered charcoal to the sole and sides of my boots. I only go in a small fraction of an inch, maybe an eighth of an inch. But I can see the footprints of my boots in the treads in the fine sandy particles."

After 19 minutes of Mr. Armstrong's testing, Colonel Aldrin joined him outside the craft.

The two men got busy setting up another television camera out from the lunar module, planting an American flag into the ground, scooping up soil and rock samples, deploying scientific experiments and hopping and loping about in a demonstration of their lunar agility.

They found walking and working on the moon less taxing than had been forecast. Mr. Armstrong once reported he was "very comfortable."

And people back on earth found the black-and-white television pictures of the bug-shaped lunar module and the men tramping about it so sharp and clear as to seem unreal, more like a toy and toy-like figures than human beings on the most daring and far-reaching expedition thus far undertaken.

During one break in the astronauts' work, President Nixon congratulated them from the White House in what, he said, "certainly has to be the most historic telephone call ever made."

"Because of what you have done," the President told the astronauts, "the heavens have become a part of man's world. And as you talk to us from the Sea of Tranquility it required us to redouble our efforts to bring peace and tranquility to earth.

"For one priceless moment in the whole history of man all the people on this earth are truly one—one in their pride in what you have done and one in our prayers that you will return safely to earth."

Mr. Armstrong replied:

"Thank you, Mr. President. It's a great honor and privilege for us to be here representing not only the United States but men of peace of all nations, men with interests and a curiosity and men with a vision for the future."

It was man's first landing on another world, the realization of centuries of dreams, the fulfillment of a decade of striving, a triumph of modern technology and personal courage, the most dramatic demonstration of what man can do if he applies his mind and resources with single-minded determination.

The moon, long the symbol of the impossible and the inaccessible, was now within man's reach, the first port of call in this new age of spacefaring. ■

AUGUST 1, 1961

Carriageless 'Selectric' Typewriter Can Accommodate Six Fonts

An IBM electric typewriter, 1965.

An electric typewriter that eliminates type bars and movable carriages and that can use six interchangeable type faces was introduced by the International Business Machines Corporation yesterday.

Instead of a movable carriage, the typewriter, called the Selectric, uses a sphere-shaped element containing the letters, numbers and punctuation symbols. The element types out the various characters as it moves from left to right across the page.

Changing to a different type font can be accomplished by removing the sphere-shaped element and replacing it with another carrying another type style. The six type faces now available are designed for billing, personal and general correspondence and script typing.

The typewriter also permits easier and faster changing of ribbons. Instead of a ribbon spool on each side of the machine, as in conventional typewriters, the new machine uses a ribbon cartridge that is mounted on the carrier. To change ribbons, the typist lifts the cartridge off the carrier and snaps a new one into place.

The company said the Selectric models now on the market came in two sizes, with the smaller unit selling for $395 and the larger one for $445.

FEBRUARY 26, 1962

NEW TOOTHBRUSH WORKS BY BATTERY

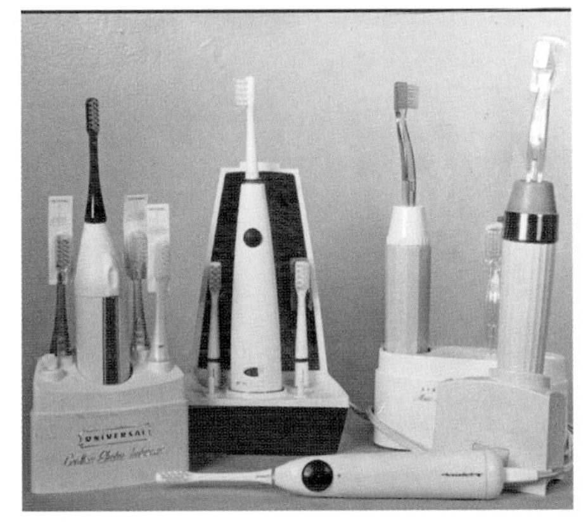

Battery-operated electric toothbrushes, mid-1960s.

The newest gadget in a gadget-minded era is an automatic toothbrush. The General Electric Company, the manufacturer, says that the toothbrush brushes the teeth up and down instead of across and also massages the gums.

The brush reportedly makes 2,000 strokes a minute, each stroke three-sixteenths of an inch long.

The brush itself looks like any other, but it is inserted in a cylindrical handle that is a battery. The battery is charged from a holder that can be plugged into any wall socket (110 or 120 volts, AC). Thus, no electrical cord is attached to the toothbrush itself.

It should be noted that bathrooms with plugs only in a light socket will not keep the battery charged unless the light is continually on.

The toothbrush comes with four brush inserts in different colors. It is $19.95 complete, 69 cents each for additional brush replacements, in the street-floor drug department at Gimbels. ■

MARCH 30, 1962

TV, VIA SATELLITE, TO SPAN ATLANTIC

Jack Gould

The first live television broadcasts across the Atlantic, serving viewers from Los Angeles to Moscow, are being planned for early summer.

Programs of ten to twenty minutes will be exchanged between the United States and Europe by means of the communications satellite Telstar, now scheduled for launching in late May or early June.

Preparation of the historic TV presentations is proving a matter of delicate negotiations involving scores of different countries.

Members of the European Broadcasting Union, embracing TV systems throughout the Continent, will meet next Thursday in Seville, Spain, to work out their part of the exchange.

Whether the Soviet Union would be accorded a direct voice in the exchange could not be ascertained last night. Technically, Russian viewers can be linked to Eurovision, the network that has previously connected Moscow and London in live TV exchanges.

In some quarters it was noted that the imminence of trans-Atlantic TV conceivably might pose a problem for Soviet authorities in deciding what Western programs to accept. Up to now TV exchanges between the Soviet Union and European democracies have been largely limited to sports or ceremonial events.

To capitalize on the prestige for the West in inaugurating trans-Atlantic live TV, the inclusion of President Kennedy in the ceremonies was automatically suggested. Some European broadcasters delicately noted that they would be left with a thankless task: which head of state should they choose to speak from Europe?

Broadcasters on both sides of the Atlantic similarly were wondering whether the satellite would orbit over the ocean in prime evening time for Europe or prime evening time for the United States. In June there would be a six-hour time difference between New York and London.

It was understood that the programs, in part at least, would consist of live scenes of landmarks on both the North American and European continents, a format that would reduce controversies and still assuage the maximum number of national prides.

The communications satellite Telstar, financed by the American Telephone and Telegraph Company, will be put aloft in cooperation with the National Aeronautics and Space Administration.

Neither American nor European broadcasters were even thinking last night of such matters as cost, regularity of service or the nature of any long-range programming. Apparently on both sides of the Atlantic there has been general agreement to withhold formal comment lest an untoward observation jeopardize the worldwide cooperation needed to make a success of the venture.

In a dispatch from London, United Press International said it had learned that Prince Philip might broadcast the initial live transoceanic message to the United States, with President Kennedy expected to "return the compliment." ■

JULY 28, 1963

NETWORK IN SPACE

Launching of Syncom Advances Worldwide Communications

William L. Laurence

The launching last week into a high altitude, near synchronous orbit of Syncom II marks another step toward the realization of an important milestone in the space age—that of a world-wide communication system, in which satellites orbiting thousands of miles above the earth will serve as a network of microwave radio-relay stations for transmitting and receiving television, telephone, telegraph, teletype, facsimile, photographs and other types of instantaneous communication.

Syncom may be said to be the prototype of the global communications satellite of the future, though a number of years may pass before it becomes operational. The Syncom type will orbit around the equator at an altitude of 22,300 miles. In that position it will make a complete orbit around the earth in exactly the time it takes the earth to make a complete turn around its axis. The satellite will thus appear to be stationary above a given point on the equator.

Satellites of the Telstar and Relay type, which are designed to orbit at lower altitudes than Syncom, call for as many as 50 vehicles to be placed in orbit to link all points of the globe. This insures that as one disappears below the horizon another will move within range of the ground communications stations. With the Syncom high altitude type, only three satellites, equally spaced in an equatorial orbit, would relay television voice and other forms of communication between any points on earth, except for the remotest polar regions.

In addition to requiring a much smaller number of satellites, the synchronous satellite has another advantage in that it requires less elaborate and costly ground equipment. A synchronous satellite can operate on solar power most of the time, since it is in sunlight 99 percent of the time. Also, no active temperature control system is needed and fewer batteries are required, thus resulting in reduction in weight.

The launching of a synchronous satellite, however, must await the perfection of methods for placing it into a precise 22,300-mile orbit and for keeping it in proper position. Because of the lack of powerful enough boosters, Syncom II was not placed in an equatorial orbit but rather in an orbit inclined about 30 degrees to the equator. It is thus not completely synchronous, but will appear to trace an elongated figure 8 every twenty-four hours over a line at longitude 55 degrees west, beginning in the Atlantic Ocean southeast of Bermuda and ending at the southern tip of Brazil. It will travel from about 30 degrees north of the equator to 30 degrees south, but will always stay within a few degrees of longitude.

Scientists believe that our present technical capabilities have reached the stage of development that will make possible commercial operation of an intermediate system of communication satellites by 1967, if a major effort is made to achieve that goal. ■

SEPTEMBER 8, 1963

THE LASER LIGHTS UP THE FUTURE

Maya Pines

A laser beam being tested during a laboratory experiment at Trion Instruments, Ann Arbor, Michigan, December 1962.

The hottest treasure hunt in the scientific world today involves a small device with the odd name of "laser" and such impressive potentialities that few companies in electronics, optics or space research dare to be left out of the race. The laser (an acronym for "light amplification by stimulated emission of radiation") stands for an entirely new conception of what light can do.

Its invention is comparable to the invention of the vacuum tube with all the developments of radio, radar, TV and transistors yet to come.

With the laser's help, light stops being just something to see by. It becomes a powerful tool able to carry messages over gigantic distances, perform delicate surgery, make radar 10,000 times more precise and weld microscopic wires. When properly focused over a short distance, the narrow, intense beams of laser light have an even more startling property: they can vaporize any known material.

Lasers make it possible to generate light in much the same fashion as radio, TV or radar waves, over which light has certain breath-taking advantages. Since laser light starts out in waves that are almost perfectly parallel, its rays never diverge seriously, regardless of distance. Furthermore, light waves are tens of thousands of times shorter than radio waves, which means that even a narrow band of visible light can hold trillions of cycles per second and thus transmit enormous amounts of information. It has been calculated that, under the right conditions, a single laser beam could carry as many messages—radio, telephone, teletypewriter and TV—as all communications channels in existence today.

Even now radio and TV frequencies are crowded; but the present electronic traffic jam is nothing compared with that forecast for the near future. Communications experts believe that the message load will double within the next ten years. This is why so much interest has centered on the laser's promise in the communications field, though its immediate uses there are still very few.

Radar based on laser light is also a possibility. One practical use will be in tracking earth satellites. The time it takes laser beams to reach the satellite and come back, as well as the angles of the reflected light, will serve to calculate the satellite's position.

Besides their narrowness, laser beams have another useful characteristic: the immense power and heat they can mobilize when focused on small areas at close range. A beam from a ruby laser can be millions of times hotter than the sun's surface.

This searing heat can be put to work in ultra-delicate surgery. Eye specialists at Columbia-Presbyterian Medical Center have used laser beams to destroy tiny tumors on a patient's retina instantly and painlessly.

Despite the extraordinary progress of lasers in less than three years, many scientists believe that their real impact will not be felt for another decade. By then it may be found that their greatest achievements lie in research on the frontiers of chemistry, biology or physics.

Dr. Arthur L. Schawlow has remarked, "With the advent of the laser, man's control of light has reached an entirely new level. Indeed, one of the most exciting prospects for workers in the field is that this new order of control will open up uses for light that are as yet undreamed of." ■

SEPTEMBER 20, 1964

A Shift to All-Electronic Phones Is Biggest Step Since Dial

Robert Alden

The country's telephone network is beginning to convert to an electronic system that one of its executives calls "the greatest step forward in telephone communication since the introduction of the dial telephone."

When the changeover is complete, a housewife will be able to turn on her oven while away from home by using her telephone, a couple out for an evening of bridge will be able to have their calls switched automatically to their host's home, and an office worker's call to a line that is busy will be completed automatically when the line is free.

Frederick R. Kappel, chairman of the American Telephone and Telegraph Company, estimates that the changeover to electronic switching in every part of the country will cost $12 billion and take up to 35 years.

Electronic switching will mean that each user will be able to tailor his telephone

(cont'd. on next page)

(cont'd. from previous page)

service to his own needs. In effect, each subscriber will be able to record his particular orders on a magnetic scratch pad in the central office.

When he leaves his own telephone to visit a friend, for example, he will dial a double-digit code number and the telephone number of the friend. Thereafter all telephone calls going to his home will automatically be transferred to the friend's home until new instructions are dialed.

Numbers dialed frequently can be coded on the magnetic scratch pad. These can then be reached by dialing three numbers, instead of the normal seven for a local call or 10 for an out-of-town call.

When a telephone number is busy, the electronic system can serve a particularly useful function. The caller can hang up and when the telephone called is free, both the caller's phone and the phone that had been busy will ring. The call will then be completed.

With the new electronic system, a person will be able to talk to three or four persons at the same time without setting up a conference call through an operator.

As a twin development, touch-tone telephones, using buttons instead of dials, are available now at three exchanges in Queens and one at Glen Cove, L.I. The cost of these telephones is $1.90 extra a month for residential services, $2.75 for business service.

The convenience of a push-button telephone, apparent to those who have used them at the World's Fair, is only a minor advantage in comparison with its potential applications.

Electronic switching will mean that each user will be able to tailor his telephone service to his own needs.

The touch-tone phone communicates with the switchboard by emitting an electronic beep of varying tone. Once the number called is reached, this electronic beep can then be used to communicate between man and a machine at the other end.

Additionally, with the expansion of underseas telephone cables and orbiting satellites, direct-distance dialing to any point in the world by an individual subscriber is now on the horizon.

United States telephone operators are already able to dial directly into the telephone systems in Belgium, France, Germany, England, the Netherlands and Switzerland.

The next step will be for the telephone user to do the direct dialing himself.

In preparation for worldwide direct dialing, telephone code numbers have been assigned to every country in the world.

The electronic switchboard will facilitate the introduction of worldwide direct dialing.

The growth and development of a worldwide telephonic communications system has come with astonishing speed. It was only 88 years ago, in 1876, that the telephone was patented by Alexander Graham Bell. ■

JULY 1, 1966

NEW TAPE SYSTEM MOVES TOWARD STANDARD CARTRIDGE

Gene Smith

North American Philips, Inc., made a major move yesterday towards standardizing tape-recorder cartridges.

Pieter Vink, president, told a news conference in the Regency Hotel that 39 major manufacturers and marketers of tape-recorder equipment in various countries had adopted the new Philips compact cassette (cartridge) system.

Among the companies committed to the system are General Electric, Revere-Wollensak, Mercury Records, Sony, Panasonic (Matsushita), Toshiba and Hitachi, he noted.

Mr. Vink termed the cassette development "a significant breakthrough" and predicted it would "greatly accelerate the growth of the quality tape recorder industry in the United States."

Wybo Semmelink, assistant vice president and manager of the high-fidelity products department, said a prerecorded library of "musicassettes" would be introduced at the upcoming Music Show in Chicago. He declined to identify the recording company or the new label.

The Philips cassette system uses principles similar to standard reel-to-reel tape recording but the operation is permanently contained within the miniature cassettes. The tape itself is less than one-quarter of an inch wide and plays at a speed of 1-7/8 inches a second.

Mr. Semmelink said that each of the pretaped units would provide playing time equal to that of a 12-inch long-playing record. He added that prices would be "comparable to those of good LP records."

The company also showed a new cassette of the same size but with 90 minutes of playing time. This was the result of thinner tapes. Work is also progressing on a third tape that would have 120 minutes of playing time on the same size cassette.

During yesterday's press showing, Mr. Semmelink took a standard tape cartridge of the type used in automobiles, emptied it from the container and proceeded to place four new cassettes inside.

"We offer 360 minutes of tape against 80 minutes in the units that are being sold at greater costs in this country today," he said.

MARCH 19, 1967

New Photo Technique Projects a World of 3-Dimension Views

Walter Sullivan

Two perspectives of a hologram projected on two screens when a laser passes through the hologram at different places.

Imagine a picture window set in what is actually the inside wall of a city apartment. In it one sees, in brilliant color and three dimensions, a garden abloom with spring flowers.

If one wishes to see beyond a statue in the foreground, one need only walk to one corner of the "window" and peer behind it, bringing into view more greensward and flowering shrubs. It is, in fact, a picture backed by solid masonry. Yet it is indistinguishable from the original view except that the bird on the branch is without song and the leaves do not move.

This is but one of the wonders that may come about—or have already done so—through a new technique known as holography. It has led to a race for the discovery of new applications reminiscent of what followed such electronic landmarks as the invention of the transistor and the laser.

The goals range from three-dimensional television and moving pictures, viewed without special glasses, to a variety of secret military applications. Soviet scientists have helped pioneer the field so it is likely that they, too, are highly active in this area.

In holography, a beam of coherent light—that is, an ordered succession of waves of one color or frequency—is split, for example by a mirror. One part shines on the object to be photographed, the other is directed toward an emulsified plate.

Light waves reflected from the object meet the waves arriving from the light source. The interaction of the waves produces submicroscopic patterns of dark and light areas. These so-called interference patterns encode in the emulsion all the characteristics of the waves reflected from the object.

An interference pattern occurs when coherent waves of the same frequency meet one another. Where the wave crests from the two beams coincide, there are bright spots. Where the waves are out of phase with one another, there are varying shades of dark.

After the plate has been developed in the manner of ordinary photographic film and coherent light is applied, the waves of this light are altered by the interference pattern so that it reaches the eye with all the directional and brightness characteristics of the light reflected from the object.

(cont'd. on next page)

NOVEMBER 2, 1965

JAPANESE CLAIM WORLD RECORD FOR HIGH-SPEED TRAIN

TOKYO, Nov. 1—Japan laid claim to the world's fastest train service today.

Beginning this morning, the streamlined electric Bullet Trains of the Japan National Railways' new Tokaido line will make the 322-mile run between Tokyo and Osaka at an average speed of 103 miles an hour. The journey takes 3 hours 10 minutes, including stops at Kyoto and Nagoya.

Railway officials announced that the Bullet Train was approximately 20 miles an hour faster than France's famed Mistral Express between Paris and Dijon, which was credited with the previous record.

Trains on the high-speed line, which was opened 13 months ago, were held to an 80-mile-an-hour average till now to allow the roadbed to settle and harden. They will travel at a top speed of 126 miles an hour on straight stretches.

(cont'd. from previous page)

Therefore, it is possible to "see" the object even though it is no longer present.

Among the applications of holography proposed in recent months or under development are the following:

- Radar systems enabling an airport traffic controller to look into a three-dimensional scope and watch all aircraft in the area, much as one watches fish in a glass-walled aquarium.
- Scanners that can map distant planets or enable engineers to see stress patterns in a whirring propeller.
- Computers that display their solution of engineering problems as three-dimensional images. The "object" that is displayed can be examined from one side or the other, as if it were really there, yet it exists only in the "imagination" of the computer.
- Photographs of fog or dust clouds that can be projected into space in three-dimensional form so that each particle can be examined, classified and counted by microscope. This makes possible for the first time the direct examination of such clouds.
- Machines that can process hundreds of thousands of pictures, picking out rapidly all patterns that conform to certain criteria. Such devices are already being used to find the signatures of oil-bearing geologic formations from explosion soundings of the earth's interior. The same system can be used to screen electrocardiograms and fingerprint files or search aerial photographs for missile sites.
- Side-looking radars that enable aircraft flying offshore to map in detail cloud-covered installations along a coastline.
- Microscopes that can display directly the three-dimensional structure of proteins and other complex molecules formed from millions of atoms. Such a capability would revolutionize the development of new drugs. ■

FEBRUARY 10, 1969

'JUMBO JET' FLIES FIRST TIME

Robert Lindsey

A Boeing 747 at the Le Bourget Airport during the 1969 Paris Air Show.

EVERETT, Wash., Feb. 9—Boeing's huge new 747, the first of the "jumbo jets" that promise a revolution in mass air travel and new standards of comfort in the air, made its first flight today.

The flight, scheduled to last at least two hours, was cut short after 1 hour and 16 minutes because of what was later described as a "minor problem" in the plane's right wing flap.

There was an icy wind blowing in from the Puget Sound as the 747, twice as big as any airliner before it, accelerated down a rain-soaked runway at the Boeing Company's plant here, 30 miles north of Seattle.

Rain kicked up from the wet runway by the plane's four powerful turbofan engines formed a misty shroud that almost enveloped the 747 as it reached its lift-off speed of 170 miles an hour, then soared gracefully into the gray sky.

Most observers on the ground agreed the 747 was quieter than any of today's airliners, and it produced almost no exhaust smoke.

After the flight, the test pilot, Jack Waddell, a 45-year-old Montanan who piloted the plane in a light-green business suit, told a reporter:

"It handled magnificently. It's a pilot's dream."

Later, at a news conference, he said: "Our chase plane [a small jet following the 747] reported some turbulence up there, but we could hardly feel it. We think the passengers in this plane will have a comfortable ride because it seems to cushion the turbulence."

"When we were making our landing approach," Mr. Waddell added, "it just seemed to sit up there like a stable platform. All the pilot has to do is leave it alone. It almost lands itself, literally."

The 747 is the first of a generation of "wide bodied" jets that for the first time will take the "tube look" away from airliners.

With a cabin 20 feet wide, the plane is more than 60 percent wider than the biggest of today's airliners. The result is a passenger cabin that looks more like a long, spacious room than a tunnel.

Twenty-eight airliners have ordered 167 of the $21.4-million 747's. Pan American Airways said it planned to inaugurate the first service with the plane late this year.

"It handled magnificently. It's a pilot's dream."

No passengers were carried in the plane's first flight today, only test instruments and 176 55-gallon barrels of water ballast that, to one observer, looked like a cargo of beer kegs.

Although the 747 can hold up to 490 passengers, most airlines plan to carry about 360, giving the passengers more elbow room than in today's planes. ■

MAY 1, 1960

MINNESOTA REPORTS ON USE OF ELECTRONIC PACEMAKER

The human heart takes its cues from natural electrical impulses. These imperceptible little shocks, conveyed through a band of muscle and nerve tissue called the "bundle of His" (after the German researcher who identified it), maintain the heart's proper rhythm. They insure that the upper chambers (the atria) and the main pumping chambers (the ventricles) contract and relax in proper sequence. Thus a natural "pacemaker" keeps the four chambers working together smoothly in the crucial job of pumping blood through the body.

For most people the electrical pulses continue—uninterrupted, unnoticed, but indispensable—throughout life. But in some persons disruptions occur, the chambers beat independently and the pump loses much of its effectiveness. This is known as heart block.

Within recent years specialists have developed artificial electronic pacemakers which send regular pulses to the heart to buoy up the natural system when it falters or fails.

In the latest issue of the Journal of the American Medical Association, Dr. C. Walton Lillehei, one of the pioneers of heart surgery, and his colleagues at the University of Minnesota Medical School have made a report which confirms significantly the value of such devices.

Transistorized electronic pacemakers not much larger than a pack of cigarettes were used not only as temporary aids after surgery but also for the long-term maintenance of non-surgical patients.

One of the latter has already been using such a device for over fifteen months, according to the report. Another, a 38-year-old engineer who had been unable to work since 1957 because of his condition, is now back at work.

The miniature pacemaker is carried in a light sling suspended from the shoulder. Tiny stainless steel wire electrodes insulated with a synthetic fiber are implanted surgically in the muscle of one of the ventricles. The electrodes connect the electronic device to the patient's heart.

The light, steady pulsing of the device supports the heart's action when its natural stimulus falters. While its rate does not adjust automatically to the body's changing needs as does the normal heart, other natural mechanisms compensate within reasonable limits.

"Not only has the threat of sudden death in the patients been removed," the report declared, "but their physical and emotional rehabilitation has been dramatic."

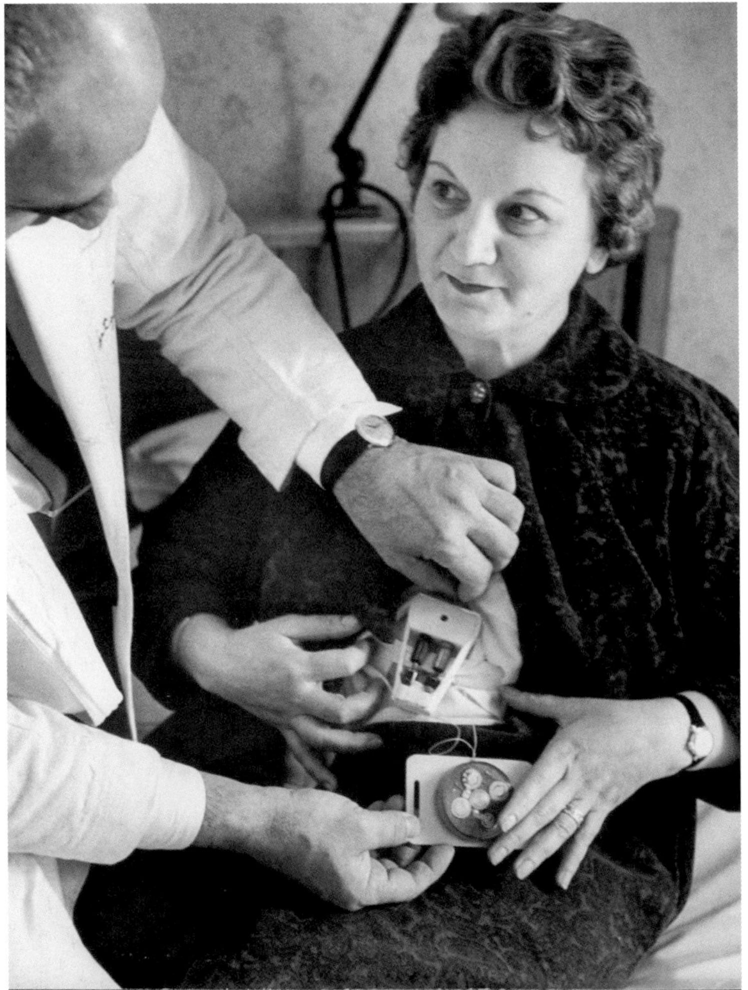

Doctor examining the battery operated exterior pacemaker of heart patient Rose Cohen, March 1961.

APRIL 12, 1962

DEFORMED BABIES TRACED TO A DRUG

Robert K. Plumb

PHILADELPHIA, April 11—The birth of thousands of deformed babies in Europe has led an American physician to appeal for stricter Federal regulations on the introduction of new drugs in this country.

The appeal was made to the American College of Physicians at its annual meeting here. It is based on a new study of several thousand deformed babies born to European mothers who took a common prescription sleeping pill that had long been considered harmless.

The babies are born with useless short stub-like arms and legs to mothers who took, often before they knew they were pregnant, a sleeping compound with the chemical name thalidomide. The drug has been widely sold in West Germany and in Britain since 1958. It was taken off the market last November. It has not been sold in the United States.

The appeal was made last night at a special session of the College of Physicians here by Dr. Helen B. Taussig, Professor of Pediatrics at the Johns Hopkins Hospital, who has just returned from a six-week inspection tour of German and British medical centers. She also held a news conference today.

"This compound [thalidomide] could have passed our present drug laws," Dr. Taussig reported. "There is no question but what we must strengthen our food and drug regulations to include routine testing of new compounds on pregnant animals."

Thalidomide, Dr. Taussig said, appeared to be the greatest sleeping pill ever devised. It worked quickly and left no hangover.

However, the American concern, the William S. Merrill Company of Cincinnati, did not obtain Federal approval to sell the drug here because officials were suspicious of it. Nonetheless, it could have been passed, Dr. Taussig emphasized in demanding stiffer United States drug regulations.

She pointed out that the drug-caused deformation of the babies, known medically as phocomelia, "is the most ghastly thing you have ever seen." ■

MAY 13, 1962

A.M.A. FEARS NEW AGED CARE PLAN IS STEP TO SOCIALIZED MEDICINE

Marjorie Hunter

WASHINGTON, May 12—The American Medical Association and the Kennedy Administration were locked in battle this week over the issue of medical care for the aged.

The fight is not a new one. Doctors and the Federal Government have been sparring over this matter for some years. But this time, both sides are determined to win.

Congressional leaders are predicting that the Administration bill on the issue will become law, possibly with minor modifications.

The bill would increase Social Security taxes to finance hospital and nursing-home care for persons 65 years of age or older. Doctors' bills would not be covered.

The Administration both wants and needs its bill. Most polls have shown it is popular with the public—and this is an election year.

The American Medical Association, mortally fearful of any step toward socialized medicine, believes that if the bill is to be headed off, this is the year it must be done.

The A.M.A. opposes any new legislation to provide medical care for the aged. It contends that those who need help are taken care of under the Kerr-Mills Law, a Federal-state program for the medically indigent.

The combination of Administration and grass-roots pressure finally showed signs of paying off in the one place that mattered: the House Ways and Means Committee.

The committee line-up had been fifteen to ten against the bill when Congress convened in January. In recent weeks, several conservative Democrats who had been counted against the bill indicated they now favored the Social Security approach and would be willing to consider some modifications of the Administration bill.

Up to that point, campaigning on both sides of the issue had been noisy but fairly polite.

The A.M.A. had been fighting back with cries of "socialized medicine." Doctors had been distributing pamphlets, ringing doorbells of their patients and inserting full-page advertisements in newspapers.

Then, last week, a group of New Jersey doctors threatened to boycott patients seeking hospital care under the Administration bill if it became law.

The spokesman for the doctors, Dr. J. Bruce Henriksen of Point Pleasant Hospital, said: "Let's put it this way. Would you like your money to go for President Kennedy's father's hospital bills?"

The Administration came up fighting.

Abraham A. Ribicoff, Secretary of Health, Education and Welfare, termed the doctors' threat an attempt to "blackmail Congress and the American people."

Some favor supporting the Administration bill. Some favor another approach, suggested by Governor Rockefeller of New York. This would let older citizens draw cash benefits if they already had adequate private health insurance.

Some Republicans are determined to fight off all medical-care bills.

Despite the split within the ranks, the Republican National Committee, official voice of the G.O.P., has continued to hammer away at the Administration's measure.

Just this week, the Republican National Committee charged that backers of the Administration bill were circulating "a pack of lies" among elderly persons of Chinese ancestry in New York City by contending that the bill would also provide money for rent, clothing and doctor bills.

The Administration is not without allies. Probably its strongest support comes from an organization called the National Council of Senior Citizens for Health Care Through Social Security.

Operating out of four small rooms near the Capitol, the council has done most of the grass-roots work. Its biggest project will be coordinating thirty-five or more rallies to be held in major cities May 20 in support of the medical-care bill.

Stepping up its own campaign, the A.M.A. has issued a twelve-page booklet entitled "The Case Against Socialized Medicine." ■

MARCH 22, 1963

2 MEASLES VACCINES LICENSED; U.S. SEES END OF DISEASE IN 1965

WASHINGTON, March 21—The Government licensed today two vaccines against measles in the hope of eradicating this No. 1 childhood disease.

One variety, a "killed vaccine," will be available immediately in limited amounts. The other, a "live vaccine," is to be on the market within a few weeks. Both were expected to be generally available from the two licensed drug manufacturers within several months.

Surgeon General Luther L. Terry, chief of the Public Health Service, said the first drop in the rate of measles could be expected next year. More than 4,000,000 cases occur annually in the United States, he estimated. There are relatively few deaths—about 400 a year—but sometimes crippling complications of deafness and mental defects occur.

The disease might be eliminated from the nation in two years under ideal conditions, Dr. Terry said. This was an "attainable goal," rather than an expectation, he emphasized.

Measles kill about 50 percent of the children in other nations who catch it, Dr. Terry said. The disease probably accounts for 25 to 50 percent of all deaths among children in underdeveloped countries.

The vaccines represent "the most significant advance in recent years toward eliminating this infectious disease from our population," Dr. Terry told a news conference.

Both vaccines were outgrowths of pioneering studies by Dr. John Enders, a Nobel Prize winner at Harvard University, and an associate, Dr. Thomas Peebles. They isolated the measles virus for the first time in 1954.

The rational reason for licensing both types of vaccines was that they have different characteristics. In general, the live vaccine produces greater and faster protection, but it also has more side effects than the killed type, according to tests on about 50,000 persons.

The live vaccine provided immunity after one injection in more than 95 percent of the susceptible children tested. This immunity remains for at least four years. However, 30 to 40 per cent of the inoculated children experienced fevers as high as 103 degrees, and 30 to 60 percent had a modified measles rash.

When the live vaccine is given with a simultaneous injection of gamma globulin, as will probably be the practice, this blood derivative puts down the cases of fever to 15 percent and reduces the duration of the fever and the rash.

In contrast, injections of the prescribed pre-shot program of killed vaccine over a period of at least two months cause the development of antibodies in 90 percent of the children. This declines to undetectable levels within a year, and a booster shot may later be required. However, there are no adverse reactions to this vaccine.

It appears that one shot of live vaccine and one shot of killed vaccine may work best, according to a report by the Surgeon General's Advisory Committee on Measles.

Since over 90 percent of all children get measles, Dr. Terry would like to see infants vaccinated between the age of 9 months and one year. Children usually come down with the disease between the ages of 2 and 6.

Hypodermic needles containing new measles vaccines, 1965.

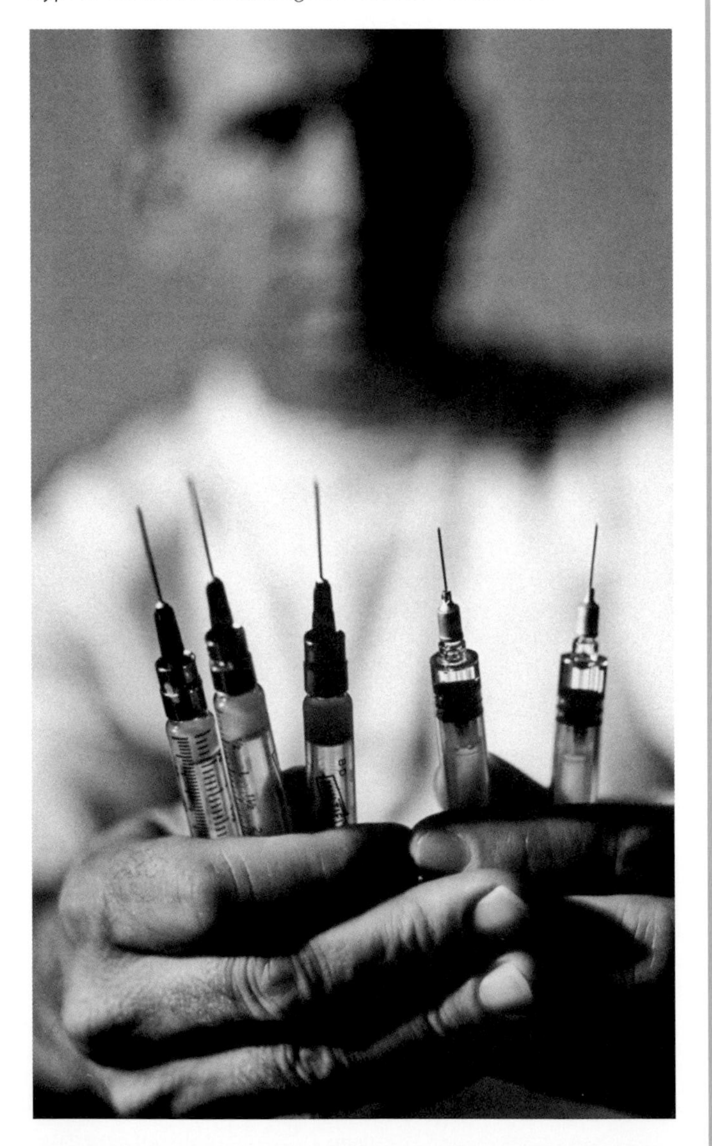

APRIL 17, 1963

LUNG TRANSPLANT SEEN WITHIN YEAR

Harold M. Schmeck Jr.

ATLANTIC CITY, April 16—The first human lung transplantation may be attempted within a year, a surgeon told a scientific meeting here today.

The needed surgical techniques have been thoroughly worked out in experiments on animals at several research institutions, Dr. James D. Hardy said. He is professor of surgery at the University of Mississippi.

The speaker said that surgeons at several institutions were now waiting for a suitable patient and a suitable opportunity.

Dr. Hardy described experimental transplantations in dogs at a session of the Federation of American Societies for Experimental Biology, at the Traymore Hotel.

Scientific sessions elsewhere heard several reports on experimental artificial hearts and heart-booster devices that have been tried in animals. None of these is now considered suitable for application to man.

One Japanese research team from Hokkaido University School of Medicine, however, did report on the experimental use in four patients of what might be considered an artificial liver. The clinical impression was that the condition of three of the patients was improved by the attempt. The device perfused substances produced by foreign liver cells into the patient's circulation.

In the report on dog lung transplantations, Dr. Hardy said that the animals were treated with an anticancer drug to extend the transplant's survival time.

During most of that time the transplanted lung functioned but with only half the efficiency of the normal lung. He said, however, that this was enough lung function to be useful.

Ordinarily the body's immunological defenses attack transplants and cause their prompt rejection. In the lung experiments, Dr. Hardy said, dogs treated with the drug kept their transplanted lungs for 30 days on the average, while untreated dogs rejected them in a week.

The reports on artificial heart devices were given to the American Society for Artificial Internal Organs at the Hotel Claridge. A heart-booster device that has been used successfully in dogs for as long as nine months was reported by a group led by Dr. Adrian Kantrowitz of Maimonides Hospital in Brooklyn. It is made of biologically inert plastic and consists of an open shunt across the arch of the aorta—the body's main artery leaving the heart. When the dog's heart pumps blood out through the aorta, some of this flows into the shunt cavity.

Since the pressure here is low, the heart's work in pumping is reduced. Once the heart's stroke is finished and the aortic valve has closed, the shunt is contracted pneumatically, giving an added impetus to the circulating blood. The device, which is timed by the electrical activity of the dog's heart, was developed in cooperation with Avco-Everett Research Laboratory in Everett, Mass. Dr. Kantrowitz said that it is not planned to use the device on humans because the power source had not been sufficiently miniaturized. Co-authors of the report were Dr. Yukihiko Nose and Dr. Martin Schamaun. ■

AUGUST 4, 1963

BIRTH PILL'S SALE UPHELD BY U.S.

Robert C. Toth

Birth control pill container, 1963.

WASHINGTON, Aug. 3—The Food and Drug Administration said today that Enovid, the popular birth control pill, could remain on the market but that doctors should prescribe it with caution, particularly for women over 34 years old.

A detailed study by a special advisory panel of experts found no direct evidence showing that the drug causes blood clots in women. However, the rate of deaths from clotting among women over 34 was significantly greater if they took the pills, the panel reported.

As a result, the F.D.A. has requested the manufacturer, G.D. Searle & Co., to put on the drug's label information on the "apparent hazard" to older women. The labels will also caution against use in women with certain cancers, liver diseases, and those with a history of clotting in veins and lungs.

About 1,200,000 American women took Enovid last year, and more than 2,000,000 are currently using it or another oral contraceptive that is on the market.

Since 1961, however, blood clots have been reported in 350 women who were taking or had taken Enovid. Thirty-five of the women died. These cases led the F.D.A. to set up its panel of experts, headed by Dr. Irving S. Wright, five months ago.

The committee found that Enovid produced some changes in the uterus similar to those occurring during pregnancy. A pregnant woman has more clotting substances in her blood, and blood clots are four to six times more common in women shortly after they deliver their babies than during pregnancy.

However, the committee found that the data neither established nor excluded the possibility that Enovid directly increases the clotting tendency of a woman's blood.

For women 35 to 39, the death rate was 2.4 times greater for women taking Enovid, and for the 40-to-44 age group, the rate was 3.8 times greater. These differences in rates were termed "highly significant" by the committee.

"The reasons for this [statistical link] are not clear at this time," the committee said. It called for carefully planned studies in this area, plus investigations of possible effects of Enovid on the coagulation properties of the user's blood.

The agency stated that physicians must now weigh the apparent risk in older women against the "demonstrated hazard" of pregnancy in those women before deciding whether to prescribe Enovid for them. The agency said that in general the drug was recommended only for short-term use of two to four years. ■

JANUARY 12, 1964

CIGARETTES LINKED TO CANCER, U.S. REPORT CONCLUDES

Walter Sullivan

Surgeon General Luther L. Terry at a press conference, holding report made by government on smoking and health.

WASHINGTON, Jan. 11—The long-awaited Federal report on the effects of smoking found today that the use of cigarettes contributed so substantially to the American death rate that "appropriate remedial action" was called for.

The committee that made the report gave no specific recommendations for action. But health officials said that possible steps might include educational campaigns, the requirement that cigarette packages carry warnings and control of advertising.

The report dealt a severe blow to the rear-guard action fought in recent years by the tobacco industry. It dismissed, one by one, the arguments raised to question the validity of earlier studies.

Combining the results of many surveys, the study panel found no doubt about the role of cigarette smoking in causing cancer of the lungs.

In men who smoke cigarettes, the death rate from that disease is almost 1,000 percent higher than in nonsmokers, it said. Lung cancer has become the most frequent form of cancer in men.

Such smoking was also found to be "the most important" cause of chronic bronchitis, increasing the risk of death from that disease and from emphysema, a swelling of the lungs due to the presence of air in the connective tissues. Emphysema is a disease of increasing incidence.

As to coronary artery disease, a frequent cause of heart failure and the leading cause of death in this country, mortality is 70 percent higher for cigarette smokers than for nonsmokers, the report said.

The role of smoking as a cause of the disease, it said, "is not proved." However, it said, the study committee considers it "prudent" from the public health viewpoint to assume such a cause-and-effect relationship rather than wait until such a relationship has been established beyond doubt.

The Tobacco Institute rejected the report, saying it was not the last word on smoking and health. The three major broadcasting networks said they would review their policies on tobacco advertising in the light of the report.

The report was prepared on the initiative of President Kennedy to help the Government decide what to do about the smoking question. The committee was formed by Dr. Luther L. Terry, Surgeon General of the Public Health Service.

At a press conference in the State Department Auditorium, where the report was released, Dr. Terry said that the Public Health Service would move "promptly" to determine what steps should be taken.

A spokesman for the committee told the press conference there was no valid evidence that filters helped reduce the harmful effects. The report also said that nicotine substitutes, such as lobeline, used in so-called "withdrawal pills," seemed ineffective in breaking the smoking habit.

The committee said that smoking was a "psychological crutch" for a large part of the 70 million Americans who were smokers in 1963. This posed the question: What would happen if this prop were suddenly pulled out from under them?

Smoking, the report said, is a habit, rather than a form of addiction. Withdrawal does not produce a characteristic illness, as it does with addicts, and is best accomplished by psychologically replacing the prop, the committee said.

"Cigarette smoking is a health hazard of sufficient importance in the United States to warrant appropriate remedial action," said the report, entitled "Smoking and Health." ■

JULY 31, 1965

PRESIDENT SIGNS MEDICARE BILL; PRAISES TRUMAN

John D. Morris

INDEPENDENCE, Mo., July 30—President Johnson flew to Independence today and signed the medicare-Social Security bill in a moving tribute to former President Harry S. Truman.

Mr. Truman, beaming, sat beside Mr. Johnson on the stage of the Harry S. Truman Library auditorium. More than 200 persons, including Vice President Humphrey, Congressional leaders and Administration officials, witnessed the ceremony.

President Johnson chose Independence for the signing because Mr. Truman was the first President who proposed a Federal program of health insurance under Social Security.

"The people of the United States love and voted for Harry Truman," the President said, "not because he gave them hell but because he gave them hope.

addiction

"I believe today that all America shares my joy that he is present now when the hope he offered becomes a reality for millions of our fellow citizens."

The 81-year-old former President, opening the ceremonies with a brief talk, said, "I am glad to have lived this long and to witness today the signing of the medicare bill."

In his address at the signing ceremonies, Mr. Johnson said:

"No longer will older Americans be denied the healing miracle of modern medicine. No longer will illness crush and destroy the savings that they have so carefully put away over a lifetime so that they might enjoy dignity in their later years."

The Senate completed Congressional action on the bill Wednesday, capping a 20-year effort to steer such legislation to final passage.

The bill expands the 30-year-old Social Security insurance program to provide hospital care, nursing home care, home nursing services and out-patient diagnostic service for all Americans over 65 years old.

It covers 17 million persons eligible for Social Security and 2 million others who do not fall under Social Security's present old-age, survivors and disability insurance program. Medical benefits to the latter group will be paid for by appropriations from general revenues, not from Social Security funds.

The new law extends Social Security coverage to self-employed physicians and to hospital interns, the last major group that had been exempt from coverage.

President Johnson used 72 pens to sign the measure and passed them out to members of Congress, labor leaders, Administration officials and others who filed across the stage and shook his hand.

Mr. Johnson and Mr. Truman chatted privately for a few minutes before and after the ceremony. ■

NOVEMBER 27, 1965

LENSES MADE PLIABLE BY PLASTIC

Stacy V. Jones

WASHINGTON, Nov. 26—A soft plastic invented by two Czechoslovak scientists is hailed as offering comfort to the wearers of contact lenses.

Promoters of the innovation expect two or more United States companies to begin production of the pliable lenses in January. Patent 3,220,960 will be issued next week to Prof. Otto Wichterle, director of the Institute of Macromolecular Chemistry in Prague, and Dr. Drahoslav Lim, a research scientist at the institute.

The National Patent Development Corporation, New York, which holds a license for the Western Hemisphere, said this week that it had already granted sublicenses to two lens makers and was negotiating with others.

The material is produced by the Princeton Chemical Research Corporation in New Jersey.

According to the patent, the plastics, called hydrogels, are suitable for body implants as well as contact lenses. They can be sterilized in boiling water.

The patent material is hydrophilic ("water-loving") and becomes saturated with the lens wearer's tears.

Dr. Allan A. Isen, an optometrist, has been conducting clinical tests of the flexible lenses with his patients in Buffalo. He said this week that when the usual hard plastic is used, the upper eyelid presses against the lens and through that against the cornea. With the soft material, there is almost no sensation in lid or cornea.

Dr. Isen is president of Isen/Frontier Contact Lens Laboratories, Inc., at Buffalo.

The inventors plan to assign next week's patent, which covers lenses and other shaped bodies, to the Czechoslovak Academy of Sciences. In 1961, they received a related patent on methods of preparing the hydrogels.

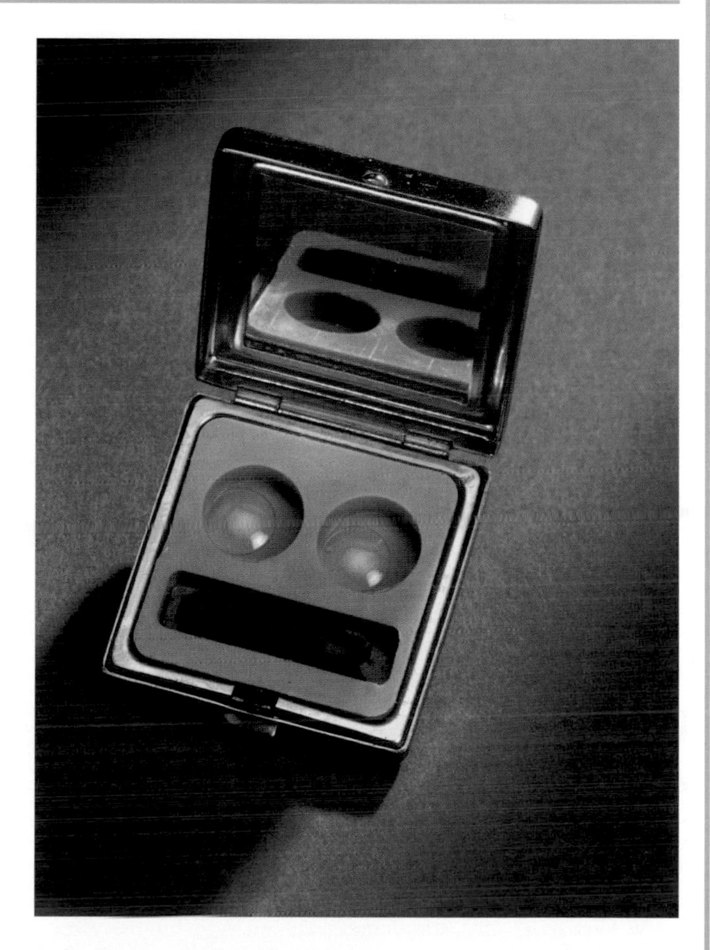

A plastic contact lenses and case, 1964.

APRIL 18, 1966

Research Into Sex Disclosed After 11-Year Inquiry

John Corry

The results of an 11-year inquiry into the physiology of sex were disclosed today with the publication of "Human Sexual Response." The inquiry involved the direct observation of 382 women and 312 men as they engaged in coitus and masturbation.

The book, published by Little, Brown & Co., was written by Dr. William H. Masters and Virginia E. Johnson. Dr. Masters, a gynecologist, is director of the Reproductive Biology Research Foundation in St. Louis. Mrs. Johnson, a clinical psychologist, is his research associate.

They wrote the book, they say, in the hope that it will offer medical and behavioral scientists information that they will adapt to treat problems of sexual inadequacy.

They consider sexual performance an integral part of sexuality, and they write that "sexuality is a dimension and an expression of personality."

They have taken pains to purge the book of anything that might be considered salacious.

Neither Dr. Masters nor Mrs. Johnson believes, and the book does not suggest, that sex is merely a physical response. But they do believe that physical responses to sex can be measured with a fair degree of accuracy, and that the community of volunteers they selected, although not a cross-section of the population, was large enough to establish a physical norm.

Perhaps their most dramatic finding has been in identifying the biophysical source of vaginal lubrication. In the past it has been traced to the uterine cervix and to the Bartholin glands, which are on each side of the vagina.

However, Dr. Masters and Mrs. Johnson have found that the vagina itself is the source of lubrication. "Human Sexual Response" describes the fluid as arising from a "sweating phenomenon."

The study has also produced photographic evidence of the failure of contraceptive agents and intravaginal diaphragms. Pictures have been taken of foams that did not foam, suppositories that did not spread and diaphragms that did not stay in place.

The inquiry was the most extensive ever undertaken on the effect of sexual activity on the cardiorespiratory system.

"In the past," says Mr. Mary C. Calderone, executive director of the Sex Education and Information Council of the United States, "doctors have told post-coronary males only to 'take it easy,' whatever that means, in their sexual activity. Masters and Johnson at least provide some basis for cardiologists to act upon."

What the two researchers have done is perfect the techniques for measuring heart stress during sexual activity, and the results of this research will now be available to heart specialists.

However, Dr. Masters and Mrs. Johnson think that the most significant result of their study may be in the adaptation of their conclusions for the treatment of sexual inadequacy. Certainly, some of their findings challenge the conventional wisdom about sex.

Psychiatrists have noted, for example, that a small genital organ in a male may cause a severe trauma for him. Dr. Masters and Mrs. Johnson have established that size of the organ has no relationship to sexual ability.

Their study also showed that there was no anatomic reason why men and women in their 70's and 80's could not respond effectively. This supposes, of course, they wrote, that both partners are in good health and mutually responsive.

Women in general, they found, respond more intensely and longer to sexual stimulation than do men.

SEPTEMBER 7, 1966

HEART PUMP PATIENT LEAVES HOSPITAL IN HOUSTON

Martin Waldron

HOUSTON, Sept. 6—A 37-year-old Mexico City woman who survived heart surgery with the aid of an experimental heart pump was released from the Methodist Hospital here today.

The patient, Mrs. Esperanza del Valle Vasquez, departed almost immediately by plane for her home in Mexico.

"We are thrilled and pleased by the results of the operation," said Ted Bowen, Methodist Hospital administrator, in introducing Mrs. Vasquez at a news conference. Dr. Michael E. DeBakey, the surgeon who helped design the heart pump, was not present, and hospital officials would not say why.

Mrs. Vasquez is the first person known to have survived after being fitted with one of the heart pumps, which are designed to relieve the heart of part of its load during recovery after surgery.

The DeBakey pump, technically known as a left ventricular bypass, assumed as much as 60 percent of the pumping action of Mrs. Vasquez's heart during the 10 days it was used, Mr. Bowen said.

The Methodist Hospital, Dr. DeBakey and Rice University—which built the pump—did not charge Mrs. Vasquez for the operation or for her stay at the hospital. Mr. Bowen said the operation was considered to be a clinical experiment and that all costs were borne by the various institutions involved and by the United States Public Health Service. Part of the cost of the development of the heart pump has been paid by the Federal Government under medical research grants.

Mrs. Vasquez said she hoped to return to her work as a beautician in Mexico City.

Mr. Bowen said Mrs. Vasquez was referred to Dr. DeBakey by a physician in Mexico City after a flareup of a previous heart condition for which she had surgery on the mitral valve.

Tests showed a need to replace the

mitral and aortic valves, Mr. Bowen said. After the purpose of the heart pump was explained to her, Mrs. Vasquez agreed to its use, the administrator said, and Dr. DeBakey performed the operation on Aug. 8.

Twice during the 10 days the pump was in use the patient's condition showed signs of worsening, Mr. Bowen said. When the pump's workload was increased Mrs. Vasquez's condition quickly improved, he added.

Mrs. Vasquez looked chipper as she awaited discharge from the hospital, and she moved about freely. She told doctors she had not felt so active in years.

Dr. DeBakey has avoided making public statements about the heart experiment since April, when he was criticized by other physicians for allowing publicity during his first tests of the heart pump on a human.

That first patient and a subsequent one died. The Methodist Hospital said each time that the operation and the pump were successes, but that the patients died from complications. Both of these patients were much older than Mrs. Vasquez. ■

SEPTEMBER 7, 1966

MARGARET SANGER IS DEAD AT 82;

Led Campaign for Birth Control

TUCSON, Ariz., Sept. 6—Margaret Sanger, the birth control pioneer, died this afternoon of arteriosclerosis in the Valley House Convalescent Center. She would have been 83 years old on Sept. 14.

As the originator of the phrase "birth control" and its best-known advocate, Margaret Sanger survived Federal indictments, a brief jail term, numerous lawsuits, hundreds of street-corner rallies and raids on her clinics to live to see much of the world accept her view that family planning is a basic human right.

The dynamic, titian-haired woman whose Irish ancestry also endowed her with unfailing charm and persuasive wit was first and foremost a feminist. She sought to create equality between the sexes by freeing women from what she saw as sexual servitude.

Trained as a nurse, Mrs. Sanger's life work began after she and her husband moved to New York in 1912. It resulted from her job as a nurse for maternity cases, principally on the Lower East Side. Many of her patients were wives of small shopkeepers, truck drivers and pushcart venders. Others were from a lower stratum of society.

The young nurse saw them, weary and old at 35, resorting to self-induced abortions, which were frequently the cause of their deaths.

Mrs. Sanger soon renounced nursing forever.

For nearly a year the ex-nurse read every scrap of material on contraception. In 1913, she went to France and Scotland to study birth control conditions, returning the following year.

Her magazine, Woman Rebel, was the spearhead of her movement. In an early issue she specified seven circumstances in which birth control should be practiced.

The articles adhered to New York's Comstock law, which made it a crime to offer contraceptive information. Nevertheless, most of the issues of the Woman Rebel were banned by the New York Post Office.

In August 1914, Mrs. Sanger was indicted on nine counts of sending birth control information through the mails and was made liable to a prison term of 45 years. The indictment was quashed in 1916. But Mrs. Sanger found that the indictment had aroused worldwide interest in the movement and she decided to take a step beyond the propagandizing then carried on by the National Birth Control League.

Mrs. Sanger and a sister, Mrs. Ethel Byrne, a trained nurse, opened a birth control clinic on Oct. 16, 1916, in the Brownsville section of Brooklyn. The clinic, at 46 Amboy Street, was the first birth control clinic in the United States.

Despite continued legal harassment, Mrs. Sanger's work was increasingly accepted. In 1937, a year after the Comstock law was reinterpreted to provide for distribution of contraceptive information, the American Medical Association adopted a report that recognized birth control as part of legitimate medical practice.

Mrs. Sanger's American Birth Control League, established in 1921, became the Planned Parenthood Federation of America in 1946 and led to the establishment of more than 250 Planned Parenthood Centers in 150 cities throughout the country.

MARCH 20, 1967

WEIGHT WATCHERS: TALKING THEIR WAY OUT OF OBESITY

Nan Ickeringill

"You look marvelous," a friend told Mrs. Marty Nidetch. "When are you due?"

"I wasn't pregnant," Mrs. Nidetch recalled recently. "But I did weigh 214 pounds."

That was in 1961. Today Jean Nidetch, who is 5 feet 7 inches tall, weighs 142. She has changed from bulky to slinky, also from brunette to blonde, and from a simple Little Neck housewife to founder and president of Weight Watchers, Inc.

Like most fat people (she considers fat a realistic, not a dirty word), Mrs. Nidetch had been a professional dieter. She tried all the fashionable crash diets, always lost weight—and always gained it back, with some to spare.

After being mistaken for an expectant mother, she tried the high-protein diet recommended by the New York City Board of Health.

When trying to follow the Board of Health diet became difficult, she bolstered her morale by inviting six fat friends to her house to discuss their weight problems.

"It seemed to help," she continued.

When Mrs. Nidetch, with the aid of dieting and her special brand of group therapy, succeeded in losing 72 pounds, she wanted other people to benefit from her

(cont'd. on next page)

(cont'd. from previous page)
experiences. So she started lecturing to various groups, free of charge.

"Finally Albert Lippert, a businessman who lost 40 pounds, encouraged me to incorporate," Mrs. Nidetch recalled.

In May 1963, Weight Watchers, Inc., came into existence. It has four officials—Mr. and Mrs. Lippert and Mr. and Mrs. Nidetch. Mr. Nidetch gave up bus driving and 69 pounds of fat.

Mrs. Nidetch estimated that half a million dieters had lost more than 10 million pounds with the help of Weight Watchers. There are 297 classes a week in New York City and 25 franchise operations in 16 states. Weight Watchers International is already operating in London and Tel Aviv and is training people to open branches in South America and South Africa.

Members pay $3 for registration and $2 a week to attend meetings conducted by former weight watchers. The meetings consist of a private weigh-in, lecture and open discussion of problems. New members are given a list of foods they should eat (such as plain-cooked fish, meat, vegetables and raw fruits) and foods they should not (such as cakes, cookies and potatoes). Neither alcohol nor diet pills are allowed, and a doctor's permission to diet is required.

Physicians, psychiatrists, nurses, lawyers, politicians, teachers, teenagers and a 79-year-old woman have lost weight with Weight Watchers, she said. Many have lost more than 100 pounds and a 19-year-old boy, who joined at 423, has lost 224 pounds and is still shedding weight.

Mrs. Nidetch knows of at least two Weight Watcher weddings. She hopes the bride and groom resisted the cake. ■

Weight Watchers founder Jean Nidetch with a photo of herself before her weight loss, 1967.

DECEMBER 10, 1967

MANY PROBLEMS REMAIN DESPITE BREAKTHROUGH IN HEART TRANSPLANTS

Howard A. Rusk, M.D.

The announcement of the first successful heart transplant made last Sunday a day of excitement, caution and skeptical optimism among the world's scientific community.

The announcement last Wednesday of a second transplant in a 2 1/2-week-old infant accelerated the excitement and interest.

To patients with severe and critical heart disease these reports were straws to be grasped with hope, the fear of disillusionment and the knowledge that probably this new breakthrough would be too late for them.

The report from the Groote Schuur Hospital in Capetown, South Africa, by the chief surgeon, Dr. Christian Neethling Barnard, and his associates of this first successful transplantation of the human heart was a blow-by-blow account of the greatest achievement in organ transplantation in our time.

Unfortunately, the second patient, operated on by Dr. Adrian Kantrowitz, a distinguished cardiac surgeon, at Maimonides Medical Center in Brooklyn, survived only 6 1/2 hours. Dr. Kantrowitz pointed out the increased technological and emotional problems in performing such surgery on infants. He and his staff are investigating the possible causes of failure.

The event that led to last week's dramatic crescendo began around the turn of the century when Dr. Alexis Carrel developed the techniques for the suturing of the blood vessels. This early basic work broke the trail to the long and painstaking approach toward organ transplantation.

The extent of the research effort is exemplified in the reported proceedings of

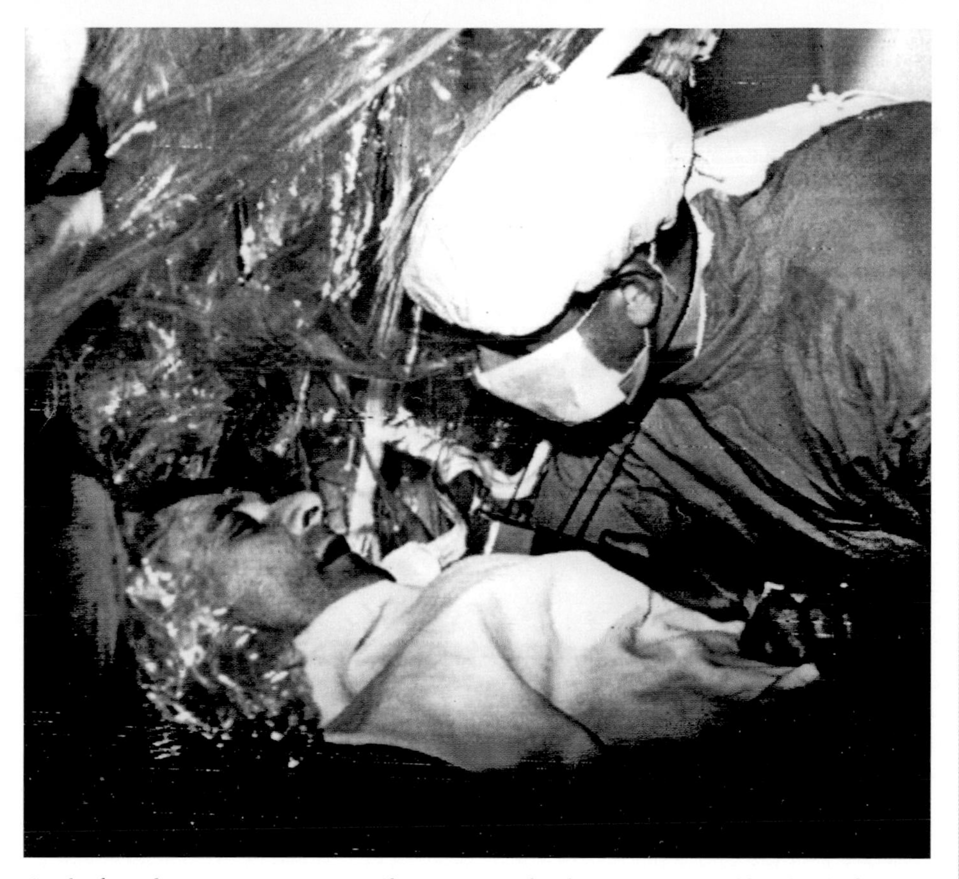

South African heart surgery pioneer Dr. Christian Barnard with patient Louis Washkansky, the first man to survive a heart transplant operation, December 6, 1967.

the seventh International Transplantation Conference that met at the New York Academy of Sciences in 1966. The report was 884 pages long and included contributions of more than 200 scientists.

The pooling of such scientific knowledge through the years culminated in the operation in which the heart of Miss Denise Ann Darvall, 25 years old, who was fatally injured in a traffic accident in Capetown, was transplanted into the body of Louis Washkansky, 55, a merchant dying of uncontrollable heart failure.

A team of surgeons, scientists, nurses, physiologists and technicians had been on standby alert for weeks awaiting a suitable set of circumstances that would provide the opportunity for transplantation.

It is most important that sufferers from heart disease throughout the world and their families must realize that this procedure is still in early experimental stages and that as the techniques are developed and refined there will be tremendous problems in obtaining organs for transplantation that involve time, type and a further unraveling of the body's complicated immunologic mechanism.

There are also certain moral and ethical problems that must be better understood and resolved.

. . . this procedure is still in early experimental stages . . .

It should be of great comfort to the grief-stricken father of Miss Darvall, who lost not only his daughter but also his wife in the fatal accident, to know that his understanding and compassion has given an opportunity for life to two doomed human beings and that, in a way, she lives on through the lives she saved. ■

DECEMBER 10, 1967

ROAD ACCIDENTS CUT SINCE BRITAIN BEGAN USE OF BREATH TESTS

LONDON, Dec. 9—A sharp drop in late night traffic accidents in London has been reported since the introduction on Oct. 9 of the Breathalyzer test for drunken driving.

Figures issued by Scotland Yard showed that the number of fatal or injurious accidents between 10 P.M. and 1 A.M. fell in October by 324, or 41.9 percent, compared with the period last year, when 773 accidents were recorded.

Similar reductions in the accident rate were reported throughout Britain.

Although the most striking decline was during the late night hours in London, the number of accidents for all hours in October also was considerably lower.

Accidents causing fatal, serious or slight injuries totaled 5,110, a drop from October 1966, of 577, or 10.1 percent. Deaths in the month fell by 28, from 82 to 54. The number of serious injuries dropped from 937 to 835, and the figures for those slightly injured went from 4,668 to 4,221.

Officials are cautious about directly attributing the decline in accidents to the Breathalyzer test, which measures the amount of alcohol a person has consumed. They noted that preliminary indications showed a substantial reduction in Friday and Saturday night traffic since the new Road Safety Act went into effect in October.

A group of pubkeepers from the Midlands descended on London last month in an attempt to persuade Parliament to rescind the law. They said their business had dropped by as much as 30 percent and that the social life of their communities had been seriously disrupted.

The hardest hit pubs were in country areas and largely dependent on motorists.

Although there have been few convictions, the law tends to act as a deterrent to those who think they might be stopped by the police after leaving a pub. ■

JUNE 10, 1969

RUBELLA VACCINE LICENSED BY U.S.

Harold M. Schmeck Jr.

WASHINGTON, June 9—The Government licensed today a vaccine against rubella, thus winning a race against the next nationwide epidemic of this virus infection, which is an important cause of human birth defects.

The manufacturer hopes to provide more than 18 million doses of the vaccine during the next 12 months for use by private physicians and in Government immunization programs. The license was given to Merck Sharp & Dohme of West Point, Pa., for a vaccine manufactured from a virus strain developed by scientists of the National Institute of Health.

The last nationwide epidemic of the disease, also known as German measles, occurred in 1964 and 1965. It is estimated that there were more than 30,000 fetal deaths and more than 20,000 babies born with serious birth defects after mothers were infected early in pregnancy during that major outbreak.

Nationwide epidemics seem to occur in cycles of roughly seven to 10 years. For this reason, public health experts think a substantial rise in the number of cases might occur in late 1970 or early 1971.

"This initial licensing brings to fruition a seven-year Government and industry effort to develop and make available a vaccine against German measles, before 1970," Robert H. Finch, Secretary of Health, Education and Welfare, said in announcing approval of the license today.

Recommendations of the United States Public Health Service's Advisory Committee on Immunization Practices call for primary emphasis on vaccinating school-age children against the disease. This would diminish the risk that pregnant women would be exposed to the infection.

It has been estimated that a nationwide vaccination program could produce a substantial reduction in the number of rubella cases within three years.

The Public Health Service hopes to mount a national program against the virus disease, but no money has yet been made available for the purpose.

The vaccine, the first of several expected to be licensed, is based on a rubella virus strain called HPV-77. Research by Dr. Maurice R. Hilleman and Eugene B. Buynak led to the development of the vaccine licensed today. The Government announcement said the product had been administered to more than 18,000 children and adults in tests of its safety and efficacy.

The possibility of developing a vaccine against the disease first became apparent in 1961, when two teams of scientists independently isolated rubella virus for the first time. The men were Dr. Thomas H. Weller and Franklin A. Neva of Harvard and Dr. Parkman, Dr. Edward L. Buescher and Dr. Malcolm S. Artenstein, who were then working in virus research at the Walter Reed Army Medical Center.

Life & Style

Lifestyle and fashion were inspired by the hippies and rock stars and images of swinging London, and the birds thereof, even in the airier reaches of high society and the mass-market, middle-class emporiums one might have thought untouched by such street-level mores.

Hippies, with their shaggy clothes, shaggier hair, flower power, ethnic jewelry and micro-minis (oddly combined with granny dresses) filtered up into fashion and even affected areas of the country (like the South) seemingly hostile to their ways. London—led by models like Jean Shrimpton and Twiggy, designers like Mary Quant and, of course, the all-conquering Beatles—brought with them miniskirts, wire-rim glasses, Nehru jackets and ornately brocaded menswear. Black power influenced fashions, and not just among blacks; some whites sported enormous Afros, too.

Marijuana was everywhere, as it is today. But there were also speed and cocaine and all manner of psychedelics, chemical (LSD, STP) and natural (mushrooms), led by Timothy Leary and Owsley, that mysterious West Coast mastermind. There was heroin, too, even if it wasn't quite the advertised hellish destination for anyone who dared indulge in a toke. For those terrified of a drugged-out nation and world, popular culture seemed to glorify drug use, from "Lucy in the Sky with Diamonds" to ganja as a sacrament for reggae stars. The Times, it should be noted, was slow to pick up on hippies and rock and drugs. The paper didn't take notice of skateboards, a Southern California phenomenon, until they reached Wesleyan. Some of the stories emanating from the San Francisco Bay Area read today like clueless anthropologists let loose in the exotic wild.

Amazingly, life went on apart from the hippie revolution. Yves St. Laurent, himself not untouched by hippie influences, became the new darling of French fashion. The Times took many of its style hints from the big department stores, which paid for a serious chunk of the paper's advertising and were the sites of many fashion shows of the day. Audrey Hepburn and Jackie Kennedy brought slim, elegant upper-class style to the nation's consciousness. Jackie's televised tour of the refurbished White House added to the impetus for elegance. But she broke the hearts of her fans—and that of Maria Callas, the discarded mistress—when she married down to Aristotle Onassis.

Sex was everywhere, not least with those miniskirts, vinyl boots (some made for walking) and white lipstick. The birth control pill encouraged free sex, as did the pro-sex wing of feminism (the anti-sex wing regarded sex as an imposition on women by rutting males). There was gay sex, too, striding out from the closet, as in Andy Warhol's drag "superstars" and, eventually, the Stonewall riots in Greenwich Village in 1969, widely regarded as the true beginning of gay liberation. With no AIDS yet and less dire sexual diseases mostly controllable, it was a golden age for sexual libertinism. Or for loving sex.

Not everything in 60's interior design was tasteful neo-French décor (or cuisine, either: LBJ fired the Kennedys' French chef in favor of barbecue). Lucite, inflatable furniture and waterbeds, another hippie influence, were the rage in some quarters. Muscle cars ruled the roads. Barbie met Ken, unfazed by G.I. Joe. Fast food (pizza chains, TV dinners) proliferated, as did diet sodas and all manner of artificial sweeteners, some now banned. Julia Child, on the page and on TV, began refining home cooking, abetted by the arrival in 1963 of Craig Claiborne as The Times's food critic. (Alden Whitman, another 60's arrival, turned obituaries, some of them parceled throughout this book, into a kind of literature.) Older, stuffier French restaurants in New York, like Le Pavillon, faded, though Lüchow's held on and newcomers, like Lutèce, arrived on the scene. Nouvelle cuisine, leaner and healthier, became the rage both in France and in America, and Chez Panisse and the American regional food movement—another post-hippie influence—were poised to enter from the wings. A serendipitous side effect of the relaxation of United States immigration quotas in 1965 was an influx of Asian (and South American, and even African) chefs who revolutionized the restaurant culture of New York, Los Angeles and beyond.

AUGUST 6, 1961

World Tensions Aid Sales Outlook for Shelters

Alexander R. Hammer

The Berlin crisis and the vast expenditures for defense needs requested from Congress by President Kennedy are revitalizing sales prospects for underground, above ground, basement blast and fall-out shelters.

Industry sources estimate that shelter sales in the United States last year amounted to about $15,000,000. The greater part of this total went mostly for do-it-yourself or company-installed basement shelters. Sales of the underground and above ground type accounted for about $2,000,000.

However, the picture has changed considerably in recent weeks as a result of the Berlin situation. One manufacturer, the Lancer Survival Corporation, a subsidiary of Lancer Industries, Inc., Mineola, L.I., has received almost 3,000 inquiries about its blast and fall-out shelters since the President's preparedness speech on the Berlin crisis about two weeks ago. From these inquiries the company has made almost 200 sales.

Sales of the Wonder Building Corporation of Chicago, which also makes a community-type shelter holding 200 persons, have increased ten-fold in the last month, according to Leo A. Hoegh, executive vice president.

Civil defense officials also report a big increase in requests for plans on how to build and stock shelters. Manufacturers who outfit shelters with needed supplies are accelerating research programs in this field. For instance, the Universal Container Corporation announced last week that it was seeking to determine the most suitable materials to line fifty-five gallon steel drums to handle a wide variety of wet and dry food products.

The General Foods Corporation, General Mills, Inc., and other major manufacturers are experimenting with and marketing dry-packed foods for shelters to include a varied diet of major proportions.

Sales prospects of shelter manufacturers also were considerably brightened last week by the announcement of the Federal Housing Administration that it would insure easier-term loans for construction of nuclear fall-out shelters in homes.

Some forty shelter manufacturers are operating in the United States with the majority making reinforced concrete shelters. Others make steel, corrugated-metal, aluminum, fiber-glass and fiber-glass-and-concrete types.

Shelters vary in price depending on the equipment installed. Some sell for more than $4,000, while the average can be bought for about $2,000. Usually they are designed to hold six persons.

Included in the price of the lower-price models are chemical toilets, air filters and an emergency escape hatch. The more expensive models include items such as food, auxiliary lights, special fall-out clothing, water supply containers, batteries, tools, fire extinguishers, radiation detection devices, a radio and other equipment. ■

Barbie and Ken in formal wear, 1964.

APRIL 21, 1963

BARBIE: Getting Serious About Ken?

Brock Milton

In an era of pre-teen dating and teen-age marriages, it is perhaps inevitable that a realistic boy doll called Ken should achieve popularity. And this seems to suggest the revolutionary idea that little girls today are viewing their girl dolls increasingly as themselves and not as their babies.

Ken is a clean-cut teen-ager. (He might even be 22.) If clothes make the man, he is clearly old enough to be not only a college graduate but also a yachtsman, a physician *(Ken Casey)* and, of course, a bridegroom. He has broad shoulders, a tapered waist and somewhat more muscle in this—his third season—than originally, when his makers kept him on the scrawny side to make him easier to dress.

Dolls are among the oldest of human institutions and representations of male figures are certainly not new. But the "play" doll has most often been a female, particularly a baby.

The symbol of the "little mother" rocking her doll to sleep is one of the sacred images of the playroom. The brief but spectacular story of Ken tends to jolt that image pretty hard. For Ken literally was summoned into being by a realistic, teen-age girl doll named Barbie. What Barbie needed, according to hundreds of letters from children, was a boy friend to take her on that date.

(cont'd. on next page)

(cont'd. from previous page)

Thus Ken, unlike Adam, was created *after* his mate. Barbie hit the market in 1959 and has sold in the tens of millions. Ken followed two years later. The sales ratio is said to be about three Barbie dolls for every Ken (a statistic that impelled one unmarried woman in the doll business to remark, "Isn't that about the way it is in life?").

But this summer a new development may raise all sorts of questions. For Mattel, Inc., the makers of Barbie and Ken, will offer a "Barbie Baby-sits" outfit. The set includes an apron, a tiny phone, a soft drink, pretzels, school-books, a baby bottle *and* a baby.

There is more to the baby than meets the eye. Even in a society where a mother has been heard to remark of her daughter, "I wouldn't mind her being married at 16 nearly as much as I would her *not* being married at 18," doll makers are understandably chary about having their miniature teen-agers produce offspring.

"If the child wants to marry them, it's up to the child," said Mrs. Ruth Handler, the dynamic gray-haired woman who with her husband runs Mattel and who by no strange coincidence has children named Barbie and Ken. "We dared not give Barbie and Ken a baby of their own. Barbie can baby-sit. What the child does with the baby is up to her."

The concept of the boy doll "came from the fans," Mrs. Handler says. Finally, she persuaded her husband that the success of the girl doll—although she had been a financial risk at the start—now made it possible for the company to take a flyer on Ken. In March, 1961, Ken made his debut.

She is sold in a bathing suit; he in swim trunks. Nine new Ken outfits for 1963 include a sailor costume, air-force man, skier, football player and a "sleeper set" (pajamas, a tiny glass of milk, sugar bun and alarm clock). The "doctor" (No. 793) includes hospital whites with a head-mirror on the cap and a black instrument bag. Barbie (No. 991) had previously appeared as a nurse. And, of course, Ken has his tux.

But although Barbie-Ken weddings seem to be inevitable (perhaps, after this summer, even necessary) the bridal gown and tuxedo are not the company's best sellers—possibly because they are among the more expensive items. Barbie's best-selling ensemble is a sweater and skirt; Ken's a sweater and slacks. In other words, the image they project is as so many tots have phrased it in letters: "Two teen-agers going steady." ■

MARCH 9, 1964

ONLY SMALL NUMBER OF STUDENTS USE MARIJUANA

Walter Carlson

According to a 1964 study, about 5% of students used marijuana.

The young college student leaned somewhat nervously against the wall, shifting his weight from one foot to the other, and talked. He talked freely, if haltingly, about why he smokes marijuana.

He talked about being "high" and the sensations of tingling and numbness that being "high" can bring. He talked about a feeling of well-being and an easing of pressures. He frankly admitted that smoking "pot" was an escape for him.

In his use of marijuana, as well as his experiments with other hallucinogens, he certainly is not typical of today's college student. Nor is he representative of a very large segment of today's college campus population.

But neither is he an isolated case, on his campus or on others throughout the country.

There have been incidents of students smoking marijuana that have come to public attention either through school or police action at, most recently, the University of Toledo, New York University, the University of Massachusetts and the University of Colorado and, last year, at Columbia, Brandeis, Cornell and the University of Wisconsin.

Marijuana usually produces a feeling of mild excitation with distortions of time and space. Giggling, reddened eyes, drooping eyelids and a peculiar odor on the breath characterize the habitual user.

There are no withdrawal symptoms from marijuana, which is not a narcotic. A narcotic is generally defined as a chemical that depresses the nervous system and relieves pain.

The students said they saw nothing morally wrong with trying new experiences, since, as one Brandeis student put it, "college is the place where experimentation is encouraged."

The students said that it was a relatively small group that indulged with any frequency. They said there were many others who had tried marijuana "maybe once or twice or so." Their number was estimated at one college at 5 per cent of the student body.

According to one Harvard student, the fact that the inner circle of devotees of "pot" is small makes marijuana relatively easy to obtain.

"To get it," he said, "you need only know someone who knows someone."

"It's the thing to do at college," one Cornell coed explained, though she added she "never really got the hang of it" and never really enjoyed it. She doesn't use it any more, partly because of the eight suspensions there last year and partly because she now associates with a different group.

The group that appears to be most centrally involved in experimentation is the one connected with the creative arts, although by no means is that its boundaries. Some students refer derisively to the users as "beatniks," others, as, "you know, the arty kind."

According to Dr. Graham B. Blaine Jr., psychiatrist to the Harvard and Radcliffe Health Service, the students involved are, for the most part, bright students.

"They are usually the ones who do not feel challenged," he said, "and are looking for something that has more grab and more bite to it. They are apathetic, usually noncommitted, those who are contemptuous of the organization man." ■

APRIL 17, 1964

NEW MUSTANG COMBINES SPORTS AND SEDAN LINES

Joseph C. Ingraham

A promotional photo of a 1964 Ford Mustang convertible.

The Ford Motor Company's new Mustang, a cross between a sports car and a family sedan, will make its debut today in dealers' showrooms after one of the most extensive publicity campaigns in automotive history.

In the opinion of Ford executives, the design and optional features are so flexible that the Mustang is "three cars in one." For the economy buyer the car can be had with a six-cylinder 101-horsepower engine and a minimum of trappings for $2,368, F.O.B. Detroit. With selected options for sporting trim and conveniences the price goes up to about $3,500. With luxury garnishing and a 300-horsepower V-8 racing engine and other extras the bill comes to more than $4,000.

The Mustang is a four-passenger vehicle with bucket front seats, a padded dashboard, carpeting and a three-speed floor-mounted manual gear shift as standard equipment. There are 50 optional accessories, from an outside rear-view mirror at $2.25, to a variety of engines costing up to $438 extra.

The car has a short rear deck and a long hood. It is on a 108-inch wheelbase and the over-all length is 181.6 inches. The height is 51 inches and the width 68 inches.

The Mustang is virtually a technical reproduction of Ford's Falcon Sprint, and one question is whether it will cut more into its sibling than into the competition, as represented by Chevrolet's Corvair Monza and Chrysler's new Barracuda. Even American Motors, apostle of the economy compact, is coming out with a sporty model featuring the sloping roof line that is high automotive fashion now.

There are two models in the Mustang line, the two-door hard-top, at the lower price, and a convertible at $2,587.

Ford officials say the Mustang was built from scratch to be a sports car with initial production pegged at 20,000 a month. The total "launching cost" was set at about $50 million.

The prosperity of the auto industry augurs well for the Mustang, market experts say, in contrast to Ford's ill-starred Edsel, which bowed out when sales were slumping in the fall of 1957.

While sports cars are in demand now, the industry also is wondering what will happen this fall when the 1965 models bow. The biggest changes will be in the standard-size cars that are getting a reported $800 million of styling and mechanical changes. They also will grow three to six inches.

The squared-off slab-sided appearance introduced by Lincoln-Continental reportedly is the new styling concept. Even Cadillac is said to be losing its tail fins after 16 years. ■

MAY 3, 1965

SKATEBOARDS TAKE THE SPOTLIGHT AT WESLEYAN

Bernard Weinraub

MIDDLETOWN, Conn., May 1—After a long, cold winter of Edmund Wilson's lectures on American literature, John Cage's recitals of avant-garde music and Francois Truffaut's new-wave films, the students at Wesleyan University have donned their oldest sneakers, grabbed their skateboards and fled to the outdoors.

Clattering along the campus's sloping, concrete walks, the students confidently decided last week to show their rivals at Williams and Amherst that not all Wesleyans are indoor-types taking such courses as "Study Group in Javanese Gamelan." They invited the two schools over the weekend for "the sporting event of the spring season"—the Little-Three Skateboard Championship.

The sport, a big hit with the 9- and 10-year-olds, had obviously spread to the collegiate set. The students balanced on their flat oak boards mounted on roller skate wheels, weaving in and out of a slalom of two dozen black and red camouflaged beer cans, zipping along walks, gliding around the campus's 19th-century brownstones, moving blithely—and, at times, not too blithely—beneath budding elm trees.

"What Cooperstown is to baseball," Barton Bean, a government major at Wesleyan, remarked soberly yesterday afternoon as shirtless and shoeless students began lining up for the first slalom, "Wesleyan will be for skateboarding. It's obvious!"

"All these Williams and Wesleyan guys can take this stuff so seriously," insisted Chuck Bunting, a 22-year-old Amherst senior. "We all went to bed at 4 in the morning. They probably went to bed at 10."

Seriousness and fervor did not go unrewarded, however, as the Williams team narrowly defeated Wesleyan and won the day's coveted award—a hot dog mounted on an aluminum foil plate.

A spokesman for Wesleyan explained that the hot dog was a symbol, in surfer terms, of expertise and style. The Amherst team, which came in a very poor third, were immediately classed gremis, or beginners.

"O.K., the big event is about to begin," Dave Putnam, Wesleyan, '66, called over a loudspeaker. "First of all, the big hot dogs from Williams."

Scattered applause broke out among the 300 students, teachers, high school girls and coeds (from Smith, Radcliffe and Mount Holyoke) as eight unsmiling skateboarders wearing surfer polo shirts and white pants glided down the 60-foot concrete walk in an overture that reverberated of clattering cans, whirring wheels and screeching turns.

The competition included a slalom (60 yards), a giant slalom (150 yards) and a cross-country (400 yards). A few students even volunteered to perform handstands or gymnastics on the boards.

For the uninitiated and unbiased, it was made immediately clear that the eight-man Wesleyan team had the most finesse, Williams had the most fervor and Amherst the most fun.

The unshaven and sleepy-eyed Amherst crew arrived late, three men and two skating boards short. One member of the team was a bearded 19-year-old Stamford University dropout who remarked that he had stopped in to visit Amherst and was immediately drafted for the sidewalk surfing team.

For several alumni who were on hand, the match was greeted with amusement and just a shade of dismay. Standing near a Gothic-style building on the campus, John Marquand, Wesleyan '62, and a graduate student in medieval history at Harvard, brushed a fleck off his brown tweed sports jacket.

"They certainly don't do this at Harvard," he said, smiling.

The first intercollegiate skateboarding championship at Wesleyan University, 1965.

JULY 24, 1965

G.I. Joe Doll Capturing New Market

Joan Cook

Although it is assiduously promoted as a soldier, "America's Movable Fighting Man," the fact is that Hasbro's increasingly popular G.I. Joe is a doll—a fully jointed, 11-inch-high doll. And as such, it is the first to score with small boys since Raggedy Andy.

In the toy field, as fiercely competitive as the Harvard-Yale game and with considerably higher stakes, G.I. Joe has scored on two counts. It has succeeded with boys despite its generic origin as a doll and, in so doing, has extended what the trade refers to as the "open end concept" in toys.

Translated, this means that in addition to revenue acquired from the original sale of G.I. Joe, cash registers continue to jingle as the money rolls in for a seemingly endless number of accessories.

To stimulate the young to further excess, new ideas are constantly being generated. Among them is the G.I. Joe Club, which attracts 3,000 new members weekly, according to a spokesman for the concern.

For a nominal fee, a member is entitled to a plastic dog-tag imprinted with name, rank and serial number, an iron-on transfer, a wall certificate, a wallet-size identification card, a copy of the monthly newspaper and, last, but not least, a copy of the G.I. Joe catalogue.

Further plans are afoot for a G.I. Joe candy bar, a movie magazine, sneakers and other assorted articles of clothing, including dungarees and a watch. A G.I. Joe comic book is already in existence.

The first to explore the open end concept in depth was Mattel with the introduction of the Barbie Doll. As Barbie's popularity spread, so did her circle of friends to include a Ken Doll, her boy friend; Allan, his sidekick; and Midge, the inevitable girl next door. And so did her and their accessories, with the sales increasing accordingly.

Because G.I. Joe comes in four versions—soldier, sailor, pilot and Marine—the initial sales potential is merely the beginning.

The idea originated in 1962 with Don Levine, Hasbro's vice-president in charge of creativity, and was formally introduced at the 1964 Toy Fair in New York.

The concept took form when Mr. Levine passed an art supply store and saw a sculptor's model figure in the window. Out of this grew the "fully articulated" figure of G.I. Joe. That means it bends.

The face was made up of a composite of 20 Congressional Medal of Honor winners, Mr. Levine said, and the small scar cut into it to give it distinction.

The company is said to have produced more than 2 million G.I. Joes to date and hopes to produce 6 million more before the year is out.

Merrill Hassenfeld, president of Hasbro, which is actually part of Hassenfeld Brothers, Inc., a 50-year-old, family-controlled business, says of his best-selling protégé:

"I have always been a firm believer that there can be no civilization without the soldier. He represents a civilizing rather than a destructive force."

Or, as another executive said with pride, "We have the largest standing army in the world." ■

OCTOBER 2, 1966

NOW THE TIGER WEARS A SEATBELT

Jeffrey O'Connell

President Johnson, signing into law on Sept. 9 the new Highway and Traffic Safety Acts of 1966, said: "The automobile industry has been one of our nation's most dynamic and inventive industries. I hope—and I believe—that its skill and imagination will be able to build in more safety."

On the same occasion, Ralph Nader, the crusading young lawyer who was so instrumental in building public and Congressional support for the new auto safety legislation, expanded on the President's theme: "The auto companies should compete dynamically to give people the maximum safety standards...Vibrant competition will do wonders for highway safety."

Ford and General Motors, meantime, began debating publicly about safety features on their cars. Ford announced that its 1969 models would include collapsible front structures designed to reduce the force generated in collisions. This, in turn, would supposedly reduce the severity of the so-called second collision—between a motorist and the interior of his car. Essentially, a collapsible front end is designed to fold up at a controlled rate, much like an accordion, if a car strikes an object head on.

G.M. disparaged this innovation. Louis G. Lundstrom, director of automotive safety engineering for G.M., said: "A breakthrough in 'front crush control' which might change traffic injuries significantly is not apparent now." He added that regardless of a car's front-end construction, an unbelted motorist in a 30-mile-an-hour crash against an immovable barrier would get no benefit from the collapsing front structure.

The public debate between Ford and G.M. is highly gratifying to the many authorities who believe that our best hope for safer cars lies in open competition among the auto companies over whose models are safest. Safety is a feature in next year's Detroit models. They will have steering columns that telescope on impact; dual braking systems with two hydraulic fluid lines instead of one (so that emergency braking power will remain if one line is damaged); and anchorages for shoulder harnesses for front-seat occupants.

Plans for another prototype safety car were introduced in January of this year at a state-sponsored hearing on auto safety conducted by Iowa Attorney General Lawrence Scalise. According to the car's designer, Dr. Carl Clark, a biophysicist at the Martin Company of Baltimore, Md.,

(cont'd. on next page)

(cont'd. from previous page)
tests have shown that motorists in such a car could survive a 45-mile-an-hour impact into a bridge abutment or a 90-mile-an-hour rear-end collision with another vehicle standing still.

Perhaps the most intriguing and promising feature of Dr. Clark's safety car is its air-bag restraint system—plastic bags inside the car inflate instantly to cushion the car's occupants in the event of a crash. Dr. Clark first developed this restraining device for astronauts. The bags are capable of expanding on impact at about 30 milliseconds (a millisecond is one-thousandth of one second), and thus could restrain motorists after a collision had begun. According to Dr. Clark, Detroit has experimented with air-bag systems but considers them visionary and impractical.

It is Detroit's failure to move fast enough along the safety road that causes most observers to be skeptical about relying heavily on voluntary safety innovations by the industry. There are indications today that the car makers are waiting for this storm to pass. Asked to comment on this year's safety furor, Chrysler's chairman of the board, George A. Love, replied: "I think the public is getting fed up with it. They are getting sick of it as a public political issue." ■

FEBRUARY 23, 1967

LSD SPREAD IN U.S. ALARMS DOCTORS AND POLICE

Gladwin Hill

LSD, or acid, being sold at the second Sky River Rock Festival a rock music and ballooning festival near Tenino, Washington, 1969.

LOS ANGELES, Feb. 22—"We just don't know how to cope with it..."

The speaker was one of the leading psychiatrists who has been battling with the nation's newest scourge: the hallucinatory drug LSD.

His admission of helplessness is seconded by an array of other medical men and law enforcement officers who have watched aghast as the use and depredations of the drug have spread during the last year.

A few months back an LSD victim in Los Angeles, gripped by the horrible psychoses the drug may induce, knew he could stagger to the Neuropsychiatric Institute at the University of California here, where there is 24-hour emergency service for the mentally disturbed.

"But we had to shut the door on him," said Dr. J. Thomas Ungerleider, one of the nation's foremost LSD researchers. "It just became too much. We're basically a teaching institution, and we didn't have enough beds for all these people. Now we just tell them to go to the County Hospital."

"Heaven knows we've got enough cases to study," the white-jacketed psychiatrist said grimly. "We've got an outpatient, huddled in his room near here, who thinks he's an orange, and that if anybody touches him he'll squirt juice."

One LSD expert, Dr. Donald Louria of New York's Bellevue Hospital, guesses that LSD use has extended to "no more than" 1 per cent of the population. That figure would represent 2 million persons—an alarming number, in view of what is becoming known about the drug.

"I don't think it's particularly a West Coast problem," says Dr. Ungerleider. "I think it's more of a national problem—a metropolitan problem. Wherever you have a big city, where conditions are favorable for making and distributing the stuff, I think the problem is about the same."

LSD has been publicized as a compound that essentially just heightens sensory perceptions, often to the point where they are weirdly distorted. This has been depicted as having the beneficial potential of "opening up the mind," even to the extent of awakening latent talents.

Four teen-agers were arrested in Hermosa Beach, near Los Angeles, in mid-January after their car rammed a house, killing a 3-year-old child. The police chief said the driver seemed to be in a trance and kept trying to climb the jail cell wall, yelling, "I'm a graham cracker—oops, my arm crumbled off..."

LSD—lysergic acid diethylamide—is a compound involving one of the principal ingredients of ergot, a fungus that grows on rye.

It can be made by someone with just an elementary knowledge of chemistry—although some of the bad effects may be resulting from unknown extraneous substances that are introduced during the process of amateur manufacture. Pure LSD can have drastic physical effects.

Dr. Ungerleider described its impact as follows:

"LSD has been called a consciousness-expanding drug. In fact it is quite the reverse. It decreases one's ability to select and pay attention. Therefore it decreases conscious functions. Sensations do become intensified. Perception, however, is not enhanced, and visual and auditory acuteness are not revolutionized but rather are distorted."

Burnell Blanchard, Southern California director of the State Bureau of Narcotics Enforcement, painted this picture:

"This LSD problem is a serious one," said Mr. Blanchard, an official of national repute who has been in drug-law enforcement for 25 years. "Our insane asylums are going to be filled if the young people continue to use it." ■

MAY 5, 1967

ORGANIZED HIPPIES EMERGE ON COAST

Martin Arnold

The Haight-Ashbury disctrict in San Francisco, California, the epicenter of the summer of love, 1967.

SAN FRANCISCO, April 30—The hippies are becoming more and more organized. They have two newspapers and a civic association.

If this trend continues the hippies won't be hippies anymore, hippie admirers feel, and this city's Haight-Ashbury section, the hippie capital, will turn into just another East Village in New York.

Villagers are for things: non-involvement in Vietnam and Negro civil rights. Hippies are for nothing. "Why can't I stand on a street corner and wait for nobody? Why can't everyone?"

Or, as Claude Haywood, a married 21-year-old hippie with shoulder length hair, said, "The world is going to chew you up, so why bother? Just wait until it does." Mr. Haywood migrated here from New York four years ago.

They have no malicious intent, but they don't dig the civil rights movement. David Simpson, 26, a hippie who came here from Chicago four years ago, summed it up this way: "The Negroes are fighting to become what we've rejected. We don't see any sense in that."

Haight-Ashbury is a lower middle class section of San Francisco. Its residences are mostly three- and four-story homes that have been converted into apartment houses, as the brownstones were converted in New York.

Most of the area's residents have learned to live with the 15,000 or so hippies for neighbors. But despite the hippies' almost total noninvolvement there are some things hippies do actively like, and these bother not only their neighbors but the San Francisco police as well.

Hippies like LSD, marijuana, nude parties, sex, drawing on walls and sidewalks, not paying their rent, making noise, and rock 'n' roll music.

There are two philosophical trends in hippiedom, and as the hippies become organized, those who adhere to one or the other hippie concept tend to become less tolerant of the other.

The old-line hippies are definitely religious in a general sense. "God is Love," is the basic tenet of their subculture. They whisper that to passersby on the street, are always calm and friendly, and they will demonstrate their love for humanity by throwing flowers at the police who harry them. Flowers and bells are their cross and crown.

But younger hippies have a slightly different "thing" or way of life, which was summed up by one of them this way: "Think what you want, but the number one rule is that you can't force your thing on other people."

"It will take two months before we go through the courts," one staff member said. "We'll have two months of free living. That's part of our thing anyhow. We're teaching people how to survive, be fed and clothed, without having any money."

All pure hippies, both boys and girls, have long and dirty hair. And though many of them work—a number of them are postmen—and have cars, they do not like to pay their bills, so often the water is shut off in their pads, making it difficult for them to wash.

While the hippies insist they love just about everyone, nobody here loves the hippies. But they have become a tourist attraction, and traffic jams are not uncommon in Haight-Ashbury as people drive slowly through the area gawking at the hippies, who have, for example, put dimes in the parking meters and lain in the parking space on the street.

One bus line has put on a daily tourist tour billed as the "Hippie Hop" through the "Sodom" of Haight-Ashbury. ■

JUNE 28, 1967

A DRUG MORE POTENT THAN LSD IN CALIFORNIA

Richard D. Lyons

A new hallucinogenic drug, described as much more powerful than LSD and similar in effect to a secret military nerve gas, is in widespread distribution in California.

The drug, called STP, has caused at least 12 persons to be hospitalized in San Francisco and Ontario, Calif., in the last 10 days. The death of a 25-year-old Ontario man last Sunday is also suspected as having been caused by the new drug.

Those using STP have described it as being a "mega-hallucination" and "the caviar of psychedelics." They said it takes three to four days to "come down" off a dose of STP, as opposed to 8 to 12 hours for LSD.

John Finlator, director of the F.D.A.'s Bureau of Drug Abuse Control, said samples of STP tablets "are being examined by F.D.A. chemists and that so far the analyses show that the chemical configuration is similar to that of certain known materials." He refused to say what those materials were.

An F.D.A. agent in New York said the agency had received scattered reports of STP use here. But he said he doubted that STP was widely used on the East Coast.

"The word has spread among the hippies about STP and some promoters apparently are passing off anything they have as STP when it's some other substance," the agent said.

Dr. Frederick H. Meyers, professor of pharmacology at the University of California Medical Center, San Francisco, stated in a telephone interview yesterday that STP users "can really get wild."

In the last 10 days, Dr. Meyers said, 11 persons have been admitted to San Francisco General Hospital because of STP intoxication.

"They have more excitement and mania on STP than LSD," Dr. Meyers said. "The STP users we have seen have had dilated pupils, rapid pulse, dry mouth and blurred vision and give a good picture of atropine poisoning."

Law enforcement agents familiar with hallucinogenic drugs have been following the activities of Augustus Owsley Stanley 3rd, a grandson of a former United States Senator. Stanley, whose present whereabouts are unknown, is reputed to be a major supplier of both STP and LSD in the United States.

Stanley, 32 years old, who lives in the Haight-Asbury section of San Francisco, was arrested on April 4, 1967, near Putnam Valley, N.Y., on a traffic violation. He was subsequently charged with possession of narcotics and he is now free on bail.

Stanley—he customarily uses only his middle name—is known to be a friend of Dr. Timothy Leary, the psychedelic prophet who is a former lecturer on clinical psychology at Harvard University.

In an interview on television station WNDT on May 31, Dr. Leary said, "LSD is somewhat old hat. There are now currently available in certain larger cities and on certain chemical laboratories, drugs more powerful which last longer than LSD." He did not name the drugs.

The letters STP appear to stem from a motor fuel additive named STP, which means scientifically treated petroleum. Most of those familiar with STP use said the drug started being seen on a wide scale on the West Coast only about a month ago. ■

OCTOBER 20, 1967

PSYCHIATRISTS GET VIEWS OF HIPPIES

Sidney E. Zion

Like so many Clarence Darrows, a handful of hippies charmed, delighted and seemingly convinced a hall full of psychiatrists Wednesday night that their life-style was not only beautiful but good, orderly and sturdy.

The occasion was a scientific meeting of the Society for Adolescent Psychiatry billed as "The Hippie Scene: As Seen by the Hippies." The six hippie panelists drew a packed house of some 500 psychiatrists and their wives and friends at the Alumni Hall of the New York University School of Medicine, at 550 First Avenue.

After three hours of explaining their "thing," it was clear that the four men and two girls had surprised and enchanted the doctors with their articulation, manner and philosophy.

Running directly against the hippie image, the panelists played down drugs ("we have evolved from heavy drug usage to normal, minimal drug usage"), flower power ("a bunch of noise—if a guy hit me, I wouldn't answer him with flowers"), and the Love Generation ("the whole love thing is bull").

"You're not hippies; you've made it," said Dr. Edward Hornick, associate professor of psychiatry at the Albert Einstein Medical College, during the question period from the floor.

"We want to talk to you as elder statesmen of the hippie movement," he asserted. "We have a feeling we're not very close to the teen-agers we're treating. We want you to tell us how we can be of more help."

"Let your hair grow and come on down to the Village and do the thing, come on down and turn on," answered Richie, a long-haired digger, to great applause.

Diggers are hippies who help other hippies and Richie is one of the town's top diggers, having organized the Diggers' Free Store at 264 East Tenth Street, where clothes, food and various knick-knacks are given away.

Throughout the night the panelists emphasized that their society was well-structured, orderly, kind to children and possessed of women devoted to family life in the old style.

"Our biggest desire is to be straight, meaning not being looked down on," said Roger, a beardless hippie with a gentle voice. "Our biggest trip is being interviewed by Time magazine or Hugh Downs. And like a London magazine reporter came to see us and when we told her our ideas she said she couldn't write a story, she said we were normal."

A number of the panelists said they had had bad experiences with psychiatry. Suzie, who is Richie's girl friend, said she first went to a psychiatrist at the age of 17.

"I trust people," she said. "So the psychiatrist told me I've just got to change. So I ran away. When you stop being true to yourself it's something I don't want to be."

When a psychiatrist in the audience suggested that the panelists were sturdy types who did not have to turn to the hippie life, Dr. Gould answered:

"They were not always so sturdy. Some have been in state mental hospitals and have had all kinds of diagnoses and tags placed on them that were very serious.

"Many of us admire them now and even envy them. I hope enough of that has come through tonight so that psychiatrists don't hurriedly apply labels—like schizophrenia—to people. To be different is not to be sick. To understand them is to see it in different terms than pathology."

The applause was explosive. ■

SEPTEMBER 9, 1968

There's Now Miss Black America

Judy Klemesrud

ATLANTIC CITY, Sept. 8—Saundra Williams is a 19-year-old Philadelphian who wears her hair natural, does African dances and helped lead a student strike at her college last spring. She's what the new black woman is all about—and today at 2:45 A.M. she became the first Miss Black America.

The curvy, hazel-eyed coed edged out seven other black beauties in a contest held in the Ritz Carlton Hotel to protest what its sponsors called "the white stereotype" of the Miss America Pageant. The black contest was set for midnight in the hopes that newsmen covering the white pageant four blocks up the Boardwalk in Convention Hall would drop in. Many of them did.

Unlike the watery finale at the Miss America Pageant, the 5-foot-4-inch, 125-pound Miss Williams did not shed a tear when she was crowned. But that did not mean she was not happy.

"This is better than being Miss America," she said after the pageant, still draped in her elaborately beaded cream-colored cape and clutching a red velvet scepter.

"Miss America does not represent us because there has never been a black girl in the pageant. With my title, I can show black women that they too are beautiful, even though they do have large noses and thick lips. There is a need to keep saying this over and over because for so long none of us believed it. But now we're finally coming around."

"My parents are middle-class Negroes," she said, "and I never experienced a bit of discrimination—until I got to Maryland State College."

That occurred when Miss Williams, a sociology major, learned she couldn't eat in a restaurant in Princess Anne, Md., home of the predominantly Negro college. So she helped organize a group of students called The Black Awareness Movement, which staged a "silent protest march" against the white business community.

"That restaurant is integrated now," she said, beaming.

Miss Williams endeared herself to the women in the 300-member audience when, in the question and answer session, she said husbands and wives should do the same amount of housework. "I think the male is getting awfully lazy," she said, drawing boos from the men.

Miss Williams, a member of the National Association for the Advancement of Colored People, said she had been wearing her hair natural a long time before the style became popular among black women.

As Miss Black America, she will receive a one-week vacation to Puerto Rico, a trophy and a modeling contract. But her goal is a career in child welfare and social work, not in modeling.

OCTOBER 20, 1968

'OH, JACKIE, WHY *HIM*?'

Judy Klemesrud

Shipping magnate Aristotle Onassis and Jacqueline Kennedy Onassis on their wedding day Greece, 1968.

Wherever she went, crowds gathered. They screamed "Jackee!" "Jackee!" and she was the closest thing this country has ever had to royalty.

They had many visions of her:

- Jacqueline Kennedy, whose pearls, pillboxes and princess-style fashions were copied by women around the world.
- Jacqueline Kennedy, the most glamorous First Lady since Dolly Madison, entertaining artists, writers and musicians at intimate White House dinners.
- Jacqueline Kennedy, collecting antiques and restoring the White House to its 18th and 19th century elegance.
- Jacqueline Kennedy, charming those two gruff world leaders, Nikita Khrushchev and Charles de Gaulle, during a trip with her husband to Europe.

But what probably endeared her most to them was her profile in courage after the

(cont'd. on next page)

(cont'd. from previous page)
assassination of her husband in Dallas and later at his funeral in Washington. Grasping the hands of her two children on the steps of St. Matthew's Cathedral, she presented to the world a portrait of regal serenity and resolute strength.

And when she walked away into private life, the image lingered on. She was the widow of a slain American President, still young and beautiful, a woman with that amorphous quality known as "style."

She vacationed all over the globe, wore the most expensive clothes, was escorted by handsome, dashing men. And she was worshiped. The American public, she once remarked to a friend, was ready to forgive her anything, "unless I run off with Eddie Fisher."

In the view of some Americans last week, Mrs. Kennedy had "run off" with someone even less likely than Eddie Fisher. It was announced that the former First Lady, now 39, would wed Aristotle Socrates Onassis, the 62-year-old divorced multimillionaire ship owner of Greek ancestry and Argentine citizenship.

It was almost as though an American legend had deserted her people. She had become, instead, a living and breathing woman, choosing for her husband a man old enough to be her father.

There were other things that made the match seem bizarre. He's 5 feet 5 inches tall, she's 5 feet 7. He's a foreigner—a Greek born in Turkey who lived for many years in Argentina. A jet setter. A man with his own island, his own airline and a $3-million yacht that has, among other things, a golden bidet.

In this year of morality backlash, when "law and order" is the rallying cry of the Presidential election, Americans had a hard time coping. Instant jokes were created, such as "Spiro T. Agnew for best man." There was some rejoicing, but usually it was drowned out by louder lamentations.

What irritated most was the age difference. Then came the religious difference (she's Roman Catholic; he's Greek Orthodox) and then the notion that her children might somehow suffer.

"I'm terribly disappointed," said Miss Ann Farber, 70, of the Bronx, a retired bookkeeper. "She could have done better. To us she was royalty, a princess, and I think she should have married a prince. Or at least someone who looked like a prince."

Israel Freedman, 59, of Brooklyn, a chauffeur for Carey Cadillac, shook his head, sighed and said plaintively:

"We're from the working class and she's from the upper class and we don't know what goes on in their heads. Why did she pick him? Maybe she's tired of having Secret Service agents follow her around." ■

DECEMBER 23, 1968

JULIE NIXON WED TO DAVID EISENHOWER

Charlotte Curtis

Former President Eisenhower's only grandson, Dwight David Eisenhower 2nd, and President-elect Richard M. Nixon's younger daughter, Julie, were married yesterday at a dignified but joyous Dutch Reformed ceremony with Quaker touches.

The spirited brunette bride, who once said that she and Mr. Eisenhower were historic enough without having their wedding or reception in the White House, surprised her father by suddenly leaning over and kissing him just after he had given her away in Marble Collegiate Church.

Then she surprised most of the 500 guests by eliminating the kiss the bride and bridegroom usually give one another. But when photographers teased them at a picture-taking session later at The Plaza, the newlyweds finally obliged.

Escorted by her father, the 20-year-old bride walked up the church aisle smiling with her head held high. If her hands quivered, nobody noticed. Her vows were more audible than those of her 20-year-old bridegroom. Friends said he was nervous.

Within 10 minutes after the wedding party, including the 18 smiling attendants, had gathered before him, the Rev. Dr. Norman Vincent Peale, the church's pastor and a Nixon family friend, was pronouncing them man and wife.

Julie, who considers herself a Quaker, asked Dr. Peale and her bridegroom to use the Quaker "thee" and "thou" as a substitute for "you" throughout the service.

The 114-year-old church, with its scarlet, gold and white sanctuary, cranberry-red carpeting, huge green balsam wreaths and masses of red and white Christmas poinsettias, was about as tradi-

President-elect Richard Nixon with his daughter, Julie, before her marriage ceremony to David Eisenhower, in New York City, 1968.

tionally handsome a setting for a wedding as a church can be. Yet its 1,500 seats were only about one-third full.

The Nixons said Julie wanted it that way. Aside from Vice President-elect Spiro T. Agnew and members of Mr. Nixon's Cabinet, there were few major political leaders or internationally recognized personages among the guests. That, too, was the way the bride wanted it.

The only sad note about the wedding was that former President Eisenhower and his wife could not attend. The general was recuperating from several heart attacks, and Mrs. Eisenhower had an upper-respiratory infection. Both were in Walter Reed Hospital.

But they saw the wedding in black and white as it was performed. The National Broadcasting Company televised the service exclusively for them on a closed circuit.

Those invited also included such other intimates as Johnnie Musanto, the man who delivered vegetables to the Nixons when they lived in California; Mr. and Mrs. Manuel Sanchez, the Cuban refugees who work at the Nixons' Fifth Avenue apartment; Thomas E. Dewey, former Governor of New York; and Mrs. Clare Boothe Luce, playwright and widow of Henry Luce, the publisher.

Miss Nixon and the eight bridesmaids wore pale pink silk dresses with round necklines, small puffed sleeves and belts looped through circlets.

The bride's slightly Victorian silk peau d'ange and Belgian lace dress was exactly as she had outlined it last summer. It had a high lace collar with pearl embroidery at the yoke, short puffed sleeves and a flared skirt with a chapel-length train.

The reception was held beneath the crystal chandeliers in the Plaza's gold and white ballroom with its pink and white decorations.

"We feel we are the luckiest parents in the world to get such a son-in-law as David," Mr. Nixon said. "And David is one of the luckiest boys to get such a girl."

The couple have rented a $95-a-month apartment near Smith. Mr. Eisenhower will drive the seven miles to Amherst. ■

FEBRUARY 24, 1962

TEENAGE GIRLS SHOW PREFERENCE FOR BOUFFANT

Mary Burt Baldwin

Bright lipstick was once the badge of becoming a teenager, but today there is a new status symbol: the exaggerated hairdo.

The trend among the younger set has brought a substantial increase in business to beauty salons where teen-agers are regular customers. Hairdressers welcome the new business, parents pay the bill and teen-agers revel in their new-found luxury.

"I come about once a month," a 14-year-old girl said as she watched a stylist set her hair in large rollers in a Manhattan salon. "I started coming about a year ago because this is one of the things teenagers do."

With several variations in the hairdo, one thing is constant: a high, puffed-up effect that is achieved by painstaking teasing. This is a process in which each lock is combed backward until the hair stands straight up. Then it is carefully patted into place without losing any of the height.

Those teenagers who cannot afford salon care amaze older generations by their proficiency in achieving similar results at home. They expertly roll their hair in jumbo rollers and spend up to thirty minutes teasing it into place the next morning.

The most popular style of the moment is the flip. This has the hair teased into a round puffball, swept over to one side and turned up at the ends.

"We all have the flip," a junior at Forest Hills High School said. "It's conformity. We see it on a pretty model and we all copy it."

"If it's not the flip, it's the chemise—that's a bubble with a guiche," another student said. (Translated, this means a high, smooth cap with two cheek curls.)

One private school in the Bronx outlawed beehives as inappropriate for young girls and forbade any style more than two inches high.

Parents, beleaguered by the familiar phrase, "But everyone else is doing it," find it difficult to stop their children from teasing their hair to extravagant proportions.

"What can you do?" one mother asked. "All her friends are doing the same things to their hair—I just try to make her keep it neat." ■

MARCH 28, 1962

Diana Vreeland, Dynamic Fashion Figure, Joins Vogue

Carrie Donovan

Diana Vreeland, the fashion editor of Harper's Bazaar for the last twenty-five years, will become the associate editor of Vogue magazine, its chief rival. The announcement was made yesterday by Jessica Daves, editor-in-chief of Vogue. Miss Daves said that the position had been newly created and that Mrs. Vreeland would work with the staff on all editorial aspects of the magazine.

The announcement of Mrs. Vreeland's new position ends a period of speculation within the magazine industry, which is undergoing drastic changes in many directions.

Although unknown to the public except as a name on the masthead of Harper's Bazaar over the years, Mrs. Vreeland is the most respected editor in the fashion business today. Her appearance at a fashion show is the highest accolade a designer can hope for. Along with the late Carmel Snow, editor-in-chief of Harper's Bazaar, Mrs. Vreeland is credited with shaping the image of the magazine and, in turn, the look of thousands of women.

Her own taste and fashion theories and her uncanny sense of discerning a fashion trend at its inception seeped into every page. Her fashion forecasts were often so avant-garde that they appeared bizarre to the magazine's readers. Her prophecies were usually right, however.

Fashion editor Diana Vreeland in the Vogue magazine offices, New York, 1966.

"The reader is the only person who counts and she knows a lot about fashion. I hope that what is stimulating to me will stimulate and interest her," Mrs. Vreeland said.

Mrs. Vreeland prefers to stay in the background of fashion, yet her fame has spread far and wide in the business, making her probably its most colorful personality. Her appearance is so dynamic, her manner of dressing and speaking so unusual, that she is viewed with a combination of awe and astonishment.

Her way of walking has been described as resembling a camel's gait. Her face with flat planes, brown eyes, a generous mouth and strong, aquiline nose has been compared to that of a cigar store Indian. Her colorful manner of speaking is part of the legend. Fixing the listener with a steady gaze, she rolls out declarative sentences in a booming voice that has an electrifying effect on the people around her. Outrageous as some of her utterances sometimes sound, they invariably have the effect of stimulating creative persons to new heights.

At least one word in every sentence is emphasized. A designer tells of the time he showed Mrs. Vreeland a swatch of bright pink silk of Eastern influence.

"I ADORE that pink!" she exclaimed. "It's the navy blue of India!"

Mrs. Vreeland sees the fashion editor's job today as that of encouraging and directing American women to express their own individuality within the current fashion pattern.

"And a woman should put more money into keeping fit," she said. "She should take care of herself. Get the right amount of sleep. It's her physical health that the world sees." ■

FEBRUARY 6, 1963

EXCITING FASHIONS IN ST. LAURENT'S NEW COLLECTION; BALENCIAGA'S SHOW ONE OF HIS BEST

Jeanne Molli

PARIS, Feb. 4—The French world has come to rest on the slender shoulder of Yves St. Laurent. He carries it with ease. All through couture week in Paris, the fashion professionals wait to see what St. Laurent will do. His is the last showing and the last word. This morning's collection proved once again that the young designer can surpass all the high hopes that are anxiously stored in him.

St. Laurent has curbed his bent for irresistible folly. There was no blithe madness in his spring designs. Women need not wonder for an instant whether they dare to wear his new designs. He has given them the cake of fashion excitement and the smooth penny irreproachable style.

(cont'd. on next page)

(cont'd. from previous page)

St. Laurent had no quarrel with the short hemline, but he sensed that it was time to put an end to the sleeveless dress. Other designers, including the infallible Givenchy, have tried and failed to bend the stubborn bare arms. St. Laurent did it in two ways—a short curved sleeve over the shoulders and a long cuffed sleeve just above the wrist. He remained true to his long lithe silhouette, but varied his smock top dresses of last season with narrow shirtwaist dresses, jumpers or body skimming shifts. Navy blue with touches of white pervaded the collection.

St. Laurent's dresses were excellent—the strongest point of the show. The cover-up dress at times was a long jumper with contrasting long cuffed sleeves. By evening the contrasting sleeves might be of embroidered lace or beading. The narrow dress with curved short sleeves was shaped close to the body with subtle seams. Silks were muted with blackened reds and shadings of browns and beige.

Balenciaga also showed today although the press is not admitted until the end of the month. But the buyers who saw the collection called it one of the best this great designer had ever done.

"There were no radical departures, nor did we expect them," one buyer said. "He gave us beautiful clothes with never a dull moment, and that's what we come to him for."

"A show at Balenciaga is worth a trip to Paris," another remarked. ■

MAY 12, 1963

BOOTS MAKE A SPLASH

Leonard Sloane

Boots, a seemingly unlikely prospect for fashion honors in the women's shoe industry, are making a big splash in the marketplace.

Although boots made an impact in the European fashion world as long ago as the late nineteen-fifties and a few fashion shoe designers and salons here took up the banner shortly afterward, it wasn't until last fall and winter that boots reached the American market in volume. The impression they made on the consumer was so great that they are even being sold to some extent for spring and summer. And the outlook for the coming fall is for the best boot season in history.

The transformation of boots from bulky, strictly functional foul-weather gear to an item in milady's wardrobe for both indoors and outdoors is one of the more important shoe fashion stories since modern shoe-making was born in 1862. Spurred by industry promotion of the boot, fashion-conscious women throughout the country became aware of this addition to the footwear line and gave boots a big acceptance. Within a few months, this category of women's shoes was prominently displayed by shoe stores and department stores everywhere.

Today boots are manufactured in a wide variety of materials, styles, lengths and heel heights. In addition to warmth and protection, they offer the opportunity for women to add a touch of the sporting or dashing look to their clothing.

"Boots used to be bought for function, now they are bought for fashion," Saks Fifth Avenue says. The shoe buyer for another major Fifth Avenue store notes, "Every girl in New York is going to have a pair of boots this year. Possibly instead of buying another pair of shoes, she'll buy boots. Of course, we hope she'll buy both."

As a part of this revolution in boots, designers have introduced boots that can be worn with furs as well as with swimsuits, with jewels as well as with jodhpurs.

Manufacturers, who might naturally be expected to wax eloquent about any new fashion trend that sells well, have every reason to be happy about the 1962-63 season. Herbert Levine, a manufacturer of high-fashion women's shoes, sold 4,000 pairs of boots last year in the $50 to $85 range, compared with 400 in 1961. By November 1962, he expects to sell another 6,000 boots, which will retail at $45 to $75 because of the expected increase in volume.

Golo, another leader in the fashion boot field whose shoes are sold at Lord & Taylor and other stores, reports that orders for this fall are 15 to 25 percent higher than last year. The company says boot orders from retailers are so heavy that they cannot all be filled.

DECEMBER 14, 1963

ACTRESS HAS INFLUENTIAL FASHION ROLE

Bernadine Morris

One of the most influential fashion figures of the last decade, Audrey Hepburn is the film star most women would like to emulate. Her hairdos, her style and her Givenchy clothes are widely admired. She represents a new breed of motion picture idol—scrubbed, well-groomed and neat, with no flamboyant fox coats or daring décolletages to support the image.

After her first big success, in "Gigi," the play based on Colette's novel, she told an interviewer that she did not own a fur coat and did not want one. Today, as one of Hollywood's top-salaried stars, she has a mink.

"But I never wear it on the outside," she explained. "It's a lining."

It forms the cozy interior of a raincoat by Hubert de Givenchy, the Paris couturier, which she wore earlier this week walking her Yorkshire terrier in Central Park in the snow.

Miss Hepburn discovered Givenchy in 1958. He had opened his salon the year before and was much talked about as an exciting new talent. She had convinced her studio that she should have a Paris wardrobe for her role in "Sabrina," and had gone to Givenchy. Today he occupies a role in the couture world equivalent to hers in the world of films.

His clothes for Miss Hepburn in such films as "Funny Face," "Love in the Afternoon," "Breakfast at Tiffany's" and the new release "Charade" have been one of the attractions of the films.

The shallow, wide, squared-off neckline for a dress in the first film has been called a "Sabrina" neckline on Seventh Avenue ever since.

Comfort in clothes is most important to her, and she finds all of Givenchy's clothes comfortable, never tight or awkward. The closest fit is in the bodices of evening dresses, "but they are still comfortable."

She believes good proportions are the secret of good clothes.

"I prefer very plain clothes, very uncluttered. I don't like distracting details. I like very simple gloves, shoes (mine are always low-heeled and made by Mancini in Paris) and hats. Nothing should take away from the basic line of the clothes.

"I like to wear very little jewelry for the same reason. It should never look as if the woman is wearing it to show off that she has it. I like jewelry best after 6 P.M." ■

Audrey Hepburn in the iconic black dress she wore in the opening sequence of "Breakfast at Tiffany's," 1961.

JUNE 3, 1964

Young Designers Set Pace in Britain

Bernadine Morris

In a burst of creativity that is reverberating beyond their own shores, British designers are producing a new breed of fashion. It is young, exuberant and occasionally zany. The clothes are worn by young people, often with a sense of pride in their rebelliousness, and most of the creators of the designs are under 30 years of age.

The vitality of their designs is having a rejuvenating effect on traditional British fashions, applauded in the past for superb fabrics and tailoring, and is winning a following across the channel and across the Atlantic.

"All of a sudden, we have become aware of a change in classic British clothes," said Gertrude Ziminsky, coat and suit buyer for Altman's, who has just returned from a buying trip to London. "The fabrics were always wonderful, but now the styling is younger and softer and not as dowdy as it used to be."

Ohrbach's knowledgeable coat and suit buyer, Sydney Gittler, who inspected British ready-to-wear for the first time in seven years this spring, reported that the clothes "look better, are styled better and have more elegance" than they did previously.

British fashions have always had a place in American stores because of the built-in customer acceptance of British tweeds, classically styled and suitable to life in the country. But in recent seasons, American store buyers have been aware of a new fashion force.

Mary Quant is the designer who is credited with transforming the British fashion image. She opened a shop in Chelsea in 1957, where she initiated the off-beat designs that came to be known as the Chelsea look. Fabrics were purposely mismatched, waistlines were very high or very low, colors were often violent, and hemlines of both jackets and skirts curved up in front. By 1960, she began designing clothes for a manufacturing concern, thereby disseminating the look far beyond Chelsea.

"She broke ground for the rest of the designers," said Louise Constantine, buyer for the Young New Yorker department at Lord & Taylor, which carries the Mary Quant clothes in New York.

"She gave the other kids courage to do what they liked. And the clothes are bound to get better as the youngsters get more experience. They have a rebellious quality in their designs, which appeals to the young people here as well." ■

British fashion designer Mary Quant, 1964.

JANUARY 31, 1965

GERNREICH'S PROGRESS; OR, EVE UNBOUND

Gloria Steinem

"A fashion," said George Bernard Shaw, "is nothing more than an induced epidemic." If that is so, the carriers of the moment are no longer the basic-black ladies of Park Avenue, or the tweedy post-debutantes in good little suits, or even the Hollywood queens of glamour and the tight fit.

The new *doyennes* of fashion are coltish, leggy, lank-haired and, most of all, young. They are the champions of Pop Art, *discothèques* and François Truffaut; the ones with enough nerve to wear suede evening pajamas or skirts that ride three inches above the knee, enough bosom to push up into a Renaissance neckline (but not enough to keep a Poor Girl sweater from looking poor), and enough in common with their European counterparts to make it impossible to tell (at least until they open their mouths) whether they were born in the Faubourg St.-Germain, Chelsea or the Upper East Side.

They don't watch Diana Vreeland; Diana Vreeland watches *them*. And then she reports or adapts or modifies their fashions in Vogue (as do the editors of Harper's Bazaar and Elle and Queen), where the slightly older ladies of fashion can see and snap them up. "Everybody," explained a Seventh Avenue manufacturer, "wants to look young now. About well-bred, they couldn't care less."

The American designer most responsible for this desertion of the ladylike—and the revolt against "traditional" Paris styles—is a Vienna-born Californian named Rudi Gernreich. Best-known outside the fashion world as the inventor of the Topless Bathing Suit and the No-Bra Bra, the fact is that for more than 10 years Gernreich has been producing a line of sportswear (which means, in fashion parlance, pretty much everything except wedding dresses and ball gowns) that has attracted an enthusiastic following among sleek young women on both coasts. His trademarks are simplicity of line, unusual fabrics, knock-'em-dead color combinations, unexpected glimpses of bare skin (in dresses as well as bathing suits) and an unbound, fluid look that suggests that the lady might be wearing nothing underneath. He perfected a see-through blouse, shortened skirts and made much of the Jean Harlow neckline.

The topless bathing suit was last year's most notorious fashion concoction. Photographs of the suit worn by Gernreich's favorite model, Peggy Moffitt—though taken from the back or with arms strategically crossed—were picked up by press and television all over the world. The costume was promptly banned by the Pope, and some towns along the Riviera threatened that wearing it would bring "legal repercussions."

Life and NBC-TV photographed public reaction to the sight of the topless on a department store dummy: most women, it was discovered, instinctively covered their breasts with their hands the moment they saw it. Several publicity-seeking starlets wore the suit to the beach and were promptly carted off by the police. When the furor was over, some 3,000 suits had been sold and it was clear that Gernreich's life would never be quite the same again.

Gernreich, whom Vogue has described as "remarkably quiet for all the crackle of his clothes...a shadowy figure," gave a few interviews, answered none of the letters, basked in the limelight briefly and then escaped for a rest to the forests of Finland.

Looking back on it, though, Gernreich has no regrets: if he had it all to do over again, he would. "I thought we'd sell only six or seven, but I decided to design one anyway.

"A designer stands or falls on the totality of each year's collection, not just one item. At the moment, this topless business has done nothing but take time away from my work, but in the end, I'm sure having my name known internationally will be a help. But that isn't why I'd do it again. I'd do it again because I think the topless, by overstating and exaggerating a new freedom of the body, will make the moderate, *right* degree of freedom more acceptable."

As for the future of fashion, Gernreich has no definite predictions. He feels that his designs change slowly; they evolve. "I don't like sudden change," he explained. "I don't even know what my future direction will be. It just *happens*."

AUGUST 4, 1965

College Girls Vote the Conservative Ticket—in Fashion

Angela Taylor

Who starts all those fashion fads that are supposed to be rampant in American colleges?

"Not us," say the college girls who are staffing the campus shops of department stores around town. "It's the high school kids."

Despite the general jazziness of the clothes shown during August in magazines and store windows, college girls consider themselves a pretty conservative lot. They spend their money carefully on tried-and-true fashions that will see them through four years.

The mixed-up prints, the expensive bell-bottom pants and the wildly patterned stockings are being bought by either teenagers or older career girls, the college sales clerks are noticing. As for themselves, they'll stick with last year's "poor" sweater, "wheat" jeans and A-line skirts.

"We want classics that will last," said Deirdre Henderson, Vassar '67. "We watch the fads, of course, but wait until they're a sure thing before we buy them."

Bell-bottoms, pea jackets and turtleneck sweaters are "super," "groovy" or "fab-gear" (synonyms for great), but the girls prefer the inexpensive, authentic kind bought in Army and Navy stores to the fancy ones dreamed up by sportswear manufacturers at several times the price.

They would be happier in skirts at mid-knee but feel they can't fight the trend for short. And if the girls are conservative, the men in their lives are downright reactionary.

"Boys hate patterned stockings, even the sheer ones," said dark-haired Barbara O'Connell, Wellesley '66.

Boots, all the girls agreed, are for cold weather only—"you get kidded a lot otherwise."

The Courrèges look so widely copied in the young market has perhaps a year to go, according to the group.

"We still like it, it's neat and comfortable," explained Mary Short, St. Joseph's '66. "But it's being overdone."

The British Mod influence? "Too grandstandish." Knee socks versus long stockings? "Nobody wears knee socks at Penn." Hats? Never, unless it's freezing, then a knitted cap or bonnet. "Sou'westers are great for rain," added Dana Rosen of Altman's, who is Bryn Mawr '68.

How about the thrift-shop look that Barbra Streisand made popular?

"We admire her as a singer, but not her ugly chic," explained Cornelia (Corki) Van Kleech, Wellesley '66, of the Stern's college staff.

The pierced-ear fad, which the girls thought was begun by teen-agers, is big in the East and traveling westward quickly. "I like them, you don't have to worry about losing them," said Corki.

Ear-piercing is a do-it-yourself operation in most dormitories, although the colleges are sometimes encouraging the girls to go to the staff doctor.

New fads coming up? Oriental seem to be in the lead. "My sister bought a sari at the World's Fair and wore it to her high school prom," Dana related.

"Be-yoo-ti-ful," chorused all eight girls. "Burnooses are coming in at Vassar," contributed Deirdre and got another four-syllable "beautiful"—which is the only way to pronounce it in collegese. ■

FEBRUARY 23, 1966

EVERYTHING'S COMING UP PUCCI

Enid Nemy

Designer Emilio Pucci, 1966.

The distinctive Pucci type of print is one of the strongest fashion statements brightening the tag end of winter.

Some of the prints now being shown on almost every floor of department stores are originals, designed in a Florentine palazzo and bearing the "Emilio" signature. But, more often than not, they are a strong and moderately priced echo.

The growing number of Pucci-influenced items has apparently done nothing to dampen the ardor of true aficionados.

"The more they make, the better ours look," said a representative of Jana Accessories, the concern that makes the official Pucci handbags and accessories.

On the other hand, Herbert Meyers, an executive of the Meyers Manufacturing Company, says his company's print bags, strongly reminiscent of Pucci, are "quite a phenomenon—selling well across the country and accounting for probably 25 per cent of our business.

"We would hope that these handbags won't be worn with print dresses. They are meant for plain linens and silks."

Women who wear the authentic Pucci silk jerseys pay from $140 to $170 for them.

One of the few areas left virtually untouched is the children's market. But at Rue des Enfants, the two partners—Sheila Marks and Linda Goldberg—have designed a hooded lounging outfit in Pucci-inspired fabric "for sophisticated children of sophisticated mothers."

AND NOW IT'S TWIGGY'S TURN

Gloria Emerson

LONDON—Twiggy is a 17-year-old British model who drops her h's, when she speaks at all. Twiggy earns at least $180 a day, which is considerably more than Harold Wilson, the Prime Minister, takes home. She is the successor to Jean Shrimpton, the blue-eyed British beauty whose blank look helped make her one of the most successful and richest models in the world. The Shrimp is still a star in London, but it is Twiggy's turn now.

Fashion model Twiggy in 1967.

Paris-Match has just acclaimed her. Elle magazine has used her on its cover. British fashion editors want to see more and more of Twiggy on their pages.

Right at Twiggy's angular little elbow—shooting up with her every inch of the way—is a 27-year-old Londoner who calls himself Justin de Villeneuve.

He is Twiggy's manager and mouthpiece. He discovered her 19 months ago, persuaded her to be a model, and now charts the long course ahead that she will take. There are offers coming at him from every direction. American Vogue would love to photograph Twiggy.

"But we've said no, we are not ready for New York," Justin said. "Twiggy has been the top model here for just three weeks and won't be ready until March." Twiggy shivers at the thought of going to New York in the winter.

"The sun's out, is it? Oooh, I dig that," she said. "Do I want to see New York? Dunno. I'm frightened. I won't like it. I'll miss mum and dad."

She is 5 foot 7 and her measurements are 32-22-32. Twiggy is not plump.

The model agencies in London, who resent the fact that she has a manager, call her a "phenomenon." They must say something because they have all been insisting the day of the pin-thin, offbeat looking girl is over, and Twiggy is exactly that.

Twiggy was launched last February when The Daily Express called her the face of 1966. Now Justin is worried—as 1967 draws near—that Twiggy might depreciate like a car. But he pulls himself together in those dark moments and rationally says that Twiggy has a good five years to go as the top girl.

Twiggy, whose real name is Leslie Hornby, still lives with her parents in a small house in Neasden, North London. Mr. Hornby builds television sets and was the one who thought of making Twiggy a limited company. Twiggy's parents trust Justin with their little girl and believe that he really has her interests at heart.

"An agent in America wanted her to take elocution lessons—offered her a lot of money if she would," Justin said. "Well, I said, 'I'm sorry, but we dig her the way she is.'" ■

DECEMBER 4, 1966

MINISKIRTS RAISE RETAILING EYEBROWS

Isadore Barmash

The miniskirt, the most important British import since the Beatles, has created a furor both in the apparel industry and among men who have at least normal vision.

What are miniskirts? Webster's Third New International doesn't define them, but the miniskirt is mostly a no-waistband skirt, or an A-line style, a "hipster" item (it sits on the hips) and has a belt of either matching fabric or leather.

These traits, however, are not what makes the miniskirt remarkable. It is the length, or more precisely, its lack of length.

The miniskirt often stops alarmingly at 4 inches above the knee. Recently, it has even been inching up to about 5 inches above the knee. This dimension's effect on the viewer is what causes men to stop and stare on crowded streets or creates disconcerting situations in the subways or draws curious groups when miniskirted women board taxis.

But, in the apparel industry, the truncated skirt has become both big business and a source of debate that will probably rage for some time.

The short-short skirt has assumed such proportions in sales of sportswear that industry sources predict that it will spread—and already is beginning to spread—to dresses, shifts, culottes, pants suits, coats, and even miniskirts to go over swimwear.

Despite the style's sweeping success at a time when its impact is beginning to lessen in England, the miniskirt's mother country, apparel makers in the United States are troubled by the protests of schools and even some church authorities.

As a result, numerous producers are reluctant to go off the deep end with the miniskirt, but are offering instead a modified form of the style. Crazy Horse Fashions, Inc., has not sold a regular-length skirt for almost a year, according to Larry Robbins, executive vice president, but has compromised by producing a "top of the knee" length.

"If fashion dictates that we get into the miniskirt," Mr. Robbins said, "we will, of course, go along. But the thigh-length styles appear to us to be both impractical and tending to make the wearer look promiscuous."

But a sharp exception to the "modified" concept was expressed by executives of Arnold Constable, Inc. This Manhattan-based chain of specialty stores recently embarked on a program appealing to the more youthful customer.

Arnold Constable is strongly behind the real thing, the unmodified miniskirt that zooms 5 inches above the knee.

"We think that the miniskirt is right at that length," declared Rea Lubar, vice president for sales promotion. "We think our customers, largely a young group, want the skirt at that length."

Miniskirts, the shortest version, are much in demand with younger girls, while virtually women of all ages want shorter skirts than in past seasons. Many reflect, with envy, their desire to look as young as possible, but recognize that wearing the pure miniskirt requires a strong dash of courage, not to mention good legs and a good figure.

The real effect of the miniskirt, outside of its impact on male viewers, is the excitement it has caused among consumers. It has greatly influenced the styling of other garments, even fur coats, and probably will result in the setting up of separate "Mini Shops" by numerous department and specialty stores in prime traffic locations on their floors.

Those who espouse it most among retailers and producers predict that the style's sales this spring will hardly be of "mini" proportions.

Models wearing four variations on the mini skirt, London, 1967.

APRIL 14, 1967

Would You Know A Djellaba From a Caftan?

Angela Taylor

What's a djellaba? A djiba? A caftan? A burnoose? Regine Wacht, a designer who makes all these garments, would like to set the record straight.

Mrs. Wacht, born in Marrakesh, Morocco, and married to Rennold Wacht, a New York real estate executive, showed her first collection of these designs in her Arabian Nights apartment on upper Fifth Avenue yesterday.

A djellaba is a long, loose dress, buttoned only from neck to waist, said Mrs. Wacht, and usually has a hood. A caftan is similar, but buttons all the way down and is worn either as a coat or a dress. The djiba is a kite-shaped, slip-on garment, with loose sleeves cut in one piece with the body. It is usually worn by men, sometimes with the arms inside—"it's cooler that way." The burnoose is a flowing cape with a hood. It fastens only at the throat.

"People are always misusing the words," she added, brushing back her long dark hair, which fell to the shoulders of her loop-buttoned, brocade caftan.

Along with djellabas, caftans, djibas and burnooses in embroidered crepes, gold and silver brocades and cut velvets, Mrs. Wacht introduced some even rarer garments.

There were hmidou (houseboy) pants—short, puffy bloomers of gold-embroidered gauze worn over pink or chartreuse body stockings. These were inspired by the livery of child servants in the Moroccan court, she said.

And then there were variations of a garment worn by the street acrobats in Morocco. These were straight, high-necked tunics over pants. An important feature was a triangular pocket just under the neckline.

"People drop in their coins," the designer said. "The acrobats are not considered beggars. They are orphans, who are trained as children to perform."

The styles in the collection will cost from $175 to about $900 when they get to stores. ■

AUGUST 6, 1967

HIPPIES BRIGHTEN BRITISH SUMMER

Dana Adams Schmidt

Hippies at Speaker's Corner in Hyde Park during a Legalize Pot rally in 1967.

LONDON, Aug. 5—The center of the young fashion world has been shifting from Carnaby Street to King's Road in Chelsea, which is a great place for parading. But in recent days—hot by British standards—many of the young hippies and their hangers-on migrate to the cool greenery of the parks where one can display clothes or just relax in the sun.

The migration has been especially noticeable since the "flower people" held a demonstration in Hyde Park recently to demand the legalization of "pot," or marijuana. Since then advocates of legalized marijuana have bought a full-page ad in The Times of London, and some knowledgeable people are predicting that "pot" will be legal in Britain in five years.

Meanwhile, smoking "pot" is the "in" thing for the young, and even in the park the faint, sweet smell has been known to drift from huddled groups on the grass. It is scarcely recognized among the family strollers, the picnickers and the boys fishing on the banks of the Serpentine.

The "flower people" are the first American influence since Elvis Presley to make a significant impact on youthful mores in this country, which is said to have originated long hair for boys and miniskirts.

However, the British, as observed in the parks this summer, are still setting trends of their own. Long, long hair is no longer quite the thing in London, though it is still worn long by American standards. Miniskirts are shorter than ever. Girls are wearing their hair either in short tight curls or long with bangs.

Satin jackets and shirts with frills all the colors of the rainbow are the rage for both boys and girls, along with the costumes, especially uniforms, of the past. Boys appear in outfits that could be guards' or hotel bellboys' uniforms, and girls wear their great-grandmothers' lace.

Flowers and bells are sometimes added, in accordance with the California model. One youth was seen walking in Hyde Park recently with a whole plant on his head.

While the girls vie for attention with ever shorter shirts, the emphasis is really on the male. London was always a man's town.

Typical of the trend is a model agency called "English Boy," which aspires not merely to provide male fashion models but to "change the image of British manhood" and put the boy, as opposed to the girl, on the magazine cover of the future.

The agency's 12 young male models pride themselves on being the opposite of the traditional square-jawed, pipe-smoking, hair-on-the-chest model. They are lean in the Twiggy style and look as though they need a good night's sleep. They don't smile.

The founder and manager of this organization is Sir Mark Palmer, 24 years old, who attended Eton and spent a year at Oxford, but appears determined to forget it.

One day recently he wore a soft, green, wide-brimmed velour hat, a lime-green crepe shirt with floppy sleeves, a bright green jacket, green plaid trousers and emerald-green shoes.

The clothes his "English boys" model are frequently sold in a Chelsea shop called Hung on You, from which they spread to King's Road and the parks, adding a gentle zest to Britain's summer madness. ■

APRIL 25, 1968

GORGEOUS GEORGE, SCRUMPTIOUS SAM & BROS.

Russell Baker

WASHINGTON, April 24—Men's fashions are now more exciting than women's. The Nehru jacket, the turtleneck shirt, thigh-gripper slacks, pastel pumps, beads, earrings, spit curls, bangs, Paisley underwear, Pucci sweaters—all are now becoming everyday apparel for the middle-class male.

Men are rapidly discovering, however, what women used to take as a matter of course—namely, that while it is wonderful to be gorgeous, it can also be agonizing. As recently as last year men were still going out to parties and dinners with nothing more to dread than the possibility that they would be dressed differently from all the other men in the room.

"Gosh," you apologized, if you arrived in a tuxedo and found all the other men in their blue pinstripes, white button-down collars and regimental stripes, "nobody told me not to dress."

Nowadays all that is changed. On the night of the big party, the husband goes upstairs two hours beforehand to begin his final preparations. He has already spent the afternoon in the barber chair under a hot hairnet getting his bangs set. Now he must lave his pelt in rich creamy suds, treat it with powerful deodorant ("not recommended for women") and splash cologne on his neck and wrists.

Out of the closet comes his new wardrobe. The price was outrageous, of course, and his wife will be furious when she finds out. When will women begin to understand about men's clothes?

After an endless wait by the wife, who keeps calling to ask if he is going to take all night to dress, he emerges in a stunning new saffron Nehru jacket, powder-blue turtleneck, mustard thigh-grippers and lime suede pumps, "How do I look?" he asks.

"You'll be the most beautiful man at the party," his wife says, and seizing him impulsively, gives him a warm kiss.

"Careful," he says, "you'll crush my turtleneck."

Well, imagine the psychic agony of each of eight or ten men as they approach this party. Imagine the humiliation of this particular husband when he walks in and discovers another man wearing not only the very same powder-blue turtleneck but also the same mustard thigh-grippers.

"I don't think you've ever looked more beautiful, Sam," says Cynthia. "That cologne you're wearing is bewitching, Pete," says Mary.

The women, of course, are merely being polite, and after flattering the husbands they will all congregate in one corner to talk about grocery prices and the school problem, while the men are left to themselves.

At dinner the wives break their conversation about ponderous affairs to josh the men good-naturedly about being foils of the fashion czars. "Why do you men let a handful of tyrants on Seventh Avenue make you throw out all your old wardrobes and buy new ones every six months?" they ask.

"Why are you women such slaves to dreary old convention?" the men retort. "Every generation, year in and year out, you all buy the same thing—dresses."

At dinner's end, everyone rises. The men withdraw to the host's bedroom to freshen their cologne. The women retreat to the library to discuss taxes over brandy and cigars.

APRIL 28, 1968

Topless, and No Bottoms, Either

Marylin Bender

Monique Van Vooren, the Belgian actress, international sex symbol and theatrical investor, has declared her intention of wearing her new, transparent chiffon blouse by Yves Saint Laurent to the Broadway opening of "Hair" tomorrow evening. If Miss Van Vooren follows through, there will be nothing (such as a bra or a body stocking) standing between her and any other first-nighters who happen to be looking at her.

However, if attention is what Mrs. Van Vooren hopes to attract, she's bound to be disappointed. Vogue and Rudi Gernreich, the California designer of monokini fame, have already endorsed the nipple as a high fashion accessory. And after the exposure by actresses in movies and Off Broadway plays of the 1960's, what's to shock in the sight of a bare female breast?

Besides, as tomorrow's audience already knows from previewers' word of mouth and skillfully planted gossip-column items, the first act of the rock musical ends with several healthy young men facing front and center in the altogether. Just how many stark naked males there are and whether the girl hippies are equally unclothed had been the subject of urgent dispute among those who have been attending previews of "Hair" during the last three weeks.

If the audience is as confused as eyewitnesses to a street-corner murder, it's for good cause. The finale is played in near-darkness with much of the cast writhing under a flower-printed sheer blanket before presenting themselves upright.

"Hair" started out last October as the first offering of Joseph Papp's Public Theater in the restored Astor Library down on Lafayette Street. The musical was favorably received as an honest if somewhat gangling presentation of the decade's alienated youth, with their drugs, unkempt hairdos, anti-Vietnam and anti-bourgeois sentiments and their liberated attitudes toward sex and color.

Last December, "Hair" moved uptown to Cheetah, a psychedelic, soft-drink, rock dance palace with theater attached. Michael Butler, scion of a Chicago tribe of millionaires involved with paper, aviation and real estate, had signed on as co-producer. Then Mr. Butler decided that with luck and a quarter of a million dollars he could propel "Hair" onto Broadway.

For the new production, its creators have made "Hair" yippier, more trenchantly topical about race, politics and war. And, of course, more explicitly physical and profane. And then there are those fleeting nudists in the first act finale.

During the previews the number of nudes has varied from performance to performance, not just because of revisions in text and direction but because of the time it takes to loosen actors' inhibitions.

"You have to get rid of a couple of hang-ups. I didn't do it the first couple of nights, but then I realized how groovy it could be," said Shelley Plimpton, a 21-year-old brunette who looks like a 12-year-old Alice in Wonderland. Her back is to the audience anyway.

"I'd love to [take my clothes off] but I haven't been asked to," said Sally Eaton, 21, who plays a pregnant flower child. "I suppose it might be a little too much like the National Geographic."

But is it really necessary? Or is it just a gimmick to drag in the Broadway bourgeoisie so they can be épaté-ed? ■

JANUARY 8, 1969

GIRLS IN PANTS AREN'T SENT TO THE PRINCIPAL'S OFFICE ANY MORE

Angela Taylor

When two 15-year-olds turned up wearing pants at the all-girl Washington Irving High School last fall, they spent the day in the dean's office. This week, Laura Caplin and Lauren Clausen, both sophomores, are freely attending classes in slacks. And so are 25 percent of their schoolmates.

Laura and Lauren don't look the suffragette type, they're slender and fragile-looking in their sweaters and pants. But they are the heroines of a dust-up that has clarified the standing of the pants-wearing girl in the New York high schools.

After Laura's disciplinary day on Nov. 25, she told her mother, Mrs. Ramona Ripston, co-director of the National Emergency Civil Liberties Committee. Although Dr. James E. Allen Jr., the state Commissioner of Education, had ruled in 1966 that school officials did not have the power to compel students to wear a particular kind of dress, Laura and her classmates said they were continually harassed by teachers unless they wore skirts.

Complaints filed against Gerard N. Oak, the school's principal, by the New York Civil Liberties Union and the National Emergency Civil Liberties Committee resulted in a letter last week to Mr. Oak from Superintendent of Schools Bernard E. Donovan. Dr. Donovan's letter pointed out that Dr. Allen's rule about school dress was still in effect.

So the girls of Washington Irving, which is at 40 Irving Place, are now moving freely through the corridors in everything from wide-legged "elephant" pants to run-of-the-mill blue jeans.

"They're warm," Christine Wall, a sophomore, said of her brown wool pants.

"Comfortable," added Judy Velasquez, a junior, in striped elephant pants.

"Better than tearing your dresses," commented Denise Lifsey, who was wearing a jump suit.

"Don't think it's over," volunteered one girl who asked not to be identified. She was wearing a sheer black shirt (over proper underwear) and black pants. "The teachers still give you dirty looks and say it's not lady-like. They can't stop us now, but they're going to make things rough."

George Shirkey, principal of Charles Evans Hughes High School, 351 West 18th Street, said he didn't think pants were proper school attire.

"After all, offices don't permit them," he said.

DECEMBER 9, 1969

THE FASHION DECADE: As Hems Rose, Barriers Fell

Marylin Bender

It was the decade of fashion and now it is ending. In the 1960's, fashion spilled out of the closet and into politics, the arts and big business. Politicians' wives and social climbers learned to drop designer names. The proper answer to the formerly impertinent question, "Whose dress are you wearing?" was not, as Lady Bird Johnson, Mary Lindsay and Happy Rockefeller discovered, "My own."

Neither they nor any other female public figure ever attained the influence of Jacqueline Kennedy. The brunette queen of the New Frontier became the Pied Piper of fashion for the masses as well as the darling of Seventh Avenue, the Avenue George Cinq and the Via Gregoriana.

Trends may have been set early in the decade by couturiers, later on by the anonymous young and the alienated, but Jacqueline Kennedy disseminated them to middle America. Because of her, women grew bouffant hairdos and crowned them with barren pillboxes, hid their curves in little nothing dresses, their eyes behind mammoth sunglasses.

In the fall of 1966, when Mrs. Kennedy hiked her skirts above her knees, so did cautious housewives over 30. Later, she let her hair go wild in a childish mane, dieted to a razor thinness, which she vaunted with sausage skin pants and poor boy sweaters. But these styles had been set by such younger, blond film idols, pop socialites and mannequins as Brigitte Bardot, Baby Jane Holzer and Twiggy. By then, Jackie had slipped off her pedestal with her marriage to Aristotle S. Onassis.

Fashion meant more than clothes in the sixties. It was life style, image, social prestige, an index of contemporaneity, a sales ploy.

Those white Courrèges boots were injected into advertising campaigns for refrigerators. Mods in lacy stockings promoted banks. Dressmakers lent their names to unrelated products (Yves Saint Laurent shower curtains, the Cardin interior of a Simca car) or became design empire builders like Emilio Pucci, whose 4-ounce, printed jersey dress was an international status symbol.

The sixties began without waists, bosoms and knees. At the end, nearly everything was showing. But change and reaction have set in. Fashion socialites are turning to social activism. The chic of the approaching seventies is a sweater and skirt (or pants). The new look is the non-clothes look, the no-make-up, the non-coiffure.

Sic transit fashion. ■

DECEMBER 26, 1969

ROCK FANS PLAY FASHION GAME, TOO

Judy Klemesrud

Janis Joplin, in 1969.

The straggly-haired teen-age girl in a black maxicoat turned to her girl friend in the subway shuttle in Times Square the other day and asked, in a very serious tone: "Have you decided what you'll wear to Janis yet?"

(cont'd. on next page)

(cont'd. from previous page)

Janis is Janis Joplin, the high priestess of rock, and her two young fans were discussing a subject that is of monumental importance to the rock crowd these days: Wearing the "right" clothes to a rock hero's concert.

"You just don't go to a rock concert in a skirt and sweater, because you'd be cheating everybody," said Lillian Roxon, a young Australian journalist living in Manhattan who wrote the 611-page "Rock Encyclopedia" (Grosset & Dunlap, $9.95).

"In rock, the audience is a definite part of the show," she added, "and sometimes it's the main part if what's happening on stage gets very draggy."

In spite of all their shouting about individuality and doing one's own thing, many rock crowd members march to the same drummer when it comes to the clothes they put on their backs.

Yes, the hip set has its equivalents of the little black dress. These are the "safe" fashions that can be worn without scorn anywhere. For the girls: bell-bottom blue jeans topped with an antique fur coat (never a new fur coat!). For boys: bell-bottom blue jeans worn with a suede fringed jacket.

These are the uniforms of the nonconforming. And they were paraded around in full force at Janis Joplin's near-capacity concert in Madison Square Garden last week.

There are other ways a rock fan can find social security, too. A maxicoat will do nicely for the girls—as long as it has a long, long scarf trailing from the neck, please.

And nowadays boys are even daring to venture out of their houses in non-belled blue jeans. But the jeans must be splattered with those prestigious white blotches, a sign that they've been tie-dyed—in bleach.

At the Joplin concert, several of the girls wore elaborate thrift-shop gowns. One had trimmed hers with fringe. Another had sewn Indian beads on hers. The favored fabrics appeared to be crushed velvet, with satin second.

The more daring boys wore such things as black velvet capes, leather maxicoats, and furry Afghanistan-style coats trimmed with colorful embroidery. One boy had sewn a small American flag on the back of his jacket, à la Peter Fonda in the movie, "Easy Rider."

It is Miss Roxon's theory that fashion goes from the rock stars to rock fans to Seventh Avenue designers—and then to the rest of the country.

"Janis gave us fringe and long, bushy hair," she said. "Cher [of Sonny and Cher] gave us bell-bottoms, and Sonny gave us lambs' wool vests. Jim Morrison [of The Doors] popularized leather clothes. And Carolyn Hester was the first singer to wear a mirrored vest without anything underneath it."

"Tie-dying is going to be more popular than ever," she predicted. "I was sitting in this place on Sunset Strip when John Sebastian of the Lovin' Spoonful walked in tie-dyed from head to toe. A little later, he and his friends drank a toast to tie-dying.

"In fact," she added, "a lot of rock stars are even sleeping on tie-dyed sheets now. Janis has some in satin." ■

SEPTEMBER 20, 1960

LATEST RAGE FOR DIETERS: POWDERS

June Owen

Metrecal, the liquid food substitute for reducer, poured for a customer by a soda fountain clerk.

The latest rage with those who wish to lose weight is the 900-calorie powdered food formula. Get-thin-easy schemes always have been snatched up eagerly, if only temporarily, by those who need to reduce or think they do.

Today's powdered mix has reached such peaks of popularity that some department, chain and drug stores are engaged in a price war to offer their version of the product at the lowest possible rate. The half-pound ration of the formula needed for one day now can be bought at prices ranging from 89 cents to $1.59.

Another indication of how the powdered reducing mix has swept the nation is that many drug and health food lunch counters now feature a glass of the powdered formula, mixed with water, as a substitute for a snack or a meal. Small talk at cocktail parties almost invariably turns to whether the chocolate, butterscotch or vanilla flavor of the mix is preferred.

Mead Johnson & Co., manufacturer of nutritional and pharmaceutical products, started the current craze with a product it introduced a year ago, in September 1959. Called Metrecal, it is a balanced mixture of protein, carbohydrates, minerals, vitamins and a minimum of fat.

One-half pound of the powder provides completely for the day's requirement of nutrients. It does this with only 900 calories, a quantity that should enable the user who does not cheat to lose approximately one-half pound a day.

The powder is mixed with a quart of water. It is suggested that one glassful can be taken in place of each meal with the fourth glass sipped before going to bed.

For about six months Metrecal had the field to itself, but since then many other companies have introduced similar products under other brand names. New ones are appearing every week.

Doctors questioned about the prepared powder for reducing generally agreed that it was perfectly safe for the average person to use. Dr. Alvan R. Feinstein, a specialist in obesity and assistant professor of medicine at the New York University School of Medicine, says there are some people who genuinely do not know what they should eat or how to eat to lose weight. But they are a minority.

"Most people know very well what they should not eat," Dr. Feinstein said. "Their problem is that they can't avoid eating it. They may follow a perfectly good diet but, once they have lost weight, they go back to their old eating habits, gain weight and the whole cycle begins again.

"The formula diet has value if it salvaged even a few of those people who lose weight by following it, then maintain their lower weight."

Dr. Feinstein was one of the originators of the Rockefeller Diet, a liquid formula devised at the Rockefeller Institute. Customers seized on it enthusiastically about five years ago. That diet, which Dr. Feinstein said was released to the public prematurely, was criticized for being too low in protein. Dr. Feinstein feels high protein content is not necessary in reducing diets. The present formulas are similar to the Rockefeller diet, but with a higher protein content. ■

MARCH 28, 1961

Lutèce Is Elegant and Expensive

Craig Claiborne

Lutèce was the original name of Paris. It also is the name of a recently opened restaurant in Manhattan that is at once impressively elegant and conspicuously expensive. The Lutèce is at 249 East Fiftieth Street.

There is much that is visually appealing about this establishment, including the candlelight, napery and walls, which boast a modest wealth of tapestries, paintings and a mural by Jean Pagès in colors as gay as a carousel. One of the upstairs dining rooms is equipped with a marble Victorian mantel over which rests an English mirror. The first-floor, split-level dining room opens onto a garden.

The tables at Lutèce are outfitted with neatly starched cloths, wonderfully oversized linen napkins and candelabra. The salt and pepper shakers seem trivial; pepper mills would be more fitting.

There are three dining areas in the restaurant with a seating capacity for, perhaps, sixty guests. At the entrance there is a diminutive bar to accommodate a dozen

(cont'd. on next page)

(cont'd. from previous page)
or fewer customers. The kitchen, which is open to public view, is small. André Surmain is the restaurant's proprietor.

The menus at Lutèce are opulently styled. On the cover is a print of a famous nineteenth-century painting of French roses by Redoute. The print is framed by a gold leaf border.

It is a point of interest that there are, in fact, two menus at Lutèce. One is for the host at each table, the other for the guests and there is this difference in the menus: The one presented to the host lists the cost of the various dishes; the menus presented to the guests list only the dishes.

As far as the guests are concerned, this seems to follow the philosophy attributed to the late J. P. Morgan. When a nouveau riche guest aboard his yacht Corsair asked about the operating expenses of the boat, Morgan replied to the effect, "Anybody who even has to think about the cost can't afford it."

There are approximately thirty items on each menu. There are three soups, seven first courses, nine main dishes, six vegetables, a platter of cheeses and seven desserts.

Lutèce has been opened for scarcely more than a month and perhaps it is this youth that causes an unevenness in the quality of the cuisine. A few of the dishes, a foie gras en brioche or a roast veal with kidney, for example, could qualify as superb; others, such as a poussin rôti aux girolles (squab chicken with wild mushrooms) are routine. A few of the dishes, such as a fillet of sole sampled recently, are disappointing in the extreme. It is this reviewer's opinion that the food at Lutèce could not be called great cuisine.

There is a small but adequate wine list at Lutèce and the price span is from about $8.50 for a 1958 Meursault to $14 for a 1957 Chambertin. A recent dinner for two included two aperitifs, two first courses, two main courses, salads with cheese, a bottle of 1957 Chassange Montrachet and two demitasses. The cost of the dinner was $52.30.

It is a point of passing interest that many items of fresh food are imported from France by air each week. This applies to wild mushrooms, truffles and oysters. The oysters, which are said to arrive each Monday, have a special delicacy and succulence. They are of the belon and Portugaises varieties, best enjoyed without other embellishment than, perhaps, a squeeze of lemon juice and a glass of chilled Chablis. ■

APRIL 7, 1961

White House Hires French Chef

Craig Claiborne

White House cooking chef René Verdon in Washington, 1965.

WASHINGTON, April 6—The White House has a new chef after all. He is René Verdon, a tall, 36-year-old Frenchman with an impressive culinary background here and abroad.

M. Verdon made his official debut yesterday with a luncheon given by President Kennedy for Prime Minister Harold Macmillan and sixteen other guests. The verdict after the luncheon was that there was nothing like French cooking to promote good Anglo-American relations.

Pierre Salinger, White House press secretary, said M. Verdon had been engaged on a temporary basis because of the number of foreign visitors expected in coming weeks. He said the chef, who is being paid out of the President's personal funds, would supervise the cuisine at all official functions.

The White House kitchen has rarely been known for the quality of its cuisine. Rumors that the Kennedys were trying to do something about it by hiring a new master cook have been circulating since February.

At the White House luncheon attended yesterday by Mr. Macmillan the menu was seasonal. It began with a trout cooked in Chablis wine and served with sauce Vincent, a mayonnaise seasoned with chopped watercress, spinach and capers.

The principal course was roast fillet of beef au jus and artichoke bottoms Beaucaire—filled with a fondue of tomatoes simmered in butter. Giant-sized asparagus followed as a separate course with sauce Maltaise, a version of Hollandaise sauce flavored with orange.

A vacherin (meringue-shell) filled with raspberries and chocolate ice cream was served as dessert. The latter, dubbed désir d'avril by the chef, was garnished with whipped cream and candied violets.

It is reported that following the private dinner last night the President extended his compliments to the chef.

M. Verdon was born in the village of Pouzauges on the West Coast of France in a region better known for its pasture lands and forests than for its food. His parents owned a bakery and pastry shop; thus he took, in his own words, "his first steps in the world of cuisine."

Learning the art of the cuisinier was not his earliest ambition and he says he gained the desire to become a cook through sibling rivalry. One of his older brothers was a baker, the other a pastry maker, and he chose to outdistance them both with the preparation of more complicated dishes. He attributes his appreciation of fine food to his mother.

He has worked in several fine kitchens in Paris, including the Berkeley, and at the Normandy Hotel in Deauville. He has also been a member of the kitchen staff aboard the French Line's S. S. Liberté.

M. Verdon came to America three years ago and has worked, among other posts, as assistant chef at the Carlyle Hotel and the Essex House in New York. He has gained an astonishing knowledge of such American dishes as gumbos and Philadelphia pepper pot.

It goes without saying that M. Verdon is an expert chef, adept at the preparation of magnificent creations whether they be quenelles of fish with lobster sauce, wine sauces or paragons of pastry. ■

OCTOBER 18, 1961

Art of French Cooking Does Not Concede to U.S. Tastes

Craig Claiborne

Since the turn of the century scores of books have been published in English on the subject of French cuisine. Many of these books have been written by French chefs via the test kitchens of publishing firms with myopic and underfed editors. Others have been dished up from the secret files and home oven of Tante Cécile, chez elle. Most of them have made disastrous concessions to what is considered "the American taste."

What is probably the most comprehensive, laudable and monumental work on the subject was published this week. It is called "Mastering the Art of French Cooking" (Alfred A. Knopf, $10), and it will probably remain as the definitive work for nonprofessionals.

This is not a book for those with a superficial interest in food. But for those who take fundamental delight in the pleasures of cuisine, "Mastering the Art of French Cuisine" may well become a vade mecum in the kitchen. It is written in the simplest terms possible and without compromise or condescension.

The recipes are glorious, whether they are for a simple egg in aspic or for a fish soufflé. At a glance it is conservatively estimated that there are a thousand or more recipes in the book. All are painstakingly edited and written as if each were a masterpiece, and most of them are.

There are many preparations in the cuisine that cannot be adequately described in words. To amplify and make the text more clear, there are a hundred or so clean-line drawings that supplement and speak more eloquently than words. These include sketches that show the making of an omelet and the paring of an artichoke to get at the heart.

Added to the embarrassment of riches are suggestions for wines to be served with many dishes and complete menus.

"Mastering the Art of French Cooking" was authored by three women. Simone Beck was French born and educated; Louisette Bertholle is half French and half American and was educated in both countries; Julia Child is a native of California who studied cooking in France.

In 1951 the three started a cooking school, L'Ecole des Trois Gourmandes, in Paris and it was then that the idea of the book took shape.

There are a few minor points on which a purist might take issue with the authors. They recommend, for example, the use of a garlic press, which is a gadget considered in some circles to be only one cut above garlic salt or garlic powder. It does not produce a flavor totally equal to garlic freshly chopped with a knife.

And there is a curious omission from the book. One of the bases for countless desserts and entrees in French cuisine is puff pastry, the flaky, many-leaved pastry used in making vol au vents (patty shells) or mille-feuilles (Napoleons). It is admittedly the most difficult of pastries to make, but it can be achieved by nonprofessionals. There also is no recipe for croissants.

In an over-all sense, however, it might be said that anyone with a natural bent for fine cuisine could become a refined cook in most areas of French gastronomy by following the details in "Mastering the Art of French Cooking." ■

A Litton Series 500 microwave oven from 1966.

MARCH 31, 1962

Microwaves Fail to Lure Home Cooks

Rita Reif

The electronic range is speedy in cooking but slow in gaining acceptance. Since 1955, when the first microwave ovens became available for home use, 10,000 units have been sold, although manufacturers optimistically had predicted that sales by 1960 would reach 100,000 a year.

Price has proven the biggest obstacle to sales, according to the Tappan Company, the single manufacturer of home units in the field. When the electronic range was introduced it sold for $1,195. Today, although the price has dropped to $795, the

(cont'd. on next page)

(cont'd. from previous page)
investment is still beyond the means of most families.

The initial enthusiasm for electronic cooking, which was and still is considered by many appliance and food experts as "the greatest single advance in the art of cooking," has cooled. The electronic range—as it is called—looks like an oven but performs cooking tasks ordinarily done in either a conventional oven or on top of a range. Food is cooked by electro-magnetic energy (microwaves) radiated from an electronic power tube called a magnetron.

During cooking the oven remains cool. Microwaves pass through the glass, plastic paper or china utensils in which they are prepared without heating them and are absorbed by the food. Metal pots and pans should not be used in the oven because metal reflects the microwaves.

The advantages of the appliance are said to include the speed in which foods are cooked (a baked potato cooks in four minutes and other foods are prepared from three to ten times faster than conventional ovens and ranges); rapid defrosting; greater retention of natural food juices and ease of maintenance. The appliance reportedly will not heat up the kitchen or produce smoke from spillage.

A major disadvantage of the device is that most people believe it does not fully replace the open range or the conventional range. Browning of foods, such as cakes or small roasts, does not take place in the unit because the cooking time is too short. However, the ranges come with browning elements that can be employed for this purpose. Most women find that for cooking stews or frying foods, and for other purposes, they need a small conventional oven and at least one or two burners to supplement the electronic range.

"This is not a gadget," said Mrs. John P. Docktor of Milwaukee in a recent interview.

Mrs. Docktor and six other owners of Tappan ranges were asked how they use their equipment. "The only thing I don't cook in my electronic range is coffee," Mrs. Docktor noted. "It is a timesaver because I can prepare dinner in a half an hour."

Mrs. Lawrence Zak, also of Milwaukee, is considered by Tappan to be one of the most adept cooks with its equipment. "I grasped it right away," she said. "The representative came out the first evening to cook the dinner and since then I have had a marvelous time improvising my own recipes. My most successful dinners are pheasant, which I serve with a beef sauce, and venison, which is served in a tomato sauce."

According to Mrs. Richard Herz of Lake Katonah, N.Y., one great advantage, aside from the shortened cooking time, is that cakes turn out fluffier, more moist and of greater volume when baked in an electronic unit.

"It's a joy to keep clean," Mrs. Herz noted, echoing all the women polled. "There's no spilling and the oven never becomes so hot that foods could be baked onto the sides or base." ■

APRIL 30, 1962

LÜCHOW'S TURNS 80

Craig Claiborne

When any institution in this city of the pneumatic drill celebrates an eightieth birthday, it is reason to raise a stein on high. And tomorrow Lüchow's Restaurant, 110 East Fourteenth Street, will toast the occasion.

It was eighty years ago in May—and presumably on the very first day—that August Lüchow, a 26-year-old immigrant from Hanover, bought a small German beer parlor where he had worked for two years as a waiter. That establishment consisted of one room, now the Gentleman's Bar and Grill. But soon Lüchow's expanded into six rooms and historians say that the restaurant is much the same as it was in the beginning.

There probably are thousands of New Yorkers, many with grandchildren, who remember being taken to Lüchow's during their childhood. Old-timers still contend that physically the place has not changed much with the passing of the years. There are still the handsome, dark-paneled walls, leaded stained-glass windows and black chandeliers, although today, of course, illumination is provided by electricity rather than by gas.

When Lüchow's first opened its doors, Fourteenth Street was the center of town, comparable today to Forty-second Street. Tony Pastor's Theatre, Tammany Hall, the original Academy of Music and Steinway Hall were situated across the street from the restaurant. Tom Sharkey, the prizefighter, had a restaurant almost next door.

Jan Mitchell, the restaurant's present owner, took over the proprietorship in 1949 and he has persisted in maintaining the Teutonic tradition insofar as possible. When he assumed ownership, in fact, he restored to Lüchow's menu many German dishes that unaccountably had been dropped in the past. The only major physical changes that he effected were a new floor, a remodeled and modernized kitchen and air conditioning.

Almost since its doors opened, Lüchow's has catered to the great and the near-great, celebrities in most fields of the arts, neighbors, politicians and tourists. Victor Herbert and Fritzie Scheff celebrated the opening of "Mademoiselle Modiste" there and, of course, there is a special room on the second floor of Lüchow's known as the Lillian Russell Museum.

Part of the old-fashioned, built-in charm of the restaurant is the convivial nature of the place and, at mid-meal almost any day of the week, it is noisy. It is said that a few years ago, when Christmas fell on Sunday, 4,000 guests were served within the course of the day. ■

Lüchow's during the 1962 Christmas season.

MAY 19, 1963

COLA PRODUCERS ENTER LOW-CAL FIELD

James J. Nagle

Heavy demand for low-calorie drinks has enticed the big cola makers into the field.

Coca-Cola's Tab has been test-marketed in Springfield, Mass., and will be introduced in 25 markets within two weeks.

Pepsi-Cola's Patio Diet Cola, introduced in February, is being sold in 60 markets throughout the country. Recently, the Hoffman Beverage Company, which has had a line of dietetic drinks known as Streamline for six years, introduced a new low-calorie beverage known as LoLo Cola.

Royal Crown Cola, the third largest company in the field, has had a low-calorie cola, known as Diet-Rite, for some years.

According to producers, the now soaring price of sugar has nothing to do with the increasing interest on the part of producers in low-calorie drinks, where such substitutes as sodium and calcium cyclamates and/or saccharin are used. It is becoming a profitable field.

The rise in the popularity of the family of low-calorie beverages, which cola is now joining, has been phenomenal. In terms of standard cases—24 eight-ounce bottles with 192 ounces of beverages—sales have risen from 7,500,000 cases in 1957 to more than 50,000,000 cases in 1962. Sales this year are expected to hit about 100,000,000 cases.

Probably the biggest push given to low calorie drinks, before this year, was in the nineteen-fifties when Kirsch Beverages, Inc., Brooklyn, introduced its No-Cal and began to promote it extensively. That product also utilizes calcium cyclamate as a sweetener.

Other products introduced in the nineteen-fifties included Royal Crown's Diet-Rite in cans, Dad's Root Beer and Canada Dry's Glamour and Cliquot Club.

The average soft drink is said to contain about 100 calories a six-ounce glass. The low-calorie drinks, according to their makers, contain far less. Cott says its products have only about six calories a glass; Hoffman that its LoLo Cola has about two calories an eight-ounce serving; Coca-Cola that its Tab has one calorie a six-ounce serving, and Kirsch that its low-calorie products have about one and one-half calories a serving. ■

JANUARY 26, 1964

Harried Housewife Lends Willing Spirit to Culinary Logistics

Joan Barthel

Julia Child on the set of her television series, 'The French Chef,' 1965.

When we had finished dinner, there was an awkward pause. Then my husband spoke. "Good," he said wistfully, "but not great." And I knew what I had to do.

By 7 o'clock I had laboriously trundled the television set to the kitchen and set it up facing the stove, just in time to hear the announcer sing out, "This is Channel 13, where The French Chef follows with another delightful recipe in the French style."

The French Chef turns out to be a woman with the charm of a Smith College girl and the sang-froid of an O.S.S. agent. As a matter of fact, she has been both. Her name is Julia Child, and on this Wednesday evening, as we meet for the very first time, she looks earnestly at me and makes me a promise.

"Once you learn how to make this quick-change pastry, you can make all kinds of goodies." I squirm expectantly.

She exhibits a pan of thick yellow stuff, but I am too busy to give it more than a hasty glance.

"You have to be sure that your measurements are right," Mrs. Child is saying. She sifts flour into a one-cup measure. "You know this kind of cup. When it's full up to the top, that means you've got one cup." I nod knowingly.

Stir flour into a cup of water. Make a little hole in the middle; add four eggs. Crack. Plop. Beat. Crack. Plop. Beat. Harder.

Crisis. She is stuffing the mixture into a pastry bag. I do not have a pastry bag. Grab spoon; drop pastry blobs onto cooking sheet. Too thick; it won't drop off. Push it, then! Faster.

Dart frantic glance at TV screen. Alas, it is the beginning of the end, for The French Chef is way ahead of me. I watch incredulously as she takes from the oven a tray of puffs that are already baked. She put them in ahead of time. Ah, the injustice of it.

But c'est la vie, and all that. She is going right ahead with the filling.

"I have here some canned clams with shallots and vermouth mixed in a thick cream sauce." Oh, some people are just born lucky.

But I brighten as The French Chef motions toward the thick yellow stuff again. "If you have some left over, here's something you can do with it. It's terribly useful stuff."

"We're going to use it to make potato dumplings. Here I have two cups of plain, ordinary mashed potatoes." She also has a pile of Swiss cheese, grated when I was not watching, and a pan of salted water, heated when I was not watching, and I never cared much for French cooking, anyway.

The camera follows her as she moves to a long table with candles, and flowers, and trays of beautiful things all made from that wretched pastry.

I miss her final message, because I am diverted by strands of smoke seeping from the oven. When I fling open the door, smoke gushes out, and I can barely see my husband's face peering at me over the TV set.

"I'm home," he says, "and what's for dinner?"

DECEMBER 17, 1965

JOHNSON FOOD DISAGREES WITH CHEF HIRED BY KENNEDY

Craig Claiborne

René Verdon, the famed chef engaged for the White House in the Kennedy Administration, has submitted his resignation to the present occupants, effective at the end of the year.

In an interview, the chef insisted that his withdrawal had nothing to do with the food preferences of President Johnson and his family. But his gesture has not been totally unexpected in professional circles since the appointment of Mrs. Mary Kaltman as "food coordinator" several weeks ago.

Mrs. Kaltman, a native of Cleburne, Tex., was formerly director of foods at the Driskill Hotel in Austin.

Since his debut with a luncheon given for Prime Minister Harold Macmillan, M. Verdon has catered hundreds of dinners for the world's high and mighty, most recently for Princess Margaret and the Earl of Snowdon and for President Mohammad Ayub Khan of Pakistan.

Although the chef, an amiable, portly man in his early forties, would make no comment about the dining habits of the Johnsons, it is certainly true that their taste in food is considerably less sophisticated than that of the Kennedys.

The Kennedys were partial to such dishes as quenelles de brochet, or delicate poached forcemeat balls made with pike, mousse of sole with lobster and braised chicken with champagne sauce.

The Johnsons have a widely publicized penchant for barbecues, spoon bread, popovers, fried chicken, brownies and Pedernales River chili.

Although Mr. Verdon was reluctant to discuss details of changes that had come about since the appointment of a food coordinator, he would admit that some of the dishes he had been asked by memorandum to prepare had seemed unaccustomed to his Gallic palate.

This would include a cold purée of garbanzos or chickpeas, which he described for his taste as "already bad hot." Some of the menu suggestions offered him also referred to recipes printed in the Gourmet Cookbooks, obviously well-thumbed volumes in the new food coordinators' hands.

"I am going to ask my pastry chef, who has been making Yule logs for 40 years, to look in a cookbook?" Mr. Verdon asked.

He said that he had not as yet formulated plans for his future. ■

JUNE 9, 1968

AMERICANS PUT YOGURT THROUGH CULTURAL CHANGE

James J. Nagle

Yogurt, a cultured, low-fat milk product that not too long ago was eaten only by health faddists in this country, is becoming a part of the diet of many Americans.

Consumed for centuries as a food in the Balkan countries, it did not reach America in a big way until the 1930's, and then was considered as a "health food." Nutritionally, yogurt has few calories but completely retains the full vitamin and mineral content of pasteurized milk, according to its producers in this country.

In Europe, the product gained momentum around the turn of the century when Dr. Ilyra Metchikoff, head of the Pasteur Institute in Paris and a Nobel Prize winner, successfully isolated the bacteria that produce yogurt. Up to then, it had been made by peasants in the Balkans chiefly by letting their milk sit out in the open air.

But it was not until the 1930's that yogurt was sold in any quantities in America, when it was produced here under the name of Lacto as a health food. In 1942, a Swiss immigrant named Jose Metzger and his son, Juan, emigrated here and set up shop in the Bronx under the name of Dannon Milk Products, Inc., to sell the product that was so successful in Europe, to grocery stores.

The new company immediately ran into trouble. The name yogurt meant nothing to Americans. Secondly, it was a perishable product and its taste was unusual to most citizens of this country, some of whom described it as "blah."

But through extensive advertising, sales were increased chiefly through emphasis on the healthful aspects of the product. It was not until 1946, however, that the company found the key to a really broad market—add strawberry preserves.

Another obstacle was the glass jar packaging, which required a deposit on the container. By altering the production process to manufacture yogurt in temperatures that would not melt the container coatings, a disposable plastic-coated container was put into use.

Eight years ago, the Beatrice Food Company exchanged about $3.5-million of its stock for the Dannon stockholders' interests in the company and Dannon became a subsidiary.

But there are formidable competitors in the field now. These include the Borden Company and National Dairy Products Corporation. Early in 1966, Borden started production in the United States of "fresh-like, full fruit flavor yogurt" with the fruit distributed throughout the product.

It is estimated that Americans eat 110 million cups of yogurt a year—70 million cups on the East Coast and 30 million on the West Coast, with the rest of the nation accounting for the balance. The largest maker is still Dannon, and Borden's says it is No. 2. But there are numerous regional producers throughout the country.

To make yogurt, a spokesman for Dannon explained, the company removes half the butterfat from fresh cow's milk while protein and other supplements are added. The milk goes through a continuous process of clarification, homogenization, and pasteurization. The milk is then piped into stainless steel vats, where it is injected with lactic cultures, developed in the company's laboratories.

JUNE 17, 1968

SIDEWALK CAFES BLOOM DESPITE SOOT AND NOISE

David K. Shipler

"Everybody's doing it," said Tom Sweeney, maître d'hôtel at the Montmarte Cafe, which extends onto the sidewalk on First Avenue near 61st Street.

Maybe not everybody, but more and more beer-drinkers, cocktail-sippers, magazine-readers, dog-walkers, baby-carriage-wheelers, pretty-girl-daters, sunbathers, theater-goers, socializers, people-watchers and restaurant owners are braving New York's noise and fumes to make sidewalk cafes flourish.

Twelve years ago, the city had three places with tables on sidewalks. Now there are 82, according to Mark J. Wiesner, a spokesman for the city's Department of Licenses, and more than half of them have sprung up in the last four years.

Most are clustered in three areas of Manhattan—in Greenwich Village, along First and Third Avenues in the 50's, 60's and 70's, and near Lincoln Center. But a few have also appeared recently in Brooklyn and Queens, and there is one in Harlem, on West 125th Street.

Part of the reason for the boom is the easing of licensing requirements, which were once so strict that they prevented almost any encroachment on the sidewalks.

Now the regulations are designed to encourage cafes, permitting level platforms to be placed over slanted sidewalks and no longer requiring barriers, such as picket fences, window boxes or iron grilles, between the tables and the pedestrian traffic.

"It's terrific," exclaimed Joe Snouffer, the manager of T.G.I. Friday's (the initials stand for Thank God It's) a brightly painted establishment on the northeast corner of First Avenue and 63d Street. "Our business started flourishing when the outdoor cafe went out there."

Outdoors at the St. Moritz Hotel on Central Park South, the finely dressed may sit and sip scotch and water at $1.40 a drink, but no food is served.

At the Montmarte Cafe, which opened five weeks ago, sidewalk diners eat French style meals for no more than $2.95. But the Montmarte typifies the cautiousness with which some cafes are venturing out into the muggy summer weather, the soot and the noise of the city.

Built in an old garage, the cafe has an open front with a wooden frame and floor extending onto the sidewalk. An awning serves as the roof, and the tables stand by huge plate-glass windows. The glass is removed only during dry, cool weather, Mr. Sweeney said.

He added that people who linger over their drinks frequently find tiny black bits of soot mingling with the ice cubes, and they sometimes ask to have them exchanged.

"Their trouble is their concept of cleanliness," scoffed Willis Rayle, a porter at the Cafe Figaro on Bleecker Street in the Village. "People in the Village do not expect the kind of cleanliness that people on the Upper East Side do."

Kentucky Fried Chicken founder Col. Harland Sanders.

JANUARY 5, 1969

Accidental Competitor in Chicken Game Is Winner

George Rood

"One thing we're really proud of—we've never had a franchise of ours go out of business. We've had to move a few of them to better locations, but none of our franchises has ever failed, not a single one."

John Young Brown Jr., the 35-year-old president of Kentucky Fried Chicken, Inc., who recently became its chief executive officer as well, talks with a confident tone and a smattering of a courtly Southern accent.

Nattily dressed in a gray sharkskin suit, Mr. Brown ran his right hand through his tousled hair as he pointed out that Kentucky Fried had "never been sued by a franchise holder, and that's pretty rare in this business."

Mr. Brown, who was one of three investors who took over Kentucky Fried in 1964, said he "got into the chicken game pretty much by chance."

Col. Harland Sanders had started the franchise chain in 1955 when an expressway diverted traffic from the roadside stand he had run in Corbin, Ky., for 25 years. It seems that the Colonel (the title is honorary) wanted some legal work done. Mr. Brown was a young lawyer who had worked his way through the University of Kentucky's law school selling the Encyclopedia

(cont'd. on next page)

(cont'd. from previous page)

Brittanica. The two got together and Mr. Brown was quickly impressed with the potential of Kentucky Fried Chicken and the Colonel's image as its No. 1 salesman.

"I remember I thought it would be real great if he could get on national television or something like that," he recalled. "So I got hold of a friend who then introduced the Colonel to Toots Shor, who went ahead and got in touch with John Charles Daly. The next thing we knew Colonel Sanders was on 'What's My Line?' It was great exposure."

Mr. Brown linked up with Jack C. Massey, who had operated a surgical supply house and had been an investment broker, and Leon W. Harman, a director of K.F.C. who owns a chain of restaurants on the West Coast and had been the Colonel's first franchisee.

The three men bought out Colonel Sanders for some $2-million, along with a $40,000-a-year salary for him as the company's goodwill ambassador. Colonel Sanders also retained control of franchise rights for K.F.C.'s 200 outlets in Canada.

The Colonel had built up a network of 700 franchisees by the time he sold the company. In the four years since then, K.F.C. has expanded to 2,000 take-out stores and restaurants covering all 50 states.

K.F.C. is planning to move into the Manhattan market soon. "We're going to franchise about 20 units here in the next two years," Brown said.

"All food products are bought locally," he emphasized, "although we provide the franchise with other supplies and equipment and, of course, the recipe." The recipe in question, devised by the white-bearded Colonel, who is now 78, includes a patented blend of 11 herbs and spices used to flavor the chicken. As part of its development program, K.F.C. has come up with a new automated chicken cooker that increases sharply the number of chickens that can be cooked each day. The device is being made available to franchisees through a leasing plan.

"I love the chicken business," Mr. Brown said, "even though it gets pretty hectic at times. That phone never stops ringing. Did you notice those gray hairs coming in on the sides? I didn't have them four years ago." ■

OCTOBER 19, 1969

CYCLAMATE SWEETENERS WILL BE TAKEN OFF MARKET NEXT YEAR

Harold N. Schmeck Jr.

WASHINGTON, Oct. 18—Robert H. Finch, Secretary of Health, Education and Welfare, announced officially today that the widely used artificial sweeteners called cyclamates will be withdrawn from general use by early next year.

He has ordered them removed from the list of substances recognized as safe for use in foods largely because some rats that were fed heavy doses of the artificial sweeteners during most of their lifespan developed bladder cancers.

Mr. Finch and high officers of his department emphasized, however, that there is no evidence, at present, to link the artificial sweeteners with cancers in man.

The use of cyclamate in the production of general purpose foods and beverages has been ordered discontinued immediately.

Recall of soft drinks containing the sweeteners is to be completed by Jan. 1. All other artificially sweetened food products using the substances are to be phased out of the market by Feb. 1.

"I should emphasize also that my order does not require the total disappearance from the market place of soft drinks, foods and non-prescription drugs containing cyclamates," Mr. Finch said. "These products will continue to be available to persons whose health depends upon them, such as those under medical care for such conditions as diabetes or obesity."

About 70 percent of the use of cyclamates is in the form of soft drinks such as Tab, Diet Pepsi, Diet Cola, Fresca, Like, Wink and others.

Mr. Finch said the beverages were singled out for the most rapid action because they are so widely used and because they contain relatively large quantities of the sugar substitutes.

In the news conference at which the announcement was made, the Secretary said his action should not be interpreted as an emergency measure, but a matter of prudence and legal necessity.

Much of the research on which today's decision was based was done under non-government auspices. Indeed, some of it was sponsored by Abbott Laboratories, principal American manufacturer of cyclamates. This pharmaceutical company brought its information to the attention of the National Cancer Institute last Monday.

Further evidence was compiled and reviewed during the rest of the week by government and non-government scientists. By Friday, they reached the unanimous opinion, Dr. Steinfeld said, that cyclamate induces cancer of the bladder in rats, using the dosages and under the conditions of the experiments.

The man who discovered cyclamate, Michael Sveda of Greenwich, yesterday questioned the test methods that led the Government to condemn cyclamate.

"If massive doses of it are bad, does this mean that normal doses will cause cancer?" he asked in a telephone interview last night.

"A 3 percent salt solution will kill you, too, if you drink too much of it," Mr. Sveda said. "They should have tried to find out what effect massive doses of sugar would have on the rats, too." ■

cancer

NOVEMBER 9, 1969

FOOD SAFETY A WORRY IN ERA OF ADDITIVES

Sandra Blakeslee

When a housewife strolls into a supermarket today she is confronted with a cornucopia of things she can shake 'n' bake, brown 'n' serve, whip 'n' chill or heat 'n' eat.

But now more and more shoppers are beginning to eye the labels on products with suspicion, trying to find out whether the foods they shake, brown, heat and whip are really safe to eat.

The Food and Drug Administration recently banned cyclamates, the artificial sweetener used in many diet products, after evidence of cancer was found in a few laboratory rats fed massive doses of the chemical.

And now it is examining monosodium glutamate, a popular food flavor enhancer sold under the brand name "Accent," and many other chemicals long considered safe for use in foods.

The Federal agency's action has stirred up a sweeping controversy involving the American consumer, chemical and food manufacturers, medical experts and others over whether additives are safe and adequately tested.

The controversy is of increasing importance to American consumers because their use of additives has been rising sharply in recent years—to perhaps three of the 1,400 pounds of substances the average American eats in a year.

This reflects a rising public demand for processed foods (such as frozen, canned or freeze-dried products) for special dietary and low-calorie foods, for snack foods, and particularly for so-called convenience foods (products such as TV dinners that can be prepared with a minimum of effort). All contain additives.

Other reasons for the increasing use of additives in foods include an increasingly urban population that wants its foods to last longer and stay fresh on shelves before use; a change in eating habits that reflects a more mobile American who likes to snack and run; a growing diet consciousness among often overfed Americans, and a growing taste for more exotic, seasoned dishes.

Food additives can be of two sorts, those added intentionally and those that sneak into food accidentally.

Accidental or unintentional food additives include pesticides and minute particles from food packaging that manage to "migrate," as the experts say, into the food itself.

Substances that migrate into foods from packages (cellophanes or glues from box tops, for example) are regulated by a lengthy group of laws that set limits on how much of an unintentional additive may be tolerated.

As many food experts have pointed out, more has been done to limit and control the migration of unintentional additives into food than has been done to control or limit the use of intentional additives.

Some 2,500 to 3,000 food additives are currently in use, including flavorings and colors. Some of the most commonly used additives are: 30 preservatives (to keep foods fresh); 28 antioxidants to retard the oxidative breakdown of fats and oils in foods, so as to keep shortenings, potato chips, chicken pot pies and other foods from turning rancid; 44 sequestrants (to separate trace elements from foods that might otherwise interfere with food processing); 31 stabilizers (to keep food at a uniform, smooth texture), and 85 surfactants (or wetting agents that allow two surfaces to come together by lowering their tension at surfaces of contact).

Such substances make food look better, feel better, taste better, hold together better, age better, mix better, spread better, pour better, and so on.

How valid are the industry's arguments that food additives are necessary to keep food fresh? One critic, Dr. Barry Commoner, a biologist from Washington University in St. Louis, says that the industry should do a lot more to speed up the delivery of foods, and thus lessen the need for so many additives.

"In Paris," Dr. Commoner said, "you can get fresh fish from the Mediterranean with no trouble. But in Pittsburgh, just try to get fresh fish from the Atlantic Seaboard."

APRIL 30, 1961

PANELED EFFECT

Bernard Gladstone

A 1960s wood-paneled kitchen.

To create the effect of wood paneling on any wall—without having to put up the panels—home owners now can paint on a new textured coating which looks and feels like natural wood.

Suitable for use over plaster or wallboard (painted or unpainted) or over wallpaper, this new type of paint can be put on with either a brush or a roller. The effect with each will be slightly different. It has a heavy, cream-like consistency, and leaves a three-dimensional "straight grain" pattern on the wall as it is applied. When this is stained (just as real wood is stained) later on, the surface looks so much like real wood paneling that it is difficult to tell it from the real thing.

To heighten the wood-grain effect, and to create the irregular heart-grain patterns which are a natural characteristic of real wood, curved grain patterns are painted on at irregular intervals along the wall. To create these grain patterns, the paint brush is held sideways and swirled up or down to draw deep U's or elongated O's on the wall.

This curved grain effect is brushed on after the base material has been applied first with normal vertical strokes. The brush is then re-dipped into the material, and an additional layer applied on top to work out the pattern described. Though individual preferences will vary, experience has shown that these breaks in the pattern are best spaced at least three to four feet apart horizontally—and at various heights—along the wall.

In order to create the planked effect which is characteristic of most wood paneled walls, the finish is scored with vertical lines from ceiling to floor after it has been allowed to set for one hour. These lines simulate the grooved joints which would be visible in real wood paneling. The lines are scored with a heavy carpenter's pencil, using a long straightedge as a guide. To make certain they will be vertical and parallel, the straightedge should be checked with a spirit level each time.

the surface looks so much like real wood paneling that it is difficult to tell it from the real thing.

Called Arvonwood, and manufactured by Arvon Products Company of Philadelphia, a gallon of this material sells for approximately $6. This will create a little over one hundred square feet of "paneling" on most surfaces. Assorted shades of wood stain are available from the same manufacturer for application over the textured finish after it has been allowed to dry for at least three days. The stain is applied with a cloth or roller. It creates a natural-looking wood tone effect with highlights and color variations which exactly duplicate the normal finish of stained wood paneling.

Though not absolutely essential, areas which will receive hard wear or abuse will benefit from an additional coat of a satin-finish varnish applied after the stain coat is dry. If preferred, a coat of paste wax can be rubbed on over these areas instead. ■

JANUARY 5, 1965

ARTISTS USE CRAFTS TO TURN A LOFT INTO A HOME

Rita Reif

Pop art, plywood and wit have transformed a silver-and-copper-plating factory into an ingenious, yet eminently comfortable, home.

"It was beyond wretchedness," Ivan C. Karp said the other morning in describing the condition of the 3,000-square-foot loft that he, his wife, Marilynn, and several artist-friends helped to make livable. Conquering the "state of decrepitude," Mr. Karp recalled, took four months and $3,000.

"The walls and floors were covered with an inch and a half of industrial waste," he noted.

Mr. Karp is the director of the Leo Castelli Gallery, a lecturer and author on art subjects and the founder-director of the Anonymous Arts Recovery Society, which is dedicated to the preservation of architectural sculpture and ornamentation of New York City buildings.

"Parts of the ceiling were hanging down," he said. "Piles of trash appeared in every corner, plumbing was nonexistent, and all the electrical wiring was concentrated in the front of the loft." But the $150 monthly rent of the would-be dwelling, on Beekman Street, which is on the edge of the financial district, made these problems seem surmountable.

Mr. Karp rounded up friends who were artists and, for agreed-upon fees, delegated sections of the renovation project to each.

The main work, that of carpentry and of floor scraping and refinishing, was done by Tadasky, a sculptor, and John Fischer, a painter.

The Karps mapped out a budget and kept to it stringently. The $3,000 represents roughly $1,000 for lumber, $1,000 for labor and $1,000 for kitchen equipment, furniture and plumbing.

Finding panels of tin plate to match those in the existing ceiling, where many were missing, was a relatively simple task for Mr. Karp, who spends Sundays visiting demolition sites throughout Manhattan searching for architectural fragments worth salvaging.

Most of the actual labor in the apartment, with the exception of some painting, fell to others as Mr. Karp busily created plans for additional storage walls, kitchen cabinets and the design of the built-in Dutch type of bed.

"We thought it would be drafty in winter," Mr. Karp noted, explaining the bed, an anomaly in this age of central heating. "As it turned out, the building has marvelous insulation, but the design of the bed gives the sleeping area a sense of architecture."

Mrs. Karp was far more active in the manifold labors of refurbishing. In spite of the fact that she holds a fulltime job at the Museum of Primitive Art and expects to receive her Ph.D. in physics and art from New York University's School of Education this month, the 25-year-old sculptor surfaced every inch of the plywood cabinetry and floor ("It was miles") with a plastic-based finish.

Furnishings and appliances were either purchased at sales in department stores or were bought inexpensively "with a good bit of haggling over prices" at shops that specialize in turn-of-the-century decorations in Greenwich Village and along Second and Third Avenues.

Brightening the apartment, which is equivalent in size to a six-room home, are the lions and satyrs, old pediments and columns from Mr. Karp's scavenging excursions and some pop art arranged on walls and standing on floors.

The Karps have just learned that the building is due to be razed at the end of this year, but they still feel their efforts were worthwhile.

MAY 19, 1967

LAMP DESIGNERS ARE AGLOW OVER NAKED BULBS

Rita Reif

For nearly 90 years, architects and designers have done their best to keep lighting under wraps. Now the bare bulb is making a comeback in some circles, bringing with it spaghetti-like tangles of exposed wiring.

As naked as the day it was born in 1879, the incandescent light bulb today hangs on wiggly wires from ceilings or is attached unshaded to wall, table or floor fixtures. Reasons for the return include the influence of pop art on furnishings, improvement in the design of bulbs and dimmer controls, and the problems of engineering and of shipping knocked-down fixtures from abroad.

Italian designers are leaders in creating fixtures that sprout bulbs, sockets and wiring like blossoms on a tree. In fact, two designs resembling trees showed up in the Italian section of the National Lighting Exposition held at the Coliseum earlier this month.

An aluminum floor lamp with bulbs at the ends of its branches was sent by Gino Sarfatti, designer-owner of Arteluce, a Milan lamp producer. A table lamp, which looked like a miniature tree with bulbs instead of buds decorating its twig-like arms, was shown by Studio Artemidi of Milan.

Milanese designers, such as Joe Cesare Colombo, believe that bulbs, wiring and sockets are as pleasing as the flame of a candle. However, Mr. Colombo and his associates use bulbs of low wattage and apparently have a larger selection of them than do American designers.

Besides lamp designers, architects also favor exposed bulbs and wiring in limited applications. Allan Kramer, of Kramer and Kramer, covered a wall with shelves for art objects in his New York apartment and illuminated the wall with movable spotlights that have loops of exposed wire and

(cont'd. on next page)

(cont'd. from previous page)

naked bulbs. The lighting is attached to the same tracks that hold the shelves.

"The beauty of the wiring diagram is something architects have long recognized," Mr. Kramer said. "Many architects like to have a piece of machinery on their desk top—the back of a telephone or the inside of a radio. So why not work wiring into a scheme?"

> Milanese designers . . . believe that bulbs, wiring and sockets are as pleasing as the flame of a candle.

Hugh Hardy, another New York architect, goes further; whenever asked why he left the wire dangling between the illuminated boxes containing art objects on a wall in his home, he says:

"That's what makes the boxes light up—why not show it?"

If history repeats itself, the bare bulb may be doomed before it ever achieves popularity in homes. When J. Pierpont Morgan pioneered in having his home wired for electricity in 1881, all the bulbs in the wall and ceiling fixtures, fed by a generator in the basement, were exposed.

Two years later the financier was thinking of shades—at least for the table lamp that sat on a corner of the desk in his study. The fringed, silk shade was the first attack on the bare bulb which continued down to 1958, when the first pop art sculpture of a light bulb was done by Jasper Johns.

And if time does not reverse the trend, the regulations established by the New York City Department of Water, Gas and Electricity may check the fashion. According to a spokesman for the city agency, exposed wiring that measures more than seven and a half feet in length and triple-plug sockets are outlawed for use in homes here. ■

JUNE 27, 1967

Borderless World of Design

Rita Reif

National boundaries used to divide the world of furniture design. Not so any longer, judging by the selection of German, Danish, Canadian and American furniture now arriving in stores and showrooms. The trend is dramatically apparent in one of three room settings that are now on view on Altman's seventh floor. German Plexiglas and tubular metal chairs were arranged around a table of clear and opaque Plexiglas by Neal Small of New York ($285). They look as if the same factory had made them. The chairs, by E. Schmidt of Germany, are clear plastic shells—lined with four plump pillows for the seat, sides and back—set in a curved chromed metal base. They are $549 each. The table has a clear plastic center and base and four curried leaves of opaque plastic on the perimeter ($285).

In a second setting, European skill in designing storage was obvious. Walnut and white laminated plastic are combined in a clothing and hi-fi-storage unit from Germany. It's 15 feet long and has three floor-to-ceiling, double-door clothing compartments and a low cabinet for hi-fi. The entire unit is $1,498.

Danish imports include an ingenious walnut bed design that is a combination of two single beds, a single headboard and tray-like end tables, which can go outside the beds or between them ($575).

The Danes have also produced a mobile bar, small enough to move from one room to another or from city to vacation house. Closed it looks like a doll's trunk (it locks like one too). When open, there are drawers and shelves for storing bottles and glasses and two stainless steel trays for ice. Two leaves on the top fold out to double the length of a serving surface. It measures 35 inches high, 23 wide and 17 deep when closed ($399).

From north of the border, Macy's has a collection of four chromed metal, leather upholstered chairs by Robert Kaiser, an industrial designer, for Takna Limited of Toronto. A sling of saddle leather on a cross metal base is $319. A second chair with sausage-shaped arms is $463. A desk chair is $269 and a fourth side chair, $539.

The most unusual design was Mr. Kaiser's rosewood veneered plywood chair and ottoman that come in parts to be assembled in minutes. Tufted, vinyl-upholstered pillows then snap onto the frames. The chair comes knocked down or assembled at $410, the ottoman $210. The collection will be available July 15 on the ninth floor.

A new collection of Lucite and wood designs at Vladimir Kagan's showroom, 40 East End Avenue (81st Street), is in the same international mood. Mr. Kagan's showroom is open to the public.

The German-born American designer used Lucite in many pieces, including a barrel-shaped chair supporting a fabric-covered seat ($285). A sleep sofa with a Lucite base and walnut or rosewood frame has a novel sausage-shaped back roll that is held in place by two notches on the arms of the frame. When used for sleeping, the sausage back rolls off the frame ($668, in walnut, $758 in rosewood).

JANUARY 25, 1968

INFLATABLE SOFA COULD DOUBLE AS A LIFE RAFT

Lisa Hammel

The inflatable chair, 1969.

Giddiness is the emotion one feels thinking about buying the new inflatable furniture now coming into stores in quantity. It's like doing the living room in early balloon.

Yet the clear plastic furniture has its practical side.

A gentle kick and it's across the room, when you want to vacuum the rug.

And it travels well in other ways. You can bring your own chair to a party (folded neatly under the arm) or be more comfortable than usual at picnics.

Or you could take your sofa swimming.

"You can float down the Hudson River on our sofa," a designer's representative said recently. "And it will not tip over," he added, with evident satisfaction.

The sofa—a Chesterfield—is one of the designs by Quasar Khanh. Along with two styles of armchair, a pouf and a hanging light fixture, the sofa will be at Azuma in two or three weeks.

Mr. Khanh's representative, Victor von Mallinckrodt, was in the office above Azuma at 415 Fifth Avenue the other day to make arrangements about the furniture.

Seated in one of the clear plastic armchairs—a round one with a sausage back (he had declined the offer of a wicker chair)—he explained how Mr. Khanh had come to work in clear materials.

"Quasar says, 'We don't like mysteries or secrets any more. We like to see through everything today.' So he designs in clear plastic."

Mr. Khanh, a Vietnamese-born engineer whose wife is Emmanuelle Khanh, the fashion designer, has come a long way from the pursuits of his earlier years—building dams in Canada.

Mr. Khanh has also designed an inflatable, clear plastic house. He hopes to have one blown up for himself this summer on a little property he has near Nice.

The house consists, Mr. Mallinckrodt explained, of a pyramid of clear plastic tires resting on a foundation, with a plastic flap for the door. When Mr. Khanh wants privacy, he will turn on an apparatus that blows colored smoke through tubes.

The furniture at Azuma, which will also come in translucent red and blue, is quite sturdy and practical, Mr. Mallinckrodt asserted.

It will withstand the weight of a heavy man or several bouncing children, "provided they are not using knives."

It takes about two minutes to inflate or deflate the armchairs with a vacuum cleaner or bicycle pump. Azuma will also have a simple foot pump that will sell for $1

DECEMBER 29, 1969

FURNITURE DECADE
A Revolution That Left No Room Untouched

Rita Reif

The spectacular sixties introduced such ferment in design, decoration and life style to the American home that no room was left untouched by the decade's end.

It was the era when the two-car family became the two-house family, when adult playrooms appeared in the home, when American pride in bathroom plumbing was shaken, when urbanites, both young and old, planted new roots in decaying city neighborhoods and embarked on a fever of town house renovation.

It was the first period since the nineteen-twenties when furniture design underwent a revolution both in form and substance. Plastics changed the shape, color and function of furnishings, and people bought the style.

Decorating, too, underwent drastic alterations as eclecticism escalated, patterns proliferated, supergraphics grew large on modernists' walls, and the society decorator became the new dictator of what-goes-with-what in traditional homes.

In affluent America, the vacation house became a reality for millions of middle-class families. It was part of the new life style for would-be skiers and sunbathers seeking escape from their apartment walls or suburban neighbors. And it provided many with the opportunity of experimenting with the new modern furnishings.

Spurred by a deepening concern for restoration of historic sites and a more personal desire to remain in a city rather than flee to the suburbs, families in the older cities bought century-old brownstones. Renovations rid rotting neighborhoods of unwanted rooming houses and provided personalized, custom-built backgrounds for their new owners.

In furniture, inflatables made their debut and went from zero to millions in sales,

(cont'd. on next page)

(cont'd. from previous page)
bringing profits not only to the vinyl producers, but also to the bicycle pump and adhesive tape manufacturers. Verner Panton's Danish inflatable of 1964 marked the turning point that made transparent plastics eventually a commonplace element in home decorating.

The art world had a more direct relationship to developments than it had assumed in decades. In New York and Paris, artists of all stylistic persuasions experimented with art-furnishings. And in Italy, Matta, the artist, carved the first all-foam furnishings from a huge slab of foam.

If modern was not everyone's delight—and for most people it was not—there were a host of traditional styles to choose from. Mass America opted for Mediterranean, responding enthusiastically to the bulky designs that boasted elaborately carved facades and were rooted, somewhat shakily, in the Spanish and Italian Renaissance.

Antiques, too, accelerated in popularity in an era that regularly racked up new records at auction.

Interior design in the sixties mirrored the changes in furniture taste in both modern and traditional styles. The modern living room in 1960 was dominated by that hole in the floor called the conversation pit. But a few years later even Alexander Girard, the architect who popularized the sunken and padded pen, had banished his from the adobe he calls home in Santa Fe, N.M.

And soon the new avant-garde, following another piper, were scaling the ladders of their double-decker, jungle gym-like environments.

A typical 1960s living room.

Society decorators moved into the spotlight with the inauguration of President Kennedy. The media and then the general public wanted to know how the rich revamped their homes. William (Billy) Baldwin and Mrs. Henry Parish 2nd, both of whom worked for the First Family, obliged with some reluctance.

Eclecticism flourished especially in rooms choked with patterns. The mono-patterned room, such a shock in 1964, when a single pattern covered walls, floor, ceiling and furnishings, was soon upstaged by the multipatterned room with as many as five motifs fighting for attention.

And out in the kitchen the equipment had reached such sophistication that the oven cleaned itself, the refrigerator defrosted itself and the garbage was crushed to a fraction of its former bulk. And perhaps in the seventies, a robot would operate and service the super-equipped machinery that helps make today's house a home. ■

Sports

If one image has remained emblematic of sports in the 1960's and that knit sports more integrally into the racial turmoil of the time, it is the photo of Tommie Smith and John Carlos, gold- and bronze-medal winners in the 200-meter dash at the 1968 Summer Olympics in Mexico City, raising their clenched, black-gloved fists in the "black power" salute. The closest parallel was Cassius Clay, having been reborn as Muhammad Ali, refusing induction into the United States Army in protest as a black man against the Vietnam War, stripped of his heavyweight boxing title and denied a boxing license in all 50 states for four years.

Beyond racial protests, Wilma Rudolph proved herself the fastest woman at the 1960 Olympics in Rome, winning three gold medals, and Bob Beamon beat the long-jump record by more than two feet eight years later. Jack Nicklaus became the pre-eminent golfer of the decade, Roger Maris hit 61 home runs and Sandy Koufax was the dominant pitcher, taming the mighty Yankees. Arthur Ashe won the first U.S. Open, in which professionals could compete with amateurs. Billie Jean King ruled women's tennis, as Rod Laver did men's tennis, winning his second Grand Slam in 1969. The recently formed Mets shocked the world, or at least the country (the rest of the world cared more about the World Cup), by winning the World Series; and the Jets, led by "Broadway Joe" Namath, beat the heavily favored Baltimore Colts in Super Bowl III. Vince Lombardi and the Green Bay Packers won the first two Super Bowls and prevailed in the horrific Ice Bowl in 1968. Wilt Chamberlain scored 100 points in a basketball game but couldn't dislodge Bill Russell and the Celtics, who won championship after championship in pro basketball. The Celtics' dominance was echoed at the college level by John Wooden's UCLA Bruins.

The Times, like America itself, mostly paid attention to American sports, although Brazil's long mastery in soccer ("football" to the rest of the world) was certified by its victory in the 1962 World Cup, although England interrupted Brazil's dominance with its first World Cup Victory in 1966. But for Harvard students and graduates (if not for their Yale counterparts), the football story of the decade, and maybe the century, was summarized by that famous headline in the Harvard Crimson in 1968: "Harvard Beats Yale, 29–29." Both teams were undefeated, and Yale had a seemingly insurmountable lead with only a couple of minutes to go. Harvard staged a furious, improbable comeback, with the tie score amounting to a thrilling moral victory. Harvard loyalists swarmed the field, and the Yale side slunk away despondently. For fans, sports are supposed to be fun to play and to watch, but they can be cruel, too.

SEPTEMBER 9, 1960

WILMA RUDOLPH, WORLD SPEED QUEEN

Wilma Rudolph crosses the finish line of the Olympic 100-meter dash in Rome, September 1960. She also won the 200-meter dash and was a member of the gold medal-winning relay team.

Seven years ago, in a Clarkesville (Tenn.) high school gymnasium, a skinny, 13-year-old girl stumbled over her feet, tripped on the basketball she was trying to dribble and landed in an eighty-nine-pound tangle at her coach's feet.

"A skeeter," said the coach, shaking his head. "You are a skeeter, all right. You're little, you're fast and you always get in my way." Skeeter got up and tried again. Within two years she became an all-state basketball player at all-Negro Burt High. Within five years she was a 5-foot-11-inch young lady of charm and poise.

And yesterday, after winning her third gold medal in the Rome Olympics, Wilma Glodean (Skeeter) Rudolph was acclaimed as the speediest woman in the world.

In the race to her speed laurels, Wilma got off to a poor start. She was four and a half pounds at birth and her parents were not sure she would survive. At 4, Wilma was stricken with double pneumonia and scarlet fever. She lost the use of one leg. For two years, once a week, Mrs. Rudolph would bundle her small child in a blanket and take a bus to a Nashville clinic. At 6, wearing specially constructed shoes, Wilma could hop around on one leg. Slowly, she improved.

Then, when she was 11, one of Wilma's brothers set up a basketball hoop in the yard.

"After that it was basketball, basketball, basketball," said Mrs. Rudolph yesterday. "Whenever I'd call her in to eat or to clean up around the house, Wilma would be out in the yard having a big time."

At high school, Wilma came to the attention of C. C. Gray, the girls' basketball coach. She was a tanglefoot. "I called her skeeter, short for mosquito. Always buzzing around," said Gray. "On the way to out-of-town games, she'd sit in the back of the school bus and tell jokes from one end of the trip to another."

In 1955 Wilma scored 803 points in twenty-five games, a record. That year, in the state tournament at Nashville, Miss Rudolph was discovered as a track prospect by accident. Edward Temple, the women's track coach at Tennessee A. and I. State University, asked Gray to form a girls' track team at Burt. Wilma had suddenly discovered that running was even more fun than playing basketball. In three years of high school track competition Wilma never lost. In 1957 she entered the all-Negro college.

Tennessee A. and I. is the cathedral of women's track in this country and Temple the high priest. Wilma soon became the most devoted disciple. She ran at least two hours a day while keeping up a B average in her major, elementary education, and working four hours a day in a campus office. In the summer, Temple held three workouts a day. The first was at 5 A.M. Through it all, Wilma managed to have a social life, too. "Boys seem to like her, and every so often she seems to have a new one," Mrs. Temple said yesterday.

And Gray, who had untangled a little basketball player seven years ago, was ebullient as he confided: "I'm coaching her 15-year-old sister, Charlene. She's going to be even faster." ■

MARIS HITS 61ST IN FINAL GAME

John Drebinger

Roger Maris yesterday became the first major league player in history to hit more than sixty home runs in a season. The 27-year-old Yankee outfielder hit his sixty-first at the Stadium before a roaring crowd of 23,154 in the Bombers' final game of the regular campaign.

That surpassed by one the sixty that Babe Ruth hit in 1927. Ruth's mark has stood in the record book for thirty-four years.

Artistically enough, Maris' homer also produced the only run of the game as Ralph Houk's 1961 American League champions defeated the Red Sox, 1 to 0, in their final tune-up for the World Series, which opens at the Stadium on Wednesday.

Maris hit his fourth-inning homer in his second time at bat. The victim of the blow was Tracy Stallard, a 24-year-old Boston rookie right-hander. Stallard's name, perhaps, will in time gain as much renown as that of Tom Zachary, who delivered the pitch that Ruth slammed into the Stadium's right-field bleachers for No. 60 on the next to the last day of the 1927 season.

Along with Stallard, still another name was bandied about at the Stadium after Maris' drive. Sal Durante, a 19-year-old truck driver from Coney Island, was the fellow who caught the ball as it dropped into the lower right-field stand, some ten rows back and about ten feet to the right of the Yankee bull pen. For this achievement the young man won a $5,000 award and a round trip to Sacramento, Calif., offered by a Sacramento restaurant proprietor, as well as a round trip to the 1962 World's Fair in Seattle.

Maris was fooled by Stallard on an outside pitch that he stroked to left field for an out in the first inning. He let two pitches go by when he came to bat in the fourth with one out and the bases empty. The first one was high and outside. The second one was low and appeared to be inside. The crowd, interested in only one thing, a home run, greeted both pitches with a chorus of boos.

Then came the moment for which fans from coast to coast had been waiting since last Tuesday night, when Maris hit his sixtieth. Stallard's next pitch was a fast ball that appeared to be about waist high and right down the middle. In a flash, Roger's rhythmic swing, long the envy of left-handed pull hitters, connected with the ball.

Almost at once, the crowd sensed that this was it. An ear-splitting roar went up as Maris, standing spellbound for just an instant at the plate, started his triumphant jog around the bases. As he came down the third-base line, he shook hands joyously with a young fan who had rushed onto the field to congratulate him.

Crossing the plate and arriving at the Yankee dugout, he was met by a solid phalanx of teammates. This time they made certain the modest country lad from Raytown, Mo., acknowledged the crowd's plaudits. He had been reluctant to do so when he hit No. 60, but this time the Yankee players wouldn't let Roger come down the dugout steps. Smiling broadly, the usually unemotional player lifted his cap from his blond close-cropped thatch and waved it to the cheering fans. Not until he had taken four bows did his colleagues allow him to retire to the bench.

Ruth's record, of course, will not be erased. On July 17 Commissioner Ford C. Frick ruled that Ruth's record would stand unless bettered within a 154-game limit, since that was the schedule in 1927. Maris hit fifty-nine homers in the Yanks' first 154 games to a decision. He hit his sixtieth four games later. However, Maris will go into the record book as having hit the sixty-first in a 162-game schedule.

For thirty-four years the greatest sluggers in baseball had striven to match Ruth's mark. Mickey Mantle fought Maris heroically through most of the season, but in the closing weeks he fell victim to a virus attack and his total stopped at fifty-four. ■

Roger Maris hits home run number 61 in 1961, beating Babe Ruth's record.

MARCH 4, 1962

WILT CHAMBERLAIN REACHES 100-POINT GOAL

The Associated Press

Wilt Chamberlain's entire life has been dedicated to performing as nature has forced him to live—tall.

His amazing feat of scoring 100 points in a single professional basketball game last night was simply another plateau in the 7-foot-l-inch star's ceaseless campaign to attain perfection in his field. In the Philadelphia Warriors' 169-147 victory over New York, Chamberlain set four National Basketball Association records—the 100-point total, his 36 field goals, 31 points in one quarter and 59 in one half.

Chamberlain realized early in life that he could not hide behind a pair of dark glasses.

Since he's always been as conspicuous as a movie star, he's determined to shine like one.

The Philadelphia ace claims not to mind the gawkers, that he's learned to live with his size. He really hasn't. It's almost impossible. The truth is that Chamberlain is self-conscious, even on the basketball court—so much so that he fears his own strength.

This may explain why the Philadelphia-born player rarely indulges in fighting on the court, rarely fouls out of a game. His explanation always has been that he is paid to score, not fight, but so are the rest of the stars in the league. He plays like a man who hates to demean his opponents.

A syndicate has offered more than three-quarters of a million dollars for the Philadelphia club, with a view to moving it to San Francisco. The syndicate admits it's paying for the franchise and Wilt. Whatever else comes is considered gravy.

As the most sought-after schoolboy star of his time, Chamberlain turned his back on Philadelphia and went to the University of Kansas. An all-American as a sophomore and junior, he quit college before his final year to join the Harlem Globetrotters. He said the slow college game cramped his style.

A year later, when he was eligible for the N.B.A., he joined the Warriors. He wanted to prove to the world he was a basketball player, not a "Globie" clown.

More than 700,000 people flocked to see the Chamberlain led Warriors in 1961 as the N.B.A. set an attendance record. Chamberlain set four league marks and tied one. Then he said he was going to quit pro basketball. In his usual frank manner, he said he felt he was the target of rough tactics by opponents.

The mild-mannered giant explained that if he continued to play, he might lose his equilibrium and poise. Later, however, he relented and signed a three-year contract reported to make him the highest-paid athlete in the country.

Chamberlain remains a controversial figure. Despite his individual greatness, his team has been unable to win a title. Some N.B.A. players, coaches and fans say he refuses to lend himself to a team effort, loafs on defense, actually hurts his club's chances. His coach, Frank McGuire, says it isn't so.

"True," says McGuire, "it isn't a one-man game. But we have weaknesses. Wilt has been superhuman. I hate to think where we'd be without him, with just a mere human being in his place." ■

Wilt Chamberlain scoring in his 100-point game, March 4, 1962.

OCTOBER 3, 1963

MAN WITH GOLDEN CHARM

Sandy Koufax, left-handed pitcher for the Los Angeles Dodgers, in 1963.

To a gushy Hollywood columnist he is Clark Gable, Gregory Peck and William Holden rolled into one. To his associates at work he is "a real class guy." And as he proved again yesterday while striking out 15 Yankees and setting a World Series record, Sanford (Sandy) Koufax is the best pitcher in baseball.

At 27 years old, at least by the standards of the Brooklyn that claims him, Sandy Koufax (rhymes with Go, Max) has the world by the tail. He drives around Southern California in a bronze convertible. He escorts an ever-fresh batch of Hollywood cupcakes. He makes umpires wince at the crack of his fast ball. He has a lot of money.

Koufax also is rather shy, unusually sensitive for a ballplayer, and not terribly interested in baseball. He has been pressed, on occasion, to refute the statement that he reads only Thomas Wolfe and Aldous Huxley and listens only to Beethoven and Mendelssohn.

"I don't know what's so highbrow about Mendelssohn," he says.

And to complicate matters to those who might want to use Koufax as a shining example of the American Dream come true, the only real handicaps he had to overcome on the way to the top were boredom, inexperience, immaturity and a sore finger. Time took care of them all.

Born on Dec. 30, 1935, the son of a lawyer, Sandy was just a nice Jewish middle-class boy who wanted to be an architect. He played basketball and baseball at Lafayette High, and went to the University at Cincinnati on a basketball scholarship. In the spring of his freshman year he struck out 34 batters in two consecutive games. The bird-dogs of baseball descended.

In December of 1954, Sandy signed a contract with the Brooklyn Dodgers, calling for a bonus estimated at $15,000.

Under the bonus rules of that time, he could not be sent down to the minors. For the next six years, he got off the Dodger bench only long enough to show bursts of blinding speed and unpardonable wildness. Through 1960 he managed to tie the record for most strikeouts in a nine-inning game (18) and set records for strikeouts in two consecutive games (31) and in three consecutive games (41). He also lost more games than he won.

He was frustrated, taunted by teammates (who claimed he lacked competitive fire), hampered by a lack of regular minor-league experience, and so consumed by pressure that he was a rear-back-and-fog-it-in thrower instead of a thinking pitcher. His explosion into prominence in 1961 was based on a complex of incidents.

First, there was a verbal skirmish with Buzzie Bavasi, the Dodger General Manager.

"I want to pitch," screamed Koufax, "and you guys aren't giving me a chance!"

"How can you pitch," snapped Bavasi, "when you can't get the side out?"

"Who the hell can get the side out, sitting in the dugout?"

Koufax began to get more starting assignments, and Norm Sherry, a catcher, persuaded him to stop throwing so hard, to cut down 10 percent on speed and work on control, curve balls and change-of-pace. More experience led to more confidence, time to greater maturity. "Somehow I learned to concentrate on the next pitch and forget about the last one."

In 1961 he won 18 games and set a National League mark of 269 strike-outs. In 1962 he threw the first of two no-hitters, was leading the National League in earned-run average (2.06), in strike-outs (209) and had a 14-4 mid-season record when the index finger of his pitching hand turned white and numb and the skin began to peel off.

Koufax did not win another game last year. His condition was diagnosed as Reynaud's Phenomenon, a circulatory ailment resulting from a bloodclot in his palm. But time healed the finger, too, and by the end of the 1963 regular season he had won 25 games and struck out 306.

Whatever the rest of the Series holds for him, Koufax will undoubtedly earn a rise in salary (about $30,000 now), which will go into his bulging stock portfolio, his part interests in a motel and an FM radio station, his plush bachelor house in the San Fernando Valley, his stereotape collection, and his alpaca sweaters.

OCTOBER 7, 1963

DODGERS WIN, 2-1, SWEEPING SERIES AGAINST YANKEES

Koufax Triumphs Again; New York Loses Four in a Row for First Time

John Drebinger

LOS ANGELES, Oct.6—The Los Angeles Dodgers brought the long reign of the high and mighty New York Yankees to a dramatic end today.

Behind another superb pitching effort by their brilliant left-hander, Sandy Koufax, the Dodgers downed the perennial American League champions, 2-1. That gave Walter Alston's National League champions a stunning four-game sweep of the World Series before a deliriously happy crowd of 55,912 in Dodger Stadium.

The Yankees' indomitable Whitey Ford, fighting desperately to keep the Bombers alive, pitched perhaps an even greater game than his adversary, who had defeated him so easily in the first game. Whitey allowed only two hits to six by Koufax.

But in the seventh inning, minutes after Mickey Mantle had hit a homer that matched a tremendous clout by Frank Howard in the fifth and made the score 1-1, a ghastly error by the usually flawlessly fielding Yanks plunged the Bombers to their most humiliating World Series defeat in more than 40 years.

Junior Gilliam, first up for the Dodgers in the seventh, bounced a "Baltimore chop" off the plate and down the third base line. For a moment it appeared that the ball might sail over Cletis Boyer's head.

But the Yanks' classy third baseman made a leaping catch of the ball and fired it like a bullet across the infield to first base. The ball, still traveling like a bullet, went right through Joe Pepitone, the crack young first baseman, for an error. It appeared that in the last instant Pepitone had lost sight of the ball in the glaring sun.

Before the ball could be retrieved in a corner of right field, the fleet-footed Gilliam had raced to third base. Willie Davis followed with a towering fly deep in center field, where it was caught by Mantle, who with this play was to see all of his noble effort undone. Mickey fired the ball faultlessly toward the plate, but there was no chance of heading off Gilliam as he went winging home on the sacrifice fly.

Once again in front, Koufax, who in last Wednesday's opener had set a World Series record of 15 strike-outs, refused to let the lead slip away again.

To Alston went the distinction of having piloted the Dodgers to their only three championships in 11 Series. Moreover, he achieved these in three different settings. The first, in 1955, was over the Yanks in Ebbets Field, Brooklyn. In 1959, Alston brought Los Angeles its first world championship in its second year in the major leagues. But that year the Dodgers made the Coliseum their temporary home. Today's victory came in Walter F. O'Malley's glittering temple in Chavez Ravine.

As for Ralph Houk, who had led the Yanks to three successive American League pennants three years at the helm, his defeat was perhaps one of the most crushing and humiliating in World Series history. ■

FEBRUARY 26, 1964

CASSIUS CLAY DEFEATS SONNY LISTON

Robert Lipsyte

MIAMI BEACH, Feb. 25—Incredibly, the loud-mouthed bragging, insulting youngster had been telling the truth all along. Cassius Clay won the world heavyweight title tonight when a bleeding Sonny Liston, his left shoulder injured, was unable to answer the bell for the seventh round.

(cont'd. on next page)

Cassius Clay (later known as Muhammad Ali) against Sonny Liston during their heavyweight title fight at Miami Beach, Florida, 1964.

(cont'd. from previous page)

Immediately after he had been announced as the new heavyweight champion of the world, Clay yelled to the newsmen covering the fight: "Eat your words." Only three of 46 sports writers covering the fight had picked him to win.

A crowd of 8,297, on its feet through the early rounds at Convention Hall, sat stunned during the one-minute rest period between the sixth and seventh rounds. Only Clay seemed to know what had happened; he threw up his hands and danced a little jig in the center of the ring.

The victory was scored as a technical knockout in the seventh round, one round less than Clay had predicted. Liston seemingly had injured the shoulder in the first round while swinging and missing with jabs and hooks at the elusive 22-year-old.

The fight was Clay's from the start. The tall, swift youngster, his hands carelessly low, backed away from Liston's jabs, circled around Liston's dangerous left hook and opened a nasty gash under Liston's left eye. He never let Liston tie him up for short, brutal body punches, and although he faltered several times, he refused to allow himself to be cornered. His long left jab kept bouncing off Liston's face.

The men had moved briskly into combat, Liston stalking, moving flat-footedly forward. He fell short with two jabs, brushed Clay back with a grazing right to the stomach and landed a solid right to the stomach. The crowd leaned forward for the imminent destruction of the young poet.

But the kid hadn't lied. All those interminable refrains of "float like a butterfly, sting like a bee," had been more than foolish songs. The kid was floating. He leaned back from Liston's jabs and hooks, backed into the ropes, then spun out and away. He moved clockwise around Liston, taunting that terrible left hook, his hands still low.

And then the crowd was cheering and booing, which is something like laughing and crying because it was the wildest thing they had ever seen. It didn't make sense. For weeks, Clay had played the fool and been tagged at will by unworthy sparring partners. This morning, at the weigh-in, he had acted bizarre and disturbed. And tonight, he had been cool and fast and without fear.

Until the knockout, the officials had had the fight a draw. Referee Barney Felix had scored the six rounds 57-57 on the 10-point-must system. Judge Bill Lovitt scored it 58-56 for Liston, and Judge Gus Jacobsen 58-56 for Clay.

But points didn't really matter after all. Poetry and youth and joy had triumphed over the 8-1 odds. And until it had happened (and perhaps until they can look it up) people laughed at the thought that a night like this could happen. ■

APRIL 10, 1965

Houston's Astrodome Open

HOUSTON, April 9—With President Johnson present, the Astrodome—the world's largest air-conditioned room—opened tonight with the first indoor major league baseball game. The President, accompanied by Mrs. Johnson, arrived here from Washington before going on to Johnson City, Tex., for the weekend. A bomb threat, telephoned to a local radio station, was given as the reason for an unheralded entrance by the Presidential party into the ballpark.

Few in the crowd of 47,876 knew the President was in the stadium until it was announced after the first inning of the exhibition game between the New York Yankees and the Houston Astros.

Mr. Johnson's presence enhanced an opening that had been marred earlier by the discovery that the dome's Lucite skylights so diffused the hard Texas sunlight that fly balls were all but untrackable during daylight hours. Experiments, begun today with orange baseballs, will continue tomorrow with cerise, yellow and red baseballs, specially tinted glasses and, perhaps, a new covering for the dome.

There was no problem tonight. Seated on an overstuffed yellow velvet swivel chair, the President saw Mickey Mantle hit the Astrodome's first home run. The sixth-inning smash caromed off a railing in the right center-field pavilion seats, about 400 feet away.

Although there were many empty seats, the stadium had been sold out for the event. "It's really cool," cried a white-gloved woman with gray curls, and her escort could only say, "Fabulous, really fabulous."

"When we Texans put things up," said a Santa Fe Railroad engineer, "we put them up right big." The engineer and his wife and daughter had driven 650 miles from Amarillo for the opening. He could remember back 30 years when this area, seven miles south of downtown Houston, was grazing land. Now his wife just beamed and said, "First ball game I ever been at where I enjoyed the seats." The seats are all upholstered in this park, like theater seats. Even the 3,000 bleacher chairs (called pavilion seats and sold for $1.50) have seat cushions, with rounded wooden backs.

The spectators were coming to see, among other things, the world's largest greenhouse (carpeted by 3 1/2 acres of Tifway Bermuda grass imported from Georgia), the largest scoreboard (six acres), and the longest baseball dugouts (120 feet each). The length of the dugouts is a reflection of the theory of the prime mover behind the Astrodome, Judge Roy Hofheinz, that people like to say they sat behind the dugout.

At its highest point, the dome rises 208 feet—higher than an 18-story building. Sitting up there, out in the heat, is a weather station that will control the air-conditioning, and a traffic spotter, who will radio warnings of potential tie-ups to police stations as far as five miles away.

The carpers in the crowd, however, were able to point to the 4,596 transparent Lucite rectangles in the dome and snicker. Black under the night sky, the skylights are blindingly bright in the afternoon. Yesterday, Astro outfielders stumbled and cringed under high fly balls, complaining that the baseball disappeared against the latticework rectangles of Lucite and concrete. Most subtle carpers, of course, need only say that there is nothing new under the sun, including the dome. After all, Emperor Vespasian had a domed stadium built in Rome about 1,895 years ago. The roof was a cloth awning that covered six acres of the Flavian amphitheater and stretched as high as 161 feet.

APRIL 12, 1965

NICKLAUS SUCCEEDS IN BECOMING MASTER OF HIMSELF

Gerald Eskenazi

When Jack Nicklaus was 10 years old, his father, Charlie, had a knee operation. The elder Nicklaus, a once-a-week golfer, couldn't keep up with his usual partners on the course so he invited young Jack to play, figuring his son wouldn't move so fast. It was his son's first appearance on a golf course.

Yesterday, no one kept up with Jack William Nicklaus. He scored the most convincing victory ever achieved in the Masters tournament at Augusta, Ga., as he fired a 69 to wind up with a record-shattering 72-hole total of 271.

The Nicklaus that the throngs at the Augusta National Golf Club saw was different from the methodical, unsmiling, machine-like player they had seen in the past years. One of the millions of television viewers who watched his victory said, "He looks like a happy kid."

If, in past years, Nicklaus has looked like something other than a "happy kid" it was, perhaps, because of the pressures he built for himself and the impossible standards he set.

"It was work, work, work, for Jack," Wayne Byers, a friend of Nicklaus's said by telephone from Columbus, Ohio.

"When Jack was 11 years old, he caught the bug. He would go on the course, play 18 holes—sometimes even 36—and then go to the driving range and hit five hundred to a thousand balls."

"You know," Byers continued, "it would seem he was doing it for the sheer joy of smacking them. You couldn't measure how many holes of golf he played. You had to measure the time he put in by the hours."

By the time he was 15, he had become the second youngest (to Bobby Jones) to qualify for the National Amateur tournament and had won three statewide junior tourneys.

Nicklaus divided his time among the fairways, the baseball diamonds and the basketball courts. He earned letters as a catcher on Upper Arlington High School's baseball team and as a backcourt man on the basketball squad.

Nicklaus, who was 25 years old last Jan. 21, is 6 feet tall, weighs 210 pounds and looks chubby. He was more slender in high school, but he added heft to his huge frame when he entered Ohio State. He became one of the country's outstanding amateur golfers. And then the pressures started.

"I've always had the feeling that Jack spread himself too thin," Byers said. "People were after him to turn pro while he was going to school. He finally did and then he had to worry about making a living for his family and struggling to finish college. And all the time people were bothering him. I think he turned inward then and perhaps mistrusted people."

But in his rise to the top Nicklaus mellowed. He almost had to if he were to become the successful businessman he is. He is part owner, with Arnold Palmer and Gary Player, of a paper-producing factory. He also has money invested in stocks and is the author of "My 55 Ways to Better Golf."

"He's so relaxed now. I bet they had to wake him to get him to the course," his secretary, Colleen Drew, said from Columbus.

Nicklaus was in no danger of rising late. His father, mother, sister and brother-in-law were with him as well as his wife, Barbara, who is expecting their third child. Their second son, Steve, was 2 years old yesterday.

Miss Drew said Barbara had predicted the victory. "She said 'Jack wins a Masters everytime I'm pregnant.' " Steve was born four days after Nicklaus captured the Masters in 1963.

Jack Nicklaus during the 1965 Masters golf tournament.

JUNE 9, 1966

NATIONAL AND AMERICAN FOOTBALL LEAGUES MERGE

Joseph M. Sheehan

Professional football's heated money war has ended. The 47-year-old National Football League and seven-year-old American Football League announced yesterday plans to merge into a single league of at least 26 teams in 25 cities.

It will take until 1970, after their present, separate multi-million dollar television contracts expire, for the leagues fully to implement the merger by playing a unified schedule. Meanwhile, the leagues will retain their present identities.

But the merger agreement will have many immediate benefits to the clubs of both present leagues and professional football's legion of followers—if not to the players. Under the pact, there will be a world championship game next January between the 1966 champions of each league. This will provide the first interleague confrontation on the playing field. There also will be interleague preseason play starting in 1967.

The leagues also have agreed to conduct a common draft of graduating players next January. Up to now, the leagues have conducted separate drafts, allowing players to negotiate with one team in each league—and to play them off against each other. This gave rise to a costly bidding war between the leagues for prime prospects and was a major factor in the move for peace. The common draft will drastically cut bonus payments and should appease the colleges, which have rallied against the in-season solicitation and pre-mature signings of college players attributable to the scramble for talent.

It also raised a possible restraint-of-trade issue under the antitrust laws. In Washington, the Justice Department said it would "take a close look" at the merger plan to see if it violates antitrust laws. A department spokesman said the agency "had been given some advance notice" of the merger.

The agreement requires the nine present American League clubs to pay the 15 present National League clubs a total of $518 million in principal and interest over a 20-year period. The National League clubs also will receive the franchise fees to be paid by two new clubs—one in each present league—to be added by 1968. On the basis of going franchise rates, this could add $15 million to $18 million to the National League coffers.

The National League also yielded on its one-team-to-a-city stand in permitting the American League Jets to remain in New York in addition to the National League Giants and in allowing the American League Raiders to stay in Oakland, in the same metropolitan area as the National League Forty-Niners of San Francisco.

The National League drew a record total of 4,634,021 paid admissions to its 98 regular-season games in 1965, up 70,972 from 1964, averaging 47,286 per game (which was 80 percent of available park capacity). The American League also reached a new peak last year, drawing 1,773,781 to 56 regular-season games, up 325,909 from 1964, averaging 31,675. Season ticket demand has reached a stage in the National League where at least half the member teams already are assured of capacity crowds for all their home games this year. Some American League teams, most notably the Jets here and the Bills in Buffalo, also are approaching the point of guaranteed home sellouts.

JULY 31, 1966

2 Goals in Overtime Give British First World Cup

W. Granger Blair

LONDON, July 30—England, deprived of a victory by a German goal in the last 15 seconds of regular play, broke through in overtime today and won the World Cup, emblematic of international soccer supremacy, by beating West Germany, 4-2. England's first World Cup victory was witnessed by a crowd of 100,000 in Wembley Stadium. It was a match marked by the kind of hard, clean play that had been noticeably absent from a number of the earlier games in the tournament.

When it was over and the spectators were shouting "England, England," Bobby Moore, the captain of the English eleven, led his team to the royal box to receive the solid gold cup from Queen Elizabeth.

A lesser team than England might have been demoralized by that game-tying goal in the last 15 seconds of the regulation 90 minutes, when England was leading, 2-1.

In a skirmish in front of the English goal, Wolfgang Weber, a German halfback, kicked the ball into the net for the equalizer. That the Germans were in a position to score stemmed largely from England's refusal to adopt stalling tactics to keep the ball.

Only once did the English team stall—about three minutes before the end of regulation play. The crowd began booing and the home eleven quickly swung back to the offensive, thereby giving the Germans their golden opportunity.

Eleven minutes after the 30-minute overtime period began. Geoff Hurst scored for England on a 10-yard shot. He booted in another goal on a breakaway dash in the final seconds. He had scored on a header in the opening minutes of the match.

The scoring began when Helmut Haller, the outstanding German forward, fired a low, powerful shot into the English goal 10 minutes after the opening whistle. Hurst tied it for England nine minutes later, when he headed in a nicely lofted free kick by Moore, who was chosen by soccer writers as the most valuable player of the tournament.

Ten minutes before regulation play was to end, Martin Peters, an English forward, found an opening in a melee in front of the German goal and blasted the ball past the sprawling German goalie, Hans Tilkowski. Then came the Weber goal that sent the game into overtime.

Hurst's first goal in overtime seemed doubtful for a moment. The linesman first indicated that the ball had hit the top bar, but had not gone in. But he and the referee conferred and England was awarded the goal as the crowd cheered.

Whatever doubts German fans might have had about the legitimacy of the English lead were dispelled when, with virtually the entire German team pressing on the English cage in a desperate attempt to score, Hurst broke away with the ball, drove downfield and easily beat the German goalie. ■

JANUARY 16, 1967

GREEN BAY WINS FIRST SUPER BOWL

William N. Wallace

Green Bay Packers quarterback Bart Starr drops back to pass in Super Bowl I, a 35-10 victory over the Kansas City Chiefs on January 15, 1967.

LOS ANGELES, Jan. 15—Bryan Bartlett (Bart) Starr, the quarterback for the Green Bay Packers, led his team to a 35-10 victory over the Kansas City Chiefs today in the first professional football game between the champions of the National and American Leagues. Doubt about the outcome disappeared in the third quarter when Starr's pretty passes made mere Indians out of the American League Chiefs and Green Bay scored twice.

The outcome served to settle the curiosity of the customers, who paid from $6 to $12 for tickets, and a television audience estimated at 60 million, regarding the worth of the Chiefs. The great interest had led to naming the event the Super Bowl, but the contest was more ordinary than super.

Starr, methodical and unruffled as ever, completed 16 of 23 passes, six producing first downs on key third-down plays. Seven completions went to Max McGee, a 34-year-old substitute end who was in action only because Boyd Dowler, the regular, was hurt on the game's sixth play. McGee scored two of Green Bay's five touchdowns, the first one after an outstanding one-handed, hip-high catch of a pass thrown slightly behind him.

The Packers, who had been favored by two touchdowns, knew they were in a challenging game for at least half of the 2 1/2-hour contest. Kansas City played very well in the first two quarters and the half-time score, 14-10, made the teams just about even. But that was all for Kansas City. In the second half the mighty Packer defense shut out the Chiefs, who were in the Green Bay half of the field only once—for one play. And they were only four yards into Packer territory.

For their efforts the Packer players won $15,000 each, with $7,500 going to each Chief. Gate receipts were estimated at $750,000 and the two television networks—the Columbia Broadcasting System and the National Broadcasting Company—paid $1 million apiece for the TV rights. So this was a $2,750,000 event, the richest for any American team sports event.

The Super Bowl games will now go on year after year, but it may be some time before an American League team will be good enough to win one, especially if the National League champion comes from Green Bay. ■

MARCH 27, 1967

Mighty U.C.L.A. Stands Alone As Ruler of College Basketball

Gordon S. White Jr.

LOUISVILLE, Ky., March 26—Collegiate basketball is clearly split into two divisions:

1—The University of California, Los Angeles.

2—All the other teams.

At least Dayton, trounced by U.C.L.A., 79-64, in the final of the National Collegiate championship last night, can lay claim to being the best of the others. But U.C.L.A. is king of the mountain, with unanimous backing to remain there for two more seasons.

The strategy that will be used to stop Lew Alcindor and his speedy teammates next season will be varied. Coaches can sleep on that problem for nine months.

Dayton, with Don May; Houston with Elvin Hayes and two other 6-foot-8-inch players; Southern California, which used the stall; and all of U.C.L.A.'s other victims in its undefeated season of 30 games didn't have the answer this time.

U.C.L.A. figures to continue as the national champion if the 7-foot-1 3/8-inch Alcindor remains there. He has given no indication he will leave before his scheduled graduation in 1969.

The finale of the National Collegiate Athletic Association tournament was not a thrilling game. Alcindor, good as he is, made victory so routine and easy that the excitement vanished seconds after the start.

U.C.L.A. is too good to provide exciting basketball. Though Houston, in a semifinal match, tested the Bruins for a while, the big and strong Cougars were obviously beaten by half-time.

Alcindor is a sophomore. Three of his best teammates—Kenny Heitz, Lynn Shackelford and Lucius Allen—are sophomores. Mike Warren, the best of the supporting cast, is a junior.

Next season, as if U.C.L.A. needs help, Coach John Wooden can call on another current sophomore, Dick Lynn. Up from the freshman ranks will be 6'8" Steve Patterson.

Coaches generally agreed on what it would take to beat U.C.L.A. First, two strong tall men must keep Alcindor under some restraint. Houston surrounded him with tall men who cut down the number of passes to him.

Second, fast defenders must harass the four other Bruins. This means three men must cover four Bruins, since two must work on Alcindor.

Third, excellent outside shooting is needed. No one can hit regularly inside because of the way Alcindor slaps the ball back into the shooter's face.

Finally, the conqueror of the Bruins must hope to catch U.C.L.A. on a bad night. ■

Lew Alcindor, who later changed his name to Kareem Abdul-Jabbar, played for the U.C.L.A. Bruins from 1965-1969.

APRIL 29, 1967

CLAY REFUSES ARMY OATH; STRIPPED OF BOXING CROWN

Robert Lipstyte

HOUSTON, April 28—Cassius Clay refused today, as expected, to take the one step forward that would have constituted induction into the armed forces. There was no immediate Government action.

Although Government authorities here foresaw several months of preliminary moves before Clay would be arrested and charged with a felony, boxing organizations instantly stripped the 25-year-old fighter of his world heavyweight championship.

"It will take at least 30 days for Clay to be indicted and it probably will be another year and a half before he could be sent to prison since there undoubtedly will be appeals through the courts," United States Attorney Morton Susman said.

Clay, in a statement distributed a few minutes after the announcement of his refusal, said: "I have searched my conscience and I find I cannot be true to my belief in my religion by accepting such a call." He has maintained throughout recent unsuccessful civil litigation that he is entitled to draft exemption as an appointed minister of the Lost-Found Nation of Islam, the so-called Black Muslim sect.

Clay, who prefers his Muslim name of Muhammad Ali, anticipated the moves against his title in his statement, calling them a "continuation of the same artificially induced prejudice and discrimination" that had led to the defeat of his various suits and appeals in Federal courts, including the Supreme Court.

Hayden C. Covington of New York, Clay's lawyer, said that further civil action to stay criminal proceedings would he initiated. If convicted of refusal to submit to induction, Clay is subject to a maximum sentence of five years imprisonment and a $10,000 fine.

Mr. Covington, who has defended many Jehovah's Witnesses in similar cases, has repeatedly told Clay during the last few days, "You'll be unhappy in the fiery furnace of criminal proceedings but you'll come out unsinged."

During the morning, five white youngsters from the Friends World Institute, a nonaccredited school in Westbury, L.I., who had driven all night from a study project in Oklahoma, and half a dozen local Negro youths, several wearing Black Power buttons, had appeared on the street. Continuous and sometimes insulting interviewers eventually provoked both groups, separately, to appear with signs. The white group merely asked for the end of the Vietnam war and greater efforts for civil rights. The Negroes eventually swelled into a group of about two dozen circling pickets carrying hastily scrawled "Burn, Baby, Burn" signs and singing, "Nothing kills a nigger like too much love." A few of the pickets wore discarded bedsheets and table linen wound into African-type garments, but most were young women dragged into the little demonstration on their lunch hours.

There was a touch of sadness and gross exaggeration throughout the most widely observed noninduction in history. At breakfast this morning in the Hotel America, Clay had stared out a window into a dingy, cold morning and said: "Every time I fight it gets cold and rainy. Then dingy and cool, no sun in sight nowhere." He had shrugged when Quinnan Hodges, his associate counsel, had showed him an anonymously sent newspaper clipping in which a photograph of Mr. Hodges had been marked "Houston's great nigger lawyer."

Sadly, too, 22-year-old John McCullough, a graduate of Sam Houston State College, said: "It's his prerogative if he's sincere in his religion, but it's his duty as a citizen to go in. I'm a coward, too." Then Mr. McCullough, who is white, went up the steps to be inducted. He was one of the 46 young men, including Clay, who were called to report on this day.

AUGUST 27, 1967

Plays Tennis Like a Man, Speaks Out Like—Billie Jean King

Hal Higdon

Billie Jean King after beating Ann Jones to win the women's singles title at the Wimbledon Lawn Tennis Championships, July 1967.

WHEN she first started playing in tennis tournaments, little Billie Jean Moffitt found her aggressive net-rushing style ineffectual against the "backcourters"—"the kids that are very steady, and play from the back court, and hit lobs all day" waiting for the opponent to make the first mistake. "They used to say, 'Ha, ha, all we need to do is get two or three back on you and you'll miss the fourth shot.' And I said, 'We'll see who's winning when we're 16.' "

It didn't take that long. When she was 15 she won her first big tournament with her own hard-hitting style, and since then she hasn't slackened a bit: she still plays a man's game, darting toward the net and glowering over it like an angry bear, covering the court as a fly covers a sugar bowl, slamming serves and mixing ground shots the way Juan Marichal mixes pitches.

Her hard, grueling game has led her to the top of women's amateur tennis, and following this summer's capture of the "Triple Crown" at Wimbledon—her second consecutive women's singles title, her fourth women's doubles championship and the mixed doubles title—Mrs. Billie Jean Moffitt King is now comfortably lodged as the world's No. 1 women's tennis player.

One of the few honors still to elude the dynamic Mrs. King is, oddly enough, the championship of her own country. But she will have a chance to remedy that this week when she goes into the United States Lawn Tennis Association tournament at Forest Hills beginning Friday. The odds are strong in her favor.

The world's top-ranked women's player is 23 years old, stands 5 feet 6 inches tall and weighs 140 pounds ("That is, when things are going right—I love to eat"). Unlike most men tennis players, who wear a sweat band around one wrist, Billie Jean—as if to emphasize her femininity—wears a gold bracelet which a friend gave her several years ago and which she hasn't taken off since. With short wavy brown hair, blue harlequin glasses, 5 million freckles and a Doris Day face, Mrs. King seems an ordinary attractive young lady.

But she is probably amateur tennis's most colorful and controversial player today.

"I have a tendency to say things that should be off the record," she admits. "I don't know if our men really want to be the best in the world," she once told a reporter asking about American tennis players. "There's no glory in this country!" And when a Chicago newspaperman recently approached Billie Jean with a request to interview her for a feature on the women's page, she blurted angrily: "That's the trouble with this sport. We've got to get it off the society page and onto the sports pages!"

Mrs. King is as outspoken and controversial on the court as off. "Billie Jean's a ham," says her husband Larry. "She likes to play before fans. And she lets them know when she's angry." If the call of an official displeases her, she does not hesitate to raise her voice to tell him. After one close line call in Fox Point, she snapped at the line judge: "How can you see from that position?" The line judge lifted his nose as if to indicate that he had been judging for 30 years and would do as he damn pleased, but following game point, when he thought no one was looking, he shifted his chair so he could see straight down the line.

"I have a tendency to say things that should be off the record . . ."

She admits, however, that lately her language has changed like her tennis game, to become less flamboyant and more mechanical. Billie Jean also dislikes the sepulchral atmosphere at most tennis tournaments and would like to see the fans shout and cheer and even boo for a change. The conservatives within tennis—that is, practically everybody—raise their eyebrows at this suggestion, too.

The consensus of the experts is that Billie Jean is not yet up to the level of those great tennis ladies of the past. "But," says Jack Kramer, "I think she's just about ready to jump into that group."

Meanwhile, Billie Jean figures that she has another two or three years of highly competitive tennis before time comes to settle down and raise a family. At the present she has focused her eyes on one goal: winning the grand slam. But that will have to wait at least until next year, since she did not play the Australian championships this year, being laid up with stomach trouble, and she lost the French championship.

Seated in the clubhouse of the Town Club, she speculated on her future: "You know, one tennis match to me is almost like life. There are so many ups and downs. You can be down to where you think there's no way possible you can win a match. You just keep trying step by step and finally you win. The next time you're in a position when you're ahead and you lose. It's just like life. Life's like that." ■

JANUARY 1, 1968

Ice Bowl: Starr's Packers Win Third Title in a Row

GREEN BAY, Wis., Dec. 31—There had never been a football game like this one. Everyone agreed—Vince Lombardi, the winning coach; Tom Landry, the losing coach; Chuck Howley, the Dallas linebacker who symbolized the losers; Bart Starr, the quarterback who scored the winning touchdown with 13 seconds left to play.

The Green Bay Packers, frustrated and punished for 40 of the 60 minutes it takes to play these games, won their third straight championship of the National Football League by defeating the Dallas Cowboys, 21-17, before a capacity crowd of 50,861 at Lambeau Field.

The temperature was 14 degrees below zero at the start of the game and 12 degrees below at the end. And on top of that there was a 14-knot northwest breeze blowing down from the Yukon. "It was terrible out there," said Landry, "terrible for both sides. That in itself made this game distinctive from any other."

The fact that the teams, champions of the Western and Eastern conferences of the N.F.L., were able to play such capable football was remarkable. It was remarkable too that the stadium was filled and nobody went home before the outcome was decided. The customers, who paid as much as $17 for their tickets, received full worth.

No team in the 47-year history of the N.F.L. has ever before won three straight championships. But the Packers came within 13 seconds of missing this achievement. On third down from the 1-yard line Starr drove over right guard behind Jerry Kramer's block to score the winning touchdown. This touchdown came at the end of an exciting 68-yard drive against the gallant Cowboys and the clock.

Football players are mortal like the rest of us and they have fear. "I was scared we had thrown it all away," said Henry Jordan, the Packers' defensive tackle who played a magnificent game.

Starr, pressured relentlessly by the Cowboy front four, was thrown eight times while attempting to pass, for losses totaling 76 yards.

But Bart and all the Packers have come back so many times from the depths of adversity. They did so again by mustering the last scoring drive. Starr passed to Donnie Anderson for 6 yards, to Anderson again for 12 to the Dallas 39 and then a big one to Chuck Mercein for 19 to the Cowboy 11. Mercein, a fullback, who was a New York Giants' reject, stormed to the 3. Anderson was stopped twice and then Starr tried the quarterback sneak to score.

If he had failed would the Packers have had time to kick a field goal on fourth down to tie the score and send the game into a sudden-death overtime? Their time-outs were used up. "It would have been close," said Lombardi. "We didn't want a tie. We had compassion for those spectators. We wanted to send them home right then." ■

FEBRUARY 11, 1968

PEGGY FLEMING ACCLAIMED AS BALLERINA ON ICE

Lloyd Garrison

GRENOBLE, France, Feb. 10—Peggy Fleming's victory in the Olympic figure skating tonight was not only a personal triumph, it was also a victory of the ballet over the Ice Follies approach to figure skating.

For traditional aficionados, her victory had all the ingredients of a Good Guy whipping the Bad Guys in an Italian-made Western, in which the film is no good unless the Good Guy guns down at least a posse of black-hatted hombres in the first

(cont'd. on next page)

Figure skater Peggy Fleming competing in the Olympics, February 1968.

(cont'd. from previous page)
reel. Tonight, the Colorado State college girl with a weakness for chocolate cake and whipped cream took on no fewer than 32 competitors and knocked them all dead.

Until Miss Fleming came along, the women's figure skating threatened to be dominated by those whom Dick Button calls the Diana Dorses of the sport—"the razzle-dazzle girls who are all flash and no depth."

Audrey Hepburn of Skating

Earlier tonight America's two-time Olympic winner in the men's figures described Peggy Fleming as the Audrey Hepburn of skating, "and Audrey Hepburn is not a Diana Dors and never will be. She isn't deliberately flashy. She doesn't blast you. She's subtle." The Diana Dorses are not unpretty to look at, but to observers like Button, they resemble overgrown chorus girls with the legs of a Green Bay linebacker. "You see a lot of Peggy's competition clumping around, skating fast like hockey players, flailing the ice with quick stops, trying to overpower you with gimmicks. The crowd may like it but it's not beautiful and it's not good skating."

"With Peggy, there's not a misplaced move. She's always in perfect position going in and out of her jumps."

The "Ice Follies" analogy was coined by Miss Fleming herself. "I primarily represent the ballet approach," she said the other day. "That is, where the movements are more graceful and everything blends smoothly as you flow across the ice." Being polite, she describes the "Ice Follies" school as being merely more "athletic." But the other girls got the point.

"Peggy," says Gabrielle Seyfert of East Germany, "has no weaknesses. I know I am the more athletic type and I'm trying to overcome it. Peggy lands softly and everything she does is connected. It's pure ballerina."

At 5 feet 4 inches and currently weighing only 108 pounds, Peggy has occasionally gotten up to 112—with her penchant for desserts. But such rare lapses account for her breaks in discipline in a sport with incredible physical and psychological demands.

While at times exuding a sorority girl's impishness, on the ice she's all poise, a very worldly black-haired and dark-eyed beauty. At last year's world championships in Vienna, the Austrian press tried to pin down Miss Fleming's appeal both as a skater and as a young woman. Some described her as "classic." Others compared her to a Grecian beauty. The Express finally tabbed her as "America's Shy Bambi."

Few would quibble with any one of these descriptions. But Miss Fleming is refreshingly unconcerned about image-making.

Before the finals here, she had her usual double-decker sandwich. After she had won and was finished with the interviews and the congratulations, she had her chocolate cake. And at last, with tonight's triumph, a few pounds more or less wouldn't matter. ■

MAY 29, 1968

Will Hockey Fans Warm to Baseball?

Edward Cowan

MONTREAL, May 28—Not quite calm yet from the Canadiens' Stanley Cup victory, hockey-mad Montreal quietly preened itself today on its elevation to baseball's major leagues.

The National League club owners' award last night of franchises to Montreal and San Diego caught this city of 2,436,000 people on the St. Lawrence by surprise.

Gerald Snyder, vice chairman of Montreal's Executive Committee, a body similar to New York's Board of Estimate, said Montreal would build a 55,000-seat domed stadium for the new baseball club at a cost of $35-million. Until the stadium is ready in 1971, baseball will be played in the Autostade, also called Expo Stadium, which is adjacent to the site of last year's hugely successful Expo '67. That park's capacity will be increased to 40,000 from the present 25,000 seats.

Montreal residents will probably never be as fervent about their still unnamed baseball team as they are about their ice-hockey darlings, but there were indications today that baseball may draw considerable crowds. More than one citizen remembered with pride that the Royals of the International League, now defunct, sent Jackie Robinson to the Brooklyn Dodgers in 1947. Robinson was the first Negro to play big-league baseball.

Baseball's problem in Canada is that hockey is a game of constant action. Baseball, a portly corporate board chairman said today, "is a very slow game. You sit around and then all hell breaks loose and you don't know why. Then you start talking to the guy next to you about it, and you have a big argument about what happened."

"Sure I'll go to see them," said a gray-haired clerk on the floor of the Stock Exchange. "I think it's great for us. Just let them keep the price down. They can make their money on the beer and hot dogs."

The Royals, once the flagship club of the Brooklyn Dodger farm system, emptied their lockers for good after the 1960 season, when they finished last. Attendance that year fell to 111,991 and the Dodgers, by then in Los Angeles, decided they had seen enough red ink. ■

AUGUST 29, 1968

U.S. OPEN TENNIS STARTING TODAY

Neil Amdur

After years of frustration and political procrastination, open tennis becomes a reality in the United States today. And what a show the first open promises to be.

There will be $100,000 in prize money, national television, 150 correspondents from all over the world and top amateur and professional players eager for a share of the fame and fortune that await the singles champions. A record advance ticket sale of $150,000 has been reported.

For E. C. (Ned) Potter, the 83-year-old statesman of the sport, the 11-day event at the West Side Tennis Club in Forest Hills, Queens, is vindication for an ideological struggle that began two decades ago. "Tennis is big enough and broad enough for both the true amateur and the professional," Potter wrote in the final chapter of 'Kings of the Court," his engrossing and informative history of the sport.

"No game can live if it flaunts the one and flouts the other. The future of tennis lies in a frank acknowledgment of this fact. Some day the amateur associations will admit that amateurs and professionals can walk hand in hand. Then tennis will enter upon its golden age."

The "golden age" began officially last March 30 when, in a historic reversal of policy, the International Lawn Tennis Federation endorsed open tennis and paved the way for the exciting, successful open tournaments in Europe and renewed spectator interest.

The honor of playing the initial stadium match in America's first open will go to Mrs. Billie Jean King, a pro, the world's top-ranking women's player and the sport's most energetic, refreshing thinker. Chasing a top singles prize of $6,000, Mrs. King, who won the Wimbledon singles title, will play Helen Amos at noon.

With its $14,000 jackpot, the men's singles division has several eye-catching openers today.

Before she plays, Mrs. King and her husband, Larry, will coordinate a clinic for 2,200 youngsters at the club. The clinic is part of an expanding tennis program financed by the Planters Peanut Division of Standard Brands, Inc. Planters is transporting the youngsters to the club, supplying food and drinks and free tickets for the matches.

SEPTEMBER 10, 1968

ASHE BEATS OKKER TO WIN TENNIS OPEN

Dave Anderson

Lieut. Arthur Ashe won the men's singles title yesterday at Forest Hills Stadium in the first United States open tennis championships. The triumph was the most notable achievement made in the sport by a Negro male athlete.

Serving a total of 26 aces, the slender Army officer defeated Tom Okker of the Netherlands, 14-12, 5-7, 6-3, 3-6, 6-3, but he was ineligible to receive the $14,000 top prize in the $100,000 event, the richest tournament in tennis history. As an American amateur, Ashe collected a total of $280 in expenses, at $20 per diem for 14 days, including two days of practice. As a Davis cup player, he had his room at the Hotel Roosevelt paid for by the United States Lawn Tennis Association.

The 25-year-old Ashe, who grew up in a middle-class Negro neighborhood in Richmond, also won the United States amateur singles championship Aug. 25 in Longwood, Mass.

Unfortunately, the drama of Ashe's glory was diminished somewhat by the size of the crowd. An estimated turnout of 7,100 was scattered throughout the 13,500-seat stadium for the final, postponed a day because of the rain that wiped out last Friday's program.

And for the first time since 1955, when

(cont'd. on next page)

(cont'd. from previous page)
Tony Trabert won the national amateur title in the West Side Tennis Club stadium, an American has conquered the men's field in this country's most distinguished tennis tournament.

As the curly-haired Dutchman waved helplessly at the grass-stained ball, Ashe spun, stood at a crouched attention and aimed his racquet handle at the tarpaulin-covered stadium wall. Then he turned and shook hands with Okker at the net.

Although the bespectacled bachelor later said that he "wasn't particularly excited about winning," his gestures in that moment of triumph betrayed his emotional involvement. Striding slowly behind the umpire's chair, Ashe clasped his hands and held them high, in the traditional gesture of a victorious boxer. Moments later, he cupped his hands behind his head and walked around, staring down at the turf.

Ashe's triumph over Okker was his 25th consecutive singles victory. He hasn't lost since a surprise defeat in mid-July by little-known Patricio Cornejo of Chile in the third round of the national clay-court championships at Milwaukee. ■

Arthur Ashe with Tom Okker (left) of the Netherlands after winning the U.S. Open at Forest Hills, N.Y., in 1968.

OCTOBER 17, 1968

2 Accept Medals Wearing Black Gloves

MEXICO CITY, Oct. 16—Tommie Smith wore a 'black glove on his right hand tonight to receive his gold medal for winning the final of the Olympic 200-meter dash in the world-record time of 19.8 seconds.

John Carlos, his American teammate, received the third place bronze medal wearing a black glove on his left hand. Both appeared for the presentation ceremony wearing black stockings and carrying white-soled track shoes. The two had said they would make a token gesture here to protest racial discrimination in the United States.

While the "Star Spangled Banner" was played, these most militant black members of the United States track and field squad bowed their heads and raised their blackgloved hands high.

The right-hand glove and the left-hand glove represent black unity. Smith explained later. "Black people are getting closer and closer together," he said. "We're uniting."

Smith, who suffered a thigh injury while winning his semi-final earlier in the day, said it had been "80 percent doubtful" he would be able to start in the final.

"When I was on the stretcher, I was really wondering if I could run," he said. "But this meant cverything to me. The doctor taped me up. It was okay."

Both San Jose State sprinters demonstrated a togetherness that apparently extended to the gold medal.

Explaining why he had glanced to his right near the finish. Carlos said: "The upper part of my calves were pulling pretty hard. I wanted to see where Tommie was, and if he could win it. If I thought he couldn't have won it, I would have tried harder to take it."

The bronze medal dangled by its green ribbon from Carlos's neck. The gold medal around Smith's neck was tucked inside his sweatsuit. "We are black," Smith said, "and we're proud to be black. White America will only give us credit for an Olympic victory. They'll say I'm an American, but if I did something bad, they'd say a Negro. Black America was with us all the way, though."

Carlos said: "We feel that white people think we're just animals to do a job. We saw white people in the stands putting thumbs down at us. We want them to know we're not roaches, ants or rats."

Switching metaphors, Carlos likened the white attitude toward black athletes to the relationship between trainers and show horses or elephants. "If we do a good job," he said. "they'll throw us some peanuts or pat us on the back and say, 'Good boy.'"

OCTOBER 19, 1968

BEAMON'S LONG JUMP AND EVANS'S 400 SET WORLD MARKS

Neil Amdur

MEXICO CITY, Oct. 18—Two astonishing track and field achievements—a 29-foot-24-inch long jump and a 43.8-second sprint in the 400-meter run—dramatically reaffirmed today the tenacity and competitive spirit of United States athletes.

Faced with mounting mental and social pressures that could have cost them coveted places on the Olympic awards platform, Bob Beamon and Lee Evans responded with gold-medal performances that rivaled the first 4-minute mile and the first 17-foot pole vault for breath-taking spontaneity.

The 21-year-old Evans scored a driving, determined triumph in the 400-meter run with his 0:43.8, which was an amazing seven-tenths of a second under the recognized world record and two-tenths better than Evans' pending performance at South Lake Tahoe, Calif., last month. Larry James of White Plains, N.Y., finished inches behind Evans in 0:43.9, Ron Freeman of Elizabeth, N.J., was third and the United States gained its first 1-2-3 medal sweep in track since 1960.

Beamon, 22, from Jamaica, Queens, startled the crowd of 45,000 in Olympic Stadium with an unbelievable opening attempt in the long jump. The world record for the event was 27 4 3/4, but Beamon, with his speed, height off the board and the thinner air at the 7,350-foot altitude here, flew by 27 feet, 28 feet and past 29 feet with a mark that may stand for years. Ralph Boston, Beamon's teammate, who shared the listed world record with Igor Ter-Ovanesyan of the Soviet Union, was third, behind Klaus Beer of East Germany.

"I figured the pressure was on me and Ralph, so I knew I had to go 100 percent," the 6-foot-3-inch Beamon said afterward. Beamon's best jump before today had been a wind-aided 27-6 1/2.

That Beamon and Evans performed so marvelously was a tribute to their instinctive will to win. American athletes—black and white—had been under enormous pressure in the last 24 hours as a result of a United States Olympic Committee ruling that stripped Tommie Smith and John Carlos, the two Negro sprinters, of their Olympic credentials.

Evans is a close friend of the pair and was one of the early leaders in the protest plans for an Olympic boycott by Negro athletes. Evans wore a pair of black socks as a silent sign of protest today. But once the gun sounded in the final, he moved out from lane No. 6 with the same fierce individual pride that earned him a berth on this strongest and most individualistic of American track teams.

After the three Negro runners crossed the finish line, they huddled for a few moments and then placed their left arms on each other's shoulders and walked a few more yards in unison. Beamon got tremendous height on his opening jump. His arms flapped like a bird and he seemed to take off like one. When the numbers 8.90 [meters] were placed on the scoreboard in front of the long-jump area, the metric figures corresponding to 29-2 1/4, the crowd let out an unbelieving roar and Beamon jumped up and down in front of the stands. ■

NOVEMBER 24, 1968

Crimson Tallies Twice in 42 Seconds

Steve Cady

CAMBRIDGE. Mass., Nov. 23—Unbeaten Harvard turned The Game into The Miracle today by scoring 16 points in the last 42 seconds and gaining a hysterical 29-29 tie with unbeaten Yale. If the capacity crowd of 40,280 still can't believe what it saw, it could hardly be blamed.

With the ball on the Yale 38, the score 29-13 and the Eli stands chanting "We're No. 1," most of the record corps of 400 reporters in the press box already had their accounts of the game well under way.

Then Frank Champi, a second-string Harvard quarterback who had already thrown one touchdown pass, decided that maybe he, not Brian Dowling of Yale, really was the reincarnation of Frank Merriwell, Yale's fictional superstar.

His 15-yard scoring pass to Bruce Freeman and a 2-point conversion run by Gus Crim put the Crimson within tying range. Then, on the last regular play of the game, after a fumbled onside kickoff had given the Crimson possession, Champi hit Vic Gatto with an 8-yard scoring pass.

Out came the paper in the press-box typewriters, out came articles that had begun, "Brian Dowling completed a spectacular Yale football career today by passing for two touchdowns and running for two more…"

Dowling, the 21-year-old Yale senior, was spectacular beyond the wildest expectations of his admirers. Calvin Hill, too, had a big day for Yale, for he scored one touchdown and passed the fabled Albie Booth for most points (144) in a Yale career.

In the final desperate moments it was the neglected Harvard offense that turned Yale jubilation into frustration.

Dowling flipped a screen pass from the Harvard 32 to an open receiver who started toward the goal line. But the receiver fumbled and Steve Ranere of Harvard pounced on the ball at the Crimson 14. Champi then got the Crimson going on the nine-play, 86-yard drive that resulted in the first of the miracle touchdowns. The big gainer, again reflecting the sudden turn of fortune, came on a fumble by Champi.

Fritz Reed, a junior who had been switched from end to tackle this season, grabbed the ball and took off toward the

Yale goal. He might have thought he was an end again and had just caught a pass.

(cont'd. on next page)

(*cont'd. from previous page*)

Anyway, he rambled from the Yale 32 to the 15. Nobody paid much attention, because only 42 seconds remained. In the Yale stands across the field from the press box, old Blues and young Blues waved white handkerchiefs and chanted, "We're No. 1."

But Champi must have been listening to Merriwell. On the next play, he looked for an open receiver, failed to find one, tried to lateral, dodged some white-jerseyed Elis and threw to his right. Freeman, the sophomore end, snagged the pass on the Yale 3 and went into the end zone.

The 2-point plunge by Crim, a junior fullback, reduced the volume of the "We're No. 1."

Now Harvard tried what it had to try—an onside kick. It worked. Yale fumbled the skittering kick and Bill Kelly, another Harvard sophomore, recovered on the Yale 49.

Champi, apparently trapped on a pass attempt, decided to do what Dowling had been doing with remarkable success most of the chilly, but clear, afternoon. He ran.

He went for 14 yards to the Yale 35 and a face-mask penalty against the Elis advanced the ball to the 20.

Time remaining: 32 seconds. Harvard fans: in an uproar. Yale fans: apprehensive.

Champi threw two passes into the end zone. Both were broken up. Champi surprised everybody, including Yale, by sending Crim up the middle on a draw play. It went for 14 yards to the Eli 6.

"We want 8," the Harvards screamed. Champi, trapped trying to pass, was nailed on the 8 for a 2-yard loss. Four seconds remained, enough for one play. Trapped again, the amazing substitute played ring-around-a-rosy with Yale's defenders. He tried to lateral, as he had attempted to do on the previous drive. He ran around in circles for what seemed like 10 seconds before spotting Gatto alone in the end zone. Gatto, the senior captain and the first back in Harvard history to rush for 2,000 yards, clutched the ball surely in the most dramatic moment of a dramatic career. Touchdown!

Spectators swarmed onto the field to mob the Harvard captain.

"Quiet, please!'" the public address announcer implored the fans. The field was cleared. Champi fired a bullet pass into Peter Varney's midsection.

Merriwell couldn't have done it any better. ■

MAY 7, 1969

CELTICS GAIN 11TH TITLE IN 13 SEASONS

Leonard Koppett

Jerry West of the Los Angeles Lakers attempts a reverse layup against Bill Russell of the Boston Celtics during the 1969 N.B.A. Championships.

LOS ANGELES, May 6—Unlimited praise for the Boston Celtics; honest sympathy for the frustration of the Los Angeles Lakers. Those were the basic reactions of the basketball world today to last night's remarkable game in which the Celtics won another National Basketball Association championship—more decisively than the final score of 108-106 suggests, but much less automatically than the phrase "another Boston title" implies.

Rarely in any professional sport has a team deserved its triumph as thoroughly as these Celtics. This was their 11th title in the 13 years that Bill Russell has been their center, and their second in a row in the three years he has also been their coach, but this time they won as underdogs, overcoming a more gifted opposing team and winning the final game on the road.

The true athletic virtues—determination, unflagging effort and alertness, absolutely unselfish teamwork, applied intelligence, mechanical skill and poise maintained under the greatest emotional pressure—were displayed by the Celtics in the highest degree.

They were lucky, too. But only their own positive qualities made it possible for them to be in position to benefit from the lucky break when it came. As a model of the power of pride and of dedicated hard work, the Celtics of this season rank even higher than many of their more overwhelming predecessors.

And yet, the Lakers came so close. Their three stars, Jerry West, Wilt Chamberlain and Elgin Baylor, have acquired over the years all the individual prizes, records, wealth, fame and appreciation any athlete can desire—but the one thing they really craved, a team championship (and especially one won from Boston), was denied them again.

West, even though hobbled by a leg injury during the last two games, played as brilliant a series as any player ever has. He set a record by scoring 556 points in 18 playoff games (30.9 a game). He scored 42 points in the last game, but his depression was as real and as deep as Baylor's and Chamberlain's.

"It's as if we aren't supposed to win," he said softly afterward. "It's just hard for me to believe they beat us. What makes it so hard is that I know we have a better team. In other years I could rationalize our setbacks, but this time I can't."

Chamberlain certainly should have made Los Angeles as invincible as everyone expected. However, Coach Bill Van Breda Kolff, who was such a success in his first year with the Lakers, never did solve the problem of creating a unity around Wilt (as Alex Hannum had done in Philadelphia). This friction between Wilt's assets and the freewheeling style preferred by the coach continued to the end, and the Lakers never did marshall their full resources effectively. ■

JANUARY 13, 1969

JETS UPSET COLTS IN SUPER BOWL

Dave Anderson

MIAMI, Jan. 12—In a memorable upset that astonished virtually everyone in the football realm, the New York Jets of the American League conquered the Baltimore Colts, the supposedly impregnable National League champions, 16-7, today for the Super Bowl prestige and paycheck.

Joe Namath, the quarterback whose optimism proved to be contagious to his teammates, directed the Jets to a 4-yard touchdown run by Matt Snell, the workhorse fullback, and field goals by Jim Turner from 32, 30 and 9 yards.

Equally important, the Jet defensive unit dominated the Colt offense. Led by Gerry Philbin, the Jet pass-rushers hurried Earl Morrall, selected as the N.F.L.'s most valuable player, into throwing three interceptions in the first half.

Midway in the third quarter, Morrall was benched and Johnny Unitas, the sore-armed master, took over at quarterback. With about 3½ minutes remaining in the game, the Colts scored on a 1-yard run by Jerry Hill, but by that time the Jets were in command.

In the A.F.L.'s ninth season, the Jets convinced 75,377 stunned spectators in the Orange Bowl and a television audience of perhaps 60 million that they deserved parity with the best teams in the N.F.L. and that Namath had developed into pro football's best quarterback.

Quarterback Joe Namath of the New York Jets during Super Bowl III on January 12, 1969 in Miami, Florida.

(cont'd. on next page)

(cont'd. from previous page)

In the point-spread type of betting, the Colts were favored by 18 to 20 points. Without a point spread, the Colts were a 7-to-1 choice.

The outcome put the Jets on a plateau with such other famous upsetmakers in sports as Cassius Clay, knocking out Sonny Liston for the world heavyweight title as an 8-1 underdog in 1964, and the racehorse, Upset, defeating Man o' War in 1919 for that thoroughbred's only loss.

But the upset did not surprise Namath, the Jets' positive thinker. Despite his reputation as a playboy, he also is a serious student of football. As he observed the Colts in game films during the week, he noticed weaknesses in their vaunted zone pass-defense that he hoped to exploit. It is one thing to see the weaknesses as the film is flashed on a hotel-room wall, it is quite another to penetrate that defense on the field.

Namath accomplished it with his lariat arm, a scientific split end named George Sauer Jr. and a fullback, Snell, whose power running established the ground game that enabled the celebrated $400,000 quarterback to keep the Colts uncertain as to what play he would call next.

Namath, Sauer and Snell accumulated impressive statistics, but the members of the Jets' offensive line—Winston Hill, Bob Talamini, John Schmitt, Randy Rasmussen and Dave Herman—provided the blocking that produced those statistics.

Protected from the vaunted Colt pass-rush as if he were a rare jewel, Namath completed 17 of 28 passes for 206 yards. Sauer caught eight for 133 yards, a significant statistic because the Jets' other wide receiver, Don Maynard, was shut out. Snell rushed for 121 yards and caught four passes for 40 more.

Namath was awarded a Dodge Charger by Sport magazine as the game's most valuable player, but Snell appeared to be equally deserving. So did all the offensive linemen. In the most significant victory in A.F.L. history, the battle had been won where it usually is in football—in the trenches.

SEPTEMBER 9, 1969

Laver Gains His 2nd Tennis Grand Slam

Neil Amdur

Rod Laver achieved the second grand slam of his tennis career yesterday. With all the competitive trademarks of the true champion, the 31-year-old king of the court overcame Tony Roche, his 24-year-old Australian countryman, 7-9, 6-1, 6-2, 6-2 in the final of the United States Open championship at the West Side Tennis Club in Forest Hills, Queens.

Australian tennis champion Road Laver at the U.S. Open, 1969.

Laver entered the record books as the only player to have achieved two sweeps of the Australian, French, British and American championships, the international events that make up the grand slam.

Don Budge registered the first slam in 1938. Laver completed his initial sweep in 1962, but as an amateur and with such established pros as Richard (Pancho) Gonzales, Ken Rosewall, Lew Hoad and Tony Trabert ineligible for the competition. That situation has changed with the approval of open tournaments.

"Tenniswise, winning this slam was a lot tougher because of all the good players," the modest, freckle-faced redhead said. "Pressurewise, I don't think it was any tougher. There's always pressure when you're playing for something over nine months."

The pressure began for him last January after he had beaten Emerson, Fred Stolle, Roche and Andres Gimeno en route to the Australian title. In the French and Wimbledon championships, he trailed, two sets to love, twice in the early rounds, but salvaged each match and went on to the crowns despite persistent pains in his left elbow.

In winning here at Forest Hills, Laver overcame psychological hazards as well as such quality pros as Dennis Ralston, Emerson, Ashe and Roche, his chief tormentor this year. Rain had washed out two complete sessions and delayed the final one day. His tense semifinal match with Ashe had been halted by darkness in the third set and finished the following day.

Meanwhile, in Newport Beach, Calif., Laver's wife, Mary, had also been experiencing delays. The couple's first child was three days overdue. Mrs. Laver reported yesterday by phone before her husband walked onto the stadium court for the final. "I've been telling him everything's fine and to concentrate on his tennis," she said.

One day remains in the tournament to complete the men's doubles. Naturally Laver is still playing, even though his mind is elsewhere.

"I want to get home as soon as possible," he said, flashing a familiar half-smile. "If you had a baby on the way, wouldn't you?" ■

OCTOBER 17, 1969

METS WIN THE SERIES AND A GRATEFUL CITY GOES WILD

Joseph Durso

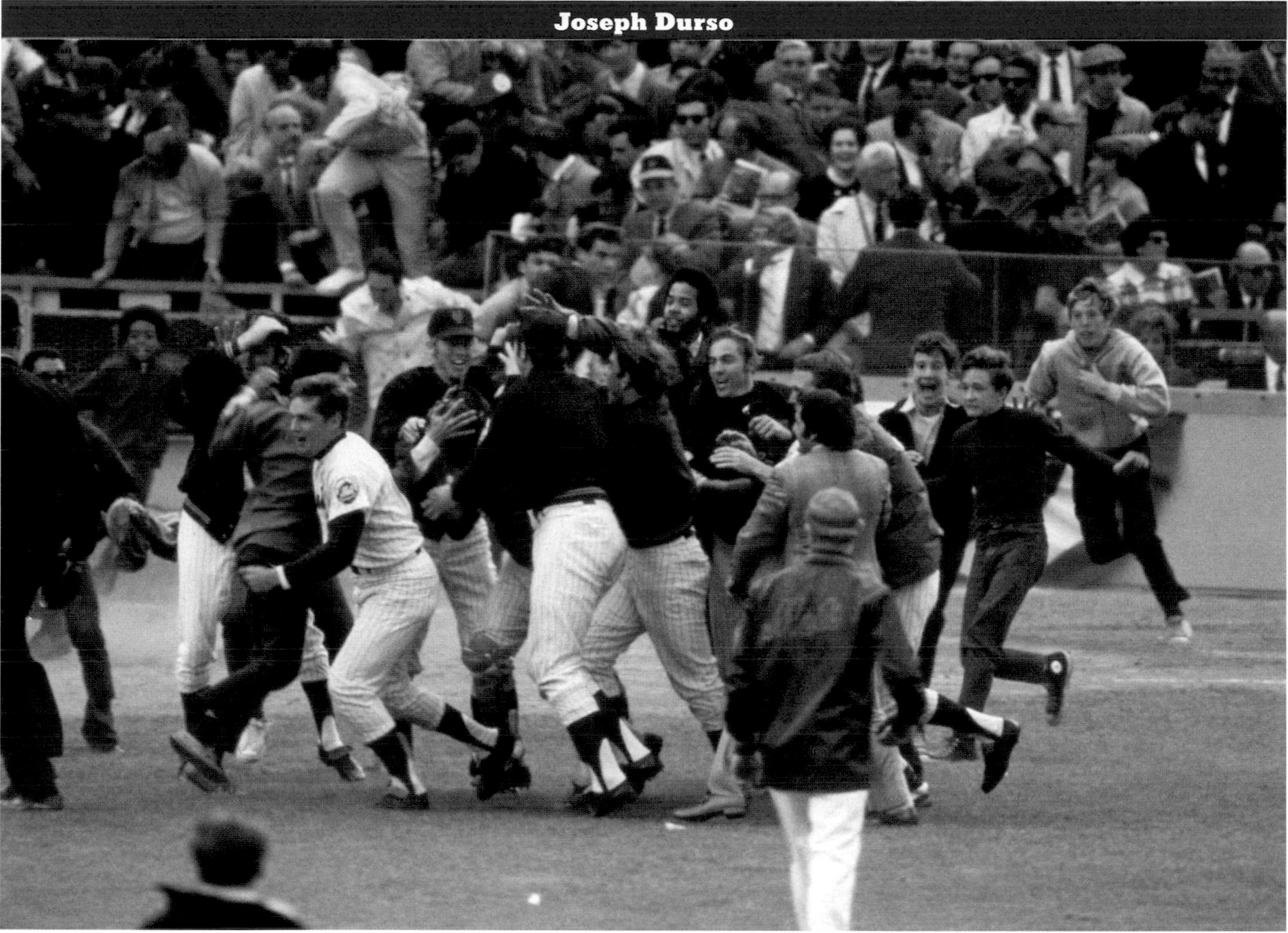

Players celebrate as jubilant fans rush the field after the New York Mets won the 1969 World Series against the Baltimore Orioles at Shea Stadium in Flushing, New York.

The Mets entered the promised land yesterday after seven years of wandering through the wilderness of baseball.

In a tumultuous game before a record crowd of 57,397 in Shea Stadium, they defeated the Baltimore Orioles, 5-3, for their fourth straight victory of the 66th World Series and captured the championship of a sport that had long ranked them as comical losers.

They did it with a full and final dose of the magic that had spiced their unthinkable climb from ninth place in the National League—100-to-1 shots who scraped and scrounged their way to the pinnacle as the waifs of the major leagues.

At 3:17 P.M. on a cool and often sunny afternoon, their impossible dream came true when Cleon Jones caught a fly ball hit by Dave Johnson to left field. And they immediately touched off one of the great, riotous scenes in sports history, as thousands of persons swarmed from their seats and tore up the patch of ground where the Mets had made history.

It was 10 days after they had won the National League pennant in a three-game sweep of the Atlanta Braves. It was 22 days after they had won the Eastern title of the league over the Chicago Cubs. It was eight years after they had started business under Casey Stengel as the lovable losers of all sports.

They reached the top, moreover, in the best and most far-fetched manner of Met baseball.

They spotted the Orioles three runs in the third inning when Dave McNally and Frank Robinson hit home runs off Jerry

(cont'd. on next page)

(cont'd. from previous page)
Koosman. But then they stormed back with two runs in the sixth inning on a home run by Donn Clendenon, another in the seventh on a home run by Al Weis and two more in the eighth on two doubles and two errors. The deciding run was batted home by Ron Swoboda, who joined the Met mystique in 1965 when the team was losing 112 games and was finishing last for the fourth straight time.

The wild, final chapter in the story was written against the desperate efforts of the Orioles, who had swept to the American League pennant by 19 games as one of the most powerful teams in modern times. The Orioles had not won since the opening game last Saturday in Baltimore and needed three straight victories to survive. In the third inning, they lashed out at Koosman with three runs and erased the memory of the six no-hit innings he had pitched against them Sunday.

But Koosman settled down after that and checkmated the Orioles on one single for the final six innings. He retired 19 of the last 21 batters, closed with a five-hitter and even swung a mean bat when the Mets began to do their "thing."

Then, in the sixth, another omen appeared. Each team argued in turn that a batter had been hit by a pitched ball. The Orioles, though, lost their argument; the Mets won theirs. And the game veered inexorably toward the "team of destiny."

When Clendenon whacked a home run off the auxiliary scoreboard on the facing of the left-field loge seats, it was his third home run in three games and putting him one short of the Series record of four shared by Babe Ruth, Lou Gehrig, Hank Bauer and Duke Snider, and putting the Mets back in business. In the next inning, Al Weis brought them even on McNally's second pitch, and finally, the stage was set for the last full measure of Met magic.

Up to bat was Swoboda and, with first base open, the Orioles might have walked him intentionally. But they elected to challenge him and Swoboda drilled the second pitch down the left-field line, where Don Buford almost made a brilliant backhand catch off the grass. But the ball dropped in for a double as Jones streaked for home to put the Mets in front, 4-3, and tumult broke out across Flushing Meadow.

Ed Charles lifted a fly to Buford for the second out. But Jerry Grote followed with a low line drive toward John Powell, and the 250-pound first baseman booted it for an error. He chased the ball, though, to his right and lobbed it to pitcher Eddie Watt, who was rushing over from the mound to cover first base. By this time, Grote was flashing across the bag and, when pitcher Eddie Watt juggled the throw and dropped it, Swoboda was flashing across the plate with the second run of the inning. That made it 5-3, and the Mets were three outs from fantasy.

There was a brief delay when Frank Robinson opened the ninth with a walk. But then Powell forced him at second base, Brooks Robinson flied out to Swoboda in right and—at 3:17 P.M.—Johnson lifted a fly to Jones in left-center.

Jones made the catch with a flourish, then he and his old high-school mate from Mobile, Tommie Agee, turned and streaked across the outfield to the Mets' bull pen in right field. They beat the avalanche by a split second and, as they ducked into the safety of the stadium's caverns, the crowd let go.

Children, housewives, mature men, all swarmed onto the field where the Mets had marched. They tore up home plate, captured the bases, ripped gaping holes from the turf, set off orange flares and firecrackers and chalked the wooden outfield fence with the signs of success. The Mets were the champions of the world on Oct. 16, 1969.

"I never saw anything like it," said Joe DiMaggio, the old Yankee, who had thrown out the first ball. ■

Arts & Entertainment

Culture played a vital role in reflecting our rapidly changing self-image as a nation. At The Times, arts coverage was in transition. A string of not-always-exciting rock critics struggled to cover the field, decisively outclassed by the Village Voice and Rolling Stone. The exception was Robert Shelton, a copy editor who loved folk music. Shelton single-handedly "discovered" Bob Dylan in 1961, at least as far as the mainstream media was concerned.

But most of the smart pop music coverage at The Times in those days, and much of the smart arts coverage in general, was engendered by an editor named Seymour Peck, who ran the Sunday Arts and Leisure section when the entire Sunday department still enjoyed a measure of independence from the daily news operation. Peck brought in all manner of promising young pop-culture writers, even when some of them (like Richard Goldstein on "Sgt. Pepper's Lonely Hearts Club Band") famously missed their marks.

In the visual arts there were the masterpieces and monuments of modernism so loyally admired by The Times. Otherwise, the 60's was the decade of minimalism and pop art, although Andy Warhol merited attention as much for his persona and entourage as his paintings. His films were mostly ignored and his house band, the Velvet Underground, went essentially unnoticed. Architecture teetered between late modernism and the flamboyance of early postmodernism.

Young American novelists flourished—Updike, Heller, Pynchon, Capote, Wolfe, Doctorow, Vonnegut, Roth. Beyond (or beneath) books, the Saturday Evening Post and the New York Herald Tribune died, but New York magazine was born.

In dance, aside from the terpsichorean cold war of defections and dueling visits by Russian and American ballet troupes and the advent of a raft of exciting experimental dancers downtown, Harvey Lichtenstein began his transformation of the Brooklyn Academy of Music into BAM, first as a magnet for dance but then for theater and music and all the performing arts.

On Broadway there were big musicals but also serious plays from a raft of young playwrights, American and British. Joe Papp proved as transformative of New York cultural life as Lichtenstein at BAM. Ellen Stewart at La MaMa and Robert Wilson began to make their marks on the experimental stage, though Wilson's plotless dreamscapes proved a mystery to The Times.

Breakthrough European film directors (Truffaut, Godard, Fellini, Bergman) may not have been greeted all that perceptively by Times critics at first, but moves were afoot in the paper by mid-decade to make the paper's film coverage more sophisticated.

A major development in television was the advent of the Corporation for Public Broadcasting and "Sesame Street." That medium reshaped news coverage in the United States but was otherwise a "vast wasteland," in the opinion of JFK's new head of the Federal Communications Commission. Still, there was a run of popular comedies and funny monster shows. There was the debut of "Star Trek," attesting to our fascination with space, as well as "Monty Python's Flying Circus," which proved that Americans did not dote on the Brits solely for their upper classes. The Pythons were a kind of comedic Beatles.

Speaking of whom, the 60's would have been unthinkable without their music. Bob Dylan, especially after he "went electric" (another Dylan moment sympathetically greeted by Robert Shelton), became the poet of white youth. Rhythm and blues escaped the ghetto of "race records" with the rise of Motown, Aretha Franklin and the Supremes. Ravi Shankar and the Nonesuch Explorer series spearheaded the new popularity of world music. There were other British rock bands as part of the British invasion, but above all there were the Beatles, who changed music, fashion and lifestyles irrevocably. I can still remember the excitement that came with every new Dylan or Beatles release, like a tablet from the mountaintop. One album could galvanize the cultural conversation.

Finally there were the landmark rock festivals, as much communal gatherings as concerts, from Monterey Pop in 1967 to Woodstock and Altamont in 1969. Despite the eventual designation of Altamont as a key marker of the end of the decade, these festivals remain the greatest symbols of what the 60's, and the hippie–rock nexus, had to offer: wonderful music and a utopian spirit that lives on to this day.

JUNE 11, 1961

IN PHILADELPHIA, AN ARCHITECT

Ada Louise Huxtable

It is quite possible that the center of the architectural world today is not one of the familiar international cultural capitals, but a more modest city—Philadelphia. This new and unexpected source of creative vitality focuses on a single remarkable man and an equally remarkable structure: Louis I. Kahn's Richards Medical Research Building for the University of Pennsylvania.

Although barely completed, Kahn's unusual work has already been accorded the recognition of a one-building show at the Museum of Modern Art, opened this week, to run through July 16; an honor not given lightly. It is a serious pilgrimage point for fellow professionals and starry-eyed students and the subject of long and thoughtful discourses in the architectural press. The museum pronounces it "an authoritative act of architecture...probably the most consequential building constructed in the United States since the war."

The object of all this interest is not, by any conventional standards, a beautiful building. It is a strong and meaningful structure, strikingly handsome, reaching beyond mere graciousness or elegance for fundamental architectural values. An exploratory building, its functional needs are studied with probing depth and courageous originality. It avoids all of the clichés, the superficial mannerisms and the easy answers that are spread sleekly and mechanically across the face of American cities and towns. Unconventional design and advanced concrete technology are integrated with intellectual and esthetic firmness. The result is a building that is architectural and architectonic in the supreme sense—a positive statement of carefully related masses and voids, of materials and structure, of needs and solutions, executed with strength, sensitivity and conviction.

As good as it is, however, the building is not without flaws. There are some bad passages; technical imperfections, facilities that might be better situated, problems of transmission of sound, too-stringent economies that reduce interiors to rock-bottom utilitarian work spaces, which, in turn, have been chaotically partitioned by staff needs.

The words that a careful study of the building inevitably evokes are old-fashioned terms of morality: honesty, integrity, truth, a dedicated search for the best artistic means to the best functional end. One hesitates to use them, for they are the same words with which Ruskin led the nineteenth century astray, down the primrose path of Venetian Gothic revival, starting an endless chain of confusion of art with morals, nostalgia with esthetics, romanticism with reality. Nevertheless, they are unavoidable here, for Kahn's "return to beginnings," his search for "what the building wants to be," is a moral as well as an esthetic act in an age that makes few moral distinctions in its operations or its architecture, accepting glittering gimmicks and flashy superficialities as the real thing.

It is Kahn's sensitive reappraisal of architectural objectives that makes his work important, even when it is imperfect or awkward, and that could be the basis of its most healthful and far-reaching influence. This one impressive building, properly understood, may well point the way to future practice. For as Kahn reminds us, "The future is now." ■

The Richards Medical Research Building at the University of Pennsylvania.

APRIL 8, 1962

JET AGE TRIUMPH

Ada Louise Huxtable

The art of the jet age is architecture, and what may prove to be one of its most significant monuments is nearing completion twenty-seven miles west of Washington.

John Foster Dulles International Airport at Chantilly, Va., the $175,000,000 Federal Aviation Agency project designed by the late architect Eero Saarinen with the engineering firm of Ammann & Whitney, is scheduled to go into service in the fall of 1962. Its 600-foot long terminal building and connecting control tower have reached their final shaping in that most expressive of twentieth-century materials, reinforced concrete, and Saarinen's revolutionary concept of air-age architecture can be clearly seen and judged.

The visitor approaching the airport across the rolling hills of the Virginia countryside receives a double impact: the realization that he is viewing a kind of architecture of a force and importance unparalleled since the unique synthesis of philosophy and style that produced the Renaissance, and that he is faced with a structure of singular beauty.

The experience is a moving one, as is

(cont'd. on next page)

(cont'd. from previous page)
the direct confrontation with any work of art of primary stature. But the spectator's emotional response to the Dulles building stems from more than fortuitous esthetics; it is an indication of the full meaning and accomplishment of architecture in our time.

We stand in the historic position of witnessing a period of spectacular architectural change and innovation of the first magnitude, and here is a landmark structure of our civilization. Only the blind or the blasé could fail to react to its expressive force.

Saarinen's airport scheme represents an important breakthrough in design. Planned from its inception for jet operation, it eliminates the increasingly cumbersome arrangement of the conventional "finger" plan, where miles of scattered, decentralized corridors stretch out to planes, and replaces them with a single, focal building and a system of "mobile lounges," which serve both as waiting rooms and a means of transportation to scheduled flights.

Most important of all, however, is the fact that these carefully studied factors of function and form have been fused into a great work of architecture by a conscious creative act—the result has been definitively molded by the taste, beliefs and purely esthetic impulses of the designer.

Therefore, we call Dulles a monument advisedly. In spite of its practical triumphs, one sees immediately that the graceful suspended arc of the terminal building's roof and its dramatic supporting pylons are conceived primarily for their stunning visual qualities. Saarinen's avowed purpose, realized beyond anyone's most optimistic hopes, was to devise a symbolic entrance to the nation. He has done so by using soaring, sculptured, 65-foot high concrete supports for a striking catenary roof, to create a dominating facade and form on a 9,800-acre flat plain.

As it stands now, still lacking window walls and finishing details, the huge shiplike structure and tower give an impression of uncompromised power and grace. It will never be so forceful again. In contemporary terms completely appropriate to its needs, it achieves an effect not unlike that of the great temples of Greece, although it does so with lively, nonstatic, nontraditional shapes.

At Dulles, a significant transmutation has taken place. For perhaps the first time, adventurous structural development per se is subordinated to a pre-selected, controlled architectural scheme, and serves it convincingly. Hazarding a guess, based on the evidence of history, this is a sign of a crystallizing style, and a great moment in art. Only when the technical means—material and structure—have developed to the point where they can further the ends—the dominating, conscious concept of the building—does any architecture approach maturity. The Dulles terminal is a mature work; a fact that underlines the tragedy of Saarinen's untimely death. ■

Dulles International Airport, Virginia, 1962.

MARCH 21, 1963

Pop Art Takes Over Guggenheim

Stuart Preston

Despite the vagueness of its title, the Guggenheim Museum's new exhibition, "Six Painters and the Object," is an all-out display of Pop art. It includes work by leading young American artists of this persuasion: Jim Dine, Jasper Johns, Roy Lichtenstein, Robert Rauschenberg, James Rosenquist and Andy Warhol. If asked Tolstoy's famous question, "What is art?" they would undoubtedly and correctly answer, "What isn't?"

If we define art as an imaginative reconstruction of reality, a process whereby what we sense and see is transformed so as to give it deeper meaning, we would have a definition that applies to everything from Michelangelo's exalted interpretations of religious subjects to a Pop artist's appropriation of the weaponry of mass media, the propaganda of the faith of the good life in mid-twentieth century America. For Pop art is an art of comment on contemporary objects of worship, something both rueful and satirical, jolting us into recognizing the hidden impact of signs and symbols we see everywhere about us, to which we all too passively submit.

Pop art draws its material from comic strips; film magazines; posters; and from objects such as flags, so familiar to us that we hardly ever look at them any more. Its strength lies in this social relevancy, in its dealing with the immediate, and its weakness—preventing it from being truly popular—lies in the fact that its most gifted practitioners are of necessity sophisticated. It is a sad irony that its public will also be a sophisticated one, comprising just the very persons searching for an amusing novelty who not so long age were delighted by such esthetic absurdities such as white-on-white non-objective paintings.

But for all its extravagance; its often silly search for ways in which to be daring, and for all that its anarchistic, anti-art attitude more devastatingly taken 50 years ago by Marcel Duchamp and later by Dada, Pop art represents a healthy reaction against the increasingly sterile esotericism of non-objective art. Pop mediates between life and art. It "connects."

If variety be the spice of a living art, the Guggenheim exhibition has the merit of showing that Pop art can be of many different kinds. We can choose here between the complex ambiguities of work by Rauschenberg and the straight-in-the-eye impact of that by Warhol and Lichtenstein. To each his own. Any culture benefits by having fun poked at its often monstrous solemnities. We can only be grateful for these genial jesters and for their pointfulness in deflating balloons. The deep, dark secret of Pop art is that it is anti-popular with a vengeance. ■

MAY 24, 1964

JOHNSON ADDS ELEGANCE TO MODERN ARCHITECTURE

Ada Louise Huxtable

This is the year of Philip Johnson, a modern architect with a difference—instead of throwing away the past, he makes use of it in new and startling ways. At 57, he has emerged as a top tastemaker, a powerful influence in the market place where all cultural styles wind up, despite the fact that he has been an architect for only 11 years, coming to the practice after a long and successful career as director of the Museum of Modern Art's Department of Architecture, architectural critic, iconoclast and rebel against "the Establishment."

Just how important a pace-setter Johnson is has become evident this spring with the unveiling of three of his newest buildings in New York City. At the World's Fair, the New York State Pavilion was immediately hailed as the architectural delight of Flushing Meadow. His design of the State Theater at Lincoln Center caused as much comment as the works performed inside it. And tomorrow the nation's First Lady, Mrs. Lyndon B. Johnson, will dedicate his rebuilt and remodeled Museum of Modern Art.

What Johnson is bringing to New York, and to a good many cities across the country, is a kind of architectural elegance that has not been seen since the turn-of-the-century days of McKim, Mead and White and the splendid "Renaissance" palaces built for the business aristocracy. But his is a new kind of elegance in completely contemporary terms—a modern architecture with the timeless values of beauty and luxury that have a universal appeal, whereas the more startling contemporary styles do not.

"I call myself a traditionalist, although I have fought against tradition all my life," he explains. "I like to be buttoned onto tradition. The thing is to improve it, twist it and mold it; to make something new of it; not to deny it. The riches of history can be plucked at any point."

In practice, the result is a frankly romantic and sensuous group of buildings which look toward the past knowledgeably, although they never copy it and can be mistaken for nothing but of the present. Johnson plays on new instruments, in new keys.

It is a controversial style, praised as a "breakthrough" by some, damned as "decorative" or "reactionary" by others, who feel that plucking the past is not a genuinely creative act and may even be something of a betrayal of modern architecture's search for completely new solutions for our time. All agree, however, that the plucking and molding are done with finesse and taste, and often result in effects of exquisite sensibility.

His houses are extravagant pleasure-palaces of carefully unostentatious richness for a Who's Who of art patrons and wealthy collectors. A Johnson house is something like the legendary Morgan yacht—if you have to ask how much it costs, you can't afford it. He is not looking for budget jobs, but he is a bit rueful that his reputation as a rich man's architect has kept away some commercial or corporate clients who consider him too expensive.

Nevertheless, he has produced at least one commercial landmark of unassailable magnificence, the Seagram Building in New York, on which he collaborated with Mies van der Rohe in 1956-58. But the building that brought him instant fame was his own glass house, which shocked his neighbors and the world when he built it in New Canaan, Conn., in 1949. Once attacked so violently, it is now preferred by some critics to his more recent historic-romantic work.

. . . a modern architecture with the timeless values of beauty and luxury that have a universal appeal . . .

Philip Johnson's style stands somewhere between the rigid boxes of the diehard functionalists and the free-form flights of fancy of the neobaroque experimenters. He has given rich, traditional materials, like marble and travertine, equal status in the modern vocabulary with contemporary steel and glass, and he has restored the backward look at history to respectability for a generation of architects that had renounced the past with an almost religious fervor.

From the glass house and the glass-walled office in the Seagram Building, Johnson continues to throw well-selected, beautifully polished stones; the royal rebel is growing gracefully into the next generation's grand old man. ■

NOVEMBER 16, 1961

MUSEUM GETS REMBRANDT FOR RECORD $2.3 MILLION

Sanka Knox

The record sale of the Rembrandt painting, "Aristotle Contemplating the Bust of Homer," at Parke-Bernet in New York, 1961.

A painting by Rembrandt was auctioned last night for the highest amount ever paid for any picture at public or private sale—$2,300,000. The painting, "Aristotle Contemplating the Bust of Homer," was purchased in four minutes of bidding by the Metropolitan Museum of Art.

From the platform of the Parke-Bernet Galleries at 980 Madison Avenue, Louis J. Marion, the auctioneer, simply announced that "an Eastern museum" had won the prize.

Later, the museum's identity was ascertained and James J. Rorimer, director of the Metropolitan, who did the bidding, disclosed that the purchase had been made possible by contributions from "several trustees and private individuals."

Mr. Rorimer said that the museum would not have been able to buy the Rembrandt out of its limited purchase funds. But, he said, as it was "considered important to add the piece to our already great collection of some thirty Rembrandts," friends of the museum offered help.

" 'Aristotle' is one of the great paintings in the world," Mr. Rorimer said, "and it would have been heartbreaking, with Wall Street so close, to have lost out on it."

"Aristotle" achieved several titles in the annals of art last night. It became the first picture in history to command an opening bid of $1,000,000. It tripled the amount paid at auction for the "Adoration of the Magi," the Rubens masterpiece that set a record of $770,000 in 1959. And, it made a crucial contribution to the highest total yield on record for an art auction—$4,679,250.

Nearly 2,000 attended the sale, most of them waiting in line on the street for an hour or two. The sale was held in four galleries. One was the main room, reserved for collectors, dealer-agents for collectors and representatives of museums.

In the other galleries, spectators witnessed the dramatic sale on closed-circuit television.

As "Aristotle" was brought on stage, the spotlights transforming the flowing sleeves of the robe into gold, the audience seemed to catch its breath, then broke into applause.

When the picture was knocked down to the Metropolitan, the applause became an ovation.

SEPTEMBER 30, 1962

New Vistas Open for Sculpture

John Canaday

This Wednesday, the Guggenheim Museum will open to the public an exhibition called "Modern Sculpture from the Joseph H. Hirshhorn Collection." Beginning at the top of the museum's ramp and easing gently down, it will summarize sculpture's part during the past hundred years of an art revolution that is still swinging along.

Without setting out to do so, the exhibition may verify a suspicion held in many quarters that sculpture, after a slow start, is on the point of replacing painting as the most significant plastic expression of our century in its second half—if, indeed, it has not already done so during its second third.

This is a radical change. A couple of hundred years or so ago, after a period of waning health, sculpture entered a period of downright invalidism during which it managed to stay alive largely as a parasite on the other arts. During the modern revolution, the painters have pretty consistently been the leaders into new territory. We think of the impressionists as fountainheads, and then of Cezanne, van Gogh, Gauguin and Seurat as great streams flowing from them, followed by the proliferation of such "isms" as expressionism, fauvism and cubism which, in turn, have now poly-proliferated (not in Webster's) into "isms" too numerous to count and recently less and less worth counting.

All this time we have been accustomed to think of sculpture as the runner-up, and indeed until about 1914 (if you chose to ignore a couple of warning signals) it was possible to generalize that modern sculpture was dependent on modern painting's innovations for such originality as it possessed. The painters would get an idea and then the sculptors would show that they could do it too. Some of the best sculpture, in fact, was done by painters on the side.

Since then, however, two primary and positive reasons have emerged to account for today's sculptural renaissance. One is technical; the other is psychological, emotional, or whatever you want to call the impulse that leads certain rational but peculiarly sensitive individuals into the precarious business of art as a way of life.

Technically, the sculptor has benefited from the flood of contemporary materials and techniques invented for utilitarian purposes but suddenly found to be adaptable as raw material for creation. Technology has offered sculptors new metals as well as old ones in new forms—endless lengths of wire, for instance, that would have amazed a Renaissance artist as something miraculously and inexplicably beautiful in its glistening surface and absolute uniformity.

The creative eye sees these highly finished machine products as new media ready for the breeding of new forms. And these forms are synonymous with new expression in the old and familiar dictum: every age supplies the artist with the materials necessary for its interpretation.

At the basis of sculpture's new vigor and positiveness is the simple, absolutely fundamental fact of sculpture—that it is a three-dimensional, literally tangible art. In an age of uncertainty, when men are wondering where they are and where, if anywhere, they are going to be next week, when there seem to be so few positive answers to such a multitude of desperate questions, the tangibility of sculpture carries with it a very direct kind of satisfaction.

Sculpture is less interested in taking over the cathartic-protest function than in implying, by its relieving tangibility, that there may be permanent values to be found and some positive responses to be shared.

This positiveness on sculpture's part need have nothing to do with new materials. The abstract sculptor is free to delight us with whatever forms he wants to invent, and may move us with whatever expressive power is inherent in those forms, with the real thing the quality of independent existence in three dimensions.

Where modern sculpture is innovational it is truly innovational. No wonder that, by example, it shows us that the movements we think of as new in painting are no longer new but an obvious rounding off, a tying up of loose ends in the last act of a play performed with such vivacity that we forget how long ago the dilemmas of the plot were presented and solved. Great art can be created in something other than a venturesome spirit, but on the premise that we are a venturesome age that demands a venturesome expression, the rest of the century may well belong to the sculptor. ■

JANUARY 10, 1963

'MONA LISA' DEBUT IS A NOISY AFFAIR

Marjorie Hunter

The opening for Leonardo da Vinci's "Mona Lisa" at the National Gallery of Art, Washington, DC. The painting was on loan from the Louvre and was displayed from Jan. 8 through Feb. 3, 1963, when it was moved to the Metropolitan Museum of Art in New York before returning to France.

WASHINGTON, Jan. 9—The "Mona Lisa" went on public display today after surviving a debut that was like a typical noisy Washington cocktail party minus the drinks.

The thousands who lined up to view the painting at the National Gallery of Art today were patient, orderly and respectful. However, the 2,000 politicians and diplomats who attended its American unveiling last night turned the debut into a virtual shambles.

They could not see because of reflections from high-powered television lights. They could not hear because the public address system was not working.

So they set up a party of their own, complete with the roaring babble without which no Washington soiree is considered a success.

André Malraux, the French Minister of Culture who had arranged the loan of the painting, looked shocked. President Kennedy, who tried without success to outshout the noisemakers, looked angry.

Secretary of State Dean Rusk, his voice hardly heard in the tumult, tried to smooth things over by explaining:

"Since the earliest days of our frontier, irreverence has been one of the signs of our affection."

Cigarette stubs ground out on the marble floors had been carefully swept away by the time the first public visitor filed past the "Mona Lisa" this morning.

The lines were not long, but they were steady throughout the day, and they moved fast—too fast for many disgruntled viewers who were told to keep moving.

A policeman stationed near the painting reported 3,185 visitors in the first hour.

"I liked it better in Paris," one woman in a fur coat whispered to a companion.

"Why, it's no bigger than a 21-inch television screen," a man said frowning. (The painting is 30 inches high and 21 inches wide.)

One woman cried when she saw the painting. Another stood in line five times and promised to come back daily. Another drove down from Pennsylvania just to see the painting.

Most visitors, after being hurried through the line, headed for a side gallery to purchase picture postcards of "Mona Lisa."

MARCH 8, 1963

PAN AM BUILDING DEDICATED IN N.Y.

The $100,000,000 Pan Am Building at 200 Park Avenue was officially added to New York's midtown skyscrapers yesterday.

The 59-story structure, although not the tallest in the city, is the largest. It is on a three-and-a-half acre site just north of Grand Central Terminal and has 2,400,000 square feet of floor space. Its size is surpassed only by the Pentagon in Washington and the Chicago Merchandise Mart.

The eight-sided building is named for its major tenant, the Pan American World Airways, which has leased 25 percent of the space. It is jointly owned by the estate of the late Erwin S. Wolfson and City Center Properties, Ltd. of London.

City, state and federal officials spoke at dedication services yesterday. They stressed the international character of the building. Governor Rockefeller said it rose over the city as a symbol of the genius and the creativity of the free enterprise system.

Mayor Wagner declared that it was an expression of "faith by the business community in this city's future." Secretary of Commerce Luther H. Hodges noted that since World War II new office buildings had added 50,000,000 square feet of rentable space in Manhattan.

Senator Jacob J. Javits and Frederick J. Erroll, president of the British Board of Trade, were other speakers.

The building was designed by Emery Roth & Sons. Walter Gropius and Pietro Belluschi were consultants.

Mr. Wolfson conceived the idea of building the structure in 1954. He died last June. A bust of him, done by Robert Berks, is welded into a center column in the vaulted lobby of the entrance. It was unveiled in the dedication ceremony.

Morgan D. Wheelock, vice president of the Real Estate Board of New York, presented a plaque on behalf of the board to Mrs. Wolfson, commemorating her husband's contribution to the real estate industry. ■

The Pan Am Building in New York City, 1963.

JANUARY 12, 1964

Questioning Pop Art's Staying Power

John Canaday

The week brought two ambitiously titled pop art shows, "Environments by 4 New Realists" at Sidney Janis and the "First International Girlie Exhibit" at the Pace Gallery.

Each of the four artists at Janis has an area to himself. Only two seem to me to have created anything like an "environment." At one end of an otherwise black-walled chamber, George Segal has erected a full-scale Plexiglas-and-metal sign, illuminated from behind, with a life-size plaster figure in front of it. The effect is altogether eerie—completely realistic and matter-of-fact in detail, but spectral, sinister and paralyzed in a kind of desperate airlessness. This is an environment indeed. Mr. Segal, whose sculptured figures look for all the world like real people who have fallen into a vat of plaster and couldn't get it wiped off before it set, and who, for all I know, may be exactly that, is a truly creative artist in a field dominated by gag men.

Nearby, Claes Oldenburg, best known for his sculptured hamburgers, has designed a bedroom ensemble consisting of a bed, chair, dresser and two bedside cabinets with lamps and shades, a clock, an ashtray and a radio. All are horrendously bastardized modern in style, and additionally are see-sawed in a way suggesting the built-in perspective of certain stage sets. The cubicle is an aseptic and synthetic corner of hell, but no more so than the originals that are its model.

James Rosenquist has something called "Door Stop," which is the plan of a three-bedroom apartment painted on the ceiling and complemented by naked electric light bulbs operated by pull-cords; something called "Capillary Action II," a Plexiglas panel painted in oil plus a tree with neon lighting, and something untitled, lying on the floor this time, which is a construction of horizontal Plexiglass panels crossed by wooden slat bridges, which you could probably walk across, plus more light bulbs. As far as I was concerned, these exhibits were crudely executed affairs devoid of environmental suggestion or any other kind of stimulus. Mr. Rosenquist and I were out of phase.

So were Jim Dine and I, although something called "The Dream No. 2" and described as "Oil on Canvas with Metal Pope and Aluminum Sheet" sounded promising, and topical, until "Pope" turned out to be a misprint for "Pipe," a tube that ran from wall to wall and—oh, why bother?

Why bother? is a question that had better be answered before going on to the Pace Gallery, since the girlie exhibition there offers no answer whatsoever. The reason for bothering with pop art is mostly the one given for climbing a mountain—because it's there. If pop art can happen, to the extent that it has already happened, and if it can produce a peripheral sculptor of the caliber of George Segal, it is not to be dismissed in spite of the fact that it already gives signs of beating itself to death.

At whatever serious level it manages to maintain, pop art is concerned with commenting on our current position in the world by imitating, in off-beat ways, objects that assault us every day as a degrading obbligato to the business of staying alive in the 20th century—billboards, signs, the thousands of objects involved in our processes of communication and the mere job of getting from one place to another. It selects its motifs from the inexhaustible and malodorous limbo of debased things that make up our landscape—the worst comic strips, the trashiest commercials, the smut magazines, the badly designed utilitarian objects, such ubiquitous paraphernalia as TV sets, and all such organic, indispensable and anonymous gear as radiators, steam pipes—anything.

Pop art, then, might serve to force us into an awareness of deficiencies and abuses that we accept in our civilization because we are accustomed to them. It might, and in an amateurish way it does, reveal Freudian morbidities within what we think of as commonplace things. (This is stale stuff.) Pop artists, it appears, do not like to be called satirists, but satire is nevertheless their commonest weapon.

But is it good satire? I do not think so. Good satire not only pokes fun, but by poking fun at weakness shows where strength lies, and by ridiculing folly points the way toward truth. Pop art does not do this. Its artists relish the inanities and perversities that they have adopted as a pictorial vocabulary; they seem to enjoy exposing what is hateful only as a compensation for something missed. The oldest dodge in the world is to be clever at the expense of your own foibles, and thus to intimate that they are not yours, but other people's.

Pop art as now practiced is an increasingly nasty spectator sport that is already tiring its audience. Whether the George Segals can fulfill themselves when subjected to such contamination is pop art's immediate question.

NOVEMBER 6, 1964

Display Unites Calder and the Guggenheim

John Canaday

Lovers are always mooning about the miracle that brought them together, and third parties, from now on, are likely to feel the same way about the Guggenheim Museum and Alexander Calder. They were made for each other, and their perfect union in a state of bliss opens for public inspection today.

The Guggenheim has never looked so good. Calder, who looks as good as ever, has never been so well displayed. His gigantic white mobile suspended within the museum's vast central space can be seen from below, from the sides and even from above. His 22-foot-high black stabile centered under it is something to stroll around in, an environmental sculpture that should make recent experimenters wonder why they ever bothered to try.

And while the space under the dome is perfect for Calder's biggest works, the niches along the ramps are ideally scaled to accommodate his most intimate ones. Everything has worked out perfectly, although the installation involved engineering problems as well as the usual harassment of coping with the building's outrageous slants, angles and warpings. The greatest tribute to Thomas Messer, the museum's director (who tied the marriage knot), is that the solutions are so successful that the difficulties seem to have vanished rather than to have been overcome.

With its walls painted white the museum sparkles with the reds, blacks, yellows and blues of the Calders that stand, hang and float about you. It is a shame that Frank Lloyd Wright can't see his building now. If he really designed it as a place to see art, he would be vindicated for the first time since the Guggenheim opened five years ago. Or if, as seems more probable, he designed it as an architectural monument with the power to defeat any effort to give proper play to the object displayed in it, he would be chastened—with the compensation that he could not but be delighted.

Everyone should be delighted. The one regretful response is that the show can't remain as a permanent installation. The perfect marriage is scheduled to break up on Jan. 10. ■

DECEMBER 14, 1964

Kennedy Family Announces Selection of Pei to Design Library

Ada Louise Huxtable

The Kennedy family announced yesterday the selection of an architect for the John F. Kennedy Memorial Library at Harvard University. At a news conference at the Hotel Pierre, Senator-elect Robert F. Kennedy named I. M. Pei, Canton-born New York architect, as the designer of the library and, in conjunction with it, of a projected institute for advanced political studies. Nathan M. Pusey, president of Harvard University, outlined plans for the Kennedy Institute, which will be connected with the Graduate School of Public Administration. Eugene R. Black, in charge of fund-raising for the library, announced that more than the original goal of $10 million had already been raised. But he said fund-raising would continue, to provide an endowment for the institute. "Contributions have come in from all over the country and the world, ranging from a few cents to a quarter of a million dollars. Over four million Americans have given something."

"No one can describe the institute before it gets started," Dr. Pusey said. "But this will be a new kind of institution in American life—a university setting to provide a meeting place between the academic world and the world of public affairs."

"The idea of the institute is to stimulate interest in politics," Robert Kennedy said.

Quoting Lord Tweedsmuir's definition of politics as "the most exciting of adventures," he explained that the purpose would be "to make young people interested in politics and government and the welfare of the country."

"This is what President Kennedy stood for, and this is what the institute will stand for," he said.

Commenting on the selection of Mr. Pei as architect for the project, Mr. Kennedy said:

"We all feel that he will be able to capture the spirit and style that we wish to express in this building."

Those who know Mr. Pei's buildings believe he may do something similar to his present work, which uses sensitively shaped and finished reinforced concrete construction to make strongly framed buildings of simple, straight lines.

Architect I. M. Pei at the Kennedy Memorial Library press conference, 1964.

Like other members of the group of leading American architects in their middle 40's, his design effects are sought through the possibilities opened up by current advances in building technology. He is not a traditionalist in any way.

"This is what President Kennedy stood for . . ."

Mr. Pei was chosen unanimously by a subcommittee of an international advisory committee of architects, after Mrs. Kennedy and the subcommittee had spent several months visiting architects' offices and studying their work, Mr. Walton said.

"Good luck, Mr. Pei," Mr. Kennedy said, with an encouraging grin. ■

FEBRUARY 28, 1965

THREE CHEERS FOR OP ART

John Canaday

"The Responsive Eye," the optical art exhibition at the Museum of Modern Art, is a brilliant show, with all the theatricalism typical of avant-garde art but with a most welcome difference. In its best and most important sections it is a display of craftsmanship in the service of a new idea as to what art should be about in this century.

The sloppiness, the shoddiness, the amateurism posing as esthetic sensibility that has marked avant-garde art for so long, gives way to art forms that demand technical perfection as an integral part of expression, and hence stand a chance of developing without the degradations that smothered abstract expressionism, assemblage and pop art in the hands of the amateur-cum-professional.

"The Responsive Eye" includes quantities of painting, but without any question the show is stolen lock, stock and barrel by the craftsmen who, with immaculate precision, have constructed devices in transparent plastics, polished alloys and other materials, that play with the eye, and cajole it, through inventions hardly related to painting and sculpture as we have known them.

I have no patience with the idea that the men who build these fascinating objects, objects where images change, move, grow, retreat, blossom and fade as the eye moves across them, are nothing more than clever display men. They are dealing with a kind of vision, a relationship between object and observer, that shows abstract expressionism to have been the poor, tired tag end of a great tradition that it was, and makes clear that pop art is now dying of the prostitute's occupational disease, exhaustion through corruption.

There is a wonderful suggestion here that, at last, we have an art form that must exist only in its own presence, as art used to exist before the process of mechanical reproduction could bring (for instance) Michelangelo to the millions in miniature reproductions that are only miniature reflections of his genius.

Optical art constructions may not be a patch on the Sistine Ceiling, when it comes to humanistic statement. But they have the glorious virtue of being free from association with the greatness of the past, with a consequent possibility of becoming expressions of the greatness of the present. They may be cold, they may be as objective as a laboratory experiment, they may say nothing about the spiritual goals that have concerned the great art of the past. But they are at least an art, or a craft, truly of our time.

Rejection of the past is of no virtue in itself. But a true and vital connection with the present is a great virtue indeed. The beautifully tooled objects that play with the laws of vision, and by playing with them may help to formulate them, may extend these laws into new areas of perception that are necessary to sanity in the present.

Keep your fingers crossed against the capacity for abuse that has killed other promises, and this may be truly a landmark exhibition. ■

MARCH 21, 1965

Not Good Taste, Not Bad Taste—It's 'Camp'

Thomas Meehan

Anyone who has lately been making the New York scene has more than likely been vaguely bewildered to hear the word "Camp" used in a context that has nothing whatsoever to do with Fort Dix, getting the children packed off to the Adirondacks for the summer or sleeping out in Bear Mountain State Park.

Among an increasing number of New Yorkers, Camp is now being used as a catch-all term to describe a previously unnamed sensibility, a third stream of taste, entirely apart from good taste or bad taste, that encompasses the curious attraction that everyone—to some degree, at least—has for the bizarre, the unnatural, the artificial and the blatantly outrageous. In short, Camp has come along to fill the singular need for a word to describe all those things that, until recently, have loosely been called "so bad they're good" (e.g., almost any Joan Crawford movie made since "Mildred Pierce"), "*too* much" (the novels of Ronald Firbank), "fantastic" (the Rockettes), or "*not* to be believed" (such headlines in The National Enquirer as "Madman Cuts Up His Date and Puts Her Body in His Freezer").

Now that one presumably has some Zen inkling of what Camp is all about, it should perhaps next be noted that the Sir Isaac Newton of Camp—that is, the person who discovered and defined the already existing phenomenon—is Miss Susan Sontag, a ubiquitous young Columbia University writer, intellectual, TV panelist and professor of philosophy who, in the fall, 1964, issue of Partisan Review, published an article entitled "Notes on 'Camp,' " in which she became the first person to discuss, seriously, Camp in print.

Of course, Miss Sontag in no way invented Camp, and, indeed, in one form or another, it's always been around—one need only think of art nouveau, Oscar Wilde, Beau Brummell, the American Negro cakewalk, certain Restoration comedies or the Hall of Mirrors in the Palace of Versailles. Nor did Miss Sontag coin the word Camp to label the phenomenon, for the word has been slangily used in that sense, especially in the New York homosexual world, since about 1950.

In any case, British philologists report that, since about 1925, the slang expression Camp has been synonymous in England with homosexual. Thus, the word apparently evolved from meaning "pleasantly ostentatious" to meaning "homosexual" and then to its current meaning. This evolution is not surprising, for Camp taste and homosexual taste are frequently the same thing. This is hastily not to say, however, that all those with Camp taste are homosexuals or that all homosexuals have Camp taste, but rather, as Miss Sontag put is, that "homosexuals, by and large, constitute the vanguard—and most articulate audience—of Camp."

(cont'd. on next page)

MARCH 24, 1966

KIENHOLZ TABLEAUS REVIVE MUSEUM'S WOES

Peter Bart

LOS ANGELES, March 23—The embattled Los Angeles County Museum of Art was plunged today into a new controversy with county officials over the display of two works of art denounced as pornographic.

The Los Angeles County Board of Supervisors voted unanimously to demand that the museum remove the controversial works, which were created by Edward Kienholz, a well known local artist. The county officials, who are empowered to order the removal of any objectionable works, termed the Kienholz exhibition "revolting."

The museum's board of trustees rejected the supervisors' demand, saying that they would support the Kienholz exhibition. They noted that his works had been shown at many outstanding museums, including the Museum of Modern Art in New York.

At the center of the controversy are two tableaus, one called "Roxy's," which depicts a room in a house of prostitution, and the second called "Back Seat Dodge," which shows a couple embracing in the back seat of an automobile. The principal critic of the Kienholz works, Supervisor Warren M. Dorn, said today that the works "were not art in the ordinary sense. My wife knows art. I know pornography."

Mr. Kienholz defended his work today and warned that he would withdraw the entire exhibition of 47 works if the two controversial ones were removed. He described his work as "a social statement in environmental associations, bringing us face to face with the unpleasant realities of everyday life."

In a statement released today the board of trustees declared:

"The board has never felt that it had the professional qualifications to pass judgment on the quality, value or character of art forms, assuming of course that they represent an honest statement by a serious artist. The board does not expect that all who view the exhibition will find it to their liking. A great museum displays and studies but does not pass judgment. Only society, present and future, can do that."

The trustees informed the supervisors that they would restrict visitors to the Kienholz display, which will open next Wednesday, to persons over 18. Supervisor Dorn rejected that concession, saying, "Pornography is not good for people of any age." ■

(cont'd. from previous page)

As one may have begun to note, many articles of Camp (beaded curtains, Tiffany lamps, Lalique glass) are old-fashioned and *démodé*, but it should be pointed out that simply because a thing is old it is not necessarily Camp. Rather, certain objects, like Tiffany lamps, which may have seemed banal and boring when they were new, somehow, to those with Camp taste, take on a luster and charm when they are old and give delight. Thus, many things that are not Camp today may ultimately become Camp, like Princess telephones, Doris Day movies or foam-rubber chairs—it's difficult to say.

Movies play a central part in the world of Camp, and the most Camp movie theater in Manhattan is the New Yorker at Broadway and West 88th Street. Indeed, the faithful of Camp have made the New Yorker one of the city's most financially successful theaters, as they've flocked there to see such Camp classics as the Busby Berkeley movies; Bette Davis in "Dark Victory"; the Marlene Dietrich-Von Sternberg films (especially "The Devil Is a Woman"); all of the Fred Astaire-Ginger Rogers movies made before "The Story of Vernon and Irene Castle"; most Lubitsch movies; "The Thing"; "Freaks"; and such Saturday afternoon adventure serials (talkies only) as Flash Gordon and Superman.

Camp not only involves finding fun and delight in things that others find banal, boring, worthless or hopelessly out-of-date, but also involves a certain amount of parody (especially unconscious parody) and what is colloquially known around New York as "the put on." Anarchic, anti-Establishment and often infuriatingly perverse, Camp is frivolous about serious things and serious about frivolous things, celebrating, as Miss Sontag put it, "the contrast between silly or extravagant content and rich form."

APRIL 17, 1966

DAVID SMITH ON TOUR

Hilton Kramer

The automobile crash that took the life of the American sculptor David Smith on May 23, 1965, brought to an abrupt and untimely end the career of one of the great artists of our time. Smith was 59 years old at the time of his death. For well over three decades he had been producing first-rate work, and in the last years of his life had entered upon a period of the most stunning productivity and accomplishment. When death struck, it struck down an artist at the height of his powers.

Thus, despite the immensity of Smith's *oeuvre*—an immensity in the sheer number of sculptures produced as well as in the esthetic quality of those sculptures—his death left one feeling tricked and deprived by the irrationality of fate.

Some time before Smith died, arrangements had been made for the International Council of the Museum of Modern Art to organize a large retrospective exhibition of his work for a tour of European museums. Last week a good part of the work—much of it drawn from Smith's own collection of his sculpture at Bolton Landing, New York—was in New York being crated for the first leg of the journey.

Smith did not live a life without public

honors. In addition to the honor that undoubtedly meant most to him—the abiding esteem of his fellow artists—he was fortunate in receiving early and intelligent recognition from the critics. He received awards of various sorts, was a familiar figure at critical symposia, and the whole public side of his career was crowned, only three months before his death, by President Johnson's appointing him to the National Council on the Arts—a body that would certainly have profited from Smith's no-nonsense grasp of the artist's real situation in this country.

Yet, all such honors notwithstanding, one sensed a certain reluctance—not only in the public at large, but even among people in a position to know better—to grant Smith his due. A measure of this reluctance is to be found in the fact that Smith was so consistently ignored by all those prestigious cultural committees—in the universities, in the corporations, and in cultural centers across the country—which in recent years have undertaken to purchase or commission large outdoor sculptures for public sites.

For all the elegance and polish of Smith's work, it never became quite as benignly respectable as Henry Moore's. Something about the scale and audacity of Smith's imagination remained too intransigent, too extreme, too difficult of access for tastes that asked to be cajoled rather than enlarged, flattered rather than challenged. And it remained so to the end. The heroic stainless steel constructions of Smith's last years—the great "Cubi" series—numbered 26 at the time of his death. A country that cared as much for its artistic heritage as it does for the endless rhetoric about cultural "explosions" would immediately have set about securing these works for public purposes. But, alas, the committees have been so busy elsewhere.

Now that an important Smith retrospective is going abroad, perhaps the distance—together with the praise the work is sure to win among European critics—will change some minds here. ■

SEPTEMBER 8, 1966

NEW WHITNEY IS HARSH AND HANDSOME

Ada Louise Huxtable

With three times the gallery space and 10 times the chic of its old building, the new, $6-million Whitney Museum promises to become this year's fashionable focus, or Whitney-a-Go-Go, of the jet art set. The new Whitney is a harshly handsome building. It also contains many sophisticated subtleties of design and detail. But the taste for its disconcertingly top-heavy, inverted pyramidal mass grows on one slowly, like a taste for olives or warm beer. It has a constant complement of sidewalk critics.

The building reveals itself as a carefully calculated design that squeezes the most out of a small, awkward 104-by-125-foot corner lot with maximum artistry and almost hypnotic skill. Tightly planned and organized, services are removed from the exhibition areas for 30,000 square feet of display space.

This structural and planning legerdemain is the work of Marcel Breuer and Hamilton Smith, working closely with the museum staff. Mr. Breuer is the internationally famous Hungarian-born architect who helped bring the modern style from Europe to America in the nineteen thirties.

Mr. Breuer's stark and sometimes unsettling structure may be less than pretty, but it has notable dignity and presence, two qualities not found uniformly in today's art. It will lend these qualities to its contents, by extension and by ambience. Occasionally, it wins hands down as a work of art itself, as when it puts sculpture to shame in the use of materials, light and forms in a striking stairwell.

The building has an extraordinary urbanity, which masquerades as a kind of "back-to-structure" crudeness. This "brutalism," as it is called in the trade, is one of the more exotic and popular forms of today's architectural estheticism.

It stresses masses of stone, largely unpolished—in this ease a truly beautiful gray granite outside and in—raw concrete complete with board marks of forms, rugged, bush-hammered concrete aggregate for interior walls, bluestone and split-slate floors.

The new building of the Whitney Museum of American Art, New York, September 27, 1966.

The trick—and again the hand is quicker than the eye—is the subtly scooped curve of a stone stair riser, the shape of a teak rail, or the juxtaposition of a rough-surfaced concrete wall with the extravagant luxury of massive, silky bronze doors. The "close-to-earth" materials have all the peasant simplicity of Marie Antoinette playing farmgirl in the hamlet at Versailles.

Add to the sophistication of this deceptive and esoteric austerity the most sophisticated technology, and the building is a total 20th-century phenomenon: a superb artificial environment for an art that maintains it is part of its time, but thrives best in hothouse isolation. The Whitney is a splendid hothouse. ■

The St. Louis Gateway Arch near completion in 1965.

OCTOBER 24, 1965

St. Louis Arch Near Completion

Ben A. Franklin

ST. LOUIS, Oct. 21—St. Louis's soaring Gateway Arch, a 630-foot stainless steel memorial to the pioneers who moved West across the Mississippi River here, comes to what construction men call the "topping out" stage next week. The city is expected to celebrate as if it had built Cheops's pyramid.

The final keystone section of the tallest national monument in the United States, a manmade landmark topped only by the Eiffel Tower, is scheduled to be pried into place late next week, closing an air gap of two feet between the gleaming, curved legs of the Jefferson National Expansion Memorial.

The name refers to Jefferson's negotiation of the Louisiana Purchase in 1803 and the surge of settlers who passed through St. Louis until about 1890.

As the arch stands now it seems in spectacular defiance of gravity, with its two 80-ton, rail-mounted "creeper cranes" perched high on its free-standing legs.

The "topping out" will mark a triumph over problems of design, engineering and construction and also over financial and organizational perils that rivaled the hazards of the pioneers whose hardihood the arch honors.

Former Mayor Bernard F. Dickman and the late Luther Ely Smith, a lawyer and civic booster, conceived the idea in 1933 of a riverfront monument to the city's role as a portal to the West. Since then the project has been beset by untold numbers of lawsuits, delays, and tribulations.

Moreover, including all the Federal

funds first paid out in the 1930s, the $7.5 million contribution of the city, and the $500,000 paid by the Terminal Railroad Association of St. Louis to relocate its tracks on the Mississippi levee, the project has cost a total of $32 million.

That figure does not include the $225,000 in architects' fees and prize money in the 1947 national competition for a memorial plan. And the finished memorial still has far to go. Another $8 million is needed for landscaping and completing the park on which it stands.

The great, glistening arch is the design of the late Eero Saarinen, who won the $50,000 first prize with his scheme of an unorthodox inverted catenary arch made of triangular sections of double-walled concrete. Five other of the 172 architects' plans submitted won $10,000 each as finalists.

In the Saarinen design, the arch was built of 12-foot prefabricated stainless steel sections, manufactured at Warren, Pa., by the Pittsburgh and Des Moines Steel Company.

Each section, after being hoisted and welded into place, had its double-walled skin filled with concrete, which was then stressed by 252 tension bars in each leg.

The slim steel rods, reaching into the foundation, were stretched taut by hydraulic jacks until the concrete had set.

Each leg is anchored in 12,000 tons of concrete in a massive triangular foundation block 90 feet on a side and sunk nearly 45 feet deep in bedrock.

When it is opened next July, the finished arch will have a 65-foot-long observation deck at the top, with service elevators and a five-car "train" for passengers in each leg. ■

NOVEMBER 6, 1966

ART OF FLORENCE DAMAGED IN FLOOD

Robert C. Doty

Irreparable damage to some of the world's great art treasures in Florence was part of the cost of the gales and floods that swept Italy yesterday and today.

At least 87 persons were known dead in floods and landslides caused by storms in Italy, Austria and Switzerland.

Torrential rains and winds up to 90 miles an hour battered the country for several hours beginning early Friday, centering on Tuscany and its capital, Florence. Venice, Grosseto and Trento were also hard hit.

The Arno River burst through its banks, flooding much of Florence to depths of up to 10 feet, cutting rail, road and wire communications and, farther downstream, inundating parts of Pisa.

"Damage is incalculable," said Mayor Piero Bargellini of Florence, who is a writer and renaissance art expert. "The war, all of the last war, probably did not do as much damage to Florence as the Arno did yesterday."

The greatest single loss yet identified was the damage to the sculptured bronze door of the Baptistry facing the city's Cathedral, Il Duomo.

Five of the ten panels of the Easy Door, or Door of Paradise, executed by the 15th-century Florentine sculptor Lorenzo Ghiberti, depicting biblical scenes, were swept off by flood waters. They were later recovered from the mud, badly scratched and marked.

Paintings and pieces of sculpture in the Uffizi Gallery, near the Piazza della Signoria, were spared, except for some works undergoing restoration in ground-floor studios, but the entire collection of more than 130,000 photo negatives of art works stored in the basement was destroyed.

Property damage was certain to be many billions of lire, perhaps as much as a billion dollars.

The 14th-century Ponte Vecchio, the only one of the Florence bridges left standing by retreating German forces in 1944, again survived, but was badly damaged.

Seventy prisoners in the Florence jail escaped during the flood and one was found dead in his cell.

DECEMBER 11, 1966

SO WARHOL STOPPED PAINTING BRILLO BOXES AND BOUGHT A MOVIE CAMERA

Elenore Lester

The girls—Andy Warhol's girls, Nico, Edie Sedgwick and International Velvet—were all living in the Chelsea area last summer. And Andy, just back from a tour with his Velvet Underground electronic rock group, wanted to make this film. So he decided to call it "The Chelsea Girls." He had no particular theme for the film, nor did he have anything that might be seriously described as a script. The idea was just to show "people doing different things." So he got the girls together with some of his other friends who were around at the time and portrayed them cutting their hair, talking, injecting dope unhygienically into the seat of their tight blue jeans, playing lethargic multi-sex games. They spent the month of August on it. Andy put about $1,500 into the thing, which is at least three times more than what is spent on most Underground films, but then it runs three-and-a-half hours and takes place on two frames simultaneously, so it is almost seven hours.

When the film came out last September, hip critics on the weeklies hailed Andy as a cross between D. W. Griffith and the Marquis de Sade.

Andy shrugs off the suggestion that the film was *cinema verité*, and that people were actually performing in a drugged state. Nobody was "turned on," he said, the whole thing was acting. "I don't believe in drugs."

How then does he get such startlingly authentic performances out of untrained actors? His method is to start with a minimal script and then let the actors go on and

(cont'd. on next page)

(cont'd. from previous page)
on until the reel ends. Andy readily admits that this method of making films might result in some boring sequences, and this is one good reason, he says, for keeping two frames going at once. "If you get bored with one, you can look at the other."

Andy's esthetic philosophy, like his personality, is simple, direct and inscrutable. He is never evasive, but always mysterious. "People go to the movies to look at people. Hollywood goes wrong in treating them like objects. They put them in beautiful countries, Rolls Royces, fly them to Egypt. You don't need all that. People are so fantastic. You can't take a bad picture."

So three years ago, when everyone suddenly discovered Pop art and Andy saw, therefore, that it was finished, he stopped painting Campbell's Soup cans and Brillo boxes and got a movie camera and trained it on people, his friends. Since then he has made more than 150 films, including such opuses as "Sleep," which runs for eight hours of a man's sleep; "Eat," which shows a man interminably eating a mushroom; and "Kiss," which etc. . . . There is no cutting, no editing, just the straightforward, sometimes endless record of what the camera sees.

Andy, who is now 36, says he has been subsidizing his film-making with the money he made on Pop paintings. He claims he can't find a backer for his movies because "People don't believe we're serious. They want to see our script first. And it seems silly to make up a script we aren't going to use just to get the money." Andy would like to be able to spend about $5,000 on a film. That would allow him to cut and edit.

But would cutting and editing spoil the rough, improvised Warhol quality—make his films slick and ordinary? No doubt Andy would find a way to keep several steps ahead of the cliché. ■

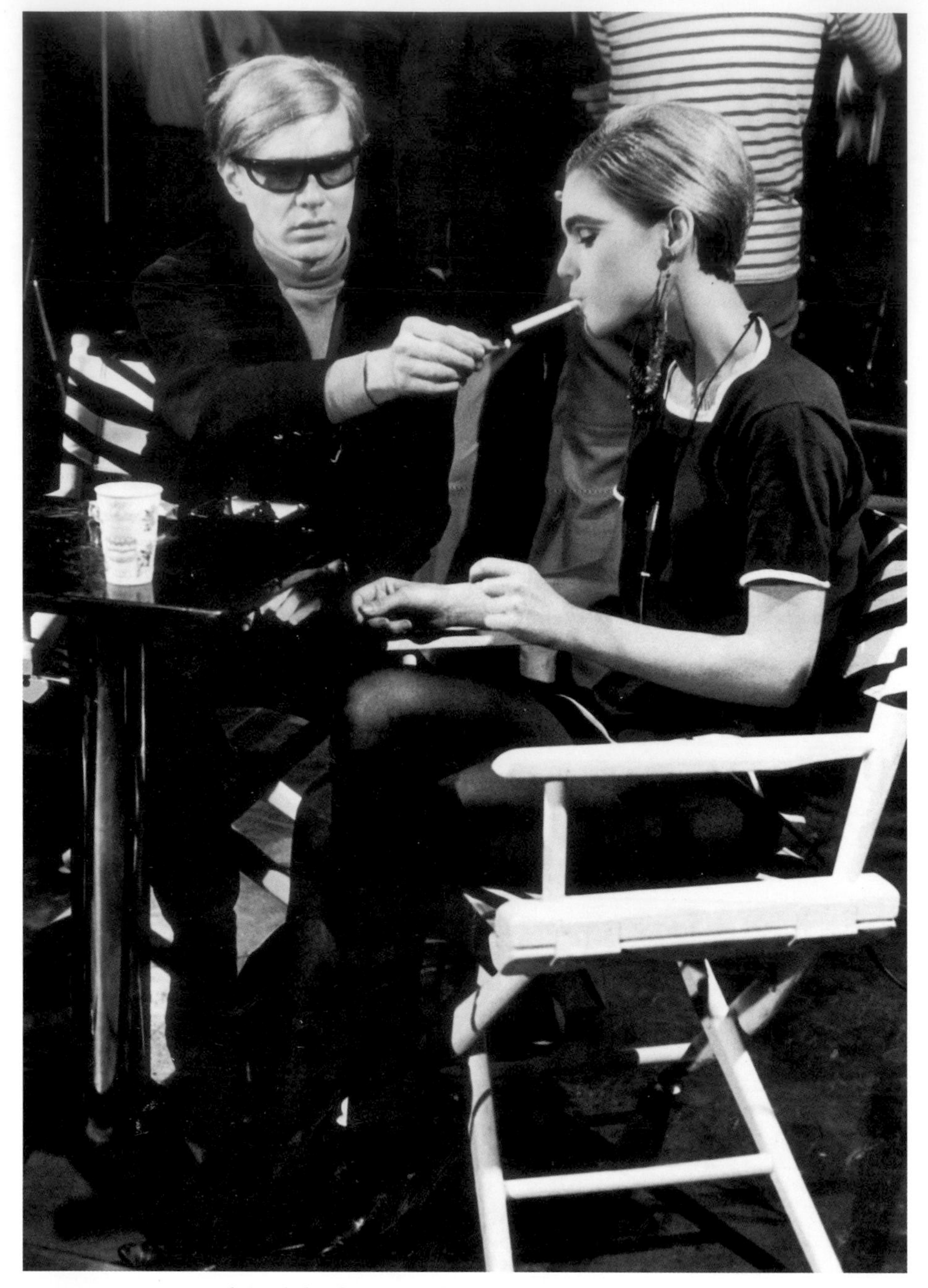

American Pop artist Andy Warhol with actress and muse Edie Sedgwick on the set of one of his films, 1966.

MAY 17, 1967

EDWARD HOPPER IS DEAD AT 84;

Painter of the American Scene

Edward Hopper, the celebrated painter of the American scene who was characterized as the painter of loneliness, died Monday in his studio at 3 Washington Square North. He was 84 years old.

Mr. Hopper attained a reputation as one of America's most distinguished and most individualistic painters. He remained resolutely determined to paint everyday subjects realistically throughout a long career that spanned numerous changes in contemporary art.

"My aim in painting," Mr. Hopper once observed, "has always been the most exact transcription possible of my most intimate impressions of nature."

His city people sitting at the all-night lunch stand, his apartment dwellers reading newspapers in barren rooms, his plain-bodied girls dressing in the morning light, his usherettes trapped in the cheap and plushy gloom of the movie palace were painted by Mr. Hopper with a respect for their right to inner privacy in the face of mass living.

While contemporaries like Rockwell Kent and George Bellows gained swift fame when American art began to veer away from conservatism early in the 20th century, Mr. Hopper declined to follow the trends and labored for years in obscurity.

Edward Hopper was born at Nyack, N.Y., July 22, 1882. He came to New York to study art in 1900, and continued to live and work here the rest of his life, except for summers in New England and short periods abroad.

During the winter of 1899-1900, he studied commercial illustration in New York. Shortly afterward he enrolled at the New York School of Art.

In 1913 the artist exhibited with other nonacademic painters at the revolutionary "Armory Show," and achieved his first sale—a canvas entitled "The Sailboat."

He continued painting in Maine during the next two summers, but in 1915 gave it up, and turned to etching. His etchings were hailed as genuine, lasting contributions to American art, and brought him awards in Los Angeles and Chicago.

Heartened by an exhibition of his watercolors at the Rehn Galleries here in 1924, Mr. Hopper resumed painting in oils. Critical interest and admiration for his works began to grow, and in 1933 he achieved major recognition—a one-man retrospective exhibition at the Museum of Modern Art.

At that time, Mr. Hopper had sold only two canvases. One of these had been bought in 1931 by the Metropolitan Museum of Art, which had previously been indifferent, if not hostile, to "modern" painters. It was "Tables for Ladies."

In 1937, the Metropolitan bought a second painting, "From Williamsburgh Bridge," from Mr. Hopper.

A wave of modernism had engulfed American realism early in the 1920s, but Mr. Hopper had persisted in painting starkly realistic though brightly colored aspects of contemporary life.

The Depression brought the attention of the abstractionists back to the American scene. They began to paint it realistically again, many in anger because of the poverty and suffering they saw.

The revival of realism brought fresh admiration to Mr. Hopper, who had been painting it all along, with steadily improving technique, deepening perception and a poet's sense of mood.

A 6-foot 5-inch lumbering man with a frank and quietly brooding face, Mr. Hopper accepted his belated success calmly. He continued to live and work in his top floor apartment studio in Washington Square North or at his summer home in Truro, Mass. Occasionally he and his wife, who also painted, would take long automobile trips around the country, during which he would make sketches for future oils and water-colors.

The retrospective exhibition of Mr. Hopper's work that was held at the Whitney Museum in 1964 covered 55 years of his painting.

JANUARY 28, 1968

A TRIUMPH OF CONSTRUCTIVISM

Hilton Kramer

The exhibition of sculpture by Louise Nevelson at the Pace Gallery is, except for her retrospective at the Whitney last year, the best exhibition of her work in some years. It is not a large exhibition but it marks a new development in her work that is going to have an influence on other sculptors and that already displays a remarkable authority and realization.

The new sculptures are constructions in Plexiglas. They are transparent, geometric, rather Miesian in their combination of a strict, unembellished syntax and a cool, detached glamour. They have distinct affinities with the current mode of Minimal sculpture, yet they stand apart from it, if only because Mrs. Nevelson's work offers the eye so much more in the way of visual incident. A maximum of visual incident—accretions of form that state and restate, that amplify and dramatize the basic structure of the work—was the principle on which Mrs. Nevelson designed her first sculptural "walls" some ten years ago.

It is interesting to look back on the changes that have overtaken Mrs. Nevelson's work in the past decade or so. A great deal of art history—both the way art is conceived and executed and the emotions it can be expected to embody—is reflected in them. Those exhibitions at the Grand Central Moderns Gallery in the nineteen fifties that won Mrs. Nevelson her first eminence were intended to overwhelm—and they did.

For those exhibitions were not mounted as discreet displays of separate objects; they were designed as spectacular sculptural environments. And indeed, the method of exhibition, which made the whole more important than the parts, led to a change in the sculptural "walls" for which Mrs. Nevelson is now best known.

The scale became architectural, but the imagery remained romantic, subjective, mysterious. There was a geometer's

(cont'd. on next page)

(cont'd. from previous page)
precision in the way forms were fitted together. But the feeling remained that of a romantic dream.

Mrs. Nevelson is a romantic by temperament, and in following what is, essentially, an antiromantic course, she has submitted her work to something stronger and more persuasive than the subjective taste to which it first gave expression—she has submitted it to the logical imperatives of its own form.

The ideal of a transparent structure, in which space, mass and light are identical and indistinguishable, in which the very syntax of the structure gives voice to the unity and inseparability of these elements—this ideal has haunted the Constructivist esthetic from its beginnings. Indeed, from before its beginnings: we find it stated as an aspiration in those crystal palaces of the nineteenth century that anticipated so much of the Constructivist idea.

. . . the best exhibition of her work in some years. . . .

I doubt if any sculptor has carried this old ideal to a more vivid realization than Mrs. Nevelson has in her new work. These transparent structures—prototypes for larger works to come—effect the final transformation of the romantic architecture of the fifties, with its Expressionist chiaroscuro, into a stunning Constructivist clarity. Everything here is open, visible, luminous. Planes dissolve into mass, and mass into light. Space is rigorously defined—for even the screws and bolts that join these Plexiglas panels provide a kind of pointillist three-dimensional drawing in space—yet it remains elusive and volatile. Ten years ago Mrs. Nevelson would have been one's last candidate for the office of redeeming the promise of Constructivist purity, yet that is precisely what her new work triumphantly accomplishes. ■

OCTOBER 6, 1968

MOVING MOTHER EARTH

Grace Glueck

A back-to-the-landscape show is burgeoning at the Dwan Gallery, though you can't exactly call it a revival of the Barbizon School. The medium (and message) is Mother Earth herself—furrowed and burrowed, heaped and piled, mounded and rounded and trenched. Called "Earth-works," the show boasts projects by nine artists who reveal their geophilia in photos, models and actual chunks of ground.

Robert Morris, for instance, has contributed a 6x6-foot pile of unsculptured terra firma. One of Claes Oldenburg's entries is a case of loam fraught with active earthworms. And Walter de Maria has sent from Germany a blown-up photo of a Munich gallery, whose floor he has carpeted wall-to-wall with dirt.

"We hope to get away from the formalism of studio art," says Robert Smithson, one of the show's prime movers, "to give the viewer more of a confrontation with the physicality of things outside. It's diametrically opposed to the idea of art as decoration and design."

Smithson, whose previous work has run to "perspective systems," has come up with a complex contribution that he calls a "non-site." It's a 5-part series of wooden bins, arranged in a perspective scheme and filled with limestone fragments from a mineral dump in Franklin Furnace, N.J. (a famous haunt for rock hounds). Shown with it is a blown-up aerial photo, pinpointing the actual sites from which the limestone was taken. The viewer can heighten his "participation" by touring them.

"This brings an abstract, rather than natural awareness of the landscape," says Smithson, who rejoices in the "dualism" between the rock (raw material) and its bins (an artificial, gallery-type scheme). "The earth to me isn't nature, but a museum. My idea is not anthropomorphic. It relates to man and matter rather than man and nature."

Even deeper into the ground thing is Mike Heizer, a 23-year-old ex-painter who comes from a family of geologists and mining engineers (his father is a digging anthropologist). Accompanying Smithson and his wife Nancy on a rock-hunt last summer in the West, Heizer put down a series of "earth liners" along a 520-mile string of dry lake beds running from Las Vegas to Oregon. His "conglomerate project" consists of eight 5-part clusters of light-catching trenches—12" deep, 12" wide, 12' long—positioned according to the sun's East-West trail.

"I refuse to draw limits because a work isn't practical," Heizer says. "In fact, my earth liners can be collected, if someone wants to put them in his yard. I did them in the desert because no one wanted them." (Actually, Heizer's desert works are "owned" by collector Robert Scull, who has already made a proprietary tour of them by helicopter.)

The "historical" work in the show is a grass-wall sculpture of 1955, done in Aspen, Colo., by 68-year-old Herbert Bayer, a versatile ex-Bauhaus man. A giant ring of turfy earth (shown in a blown-up photo) it might have been turned out by a cosmic Jello mold. "If we were a museum, of course," muses Virginia Dwan, the Minnesota Mining (hmm!) and Mfg. heiress who owns the gallery, "we could have started with the Mayans and Egyptians."

The notion for the show goes back two years, when Smithson was hired as an art consultant by Tippetts-Abbett-McCarthy-Stratton, an architectural-engineering firm working up proposals for a Dallas-Fort Worth airport. His ideas for "aerial art"—sculptured mounds of earth and gridworks viewable from low-flying aircraft—are under consideration. But so far, the airport has not got off the drawing board.

MARCH 2, 1969

ABSTRACTION AND 'THE LANDSCAPE PARADIGM'

Hilton Kramer

The large exhibition of paintings by Helen Frankenthaler which has now come to the Whitney Museum of American Art, Madison Avenue at 75th Street, will be a surprise, I think, even to many people who had reason to feel that they were well acquainted with her work. The exhibition consists of 45 paintings dating from 1952 to 1968. Not only does the work fully support the retrospective scale of the exhibition, but—what is more surprising perhaps—the scale of the exhibition is genuinely illuminating. For myself, certainly, this exhibition establishes Miss Frankenthaler as one of our best painters.

As a painter, she derives of course from the Abstract Expressionist movement, and in some respects has remained more faithful to the basic tenets of that movement—especially as they were exemplified in the work of Jackson Pollock—than any other painter of her generation. At the same time, her work forms a decisive link between the art of the Abstract Expressionists and that of the color abstractionists of the sixties.

She is a lyric landscapist who has profited—hugely—from the increased scale and confidence that came into American painting with the Abstract Expressionists. Without committing her art to the descriptive conventions of traditional landscape painting, Miss Frankenthaler has nonetheless remained within its general orbit of feeling. The kind of synthesis of landscape and abstraction that she has so successfully effected—a style at once very personal, very responsive to the articulation of an individual temperament, and yet owing much to the historical imperatives that have overtaken the methodology of painting—this sort of synthesis is only possible, perhaps, when the syntax of painting has been decisively redefined beforehand.

Beside an artist like Kenneth Noland, say, or Frank Stella, Miss Frankenthaler is indeed a more traditional composer. Pictures such as "Three Moons" (1961), "Sea Scape and Dunes" (1962), "Island Weather II" (1963), or even the more recent "Noon" (1966) and "Flood" (1967), do not require the kind of radical adjustment in our expectation of the pictorial experience that, for better or worse, is essential to an appreciation of Noland's or Stella's recent work. There is, in her work, no suggestion of a system or a formula or a doctrine that must be satisfied before the sensibility of the painter can be allowed to enact its expressive tasks. There is, on the contrary, a very evident amplitude of feeling that has found a style perfectly attuned to its freedom and intelligence. ■

American abstract painter Helen Frankenthaler in her New York studio, circa 1960.

NOVEMBER 3, 1960

LADY CHATTERLEY RULED NOT OBSCENE

Seth S. King

LONDON, Nov. 2—A jury of three women and nine men decided today that "Lady Chatterley's Lover" was not obscene.

In the first major test of Britain's new obscene publications law, Penguin Books, Ltd., received legal clearance to publish D. H. Lawrence's controversial novel without expurgation. Such a version of the narrative of an English lady's love affair with her invalid husband's gamekeeper had been banned here since it was first offered for publication in 1928.

Within the next ten days, 200,000 copies of the paperback edition will go on sale at 3s 6d (about 50 cents).

The verdict was a posthumous victory for Lawrence, who had refused to alter his original manuscript to meet the objections of his British publishers.

Under the terms of the law, which became effective last year, the jury had to decide two points: whether the book was obscene and, if it were, whether its publication was justified for the public good.

Under the previous obscenity law, the literary value of the book and its author's standing were not admissible as a defense.

Although the verdict was hailed by many British literary figures, some publishers expressed concern that it might open the way for a new flood of border-line fiction.

However, jubilant officials of Penguin Books did not agree.

Sir Allen Lane, managing director of the company, said: "The decision means that it will be extremely doubtful whether there are any more prosecutions in the future of a serious author published by a serious publisher."

Had Penguin Books been found guilty under the criminal action brought by the Crown, the company would have been liable to a fine and its directors to imprisonment up to three years.

The defense called thirty-five witnesses to testify in support of the book's literary merit and the author's importance. Among these were some of Britain's best-known writers and broadcasters, an Anglican Bishop and a Roman Catholic layman, an authority on obscene literature.

An unexpurgated version of "Lady Chatterley's Lover" was published in the United States last year by Grove Press. The United States Postmaster General ruled it was obscene and could not be sent through the mail. However, he was overruled in July of 1959 by Federal Judge Frederick van Pelt Bryan, who held the book was not objectionable on these grounds. ■

Two women outside a bookshop in Leicester Square, London, after a jury at the Old Bailey decided that "Lady Chatterley's Lover" by D.H. Lawrence was not obscene.

OCTOBER 16, 1960

The Awful Story of Hitler's Germany, Movingly Told

H. R. Trevor-Roper

THE RISE AND FALL OF THE THIRD REICH A History of Nazi Germany.
By William L. Shirer. 1,245 pp.
New York: Simon and Schuster. $10.

How can we even look objectively on the Third Reich? It was the greatest, most horrible phenomenon of the twentieth century. It dominated the lives of some of us: we cannot think ourselves free of its effects. To others it is an episode of that dark period before they were aware of events: they can never imagine its real quality or horror and easily suspect us of exaggeration. In ordinary circumstances it would be impossible, only half a generation after its end, in the twilight period between passion and documentation, to write its history. But with the Third Reich nothing was ordinary, not even its end. Adolf Hitler aimed at "world power or nothing," and after a brief period of world power ended up with nothing. In that total annihilation all the secrets of his rule were broken open, all the archives captured, their truth tested in court, their contents made public.

Now, as never before, the living witnesses can converge with the historical truth. All they need is a historian. In William L. Shirer they have found him. He was himself in Germany from 1935 to 1941—need one refer to his "Berlin Diary"? Since the war he has studied the massive documents made available by Hitler's total defeat. And now he has brought together his experience and his study in a monumental work, a documented, 1,245-page history of the whole episode of Hitler's Third Reich.

Of course, he will have some critics; every author has. I can think of points to criticize. Is he fair to Nietzsche and Gobineau? Is he still so sure about the Reichstag fire? Might he not have freed himself a little more from the day-to-day diplomacy of 1938-39 to say more of the internal structure of Nazi Germany? Might he not, in view of his own residence in Germany, have captured and conveyed a little more of the atmosphere of the time, portrayed the personalities, re-created the sense of permanent crisis in which Hitler kept the world? Perhaps he might, but these are trivial criticisms in view of the greatness of his achievement. This is a splendid work of scholarship, objective in method, sound in judgment, inescapable in its conclusions. Not that Mr. Shirer states his conclusions; he leaves them to be deduced.

First of all, Shirer points out, Hitler was a man of political genius. He does not shrink, as so many historians do, from using that term. For a long time it has been fashionable to decry Hitler as a mere puppet of impersonal forces, froth thrown up by the waves of historic change. If one says or implies that he has genius, one is accused of admiring him, of being almost a Nazi oneself. I have endured a good deal of abuse from virtuous liberals and Socialists on this score. But it is really absurd to deny Hitler's genius, though it was the genius of a devil, a genius devoted to the destruction and degradation of humanity.

Hitler, says Mr. Shirer—and how I agree with him—was "possessed of a demonic personality, a granite will, uncanny instincts, a cold ruthlessness, a remarkable intellect, a soaring imagination and—until toward the end—an amazing capacity to size up people and situations." It is worth adding also, as evidence of this genius, that Hitler, alone of great revolutionaries, both launched his revolution and commanded all its stages. Nazism devoured its children but never its begetter. He was its prophet and tyrant alike. It began and ended with him, and the rise and fall of the Third Reich are synonymous with his career.

Mr. Shirer quotes Goethe's remark, "I have often felt a bitter sorrow at the thought of the German people, which is so estimable in the individual and so wretched in the generality. A comparison of the German people with other peoples arouses a painful feeling, which I try to overcome in every possible way." We should try to overcome it too; but not by overlooking the facts. The facts are in this book: massive, proved, indisputable. If anyone is tempted, by the evidence of Hitler's political and diplomatic achievements, to admire his indisputable genius, let him read Mr. Shirer's excellent chapter of the New Order and see, and remember, the hideous purpose to which 65 million Germans either actively helped or tacitly allowed it to lead them. ■

The novelist and short story author John Updike, Massachusetts, 1960s.

NOVEMBER 6, 1960

You Cannot Really Flee

David Boroff

RABBIT, RUN.
By John Updike. 307 pp. New York: Alfred A. Knopf. $4.

At the beginning of this moving and often brilliant novel, "Rabbit" Angstrom quietly watches a group of boys playing basketball. Then, shedding his coat, he joins them at play, demonstrating superbly the virtuosity that eight years earlier had made him the star of his high school team. This opening defines the mood of nostalgia and unquiet adulthood that characterizes John Updike's "Rabbit, Run."

Rabbit is an older and less articulate Holden Caulfield. An urban cipher, he is trapped by wife, baby, an uncongenial job as demonstrator for a new kitchen utensil.

This is the stuff of shabby domestic tragedy—and Mr. Updike spares the reader

(cont'd. on next page)

(cont'd. from previous page)

none of the spiritual poverty of the milieu. The old people are listless and defeated, the young noisily empty. The novel, nevertheless, is a notable triumph of intelligence and compassion; it has none of the glib condescension that spoils so many books of this type. The characters have an imposing complexity. The local Lilith is neither a golden-hearted harlot nor an item from a sociologist's workbook, but oddly lovable, stingingly real. Rabbit's wife is no self-indulgent slattern, but a woman with a rich and tortured consciousness—her interior monologues remind one of a less lascivious Molly Bloom. And Rabbit, neither an overaged delinquent nor a casual satyr, is a seeker and a sufferer—a man in impotent rebellion against all the people "advertising their belief that the world arches over a pit, that death is final, that the wandering thread of his feelings lead nowhere."

The author's style is particularly impressive: artful and supple, its brilliance is belied by its relaxed rhythms. Mr. Updike has a knack of tilting his observations just a little, so that even a commonplace phrase catches the light. The prose is that rarest of achievements—a perfectly pitched voice for the subject.

"Rabbit, Run" is a tender and discerning study of the desperate and the hungering in our midst. A modest work, it points to a talent of large dimensions—already proved in the author's New Yorker stories, and his first novel, "The Poorhouse Fair." John Updike, still only 28 years old, is a man to watch. ■

OCTOBER 22, 1961

'AIN'T' IS IN, 'RAVIOLIS' AIN'T

Mario Pei

WEBSTER'S THIRD NEW INTERNATIONAL DICTIONARY OF THE ENGLISH LANGUAGE.
Unabridged. Illustrated. 2,720 pp. Springfield, Mass.: G. & C. Merriam Company. $47.50.

Language, like time, marches on; but language far outstrips time in its progress. Noah Webster's first unabridged dictionary, published in 1828, had 70,000 entries. The new Merriam-Webster, the third revised edition, has 450,000. Of these, 100,000 are new words and new word meanings.

All languages are potentially equal, but the extent and range of a language's vocabulary reflect the state of civilization of its speakers, the activities in which they indulge, the material objects they create and use, the abstract concepts they evolve. Far from viewing with alarm our astounding language growth within the past 130-odd years, we should rejoice over this index of material and intellectual progress. At the most, we may wonder how many 2,720-page volumes will be required for the Merriam-Webster Unabridged of the year 2000.

It is all very well to say that the average speaker knows and uses only a small fraction of the total number of words listed. The words are there, at his disposal; and a certain proportion, however small, of our vocabulary increase must perforce rub off on even the most illiterate of speakers. Merriam-Webster's publicity catch-phrase "the greatest vocabulary explosion in history" has plenty of justification. Examples of it range all the way from *breezeway* and *split-level* to *fringe benefit* and *sit-in*, from *airlift* to *no-show* to *deceleration* and *astronaut*, from *beatnik* and *den mother* to *wage dividend* and *zen*.

There are many commendable features in this latest of vocabulary offerings. Whether they are such as to justify the claim of "revolutionary techniques designed to make words meaningful to everyone" is perhaps debatable. Certain technical terms require far more than a dictionary definition to be meaningful.

This raises the question of authority, pointed up by the statement that the Merriam-Webster has been "the principal authority in courts of law, schools, and the U.S. Government Printing Office." The compilers would undoubtedly say that the dictionary's authority is based on usage, but the question insistently comes up: "Whose usage?" That of J. F. Kennedy—or that of Joe Doakes?

Ain't, we are told, gets official recognition at last as "used orally in most parts of the U.S. by cultivated speakers." With tongue in cheek, perhaps? Of course, *ain't* has a long and honorable tradition and has consistently appeared in dictionaries, both British and American; the new Merriam-Webster boasts of the fact that the label "colloquial" has been dropped, thus sanctioning the "informality of modern English."

This is all to the good, but it leaves me wondering how far the process of informality can go before it incurs the charge of outright vulgarism.

Inconsistencies in treatment appear. Why is *spaghetti* said to have a plural *s*, while *ravioli* and *rigatoni* are given *i* plurals? From the standpoint of the language of origin, all these nouns are already plural. If "usage" is alleged as a defense, then I must regretfully report that the same people who say (and write) *spaghettis* also say and write *raviolis*.

Dozens of new meanings and uses appear, and they are exemplified by an impressive series of quotes ranging from Polly Adler to Virginia Woolf, and from Police Detective to The New York Times. Yet I miss, in this new version, some of the features that appeared in my 1884 volume—sets of special tables at the end, and particularly etymologies for some personal and place names.

Despite these and other criticisms that could and will be made, "Webster's Third New International Dictionary" will enjoy a healthy life, even if not too prolonged. It is the closest we can get, in America, to the Voice of Authority. ■

language

FEBRUARY 4, 1962

"CUCKOO'S NEST" TACKLES GOOD AND EVIL

Martin Levin

Hardly a single aspect of sanitarium lore has been overlooked in this season's budget of asylum novels. Hospital bureaucracy, professional rivalries, the war between old and new therapies—you'll find them all in recent fiction, and once (in Jennifer Dawson's luminous "The Ha-Ha") or twice, as in Ken Kesey's "One Flew Over the Cuckoo's Nest" (Viking, $4.95). They occur in a work of genuine literary merit. What Mr. Kesey has done in his unusual novel is to transform the plight of a ward of inmates in a mental institution into a glittering parable of good and evil.

Bromden, the character through whose eyes one sees an off-center world, is a deeply withdrawn inmate with a persecution mania. But in truth he is also persecuted. At his most deluded, Bromden sees his ward run by a diabolist ("The Big Nurse") and her three demonic flunkies via an electronic system that saps the patients of their humanity; at his most lucid, he sees a calculated sadist and three degenerates compressing the ward into a "Therapeutic Community." Having the same common denominator, reality and illusion keep dissolving into one another in Caligari-like sequences. These have greater and greater lucidity as the "fog machine" falters and The Big Nurse begins to get her comeuppance from a prison-farm casual named McMurphy—a life-loving roisterer whose symbolic import would be visible even if he didn't have white whales emblazoned on his undershorts. The catastrophic terminus of this novel is a bit obvious. But the route traversed is so brilliantly illuminated that it is reward enough.

JUNE 24, 1962

Hapless Defiance

Morris Gilbert

A HOUSE FOR MR. BISWAS.
By V. S. Naipaul. 531 pp. New York: McGraw-Hill Book Company. $5.95.

A most gifted writer, V. S. Naipaul of Trinidad, having warmed up with short novels (glowingly received here) now turns in a major performance which reviewers of a British edition found "wonderfully funny," "very entertaining" and which, to this reader, has both those characteristics and is also heart-rending.

The scene is Trinidad, but a Trinidad that hardly a tourist on that blissfully-advertised island would recognize. The utterly bewildering affairs of one enormous, inchoate, influential Trinidadian-Hindu family, the Tulsis, dominate the narrative, with Mr. Biswas a pitiable little figure in defiant, hapless opposition. He reminds one of H. G. Wells' immortal Mr. Polly, a misfit, a sensitive creature thrust into an insensitive world. Like Mr. Polly, he is a child of misfortune. All the omens at his birth were bad.

His one purpose in life was to have a house of his own, and thus avoid the insolent patronage of the Tulsis. Time and again he tried, in this tale of desperate frustration; and his progress from appalling beginnings to a rickety, but at least ostensibly presentable, home is the gist of the narrative.

The story of Mr. Biswas is told with virtually filial tenderness and understanding. The picture of the Hindu community of Trinidad, its mixture of peasant brutishness and quick, nervous brilliance, its unrooted bewilderment in a world still alien to it, is engrossing. This big, ludicrous, fascinatingly detailed novel has great quality. ■

SEPTEMBER 23, 1962

DANGERS IN PESTICIDES VIVIDLY PICTURED

Lorus and Margery Milne

SILENT SPRING.
By Rachel Carson. Drawings by Lois and Louis Darling. 368 pp. Boston: Houghton Mifflin Company. $5.

Poisoning people is wrong. Yet, for the sake of "controlling" all kinds of insects, fungi and weed plants, people today are being poisoned on a scale that the infamous Borgias never dreamed of. Cancer-inducing chemicals remain as residues in virtually everything we eat or drink. A continuation of present programs that use poisonous chemicals will soon exterminate much of our wild life and man as well. So claims Rachel Carson in her provocative new book, "Silent Spring."

"Silent Spring" is a cry to the reading public to help curb private and public programs which by use of poisons will end by destroying life on earth.

Know the facts and do something about the situation, she urges. She intends to shock and hopes for action. She fears the insidious poisons, spread as sprays and dust or put in foods, far more than the radioactive debris from a nuclear war.

Her account of the present is dismal. It is not hopeless—at least not yet. But she demands a quick change in "our distorted sense of proportion." How can intelligent beings seek to control a few unwanted species by a method that contaminates the entire environment and brings the threat of disease and death even to our own kind?

Miss Carson gives most of her attention to insecticides, herbicides and fungicides, since these are the most dangerous poisons. She shows the futility of relying on them or any new substitutes offered to counteract the swift evolution of immunity to chemical control shown by more and

(cont'd. on next page)

(cont'd. from previous page)

more insects and fungus diseases. She quotes an authority on cancer, Dr. W. C. Hueper of the National Cancer Institute, who has given "DDT the definite rating of a 'chemical carcinogen'"—a cancer inducer. Other modern insecticides are still more deadly. Nor did the discovery of their poisonous character "come by chance: insects were widely used [during World War II] to test chemicals as agents of death for man."

Those who grow and store food and other products that can be hurt by pests will surely accuse "Silent Spring" of telling only part of the story. They will claim that today efficiency in raising and distributing food and wood depend upon the use of poisons. If biological control methods were relied upon or hand labor required, the yield would be smaller and the market price higher. They might ask, "Do you want wormy apples and buggy flour, or traces of pesticides that by themselves have not yet been proved harmful?"

"Silent Spring" is so one-sided that it encourages argument, although little can be done to refute Miss Carson's carefully documented statements.

In answer to the charge that the balance of nature has been upset, it has been pointed out by some members of the chemical industry that modern medicine is equally upsetting. This sort of defense merely invites a pox on both the biocide and the drug industries. It is high time for people to know about these rapid changes in their environment, and to take an effective part in the battle that may shape the future of all life on earth. ■

JANUARY 31, 1963

A Negro in White America

Sheldon Binn

Author James Baldwin in 1962.

"You must put yourself in the skin of a man..." writes James Baldwin as he seeks to translate what it means to be a Negro in white America so that a white man can understand it.

Despite the inherent difficulties of such a task, his translation in his latest book, "The Fire Next Time," is masterful. No matter the skill of the writer, and Mr. Baldwin is skillful, one can never really know the corrosion of hate, the taste of fear or the misery of humiliation unless one has lived it. Only James Meredith knows what it really means to be James Meredith. But if the actuality cannot be known, it can be related.

On one level it can be related so the listener becomes more or less curious, mildly interested and intellectually aware of what he is hearing.

On another and higher level, it can be related so the listener becomes virtually part of the experience, intensely feels the hurt and pain and despair, and yes, even the hope. The listener can be transformed, as far as words will take him, into the skin of the teller.

He has pictured white America as seen through the eyes of a Negro.

What he has drawn will not sit well with even some whites who count themselves as friends of the Negro. But he has not written this book of two essays to please.

"The brutality with which Negroes are treated in this country simply cannot be overstated, however unwilling white men may be to hear it," he writes.

Thus he has written from a heart which has felt a unique kind of hurt and a brain which has desperately sought hope in the face of what often seems to be the merciless logic of despair. He has fashioned his plea to America out of the past he has known, from the ferment of the present and the possibilities of the future.

Mr. Baldwin pleads: "If we—and I mean the relatively conscious whites and the relatively conscious blacks, who must, like lovers, insist on, or create, the consciousness of others—do not falter in our duty now, we may be able, handful that we are, to end the racial nightmare, and achieve our country, and change the history of the world."

Otherwise, the next time fire.

But if the facts he adduces are damning, his transcendent hope remains.

"I think we must *believe* it is possible," he writes. ■

MARCH 6, 1963

Women 'Educated' Out of Careers

Fred M. Hechinger

NEW YORK—Manpower experts have long been complaining that loss of womanpower seriously drains our national pools of talent. Mathematicians have charged that even mathematically brilliant girls are discouraged in early childhood from pursuing that "unladylike" study. Engineering experts say that mistaken notions about women's roles and goals have chased promising girls away from engineering careers. Now, in a frank chapter of her new book, "The Feminine Mystique" (W.W. Norton & Company; $5.95), Betty Friedan puts a major share of the blame on "The Sex-Directed Educators."

The author documents the disturbing facts on today's college campuses and in the high schools. Although more American women have been going to college during the fifties than ever before, fewer of them were going on from college to become physicists, philosophers, poets, doctors, lawyers, stateswomen, social pioneers or even college professors. Increasing numbers of girls—women's college students as well as coeds—"seemed suddenly incapable of any ambition, any vision, any passion, except the pursuit of a wedding ring," the book says.

American actress Ava Gardner with a copy of "The Feminine Mystique" by Betty Friedan, 1963.

The indictment is uncompromising and occasionally extreme. But while the case may be somewhat overstated, the symptoms of a dangerous trend have in no way been misstated. In fact, the book confirms and drives home with editorial passion many dangers that educators themselves often warn against privately.

Mrs. Friedan cites a report on students in high-quality women's colleges: "Strong commitments to an activity or career other than that of a housewife is rare." She quotes a psychology professor at an equivalent institution: "I couldn't schedule the final seminar for my senior honor students. Too many kitchen showers interfered."

But she also asked the students themselves. A senior in cap and gown told her: "Our parents expect us to go to college. Everybody goes...But a girl who got serious about anything she studied...would be peculiar, unfeminine."

The girls, said Mrs. Friedan, behaved as if college were an interval to be gotten through impatiently, efficiently, bored—so that the "real"—meaning feminine and married—life could begin. Is this the fault of the students? Mrs. Friedan says No. Society's pressures (discussed in other chapters) play an important part; but educators are guilty of going along with a trend, and often even pushing it.

What are the consequences of all this? Mrs. Friedan concludes that it actually prevents many girls from preparing for a realistic career or intellectual commitment. It hides the fact that most modern women will spend 25 or more years of their adult lives on jobs or activities outside the home. It seduces girls into "seeking security in the man," with a subsequent loss both to themselves and to their families. It fosters preoccupation with boys, dates and sex that becomes not a real interest at all, but a defense against intellect.

This leads to flight into marriage—ever earlier marriage.

The account of what is wrong gives important hints as to what might be right. The young people—women as well as men—who commit themselves to serious study, possibly graduate or vocational work, have a far better chance of finding security in their own accomplishments and strength in their disciplined minds rather than their immature emotions. When they marry, they are more likely to find, along with love, a basis for mutual respect. ■

MARCH 19, 1963

"A Clockwork Orange" Is a Tour de Force in Nastiness

Brian O'Doherty

"A Clockwork Orange" is a brilliant novel. In young Alex, Anthony Burgess has created the most interesting delinquent since Pinky in Grahame Greene's "Brighton Rock." Alex is vicious, depraved, anarchic, a pure little monster, and the purity of his dedication to evil keeps lighting his deeds like some grotesque halo.

Alex's choice of evil is total and enthusiastic; his aimlessness is electric, like a shark switching around to the nearest scent; his intelligence is sharply practical and of a high order. The novel is about this individual versus the State, which removes his capacity for choice, turning him into a mass of conditioned reflexes, all wholesome and good. It is a weird little morality tale, told in a taut, telescoped style that gives the effect of a continuous close-up. The narrator is Alex himself.

The chilling thing about Mr. Burgess's approach is that his novel is an intimate memoir from the future. For Alex lives in a world that is all one, that had conquered space, that has no problems except social cancer. As we look out through Alex's eyes on the immediate present (like an animal Alex has little sense of past or future), the author suggests the total condition of the strange new world outside, a world inimical to and yet favoring Alex and his hoodlum-beatniks.

The "hip" language that Alex and his "droogs" (gangmates) speak is a further development in the lingo of the outsiders. It lights up page after page in pin-ball machine fashion, and midway through the book you can understand it as well as Alex. Fighting a rebellious droog, Alex says, "I had just ticklewickled his fingers with my britva (knife), and there he was looking at the malenky (little) dribble of krovvy (blood) that was reddening out in the lamplight." This device could easily have become a bore, but Mr. Burgess handles it with intelligence and for a purpose. The neologisms are provocative, their logic often ironically apparent (cigarettes are called "cancers"), and by the end of the book one is left with a satisfactory sense of having learned a language and become part of an in-group, which is exactly Mr. Burgess's purpose.

The main moral is that evil chosen is superior to unchosen good. The point that Alex's initial evil is as much a result of conditioning by society as it is his own free choice, is ignored. Fortunately Mr. Burgess does not weaken his book by offering answers to the individual's anti-social perversions or to collective surgery on the individual's free will. He tells an abruptly fascinating story that lands again and again on these two large targets. In fact his eagerness to hit his targets runs a little away with him in the second half of the book; instead of allowing the irony to grow from his situations he tends to force it on them, occasionally blunting the slicing edge of his prose. But all in all, "A Clockwork Orange" is a tour-de-force in nastiness, an inventive primer in total violence, a savage satire on the distortions of the single and collective minds.

APRIL 21, 1963

PYNCHON'S V: MATA HARI WITH A CLOCKWORK EYE

George Plimpton

Since the war a category of the American novel has been developed by a number of writers: American picaresque one might call the archetype, and its more notable practitioners would include Saul Bellow with "The Adventures of Augie March"; Jack Kerouac, "On the Road"; Joseph Heller, "Catch-22"; Clancy Sigal, "Going Away"; and Harry Mathews, who last fall produced a generally overlooked though brilliant novel entitled "Conversions."

Such novels are invariably lengthy, heavily populated with eccentrics, deviates, grotesques with funny names (so they can be remembered), and are usually composed of a series of bizarre adventures or episodes in which the central character is involved, then removed and flung abruptly into another. Very often a Quest is incorporated, which keeps the central character on the move.

For the author, the form of the picaresque is convenient: he can string together the short stories he has at hand (publishers are reluctant to publish short-story collections, which would suggest the genre is perhaps a type of compensation). Moreover—the well-made, the realistic not being his concern—the author can afford to take chances, to be excessive, even prolix, knowing that in a work of great length stretches of doubtful value can be excused. The author can tell his favorite jokes, throw in a song, indulge in a fantasy or so, include his own verse, display an intimate knowledge of such disparate subjects as physics, astronomy, art, jazz, how a nose-job is done, the wildlife in the New York sewage system. These indeed are some of the topics which constitute a recent and remarkable example of the genre: a brilliant and turbulent first novel published this month by a young Cornell graduate, Thomas Pynchon. He calls his book "V."

"V" has two main characters. One of them is Benny Profane—on the loose in New York City following a Navy hitch and a spell as a road-laborer. His friends are called the Whole Sick Crew, a fine collection of disaffected about whom one observer says "there is not one you can point to and say is well."

Set in contrast to Profane is a young adventurer named Stencil. He is active as opposed to passive, obsessed by a self-imposed

MAY 20, 1963

HAUSNER CRITICIZES ARENDT BOOK ON EICHMANN

Irving Spiegel

Gideon Hausner, Israel's prosecutor of Adolf Eichmann, voiced sharp criticism last night of those he said had "twisted and distorted" the facts of the Nazi criminal's trial in Jerusalem.

Specifically, he criticized Hannah Arendt for her book, "Eichmann in Jerusalem: A report on the Banality of Evil."

Miss Arendt, a former Zionist who holds a Ph.D. degree from Heidelberg University, wrote of various legal aspects of the Eichmann trial, which she witnessed, of the behavior of various governments concerning Jews during the Hitler period and the behavior of Jewish victims themselves.

She reported that Eichmann "to a truly extraordinary degree" had the "cooperation" of Jews in their own destruction. Eichmann was found guilty of the mass murder of Jews and hanged in Israel on May 31, 1962.

Mr. Hausner, former Attorney General of Israel, asserted that the reason the "Eichmann trial shook the conscience of the world was because the bare facts were exposed for all to see…and they cannot be twisted and distorted by some who want to rewrite history."

"There are now some historians," he said, "fortunately few in number, who for one reason or another cruelly and falsely blame the Jews and their leaders for 'letting themselves' be slaughtered."

These writers, he added, "blatantly distort facts and evidence."

Miss Arendt's book has evoked sharp controversy in Jewish religious and secular circles. In sharply rejecting the thesis that Jewish victims in the Hitler period had behaved passively, Mr. Hausner cited several instances of Jewish heroism, which had been depicted at the Eichmann trial in Jerusalem.

He pointed to the heroic resistance of Jewish men, women and children in the town of Bialystok, Poland. Here, he said, the Jews, under the command of Mordecai Tennenbaum, resisted "with only a handful of weapons" until they were killed. ■

duty which he follows, somewhat joylessly—a Quest to discover the identity of V., a woman's initial which occurs in the journals of his father, a British Foreign Office man, drowned in a waterspout off Malta. The search for V., a puzzle slowly fitted together by a series of brilliant episodic flashbacks, provides the unifying device of the novel—a framework encompassing a considerable panorama of history and character.

The identity of V., what her many guises are meant to suggest, will cause much speculation. What will be remembered, whether or not V. remains elusive, is Pynchon's remarkable ability—which includes a vigorous and imaginative style, a robust humor, a tremendous reservoir of information (one suspects that he could churn out a passable almanac in a fortnight's time) and, above all, a sense of how to use and balance these talents. True, in a plan as complicated and varied as a Hieronymous Bosch triptych, sections turn up which are dull—the author backing and filling, shuffling the pieces of his enormous puzzle to no effect—but these stretches are far fewer than one might expect.

. . . a brilliant and turbulent first novel . . .

Pynchon is in his early twenties; he writes in Mexico City—a recluse. It is hard to find out anything more about him. At least there is at hand a testament—this first novel "V."—which suggests that no matter what his circumstances, or where he's doing it, there is at work a young writer of staggering promise. ■

APRIL 21, 1964

Cornwell (Alias Le Carré) Submits to Interrogation

Harry Gilroy

Mark this CONFIDENTIAL. The man under investigation is a certain David Cornwell. He writes books under a pseudonym, John Le Carré. The last one, "The Spy Who Came in From the Cold," has sold 140,000 copies in the United States and a lot in England.

Yesterday, Mr. le Carré (or Mr. Cornwell) was subjected to interrogation. The interrogators were a shrewd lot who said they were Press.

He does not look like a spy, which struck the interrogators as rather suspicious in itself.

In his book, British Intelligence sacrifices a loyal British agent to protect an ex-Nazi German double agent. Was the purpose of the book to make Intelligence look like a shabby organization?

"No," he said lightly, "that was to show they were a highly efficient organization." He added that he wanted to show a paradox of the Cold War. The East holds ideology more important than individuals; the West holds the opposite, but his story shows an organization in the West abandoning the Western spirit to defend the West.

What was his own job? He was second man in the internal political division of the British Embassy at Bonn. He went frequently to Berlin in the summer of 1961 when the wall was being built.

How does he know about spying? His sources are the books he reads and spy case reports that have been published. One book he has read is "Ashenden," by W. Somerset Maugham, which told of Mr. Maugham's experiences in British Intelligence in World War I when he lived in Switzerland with the profession of novelist as his cover.

Where is he living now that he has resigned from the Foreign Service? Crete. And what is he doing there? Living there with his wife and three small sons and writing another novel.

There, in summary, were the suspicions, and the curious little facts and the curiously little information that showed up in the interrogation. ■

OCTOBER 23, 1964

SARTRE REJECTS NOBEL PRIZE

Writer and philosopher Jean-Paul Sartre in Paris, 1964.

STOCKHOLM, Oct. 22—The Nobel Prize for Literature was awarded today to Jean-Paul Sartre, who promptly refused the honor and the $53,000 that accompanies it.

The 59-year-old French writer, philosopher and exponent of existentialism said a writer must not accept official awards, because to do so would add the influence of the institution that honored his work to the power of his pen. That is not fair to the reader, he said.

Sartre had forewarned the Swedish Academy, which makes the literature award, that he did not want it. Nevertheless, the academy members felt that he was the only possible recipient this year.

He is the first to turn down the award fully and freely.

In 1925, George Bernard Shaw rejected the prize, then decided to accept, with the money going toward the translating of Swedish literature. Boris Pasternak refused the 1958 award under evident Soviet pressure.

The academy's secretary, Kari-Ragnar Gierow, said: "If Sartre does not collect the prize, the money will be returned to the Nobel Prize funds. The academy's award is not guided by the possible winner's wishes but only by the decision of the academy's 18 members."

The academy chose Sartre for his "authorship, which has always been rich in ideas and which has had a vast influence on our times, mainly through its spirit of liberty and quest for truth."

Sartre has taken a vigorous part in most of the great contemporary controversies. He has dealt, for example, with the American Negro problem, what he considers to be unnecessary fears of Communism, French treatment of Algerian freedom fighters and West German prosperity.

JANUARY 5, 1965

T. S. Eliot, the American-born Poet, Dies in London at 76

LONDON, Jan. 4—T. S. Eliot, the quiet, gray figure who gave new meaning to English-language poetry, died today at his home in London. He was 76 years old.

Eliot was an American, born in St. Louis. He moved to England at the beginning of World War I and became wholly identified with Britain, even becoming naturalized in 1927.

Nevertheless, when President Johnson recently awarded the Medal of Freedom to leaders in American literature and public life, Eliot was among those honored. He did not make the trip to the United States, however, to receive the award.

The influence of Eliot began with the publication in 1917 of his poem "The Love Song of J. Alfred Prufrock." Perhaps his most significant contribution came five years later in the lengthy poem "The Waste Land."

From time to time Eliot would give readings of his poetry in public. He read softly, but when he ended "The Waste Land" in a quick rush of words audiences were always moved.

Eliot was a convert to Anglo-Catholicism and his religious belief showed up strongly in his later works.

Eliot won the Nobel Prize for Literature in 1948 and was awarded the Order of Merit by Britain in the same year.

This is the way the world ends
This is the way the world ends
This is the way the world ends
Not with a bang but a whimper

These four lines by Thomas Stearns Eliot, written as the conclusion to "The Hollow Men" in 1925, are probably the most quoted lines of any 20th-century poet writing in English. They are also the essence of Eliot as he established his reputation as a poet of post-World War I disillusion and despair.

They were written by an expatriate from St. Louis, a graduate of Harvard College, who had chosen to live in London and who was working as a bank clerk.

The "bang and the whimper," together with "The Waste Land" published three years earlier, established Eliot as a major poet. From there he went on to mellowness, fame, financial independence and a Nobel prize, but he always remained, in the layman's view, the poet of gray melancholy.

In his later years he had an office in London in the publishing house of Faber & Faber, of which he was a director. There he carried on his business, writing letters and articles, somewhat like the clerkish type he resembled.

In appearance he was then, as he was in early life, a most unlikely figure for a poet. He lacked flamboyance or oddity in dress or manner, and there was nothing of the romantic about him. He carried no auras, cast no arresting eye and wore his heart, as nearly as could be observed, in its proper anatomical place.

"This is the way the world ends"

His habits of work were equally "unpoetic," for he eschewed bars and cafes for the pleasant and bourgeois comforts of an office with padded chairs and a well-lighted desk.

Eliot's dress was a model of the London man of business. He wore a bowler and often carried a tightly rolled umbrella. His accent, which started out as pure American Middle West, did undergo changes, becoming over the years quite British U.

The U was complete and unfeigned, "I am," he said stoutly, "an Anglo-Catholic in religion, a classicist in literature and a royalist in politics."

Even so, his ascetic austerity drew the line at gin rummy, which he delighted to play of an evening. He also kept a signed photograph of Groucho Marx, cigar protruberant, in his study at home.

These touches lend credence to Eliot's attempts in later years to soften some aspects of his credo. His religious beliefs, he asserted, remained unchanged and he was still in favor of monarchy in all countries having a monarch, but the term classicism was no longer so important to him.

MAY 11, 1966

HELLO, ELECTRIC AGE

Eliot Fremont-Smith

The hottest ticket in town last weekend was to a showing of Herbert Marshall McLuhan, author, lecturer, philosopher, critic, celebrity, director of the Center for Culture and Technology at the University of Toronto, and by-now legendary interpreter of new media phenomena to those who would be with it. The event took place at the Kaufmann auditorium of the 92nd Street Y.M.-Y.W.H.A. Mr. McLuhan, a tall, slender man whose voice betrays neither emotion nor personal origin, delivered a stream of metaphorical allusions, natty epigrams and throw-away jokes, all presumably redolent with the revolutionary implications of "the electric age" (what he says we are in but don't know it) to a sell-out crowd remarkable for its conservative dress, attentive manner and approaching middle-age. Outside the auditorium, in an adjoining gallery, Mr. McLuhan's image mouthed a similar patter through the medium of TV circuitry to those who couldn't get in for the live show.

Mr. McLuhan's central thesis, out of Buckminster Fuller, is that the environment man creates becomes his media for knowing it and defining himself, his role in it—that it serves as an extension of his central nervous system for the purpose of receiving and communicating information. The "content" of this information is at once about the environment and determined, or altered, by it, according to which sense is activated.

In "Understanding Media: The Extensions of Man" (1964), McLuhan argues that through electric technology the aural sense has once again become pre-eminent, that the extraordinary speed-up of information processing and retrieval (data computers) and communications (TV, Xerography) has both narrowed the gap between thought and action and forced us into immediate and intense social involvement with each other: "As electrically contracted, the globe is no more than a village."

This he finds is good (and one may trace his own movement from outrage to contentment in his books) because "feedback"—the effects of individual influence on the organization of environment—is once again possible.

It is all, also, quite baffling to the rest of us still traumatized by sequential thought and unaware of the nature of the revolution we do sense is going on. In fact, Marshall McLuhan may be the first electronically-thinking man. His style suggests it—part Bob Hope, part professor, part trivia machine, part analyst and oracle, spouting ideas, insights, contradictions, quotations, eccentricities, half-truths and prophecies all at once and tonelessly. It is baffling, and it is eerie; whether he needs some critical feedback or whether we need to catch up fast is, rather startlingly, an open question.

I am by nature leery of prophets, particularly when they come on like stand-up comics; but this one I have not quite been able to chuckle off. Not yet. ■

FEBRUARY 17, 1967

World Sale of 'Little Red Book' Brisk

"Quotations from Chairman Mao Tse-Tung," a chapbook for China's Red Guards, has been making its appearance in the bookstalls of the world and has already topped a best-seller list in France.

It is a mandatory smashing success in China, where the Red Guards brandish it during demonstrations and use it as a handy guide to attitude on all occasions.

United States importers report heavy demand and in France, a Paris publishing house, Editions du Seuil, a leftist Roman Catholic concern, has put out its own edition. This is reported to have sold 60,000 copies and is going into a third printing.

In Tokyo, editions translated and printed locally are among the current best-sellers. The several hundred copies available in London have sold out. The main demand seems to come from students, intellectuals, and those who follow Chinese developments.

(cont'd. on next page)

(cont'd. from previous page)

In the United States, where two companies import the Peking edition under Treasury Department licenses, "Quotations" has been available for the last three or four weeks in modest supply, with indications of bigger business to come.

The work that is attracting all of this attention comes, in its official Peking printing, in a bright red plastic cover with a matching fabric bookmark to keep the place in its pages made of sturdy paper. Mr. Mao's thoughts are grouped under 33 headings. Among these are "The Communist Party," "War and Peace," "Imperialism and All Reactionaries Are Paper Tigers," "Education and the Training of Troops," "Building Our Country Through Diligence and Frugality" and "Culture and Art."

There is a picture of Mr. Mao in the front; one page bearing the slogan, "Workers of All Countries, Unite!", and advice from Lin Piao, Defense Minister, to "Study Chairman Mao's writings, follow his teachings and act according to his instructions."

Each quotation is followed by a detailed bibliographical reference to the speech or written work from which it is taken. Some of the utterances are several hundred words long, some are brief maxims. Some are specific and direct and some have a platitudinous quality of words by a Communist Ben Franklin. ■

MARCH 1, 1967

Henry Luce, 68, Dies Created the News Magazine

Alden Whitman

A man of missionary zeal and limitless curiosity, Henry Robinson Luce deeply influenced American journalism between 1923, when he and the late Briton Hadden founded Time The Weekly Newsmagazine, and 1964, when he retired as head of one of the world's largest and richest publishing empires.

Mr. Luce created the modern news magazine, fostered the development of group journalism, restyled pictorial reporting, encouraged a crisp and adjective-studded style of writing and initiated the concept of covering business as a continuing magazine story.

In the process, the tall, lean man with heavy eyebrows grew to be one of the nation's wealthiest men, rose to a position of vast and pervasive economic, political and social influence and helped shape the reading habits, political attitudes and cultural tastes of millions. Nonetheless, he tried to remain inconspicuous as a public figure. In private his manner of living was notably inconspicuous.

"We tell the truth as we see it," Mr. Luce once explained when his magazines took sides on controversies. And he was accustomed to urge his editors to make a judgment. He believed that objectivity was impossible. "Show me a man who claims he is objective," he told an interviewer, "and I'll show you a man with illusions."

To a remarkable extent during the peak of his total involvement with his magazines--Time, Fortune, Life and Sports Illustrated--the judgments and opinions that were printed reflected the focus of Mr. Luce's own views--and these encompassed virtually every facet of human endeavor.

He was a stanch Republican, a defender of big business and free enterprise, a foe of big labor, a steadfast supporter of Chiang Kai-shek, an advocate of aggressive opposition to world Communism. He was also an Anglophile, but he believed that "the 20th century must be to a significant degree the American century."

As with many who achieve eminence, Mr. Luce was lauded by those he benefited; he was cursed by those who felt injured by him and, sometimes, even by those men whose careers he had made.

Virtually no one viewed him temperately, yet admirer and critic respected his business accomplishments, his ingenious brain, his insatiable curiosity, his editorial prescience. For example, he anticipated an American appetite for tersely packaged news, for the photojournalism of Life magazine and for the easy-to-grasp pictorial essay on such topics as "The World We Live In," "The World's Great Religions" and "The Human Body."

Mr. Luce was not gregarious, especially convivial or given to mixing with those he considered his intellectual inferiors. "He lived well above the tree line on Olympus," one of his editors remarked.

Attempting to explain the difference between the dour Mr. Luce and the puckish Time magazine, a friend said:

"Time is a side of Luce called forth by the magic of the written word."

The Luce enterprises, which had an annual revenue of $503-million in 1966, were started on an $86,000 shoestring in 1923 by Mr. Luce and Mr. Hadden. The two, schoolmates at Hotchkiss and Yale, had for a long time discussed the idea of getting out a weekly magazine capsulizing the news for readers who wanted a condensed account of events.

Mr. Luce wrote little about himself for publication and was seldom quoted in his own publications. In his travels he talked to presidents, premiers, popes, cardinals, ambassadors, bankers, political leaders, industrialists, generals and admirals.

Many in Time, Inc., close to Mr. Luce were impressed by his ranging interests. Hedley Donovan, who succeeded Mr. Luce as editor in chief, recalled that his superior had "an extraordinary zeal for new ideas, not only as inspiration for new modes and vehicles of journalism but as a subject matter for journalism."

MAY 23, 1967

LANGSTON HUGHES, WRITER, 65, DEAD

Chronicled Negro Life in Poems, Plays and Novels

Langston Hughes, the noted writer of novels, stories, poems and plays about Negro life, died last night in Polyclinic Hospital at the age of 65.

Mr. Hughes was sometimes characterized as the "O. Henry of Harlem." He was an extremely versatile and productive author who was particularly well known for his folksy humor.

In a description of himself written for "Twentieth Century Authors," a biographical dictionary, Mr. Hughes wrote:

"My chief literary influences have been Paul Laurence Dunbar, Carl Sandburg and Walt Whitman. My favorite public figures include Jimmy Durante, Marlene Dietrich, Mary McLeod Bethune, Mrs. Franklin D. Roosevelt, Marian Anderson and Henry Armstrong."

"I live in Harlem, New York City," his autobiographical sketch continued. "I am unmarried. I like 'Tristan,' goat's milk, short novels, lyric poems, heat, simple folk, boats and bullfights; I dislike 'Aida,' parsnips, long novels, narrative poems, cold, pretentious folk, buses and bridges."

It was said that whenever Mr. Hughes had a pencil and paper in his hands, he would scribble poetry. He recalled an anecdote about how he was "discovered" by the poet Vachel Lindsay.

Lindsay was dining at the Wardman Park Hotel in Washington when a busboy summoned his courage and slipped several sheets of paper beside the poet's plate. Lindsay was obviously annoyed, but he picked up the papers and read a poem titled "The Weary Blues."

As Lindsay read, his interest grew. He called for the busboy and asked, "Who wrote this?"

"I did," replied Langston Hughes.

Lindsay introduced the youth to publishers who brought out such works by the rising poet and author as "Shakespeare in Harlem," "The Dream Keeper," "Not Without Laughter," "The Ways of White Folks," "The Big Sea" and "Pope and Fifina" as well as the initial "The Weary Blues."

"My writing," Mr. Hughes said, "has been largely concerned with the depicting of Negro life in America."

James Langston Hughes, who dropped his first name, was born in Joplin, Mo., on Feb. 1, 1902. His mother was a school teacher and his father was a storekeeper.

After his graduation from Central High School in Cleveland, he went to Mexico and then attended Columbia University for a year. Mr. Hughes held a variety of jobs, including seaman on trips to Europe and Africa, cook in a Montmartre nightclub in Paris and then busboy at the Washington hotel where he presented his poetry to Lindsay.

His first book, "The Weary Blues," was published by Alfred A. Knopf in 1925.

JUNE 8, 1967

Dorothy Parker, 73, Literary Wit, Dies

Alden Whitman

Dorothy Parker, the sardonic humorist who purveyed her wit in conversation, short stories, verse and criticism, died of a heart attack yesterday afternoon in her suite at the Volney Hotel, 23 East 74th Street. She was 73 years old and had been in frail health in recent years.

In print and in person, Miss Parker sparkled with a word or a phrase, for she honed her humor to its most economical size.

Many of Miss Parker's writings appeared in The New Yorker magazine, to which she was a contributor from its second issue, Feb. 28, 1925, until Dec. 14, 1957.

The best of Miss Parker's humor was wry and dry, antic and offbeat, even that about herself. For her epitaph she suggested "Excuse My Dust," and of her poetry she said, "I was following in the exquisite footsteps of Miss Edna St. Vincent Millay, unhappily in my own horrible sneakers."

After she had by chance sent some of her verses to Vogue magazine, she was hired at $10 a week to write picture captions. At the same time, Franklin P. Adams, who was generally known by his initials of F.P.A., published some of her poetry in his column, then appearing in The Daily Mail.

Miss Parker worked for Vogue until 1920, when, during an office reorganization, she resigned. It was during the following five years that she attained her celebrity for sizzling, off-the-cuff wit from her repartee at the Algonquin Round Table.

Miss Parker, Robert Benchley and Robert E. Sherwood were the founders of the group when they all worked at Vanity Fair.

The group rapidly expanded, and Frank Case, the hotel's proprietor, provided a round table for it. The group, usually about 10 a day, lunched together for about a decade. At one time or another it included George S. Kaufman, Harold Ross, Donald Ogden Stewart, Russel Crouse, Edna Ferber, Heywood Brown, Ruth Gordon and, of course, F.P.A., and the three founders.

As a short-story writer, Miss Parker produced several that were more than merely excellent: "Big Blonde," which won the O. Henry Memorial Award in 1929; "Telephone Call"; "Soldiers of the Republic" and "Arrangement in Black and White."

The latter is a particularly mordant satire of a woman explaining her own and her husband's attitude toward Negroes. Its most memorable passage reads:

"But I must say for Burton, he's heaps broader-minded than lots of these Southerners. He's really fond of colored people. Why, he says himself he wouldn't have white servants."

NOVEMBER 7, 1967

New Owners Will Publish The New York Magazine

The New York Magazine, which ceased publication as the Sunday supplement of The World Journal Tribune when the paper failed six months ago, is being revived under new ownership.

The editors of the magazine will announce today that they have found new sponsors and will resume publication on March 1.

Clay Felker, who edited the magazine first for The Herald Tribune and later for The World Journal Tribune, will again head the editorial board. He acquired, from John Hay Whitney, publisher of The Herald Tribune, the right to use the magazine's name.

The ownership of the new weekly will be shared by the editorial board and a group of financial backers headed by Armand G. Erpf, a partner in the investment company of Loeb, Rhoades & Co.

The editorial board will include Tom Wolfe, Jimmy Breslin, George Goodman, a financial writer who uses the pen name "Adam Smith," and Milton Glaser, art director. All were associated with the magazine in the past.

George A. Hirsch, a former executive of Time Inc., will be the new publisher. He and Mr. Felker said yesterday that the magazine would be politically independent and concentrate on news about the arts, economics and social problems "for the sophisticated, intelligent reader who is not afraid of colorful, impressionistic journalism."

MARCH 13, 1968

Cleaver's Journey Into the Interior

Thomas Lask

SOUL ON ICE.
By Eldridge Cleaver. 210 pages. A Ramparts Book. McGraw-Hill. $5.95.

Eldridge Cleaver's "Soul on Ice" is part autobiography, part commentary. Yet so closely are these braided, so subtly does one lead from one to the other that it would be hard to say which is the life, which the thought. The events he tells about brought a new awareness of what he was, new insights into his situation as a black man and as an individual black man. The new ideas altered the motives and thrust of his life. It is intriguing to watch the blossoming of his mind and to be provoked, not always happily, by the fruits of it. Mr. Cleaver's thoughts on the Negro in America, on black power, on white and black sexuality, on people such as the Rev. Dr. Martin Luther King, James Baldwin, Muhammad Ali and others will stimulate all those remotely concerned with the position of black and white people in the United States today. The response will certainly not be unanimous. What will be agreed is that it is an exceptional volume both in what it says and how the author came to say it.

Mr. Cleaver does not tell us everything about himself, only what counts. In 1954, at the age of 19, he was in jail in California for possession of marijuana. For Mr. Cleaver in those years, using the drug was natural, no more reprehensible than drinking alcohol. It was, he said, necessary if Negroes were to maintain their sanity in an environment that continually attacked their dignity and manhood.

He was released, but a rape charge took him back to jail, this time for a much longer stay. Once there, he began to take stock of himself. He began to read, to attend classes, given by an unusual and unusually able teacher. The more he learned the more his appetite grew, increasing by what it fed upon. He tells without tears the petty ways the prison authorities managed to prevent the acquisition of those books they didn't want the men to have. He tells also of what it is like to be forever on guard, never to be able to let yourself go. He praises the cells that locked him into peace and safety.

Eventually he became a Black Muslim, especially a follower of Malcolm X, whom he eulogizes in a moving and eloquent passage. In time, after the assassination of Malcolm X, he moved away from black separatism. He now sees the problem of the Negro in America as tied in with the problem of colonial peoples everywhere. His essay on Vietnam is, as might have been predicted, scornful and bitter. It is not only an unjust and oppressive war, he argues, but the Negro, who he says makes up 16 percent of the fighting force, is being used by the white power structure to disguise the fact that white people are killing people of color. It is an attempt by the white establishment to take the onus off the war by having a large proportion of Negroes in the American ranks.

Indeed wherever Mr. Cleaver thinks he sees a black man cooperating or giving in to the white Establishment, he rakes him over the coals. Even Dr. Martin Luther King comes in for harsh criticism.

There are also a handful of essays, sometimes written in symbolic and abstract language, that deal with the four-cornered relationship of black and white sexuality. They contain many striking psychological insights and conclusions that will provide plenty of debate in smoky rooms and in print. Mr. Cleaver gives them great weight in his book. I wonder, however, whether by doing so he isn't feeding the prejudices of all those who deny the essential economic and political character of the rights movement. He has provided a couple of handy chapters for those people who argue blindly that the aim of Negroes is not to live decently but only to be able to mix intimately with the whites. It is a tricky business to raise a personal preference to a law of the land. ■

AUGUST 12, 1968

FREAK-OUT IN DAY-GLO

Eliot Fremont-Smith

Tom Wolfe, in his signature white suit and shoes, in New York City, 1968.

THE ELECTRIC KOOL-AID ACID TEST.
By Tom Wolfe. 416 pages. Farrar, Straus and Giroux. $5.95.

Zonked—and it's not a bad feeling, not bad at all. A genuine raz-daz high, courtesy of Tom Wolfe. And it's done with words. What Ken Kesey could not quite manage, an "acid graduation," a great turn-on without drugs, Mr. Wolfe brings off. Fantasy. Vibrations. History. Wow.

History: "The Electric Kool-Aid Acid Test" is the history—complete with fantasy, vibrations—of the great freak-out of the nineteen sixties, the trip to "the raggedy raggedy edge" of Ken Kesey and his Merry Pranksters. It is not simply the best book on the hippies, it is the essential book.

Mr. Wolfe seems to have gotten right into the pulsing, ballooning heart of the matter, in terms both of subject focus and style. The book is printed in black and white, but the words come through in crazy Day-Glo—fluorescent, psychedelic, at once energetic and epicene. Was Ken Kesey really the guru son king of the whole hippie thing? Maybe not. It doesn't matter. The vibrations are there, and that's what counts. And the bus.

The bus was a 1939 International Harvester schoolbus that Mr. Kesey bought second-hand around 1962; he and his Merry Pranksters painted it in swirls of Day-Glo colors and wired it for total mind-blowing sound and traveled around the country in it, mostly California. This was after Mr. Kesey had gotten on to LSD, as a volunteer in some medically supervised neuropharmcological experiment at Menlo Park. Mr. Kesey had simply taken over the drug scene from the medical men, and was already heading toward a new religion, what Mr. Wolfe called "Edge City," and taking with him a group of young men, coalesced around him, the self-dubbed Merry Pranksters.

It is a fascinating story, for it brings together both the free-wheeling, Captain Marvel, 400-horse power "feel" of the movement (only in America!) and its history, the chronology of the whole drop-out phenomenon. Mr. Kesey's group was the center, the mainstring, with lines into it from affluent suburbia, the Beats and the Hell's Angels and lines out of it to the great put-ons, love-ins and freak-outs, to acid rock, communal living, mixed media, orgy, the yippies and beyond. And one comes away convinced; yes, Kesey was the son king. ■

AUGUST 14, 1968

The Sorcerer's Apprentice

Charles Simmons

THE TEACHINGS OF DON JUAN
A Yaqui Way of Knowledge.
By Carlos Castaneda. 196 pages. University of California Press. $5.95.

This is the beginning, not of a novel, but of a doctoral thesis by Carlos Castaneda:

"In the summer of 1960, while I was an anthropology student at the University of California, Los Angeles, I made several trips to the Southwest to collect information on the medicinal plants used by the Indians of the area. The events I describe here began during one of my trips. I was waiting in a border town for a Greyhound bus, talking with a friend who had been my guide and helper in the survey. Suddenly he leaned toward me and whispered that the man, a white-haired old Indian, who was sitting in front of the window was very learned about plants, especially peyote. I asked my friend to introduce me to this man."

The Indian was don Juan, from the Mexican province of Sonora. He listened to Castaneda chatter on about peyote. Then, without comment, he boarded his bus and rode away. The young man persisted, found out where don Juan lived and eventually became his friend. Still the old man would not discuss peyote.

One evening, however, don Juan told Castaneda to find, on the 8-x-12-foot porch, his own "spot," a place where all fatigue would disappear and where he would feel safe. For over six hours Castaneda searched without luck. He did find "the other spot," an inimical place that filled him with anxiety, and, exhausted, fell asleep a few feet away. The next morning don Juan told him that he had found his spot by falling asleep on it.

Pleased with the young man's willingness to work, don Juan finally introduced him to peyote, the hallucinogenic cactus, or, as the old man preferred to call it, *Mescalito*. Under his direction, Castaneda chewed seven *mescalitos*. The effects were various and profound, but centered on Castaneda's frolicking with a luminescent dog, which don Juan later claimed was Mescalito himself, the quasi-divine personification of peyote.

Don Juan was again pleased with his initiate. "I've made up my mind and I am going to teach you the secrets that make up the lot of a man of knowledge."

There are four enemies of a man of knowledge. The first is fear, "a terrible enemy—treacherous, and difficult to overcome." Then clarity, "which is so hard to obtain, dispels fear, but also blinds." Third, power, "the strongest of all enemies. [It turns] him into a cruel, capricious man." Finally, if he conquers these three, "the man will be, by then, at the end of his journey of learning, and almost without warning he will come upon the last of his enemies: Old age!"

(cont'd. on next page)

(cont'd. from previous page)

As Castaneda followed the way of knowledge, he had many visions under the influence of Mescalito, Jimson weed and an hallucinogenic mushroom, probably *Psilocybe Mexicana*. The central vision was not anthropological, but Freudian: "My father and I were standing by a fig tree. I embraced my father and hurriedly began to tell him things I had never been able to say....I said staggering things about my feelings toward him, things I would never have been able to voice under ordinary circumstances. My father did not speak. He just listened and then was pulled, or sucked, away. I was alone again. I wept with remorse and sadness."

Castaneda suffered the same ambivalence toward don Juan, his surrogate father, and finally was forced to explain to him that he was experiencing recurrent, spontaneous states of nonreality. Planes flying overhead caught his attention and seemed to carry him away. Don Juan diagnosed loss of soul and set up a night of combat, warning Castaneda that he must stay, whatever comes, on his spot. Then throughout the night—described in a remarkable passage—don Juan, imitating enemies imitating himself, attempted to lure Castaneda off his spot. Castaneda stuck, and according to don Juan the next morning, thereby regained his soul.

But the apprenticeship was over. "Although don Juan has not changed his benefactor's attitude toward me, I do believe that I have succumbed to the first enemy of the man of knowledge." Thus ends a book I don't have the background to judge as anthropology. However, it is an extraordinary spiritual and psychological document. Its style is so severe and yet easy, its narrative effects so expert, that if it had been published as a novel it would be, I think, destined for fame. ■

DECEMBER 21, 1968

John Steinbeck Dies at 66

Alden Whitman

John Steinbeck, one of six Americans to have won the Nobel Prize for literature, died late yesterday afternoon of severe coronary and valvular heart disease at his home, 190 East 72nd Street. He was 66-years old.

Mr. Steinbeck, who had been in failing health since Memorial Day, had moved into the city at that time from his country home in Sag Harbor, L.I.

Of Mr. Steinbeck's 24 works of fiction, one novel, "The Grapes of Wrath," was the anchor of his fame. A compassionate, realistic and deeply emotional account of a farm family's forced migration from the Depression dustbowl of Oklahoma to the exploitative migrant labor camps of California, the book, published in 1939, brought its 37-year-old author overnight praise and denunciation.

The acclaim was for the novel's lucid and powerful narrative of the Joads and their fellow Okies and migrants, whose human frailties made more poignant their desperate struggle to survive. Their survival was not a triumph of heroic individualism but the result of a painfully learned lesson in the importance of cooperation to achieve a common purpose. This was a story—and a theme—that was especially congenial to Depression-era readers, many of whom had jettisoned the concept of rugged individualism.

The criticism was for Mr. Steinbeck's apparent attack on capitalism and his suggestion that it could produce the poverty and the dislocation that all but swept the Okies under. Many of these critics were certain that the writer was a Communist (he was not), and his book was banned as subversive by a number of libraries. Actually, "The Grapes of Wrath" contains a specific defense of private property and private enterprise, although this was overshadowed by the book's denunciation of big business as irresponsible.

Zealously guarding his privacy, Mr. Steinbeck took little part in the public literary life of his time. He rarely served on committees, signed appeals, attended parties, lectured at colleges or commented on the work of other writers. He lived simply, inconspicuously and off the beaten track—in a ranch house in California, in a cottage in Long Island, in a nondescript brownstone on New York's Upper East Side.

Because Mr. Steinbeck isolated himself so much, he was considered reserved and difficult to get to know really well. "John always seemed occupied with his inner thoughts," an acquaintance of many years said recently. "He had a way of putting you off if you tried to probe him and a way of making you feel as if you were being observed under his microscope."

In another view, Mr. Steinbeck was accounted a delightful companion in a small circle of intimates that include Nathaniel Benchley, Elia Kazan, Arthur Miller, Edward Albee, Abe Burrows, John Huston and Thomas Guinzburg, his publisher.

"John was a very soft man, once you got to know him," Mr. Guinzburg said. "He was wonderfully kind. He was pleased by small things, just like a big kid."

Mr. Steinbeck felt very much at home with people of no pretension—the Okies among whom he lived and worked for a while, workers in a fish-canning factory, ranch hands, apple pickers and paisanos. He delighted to talk with them, drink with them and worry over their day-to-day problems. And for their speech he developed a marvelously accurate ear and for their ways a keen eye.

FEBRUARY 23, 1969

PORTNOY'S COMPLAINT

Josh Greenfeld

Philip Roth in 1968.

Guilt-edged insecurity is far more important when it comes to the making—and unmaking—of an American Jew than, say, chicken soup or chopped liver. So, not surprisingly, a special blend of guilt-power usually fuels the American-Jewish character in fiction, sends him soaring to his manic highs and plummeting to his abject lows.

But while the American-Jewish novelist has thus had a subject, though he has been searching diligently, questing imaginatively, he has lacked an ideal form. Now, with "Portnoy's Complaint," Philip Roth ("Goodbye Columbus," "Letting Go," "When She Was Good") has finally come up with the existentially quintessential form for any American-Jewish tale bearing—or baring—guilt. He has done so by simply but brilliantly casting his American Jewish hero—so obviously long in need of therapy—upon a psychoanalyst's couch (the current American-Jewish equivalent of the confessional box) and allowed him to rant and rave and rend himself there. The result is not only one of those bullseye hits in the ever-darkening field of humor, a novel that is playfully and painfully moving, but also a work that is certainly catholic in appeal, potentially monumental in effect—and, perhaps more important, a deliciously funny book, absurd and exuberant, wild and uproarious.

His adventures—and misadventures—involve a penchant for unseemly masturbation, a fetish for untimely fellatio, and even the staging of a mini-orgy in Rome. He also manages to squeeze by a succession of picturesque girl friends.

But what finally drives Portnoy to the analyst's couch is a traumatic sojourn in the State of Israel ("Hey, here we're the WASPS!"). For there he meets his bête noire, his undoer, a Jewish Pumpkin, physically reminiscent of his mother, whom he tries to ravage only to be rendered impotent in the process.

And the novel ends at a beginning, with the straight-man analyst speaking his only line: "So. Now vee may perhaps to begin. Yes?"

I feel very much the same way about the ultimate significance of this much ballyhooed, eagerly awaited novel. If viewed as the apotheosis of a genre, the culmination of a fictional quest—and it is, I think, as I've tried to say, the very novel that every American-Jewish writer has been trying to write in one guise or another since the end of World War II—then it may very well be what is called a masterpiece—but so what? It could still also be nothing more than a cul-de-sac.

However, if by this definitive outpouring into a definitive vessel of a recurring theme, thus guilt (screaming, strident, hysterical, hyperbolic, hyperthyroid) has been successfully expatiated, and future American-Jewish novels will be all the quieter, subtler, more reflective and reasoned because of it, then this novel can truly be judged a milestone.

Whether a dead-end auto-da-fé or open-end bar mitzvah peroration on the road to cultural manhood—read "Portnoy's Complaint." And don't feel the least bit guilty about enjoying it thoroughly: I know not since "Catcher in the Rye" have I read an American novel with such pleasure.

MARCH 30, 1969

POSTMORTEM ON SATURDAY EVENING POST

Philip H. Dougherty

In an upstairs room of the Lexington Hotel one recent afternoon there was a wake—a wake for The Saturday Evening Post.

Words, some bitter, some sad, some sarcastic and some constructive, were spoken by William Emerson, who had been editor of the 148-year-old American institution; Herb Lubalin, the design consultant who had twice redesigned what had once been the country's leading carrier of national advertising; and John J. Meskil, vice president and media director of Warwick & Legler.

At this luncheon of the Society of Publication Designers, Mr. Meskil, media man, spoke of a magazine that died "because it no longer served the needs of today's society," because it failed to change the frequency of publication, because of the competition from Life, Look and the Reader's Digest for advertising dollars that just wouldn't spread around.

Although Mr. Emerson said that "anybody who read us understands what we were at the end," Mr. Meskil said, as many other media men have said, The Post had lost its niche.

Mr. Lubalin defined that niche as "a great middle class, sort of semi-sophisticated literary magazine during the 1900s, the 1920s and the 1930s and it had a place in our society." Then along came Life and Look, he said, and Curtis gave up its niche, tried to compete and couldn't.

Mismanagement is a reason that always comes up when ad industry people talk of this magazine. And Herb Maneloveg of Batten, Barton, Durstine & Osborn, writing in Advertising Age, spells it out, saying it was "an accumulation of a hundred sins of omission and commission, of lost opportunities, of financially foolhardy blunders and misspent directions too numerous to recount."

And the competition from other mass magazines and the terrible tube cut deeply into The Post's advertising picture.

(cont'd. on next page)

(cont'd. from previous page)

None of these media men could convince Bill Emerson that The Post wasn't a good place for advertising.

"I think it was a damn good vehicle for advertising. I think we had a higher renewal rate, we had better reports on readership than the competition."

And at one point, he said with understandable bitterness, "I hope that all the one-eyed critics will lose their other eye."

But it was Jack Golden, president of the Publication Designers group, who said the words that were on minds of many in his audience whose livelihood is derived from the magazine business.

"We have come here today not to mourn the passing of a great magazine, but to find out why it died," he said. "We believe the demise of The Post is of far greater reaching significance than may be apparent at the moment." ■

APRIL 15, 1969

Latin Writers Stir U.S. Publishers' Interest

Henry Raymont

Harper & Row believes it has a best seller on its winter list with a novel by the Colombian author Gabriel García Márquez, "One Hundred Years of Solitude." It has already caused a literary furor in Latin America and Europe.

Farrar, Straus & Giroux has overcome political barriers to acquire the first novel of one of Cuba's leading writers, José Lezama Lima's "Paradiso."

E. P. Dutton is planning to publish next fall the first of eight volumes containing the complete works of Argentina's best-known essayist, Jorge Luis Borges.

These are but three examples of a new and growing interest by publishers here in Latin-American authors, particularly in the younger generation, which includes such intellectual revolutionaries as García Márquez, Carlos Fuentes of Mexico and Mario Vargas Llosa of Peru.

Because of the language hurdle and a relative lack of interest in Latin America until a few years ago most of the area's writers were the domain of Alfred A. Knopf and a few university presses. But now a dozen other major publishing houses are vying for Latin-American authors with the same eagerness that had been shown for the works of Jean-Paul Sartre, Albert Camus, Günter Grass and Max Frisch.

"We are certain that Garcia Marquez will cause the same sensation as some of the postwar French and German writers brought to the American literary scene," Cass Canfield Jr., his editor at Harper & Row, said yesterday.

"One Hundred Years of Solitude" is a witty fantasy about a mythical rural community in Colombia founded by a Col. Aureliano Buendia who tells his story in the style of the Arabian Nights.

In addition to publishing the collected works of Mr. Borges, Dutton is preparing "The Treason of Rita Hayworth," Manuel Puig's novel about the fantasies of a young boy in an Argentine town, an anthology of Mexican poetry and a new work by José Donoso.

Much of the upsurge in publishing Latin-American writers has been stimulated by the Center for Inter-American Relations and the Ford Foundation, which have helped finance translations and provide editorial advice to a number of publishing houses.

"All that was really required was an initial impulse," José Castillo, director of the center's literature program, said yesterday. "There is an immense interest in Latin America now that the American publishers have realized that our authors are not only good writers but also relevant to the contemporary scene."

APRIL 27, 1969

AT COSA NOSTRA, BUSINESS WAS BOOMING

Dick Schaap

The Godfather
By Mario Puzo.
446 pp. New York:
G. P. Putnam's Sons. $6.95.

There are strong similarities between Michael Corleone and Alexander Portnoy. Neither of them, for instance, wishes to enter his father's line of work. Each of them falls for a White Anglo-Saxon Protestant girl. Of course, there are some differences, too. When Alexander Portnoy's father is frustrated, he gets constipated; when Michael Corleone's father is frustrated, he gets someone killed.

"The Godfather" is the coming of age of Michael Corleone in a world that Philip Roth never knew. It is the world of the Mafia in America, and the dialogue and the logic of "The Godfather" ring true enough to raise the suspicion that, at least by hearsay, Mario Puzo knows his subject well.

If Philip Roth has created a Jewish mother who can actually give you heartburn, Mario Puzo has created a Sicilian father who will make you shiver every time you stroll on Mulberry Street. And, with loving care and detail, what Roth has done for masturbation, Puzo has done for murder.

Yet it is unfair to carry the analogy too far. "The Godfather" is not written nearly so artfully as "Portnoy's Complaint." Nor does it approach the humor of Roth's work. Yet "The Godfather" is such a compelling story, the truth—disguised and distorted—as fiction genre, that any day now, I am certain, the Portnoy family and the Corleone family will end up sharing the heady heights of best-sellerdom as comfortably as the Jews and the Italians have long shared the pleasures of salami.

The plot revolves around gang warfare,

and the names of the antagonists might as well read Anastasia and Genovese and Gallo and Profaci because almost all of the incidents spring straight from the headline on page 3 of The Daily News (or page 87 of The Times, for that matter). For the most part, they only kill each other; as far as I can recall, only two innocents get killed in the entire book, and one of them is a horse—a magnificent horse, to be sure. The incidents—from a gangland kidnapping in Manhattan to an Appalachian-type sitdown to a murder on the Southern State Parkway—guarantee the pace of the narrative; the deeper strength of the narrative comes from examinations of the Mafia mind, a dedication to a peculiar kind of professionalism, a conviction that street justice is more equal and more honest than the justice practiced in the courts.

"The Godfather" is weakest when Puzo reaches out to drag in dramatic scenes that advance neither his plot nor his characters. Obviously, he has collected vivid vignettes, based partly or wholly on fact, that he could not resist throwing in. I can't particularly blame him; some of the extraneous Hollywood and Las Vegas scenes are wonderful little anecdotes that would brighten even the most blasé cocktail party; it would have taken a very strong-willed man to keep them out of "The Godfather."

Allow for a touch of corniness here. Allow for a bit of overdramatization there. Allow for an almost total absence of humor. Still Puzo has written a solid story that you can read without discomfort at one long sitting. Pick a night with nothing good on television, and you'll come out far ahead. ■

OCTOBER 22, 1969

JACK KEROUAC, NOVELIST, DEAD;
Father of the Beat Generation

Joseph Lelyveld

Jack Kerouac, the novelist who named the Beat Generation and exuberantly celebrated its rejection of middle-class American conventions, died early yesterday of massive abdominal hemorrhaging in a St. Petersburg, Fla., hospital. He was 47 years old.

"The only people for me are the mad ones, the ones who are mad to live, mad to talk, desirous of everything at the same time," he wrote in "On the Road," a novel he completed in only three weeks but had to wait seven years to see published.

When it finally appeared in 1957, it immediately became a basic text for youth who found their country claustrophobic and oppressive.

Mr. Kerouac's admirers regarded him as a major literary innovator and something of a religious seer, but this estimate of his achievement never gained wide acceptance among literary tastemakers.

The Beat Generation, originally regarded as a bizarre bohemian phenomenon confined to small coteries in San Francisco and New York, spilled over into the general culture in the nineteen-sixties. But as it became fashionable to be beat, it became less fashionable to read Jack Kerouac.

As he painstakingly informed his readers in his long series of autobiographical works—which he intended to be read, ultimately, in sequence as one novel—Jack Kerouac was born in Lowell, Mass., on March 12, 1922, the son of a French-Canadian printer.

He spoke French before he spoke English and still had an accent when he made up his mind while still in high school to become a major American writer. But it was as a football player, a fast, agile fullback, that he first won any kind of recognition.

In 1939 he entered Horace Mann School in the Riverdale section of the Bronx, with the promise of a football scholarship to Columbia University if he could prove himself academically.

His football career ended in spring practice of his freshman year when the coach, Lou Little, (later to appear in a Kerouac novel as "Lu Libble") told his young fullback to stop malingering after he was injured on a play. The injury, as Mr. Kerouac told the story, was a broken leg.

He lost his scholarship to Columbia after the career-ending injury, but World War II would have interrupted his studies in any case. He served first in the merchant marine, then briefly in the Navy, from which he was discharged as "a schizoid personality."

It was immediately after the war that he had had the experiences that shaped him decisively as a writer. He returned to New York and became close to Allen Ginsberg, then a Columbia undergraduate, and William Burroughs, the scion of a wealthy St. Louis family. Mr. Kerouac was later to give them the titles of their best-known works—"Howl" and "Naked Lunch."

In those years, Mr. Kerouac was constantly on the move, from New York to Denver, then on to San Francisco, down to Mexico City, and back to New York. This was his discovery of America, the basis for "On the Road."

Much of his traveling was done in the company of a young drifter from Denver named Neal Cassady, who had a hunger for experience and a taste also for theology and literature. Inevitably, he became a main character of "On the Road," but he became much more—a literary model, supplanting Thomas Wolfe, Ernest Hemingway and William Saroyan.

Cassady had never been published, but he wrote voluminous letters—"fast, mad, confessional, completely serious, all detailed," Mr. Kerouac later recalled—that gave the aspiring novelist his idea of spontaneous style. Specifically the inspiration for "On the Road" was a letter from Cassady that ran to 40,000 words.

He shunned literary society and spent most of his last years in a withdrawn existence in places like St. Petersburg, Northport, L.I., and his hometown of Lowell, where he maintained a residence in a ranch-style house with his invalid mother and his third wife, Stella.

JUNE 17, 1961

BALLET STAR NUREYEV DEFECTS IN PARIS

PARIS, June 16—A principal male dancer of the Kirov Opera ballet group of Leningrad sought asylum in France today.

The dancer, 23-year-old Rudolf Nureyev, broke away from the ballet company as it was preparing to board a plane at Le Bourget Airport to fly to London.

Mr. Nureyev and the Kirov troupe enjoyed a considerable success here after arriving last month to stage performances at the Paris Opera and the Sports Palace. Mr. Nureyev, who has been with the Kirov ballet corps for ten years, was promoted to lead male dancer a year ago.

It was understood that the Russian had come to Paris with the idea of defecting and had discussed his plans with certain French friends. His fellow dancers were said to have been considerably disturbed when word of his action spread through the troupe.

The defection occurred this morning as the dancers were going through customs formalities at the airport north of Paris. An unusually large number of Soviet Embassy officials were present to see the troupe off.

Shortly before the time to board the plane, Mr. Nureyev was approached by two unidentified members of the troupe. They were reported to have been acting in a "semi-official" capacity for Soviet officials, who perhaps did not want to call attention to the situation.

His two colleagues advised Mr. Nureyev to return to Moscow immediately but he rejected the advice. He then went into the airport bar with members of the troupe and the Soviet officials. A few minutes later he dashed out of the bar and, shouting "Protect me!" ran toward some airport policemen.

The defecting Russian was escorted to the airport police office. There, in the presence of the Soviet officials, he declared that he had made his decision in "full liberty" and under no pressure.

Before leaving in a police car for the Ministry of Interior in Paris, he again stressed to newsmen that he had acted in complete freedom.

It is unlikely that his request for asylum will be turned down. ■

Rudolf Nureyev performing in "The Sleeping Beauty" in Paris, May 1961.

DECEMBER 16, 1963

Ford Fund Allots 7.7 Million to Ballet

Allen Hughes

The Ford Foundation announced yesterday that it had made grants totaling $7,756,750 to eight organizations to further the development of professional ballet in the United States over a 10-year period.

This is the largest sum any foundation has ever allotted at one time to one art field.

Under the plan on which the grants are based, performing companies, ballet schools, private teachers and students will benefit in various ways as projected programs are carried out.

Of the total amount, $5,925,000 will go to two affiliated institutions in New York: the New York City Ballet and the School of American Ballet, both headed by George Balanchine and Lincoln Kirstein.

The other grants have been made to the following companies: San Francisco Ballet,

APRIL 25, 1964

'A Midsummer Night's Dream' Danced at New Theater

Allen Hughes

Magnificent is the word for the impression the New York City Ballet made in its formal debut last night at the glittering new New York State Theater at Lincoln Center for the Performing Arts.

The splendors of the building itself might have overwhelmed a performance of less than first-class quality or a production of minimal visual attractions. But the company's new presentation of George Balanchine's "A Midsummer Night's Dream" was beautiful enough to hold its own in Philip Johnson's splendid structure.

The substance of the work has not been appreciably altered for the transplantation from the adequate stage of the City Center to the marvelously spacious one in the New York State Theater, but David Hays has created new sets that are bigger and grander in every respect than the old.

The dancing of the evening seemed altogether excellent. Nearly everyone (except Bottom and his companions, who are supposed to be rough) seemed touched by uncommon sensitivity and grace.

Suzanne Farrell was a lovely Titania, Edward Villella was brilliant and kingly as Oberon, and Jacques d'Amboise and Patricia Wilde were authoritative in the divertissement. The part of Puck was acted and danced as usual by Arthur Mitchell, which means that it was about as nearly perfect as it could be. How he retains the spirit of freshness that imbues his every appearance in the role, is a secret known only to him.

Suzanne Farrell in the New York City Ballet production of "A Midsummer Night's Dream" choreographed by George Balanchine at the New York State Theater, 1964.

It is good to report that the New York City Ballet Orchestra, conducted by Robert Irving, sounded very good in the new theater. It would seem that the acoustical problem that has plagued Philharmonic Hall has not traveled across the Lincoln Center Plaza. The acoustical demands are not the same for a ballet and musical-comedy theater as for a concert hall, of course, but decent, balanced sound is a must, and Mr. Johnson seems to have achieved it. The business of acoustics, however, is like marriage; audience and hall must live together a little time before their virtues and flaws become apparent.

Speaking of music, the ballet was preceded by the playing of a new fanfare composed last month by Igor Stravinsky for the new theater and dedicated to Mr. Balanchine and Lincoln Kirstein, the general director of the company. Following the fanfare, a chorus from the High School of Music and Art sang "The Star-Spangled Banner" in Mr. Stravinsky's controversial harmonization.

It was, therefore, an unusual and memorable evening from start to finish. ■

$644,000; National Ballet, Washington, $400,000; Pennsylvania Ballet, Philadelphia, $295,000; Utah Ballet, Salt Lake City, $175,000; Houston Ballet, $172,750; and Boston Ballet, $144,000.

All grants except those to the School of American Ballet and the Boston Ballet are made with the provision that the organizations match or augment them with specified sums to be raised independently.

In announcing the grants, Henry T. Heald, president of the Ford Foundation, said, "This new program for the long-range professional development of ballet may be regarded as of comparable significance to that undertaken last year by the foundation to strengthen professional resident theater in the United States."

The growth of interest in ballet in the United States can be measured in part by the post-World War II efflorescence of nonprofessional ballet companies throughout the country. Most observers agree that some are good, that many are weak but that all indicate that ballet is increasingly attracting the attention of Americans everywhere.

The program announced yesterday is restricted to classical ballet, but W. McNeil Lowry, director of the foundation's humanities and arts program, said that future assistance for "modern" dance was not ruled out. ■

FEBRUARY 9, 1963

Dancers Explore Wild New Ideas

Allen Hughes

There is a door marked "Push" in the gymnasium of the Judson Memorial Church in Greenwich Village, and in front of that door one evening last week, a number of young people did all sorts of zany things in their efforts to push away the barriers they find impeding the progress of the dance.

Perhaps it would be more accurate to say that they are concerned with the performing arts in general rather than the dance alone, for in the course of their often antic efforts, they flailed away at a number of allied theater arts. Still, most of these young people were dancers, and the title of their program was "A Concert of Dance #3."

Most of the participants were familiar from previous "far out" programs. Yvonne Rainer, for example, is invariably in the middle of the wildest and woolliest goings-on in the name of dance. She is of the sort that makes Merce Cunningham look like the stuffiest reactionary and gives the Alwin Nikolais crowd down at Henry Street Playhouse the appearance of antiquated relics.

Anyone familiar with Cunningham and Nikolais performances knows that these two men, among a number of others, have not dragged their feet in exploring new dance theater idioms, but Miss Rainer and her chums are way ahead of them.

Before we go further, however, let us remind ourselves that we are not talking about quality of product. What we are talking about is the unleashing of ideas, and an almost uncritical unleashing in the case of Miss Rainer, Carolee Schneeman, William Davis, to mention a few "choreographers" involved in the gymnasium romp at Judson Church.

We must understand, too, that we cannot dismiss everything they did as embarrassing hi-jinks perpetrated by aging juveniles. This is too easy an out for people who would rather not have their lazy habits of thought disturbed.

What, then, must we consider for a moment?

Well, did you ever see a dance accompanied, decorated and—in a sense—dictated by the shedding of newspapers? I am not sure I have either, but in this program Miss Schneeman had a number of dancers involved in what was titled "Newspaper Event," and I assume she thought what they did was dancing. Perhaps it was.

In any case, it was surprisingly intriguing visually, and it actually—if accidentally—built to a climax despite its improvisational character.

In Miss Rainer's "We Shall Run," 12 dancers ran to a movement from Berlioz' "Requiem." Sometimes they ran as a pack, sometimes they divided into groups, sometimes they huddled for an instant, but only as a respite from the gentle, rhythmic running that almost became hypnotic before it ended. And all the while, the singing of Berlioz went on. Crazy you think? Non-dance? Who's to say? If it isn't dance, what is it?

they are concerned with the performing arts in general rather than the dance alone

Did it ever occur to you that a pas de deux might be done to whatever emanated from transistor radios hung on the belts of two performers? It occurred to William David, who choreographed "Field," and he and Barbara Lloyd did some beautiful balletic adagio dancing while his set was tuned to WABC and hers to WINS. Somehow, the two managed to correlate their movements to the rhythms of the music that came from her station (there was talk on his), and this must have taken a bit of doing on the spur of the moment. Nonsense?

It was, you see, an unusual evening all the way around, and perhaps not so mad as this sketchy summary may make it seem. At the very least, it proved that we have by no means come to the end of the line in so far as experimentation is concerned. That in itself is enough to remind even the most pessimistic among us that dance theater is not necessarily dead yet. ■

JUNE 16, 1966

AMERICAN BALLET OPENS IN MOSCOW

Raymond H. Anderson

MOSCOW, June 15—The Soviet and United States flags hung side by side tonight in Moscow's Operetta Theater at American Ballet Theater's six-week cultural exchange tour of the Soviet Union. The mood, however, differed strongly from the atmosphere during the ballet company's appearance in Moscow in 1960, when former Premier Nikita Khrushchev attended a performance and later, at a midnight supper, raised a toast to the American dancers and to "art and friendship." No high-level Soviet leaders were in the audience tonight.

The opening number, "Interplay," a lighthearted ballet based on children's games, choreographed by Jerome Robbins to the music of Morton Gould, brought polite applause but little enthusiasm from the audience.

However, by the time the curtain fell on the final ballet, "Etudes," by Harald Lander, the Russians had warmed considerably, and with rhythmic applause brought the dancers back for repeated bows.

The favorite of the evening was Toni Lander, a Danish dancer who joined the American Ballet Theater in 1960.

There had been some uncertainty whether the company's performance of "Pillar of Fire," choreographed by Antony Tudor to music by Arnold Schoenberg, might be a bit gamy for a Russian audience, with its theme of lust and seduction. The audience took it in stride and applauded strongly at the conclusion.

Russian ballet dancers in the audience were overheard during intermission praising the technical skill of the Americans. Some objected to what they regarded as "virtuosity," which is not considered good form in ballet circles here.

The 56 dancers and the administrative staff of the American Ballet Theater arrived in Moscow Monday, giving little time for rehearsals and adjustments to the Operetta Theater's stage. The ballet company, after six performances in Moscow, is scheduled to go to Minsk, Leningrad, Yalta and Kharkov returning to the United States July 24. ■

APRIL 17, 1967

Appraising Balanchine's 'Jewels'

Clive Barnes

Curiously enough, I have never felt any particular emotions about jewels—colored glass suits me almost as well. Yet George Balanchine's new three-act ballet, "Jewels," delights me. Although its acts are called "Emeralds," "Rubies" and "Diamonds" and Karinska has decked out her costumes in appropriately colored glass, the ballet has nothing at all to do with precious gems or, indeed, with anything else. It is simply a ballet about music and dancing. And what dancing it is! The company's members go at it like lovely greyhounds. It is a wholehearted spectacle not to be missed.

"Emeralds," the first section, is set to music by Fauré—it is the least flamboyant part of the ballet, but in some respects the most perfect. The Fauré music—parts of the incidental music written for "Pelléas et Mélisande" and "Shylock"—wraps its way around the dancers, who move in its atmosphere with a chic grace.

It would be easy to think of "The Jewels" as three separate ballets held together merely by Karinska's variously colored but basically similar costumes and by Peter Harvey's hideous (to be generous to it) basic permanent set. However, apart from these visual devices and the ghost of a common gem-like theme, the sections do possess a certain stylistic similarity.

For example, some of the straight-legged leaps you admire in "Emeralds" recur in "Rubies," as does a very distinctive partnering device, where the girl is supported by the crook of the elbow rather than the hand. So, perhaps contrary to first impressions, either Mr. Balanchine has attempted to create some stylistic unity through the ballet, or the fact that the parts are all products of the same creative impulse has left its unplanned mark.

"Rubies" is the most scintillating of the three pieces; it is witty, off-beat, and choreographed in that special style of character-classicism that started with the strange visual harmonies of "The Four Temperaments."

After the asperity of Stravinsky's "Capriccio," in which Gordon Boelzner was the deft piano soloist, the music moves to Tchaikovsky's Third Symphony, for the final episode, "Diamonds." Here Mr. Balanchine seeks a broader style of dance, expansive and imperial. Although I think he has tried to get too many persons on stage in the finale, the dancing is as sumptuous as Mr. Balanchine's conception.

In the ballerina role, Suzanne Farrell is as smooth as cream, and moves like a princess who has never heard of revolution. Her movements cut the air imperiously, and her smile has the slight reserve of graciousness—even, you feel, her blush would have a tinge of blue blood suffusing it. Partnering her, Jacques d'Amboise looks altogether more democratic. But his partnering is totally secure and gallant, his dancing lithe and exciting. ■

JANUARY 14, 1969

CUNNINGHAM ON BROADWAY

Clive Barnes

It has taken a lot of time and a special Ford Foundation grant to bring Merce Cunningham and his company to the bright lights and loud noise of Broadway. And once here it must be admitted that their lights are brighter and noise louder than any of the competition.

Mr. Cunningham and his troupe were at the Billy Rose Theater last night, launching the month-long season of Theater 1969 Dance Repertory. Mr. Cunningham will appear for a week, then José Limón, then Alvin Ailey and finally there is to be a week given over to four avant-gardist troupes, those of Twyla Tharp, Meredith Monk, Yvonne Rainer and Don Redlich.

Clearly Mr. Cunningham decided to let his new-found Broadway audience off lightly for an introduction, by opening this first program with one of the most immediate of his recent works, "Rainforest." It remains a dreamily engrossing work, gentle in an appropriately miasmic way, with dances that appear sinuously uninvolved both with one another or with the rain forest itself suggested by the steamily drifting and dripping music of David Tudor and the mysterious helium-filled and floating silver pillows provided by Andy Warhol by way of décor.

"Place," first created rather more than a couple of years ago, is Cunningham in his harsher, less indulgent mood. The music by Gordon Mumma is a web, a bleb, of electronic sound, pounding against the eardrums, providing a kind of tunnel of noise inside which the dancers move. The dances are disconsolate, their images are desolate, and the anguished, neurotic choreography suggests pain and dissension.

At times the bustle of urban living seems to indicate that the place of Mr. Cunningham's title is the wastage of our cities. At other times some more personal yet no less ravaged landscape appears to be evoked. At the end—with a remarkable dramatic gesture—Mr. Cunningham simply shows a man struggling unsuccessfully to get out of a plastic bag. Like a grotesque puppet, he fights desperately and horridly.

The program ended with the old Cunningham-John Cage favorite, "How to Pass, Kick, Fall and Run." This is a kind of demonstration of the Cunningham style, yet typically it is a demonstration with a difference.

Instead of being set to music, it is set to readings from John Cage's book "Silence." Two readers, David Vaughan and Mr. Cage himself, sit on each side of the stage, sipping champagne and gazing at the dancers. And they read—selections prearranged by themselves but not known to each other—keeping the reading of each excerpt in the same time slot. Sometimes both Mr. Vaughan and Mr. Cage are talking antiphonally to each other. Quite often they select, always at different times, the same anecdote to tell. To this speech, or rather against this speech, Mr. Cunningham and his dancers perform, now and again suggesting certain sporty motifs and movements, but usually just dance.

Mr. Cunningham himself was in fine form, lithely happy, and always keeping his cool very cool. Mr. Cage, as impassive as a monument imminent for erosion, tells his stories with his "brut reservé" voice, well-matched by the quieter, more querulous tones of Mr. Vaughan. It was a pity, however, that they had to sit up in boxes. There seems to be more contact between them and the dancers when they are on the stage with them. ■

MAY 4, 1960

'Fantasticks' Opens Off Broadway

Brooks Atkinson

Having won a lot of admirers with a short version of "The Fantasticks," Tom Jones has expanded it for the production that opened at the Sullivan Street Playhouse last evening.

Although it is ungrateful to say so, two acts are one too many to sustain the delightful tone of the first. After the intermission, the mood is never quite so luminous and gay.

The remark is ungrateful because the form of a masque seems original in the modern theatre. Harvey Schmidt's simple melodies with uncomplicated orchestrations are captivating and the acting is charming. Throughout the first act "The Fantasticks" is sweet and fresh in a civilized manner.

According to the program, it is based on Rostand's "Les Romantiques." In the form of a dainty masque, designed in modern taste by Ed Wittstein, it is a variation on a Pierrot and Columbine theme. A boy and a girl, who are neighbors, are in love as long as a wall separates them and they believe that their fathers disapprove. Actually, their fathers want them to marry. To create an irresistible romantic mood, the fathers arrange a flamboyant abduction scene in the moonlight.

Although the story is slight, the style is entrancing in Word Baker's staging. It seems like a harlequinade in the setting of a masque. The characters are figures in a legend, acted with an artlessness that is winning. As the Narrator, the Girl and the Boy, Jerry Orbach, Rita Gardner and Kenneth Nelson, respectively, sing beautifully and act with spontaneity, not forgetting that they are participating in a work of make-believe.

After the intermission the author substitutes sunshine for moonlight. Disillusion destroys the rapture of the introductory scene. Pierrot and Columbine have combed the stardust out of their hair. But it seems to this theatergoer that the second act loses the skimming touch of the first. As an aging ham actor, Thomas Bruce is not so funny as he is in his first appearance, and the conceits of the staging become repetitious.

Perhaps "The Fantasticks" is by nature the sort of thing that loses magic the longer it endures. Any sign of effort diminishes it. But for the space of one act it is delightful. The music, played on piano and harp, has grace and humor. All the actors are thoroughbreds. ■

JULY 31, 1960

What Off Broadway Has—and Hasn't—Accomplished

John Gassner

The off-Broadway play, "Little Mary Sunshine," 1960.

After a discouraging Broadway season, it is consoling to consider the off-Broadway theatre of the same period. The little theatres presented approximately the same number of productions as Broadway. Their range of interest was at least as wide, and they exercised a decidedly happier choice in the plays they produced with general competence and occasional distinction.

More remarkably, the off-Broadway enterprise began at last to satisfy its critics' appetite for provocative new works. As the season advanced, New Yorkers could make one gratifying discovery after another with no greater effort than it takes to leave the Times Square area. Young American writers contributed "The Connection," "The Zoo Story" and "The Prodigal" while European avant-gardists supplied "Krapp's Last Tape," "The Balcony," "The Killer" and "Between Two Thieves." It was almost possible to believe that Jack Gelber, Edward Albee and Jack Robertson, on our side of the Atlantic, and Beckett, Genet and Ionesco from Paris were ushering in a small renascence in playwriting.

The off-Broadway theatre also accounted for most of the originality of the past season's musical entertainment. The liveliness of "Little Mary Sunshine," the loveliness of "The Fantasticks" and the charm of "Ernest in Love" brought relief from the mammoth musicals of midtown show business.

With its successes, and even with some distinguished failures such as Ionesco's political fantasia "The Killer," Off Broadway performed the near-miracle of making theatre in New York look like a living art rather than an animated corpse.

With so much to be grateful for, it would be ungracious to draw up a bill of charges against the noble enterprise. One could wish, however, that the off-Broadway theatre as a whole were less marked by tentative efforts, scattered aims and a temporizing spirit. Its operations tend to be a harum-scarum as the opportunist ventures of the Broadway supermarket, where patronage becomes the sole test of value.

It is a compliment to say so, of course, but I look for artistic leadership from the off-Broadway stage. New Yorkers previously found this leadership among the new theatre groups of the nineteen thirties and in the earlier "little theatre" vanguard of the Provincetown Players, the Neighborhood Playhouse, the Greenwich Village Players and the young Theatre Guild. Aware as I am of the difficulty of realizing the expectations aroused by these earlier ventures, I cannot, nevertheless, reconcile myself to a condition of drift in present avant-garde circles. To my mind, even a disengaged or despairing point of view, which ultimately proves desiccating, is preferable to no point of view at all.

But I have hankered for fresh dramatic forms and production styles from the off-Broadway theatre no less than for a sense of direction in the plays it introduces or revives. The mere use of some kind of "arena theatre" has hardly any esthetic significance. Give a theatre-in-the-round production to "Three Men on a Horse," for example, and the play remains the same sort of farce it was, when it first appeared on Broadway. A vital sense of style has yet to be achieved in the off-Broadway operation as a whole, although exemplary efforts have appeared in José Quintero's individually-styled work at the Circle in the Square and Judith Malina's and Julian Beck's experiments at The Living Theatre.

Having aired such extravagant expectations, this writer might as well blurt out his remaining dreams. One of these is that the best results of off-Broadway enterprise should reach the rest of the country. I also hope that the best producing groups will be able to follow The Living Theatre's example of keeping some plays in repertory. I could wish, too, that it were possible to assure the return of some of the season's memorable productions such as "W.S.A.," "Machinal," "A Country Scandal" and "The Fantasticks" after the conclusion of their original runs. At present, the off-Broadway theatre appears to have no more memory than Broadway does.

I entertain, in conclusion, two dreams impossible of realization without some form of subsidy from private or public sources. The first is that it will be possible for off-Broadway productions to provide their personnel with a living, and the second that the price scale can be kept low enough to secure the patronage of the young playgoer and the "common," but uncommonly interested, man. For many individuals who fit this description, the off-Broadway theatre is already overpriced.

If it cannot become a "people's theatre" in the full sense of the term, it should at least be kept accessible to slender purses. It is already apparent that only a few highly touted presentations thrive downtown while the rest expire from public neglect. The off-Broadway stage has begun to suffer from the same condition of "surfeit or starvation" that prevails on Broadway and deprives it of cultural significance. ■

OCTOBER 15, 1961

BROADWAY'S STARS COME WITH CONDITIONS

Milton Esterow

With a new Broadway season under way amid much ballyhoo, thousands of contracts have been signed without hoopla between the producer and the author, actor, director, scene designer, costume designer, composer, lyricist, choreographer, orchestrator, arranger, lighting expert and others. A number of these documents embody whims that range from insisting on the color of dressing-room draperies to specifying the level of temperature to be maintained on stage. All of them are as closely guarded as the private papers of the White House.

"If someone has something, the next one hears about it and wants the same thing," explains a company manager.

Some contracts consist of as many as half a dozen pages and, says Richard Maney, elder statesman of Broadway's drum-beaters, read like codicils to the Magna Charta. Billing clauses, which stipulate such things as thickness, boldness, prominence and size of the printer's type, especially make producers turn to the tranquillizer bottle. The desire for what they consider proper billing is so intense that actors have been known to take a decrease in salary to get it.

A billing problem has already been solved this season in Tennessee Williams' "The Night of the Iguana." The two stars—Bette Davis and Margaret Leighton, or Margaret Leighton and Bette Davis—will have alternate top billing on the marquee and in the advertisements and theatre programs. When such a treaty is reached, stars seldom fail to notice if they get a bad count. One actress complained to her producer not long ago, "She's [her co-star] been on top twenty-four times to my eighteen."

Last season, when Michael Rennie signed to appear with Barbara Bel Geddes and Barry Nelson in "Mary, Mary," he felt his name deserved equal prominence on the marquee. Since all three names couldn't be squeezed into one line above the play's title—the hallowed ground reserved only for stars—a settlement was reached whereby Mr. Rennie would have a second line all to himself.

"Sole star billing" is not uncommon. This means that no one else can have his name on the marquee or within 50 percent of the size of the star's in advertising or programs. Some players demand that their names be the same size as the title.

Among stars, requests for maids, hairdressers, valets and chauffeured limousines to and from the theatre are fairly common. Approval by a star of all photographs taken by

(cont'd. on next page)

(cont'd. from previous page)
a star of all photographs taken by the show's photographer is viewed by producers as understandable. Less understandable was the actor who asked that a chauffeured limousine be put at his disposal at all times.

Several directors have stipulated that the cast must not receive outside coaching during rehearsals. "They slip off to teachers who run over the scenes with them and then they come back with an entirely different interpretation," says a prominent director.

English actors are considered in some quarters to be the worst offenders. "Some of them make it clear that they wouldn't set foot here if it weren't for the money," says a producer. "Many like to have the temperature at a certain degree. They like the stage to be quite cool." What if it gets hot? "All they can do then is yell and perspire a little more." ■

MARCH 30, 1962

NEW THEATRE IN CENTRAL PARK NO SURPRISE TO ITS DIRECTOR

Brooks Atkinson

Shakespeare's "The Winter's Tale" in Central Park, New York, 1962.

No one is less astonished than Joseph Papp by the new outdoor theatre that is rising in one of the loveliest corners of Central Park. He regards it as a logical part of his New York Shakespeare Festival.

The theatre on the shore of Belvedere Lake looks as though it were going to have the most useful Shakespeare stage in the country. It will consist of "about 2,500 planks and a passion," Mr. Papp says in a sardonic variation on the familiar "two planks and a passion." The chairs are to be fastened permanently to green-painted planks, which, in turn, are fastened permanently to the steel framework.

Naturally, Mr. Papp, now 40 years of age, is pleased by this proof that his free Shakespeare in Central Park has become a permanent institution. His progress from a wildcat operation on the Lower East Side in 1955 has been thoughtful and relentless. No one has ever fought harder to give New York something free. Through all the crises, which included Robert Moses in his most irascible proconsul mood, no one has been less excitable than Mr. Papp. He has always believed that free performances of Shakespeare out of doors would become essential to the cultural life of thousands of New Yorkers—probably 150,000 this year.

To most of us, the fact that he insists on giving the performances free on a first-come, first-served basis is the most astonishing factor in the enterprise. But Mr. Papp does not feel like a public benefactor. He feels like a professional stage director. Now that his theatre is established he finds himself reverting to his original interest in problems of Shakespearean acting. This year he will direct "The Merchant of Venice," with George C. Scott as Shylock, and "King Lear," with Frank Silvera in the title role.

If Shakespeare in the Park has become a permanent institution it is primarily because the productions, good or bad, invariably glow with vitality. Among the actors who have flourished in the Park productions are some now recognized as New York's ablest—Colleen Dewhurst, George C. Scott, J. D. Cannon, Rex Everhart, Staats Cotsworth, Robert Gerringer, Donald Madden, Gerry Jedd, Nan Martin, Albert Quinton, Nancy Wickwire, Ray Reinhardt. Incidentally, the weekly salary scale is now $100, $75 and $45, according to the importance of the role. Originally, the salary scale was zero.

In 1957 the budget was $33,845. This year it will be $263,466—reflecting the growing professionalism of the work. The city has been asked to contribute $100,000. Whatever the city does not give, a fund-raising committee appointed by Mayor Wagner must coax and wheedle out of citizens and private foundations. Every year Mr. Papp has to face this Sisyphian labor. Being an optimist he never seems to worry about it, and now he has accumulated friends who pitch in and help.

Meanwhile, he is casting actors for rehearsals that will begin on May 17. On June 18, when the season opens, the first 2,300 people on line will throng into a beautiful theatre that will come to life when actors mount the stage. ■

MAY 9, 1962

'A Funny Thing Happened'. . . and Another and Another

Howard Taubman

Know what they found on the way to the forum? Burlesque, vaudeville and a cornucopia of mad, comic hokum.

The phrase for the title of the new musical comedy that arrived at the Alvin last night might be, caveat emptor. "A Funny Thing Happened on the Way to the Forum" indeed! No one gets to the forum; no one even starts for it. And nothing really happens that isn't older than the forum, more ancient than the agora in Athens. But somehow you keep laughing as if the old sight and sound gags were as good as new.

A plastic-faced, rolling-eyed, Falstaff-like character like Zero Mostel playing zany follow-the-leader with three centurions ordered to keep an eye on him? A rubber-faced, murmurous David Burns playing an enamored old goat and cooing like an antiquated turtle dove? A bewigged and fluttering Jack Gilford got up in a shimmering white gown and pretending to be a dead, yet agitated, virgin? A lank, deep-voiced Shakespearean like John Carradine pretending to be a timid though agile dealer in courtesans?

If stuff like that doesn't joggle your funny bone, keep away from the Alvin. For the rest of us who were young and risible in the days when comedians were hearty and comedy was rough and tumble and for the new generations who knew not the untamed gusto of this ancient and honorable style of fooling, it will be thumbs up for this uninhibited romp.

Burt Shevelove and Larry Gelbart, authors of the book, are willing to pay full credit, if not royalties, to Plautus, their distinguished antecedent. Their book resorts to outrageous puns and to lines that ought to make you cringe.

George Abbott, who has been around a long time but surely staged nothing for the forum mob, has forgotten nothing and remembered everything. He has engineered a gay funeral sequence to a relentlessly snappy march by Stephen Sondheim. He has used mixed identities, swinging doors, kicks in the posterior, double takes and all the rest of the familiar paraphernalia with the merciless disingenuousness of a man who knows you will be defenseless.

Mr. Sondheim's songs are accessories to the pre-mediated offense. With the Messrs. Mostel, Gilford, Burns and Carradine as a coy foursome, "Everybody Ought to Have a Maid" recalls the days when delirious farceurs like the Marx Brothers could devastate a number. When Mr. Mostel, the slave with a nimble mind and a desire to be free, persuades Mr. Gilford, the nervous straw boss of the slaves, to don virgin's white, the two convert the show's romantic and pretty "Lovely" into irresistible nonsense.

Say all the unkind and truthful things you wish about "A Funny Thing." It's noisy, coarse, blue and obvious like the putty nose on a burlesque comedian. Resist these slickly paced old comic routines, if you can. Try and keep a straight face as Zero Mostel explains to the sacrificial Jack Gilford that an impending pyre is only "a fire pyre." ■

OCTOBER 15, 1962

WHO'S AFRAID OF EDWARD ALBEE?

Howard Taubman

Thanks to Edward Albee's furious skill as a writer, Alan Schneider's charged staging and a brilliant performance by a cast of four "Who's Afraid of Virginia Woolf?" is a wry and electric evening in the theatre.

You may not be able to swallow Mr. Albee's characters whole, as I cannot. You may feel, as I do, that a pillar of the plot is too flimsy to support the climax. Nevertheless, you are urged to hasten to the Billy Rose Theater, where Mr. Albee's first full-length play opened Saturday night.

For "Who's Afraid of Virginia Woolf?" is possessed by raging demons. It is punctuated by comedy, and its laughter is shot through with savage irony. At its core is a bitter, keening lament over man's incapacity to arrange his environment or private life so as to inhibit his self-destructive compulsions.

Mr. Albee carries along the burning intensity and icy wrath that informed "The Zoo Story" and "The American Dream." He has written a full-length play that runs almost three and a half hours and that brims over with howling furies that do not drown out a fierce compassion. After the fumes stirred by his witches' cauldron are spent, he lets in, not sunlight and fresh air, but only an agonized prayer.

Although Mr. Albee's vision is grim and sardonic, he is never solemn. With the instincts of a born dramatist and the shrewdness of one whose gifts have been tempered in the theater, he knows how to fill the stage with vitality and excitement.

Sympathize with them or not, you will find the characters in this new play vibrant with dramatic urgency, in their anger and terror they are pitiful as well as corrosive, but they are also wildly and humanly hilarious. Mr. Albee's dialogue ripples with a relish of the ludicrous. His controlled, allusive style grows in mastery.

In "Who's Afraid of Virginia Woolf?" he is concerned with Martha and George, a couple living in mordant, uproarious antagonism. Married for more than 20 years, they claw each other like jungle beasts. In the dark hours after a Saturday midnight they entertain a young married pair new to the campus, introducing them to a funny and cruel brand of fun and games. Before the liquor-sodden night is over, there are lacerating self-revelations for all.

Mr. Albee would have us believe that for 21 years his older couple have nurtured a fiction that they have a son, that his imaginary existence is a secret that violently binds and sunders them and that George's pronouncing him dead may be a turning point. This part of the story does not ring true, and its falsity impairs the credibility of his central characters.

If the drama falters, the acting of Uta Hagen and Arthur Hill does not. As the vulgar, scornful, desperate Martha, Miss Hagen makes a tormented harridan horrifying believable. George Grizzard as a young biologist on the make shades from geniality to intensity with shattering rightness. And Melinda Dillon as his mousy, troubled bride is amusing and touching in her vulnerable wistfulness.

Mr. Albee's new work, flawed though it is, towers over the common run of contemporary plays. It marks a further gain for a young writer becoming a major figure of our stage. ■

JANUARY 17, 1964

CAROL CHANNING STARS IN 'HELLO, DOLLY!'

Howard Taubman

As a play Thornton Wilder's "The Matchmaker" vibrated with unheard melodies and unseen dances. Michael Stewart, Jerry Herman and Gower Champion apparently heard and saw them, and they have conspired ingeniously to bring them to shining life in a musical shot through with enchantment.

"Hello, Dolly!," which blew happily into the St. James Theater last night, has qualities of freshness and imagination that are rare in the run of our machine-made musicals. It transmutes the broadly stylized moon of a mettlesome farce into the gusto and colors of the musical stage. What was larger and droller than life has been puffed up and gaily tinted without being blown apart. "Hello, Dolly!" is the best musical of the season thus far.

It could have been more than that. Were it not for lapses of taste, it could have been one of the notable ones. But Mr. Champion, whose staging and choreography abound in wit and invention, has tolerated certain cheapnesses, like the vulgar accent of a milliner's clerk, like the irritating wail of a teenager crying for her beau, like the muddled chase in the midst of a series of tableaux vivants. Mr. Stewart's book has settled for some dull and cheap lines the musical would not miss.

It is a pity because "Hello, Dolly!" does not need such crutches. But enough of peevishness. Let us rejoice in the blessings "Hello, Dolly!" bestows.

The conception as a whole, despite an occasional excess of exuberance that turns into turbulence, is faithful to the spirit of Mr. Wilder's broad, chuckling jest. Mr. Stewart's book holds fast to Mr. Wilder's atmosphere and style even if it trots off into Broadwayese now and then. Mr. Herman's songs are brisk and pointed and always tuneful.

The basic story, deliberately calculating in its simplicity, is unchanged. Here in a shrewdly mischievous performance by Carol Channing is the endlessly resourceful widow, Mrs. Dolly Gallagher Levi, matchmaker and lady-of-all-trades, who sets her enormous bonnet crested by a huge pink bird for the half-millionaire, Vandergelder, and lands him on her pleasure-loving terms.

Resplendent in scarlet gown embroidered with jewels and a feathered headdress, and looking like a gorgeous, animated kewpie doll, Miss Channing sings the rousing title song with earthy zest and leads a male chorus of waiters and chefs in a joyous promenade.

Here is David Burns as the curmudgeon Vandergelder, bellowing nasally like W. C. Fields redivivus. Charles Nelson Reilly and Jerry Dodge as two of Vandergelder's oppressed clerks loose on the town sing and dance agreeably, and their buffoonery would be funnier if it were toned down. Eileen Brennan is as pretty and desirable a Widow Molloy as one could wish—with a voice, too.

What gives "Hello, Dolly!" its special glow is its amalgamation of the lively theater arts in the musical numbers. Mr. Champion has provided fragments of dance for the overtureless opening that are all the more attractive because they are spare and unexpectedly spaced.

When he fills the stage for the ebullient "Put on Your Sunday Clothes" at the Yonkers Depot and has his lavishly garbed cast promenading along the oval runway out front, the theater throbs with vitality. For a 14th Street parade Mr. Champion has deployed his forces in a cheerful old New York version of medieval guilds. To a bouncing gallop by Mr. Herman, Mr. Champion has set a corps of waiters with trays, spits and jeroboams at the ready, dancing a wild, vertiginous rout.

Making the necessary reservations for the unnecessary vulgar and frenzied touches, one is glad to welcome "Hello, Dolly!" for its warmth, color and high spirits.

MARCH 25, 1964

Hatred Explodes in 'Dutchman'

Howard Taubman

Everything about LeRoi Jones's "Dutchman" is designed to shock—its basic idea, its language and its murderous rage.

This half-hour-long piece, the last of three one-act plays being performed at the Cherry Lane Theater, is an explosion of hatred rather than a play. It puts into the mouth of its principal Negro character a scathing denunciation of all the white man's good works, pretensions and condescensions.

If this is the way the Negroes really feel about the white world around them, there's more rancor buried in the breasts of colored conformists than anyone can imagine. If this is the way even one Negro feels, there is ample cause for guilt as well as alarm, and for a hastening of change.

As an extended metaphor of bitterness and fury, "Dutchman" is transparently simple in structure. Clay, a Negro who wears a three-button suit and is reserved and well-spoken, is accosted by a white female on a train. Lula is a liar, a slut, essentially an agent provocateur of a Caucasian society.

After she disarms Clay with her wild outbursts and sinuous attentions, she turns on him in challenging contempt. His answer is to drop the mask of conformity and to spew out all the anger that has built up in him and his fellow Negroes. When this outburst of violent resentment has finished and Clay has left the train, Lula notices that another Negro has boarded and she sets her slinky charms for him.

Mr. Jones writes with a kind of sustained frenzy. His little work is a mélange of sardonic images and undisciplined filth. The impact of his ferocity would be stronger if he did not work so hard and persistently to be shocking. ■

MARCH 27, 1964

STREISAND SHINES IN 'FUNNY GIRL'

Howard Taubman

Barbra Streisand, star of "Funny Girl," in 1965.

Who wouldn't want to resurrect Fanny Brice? She was a wonderful entertainer.

Since Fanny herself cannot be brought back, the next best thing is to get Barbra Streisand to sing and strut and go through comic routines à la Brice. Miss Streisand is well on her way to becoming a splendid entertainer in her own right, and in "Funny Girl" she goes as far as any performer can toward recalling the laughter and joy that were Fanny Brice.

If the new musical that arrived last night at the Winter Garden were dedicated entirely to the gusto and buffoonery of Fanny Brice, all would be well nigh perfect this morning. But "Funny Girl" also is intent on telling the story of how Fanny loved and lost Nick Arnstein, and part of the time it oozes with a thick helping of sticky sentimentality.

But that's show-business sagas for you. They rarely can untrack themselves from the hokum and schmaltz that authors and, for all one knows, show people consider standard operating procedure. As for the public, it often is a pushover for the glamour of the stage and the romances of show folk.

"Funny Girl" is most fun when it is reveling in Fanny's preoccupation with show business. Miss Streisand as a young Brice bursting with energy and eagerness to improve her routines is an impudent dancing doll who refuses to run down. Miss Streisand imagining herself in a radiant future in "I'm the Greatest Star," an appealingly quirky song, is not only Fanny Brice but all young performers believing in their destinies.

For an evocation of the stately Ziegfeld Follies, which Miss Brice brightened with her exuberance, there are two big nostalgic numbers.

Miss Streisand hamming it up in her first rendezvous with Sydney Chaplin in a private room in a swank restaurant is almost as funny as the funny girl herself might have been. She uses a fan with mock coyness; she arranges herself on a chair like a rachitic femme fatale; she walks across the room with a wiggle Mae West would envy.

Isobel Lennart's book skirts sentimentality reasonably well until Fanny and Nick turn serious, get married and run into troubles. By the end "Funny Girl" is drenched in tears.

The true laughter in this musical comes from the sense of truth it communicates

Fortunately, Miss Streisand can make a virtue out of suffering, if she is allowed to sing about it. Jule Styne, who has written one of his best scores, has provided her with bluesy tunes like "Who Are You Now?" and she turns them into lyrical laments.

Mr. Chaplin is a tall, elegant figure as Nick, gallant in courting and doing his best when he must be noble. Kay Medford, who seems to be a stage mother every time you see her in a musical, is dry and diverting as Fanny's shrewd parent. Danny Meehan is agreeable as a hoofer who befriends the young Fanny.

It's the authentic aura of show business arising out of Fanny Brice's luminous career that lights up "Funny Girl." Much of the spoken humor is homespun—that is, East Side homespun. The true laughter in this musical comes from the sense of truth it communicates of Fanny Brice's stage world. And Fanny's personality and style are remarkably evoked by Miss Streisand. Fanny and Barbra make the evening. Who says the past cannot be recaptured? ■

SEPTEMBER 23, 1964

MOSTEL AS TEVYE IN 'FIDDLER ON THE ROOF'

Howard Taubman

It has been prophesied that the Broadway musical theater would take up the mantle of meaningfulness worn so carelessly by the American drama in recent years. "Fiddler on the Roof" does its bit to make good on this prophecy.

The new musical, which opened last night at the Imperial Theater, is filled with laughter and tenderness. It catches the essence of a moment in history with sentiment and radiance. Compounded of the familiar materials of the musical theater—popular song, vivid dance movement, comedy and emotion—it combines and transcends them to arrive at an integrated achievement of uncommon quality.

Zero Mostel and Maria Karnilova in "Fiddler On The Roof," 1964.

The essential distinction of "Fiddler on the Roof" must be kept in mind even as one cavils at a point here or a detail there. For criticism of a work of this caliber, it must be remembered, is relative. If I wish that several of the musical numbers soared indigenously, if I find fault with a gesture that is Broadway rather than the world of Sholem Aleichem, if I deplore a conventional scene, it is because "Fiddler on the Roof" is so fine that it deserves counsels toward perfection.

But first to the things that are marvelously right. The book that Joseph Stein has drawn from the richly humorous and humane tales of Sholem Aleichem, the warm-hearted spokesman of the poor Jews in the Russian villages at the turn of the century, is faithful to its origins.

Although there is no time in a musical for a fully developed gallery of human portraits, "Fiddler on the Roof" manages to display several that have authentic character. The most arresting, of course, is that of Tevye, the humble dairyman whose blessings included a hardworking, if sharp-tongued, wife, five daughters and a native philosophical bent.

If Sholem Aleichem had known Zero Mostel, he would have chosen him, one is sure, for Tevye. Mr. Mostel looks as Tevye should. His full beard is a pious aureole for his shining countenance. The stringy ends of his prayer shawl hang from under his vest; the knees of his breeches are patched, and his boots are scuffed.

A man of goodwill, Mr. Mostel often pauses to carry on a dialogue with himself, arguing both sides of a case with equal logic. He holds long conversations with God. Although his observations never are disrespectful, they call a spade a spade. "Send us the cure," he warns the Lord, "we got the sickness already." Mr. Mostel does not keep his acting and singing or his walking and dancing in separate compartments. His Tevye is a unified, lyrical conception.

The score by Jerry Bock and the lyrics by Sheldon Harnick at their best move the story along, enrich the mood and intensify the emotions. "Sabbath Prayer" is as hushed as a community at its devotions. "Sunrise, Sunset" is in the spirit of a traditional wedding under a canopy. When Tevye and Golde after 25 years of marriage ask themselves, "Do You Love Me?" the song has a touching angularity. But several of the other romantic tunes are merely routine.

Jerome Robbins has staged "Fiddler on the Roof" with sensitivity and fire. As his own choreographer, he weaves dance into action with subtlety and flaring theatricalism.

Richness of flavor marks "Fiddler on the Roof." Although it does not entirely eschew the stigmata of routine Broadway, it has an honest feeling for another place, time and people. And in Mr. Mostel's Tevye it has one of the most glowing creations in the history of the musical theater. ■

JANUARY 29, 1965

PLAY TO CHARGE $7.50—NEW HIGH PRICE

Sam Zolotow

Neil Simon's incoming comedy, "The Odd Couple," starring Art Carney and Walter Matthau, will charge the highest top price asked for any straight play thus far this season. Orchestra tickets from Monday through Saturday nights will be $7.50 at the Plymouth, where the play will open March 10.

Usually straight plays have a top of $6.90 from Monday through Thursday nights, rising to $7.50 on Friday and Saturday nights.

Reached in Wilmington, Del., where "The Odd Couple" is trying out, Saint Subber, the producer, said:

"With two stars of the caliber of Mr. Carney and Mr. Matthau, it's an enormously expensive play to operate. If the stars are worth it, a producer doesn't mind paying those salaries."

"Those salaries" were not specified by Mr. Subber, but elsewhere it was disclosed that Mr. Carney receives 10 percent of the weekly gross, with a minimum guarantee of $2,500. In addition, he gets 7 1/2 percent of the profits for the first six months and 10 per cent thereafter.

Mr. Matthau, who is paid 7 1/2 percent of the gross against a guarantee of $2,000, has a stake of $10,000 in the venture. Two of the other investors are Gustave Berne, the largest with $37,500, and Mike Nichols, director of "The Odd Couple," with $10,000.

The weekly expenses at the 1,063-seat Plymouth are said to be about $30,000. At capacity business, the weekly gross will be $47,000 for the one-set attraction, capitalized at $150,000.

Paramount is acquiring the film rights at an advance of $175,000 toward a maximum payment of $500,000. The difference will be paid by Paramount at the rate of 10 percent for every profitable week of the engagement.

The Plymouth has been leased from the Shuberts by David J. Cogan, owner of the Biltmore and Eugene O'Neill Theaters. "Barefoot in the Park," written by Mr. Simon, directed by Mr. Nichols and produced by Mr. Subber, is in its second year at Mr. Cogan's Biltmore. ■

MARCH 11, 1965

Skillful Comedy in Neil Simon's 'Odd Couple'

Howard Taubman

The opening scene in "The Odd Couple," of the boys in their regular Friday night poker game, is one of the funniest card sessions ever held on a stage.

If you are worried that there is nothing Neil Simon, the author, or Mike Nichols, his director, can think of to top that scene, relax. The main business of the new comedy, which opened last night at the Plymouth Theater, has scarcely begun, and Mr. Simon, Mr. Nichols and their excellent cast, headed by Art Carney and Walter Matthau, have scores of unexpected ways prepared to keep you smiling, chuckling and guffawing.

Mr. Simon has hit upon an idea that could occur to any playwright. His odd couple are two men, one divorced and living in dejected and disheveled splendor in an eight-room apartment and the other about to be divorced and taken in as a roommate.

One could predict the course of this odd union from its formation in misery and compassion through its disagreements to its ultimate rupture. Mr. Simon's way of writing comedy is not to reach for gimmicks of plot; he probably doesn't mind your knowing the bare outline of his idea.

His skill—and it is not only great but constantly growing—lies in his gift for the deliciously surprising line and attitude. His instinct for incongruity is faultless. It nearly always operates on a basis of character.

Begin with that poker game. Mr. Matthau, the slovenly host, is off stage in the kitchen fixing a snack while Nathaniel Frey, John Fiedler, Sidney Armus and Paul Dooley are sitting around the table on a hot summer night, sweating and grousing at the luck of the cards.

Mr. Matthau walks in with a tray of beer and white and brown sandwiches. The sixth member of the Friday night regulars, Mr. Carney, is missing. Evidently he has been away from his known haunts for 24 hours, and a phone call from his wife informs his friends that she hopes he never turns up. Since they know that he is a man who takes such blows seriously, they fear that he will do something violent to himself.

With Mr. Carney's arrival as Felix, the discarded husband, the principal action begins. Mr. Carney is truly bereaved, a man of sorrows. His eyes are stricken, his lips quiver, his shoulders sag. Even poker gives way before his desolation. When the players go home, they depart softly and gravely like chaps leaving a sick room.

Mr. Matthau as Oscar, the host, consoles Felix, massaging away the spasms in his neck and enduring the moose calls with which the unfortunate fellow clears ears beset by allergies. Nothing much happens during the rest of the act except that these two inevitably blunder into a domestic alliance, but there is scarcely a moment that is not hilarious.

The unflagging comedy in the remainder of the play depends on the fundamental switch—of the odd couple. Felix is a compulsive house keeper, bent on cleaning, purifying the air and cooking.

Mr. Matthau for his part is wonderfully comic as a man who finds his companion's fussy habits increasingly irksome. He walks about with a bearish crouch that grows more belligerent as his domestic situation becomes both familiar and impressive.

Mr. Nichols's comic invention, like Mr. Simon's, shines through this production and the comfortable Riverside Drive apartment invoked by Oliver Smith's set.

"The Odd Couple" has it made. Women are bound to adore the sight of a man carrying on like a little homemaker. Men are sure to snicker at a male in domestic bondage to a man. Kids will love it because it's funny. Homosexuals will enjoy it—for obvious reasons. Doesn't that take care of everyone? ■

JANUARY 31, 1966

Stanley Kauffmann

It is Bob Fosse's evening at the Palace. That newly refurbished theater, clad in several becoming shades of red, re-opened on Saturday night with a musical called "Sweet Charity." The show's chief attractions are the staging and the dances by Mr. Fosse, which have style and theatrical vitality. The same cannot be said for the book or the score.

The book was adapted from Federico Fellini's film "Nights of Cabiria" (1957), to which it has retained some resemblances. The heroine has been changed from a sentimental Roman tart to a sentimental New York dance-hall hostess, but the story begins and ends with her abandonment by a man; she spends one evening with a famous actor; there is a "religious" pilgrimage to a jazz revival meeting.

Beyond that, the material has been supplied by Neil Simon and, in the main, without the wit—or even the wisecracks—that

(cont'd. on next page)

(cont'd. from previous page)
have previously marked his comedies. Possibly Mr. Simon is hampered by working on someone else's ideas. In any event, the result is a series of pattern scenes, generally with pattern characters filling in the shape of the scene with pattern dialogue.

The occasional good line is poorly treated. A man who is trapped in a stalled elevator begins to panic, and says: "I'd be all right if I could just get out for a few minutes." As we laugh, we hear the joke being explained into the ground—and we stop laughing.

But the chief trouble with the show is that it is so patently designed from Moment One to be a heart-tugger. Gwen Verdon, in the name role, appears in silhouette and dances forward as title "credits" are lowered from the files. The signs read: "The Story of a Girl Who Wanted to be Loved." It is a typographical error: this is the story of a show that wants to be loved.

Miss Verdon, as Charity, has a marathon role in which she is rarely off stage. She is a first-class performer: a good singer, an excellent dancer, a thorough, stage-taking professional. But—and this is partly Mr. Fosse's fault—she plays so unremittingly in the brave-pathetic vein that, abetted by a narrative, nondramatic script, she frequently repeats effects.

Mr. Fosse's staging of numbers is often superb. Cy Coleman here joins the company of the many current show composers who supply appropriate rhythms but no tunes that can be remembered. Dorothy Fields's lyrics are no more than serviceable.

"Sweet Charity" grows tedious between its brightest numbers, despite Mr. Fosse's work and Miss Verdon's professionalism, because it so heavily emphasizes the adjective in the title. The good-hearted dumb broad is one of the oldest of stage clichés.

Not to ask too much of a musical, we can still note a quickly implanted sense that Charity is merely a theatrical device. No one connected with this show persuades us that she is anything more than a mechanism with which they hope to "get" the audience. Despite all the heat and skill applied, the mechanism remains mechanical. ■

MAY 25, 1966

'MAME' IS BACK WITH A SPLASH

Stanley Kauffmann

"Mame" is back, with music—probably to stay as long as last time when it was "Auntie Mame," without music. As show biz goes, this is good news. It opened last night in a splendidly splashy production. Even the scenery is entertaining.

There may be a few benighted Eskimos who still need to be told that the story comes, originally, from Patrick Dennis's novel. It concerns (dear Eskimo readers) a zesty Manhattan lady of the nineteen twenties, wealthy and ingratiatingly wild, who inherits a young nephew from her deceased brother and shortly afterward inherits the Depression.

This star vehicle deserves its star, and vice is very much versa. No one can be surprised to learn that Angela Lansbury is an accomplished actress, but not all of us may know that she has an adequate singing voice, can dance trimly, and can combine all these matters into musical *performance.*

In this marathon role she has wit, poise, warmth, and a very taking coolth. The visceral test, I suppose, is whether one is jealous of little Patrick growing up with an aunt like that. I was green.

Then there is little Patrick himself. Frankie Michaels, as Patrick, is fine: no saccharin, complete conviction, a good enough singer, and he even dances a little (a tango!). I'm sure that Miss Lansbury would be the first to assert how difficult her job would be with a lesser nephew.

Beatrice Arthur gives a caustic musical-comedy performance as a bosom pal of Mame's that is fluent in skill and superb in timing. Jane Connell is Agnes Gooch, the comic secretary, and this part, as written, is still too broad for me, particularly in the change from chastity to chase. But Miss Connell, another singing actress, plays it better than it deserves, with the caricature rather than character that it asks.

Messrs. Lawrence and Lee have applied a neat distilling touch to their original play-script, allowing for what is supplied by songs and dances. Jerry Herman's score has music that is strongly rhythmic and sufficiently tuneful, and lyrics that are generally deft. I could have done with one less cheer-up number in the first act ("We Need a Little Christmas"). My own favorite is Mame's solo, "If He Walked Into My Life," in which she wonders whether she is responsible for the grown Patrick's mistakes—a good song well done by an *actress.*

This star vehicle deserves its star . . .

Like some other recent musicals, "Mame" is a bit too long, particularly in the first act—which puts an extra burden on the second act. Like most others, it comes to our ears through an amplifying system of which we are never unaware. Like most others, it is, fundamentally, one more trip through material that most of us know very well already; and this is not necessarily a cheery comment on the State of the Theater or the State of Us.

But, whatever those truths may be, the present truth is that "Mame" does its job well with plenty of effective theatrical sentiment, laughs and vitality.

And with Miss Lansbury.

NOVEMBER 21, 1966

'CABARET' OPENS AT THE BROADHURST

Walter Kerr

Joel Grey (rear center, in black tuxedo) and cast in the Broadway musical "Cabaret," New York, 1966.

"Cabaret" is a stunning musical with one wild wrong note. I think you'd be wise to go to it first and argue about that startling slip later.

The first thing you see as you enter the Broadhurst is yourself. Designer Boris Aronson has sent converging strings toward a vanishing point at upstage center. Occupying the vanishing point is a great geometric mirror, and in the mirror the gathering audience is reflected. We have come for the floor show, we are all at tables tonight, and anything we learn of life during the evening is going to be learned through the tipsy, tinkling, angular vision of sleek rouged-up clowns, who inhabit a world that rains silver.

This marionette's-eye view of a time and place in our lives that was brassy, wanton, carefree and doomed to crumble is brilliantly conceived. The place is Berlin, the time in the late 20s when Americans still went there and Hitler could be shrugged off as a passing noise that needn't disturb dedicated dancers. The story line is willing to embrace everything from Jew baiting to abortion, but it has elected to wrap its arms around all that was troubling and all that was intolerable with a demonic grin, an insidious slink, and the painted-on charm that keeps revelers up until midnight making false faces at the hangman.

Master of Ceremonies Joel Grey is cheerful, charming, soulless and conspiratorially wicked. In a pink vest, with sunburst eyes gleaming out of a cold-cream face, he is the silencer of bad dreams, the gleeful puppet of pretended joy, sin on a string.

Under choreographer Ronald Field's beautifully malicious management, Mr. Grey is superb, as are the four girls who bang at instruments and call themselves the Kit Kat Klub Kittens, and the unending supply of tenors to give an Irish lilt ("Tomorrow Belongs to Me") to a contrapuntal pause in the tacky, rattling, bizarre and bankrupt goings-on. With the exception of an unlucky last song for landlady Lotte Lenya, the John Kander-Fred Ebb tunes snatch up the melodic desperation of an era and make new, sprightly, high-voltage energy of it.

Miss Lenya has never been better, or if she has been, I don't believe it. Her suitor, Jack Gilford, makes his first-act wrap-up, a rapid-fire comic turn called "Meeskite," one of the treasures of the occasion.

We are left now with the evening's single, and all too obvious, mistake. One of the cabaret tables is empty, the table reserved for heroine Sally Bowles. Sally Bowles, as the narrative has it, is a fey, fetching, far-out lassie with a head full of driftwood and a heart she'd rather break than shackle. She is a temperament, and she needs a temperament to play her.

Producer-director Harold Prince, in a totally uncharacteristic lapse of judgment, has miscast a pretty but essentially flavorless ingenue, Jill Haworth, in the role. She is trim but neutral, a profile rather than a person, and given the difficult things "Cabaret" is trying to do, she is a damaging presence, worth no more to the show than her weight in mascara.

The style is there, though, driven like glistening nails into the musical numbers, and I think you'll find they make up for what's missing. ■

OCTOBER 6, 1967

'VILLAGE' THEATER NEARING REALITY

Lawrence Van Gelder

Between East Village and West, Joseph Papp is herding another idea through the gap between dream and reality. Behind the ancient red facade of the Astor Library at 425 Lafayette Street, the impresario of the New York Shakespeare Festival's Public Theater is casting a once moribund civic landmark in the role of a busy, living hive of theater and art.

On Oct. 17, with the opening of the rock 'n' roll musical "Hair," one third of Mr. Papp's structural goal for the old library—spared from demolition by the Landmarks Preservation Commission—will have been realized. "Hair" will play in the new 299-seat Florence Sutro Anspacher Theater, one of three that Mr. Papp hopes to have in operation inside the 249-foot-long building within the next 18 months.

If all goes according to plan, the Anspacher Theater, a three-quarter-round playhouse with a thrust stage and grid, will be joined by the 299-seat Estelle R. Newman Theater whose non-proscenium open stage—45 feet wide and 40 feet deep—will rival those of the Broadway theaters deemed best for musicals. In addition, there will be an experimental theater, which Mr. Papp now refers to as the Third Theater, with flexible seating for 150 to 175 people and a variety of lighting positions.

There are actors' tunnels circling the theater, prop spaces, a Green Room used for rehearsals, and a dressing room whose design reflects Mr. Papp's solicitude for his actors. Nearby are costume shops.

Correspondingly, there is a North Hall, in beige and white, with fine acoustics for music—especially strings—to be used for chamber and dance programs.

Mr. Papp also speaks of having a "jazz cave" somewhere in the building, and on a typical night when all is ready, audiences will have available an experimental play at twilight, two others in the Newman and Anspacher Theaters and art exhibitions and concerts.

Papp recalls that when he was campaigning for free Shakespeare in Central Park, he used to compare the idea to that of free public libraries. Now the headquarters of free Shakespeare and the home of the free library are one and the same.

"Maybe it's fate," said Mr. Papp. ■

OCTOBER 17, 1967

'Rosenkrantz and Guildenstern Are Dead': Worm's-Eye View of Tragedy

Clive Barnes

It is not only Hamlet who dies in "Hamlet." They also serve who only stand and wait. Tom Stoppard's play "Rosencrantz and Guildenstern Are Dead" is a very funny play about death. Very funny, very brilliant, very chilling; it has the dust of thought about it and the particles glitter excitingly in the theatrical air.

Mr. Stoppard uses as the basis for his play a very simple yet telling proposition; namely that although to Hamlet those twin-stemmed courtiers Rosencrantz and Guildenstern are of slight importance, and that to an audience of Shakespeare's play they are little but functionaries lent some color by a fairly dilatory playwright, Rosencrantz and Guildenstern are very important indeed to Rosencrantz and Guildenstern.

This theme is the play of "Hamlet" not seen through the eyes of Hamlet, or Claudius, or Ophelia or Gertrude, but a worm's-eye view of tragedy seen from the bewildered standpoint of Rosencrantz and Guildenstern.

From the start, the conversation of the title characters, full of Elizabethan school logic and flashes of metaphysical wit, is amusing but deliberately fatuous. Rosencrantz and Guildenstern are fools. When you come to think of it, they would have to be. Otherwise they might have been Hamlet.

As they talk, the suspicion crosses the mind (it is a play where you are encouraged to stand outside the action and let suspicions, thoughts, glimmers and insights criss-cross your understanding) that Mr. Stoppard is not only paraphrasing "Hamlet," but also throwing in a paraphrase of Samuel Beckett's "Waiting for Godot" for good measure. For this is antic lunacy with a sad, wry purpose. Like Beckett's tramps, these two silly, rather likable Elizabethan courtiers are trying to get through life with a little human dignity and perhaps here and there a splinter of comprehension.

Mr. Stoppard seems to see the action of his play unfolding like a juicy onion with strange layers of existence protectively wrapped around one another. There are plays here within plays—and Mr. Stoppard never lets us forget that his courtiers are not only characters in a life, but also characters in a play.

It is impossible to re-create the fascinating verbal tension of the play—Mr. Stoppard takes an Elizabethan pleasure in the sound of his own actors—or the ideas, suggestive, tantalizing that erupt through its texture. All this is something you must see and hear for yourself.

To an extent, the original British National Theater version has been reproduced here by its original and brilliant director, Derek Goldby. Helped by the tatterdemalion glories of Desmond Heeley's setting, the richness of his costumes, and Richard Pilbrow's tactfully imaginative lighting, the play looks very similar. But whereas the supporting players in London—the Hamlet, Claudius and the rest—could well have played their roles in Shakespeare as well as in Stoppard, here there is understandably less strength.

However, the mime roles of the players (expertly devised by Claude Chagrin) are superbly done, Paul Hecht is remarkably good as the chief Player (although I would have welcomed a touch more menace) and Brian Murray and John Wood provide virtuoso portrayals as Rosencrantz and Guildenstern.

This is a most remarkable and thrilling play. In one bound Mr. Stoppard is asking to be considered as among the finest English-speaking writers of our stage, for this is a work of fascinating distinction. Rosencrantz and Guildenstern LIVE! ■

OCTOBER 4, 1968

'GREAT WHITE HOPE' STARS JAMES EARL JONES

Clive Barnes

Howard Sackler's play "The Great White Hope" came into the Alvin Theater last night like a whirlwind, carrying with it, triumphantly, James Earl Jones. Indeed, to be honest I'm not sure that the whirlwind was not on the other foot, and that it was Mr. Jones who was doing some of the carrying—but about the triumph make no mistake.

Mr. Sackler has written a great part—a tragic hero, cheated, degraded and at last brutally beaten. But more than this, Mr. Sackler has used his hero, Jack Jefferson, a figure based closely on the first black heavyweight champion of the world, Jack Johnson, as a symbol in part of black aspiration. And white audiences are bound to feel white guilt—a guilt hardly lessened by the treatment meted out to the present Black Muslim heavyweight champion, Muhammad Ali.

The play has an epic scope and range to it. It picks up the Johnson story soon after that Australian day in 1908 when Johnson whipped Tommy Burns to win the championship and takes it to Havana in 1915, when Jess Willard, the great white hope, won it back for the whites—at least for a time.

Very properly Mr. Sackler does not stick to the letter of history—at the end, for example, his hero, all but battered to a pulp, is fairly and squarely beaten, having resisted offers to throw the fight. Certainly Willard did not beat the real Johnson so effectively, yet Mr. Sackler is here dealing with playwriting and not prizefighting and he is right.

He has also whitewashed his hero, and it is here perhaps a fault of the play that, apart from his pride, Jack Jefferson is almost too good, too noble, to be true. And while we are fault-picking the play—although trimmed a little since I first saw it at the Arena Stage in Washington—is still too long, and sprawlingly constructed. But this now hardly matters at all in the face of the play's tempestuous merits, and the opportunities it gives not only to its baffled bull of a hero but also to the white girl who chooses to share his degradation.

It is in this relationship, warm and yet finally corrosive, that the play finds its heart, for it lies at the nub of Jack's anger and rejection. This forbidden love is also the visible gesture of defiance that Jack throws out to the white world and—through a Mann Act prosecution—his downfall.

> **The play has an epic scope . . .**

The play moves faster and crisper than it did in Washington, although the director, Edwin Sherin (who shares fully in the triumph with Mr. Sackler and Mr. Jones), is the same, as, very rightly, is much of the cast. It is Mr. Sherin's sheer skill that keeps the play interlocking so neatly, adding up to a fast series of something like cinematic takes, and he uses this pace to build up a fine and oddly convincing picture of America and Americans at the beginning of the century.

Of the vast supporting cast—the play is the size of a musical—two splendid characterizations stand out, Lou Gilbert as the seedy but decent little Jewish manager and, most remarkably, Jane Alexander as Jack's girl Ellie.

As I was leaving the theater Mr. Jones was receiving a standing ovation of the kind that makes Broadway history. If I had had the time I would have stayed to cheer. He deserved it.

MARCH 30, 1969

Mother Is at Home at La Mama

Patricia Bosworth

The other afternoon, in a grimy little coffee shop on East 4th Street, Ellen Stewart sat talking with some of her La Mama playwrights. Whenever their voices rose, she would hold up her hand so that a dozen gold bracelets slid down to her elbow, and she would say, "You listen to Mother, hear?" And the playwrights would stop arguing and listen.

Everybody in the East Village knows that Ellen Stewart, doyenne of Off Off Broadway, has been having urgent financial problems with her theater. Every struggling actor and poet knows that for the past eight years, in spite of those financial problems plus a few with Equity and the building authorities, Miss Stewart has managed to put on workshop productions of 200 new plays in her avant-garde theater "club." Audiences have gladly paid $1 "membership dues" to see shows like Rochelle Owens's "Futz," Jean-Claude van Itallie's "America Hurrah," Lanford Wilson's "The Rimers of Eldritch" and Megan Terry's "Viet Rock."

The original Cafe La Mama was a basement, the second a loft, the third a rehearsal hall. Last year, when the Ford and Rockefeller Foundations came through with grants totaling $90,000, Miss Stewart was able to move from her cramped quarters above a dry cleaners at 122 Second Avenue and achieve her dream—a permanent headquarters—in a spacious building at 74 East Fourth Street. There she will have not one but two theaters; the first will open Wednesday night, the second Thursday.

Four months ago, Miss Stewart became seriously ill and went into the hospital. When she was released, she discovered that work on her new building was nowhere near completion and the foundation money had long since been used up. All over the city actors were rehearsing plays to be done at La Mama but the building contractors weren't promising to have it ready. Even more upsetting, in her absence, some of the La Mama troupe had begun

(cont'd. on next page)

(cont'd. from previous page)
squabbling among themselves. "We can take anything," said actress-playwright Julie Bovasso, "No food, very little sleep and poor rehearsal conditions but we need to know *she's* around."

Rochelle Owens put it this way: "Ellen is the love-energy of La Mama."

So that afternoon Miss Stewart met with her playwrights in the East Fourth Street coffee shop and let loose some "love energy." Eventually all the problems were solved and Miss Stewart seemed relieved. "Did I forget anything?" she demanded. No answer. "All right, then, happy now? Shoo!" Everybody got up, collected scripts and pencils, and left her to her coffee.

"This is part of my day," she explained. "Dealing with my children. I call them my children, my babies, my biddies. My playwrights. I possess them until they don't need me any more. Playwrights should be treated with utmost care, you know, or they can die. They are such delicate, perishable creatures.

"In our culture playwrights can be eaten alive by the success-failure syndrome. I've never believed in long runs for that reason. The ability to create is a dangerous and wonderful thing."

She paused reflectively. "What does La Mama need most?" I asked. She laughed. "Money," she said, "$25,000. We need, we need, we need!"

"I remember when Sam Shepard and Paul Foster and I repaired the plumbing in one of the La Mama theaters and then everything flushed the wrong way. I remember when the Buildings Department gave me 9 days to put in $9,000 worth of electrical wiring, so Robert Patrick got 30 playwrights to write 3-minute skits for a show to raise the money. The revue was entitled 'Bang' and everybody stayed up 5 days straight rehearsing and then between performances the actors would come out and literally beg the audience for money.

"But I'm proud of what's come out of it all," said Miss Stewart. "I'm proud that Lanford Wilson's 'Balm in Gilead' has been published and 'Futz' is being made into a movie and Tom O'Horgan's direction of 'Hair' on Broadway has been so innovational. Isn't that the point of La Mama—to see projects bear fruit? I guess you could say La Mama is my raison d'étre. Living a life is a great privilege. To find out your *reason* for living—I'm very lucky." ■

APRIL 30, 1968

'Hair' Is Fresh and Frank

Clive Barnes

A scene from the Broadway musical "Hair," 1968.

What is so likable about "Hair," that tribal-rock musical that last night completed its trek from downtown, via a discothèque, and landed, positively panting with love and smelling of sweat and flowers, at the Biltmore Theater? I think it is simply that it is so likable. So new, so fresh and so unassuming, even in its pretensions.

The authors of the originally dowdy book—and brilliant lyrics—have done a very brave thing. They have in effect done away with that book altogether. "Hair" is now a musical with a theme, not with a story. Nor is this all that has been done in this totally new, all lit-up, gas-fired, speed-marketed Broadway version. For one thing it has been made a great deal franker. In fact it has been made into the frankest show in town—and this has been a season not noticeable for its verbal or visual reticence.

A great many four-letter words, such as "love," are used very freely. At one point—in what is later affectionately referred to as "the nude scene"—a number of men and women (I should have counted) are seen totally nude and full, as it were, face.

Frequent references—frequent approving references—are made to the expanding benefits of drugs. Homosexuality is not frowned upon. The American flag is not desecrated—that would be a Federal offense, wouldn't it?—but it is used in a manner that not everyone would call respectful. Christian ritual also comes in for a bad time, the authors approve enthusiastically of miscegenation, and one enterprising lyric catalogues somewhat arcane sexual practices more familiar to the pages of the "Kama Sutra" than The New York Times. So there—you have been warned. Oh yes, they also hand out flowers.

This is a happy show musically. Galt MacDermot's music is merely pop-rock, with strong soothing overtones of Broadway melody, but it precisely serves its purpose, and its noisy and cheerful conservatism is just right for an audience that might wince at "Sergeant Pepper's Lonely Hearts Club Band," while the Stones would certainly gather no pop moss.

Yet with the sweet and subtle lyrics of Gerome Ragni and James Rado, the show is the first Broadway musical in some time to have the authentic voice of today rather than the day before yesterday. Robin Wagner's beautiful junk-art setting is as masterly as Nancy Potts's cleverly tattered and colorful, turned-on costumes. And then there is Tom O'Horgan's always irreverent, occasionally irrelevant staging—which is sheer fun.

Mr. O'Horgan makes the show vibrate from the first slow-burn opening—with half naked hippies statuesquely slow-parading down the center isle—to the all-hands-together, anti-patriotic finale.

But the essential likability of the show is to be found in its attitudes and in its cast. You probably don't have to be a supporter of Eugene McCarthy to love it, but I wouldn't give it much chance among the adherents of Governor Reagan. The attitudes will annoy many people, but as long as Thoreau is part of America's heritage, others will respond to this musical that marches to a different drummer. ■

DECEMBER 20, 1969

Dr. Freud Depicted in Dance

Don McDonagh

During the first act Thursday night I thought that I had stumbled in on a stranger's group therapy session. During the second, I recognized Meredith Monk's mother talking to herself and was reassured that it indeed was the Brooklyn Academy of Music and Robert Wilson's production "The Life and Times of Sigmund Freud."

The work described itself as a dance play in three acts but any resemblance to plays was purely coincidental. A stranger strolled by during the first intermission and asked whether I had any idea of what was going on. "Very little," I had to confess.

The dance play was divided into three parts, like Gaul, the unconscious mind and most traditional plays. Each was laid out in a surrealistic manner that at times showed a keenly sensitive eye for striking visual balances—like a Dali painting come to life—but over-all was baffling.

The first part was a beach scene at the dawn of the world or some other momentous time, and people wandered back and forth and a turtle was dragged through the sand. The procession of people was made with slow and weighty movement. At the end of the act a woman in black placed an Egyptian figurine on a table.

In the second act, set in a large study, a figure sat in a chair with his back to the audience. The room slowly filled with people doing their individually nutty thing: Three men were intent on a nonsensical board game and changed sides to keep any advantage in position to a minimum. And a woman played the piano. At the end, a lumbering set of four hairy legs promenaded across the stage after which the man in the chair placed a Chinese figurine on the waiting table.

The last section was set in a Dada-esque barn full of bears, tigers and other wildlife. It ended with a little boy crying and Sigmund Freud staring at the objects that had been left on the table. He wandered in through every scene and at last came to rest. The staging had a bizarre charm but the story line I think would only be clear to an analyst.

SEPTEMBER 26, 1960

NIXON AND KENNEDY CLASH IN TV DEBATE ON SPENDING, FARMS AND SOCIAL ISSUES

Russell Baker

Richard Nixon and John F. Kennedy during the first televised presidential debate, 1960.

CHICAGO, Sept. 26—Vice President Nixon and Senator John F. Kennedy argued genteelly tonight in history's first nationally televised debate between Presidential candidates.

The two men, confronting each other in a Chicago television studio, centered their argument on which candidate and which party offered the nation the best means for spurring United States growth in an era of international peril.

In one of the sharper exchanges of the hour-long encounter, Mr. Nixon charged that the Democratic domestic program advanced by Senator Kennedy would cost the taxpayers from $13,200,000,000 to $18,000,000,000.

This meant, Mr. Nixon contended, that "either he will have to raise taxes or you have to unbalance the budget."

Unbalancing the budget, he went on, would mean another period of inflation and a consequent "blow" to the country's aged living on pension income.

"That," declared Senator Kennedy, in one of the evening's few shows of incipient heat, "is wholly wrong, wholly in error." Mr. Nixon, he said, was attempting to create the impression that he was "in favor of unbalancing the budget."

In fact, Mr. Kennedy contended, many of his programs for such things as medical care for the aged, natural resources development, Federal assistance to school construction and teachers salaries could be financed without undue burden on the taxpayer if his policies for increasing the rate of economic growth were adopted.

"I don't believe in big government, but I believe in effective government," Mr. Kennedy said. "I think we can do a better job. I think we are going to have to do a better job."

For the most part, the exchanges were distinguished by a suavity, earnestness and courtesy that suggested that the two men were more concerned about "image projection" to their huge television audience than about scoring debating points.

Senator Kennedy, using no television makeup, rarely smiled during the hour and maintained an expression of gravity suitable for a candidate for the highest office in the land.

Mr. Nixon, wearing pancake makeup to cover his dark beard, smiled more frequently as he made his points and dabbed frequently at the perspiration that beaded out on his chin.

The debate was carried simultaneously by all three major television networks, the American Broadcasting Company, the National Broadcasting Company and the Columbia Broadcasting System. It was also carried by the radio networks of all three and that of the Mutual Broadcasting System.

The first debate, produced by C.B.S., took place in a big studio at the C.B.S. Chicago outlet, Station WBBM-TV. Studio One, in which they met, was sealed off from the hundreds who swarmed through its corridors and sat in adjoining studios to watch the show on station monitors.

When the debate was over, the two candidates were spirited out of the studio through a freight driveway. At his hotel later, Mr. Nixon was noncommittal about how well he thought he had done. "A debater," he said, "never knows who wins. That will be decided by the people Nov. 8."

Mr. Kennedy was not available for comment, but his advisers said they were elated over his performance.

The only persons permitted in the studio besides television crewmen were two wire service reporters, three photographers and one aide to each candidate.

When the show ended, each man was asked how he felt about the outcome.

"A good exchange of views," said Mr. Nixon.

"We had an exchange of views," Mr. Kennedy agreed. ■

OCTOBER 4, 1960

Andy Griffith Down Home

Homespun humor and an occasional heart-throb are the principal ingredients in "The Andy Griffith Show," which began last night over Channel 2. The humor is entrusted chiefly to Mr. Griffith, portraying an amiable country sheriff; Don Knotts, a timid deputy; and Frances Bavier, a baffled housekeeper. Ronny Howard, as a mischievous, motherless boy, provides the poignancy, and he's a clever little scene-stealer. Altogether, however, "The Andy Griffith Show" appears to be only mildly entertaining.

Andy Griffith as Sheriff Andy Taylor, Jim Nabors as Gomer Pyle, Ron Howard as Opie Taylor and Don Knotts as Deputy Barney Fife in "The Andy Griffith Show."

MAY 10, 1961

F.C.C. HEAD BIDS TV MEN REFORM 'VAST WASTELAND'

Val Adams

WASHINGTON, May 9—Newton N. Minow, the new chairman of the Federal Communications Commission, presented a scorching indictment of contemporary television at the National Association of Broadcasters convention today.

Addressing more than 2,000 broadcasters, Mr. Minow described TV's program output as a "vast wasteland." He excoriated the amount of violence and mediocrity in shows and said the F. C. C. would no longer automatically renew station licenses.

He called upon viewers to speak up at public hearings that he plans to hold at the community level when a station's license is up for renewal. Calling for diversification in programming, Mr. Minow invited each station operator to view his station's programs for one day, from sign-on to sign-off.

"You will see," he said, "a procession of game shows, violence, audience participation shows, formula comedies about totally unbelievable families, blood and thunder, mayhem, violence, sadism, murder, Western bad men, Western good men, private eyes, gangsters, more violence and cartoons. And, endlessly, commercials—many screaming, cajoling and offending. And most of all, boredom. True, you will see a few things you will enjoy. But they will be very, very few."

Mr. Minow acknowledged that a Western show draws a larger audience than a symphony, but said "it is not enough to cater to the nation's whims—you must also serve the nation's needs."

"For every hour that the people give you—you owe them something," the F. C. C. chief told the broadcasters. "I intend to see that your debt is paid with service."

Many broadcasters admitted that they were indignant over the speech, but many reserved comment until they had studied its text. The only network comment came from Leonard H. Goldenson, president of American Broadcastings-Paramount Theatres, owner of the American Broadcasting Company.

(cont'd. on next page)

(cont'd. from previous page)

He said it was a "courageous speech" and expressed the hope that the F. C. C. would enhance competition by authorizing more outlets in cities with only two TV stations.

The 35-year-old Mr. Minow, a former law partner of Adlai E. Stevenson, asserted that "the squandering of our air waves is no less important than the lavish waste of any precious natural resource."

Declaring that children spend as much time watching television as they do in the schoolroom, Mr. Minow told broadcasters they should do more to "enlarge the capacities of our children."

"If parents, teachers and ministers conducted their responsibilities by following the ratings," Mr. Minow said, "children would have a steady diet of ice cream, school holidays and no Sunday school. What about your responsibilities? Is there no room on television to teach, to inform, to uplift, to stretch, to enlarge the capacities of our children?"

In discussing his plan for community hearings on the renewal of a TV license, Mr. Minow said:

"When a renewal is set down for hearing, I intend—whenever possible—to hold a well-advertised public hearing, right in the community you have promised to serve. I want the people who own the air and the homes that television enters to tell you and the F. C. C. what's been going on."

Looking ahead to global television, Mr. Minow said that we cannot permit television in its present form to be our voice overseas."

"What will people of other countries think of us when they see our Western badmen and good men punching each other in the jaw in between the shooting?" he asked. "What will the Latin-American or African child learn of America from our great communications industry?" ■

NOVEMBER 21, 1962

Merv Griffin Enlivens Daytime

Jack Gould

Television host Merv Griffin talking with audience members, 1963.

Much the liveliest interlude in daytime television this season is the 55-minute period with Merv Griffin, the gentleman of engaging manner who somehow manages to persuade all types of celebrities to come out in the midday overcast.

It will be recalled that during the interval between Jack Parr and Johnny Carson on the "Tonight" show it was Mr. Griffin who far and away was the most successful stand in. Now at 2 o'clock, Mondays through Fridays, on Channel 4, he is fulfilling the same role in his own behalf and bringing to the drabness of early-afternoon video a touch of substance, fun and glamour.

In format, Mr. Griffin's show is identical with "Tonight" save for the number of commercials, which seems even greater. But Mr. Griffin has his own attributes; he can sing a bit on the side but more especially he is an alert interviewer with a feeling for the possibility of a gag, is good at asking questions that may lead somewhere and is particularly adept at keeping conversation afloat.

Presumably, the National Broadcasting Company is showing a generous budgetary attitude toward Mr. Griffin because the hour is one way to demonstrate color-TV sets in department stores. But on his own, the host has managed to make the program something of a stopping place for a wide variety of individuals, apparently because it does enjoy a relaxed leeway in subject matter.

On several occasions, Danny Kaye has disported himself to fine effect on the show, and Merriman Smith, the White House correspondent for United Press International, has demonstrated that a newspaperman, after all, can be as amusing on his feet as on paper. This afternoon Pierre Salinger, the White House press secretary, is scheduled to be the guest.

Yesterday afternoon's program was typical of a guest line-up decidedly unusual in daytime variety. Anne Bancroft, the actress, talked of her pride in the Actors Studio and her singing contributions to the Perry Como Show; actress she is and, now it may be added, siren as well. Harvey Lembeck amusingly resisted any and all plugs for the Actors Studio.

Florence Henderson was on hand for a delightful song, and a young comedian, Stanley Miron Handelman, for a patter of calculated hesitancy. Xavier Cugat led the orchestra with his pipe in his mouth; the corncob rhumba, as it were. ■

JUNE 21, 1964

'FUGITIVE' IS SOMEONE TO ROOT FOR

Paul Gardner

Two handcuffed men sit side-by-side on a rushing train. The fellow with the worried look is Dr. Richard Kimble, accused of slaying his wife and now en route to the Big House. Suddenly the train leaps off the track, passenger cars plow into each other and Kimble, miraculously freed, is running breathlessly away.

For the last nine months, Kimble, the hero of the American Broadcasting Company's weekly series, "The Fugitive," has been running across the country in a chase-within-a-chase story that has all the built-in suspense of the old time serials at the neighborhood movie palace. Viewers presumably can be confident that the fleeing physician will not be caught for years since "The Fugitive" has emerged as one of the season's durable shows.

Always keeping one jump ahead of his pursuer, Kimble, who would like to establish his innocence, never has the time: Besides being in search of a one-armed man who he believes did away with Mrs. Kimble, the hardy physician is constantly involved with maidens in distress, mentally disturbed husbands, hoodlums and assorted individuals determined to make his life a sporting one.

The success of "The Fugitive," filmed on appropriately spooky ranches, roads, harbors and construction sites, lies in the All-American paradox. An honest man is on the run from the law and society. His personal happiness is constantly threatened by outside forces, so he must, by choice, be a loner.

This theme appeals to male viewers trapped in their own Big House. Within these suburban prisons, inmates can feel rapport with the unjustly accused underdog; he is someone to root for.

In the upcoming episode on Tuesday at 10 P.M., Kimball, played by David Janssen, is quietly trying to lose himself in a construction gang. Danger arises when a retarded teenage youth seeks his sympathy and once again Kimball must be on the run.

"People identify heavily with Kimball," says producer Alan Armer. "We get letters asking us to give him a second chance, to let him find the one-armed man and return to his medical practice. And I've never worked on a show before that brought in so many unsolicited scripts. Everyone seems to have escape ideas, especially little ladies. If only some of the stories were any good!"

Next season "The Fugitive" will explore the circumstantial evidence that would have sent Kimball to jail, a situation remarkably similar to the real-life Samuel Sheppard murder trial in which a bushy-haired man allegedly figured as the missing assailant instead of a one-armed killer.

"The Fugitive" has done as much for Janssen's career as "Ben Casey," "Gunsmoke" "Wyatt Earp," and "Have Gun, Will Travel," did for Vince Edwards, James Arness, Hugh O'Brian and Richard Boone, respectively.

Like Janssen, these actors flopped in Hollywood, were relegated to B-pictures, and finally found their metier as heroes of TV serials. This year Janssen and "The Fugitive" won TV Guide's popularity poll.

Publicists for the program claim that Kimble is a living person to Janssen, who is quoted as saying, "I must put myself completely into the character to make him believable." Even TV stars are obviously aware of The Method. ■

JULY 15, 1964

TV IS PREPARING A MONSTER RALLY

Paul Gardner

The situation horror show apparently will set the trend this fall in competing with television's situation comedies.

Two tongue-in-check monster serials, "The Munsters" and "The Addams Family," and one comedy about witchcraft, "Bewitched," will be given their debuts In September. In "The Living Doll," Julie Newmar will portray a robot designed by a diabolical scientist.

The executive producer of "The Munsters" said yesterday that the horror shows were probably going to become the new vogue. "Horror films have enjoyed a big success in movies," Joseph Connelly said, "and I think they'll go on TV."

The characters in "The Munsters" include Dracula, Dracula's daughter, Frankenstein and his beautiful niece. "They are contemporary people—good people," Mr. Connelly added. "Their problem is the way they look."

"The Munsters" will be carried by the Columbia Broadcasting System. One of the little Munsters, who disapproves of Thanksgiving dinner rituals, asks, "Whoever thought of sitting around and eating a dead bird?"

The American Broadcasting Company will produce "Bewitched" and "The Addams Family." Carolyn Jones will play Morticia Addams, the ashen-faced heroine.

"Ours really isn't a horror show," David Levy, executive producer insisted. "Our people have red blood. They're—well, bizarre. We aren't giving the Addams house an excessively cobwebby look. The atmosphere is pleasant. We are reaching for an audience of children and adults." The characters are based on the cartoon figures of Charles Addams.

In "Bewitched," Elizabeth Montgomery will play a housewife who is a witch—in the literal sense. Her husband is an ordinary mortal.

"We see it as a very human comedy about a marriage," Harry Ackerman, executive producer, reported. "Except, in this marriage, the poor wife is trying to kick the witching habit." ■

witchcraft

SEPTEMBER 15, 1964

JOHNSON AND GOLDWATER LAUNCH TELEVISION CAMPAIGNS

Nan Robertson

WASHINGTON, Sept. 14 — Shortly before 11 Saturday night, a little girl licking an ice cream cone appeared on millions of television screens all over America.

While the little girl concentrated on her ice cream, a woman's voice, tender and protective, told her that people used to explode atomic bombs in the air, and that the radioactive fallout made children die.

The voice then told of the treaty preventing all but underground nuclear tests, and how a man who wants to be President of the United States voted against it.

"His name is Barry Goldwater," she said. "So if he's elected, they might start testing all over again."

A crescendo of Geiger-counter clicks almost drowned out the last words; then came the male announcer's tag-line:

"Vote for President Johnson on November third. The stakes are too high for you to stay home."

The war of political television commercials has begun, with the first Democratic spot in the same vein last Monday, the second Saturday night. The Republican National Committee began its TV campaign today.

All indications are that the Democrats are first trying to scare the voters with the idea that Senator Goldwater, the Republican nominee, opposed the nuclear treaty, and then to impress them with the Democratic record; and that the Republicans will first try to soothe the mothers about Mr. Goldwater and then impress them with the Republican record.

Today the Republicans led off with a five-minute TV spot seen in 187 cities. The theme was that their party was "the party of peace through strength." An announcer's voice mentioned "failures at the wall of shame in Berlin," and failures at the Bay of Pigs in Cuba and in Vietnam. Senator Goldwater then came on to declare that "Communism is the only great threat to the peace."

"Some distort this proper concern to make it appear that we are preoccupied with war. There is no greater political lie," he said.

"I am trying to carry to the American people this plain message. This entire nation and the entire world risk war in our time unless free men remain strong enough to keep the peace."

The Republicans have based their entire advertising campaign on the conviction that television is Senator Goldwater's best medium and President Johnson's worst. They are thus planning extensive use of television in the campaign.

Only three spots have been seen so far by the public, but the attacks on the advertising have already begun. The Republicans have charged that the Democrats are presenting "horror-type" commercials that frighten and disgust adults. The advertisement of Monday night a week ago began with a little girl plucking daisy petals and ended with a nuclear blast.

Today, the Republican National Chairman Dean Burch filed a formal complaint with the Fair Campaign Practices Committee about last Monday's spot.

"This horror-type commercial is designed to arouse basic emotions and has no place in this campaign," he said. "I demand you call on the President to halt this smear attack on a United States Senator and the candidate of the Republican party for the Presidency."

The Democrats have replied that everything Mr. Goldwater has said and done on the subject of atomic weapons and their control is terrifying enough.

However, even viewers describing themselves as "loyal Democrats" have written the national committee complaining that the first television spot was "too hard-hitting."

Mr. Wright said that the Democratic advertisements would move soon into the positive area of President Johnson's accomplishments—"peace, prosperity and legislative progress."

The Republicans plan to stress the idea of "Peace Through Strength" and that Mr. Johnson has not debated with Mr. Goldwater on television. ■

SEPTEMBER 25, 1964

'THE MUNSTERS': HORRIBLY ENGAGING

Jack Gould

There is not the slightest doubt how youngsters and probably a good many of their elders will begin their television viewing on Thursday night; it will be with "The Munsters" and, more particularly, with Fred Gwynne as the most engaging and amusing Frankenstein monster ever to reach the screen.

The filmed series is inspired offbeat nonsense that will disarm everyone who thought an era of horror might be descending on TV; "The Munsters" is designed for fun and offers classic spooks in a new dimension. The ghouls who made their debut last night on the Columbia Broadcasting System are an eminently wholesome lot in search of nothing more than a congenial family life in the suburban community to which they have moved. It is the rest of the world that doesn't understand their distinctive problems.

The creators of "The Munsters"—Norm Leibmann, Ed Haas, Al Burns and Chris Hayward—have the right approach, the approach that was so completely missing from "The Addams Family." Herman Munster, the head of the house; Lily, the vampire-looking spouse beset by household chores, and Grandpa Munster, an erstwhile Dracula who does not realize he has passed his prime, take their physical appearances for granted and see nothing unusual in the grotesque and macabre decor that distinguishes their home. In never suggesting its premise needs an explanation, "The Munsters" has a head start. A workable subplot enables the Munsters to bridge plausibly the gap between their existence and the more familiar life of their neighbors. Marilyn Munster, played by Beverly Owen, is a highly videogenic niece who is at ease in both worlds and finds herself caught in the midst of the conflicting interpretations of normality. In the weeks ahead the device should enable the program to make unlimited commentary on

SEPTEMBER 8, 1967

SALLY FIELD PORTRAYS A 'FLYING NUN'

Jack Gould

The program with an instant box-office title, "The Flying Nun," looks headed for a downdraft. The idea of doing a situation comedy about a sprightly novice in and around a Puerto Rican convent is strong on novelty value and not without considerable possibilities for obtaining winning qualities of amusement and charm; these potential values are still there.

But the addition of the gimmick of having the nun fly through the air like an ecumenical glider turned last night's premiere into basically a one-joke event. If a viewer has seen a single installment of "The Flying Nun" there would seem the danger that he has seen them all.

The new attraction of the American Broadcasting Company's network is derived more or less from "The 15th Pelican," a short novel by Mrs. Tere Rios. With the success of the airborne Mary Poppins obviously in mind, the producer decided to combine the enduring appeal of a nun with aeronautical make-believe. The pitfall occurred when Sister Bertrille went aloft and the dividend was only a gimmick followed by stereotyped Hollywood goings on. The program's creators and writers succumbed at the crucial moment to the most prevalent of popular TV's failings: the use of a larger than life stunt to avoid hard work at the typewriter.

The perky Sally Field is portraying the 90-pound American novice who discovers that the birdlike design of the coronet of the convent order permits a takeoff when the wind is right. She uses her flight capabilities for generally noble purposes but predictably suffers a forced landing in a secret American military base on a remote island.

Thereafter the sprouting of melodramatic corn knows no denominational distinctions.

On the ground, the ebullient Miss Field's portrayal of Sister Bertrille has decided long-range potential. In the young novice's unorthodox pep and vigor in enlisting the outside world's support for the convent's educational and hospital endeavors, there are the makings of a pleasant and diverting demonstration of the adaptability of the church to the modern age. In the byplay with a bemused senior nun, played very effectively by Marge Redmond, and in the compassionate sternness of the mother superior, played by Madeleine Sherwood, there are the ingredients for a very human comedy in an uncommon environment.

In the earthbound sequences, which largely revolve around Sister Bertrille outwitting a rich Caribbean playboy preoccupied by long weekends with delectable dishes, the dialogue did contain a few light, offbeat lines that capitalized on the religious setting without offense. With many factors working in favor of "The Flying Nun," a viewer can only hope that the business of self-propelled flight does not overshadow all else. ■

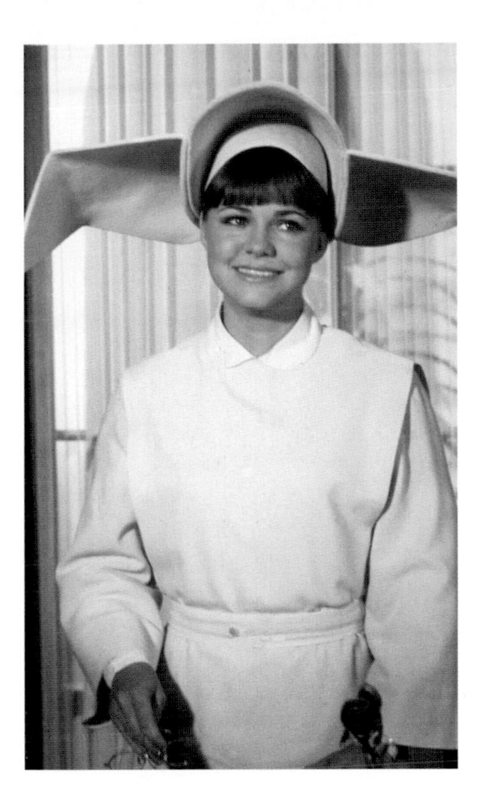

Sally Field as Sister Bertrille in "The Flying Nun," 1969.

SEPTEMBER 12, 1967

Carol Burnett Outshines Her Writers

George Gent

Carol Burnett and guest star Lucille Ball on "The Carol Burnett Show," September 23, 1967.

Carol Burnett, whose new show made its debut on the Columbia Broadcasting System last night (Channel 2 at 10 P.M.), is luckier than most of her brothers and sisters in the new situation comedy series.

(cont'd. on next page)

NOVEMBER 8, 1967

Johnson Signs Bill Creating Nonprofit TV Agency

Robert B. Semple Jr.

WASHINGTON, Nov. 7—President Johnson signed into law today a bill creating a nonprofit public corporation to accelerate the growth and improve the quality of noncommercial television.

The bill, which is regarded in Government and in industry circles as a measure of immense potential significance for the medium, establishes a Corporation for Public Broadcasting. The corporation's first major responsibility will be to channel funds to noncommercial radio and television stations, program production groups and educational television networks to stimulate the further development of programs of high quality.

The bill authorizes $9 million in fiscal 1968 for this purpose. The money, however, has not actually been appropriated by Congress. But if the funds are, in fact, made available—and the President and his aides are cautiously hopeful that they will be—they would represent the first Federal funds earmarked specifically for the support of the operation of noncommercial television stations and the content of their programs.

Mr. Johnson was in good humor, mixing solemn judgments on the significance of the measure with an occasional quip. He was effusive in his praise for the members of Congress, Administration officials and private citizens who had worked for noncommercial television.

The President announced after his remarks the appointment of the first two members of the board. They are Dr. Milton Eisenhower, brother of former President Eisenhower and president emeritus of John Hopkins University, and Dr. James Killian, chairman of the Corporation of the Massachusetts Institute of Technology.

The major question that pervaded the day's ceremonies was the unspoken question of money. There has been some feeling here that Mr. Johnson's requests may be caught in the economy wave and the legislative turmoil generated by the war in Vietnam.

However, the corporation is authorized to receive private contributions, and when Mr. Johnson finished his talk the president of the Carnegie Corporation of New York, Alan Pifer, rose and announced that his organization was pledging $1 million to support the new broadcasting corporation. A similar contribution had also been pledged earlier by the Columbia Broadcasting System. The United Auto Workers have also pledged $25,000 and the Communications Workers of America $100,000. ■

(cont'd. from previous page)
She can, if she so chooses, escape from the cage of banality her Hollywood-based writers have prepared for her.

On the record, Miss Burnett was at her best during her opening dialogue with members of the audience, where her imaginative comic talents were allowed free rein and she was able to improvise as the situation warranted.

Miss Burnett, who has more stops in her comic lute than most of the high-priced funny men around, got only minimal help from her writers during the rest of the show, although she did perform a devastating and hilarious take-off of Shirley Temple that the California Democrats might consider using as a campaign document. Jim Nabors, the star of C.B.S.'s "Gomer Pyle, U.S.M.C.," contributed his fine baritone to several numbers on the show and assisted in several skits. But the show depends entirely on Miss Burnett's multiple talents, and these may not be enough if she doesn't get some help from her writers. ■

APRIL 14, 1968

FAR RIGHT, FAR LEFT—FAR OUT

Calvin Kentfield

"Let's face it, we've got a hit show." The speaker was Dan Rowan, "straight man" of the team of Rowan and Martin, whose prime-time (Mondays at 8 P.M.) comedy hour, "Rowan and Martin's Laugh-In," has N.B.C. brass in helpless giggles. The brass may not like the jokes but they love the ratings, which currently put the two comics and their crew in fifth place. Dick Martin, the "dumb" partner, was dressed in casual white, including a white turtleneck draped with a rawhide thong supporting a large brass ankh-like ornament—a gift from Sammy Davis and an emblem of the marijuana cause. Rowan wore a huge embroidered Peace symbol on his blue blazer, instead of an old-school or family crest.

Martin passed me the latest statistical intelligence from N.B.C. announcing that their particular Monday-night silliness was once again preferred by viewers over the silliness available on C.B.S. ("Gunsmoke" and "The Lucy Show") and A.B.C. ("Cowboy in Africa" and "Rat Patrol"). Knocking out Lucy has been a rough go, but everybody's happy now.

"How long do you think this will last?" I asked.

The answer was a shrug. Two shrugs.

The fact that they are doing what they call "just comedy" is the very thing that has shoved them so precipitately from the pan into the red-hot coals of success. That and George Schlatter, their producer, who really got the show going and keeps it going. "We could have done a usual," Rowan said. "You know, guest singers, those dancers—but what's the point? We got all these crazy kids and writers and put them all together and came up with a show that's strictly television. It couldn't be anything else. And the pace of the show. It never stops. I think that's the secret, you never know what's going to happen."

For anybody who has never witnessed a "Laugh-In," it can come as quite a shock. Even Jonathan Winters (who, given his head, can be the funniest man alive) has been tamed and contained by a big time network format that gives him little chance to cut loose, whereas the "Laugh-In" seems truly wild and uninhibited by comparison. And it really is the "Laugh-

NOVEMBER 23, 1969

This 'Sesame' May Open the Right Doors

Jack Gould

The new program called "Sesame Street" understandably and deservedly has prompted cheers from the parents of preschool children. With high professional skill in using the techniques of television to woo youngsters into an awareness of the alphabet, numbers, healthy social relationships, lessons in logic and thoughtful behavior, the Children's Television Workshop has embarked on a six-month experiment that quite conceivably could have a larger influence on the home screen.

With the initial support of Alan Pifer, president of the Carnegie Corporation, the lively and attractive Mrs. Joan Ganz Cooney, executive director of the Workshop, quietly junked all the accepted norms of video and embarked on a pioneering course. Now financed to the tune of $8 million over two years, with $1 million sensibly set aside to evaluate the end results, the Workshop set out to discover what was a public TV need from the social and educational standpoint, rather than surrender to the typed TV that just drifts along with the mob in hopes of garnering high ratings and income.

"Sesame Street" has the inherent excitement of a bold and constructive venture aimed at ascertaining some facts about the wants and interests of preschoolers, but it is with a feeling of helplessness that an adult tries to assess the potential impact of the Children's Television Workshop. When dealing with 12 million prekindergarten youngsters, generalizations simply don't work. The children of highly educated and affluent parents may have quite a different reaction from underprivileged youngsters whose mothers and fathers may have difficulty in reading.

On a large scale, the country's reward may be a social document of infinite value in education. Were the goals of "Sesame Street" to be duplicated on a classroom basis the cost would run upward of $3 billion, the project would take years and there would never be enough trained teachers.

What Mrs. Cooney has done is take the mobile appeal of television and adapt it to techniques that have been used for generations in books for preschoolers. The program is rather clearly intended for the underprivileged child whose family cannot afford private nurseries, though it is also being shown in publicly operated day-care centers. The use of a cast of blacks and whites is one of its most attractive features. Children are the true nobility of interracial tolerance—theirs is the rapport of honest

(cont'd. on next page)

The cast members of "Sesame Street" during their inaugural season. From left, Will Lee, Matt Robinson, Bob McGrath and Loretta Long with puppets (from left) Big Bird, Cookie Monster, Grover, Ernie, Bert and Oscar the Grouch.

In" that comes through because, although Rowan and Martin are the stars, they happily restrict their exposure and put on view any number of funny people who keep things going.

"You make jokes about political issues, morality, religion, race, etc.," I said. "Has the network ever objected?"

"Not yet," Martin said. "We use a lot of sexual jokes. I, personally, have always thought sex was funny, a good subject for comedy. I think it's one of those things that never wear out."

"And politics," Rowan said. "You take the Smothers Brothers—they use a lot of political material, but it's all slanted. We don't slant ours. If we knock LBJ or the Vietnam war, we knock Ronnie Reagan too. Our writers, for instance—and we've got about 10 of them—run from right to left. Our chief writer writes speeches for Richard Nixon."

The thing, the "Laugh-In," whatever it is, comes off, or on, like a combination in a new medium of "Hellzapoppin" and Peter Sellers' old "Goon Show" on the B.B.C. And as long as world leaders and human institutions continue to perform in the hilarious manner we've come to expect ("We all want this war to end," cast member Judy Carne said on one recent show, "so we can bring our boys home from Canada") there will be no end of material for the 10 writers to draw from and the show could go on forever—or at least until the first Bomb falls. ■

(cont'd. from previous page)
individualism and "Sesame Street" will warm the hearts of all those who believe such an accord should be started at the earliest moment.

"Sesame Street" makes extensive use of stocking puppets. Oscar, the drudge in the ash can, has a touch of beguiling attraction, but the others seem distressingly bland. One yearns for Burr Tillstrom and Kukla and Ollie. "Sesame Street" also could do with more outright laughter, a vital insurance policy on a 26-week series.

Only time will tell how "Sesame Street" does over the long haul; the value of novelty can subside. Some of its supporters have been a shade haughty about children "wasting their time" on trite commercial fare, notably Saturday morning cartoons. This argument should not be carried too far. There is a place for time-wasting and a place for something more substantial. Balance between the two is the criterion and, in the last analysis, parental responsibility along with broadcaster responsibility must play their share in its achievement. ■

DECEMBER 15, 1969

Inside-Out Dreams from London

Alan Brien

Monty Python's Flying Circus creators and cast members, from left, Terry Jones, Graham Chapman, John Cleese, Eric Idle, Terry Gilliam and Michael Palin.

LONDON—The new late-night comedy series transmitted every Sunday evening by the British Broadcasting Corporation is called "Monty Python's Flying Circus" but its name, say its authors, is "not supposed to mean anything." Working titles range from "Socks and Violence" to "Wodge Wodge Boodley Oodle Poo." The aim was to frustrate expectation. Childlike yet sophisticated, surrealist and simple-minded, it provides an outlet for the team's personal obsessions, group fantasies and nightmarish anecdotes.

A word they all hate is "satirical." The connection linking their involved sketches, silent-film action sequences and animated graphics with the real world is oblique and tenuous. But the inside-out dream logic nevertheless exists.

The spate of articles, picture spreads and documentary TV features on teenage hoodlums provokes the team to mount an investigation into a provincial town terrorized by senile delinquents. Old ladies in black silk and old lace race their motorcycles through the shopping center with "Hell's Grannies" painted on their backs. They picket high schools with signs demanding "Make Tea, Not Love." They rip up seats during performances of "Sound of Music."

Accusations of police violence lead them to show a typical lovable flatfoot confiding, "It's the uniform they respect. That, and my bad breath." Mass-media adulation of mediocre actors inspires them to insert a caption reading, "The part of David Hemmings was played by a piece of wood" and an end-of-program acknowledgment: "David Hemmings appeared by permission of the National Forestry Commission."

There is the verbal comedy of the topsy-turvy situation—an enlisted man complains to his colonel that the recruiting advertisements promised water-skiing, polo and tropical sun-bathing, but now he finds there are real bullets in the rifles. "Good God, you're not a pacifist?" demands the officer.

Animated segments featuring grotesque, hilarious, often beautiful images are supplied by Terry Gilliam, a 29-year-old American illustrator. He dubs all his own voices and produces all his own sound effects, working a seven-day week to fill his 10 minutes or so of the program.

The other five actor-writers are all "Oxbridge" graduates under the age of 30—John Cleese, Terry Jones, Michael Palin, Eric Idle and Graham Chapman. Chapman, like Jonathan Miller before him, is a doctor of medicine. One of the ancestors of "Monty Python's Flying Circus" is obviously "Beyond the Fringe," the revue in which Mr. Miller appeared, though the humor is much less intellectual, closer to the nonsense tradition of Lewis Carroll. Another strand in its genealogy is the now almost legendary "Goon Show," which, first on radio and then on TV, pioneered a zany, very English brand of schizoid fooling in the fifties and first made Peter Sellers a household name. There is even something in the show's confident, audience-mocking style that echoes "Laugh-In."

Despite the heated public debate over the B.B.C.'s plans for the future, with its critics accusing it of lowered standards and tasteless competition in order to avoid a $20-million debt by 1971, it is hard to imagine that any commercial TV network would have the courage and imagination to back "Monty Python." ■

APRIL 5, 1960

'BEN-HUR' TAKES RECORD 11 AWARDS

Murray Schumach

HOLLYWOOD, Calif., April 5—The movie industry opened its most important ballot box last night and learned that it had chosen "Ben-Hur" as its best film of 1959 and had given to this Metro-Goldwyn-Mayer picture more awards than any movie has ever received.

The selection was the climax of the thirty-second annual Oscar awards by the Academy of Motion Picture Arts and Sciences, which honored all branches of movie work here and abroad, with eleven citations for "Ben-Hur." The previous record-holder was "Gigi," with nine Oscars.

For the finest acting performances of the year, the industry voted Oscars to Charlton Heston, star of "Ben-Hur," and to Simone Signoret, who won critical acclaim in "Room at the Top."

The other top awards went to William Wyler for directing "Ben-Hur"; Shelley Winters as best supporting actress in "The Diary of Anne Frank"; and Hugh Griffith for the best supporting performance by an actor, for his role in "Ben-Hur."

"Black Orpheus," a French-made adaptation in color of the classic Orpheus legend, filmed in Brazil, largely with a native cast, was chosen as the best foreign-language feature.

Miss Signoret, a French star, was honored for her work as the married, ill-fated sweetheart of an ambitious young Yorkshireman. This marked the first time that the top prize was given to a feminine star in a British movie.

Mr. Heston accomplished the feat of winning an Oscar on his first nomination. The award for directing was nothing new to Mr. Wyler, who had received Oscars for "Mrs. Miniver" in 1942 and for "The Best Years of Our Lives" in 1946.

The awards, far from being overshadowed by the strike by actors that has ended movie production in seven of eight major studios here, were used as an excuse to make jokes.

Thus, during his master-of-ceremonies patter, master-of-ceremonies Bob Hope remarked:

"Who else but actors would give up working for Lent?"

At another time, he referred to the gathering of distinguished movie personalities as "the most glamorous strike meeting." ■

Janet Leigh in the iconic shower scene in Alfred Hitchcock's "Psycho," 1960.

JUNE 17, 1960

SUDDEN SHOCKS

HITCHCOCK'S 'PSYCHO' BOWS AT 2 HOUSES

Bosley Crowther

You had better have a pretty strong stomach and be prepared for a couple of grisly shocks when you go to see Alfred Hitchcock's "Psycho," which a great many people are sure to do. For Mr. Hitchcock, an old hand at frightening people, comes at you with a club in this frankly intended blood-curdler, which opened at the DeMille and Baronet yesterday.

There is not an abundance of subtlety or the lately familiar Hitchcock bent toward significant and colorful scenery in this obviously low-budget job. With a minimum of complication, it gets off to a black-and-white start with the arrival of a fugitive girl with a stolen bankroll right at an eerie motel.

Well, perhaps it doesn't get her there

(cont'd. on next page)

(cont'd. from previous page)

too swiftly. That's another little thing about this film. It does seem slowly paced for Mr. Hitchcock and given over to a lot of small detail. But when it does get her to the motel and apparently settled for the night, it turns out this isolated haven is, indeed, a haunted house.

The young man who diffidently tends it—he is Anthony Perkins and the girl is Janet Leigh—is a queer duck, given to smirks and giggles and swift dashes up to a stark Victorian mansion on a hill. There, it appears, he has a mother—a cantankerous old woman—concealed. And that mother, as it soon develops, is deft at creeping up with a knife and sticking holes into people, drawing considerable blood.

That's the way it is with Mr. Hitchcock's picture—slow buildups to sudden shocks that are old-fashioned melodramatics, however effective and sure, until a couple of people have been gruesomely punctured and the mystery of the haunted house has been revealed. Then it may be a matter of question whether Mr. Hitchcock's points of psychology, the sort highly favored by Krafft-Ebing, are as reliable as his melodramatic stunts.

Frankly, we feel his explanations are a bit of leg-pulling by a man who has been known to resort to such tactics in his former films.

The consequence is his denouement falls quite flat for us. But the acting is fair. Mr. Perkins and Miss Leigh perform with verve, and Vera Miles, John Gavin and Martin Balsam do well enough in other roles.

The one thing we would note with disappointment is that, among the stuffed birds that adorn the motel office of Mr. Perkins, there are no significant bats.

FEBRUARY 8, 1961

'BREATHLESS' SORDID VIEW OF FRENCH LIFE

Bosley Crowther

As sordid as is the French film, "Breathless" ("A Bout de Souffle")—and sordid is really a mild word for its pile-up of gross indecencies—it is withal a fascinating communication of the savage ways and moods of some of the rootless young people of Europe (and America) today.

Made by Jean-Luc Godard, one of the newest and youngest of the "new wave" of experimental directors who seem to have taken over the cinema in France, it goes at its unattractive subject in an eccentric photographic style that sharply conveys the nervous tempo and the emotional erraticalness of the story it tells. And through the American actress, Jean Seberg, and a hypnotically ugly new young man by the name of Jean-Paul Belmondo, it projects two downright fearsome characters.

This should be enough, right now, to warn you that this is not a movie for the kids or for that easily shockable individual who used to be known as the old lady from Dubuque. It is emphatically, unrestrainedly vicious, completely devoid of moral tone, concerned mainly with eroticism and the restless drives of a cruel young punk to get along. Although it does not appear intended deliberately to shock, the very vigor of its reportorial candor compels that it must do so.

On the surface, it is a story of a couple of murky days in the lives of two erratic young lovers in Paris, their temporary home. He is a car thief and hoodlum, on the lam after having casually killed a policeman while trying to get away with a stolen car. She is an expatriate American newspaper street vendor and does occasional stories for an American newspaper man friend.

But in the frenetic fashion in which M. Godard pictures these few days—the nerve-tattering contacts of the lovers, their ragged relations with the rest of the world—there is subtly conveyed a vastly complex comprehension of an element of youth that is vagrant, disjointed, animalistic and doesn't give a damn for anybody or anything, not even itself.

All of this, and its sickening implications, M. Godard has got into this film, which progresses in a style of disconnected cutting that might be described as "pictorial cacophony." A musical score of erratic tonal qualities emphasizes the eccentric moods. And in M. Belmondo we see an actor who is the most effective cigarette-mouther and thumb-to-lip rubber since time began.

Say this, in sum, for "Breathless": it is certainly no cliché, in any area or sense of the word. It is more a chunk of raw drama, graphically and artfully torn with appropriately ragged edges out of the tough underbelly of modern metropolitan life. ■

OCTOBER 6, 1961

Audrey Hepburn Stars in 'Breakfast at Tiffany's'

A. H. Weiler

A viewer is always aware that he is intermittently guffawing and constantly being amazed by a succession of surprises in "Breakfast at Tiffany's," which, gleaming like a $50,000 bauble from that haughty institution, landed at the Music Hall yesterday. And, like that storied novella by Truman Capote from which it stems, it is a completely unbelievable but wholly captivating flight into fancy composed of unequal dollops of comedy, romance, poignancy, funny colloquialisms and Manhattan's swankiest East Side areas captured in the loveliest of colors.

Above all, it has the overpowering attribute known as Audrey Hepburn, who, despite her normal, startled fawn exterior, now is displaying a fey, comic talent that should enchant Mr. Capote, who created the amoral pixie she portrays, as well as movie-goers meeting her for the first time in the guise of Holly Golightly.

But comparisons between the book and the script cannot be avoided and, while scenarist George Axelrod and the producers cleaved fairly closely to the pages of Mr. Capote's work, they erred, it appears to an observer who has read the original, in changing the character of Paul Varjac, Holly's writer-neighbor.

In transforming him from a dispassionate admirer, as amoral as Holly, into a gent being subsidized, for purely romantic purposes, by a rich, comely woman, the character loses conviction. Why, one wonders, should he give up a good thing, especially if Holly doesn't seem to be interested in love for love's sake? "Breakfast at Tiffany's" loses momentum as it heads toward that happy ending, and that ending is not patterned after Mr. Capote's design. But it may be allowed. It seems downright ungentlemanly to short-change as resolutely cheerful a sprite as Holly, who deserves a handsome husband after being cheated out of the Brazilian millionaire for whom she has set her cap.

Miss Golightly, is, as her one-time Hollywood agent declares, "a phony, but a real phony, understand Fred, baby?" She is, in short, "a wild thing." All the quick-silverish explanations still leave the character as implausible as ever. But in the person of Miss Hepburn, she is a genuinely charming, elfin waif who will be believed and adored when seen.

A word must be said for the wild party thrown by Miss Hepburn and her visit to Tiffany's in which John McGiver, as a terrifyingly restrained clerk, solicitously sells her a trinket for under $10. Both scenes are gems of invention. If all of "Breakfast at Tiffany's" doesn't measure up to these high standards, there are always Miss Hepburn and enough other ingredients to make it a pleasantly memorable entertainment. ■

'SPLENDOR IN THE GRASS' IS FEROCIOUS SOCIAL DRAMA

Bosley Crowther

Sex and parental domineering again confound two romantic high-school youngsters in Elia Kazan's and William Inge's new film, "Splendor in the Grass."

But where these conventional homely hazards to the tranquility and freedom of youth have been frequently calculated to an obsessive degree in previous films, they are put rather fairly in focus and dramatic rationality in this. They are made to appear congenial forces that misshape the lives of two nice kids, played with amazing definition by Warren Beatty and Natalie Wood.

This is not to suggest that the hazards are hidden within a euphemistic haze or that the social and moral implications of their presence are tactfully glazed. Mr. Inge had written and Mr. Kazan has hurled upon the screen a frank and ferocious social drama that makes the eyes pop and the modest cheek burn.

Petting is not simply petting in this embarrassingly intimate film. It is wrestling and chewing and punching that end with clothes torn and participants spent. And boozing is not simply boozing with adults, and also with kids. It is swilling and reeling and hollering and getting disgustingly sick.

But where these might sound exaggerations and seem sensationalisms in other films, they are reasonable, plausible, convincing and incisively significant here. For the turmoil of sex-starving youngsters is set within the socially isolated frame of a Kansas town in the late nineteen twenties—a town raw, rich and redolent with oil, with the arrogance of sweaty money-grubbers and the platitudes of corn-belt puritans. The torment of two late-adolescents, yearning yet not daring to love, is played against the harsh backdrop of cheapness, obtuseness and hypocrisy.

There are times when the heat gets too oppressive, when Mr. Kazan lays the purple on too thick, when you get a sneaking suspicion he is playing to the mob for effect. He has made a depraved flapper sister of the boy such an absolute mess that you cringe when she's flaming like a bonfire and are relieved when she disappears. Barbara Loden's performance is all fireworks and whirling razor blades.

Warren Beatty, as Bud Stamper, and Natalie Wood, as Wilma Dean Loomis, in "Splendor In The Grass," directed by Elia Kazan, 1961.

But the milieu is generally terrific—right on the beam and down Main Street, ugly and vulgar and oppressive, comical at times and sad. Pat Hingle gives a bruising performance as the oil-wealthy father of the boy, pushing and pounding and preaching, knocking the heart out of the lad. Audrey Christie is relentlessly engulfing as the sticky-sweet mother of the girl, and Fred Stewart, Joanna Roos and John McGovern are excellent in other adult roles.

In the end, however, the authority and eloquence of the theme emerge in the honest, sensitive acting of Mr. Beatty and Miss Wood. The former, a surprising newcomer, shapes an amiable, decent, sturdy lad whose emotional exhaustion and defeat are the deep pathos in the film. Except that he talks like Marlon Brando and has some small mannerisms of James Dean, Mr. Beatty is a striking individual. He can purge himself, if he will.

And Miss Wood has a beauty and radiance that carry her through a role of violent passions and depressions with unsullied purity and strength. There is poetry in her performance, and her eyes in the final scene bespeak the moral significance and emotional fulfillment of this film. ■

MARCH 18, 1962

'New Wave' Coups by Truffaut, Malle

Cynthia Grenier

PARIS. Local moviegoers and critics have been discovering during the past month that they were premature in thinking all the directorial talents tossed up by the "New Wave" were finished. Both François Truffaut and Louis Malle—just turned 30—were bringing the public out in droves to see how they had handled two of France's favorite actresses—Jeanne Moreau and Brigitte Bardot.

The fact that both women—who these days can pick and choose just about any director their hearts desire—decided to have the likes of Malle and Truffaut indicated to most critics that the New Wave is no longer a rebel movement, but, on the contrary, has become an integral part of the French movie world. Indeed most critics agree that the term New Wave has no more meaning, except for film historians, and should henceforth be eliminated when speaking of Truffaut and his compeers.

The Truffaut film, "Jules et Jim," an adaptation by Truffaut himself of the one novel written by a 76-year-old man a few years before his death in 1958, went over so much more successfully than anyone had imagined that its distributors had to open it in a second theatre to meet the demand. The film, black-and-white and 'Scope, earned Truffaut about every superlative in the book, for directorial imagination and inventiveness. As for Mlle. Moreau, whose comment, "This is my favorite film," is blazoned in neon on the marquees playing "Jules et Jim," Paris critics, who are exceedingly partial to her anyway, gave up, running heads like "Jeanne Moreau—sublime."

Malle's high-priced, Eastman-color picture, "La Vie Privée," ("Private Lives"), the top box-office draw in Paris these last few weeks, suffered, as far as the critics were concerned, from massive advance overexposure, largely because it starred Mlle. Bardot, supposedly playing her own real-life personage. The result was that the critics subjected the film to particularly close scrutiny before according it their reserved approval. ■

AUGUST 6, 1962

MARILYN MONROE DEAD, PILLS NEAR

Marilyn Monroe, a few weeks before she died on August 5, 1962, at the age of 36.

HOLLYWOOD, Calif., Aug. 5—Marilyn Monroe, one of the most famous stars in Hollywood's history, was found dead early today in the bedroom of her home in the Brentwood section of Los Angeles. She was 36 years old.

Beside the bed was an empty bottle that had contained sleeping pills. Fourteen other bottles of medicines and tablets were on the night stand.

The impact of Miss Monroe's death was international. Her fame was greater than her contributions as an actress.

As a woman she was considered a sex symbol. Her marriages to and divorces from Joe DiMaggio, the former Yankee baseball star, and Arthur Miller, the Pulitzer Prize playwright, were accepted by millions as the prerogatives of this contemporary Venus.

The events leading to her death were in tragic contrast to the comic talent and zest for life that had helped to make "Seven Year Itch" and "Some Like It Hot" smash hits all over the world.

Miss Monroe's physician had prescribed sleeping pills for her for three days. Ordinarily the bottle would have contained forty to fifty pills.

The actress had also been under the care of a psychoanalyst for a year, and had called him to her home last night. He had suggested she take a drive and relax. She remained home, however.

After an autopsy the Los Angeles coroner reported that Miss Monroe's "was not a natural death." Pending a more positive verdict by Dr. Theodore J. Curphey, the coroner, the Los Angeles police refused to call the death a suicide.

During the last few years Miss Monroe had suffered severe setbacks. Her last two films, "Let's Make Love" and "The Misfits," were box-office disappointments. After completion of "The Misfits," written by Mr. Miller, she was divorced from him.

On June 8 Miss Monroe was dismissed by Twentieth-Century-Fox for unjustifiable absences during the filming of "Something's Got to Give," in which she was starred. Filming on the picture has not resumed.

In low spirits she withdrew to her one-story stucco house in an upper middle-class section, which was far different from the lavish suites of the Beverly Hills Hotel that had been more typical of her. She died in the house at 12305 Fifth Helena Drive.

The last person to see her alive was her housekeeper, Mrs. Eunice Murray, who had lived with her.

In the last two years Miss Monroe had become the subject of considerable controversy in Hollywood. Some persons gibed at her aspirations as a serious actress. They considered it ridiculous that she should have gone to New York to study under Lee Strasberg.

Miss Monroe's defenders, however, asserted that her talents had been underestimated by those who thought her appeal to movie audiences was solely sexual.

Miss Monroe wound up as a virtual recluse. Hardly any of her neighbors had seen her more than once or twice in the six months since she had moved into her two-bedroom bungalow, which is modest by Hollywood standards.

OCTOBER 25, 1962

BRAINWASHING IS THEME OF 'THE MANCHURIAN CANDIDATE'

Bosley Crowther

With the air full of international tension, the film "The Manchurian Candidate" pops up with a rash supposition that could serve to scare some viewers half to death—that is, if they should be dupes enough to believe it, which we solemnly trust they won't.

Its story of a moody young fellow who was captured by the Communists during the Korean campaign and brainwashed by them to do their bidding as a high-level assassin when he gets home to America is as wild a piece of fiction as anything Alfred Hitchcock might present, but it could agitate some grave imaginings in anxious minds these days, especially since it is directed and acted in a taut and vivid way.

Presumably it was intended as a thriller with overtones of social and political satire—a deliberate double-barreled shot at the vicious practice of brain-washing, whether done by foreign militarists or by fanatical politicians working on the public here at home. That was the evident purpose of the novel of Richard Condon, on which it is based.

But somewhere along in the turning of the novel into the film, the figure of the Communist-triggered killer loomed out of all proportion to the ridiculous United States Senator who is set up as his thematic counterpart.

The menace of this fellow, the hypnotized hero with a gun waiting to do the bidding of the Moscow Frankensteins, becomes so ominous and pervasive that the rabid, red-baiting senator—his stepfather, managed by his mother—becomes no more than a dunce, a joke. Whatever chance of balanced satire and ironic point there might have been in the subtle equating of these two firebrands is lost in the script of George Axelrod.

With that said, however, it must be added that the film is so artfully contrived, the plot so interestingly started, the dialogue so racy and sharp and John Frankenheimer's direction is so exciting in the style of Orson Welles when he was making "Citizen Kane" and other pictures that the fascination of it is strong. So many fine cinematic touches and action details pop up that one keeps wishing the subject would develop into something more than it does.

Laurence Harvey is impressive as the killer—a darkly moving evil force—until he has to perform the nonsense that is worked out for him at the end. Frank Sinatra is slightly over-zealous and too conspicuous with nervous tics to carry complete conviction as the army major (also a brainwash victim) who breaks the case. But Angela Lansbury is intense as the killer's mother, James Gregory is vulgar and droll as the senator (modeled after Joseph R. McCarthy) and Khigh Dhiegh plays a villain handsomely.

With so much in it that examples a dynamic use of the screen, it is too bad that "The Manchurian" has so little to put across. ■

DECEMBER 17, 1962

LAWRENCE OF ARABIA: DESERT WARFARE SPECTACLE

Bosley Crowther

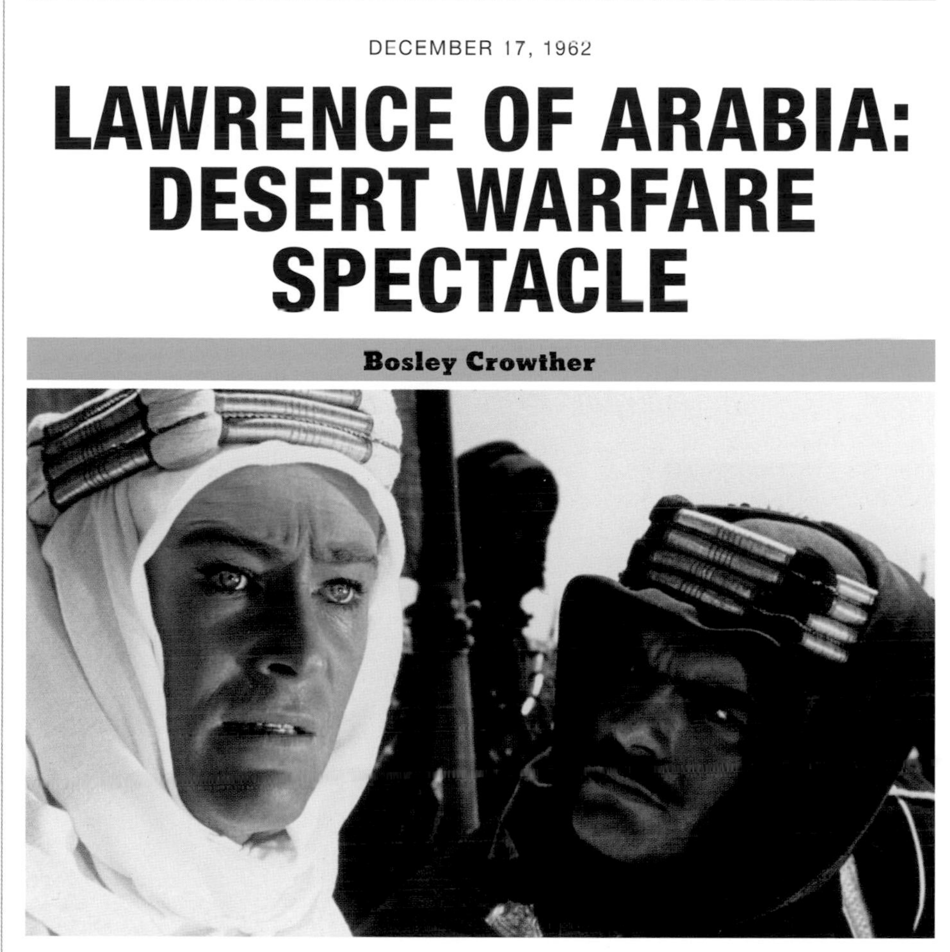

Peter O'Toole and Omar Sharif in "Lawrence of Arabia"

Like the desert itself, in which most of the action in "Lawrence of Arabia" takes place, this much-heralded film about the famous British soldier-adventurer is vast, awe-inspiring, beautiful with ever-changing hues, exhausting and barren of humanity.

It is such a laboriously large conveyance of eye-filling outdoor spectacle—such a brilliant display of endless desert and camels and Arabs and sheiks and skirmishes with Turks and explosions and arguments with British military men—that the possibly human, moving T. E. Lawrence is lost in it. We know little more about this strange man when it is over than we did when it begins.

(cont'd. on next page)

(cont'd. from previous page)

Sure, a lean, eager, diffident sort of fellow, played by blue-eyed Peter O'Toole, a handsome new British actor, goes methodically over the ground of Lawrence's major exploits as a guerrilla leader of Arab tribesmen during World War I. He earnestly enters the desert, organizes the tribes as a force against the Turks for the British, envisions Arab unity and then becomes oddly disillusioned as the politicians move in.

Why Lawrence had a disposition to join the Arab tribes is barely hinted in the film. The inner mystery of the man remains lodged behind the splendid burnoosed figure and the wistful blue eyes of Mr. O'Toole.

The fault seems to lie first in the concept of telling the story of this self-tortured man against a background of action that has the characteristic of a mammoth Western film. The nature of Lawrence cannot be captured in grand Super-Panavision shots of sunrise on the desert or in scenes of him arguing with a shrewd old British general in a massive Moorish hall.

The fault is also in the lengthy but surprisingly lusterless dialogue of Robert Bolt's over-written screenplay. Seldom has so little been said in so many words.

There are some great things in the picture—which runs, incidentally, for 3 hours and 40 minutes, not counting intermission. There is some magnificent scenery, barbaric fights, a mirage in the desert that is superb (the one episode in the picture that conveys a sense of mystery). And there are some impressive presentations of historic characters.

Alec Guinness as the cagey Prince Feisal, Anthony Quinn as a fierce chief, Omar Sharif as a handsome Arab fighter and Jack Hawkins as General Allenby stand out in a large cast that is ordered into sturdy masculine ranks by David Lean.

But, sadly, this bold Sam Spiegel picture lacks the personal magnetism, the haunting strain of mysticism and poetry that we've been thinking all these years would be dominant when a film about Lawrence the mystic and the poet was made. It reduces a legendary figure to conventional movie-hero size amidst magnificent and exotic scenery but a conventional lot of action-film cliches.

It is, in the last analysis, just a huge, thundering camel-opera that tends to run down rather badly as it rolls on into its third hour and gets involved with sullen disillusion and political deceit. ■

MAY 30, 1963

'DR. NO,' MYSTERY SPOOF

Bosley Crowther

Sean Connery as James Bond in the film "Dr No."

If you haven't yet made the acquaintance of Ian Fleming's suave detective, James Bond, in the author's fertile series of mystery thrillers akin to the yarns of Mickey Spillane, here's your chance to correct that misfortune in one quick and painless stroke. It's by seeing this first motion picture made from a Fleming novel, "Dr. No."

This lively, amusing picture, which opened yesterday at the Astor, the Murray Hill and other theaters in the "premiere showcase" group, is not to be taken seriously as realistic fiction or even art, any more than the works of Mr. Fleming are to be taken as long-hair literature. It is strictly a tinseled action-thriller, spiked with a mystery of a sort. And, if you are clever, you will see it as a spoof of science-fiction and sex.

For the crime-detecting adventure that Mr. Bond is engaged in here is so wildly exaggerated, so patently contrived, that it is obviously silly and not to be believed. It is a perilous task of discovering who is operating a device on the tropical island of Jamaica that "massively interferes" with the critical rocket launchings from Cape Canaveral.

Nonsense, you say. Of course, it's nonsense—pure, escapist bunk, with Bond, an elegant fellow, played by Sean Connery, doing everything (and everybody) that an idle day-dreamer might like to do. Called from a gaming club in London to pick up his orders and his gun and hop on a plane for Jamaica before a tawny temptress leads him astray, old "Double Oh Seven" (that's his code name) is in there being natty from the start. And he keeps on being natty, naughty and nifty to the end.

It's not the mystery that entertains you, it's the things that happen along the way—the attempted kidnapping at the Jamaica airport, the tarantula dropped onto Bond's bed, the seduction of the Oriental beauty, the encounter with the beautiful blond bikini-clad Ursula Andress on the beach of Crab Key. And it's all of these things happening so smoothly in the lovely Jamaica locale, looking real and tempting in color, that recommend this playful British film.

The ending, which finds Joseph Wiseman being frankly James Masonish in an undersea laboratory that looks like something inspired by Oak Ridge, is a bit too extravagant and silly, and likewise too frantic and long. But something outrageous had to be found with which to end the reckless goings-on.

'8 1/2': FELLINI'S CONTEMPLATION OF A DIRECTOR'S LIFE

Bosley Crowther

If you thought Federico Fellini's "La Dolce Vita" was a hard-to-fathom film, random and inconclusive, wait until you see "8 1/2," his latest.

Here is a piece of entertainment that will really make you sit up straight and think, a movie endowed with the challenge of a fascinating intellectual game. It has no more plot than a horse race, no more order than a pinball machine, and it bounces around on several levels of consciousness, dreams and memories as it details a man's rather casual psychoanalysis of himself. But it sets up a labyrinthine ego for the daring and thoughtful to explore, and it harbors some elegant treasures of wit and satire along the way.

Cannily, Mr. Fellini has chosen a character he knows as the subject of his introspection. He has chosen a director of films. A person familiar with his nature might even suspect it is Mr. Fellini himself. And he has planted this character in a milieu of luxury and toil he knows so well that you sense that every detail of the canvas must be wrenched from his own experience.

The picture begins with this fellow sitting trapped in his car in a traffic jam, immobilized among a crowd of zombies that might be dead souls crossing the River Styx. Suddenly suffocating, he struggles wildly to be released. And the next thing—he's floating upward, out of the traffic jam and above a beach, where he is magically hauled back earthward by a kite-string tied to his leg.

Thus does Mr. Fellini notify us right away that he has embarked on a fanciful excursion with a man who has barely escaped death. By the obvious implications of his pictorial imagery this would be the only release from the stagnation and deadness he feels himself to be in.

The fellow is trying to apply himself to preparing a new movie, while his mistress comes to stay nearby and swarms of idlers and job hunters persistently keep after him.

But, alas, he cannot get going. He is full of anxieties, doubts and disbelief in the value of movies. And, in this uncertain state, his mind takes to wandering off in memories and building fantasies.

Mr. Fellini does give us sufficient clues to the nature and problems of his fellow to lead us to understand—that is, if we have the patience and the prescience. And what we discover (at least, I do) is an outrageous egotist, a man of supreme romantic notions with a charmingly casual conceit, who has been attended and spoiled by women ever since he was a tot.

Mr. Fellini has managed to compress so much drollery and wit, so much satire on social aberrations, so much sardonic comment on sex and, indeed, when you come right down to it, even a bit of a travesty of Freud, that it pains me to note that he hasn't thought his film through to a valid end.

. . . a piece of entertainment that will really make you sit up straight and think . . .

Actors Mino Doro (left) and Marcello Mastrioanni (center) with director Federico Fellini on the set of "8 1/2."

He has his erratic hero, whom Marcello Mastroianni plays in a beautifully bored and baffled fashion, suddenly become aware that the trouble with him is that he has always taken but never given love. And when he grasps this, he is able to get all the people he knows to join hands and get ready to make a fine movie on the set of a rocket launching pad.

This is a romantic side-step—as romantic as the whole film, the title of which, incidentally, means simply Mr. Fellini's Opus 8 1/2. But this is, in large part, compensated by much that is wonderful—by Mr. Fellini's tremendous pictorial poetry, his intimations of pathos and longing, his skill with the silly and grotesque; by some splendid and charming performing, and much, much more. There is also another delicious Nino Rota musical score. ■

JUNE 13, 1963

'CLEOPATRA': 4-HOUR EPIC TRIBUTE TO ITS ARTISTS' SKILLS

Bosley Crowther

Elizabeth Taylor as Cleopatra, and Richard Burton as Mark Antony, in "Cleopatra," 1963.

Forget the fantastic sum that "Cleopatra" is reported to have cost. Forget the length of time it took to make it and all the tattle of troubles they had, including the behavior of two of its spotlighted stars. The memorable thing about this picture is that it is a surpassing entertainment, one of the great epic films of our day.

This may come as surprising information to those who have blindly assumed that any film of such mammoth proportions (it runs a few minutes more than four hours, excluding the intermission) and which has gone through so much storm and strife could not possibly be a cohesive, intelligent piece of work. But the slip-up in this assumption was that it didn't make due allowance for the tremendous potential of the story and the proven skill of the artists who did the job.

After all, what we know from history of the ancient Egyptian queen, who cast her spell over the two great Roman generals Julius Caesar and Mark Antony and, by her relations with them, affected the destiny of the world, is fraught with imperishable romance, adventure and tragedy. It is history of mighty dimensions, human drama on a grand and noble scale, which has fired the imaginations of poets and playwrights from Shakespeare to Shaw.

Why, then, shouldn't this tremendous story be envisioned supremely on the screen, which has the facilities for showing the true magnitude of great events, as well as the close, emotional contacts of strong personalities? There is no reason why it shouldn't. And the bright news this morning is that, thanks to the aptness of the medium, to fine photography in color and Todd-AO, and to the skill of many fine artists, it has been envisioned handsomely.

In this exciting achievement, Joseph L. Mankiewicz, as the screen playwright and director, has played the most influential role. For it is his fabrication of characters of colorfulness and depth, who stand forth as thinking, throbbing people against a background of splendid spectacle, that gives vitality to this picture and is the key to its success.

These are not obvious actors in geegaw costumes who march around in a fake world staked out by Cecil B. DeMille. (You may remember he did a "Cleopatra"—a lulu—back in 1934.) These are plausible people, maturely conceived and turned loose in a realm of political intrigues, conflicts and thrusts for personal power. They are moved by considerable forces, emboldened by well-defined desires, and they speak literate words that crackle with sophisticated imagery and wit.

Elizabeth Taylor's Cleopatra is a woman of force and dignity, fired by a fierce ambition to conquer and rule the world—at least, the world of the Mediterranean basin—through the union of Egypt and Rome. In her is impressively compacted the arrogance and pride of an ancient queen.

But she is not an ancient queen, mind you, in the quality of her thought—nor, indeed, in the modified high style of her exceedingly low-cut gowns. Mr. Mankiewicz has wisely not attempted to present us with historical copies. He and the writers who have helped him have drawn their major dramatic episodes from Plutarch, Suetonius and others. But the minds of their characters work along lines more in accord with contemporary thought, just as do those of the characters in the plays of Shakespeare and Shaw.

. . . one of the great epic films of our day.

Caesar is no fustian tyrant. Played stunningly by Rex Harrison, he is a statesman of manifest wisdom, shrewdness and magnanimity. And he is also a fascinating study in political ambiguities. He is torn by loyalty, ambition and wishes for his son. Mr. Harrison's faceted performance is the best in the film.

But Richard Burton is nonetheless exciting as the arrogant Antony—a man the very opposite of Caesar, whom he would so much like to be. He is the stubborn professional soldier, aspiring to statesmanlike deeds, but lacking the brains, the self-assurance, everything but the raw vitality. The tragedy lies in his incompetence to accomplish Cleopatra's bold design, while being inevitably locked to her—and she to him—by the bonds of love.

By virtue of brilliant staging, Mr. Mankiewicz keeps this well-known tale moving with visual excitements that increase the dramatic flow and give extraordinary insights into the characters.

There may be those who will find the length too tiring, the emphasis on Roman politics a bit too involved and tedious, the luxuriance too much. But unless you are one of those skeptics who are stubbornly predisposed to give "Cleopatra" the needle, I don't see how you can fail to find this a generally brilliant, moving and satisfying film. ■

JANUARY 30, 1964

'DR. STRANGELOVE': Kubrick Presents Sellers in 3 Roles

Bosley Crowther

Stanley Kubrick's new film, called "Dr. Strangelove or: How I Learned to Stop Worrying and Love the Bomb," is beyond any question the most shattering sick joke I've ever come across. And I say that with full recollection of some of the grim ones I've heard from Mort Sahl, some of the cartoons I've seen by Charles Addams and some of the stuff I've read in Mad Magazine.

For this brazenly jesting speculation of what might happen within the Pentagon and within the most responsible council of the President of the United States if some maniac Air Force general should suddenly order a nuclear attack on the Soviet Union is at the same time one of the cleverest and most incisive satiric thrusts at the awkwardness and folly of the military that have ever been on the screen.

My reaction to it is quite divided, because there is so much about it that is grand, so much that is brilliant and amusing, and much that is grave and dangerous.

On the one hand, it cuts right to the soft pulp of the kind of military mind that is lost from all sense of reality in a maze of technical talk, and it shows up this type of mentality for the foolish and frightening thing it is.

Some of the conversations in that War Room are hilarious, shooting bright shafts of satire through mounds of ineptitude. There is, best of all, a conversation between the President and an unseen Soviet Premier at the other end of a telephone line that is a titanic garble of nuttiness and platitudes.

Funny, too, in a mad way, is the behavior of the crew in one of the planes of the airborne alert force ordered to drop the bomb. The commander is a Texan who puts on a cowboy hat when he knows the mission is committed. Slim Pickens plays this role. He and Keenan Wynn as a foggy colonel are the funniest individuals in the film.

On the other hand, I am troubled by the feeling, which runs all through the film, of discredit and even contempt for our whole defense establishment, up to and even including the hypothetical Commander in Chief.

When virtually everybody turns up stupid or insane—or, what is worse, psychopathic—I want to know what this picture proves. The President, played by Peter Sellers with a shiny bald head, is a dolt, whining and unavailing with the nation in a life-or-death spot. But worse yet, his technical expert, Dr. Strangelove, whom Mr. Sellers also plays, is a devious and noxious ex-German whose mechanical arm insists on making the Nazi salute.

And, oddly enough, the only character who seems to have much common sense is a British flying officer, whom Mr. Sellers—yes, he again—plays.

The ultimate touch of ghoulish humor is when we see the bomb actually going off, dropped on some point in Russia, and a jazzy sound track comes in with a cheerful melodic rendition of "We'll Meet Again Some Sunny Day." Somehow, to me, it isn't funny. It is malefic and sick. ■

APRIL 14, 1964

Poitier Wins Oscar as Best Film Actor

Murray Schumach

SANTA MONICA, Calif., April 13—Motion-picture history was made tonight at the Santa Monica Civic Auditorium when Sidney Poitier became the first Negro to win an Oscar for best performance by an actor.

Mr. Poitier received the traditional gold-plated statuette at the 36th annual Oscar ceremonies for his portrayal, in "Lilies of the Field," of an itinerant construction worker who builds a chapel in the Southwest for refugee nuns.

Named best picture of 1963 was "Tom Jones," the adaptation of Henry Fielding's 18th-century novel, which satirizes English morality and literature. Its hero is a combination of gentleman, scapegoat and well-intentioned simpleton.

This choice was also significant, since it was only the second foreign-made movie to be named best picture by members of the Academy of Motion Picture Arts and Sciences. The first was Laurence Olivier's "Hamlet," in 1948.

But it was the stirring ovation for Mr. Poitier that was the dramatic highlight of the evening.

After accepting the award with a broad smile, he said somberly that "it has been a long journey to this moment."

The outburst for Mr. Poitier was recognition not only of his talent, but also of the fact that Hollywood has felt guilty about color barriers of the past, some of which still exist here.

Mr. Poitier's victory was particularly bright because it was against very strong competition. His four rivals were Albert Finney ("Tom Jones"), Richard Harris ("This Sporting Life"), Rex Harrison ("Cleopatra") and Paul Newman ("Hud").

This was the second time that Mr. Poitier was nominated for best acting. The last time was for his role as an escaped convict, chained to Tony Curtis, in "The Defiant Ones." Until tonight, the only important Oscar award to a Negro was for best supporting actress. That one went to Hattie McDaniel as Vivian Leigh's Mammy in "Gone With the Wind," in 1939. ■

OCTOBER 22, 1964

LOTS OF CHOCOLATES FOR MISS ELIZA DOOLITTLE

Bosley Crowther

Audrey Hepburn as Eliza Doolittle in "My Fair Lady," 1964.

As Henry Higgins might have whooped, "By George, they've got it!" They've made a superlative film from the musical stage show "My Fair Lady"—a film that enchantingly conveys the rich endowments of the famous stage production in a fresh and flowing cinematic form. The happiest single thing about it is that Audrey Hepburn superbly justifies the decision of the producer, Jack L. Warner, to get her to play the title role that Julie Andrews so charmingly and popularly originated on the stage.

All things considered, it is the brilliance of Miss Hepburn as the Cockney waif who is transformed by Prof. Henry Higgins into an elegant female facade that gives an extra touch of subtle magic and individuality to the film.

Other elements and values that are captured so exquisitely in this film are but artful elaborations and intensifications of the stage material as achieved by the special virtuosities and unique flexibilities of the screen.

There are the basic libretto and music of Alan Jay Lerner and Frederick Loewe, which were inspired by the wit and wisdom in the dramatic comedy, "Pygmalion," of George Bernard Shaw. With Mr. Lerner serving as the screen playwright, the structure and, indeed, the very words of the musical play are preserved. And every piece of music of the original score is used.

There is punctilious duplication of the motifs and patterns of the decor and the Edwardian costumes and scenery, which Cecil Beaton designed for the stage. The only difference is that they're expanded. Since Mr. Beaton's decor was fresh and flawless, it is super-fresh and flawless in the film.

In the role of Professor Higgins, Rex Harrison still displays the egregious egotism and ferocity that he so vividly displayed on the stage, and Stanley Holloway still comes through like thunder as Eliza's antisocial dustman dad.

Yes, it's all here, the essence of the stage show—the pungent humor and satiric wit of the conception of a linguistic expert making a lady of a guttersnipe by teaching her manners and how to speak, the pomp and mellow grace of a romantic and gone-forever age, the delightful intoxication of music that sings in one's ears.

For want of the scales of a jeweler, let's just say that what Mrs. Hepburn brings is a fine sensitivity of feeling and a phenomenal histrionic skill. It is true that Marni Nixon provides the lyric voice that seems to emerge from Miss Hepburn, but it is an excellent voice, expertly synchronized. And everything Miss Hepburn mimes to it is in sensitive tune with melodies and words.

"By George, they've got it!"

Mr. Cukor has maneuvered Miss Hepburn and Mr. Harrison so deftly in these scenes that she has one perpetually alternating between chuckling laughter and dabbing the moisture from one's eyes.

This is his singular triumph. He has packed such emotion into this film—such an essence of feeling and compassion for a girl in an all too-human bind—that he has made this rendition of "My Fair Lady" the most eloquent and moving that has yet been done.

There are other delightful triumphs in it. Mr. Harrison's Higgins is great—much sharper, more spirited and eventually more winning than I recall it on the stage. Mr. Holloway's dustman is titanic, and when he roars through his sardonic paean to middle-class morality in "Get Me to the Church on Time," he and his bevy of boozers reach a high point of the film.

Wilfrid Hyde White as Colonel Pickering, who is Higgins's urbane associate; Mona Washburn as the Higgins housekeeper; Gladys Cooper as Higgins's svelte mama; and, indeed, everyone in the large cast is in true and impeccable form.

Though it runs for three hours—or close to it—this "My Fair Lady" seems to fly past like a breeze. Like Eliza's disposition to dancing, it could go on, for all I'd care, all night. ■

MARCH 3, 1965

'The Sound of Music' Opens at Rivoli

Bosley Crowther

The fact that "The Sound of Music" ran for three and a half years on Broadway, despite the perceptible weakness of its quaintly old-fashioned book, was plainly sufficient assurance for the producer-director Robert Wise to assume that what made it popular in the theater would make it equally popular on the screen. That was a cheerful abundance of kirche-küche-kinder sentiment and the generally melodic felicity of the Richard Rodgers-Oscar Hammerstein 2nd musical score.

Julie Andrews in "The Sound of Music."

As a consequence, the great-big color movie Mr. Wise has made from it, and which was given a great-big gala opening at the Rivoli last night, comes close to being a careful duplication of the show as it was done on the stage, even down to its operetta pattern, which predates the cinema age.

To be sure, Mr. Wise has used his cameras to set a magnificently graphic scene in and around the actual city of Salzburg that lies nestled in the Austrian Alps. By means of a helicopter, he zooms over the snow-capped peaks and down into the green and ochre region, just as he zoomed down into New York's crowded streets in his memorable film of "West Side Story" (which was considerably different from this).

Julie Andrews plays the role of the postulant nun who leaves the abbey to try her hand at being governess to the seven children of the widowed Captain Von Trapp—and remains, after the standard digressions, to become their stepmother. And it is she who provides the most apparent and fetching innovation in the film.

Miss Andrews, with her air of radiant vigor, her appearance of plain-Jane wholesomeness and her ability to make her dialogue as vivid and appealing as she makes her songs, brings a nice sort of Mary Poppins logic and authority to this role, which is always in peril of collapsing under its weight of romantic nonsense and sentiment.

Despite the hopeless pretense of reality with which she and the others have to contend, especially in the last phase, when the Von Trapps are supposed to be fleeing from the Nazis and their homeland, Miss Andrews treats the whole thing with the same air of serenely controlled self-confidence that she has when we first come upon her trilling the title song on a mountain top.

Even though a couple of new songs have been added (both forgettable), Mr. Wise seems to run out of songs toward the end of the picture and repeats two or three of the more familiar ones. But the same must be said of "The Sound of Music." It repeats, in style—and in theme.

However, its sentiments are abundant. Businesswise, Mr. Wise is no fool.

DECEMBER 16, 1966

WALT DISNEY, 65, DIES ON COAST; FOUNDED AN EMPIRE ON A MOUSE

LOS ANGELES, Dec. 15—Walt Disney, who built his whimsical cartoon world of Mickey Mouse, Donald Duck and Snow White and the Seven Dwarfs into a $100-million-a-year entertainment empire, died in St. Joseph's Hospital here this morning. He was 65 years old.

His death, at 9:35 A.M., was attributed to acute circulatory collapse. He had undergone surgery at the hospital a month ago for the removal of a lung tumor that was discovered after he entered the hospital for treatment of an old neck injury received in a polo match. On Nov. 30 he re-entered the hospital for a "post-operative checkup."

Just before his last illness, Mr. Disney was supervising the construction of a new Disneyland in Florida and the renovation of the 10-year-old Disneyland at Anaheim. His motion-picture studio was turning out six new productions and several television shows and he was spearheading the development of the vast University of the Arts, called Cal Art, now under construction here.

Although Mr. Disney held no formal title at Walt Disney Productions, he was in direct charge of the company and was deeply involved in all its operations. Indeed, with the recent decision of Jack L. Warner to sell his interest in the Warner Brothers studio, Mr. Disney was the last of Hollywood's veteran moviemakers who remained in personal control of a major studio.

From his fertile imagination and industrious factory of drawing boards, Walt Elias Disney fashioned the most popular movie stars ever to come from Hollywood and created one of the most fantastic entertainment empires in history.

Where any other Hollywood producer would have been happy to get one Academy Award—the highest honor in American movies—Mr. Disney smashed all records by accumulating 29 Oscars.

Mr. Disney went from seven minute animated cartoons to become the first man to mix animation with live action, and he pioneered in making feature-length cartoons. His nature films were almost as popular as his cartoons, and eventually he expanded into feature-length movies using only live actors.

The most successful of his non-animated productions, "Mary Poppins," released in 1964, has already grossed close to $50 million. It also won an Oscar for Julie Andrews in the title role.

From a small garage-studio, the Disney enterprise grew into one of the most modern movie studios in the world, with four sound stages on 51 acres. Mr. Disney acquired a 420-acre ranch that was used for shooting exterior shots for his movies and television productions.

Mr. Disney's restless mind created one of the nation's greatest tourist attractions. Disneyland, a 300-acre tract of amusement rides, fantasy spectacles and re-created Americana that cost $50.1 million.

By last year, when Disneyland observed its 10th birthday, it had been visited by some 50 million people. Its international fame was emphasized in 1959 by the then Soviet Premier Nikita S. Khrushchev, who protested, when visiting Hollywood, that he had been unable to see Disneyland. Security arrangements could not be made in time for Mr. Khrushchev's visit.

Even after Disneyland had proven itself, Mr. Disney declined to consider suggestions that he had better leave well enough alone:

"Disneyland will never be completed as long as there is imagination left in the world." ■

FEBRUARY 2, 1967

Western Film Clichés in 'A Fistful of Dollars'

Bosley Crowther

Cowboy camp of an order that no one has dared in American films since, gosh, Gary Cooper's "The Virginian" (which is prototypical) is flung on the screen with shameless candor in the European-made, English-dubbed, Mexican-localized Western, "A Fistful of Dollars."

Just about every Western cliché that went with the old formula of the cool and mysterious gunslinger who blows into an evil frontier town and takes on the wicked, greedy varmints, knocking them off one by one, is in this egregiously synthetic but engrossingly morbid, violent film, put together as an Italian-German-Spanish co-production and shot for the most part in Spain.

There's this fellow who comes out of nowhere, laconic and steely-eyed, looking for business as a killer and fantastically swift on the draw. There are these families, the Baxters and the Rojos, locked in an ineffectual feud over who will control the smuggling business that centers in this Mexican town. There's the timid cantina proprietor, the coffin-maker waiting for clients—everything except the customary moral redemption and the naughty woman with the heart of gold.

It is notable that the lanky gringo who rides into San Miguel and virtually depopulates the area before he rides out again is in no way devoted to justice or aiding the good against the bad. He is an icy and cynical gunman whose only interest is what's in it for him.

Swiftly, he scans the situation. "There's money to be made in a place like this," he informs the cantina proprietor, and therewith sets about making it.

Clearly, the magnet of this picture, which has been a phenomenal success in Italy and other parts of Europe, is this cool-cat bandit who is played by Clint Eastwood, an American cowboy actor who used to do the role of Rowdy in the "Rawhide" series on TV. Wearing a Mexican poncho, gnawing a stub of cheroot and peering intently from under a slouch hat pulled low over his eyes, he is simply another fabrication of a personality, half cowboy and half gangster, going through the ritualistic postures and exercises of each.

His distinction is that he succeeds in

JULY 9, 1967

VIVIEN LEIGH, 53, IS DEAD IN LONDON

LONDON, July 8—Vivien Leigh, the stage and screen actress, was found dead in her London apartment this morning. Theater lights in the West End were blacked out for an hour tonight in tribute to her.

Miss Leigh, who was 53 years old, was confined to her apartment on Eaton Square, Belgravia, four weeks ago with a recurrence of tuberculosis, an illness from which she had suffered since 1945.

Sir Laurence Olivier, her former husband, spent about half an hour at the three-bedroom apartment this morning after learning of Miss Leigh's death. Sir Laurence was her second husband. They were married in 1940 and divorced 20 years later.

Behind fragile beauty and sophisticated charm, Miss Leigh harbored a feverish dedication to acting and a tough business sense that drove her to develop constantly an originally modest talent until she became one of the century's great stars.

Her fame was made worldwide early in her career by her performance as Scarlett O'Hara, in the film version of "Gone With the Wind," in which she starred with Clark Gable. For this role Miss Leigh won the first of two Oscars—the second was in the film version of Tennessee Williams's "A Streetcar Named Desire," in which she captured the complex sensitivity and desperate tragedy of Blanche du Bois.

Although Miss Leigh appeared in other films from time to time—"Waterloo Bridge," "That Hamilton Woman," "A Yank at Oxford," "Caesar and Cleopatra," "Anna Karenina," "The Deep Blue Sea," "The Roman Spring of Mrs. Stone," "Ship of Fools"—she always reserved much of her time for the stage.

Her Cleopatra to Sir Laurence's Caesar, in Shaw's "Caesar and Cleopatra," was memorable on Broadway, as well as in England. On alternating nights, they would do Shakespeare's "Antony and Cleopatra."

Miss Leigh's desire to be an actress began in childhood. She was born in Darjeeling, India, Nov. 5, 1913, to an Irish mother, Gertrude Robinson Hartley, and her English husband, Ernest Richard Hartley, a stockbroker. She was sent to a convent in London for early schooling and there, in her first school plays became certain she wanted to spend her life acting. Her schooling was continued in France, Italy and Germany as well as in England, and she began studying acting as an adolescent.

This early training was begun in the Royal Academy of Dramatic Art, where she did not do too well, and augmented by private instruction in Paris from an actress with the Comédie Française.

Miss Leigh's first stage role was in the London suburbs in 1935, a small part in "The Green Sash." Though the play never reached the West End, she attracted the attention of a producer, Sydney Carroll, who cast her as a cocotte in "The Mask of Virtue," that prepared the way for a long career.

But instead of going from one frivolous show to the next, she became involved in serious drama, with the encouragement of Mr. Olivier. She worked with the Old Vic in Shakespeare. She also toured with other groups in a wide variety of plays.

She considered comedy more difficult than tragedy. "It's much easier to make people cry than to make them laugh," she once remarked while she was in Jean Giraudoux's comedy "Duel of Angels."

To the very end, Miss Leigh kept a sense of perspective about drama. She once remarked, after having acquired her two Oscars, that though "Gone With the Wind" had greatly helped her career, her role was very shallow compared to Shakespeare's "Cleopatra."

being ruthless without seeming cruel, fascinating without being realistic. He is a morbid, amusing, campy fraud.

The other distinction of the picture is that it is full of spectacular violence. Sergio Leone, who directed from a script which we understand is a rewrite of the script of "Yojimbo," a Japanese samurai picture made by Akira Kurosawa with Toshiro Mifune, has crowded it with such juicy splashes as a big fat fellow being squashed by a rolling barrel, a whole squad of soldiers being massacred, and punctured men spitting gore.

Filmed in hard, somber color and paced to a musical score that betrays tricks and themes that sound derivative (remember "Ghost Riders in the Sky"?), "A Fistful of Dollars" is a Western that its sanguine distributors suggest may be loosing a new non-hero on us—a new James Bond. God forbid ■!

DECEMBER 12, 1967

'Guess Who's Coming to Dinner' Arrives

Bosley Crowther

"Guess Who's Coming to Dinner," which came to the Beekman and the Victoria yesterday, is a most delightfully acted and gracefully entertaining film, fashioned much in the manner of a stage drawing-room comedy, that seems to be about something much more serious and challenging than it actually is.

It seems to be about the social bias encountered by a San Francisco miss, daughter of liberal and socially prominent parents, who wants to marry a distinguished Negro scientist and suddenly finds herself opposed by her own father and the father of her fiancé. It seems to pose directly the question contained in that old hypocritical line: "I've got nothing at all against Negroes, but would you want your sister (daughter) to marry one?"

This certainly is the issue that swiftly and startlingly confronts Spencer Tracy and Katharine Hepburn when their daughter, Katharine Houghton, breezes home from a short vacation in Hawaii with beaming Sidney Poitier in tow, and bluntly announces with firm finality that they are going to be wed.

The mother of the girl, a New Deal liberal and a blue-stocking of the sort that

(cont'd. on next page)

Sidney Poitier with Spencer Tracy and Katharine Hepburn in Stanley Kramer's film "Guess Who's Coming to Dinner," 1967.

(cont'd. from previous page)

Miss Hepburn has played with crisp dexterity and assurance so many times, has plunked positively for the marriage, after her first indication of surprise, and seems almost as joyous about it as if it were her own.

The issue hangs on one big question mark—the father of the intended bride. Will he oppose the marriage? Will he bolt his liberal posture and say "No"? Or is he merely manifesting the misgivings and hesitations of any father of any girl who wants to marry a man much older than she is, whom she has known for only 10 days?.

Mr. Tracy and Miss Hepburn are superior—he the crusty, sardonic old boy who speaks from a store of flinty wisdom but whose heart overflows with tender love; and she the seemingly airy patrician whose eyes often well with compassionate tears.

Mr. Poitier is also splendid within the strictures of a rather stuffy type that might also be questioned, if one were dissecting this film, and Beah Richards is deeply touching as his mother, which is the most profound and dignified role. Isabelle Sanford gets off some nifties, in a somewhat Dick Gregoryish vein, as the family's Negro maid who has the strongest bias against mixed marriages.

"Civil rights is one thing but this here is something else," she sniffs in a burst of incisive recognition that might also characterize the blue-chip film.

One might add that it has the further value of strong personal sentiment, in that it offers Mr. Tracy so graciously in the last role he played before his death. ■

DECEMBER 31, 1967

GRADUATING WITH HONORS

Bosley Crowther

There is a particular satisfaction in being able to wind up this year—and also my occupation of the job of film critic on The Times—with a hearty salute to a film and a talent which remind me excitingly of a film and a talent that I was privileged to hail within a few months after I took over this job.

The film is Mike Nichols's "The Graduate," a funny and sharp satiric thrust at a delicate and generally neglected aspect of contemporary American society—that is, the piteous immaturity and anti-intellectualism of a large proportion of the supposedly educated and cultivated affluent middle class. And the film of which it reminds me by the nature of its fresh satiric style is Preston Sturges's "The Great McGinty," a wonderful lampoon of American machine politics.

In so many ways, this nifty picture that Mr. Nichols has made from a script by Calder Willingham and Buck Henry, based on a novel by Charles Webb, compares to that delicious entertainment with which Mr. Sturges began his career as one of the most skillful and prolific satirists ever to make films in Hollywood.

Its subject and contemplation are distinctly American, pegged to the characteristics of ways of life in the United States. Its people are recognizable as only Americans, just as the people in Alfred Hitchcock's earlier pictures were recognizable only as British or those in Marcel Pagnol's as only French. It is deftly sophisticated without in any way being above or condescending to the mass audience's intelligence and taste. And its cinematic style is energetic, aggressive and full of surprise.

It tells of the embarrassments and confusions of a solemn young man when he returns to the Beverly Hills home of his parents after graduating from one of the eastern status colleges and is tacitly expected by his parents to fall into their pattern of life. That pattern includes gay parties around the family swimming-pool, a lot of drinking, riding in sports cars, golf, and naturally, marrying a girl of one's set.

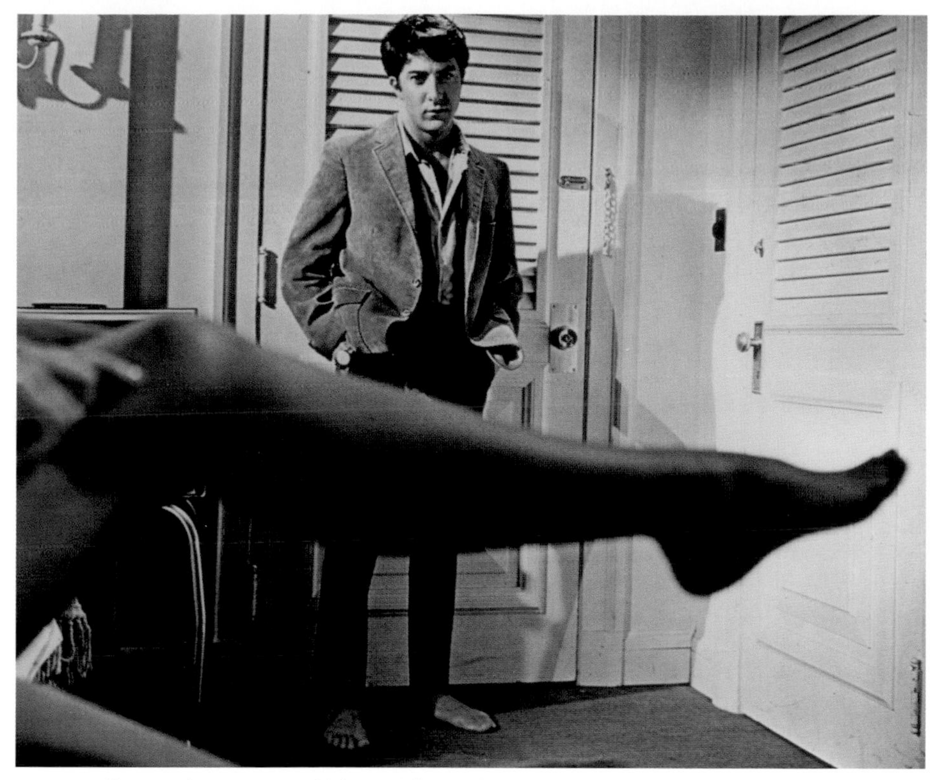

Dustin Hoffman and Anne Bancroft's leg in "The Graduate," 1967.

It presumes an ebullient spirit and a posture of youthfulness. It does not tolerate indecision or contemplation towards which this young man obviously is bent.

But it soon angles into an aspect of this affluent society that is neither funny nor vulgarly amusing, though Mr. Nichols manages to make it seem a practice of personal conduct that is full of droll grotesqueries. It is the practice of sexual infidelity, and here he has it originated and engineered by the wife of the partner of the young man's father who bluntly seduces the youth.

Mr. Nichols develops what is actually a quite sordid state of affairs into a wickedly sly, amusing and marginally poignant illumination of a fact of life. With anyone less skillful and aptly dead-panned than Anne Bancroft playing the wife and a marvelous new young actor named Dustin Hoffman playing the conscientious youth, this development in the story could be repellent. As it stands, however, it is astonishing, uproarious and pathetic because of the inadequacies and frustrations it implies.

The way Mr. Nichols ends his picture is the final satiric twist in this altogether bright and cinematic contemplation of affluent immaturity.

There is verbal dexterity and commentary in Mr. Nichols's film, fluency with camera, and sharpness and surprise in editing. He who was trained in the theater, as Mr. Sturges was, also picked his actors shrewdly and gets dandy performances from them.

. . . a wonderful lampoon of American machine politics.

Miss Bancroft and Mr. Hoffman are superior—he particularly, because he has to keep believable and sympathetic this extraordinarily sensitive, decent, foolish little guy, and he does so with amazing physical crotchets and personality pleasantries.

Especially subtle and appealing is the way background folk music is used to suggest moods and counterpoint fast humor with gentle wistfulness. The music is done by Simon and Garfunkel, whose "Are You Going to Scarborough Fair" is especially appealing and appropriate to the strain of sadness that runs through the film. ■

APRIL 4, 1968

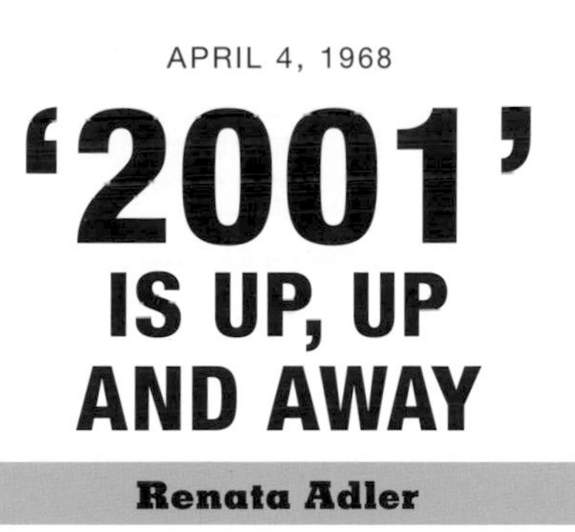

'2001' IS UP, UP AND AWAY

Renata Adler

Even the M-G-M lion is stylized and abstracted in Stanley Kubrick's "2001: A Space Odyssey," a film in which infinite care, intelligence, patience, imagination and Cinerama have been devoted to what looks like the apotheosis of the fantasy of a precocious, early nineteen-fifties city boy. The movie, on which Kubrick collaborated with the British science-fiction author Arthur C. Clarke, is nominally about the finding, in the year 2001, of a camera-shy sentient slab on the moon and an expedition to the planet Jupiter to find whatever sentient being the slab is beaming its communications at.

There is evidence in the film of Clarke's belief that men's minds will ultimately develop to the point where they dissolve in a kind of world mind. There is a subplot in the old science-fiction nightmare of man at terminal odds with his computer. There is one ultimate science-fiction voyage of a man (Keir Dullea) through outer and inner space, through the phases of his own life in time thrown out of phase by some higher intelligence, to his death and rebirth in what looked like an intergalactic embryo.

But all this is the weakest side of a very complicated, languid movie—in which almost a half-hour passes before the first man appears and the first word is spoken, and an entire hour goes by before the plot even begins to declare itself. Its real energy seems to derive from that bespectacled prodigy reading comic books around the block. The whole sensibility is intellectual fifties child: chess games, body-building exercises, beds on the spacecraft that look like camp bunks, other beds that look like Egyptian mummies, Richard Strauss music, time games, Strauss waltzes, Howard Johnson's, birthday phone calls.

The movie is so completely absorbed in its own problems, its use of color and space, its fanatical devotion to science-

(cont'd. on next page)

(cont'd. from previous page)

fiction detail, that it is somewhere between hypnotic and immensely boring. (With intermission, it is three hours long.) Kubrick seems as occupied with the best use of the outer edge of the screen as any painter, and he is particularly fond of simultaneous rotations, revolving, and straight forward motions—the visual equivalent of rubbing the stomach and patting the head.

There is also a kind of fanaticism about other kinds of authenticity: space travelers look as sickly and exhausted as travelers usually do; they are exposed in space stations to depressing canned music; the viewer is often made to feel that the screen is the window of a spacecraft, and as Kubrick introduces one piece of unfamiliar apparatus after another, the viewer is always made aware of exactly how it is used and where he is in it.

The special effects in the movie—particularly a voyage, either through Dullea's eye or through the slab and over the surface of Jupiter-Earth and into a period bedroom—are the best I have ever seen; and the number of ways in which the movie conveys visual information (there is very little dialogue) drives it to an outer limit of the visual.

The special effects in the movie . . . are the best I have ever seen . . .

And yet the uncompromising slowness of the movie makes it hard to sit through without talking—and people on all sides when I saw it were talking almost throughout the film. With all its attention to detail—a kind of reveling in its own I.Q.—the movie acknowledged no obligation to validate its conclusion for those, me for example, who are not science-fiction buffs. By the end, three unreconciled plot lines—the slabs, Dullea's aging, the period bedroom—are simply left there like a Rorschach, with murky implications of theology. This is a long step outside the convention, some extra scripts seem required, and the all-purpose answer, "relatively," does not really serve unless it can be verbalized. ■

MARCH 19, 1968

THE PRODUCERS:
Gross Hilarity

Renata Adler

"The Producers" is a violently mixed bag. Some of it is shoddy and gross and cruel; the rest is funny in an entirely unexpected way. It has the episodic, revue quality of so much contemporary comedy—not building laughter but stringing it together skit after skit, some vile, some boffo. It is less delicate than Lenny Bruce, less funny than "Doctor Strangelove," but much funnier than "The Loved One" or "What's New, Pussycat?"

It begins with Zero Mostel, overacting grotesquely under the direction of Mel Brooks, the famous 2,000-Year-Old Man and writer-narrator of the Academy Award-winning cartoon "The Critic." Mostel, as a producer who gets investors by giving old ladies "their last thrill on the way to the cemetery," is first shown in silhouette through the glass door to his office, as he nuzzles one of his elderly ladies. That is the last time. We next see him rolling about with them, being chased by them, making lewd conversation with them, and generally being as gross and unfunny as only an enormous comedian bearing down too hard on some frail, tasteless routines can be.

Gene Wilder, who pays the young bookkeeper who inspires Mostel to oversubscribe with backers a show that will close after a single night (leaving Mostel and Wilder with the amount that has been oversubscribed), is wonderful. He plays his present part as though he were Dustin Hoffman being played by Danny Kaye. Going through long, infinitely variegated riffs and arpeggios of neuroticism, he blushes and gasps, "I'm hysterical," and grins shyly and fondles his security blanket. He is forced to be as loud and as fast as Mostel (and as the crude and incredibly amateurish cutting). But he's fine.

They decide to produce "Springtime for Hitler," a play by a helmeted Nazi in Yorkville, a play true to "the Hitler you loved, the Hitler you knew, the Hitler with a song in his heart." They hire a transvestite director, whose plays have never lasted beyond the first rehearsal. As leading man, they hire a mind-blown hippie played by Dick Shawn. Mostel hires for himself a blond receptionist, who does not speak English, and who, when told to go to work, begins to dance frenetically.

Strangely enough, the first act of "Springtime for Hitler: A Gay Romp with Adolf and Eva in Berchtesgaden" is the funniest part of this fantastically uneven movie. There is just enough talent and energy to keep the blackest of collegiate humors comic. Barely.

Then, the movie makes a terrible and irreversible mistake. It allows the audience onscreen to find the play funny. This turned the real audience in the theater off as though a fuse had blown. There is nothing like having your make-believe audience catch on to a joke—and a joke that absolutely capsizes the plans of your leading characters—to make your real audience really hostile to you.

On the whole, "The Producers" leaves one alternately picking up one's coat to leave and sitting back to laugh.

JUNE 13, 1968

ROSEMARY'S BABY

Renata Adler

Mia Farrow and behind her, John Cassavetes, with some neighbors in "Rosemary's Baby."

If a person exhibits paranoid symptoms these days it would seem common decency not to report him, at least, to the persons he claims to be persecuted by, and when Mia Farrow tells what is, after all, a highly plausible story to her obstetrician in "Rosemary's Baby," it seems wrong of him to deliver her straight to a coven of witches that has designs on her baby. Lord knows how many cases of extremely accurate reporting are cured each day by psychiatrists.

The story, based on a novel by Ira Levin, and written and directed by Roman Polanski ("Repulsion," "Knife in the Water"), makes absolute sense in several ways. It is a horror film, not very scary. There are several false frights—a closet door opening ominously to reveal a vacuum cleaner, a letter in a dead woman's hands that reads "I can no longer associate myself," dropped objects in a dark cellar at the Dakota on West 72nd Street. But the only really jumpy second occurs when Miss Farrow speaks suddenly and startles a reading witch.

The story concerns a young couple, Miss Farrow and John Cassavetes, who move to the Dakota—as likely a place for horrors as any—where Miss Farrow ultimately has reason to believe that her husband, in return for success in his career as an actor, has arranged something with the people next door for her forthcoming child. Ruth Gordon overplays one rouged, elderly witch, with clear joy and overlapping, mutually interrupting sentences.

Miss Farrow is quite marvelous, pale, suffering, almost constantly on-screen in a difficult role that requires her to be learning for almost two hours what the audience has guessed from the start. One begins to think it is the kind of thing that might really have happened to her, that a rough beast did slouch toward West 72nd Street to be born. Everyone else is fine, but the movie although is it pleasant—doesn't seem to work on any of its dark or powerful terms.

I think this is because it is almost too extremely plausible. The quality of the young people's lives seems the quality of lives that one knows, even to the point of finding old people next door to avoid and lean on. One gets very annoyed that they don't catch on sooner. One's friends would have understood the situation at once. So that for most of its length the film has nothing to be excited about. It has Miss Gordon bringing herbs and cookies and Miss Farrow eating or not eating them—nothing cumulative—to fill that time with suspense. But the good side of that is that you can see the movie, and like it, without risking terrors or nightmares. ■

NOVEMBER 1, 1968

Film Industry Begins Ratings

Vincent Canby

HOLLYWOOD, Oct. 31—In their ample offices here above a Rexall drug store, Geoffrey M. Shurlock, director of the Motion Picture Association of America's Code Administration, and his five-man staff have been quietly classifying movies that go into general release beginning tomorrow.

Social historians may someday write that on Nov. 1, 1968, for better or worse, the American movie industry inaugurated its voluntary film classification system, designed to bar children under 16 from seeing movies that the industry's code people deem to be too vulgar, violent or sexy.

This means that the vast majority of movies going into commercial release will carry one of the following ratings:

G—suggested for general audiences.

M—for adults and mature young people.

R—restricted, persons under 16 not admitted unless accompanied by a parent or guardian.

X—those under 16 not admitted.

The three movies that have so far received X ratings were made abroad, including Warner Brothers-Seven Arts's "The Girl on a Motorcycle." Lending weight to the fear that the X rating may be used to exploit some films was the comment made yesterday about "Girl on a Motorcycle" by a Warner Brothers executive.

"They," he said, referring to the code staff, "asked us to make some cuts, but we decided to go ahead and take the X rating and make some money." The scenes that were left in included one explicit depiction of love making.

Harrison Starr, executive producer of Michelangelo Antonioni's "Zabriskie Point," now shooting at Death Valley, Calif., said they would probably excise from the script a four-letter word for copulation if its inclusion would result in an X. Such a rating would automatically reduce the potential earnings of a movie that is expected to be of particular interest to audiences between the ages of 16 and 25.

Proponents of the rating system see two possible ways in which the intended effect of the system may be nullified. They fear that if an X-rated film attains great success at the box office, it would stimulate the production of more films featuring even more sex and violence. They also fear that exhibitors might not enforce the rating (thus inviting local, state or Federal classifications) or they might put pressure on the code staff to limit the number of X-rated films arbitrarily.

The man responsible in large measure for the success or failure of the rating system is Mr. Shurlock, a thoughtful, classics-reading, 74-year-old man who joined the code staff in 1932 and succeeded the late Joseph I. Breen as its director in 1954.

Movies are his profession and his passion, but he has never been involved in Hollywood's social life. "What it came down to, I think, I just couldn't play cards—bridge, poker or even hearts," he said the other day. Then he added more seriously: "This has to be a bit of an ivory tower job."

In informal conversation this week, Mr. Shurlock declined to discuss the ratings made to date, explaining that his staff was "still feeling its way." Decisions are arrived at by consensus.

The new system, Mr. Shurlock stressed, recognizes the fact that all movies are not suitable for all audiences.

"I'm not really worried about there being too many R or X pictures," he said. "I'm happy that we can now exercise our responsibilities to protect children from certain movies that are obviously unsuitable." ■

DECEMBER 5, 1968

THE DEAD LIVE

Vincent Canby

"Night of the Living Dead" is a grainy little movie acted by what appear to be nonprofessional actors, who are besieged in a farm house by some other nonprofessional actors who stagger around, stiff-legged, pretending to be flesh-eating ghouls.

The dialogue and background music sound hollow, as if they had been recorded in an empty swimming pool, and the wobbly camera seems to have a fetishist's interest in hands, clutched, wrung, scratched, severed and finally—in the ultimate assumption—eaten like pizza.

The movie, which was made by some people in Pittsburgh, opened yesterday.

MAY 26, 1969

Dustin Hoffman and Jon Voight Star in MIDNIGHT COWBOY

Vincent Canby

Joe Buck is 6 feet tall and has the kind of innocence that preserves dumb good looks. Joe Buck fancies himself a cowboy, but his spurs were earned while riding a gas range in a Houston hamburger joint. Ratso Rizzo, his buddy and part-time pimp from the Bronx, is short, gimpy and verminous. Although they are a comparatively bizarre couple, they go unnoticed when they arrive at one of those hallucinogenic "Village" parties where the only thing straight is the booze that no one drinks.

Joe is a funny, dim-witted variation on the lonely, homosexual dream-hero who used to wander disguised through so much drama and literature associated with the nineteen fifties.

"Midnight Cowboy" is a slick, brutal (but not brutalizing) movie version of James Leo Herlihy's 1965 novel. It is tough and good in important ways, although its style is oddly romantic and at variance with the laconic material. It may be that movies of this sort (like most war movies) automatically celebrate everything they touch. We know they are movies—isolated, simplified reflections of life—and thus we can enjoy the spectacle of degradation and loss while feeling superior to it and safe.

Director John Schlesinger is most successful in his use of actors. Dustin Hoffman, as Ratso (his first movie performance since "The Graduate"), is something found under an old door in a vacant lot. With his hair matted back, his ears sticking out and his runty walk, Hoffman looks like a sly, defeated rat and talks with a voice that might have been created by Mel Blanc for a despondent Bugs Bunny. Jon Voight is equally fine as Joe Buck, a tall, handsome young man whose open face somehow manages to register the fuzziest of conflicting emotions within a very dim mind.

. . . its style is oddly romantic . . .

Waldo Frank's screenplay follows the Herlihy novel in most of the surface events. Joe Buck, a Texas dishwasher without friend or family, comes to New York to make his fortune as a stud to all the rich ladies who have been deprived of their rights by faggot eastern gentlemen. Instead, he winds up a half-hearted 42nd Street hustler whose first and only friend is a lame, largely ineffectual con artist.

As long as the focus is on this world of cafeterias and abandoned tenements, of desperate conjunctions in movie balconies and doorways, of catchup and beans and canned heat, "Midnight Cowboy" is so rough and vivid that it's almost unbearable. Less effective are abbreviated, almost subliminal fantasies and flashbacks. Most of these are designed to fill in the story of the young Joe Buck, a little boy whose knowledge of life was learned in front of a TV set while his grandmother, good-time Sally Buck, ran a Texas beauty parlor and lived with a series of cowboy-father images for Joe.

"Midnight Cowboy" often seems to be exploiting its material for sensational or comic effect, but it is ultimately a moving experience that captures the quality of a time and a place. It's not a movie for the ages, but, having seen it, you won't ever again feel detached as you walk down West 42nd Street, avoiding the eyes of the drifters, stepping around the little islands of hustlers and closing your nostrils to the smell of rancid griddles. ■

SEPTEMBER 25, 1969

SLAPSTICK AND DRAMA CROSS PATHS IN 'BUTCH CASSIDY'

Vincent Canby

Paul Newman and Robert Redford in "Butch Cassidy and the Sundance Kid," 1969.

"Butch Cassidy and the Sundance Kid" were real-life, turn-of-the-century outlaws who, in 1905, packed up their saddlebags, along with Sundance's mistress (a schoolteacher named Etta Place), and left the shrinking American West to start a new life, robbing banks in Bolivia.

According to the movie, their decline and fall was the sort of alternately absurd and dreamy saga that might have been fantasized by Truffaut's Jules and Jim and Catherine—before they grew up.

Butch (Paul Newman) is so amiable that it's not until he gets to Bolivia, and is more or less forced to go straight, that he ever brings himself to shoot a man. Sundance (Robert Redford) behaves like the perpetual younger brother. Although confident of his own abilities, he always defers to Butch, whose schemes end in disaster more often than success. Etta (Katharine Ross) is the kind of total woman who can cook, keep house of sorts, seldom grumbles, and, if necessary, will act as third gun.

This is an attractive conceit and much of "Butch Cassidy and the Sundance Kid" is very funny in a strictly contemporary way—the last exuberant word on movies about the men of the mythic American West who have outlived their day. Butch and Sundance have the physical graces of classic Western heroes, but all four feet are made of silly putty.

When they try to rob a train and blow open its safe, the dynamite charge destroys not only the safe but also the entire baggage car. When they can escape from a posse only by jumping from a high cliff into a raging rapids below, Sundance must admit ruefully that he doesn't know how to swim.

George Roy Hill ("Thoroughly Modern Millie," "Hawaii") who directed, and William Goldman, the novelist ("Boys and Girls Together") and occasional scenarist ("Harper"), who wrote the original screenplay, have consciously mixed their genres. Even though the result is not unpleasant, it is vaguely disturbing—you keep seeing signs of another, better film behind gags and effects that may remind you of everything from "Jules and Jim" to "Bonnie and Clyde" and "The Wild Bunch."

There is at the heart of "Butch Cassidy" a gnawing emptiness that can't be satisfied by an awareness that Hill and Goldman probably knew exactly what they were doing—making a very slick movie.

There are some bothersome technical things about the movie (the camera is all zoom, zoom, zoom) but the over-all production is very handsome, and the performances fine, especially Newman, Redford and Miss Ross, who must be broadly funny and straight, almost simultaneously. They succeed even if the movie does not. ■

APRIL 30, 1960

DICK CLARK DENIES RECEIVING PAYOLA

Anthony Lewis

WASHINGTON, April 29—Dick Clark swore to House investigators today that he had never taken payola, but the Congressmen were skeptical.

"I have not done anything that I think I should be ashamed of or that is illegal or immoral," Mr. Clark said, "and I hope to eventually convince you of this. I believe in my heart that I have never taken payola."

The House Special Subcommittee on Legislative Oversight produced figures showing that in less than three years Mr. Clark had received $167,750 in salary and $409,020 in increased stock values, on investments of $53,773.

Repeatedly the subcommittee's counsel, Robert W. Lishman, charged that this money had come to Mr. Clark because of his position as a disk jockey—the country's most influential and best paid, according to the industry.

"You say you did not get any payola," said Representative Steven B. Derounian, Republican of Roslyn, L.I. "But you got an awful lot of royola."

Mr. Clark, who is 30 years old, was smooth, slim and youthful on the witness stand. He wore his best blue serge suit and had a leather dispatch case at his side. He seemed even more self-possessed than his experienced counsel, Paul A. Porter.

The broadcasting touch was evident in his voice, which was low and casual—cool, one might say. He threw in slang and little touches of friendly informality from time to time, but mostly he was serious and sincere.

Surprisingly, there was hardly a teenager in the House caucus room. Mr. Clark's show, "American Bandstand," which appears daily on the American Broadcasting Company's television network, has a vast audience of teenagers.

Although networks do not officially announce their billings, or income from announcers, authoritative trade publications and agencies listed A.B.C.-TV's billings as $130,000,000 in 1959. This would mean that Mr. Clark's presentations brought in revenue of about $5,200,000 from sponsors.

Mr. Clark said he had picked the songs for "American Bandstand" on the basis of their popularity or their potential.

Asked why he did not play more songs by Frank Sinatra, Bing Crosby, Perry Como and other established stars instead of building up unknown names, Mr. Clark said these singers did not appeal to his teenage audience. ■

JULY 31, 1960

JAZZ PLAYED ON A PLASTIC SAX

John S. Wilson

Not since Charlie Parker began to be heard around town some twenty years ago has a jazz musician stirred up as much controversy as Ornette Coleman has during the last year. Mr. Coleman, who plays a plastic alto saxophone (originally for economic reasons, now by preference), can be described as an original in jazz, but what he is beyond that opens the doors to the controversy. His performances are expressed in irregular swoops of sound, punctuated by nervous bleats and delivered in a shrill, edgy tone that can rasp across one's nerves like chalk scratching a blackboard.

He is, he says, trying to break through to "a new, freer conception of jazz," one element of which is free group improvisation by his quartet.

"Before we start out to play," Mr. Coleman explains in his notes for his most recent disk, 'Change of the Century' (Atlantic), "we do not have any idea what the end result will be. Each player is free to contribute what he feels in the music at any given moment. We do not begin with a preconceived notion as to what kind of effect we will achieve."

This is Mr. Coleman's fourth LP. As his recorded work accumulates and the ear becomes adjusted to his unorthodox playing, two points become increasingly evident. First, and undoubtedly most important, Mr. Coleman has a strong, underlying, blues-rooted jazz feeling. The so-called "cry" that is often cited as the hallmark of the true jazz musician is very evident in much of his playing. But the freedom that

Ornette Coleman in the 1960s.

Mr. Coleman is seeking may be eluding him because he appears to have created his own set of clichés in the repetitious style to which he limits himself.

His program on "Change of the Century" typifies the problem in communication that Mr. Coleman has set for himself. On one selection, a blues called "Ramblin'," he allows the emotional projection inherent in this type of tune to influence his playing sufficiently to give it some form and substance. But the remaining six selections are grinding, jittery exercises that, except for the superb bass playing of Charlie Haden, soon become tedious. ■

MARCH 30, 1961

PETE SEEGER CONVICTED OF CONTEMPT

Philip Benjamin

Pete Seeger, the folk singer, was convicted of contempt of Congress yesterday by a jury in Federal Court. He was found guilty on all ten counts of an indictment charging him with refusing to answer questions by the House Committee on Un-American Activities.

Mr. Seeger had appeared before the committee Aug. 18, 1955, when it was in New York investigating possible Communist infiltration in the entertainment industry.

The 42-year-old singer could receive up to a year in prison and a $1,000 fine on each count. He will be sentenced next Tuesday morning at 10:30 A.M. The verdict will be appealed.

The jury, composed of eight men and four women, deliberated for an hour and twenty minutes before bringing in its verdict. Mr. Seeger was continued in $1,000 bail pending sentence.

The indictment was based on his refusal to answer ten questions at the 1955 hearing. The questions concerned alleged membership in the Communist party and participation in various Communist or Communist-front activities.

Mr. Seeger did not specifically invoke any Constitutional amendments as a basis for refusal to answer questions, but he said during a recess yesterday that the First Amendment, which guarantees freedom of speech, was implicit in his refusal.

During the three-day trial before Federal Judge Thomas F. Murphy, Mr. Seeger's attorney, Paul L. Ross, had attempted to cast doubt on the validity of the Congressional committee's investigation of the entertainment industry in New York, since no legislation had resulted from it.

In his charge to the jury yesterday, however, Judge Murphy said he had "determined as a matter of law" that the committee had conducted a valid inquiry and its questions to Mr. Seeger had been pertinent.

Irving Younger, the assistant United States attorney prosecuting the trial, said in summing up that the only issue was whether Mr. Seeger had been in contempt of Congress by refusing to answer questions.

Mr. Seeger did not take the stand. Yesterday Mr. Ross called four persons as character witnesses. They were Dr. Helen Parkhurst, an educator and founder of the Dalton School, a progressive school here; Moses Asch of Folkways Records, for whom Mr. Seeger has recorded songs; the Rev. Gerald Humphrey, a Protestant Episcopal priest from Beacon, N.Y., where Mr. Seeger lives; and Dr. Harold Taylor, former president of Sarah Lawrence College in Bronxville.

Two other persons indicted with Mr. Seeger will go on trial soon. They are Elliot Sullivan, 54, an actor, of 2 Peter Cooper Road, and Martin Yarus, an actor known professionally as George Tyne, 44, of 514 Central Park West. ■

APRIL 24, 1961

JUDY GARLAND AT CARNEGIE HALL

Lewis Funke

Judy Garland performing at Carnegie Hall, April 23, 1961.

The religious ritual of greeting, watching and listening to Judy Garland took place last night in Carnegie Hall. Indeed, what actually was to have been a concert—and was—also turned into something not too remote from a revival meeting.

From the moment Miss Garland came

(cont'd. on next page)

(cont'd from previous page)

on the stage, a stage, incidentally, on which have trod before her the immortals of music, the cultists were beside themselves. What Rev. Dr. Billy Graham would have given for such a welcome from the faithful!

They were on their feet even before the goddess grabbed the microphone, and by the time she had bestowed the first of those warm smiles, they were applauding and screaming "Bravo!" Miss Garland could have probably ended the concert right there and they would still be cheering. The fact is that at least a half dozen times more during the evening the standing ovation, plus the screaming, took place.

Whether or not this sort of unadulterated adulation was warranted is a matter a non-cultist had better not discuss in public. And whether or not so professional a performer as Miss Garland requires the ritual to put her on her mettle is questionable. But on her mettle she was last night as she went through a repertoire of favorites.

Looking trimmer and a good deal more youthful than she has in years, Miss Garland was always in control of herself. She soothed the tender songs as only she knows how to soothe tender songs, and she projected the loud ones with all the vigor at her command. With "Alone Together" or "The Man That Got Away" she wove enchantment. With "San Francisco," "Come Rain or Come Shine" or "I Can't Give You Anything But Love" she whipped the adherents into frenzies of exaltation.

It was, to be truthful, surprising that this audience was able to muster the pandemonium it let loose when Miss Garland wound up with "The Trolley Song," "Rock a Bye" and included among her encores "Over the Rainbow" and "Swanee."

Through it all she was the usual Judy, perspiring profusely ("sweat," she said candidly and more earthily), taking the usual sip of water, standing frequently in front of the microphone letting her voice convey her emotions with a minimum of gesture or movement; other times she skipped a bit, sort of dancing lightly with the rhythm, always making her audience feel—as one listener remarked—"as if she's singing just to you."

In any case, one thing is certain: old Carnegie Hall can take it and by this morning everything undoubtedly is serene again on West Fifty-seventh Street. ■

SEPTEMBER 24, 1962

ORCHESTRA'S QUEST FOR A HOME ENDS AFTER 116 YEARS

In March, 1846, members of the four-year-old New York Philharmonic Society held a meeting in the New York Coliseum. The rallying cry was "we must build a Philharmonic Hall!" Last night, 116 years later, after a migration that included at least 10 temporary homes and a steady movement uptown, the New York Philharmonic at last played in its own hall.

The hall is the Philharmonic's "own" for a number of reasons. The whole idea of Lincoln Center grew out of exploratory talks by representatives of the Philharmonic and the Metropolitan Opera with John D. Rockefeller 3d over their housing problems. The Philharmonic is represented on the Lincoln Center board of directors. It was also represented on the Philharmonic Hall subcommittee of the Lincoln Center building committee.

Philharmonic Hall will also house the orchestra's offices. No longer will the orchestra's officials have to sprint across West 57th Street to coordinate matters between the controller and the box office.

The orchestra's contract with Lincoln Center begins on Oct. 1, and runs for 24 years with three renewal options of 25 years each. Thus the orchestra tenure in its new home for at least the next 99 years.

On Dec. 7, 1842, the New York Philharmonic Society gave its first public concert, in the Apollo Rooms at 410 Broadway, near Canal Street. The orchestra then numbered 55 professional musicians, who had paid $25 for the privilege of joining the

SEPTEMBER 29, 1961

20-YEAR-OLD BOB DYLAN IS BRIGHT NEW FACE

Robert Shelton

A bright new face in folk music is appearing at Gerde's Folk City. Although only 20 years old, Bob Dylan is one of the most distinctive stylists to play in a Manhattan cabaret in months.

Resembling a cross between a choir boy and a beatnik, Mr. Dylan has a cherubic look and a mop of tousled hair he partly covers with a Huck Finn black corduroy cap. His clothes may need a bit of tailoring, but when he works his guitar, harmonica or piano and composes new songs faster than he can remember them, there is no doubt that he is bursting at the seams with talent.

Mr. Dylan's voice is anything but pretty. He is consciously trying to recapture the rude beauty of a Southern field hand musing in melody on his porch. All the "husk and bark" are left on his notes and a searing intensity pervades his songs.

Mr. Dylan is both comedian and tragedian. Like a vaudeville actor on the rural circuit, he offers a variety of droll musical monologues: "Talking Bear Mountain" lampoons the overcrowding of an excursion boat, "Talking New York" satirizes his troubles in gaining recognition and "Talking Havah Nagilah" burlesques the folk-music craze and the singer himself.

In his serious vein, Mr. Dylan seems to be performing in a slow-motion film. Elasticized phrases are drawn out until you think they may snap. He rocks his head and body, closes his eyes in reverie and seems to be groping for a word or a mood, then resolves the tension benevolently by finding the word and the mood.

Mr. Dylan's highly personalized approach toward folk song is still evolving. He has been sopping up influences like a sponge. At times, the drama he aims at is off-target melodrama and his stylization threatens to topple over as a mannered excess.

But if not for every taste, his music-making has the mark of originality and inspiration, all the more noteworthy for his youth. Mr. Dylan is vague about his antecedents and birthplace, but it matters less where he has been than where he is going, and that would seem to be straight up. ■

orchestra and sharing in its profits. Members of the orchestra served as ushers at the first concert, white gloved and carrying long, white, wooden wands.

One of the three conductors at that first concert, which included Beethoven's Fifth Symphony, several vocal selections and some chamber music, was the eccentric American violinist Ureli Corelli Hill, who had first envisioned the whole enterprise. Mr. Hill stayed with the orchestra until 1873, then played in theaters in New York until depression over finances resulted in his suicide in 1875.

During the next few years the orchestra played in five other halls. The Assembly Rooms of the Chinese Building at 541 Broadway, Niblo's Gardens at Broadway and Prince Street, Metropolitan Hall, on the same corner, and the Broadway Tabernacle on Broadway and Worth Street. On May 20, 1846, a "festival concert" was given at Castle Garden (Fort Clinton) on the Battery to raise money for Philharmonic Hall.

And so the Odyssey continued. Philharmonic concerts were given at three halls on East 14th Street—Irving Hall, the Academy of Music and Steinway Hall. When the Metropolitan Opera House opened in 1883, one of its tenants was the New York Philharmonic. The orchestra was, by that time, flourishing. From an initial three-concert season in 1842-43, it had expanded its season to five performances. Its membership had reached 80.

Then, on Nov. 18, 1892—nearly 50 years after its founding—the Philharmonic made its first appearance on the stage of Andrew Carnegie's new Music Hall. Carnegie Hall (the name was officially adopted in 1898) had opened in May, 1891.

The hall was planned largely to house the Philharmonic's then rival, the New York Symphony Society. That orchestra was founded by Leopold Damrosch in 1878, and had been since his death in 1885 by his son, Walter. The Symphony Society's parent organization was the Oratorio Society, founded in 1873 and also conducted by Damrosch father and son.

The main hall opened with a one-week festival, planned and presented by the New York Symphony Society and the Oratorio Society. The special guest for the week was Peter Ilyich Tchaikovsky, who made the journey from Russia to hear and conduct a number of his compositions. As he arose, a great roar welled up from the crowd. When he started to speak, a hush fell.

Even after its first concert at Carnegie Hall, the Philharmonic split its season that year between there and the Metropolitan Opera House. From then on, however, Carnegie Hall was "home" to the Philharmonic. The two orchestras continued as friendly rivals until 1928, when they merged into the present Philharmonic-Symphony Society. By last season the season had grown to 30 weeks, and the orchestra to 104 players. ■

Avery Fisher Hall, the home of the New York Philharmonic orchestra, at the Lincoln Center for the Performing Arts, 1962.

JULY 29, 1963

FOLK-MUSIC FETE CALLED A SUCCESS

Robert Shelton

Joan Baez and Bob Dylan at the Newport Folk Festival, Rhode Island, 1963. This was Dylan's first performance on the Newport stage.

NEWPORT, R.I., July 28—On almost every level, the three-day Newport Folk Festival of 1963, which closed tonight with more than 13,000 listeners filling Freebody Park, was an enormous success.

The 47,000 paid admissions for the event surpassed the attendance at the Newport Jazz Festival earlier this month by 11,000. Because of this turnout and the fact that more than 70 performers who appeared here since Friday worked for minimum wages, the nonprofit Newport Folk Foundation will have about $70,000 to use for enriching the field of folk music with educational projects.

The folk festival can be praised for its high esthetic level, for imaginative programming and skillful choice of performers. It can be praised for educating an audience. Amid all this, despite scorching temperatures, the weekend was truly festive. A tirelessly enthusiastic audience of teenagers and young adults, looking as fresh and wholesome as the cast of an Andy Hardy film, made the event almost as exciting as the performers did.

A listener reels away from this resort city as from a buffet of rich food. There was a cross section of the top level of professionals, and a legion of lesser-known performers. So that the audience could pick and choose, nearly 20 daytime panels and workshops, as many as four at a time, were deployed on the grass tennis courts of the Newport Casino.

To single out particularly strong performances from this marathon is difficult. Yet, one will not soon forget Bob Dylan closing the first concert singing "We Shall Overcome," with a chorus behind him made up of the Freedom Singers, Peter, Paul and Mary; Joan Baez and the Messrs. Bikel and Seeger. One will remember Doc Watson and Bill Monroe in the taut, Faustian white gospel song, "What Would You Give in Exchange for Your Soul?" One will remember Tony Saletan leading African songs, and Ian and Sylvia from Canada, and Bob Davenport from England and much, much more.

The Newport Folk Foundation will have its challenges in tightening the programming, improving the physical setup of the festival, and moving into other areas of folk tradition not covered here this weekend. But the dominant impression was one of a cooperative production by devotees more concerned with artistic purpose than commercial considerations. The audience, who enjoyed such a large ratio of ethnic music without sugarcoating, showed a maturity beyond the years of most of those who attended.

The triumph of the Newport Folk Festival this weekend should be resounding for a long time to come. Integrity in folk music had a field day at the box office.

FEBRUARY 8, 1964

BEATLES INVADE, FANS SCREAM

The Beatles (from left, John Lennon, Paul McCartney, Ringo Starr, George Harrison) arriving at John F. Kennedy Airport in New York, for their first U.S. tour, 1964.

Paul Gardner

Multiply Elvis Presley by four, subtract six years from his age, add British accents and a sharp sense of humor. The answer: It's the Beatles (Yeah, Yeah, Yeah).

The rock 'n' roll group, which may become Britain's most successful export since the bowler, arrived at Kennedy International Airport yesterday and more than 3,000 teenagers stood four deep on the upper arcade at the International Arrivals Building to greet them.

Disk jockeys who have an interest in Beatle records had urged the young people to welcome them. The quartet has sold 6 million records and earns as much as $10,000 a week for appearances. Five organizations, represented by at least 17 press agents, will share in the Beatle's American booty.

An official at Kennedy Airport shook his head and said, "We've never seen anything like this here before. Never. Not even for kings and queens."

There were girls, girls and more girls. Whistling girls. Screaming girls. Singing girls. They held "Beatles, we love you" and "WELCOME" signs. When the Beatles's plane touched down at 1:20 P.M. the girls chanted, "We want Beatles."

The Beatles are Paul McCartney, 21 years old; Ringo Starr, 23; George Harrison, 21; and John Lennon, 23. They arrived by jet with their personal manager, one Beatle wife (Mrs. Lennon), two road managers and one press agent.

The Beatles will make their first live television appearance here Sunday evening on the Ed Sullivan show. On Tuesday, they will go to Washington for a concert at the Coliseum. On Wednesday, Lincoln's Birthday, they will give two shows at Carnegie Hall.

The Beatles, who popularized rock 'n' roll in Britain, have added new gimmicks: tight pants, boots, and hair that never seems to be cut.

Danielle Landau, a 15-year-old from Brooklyn, oohed and aahed as the Beatles left the terminal. "They're different." She sighed, "They're just so different. I mean, all that hair. American singers are soooo clean-cut."

The Beatles are staying at the Plaza Hotel. They have a 10-room suite and a guard who is on duty 24 hours. They were driven into the city by four limousines—each Beatle had his own Cadillac.

Besides the screaming teenagers, the Beatles were met by 200 reporters and photographers from newspapers, magazines, foreign publications, radio and television stations, and teenage fan magazines. A press conference was bedlam.

The International Arrivals Building was filled with policemen who were buffeted by the teenagers. One policeman said, "The detail was increased. We knew it could get pretty wild." And it did. (Yeah, Yeah, Yeah.) ■

FEBRUARY 10, 1964

QUARTET CONTINUES TO AGITATE THE FAITHFUL

Jack Gould

The cyclical turnover in teenage trauma received recognition last night in the businesslike appearance of the Beatles on the "Ed Sullivan Show" over the Columbia Broadcasting System. The boys hardly did for daughter what Elvis Presley did for her older sister or Frank Sinatra for mother.

The Liverpool quartet, borrowing the square hairdo used every morning on television by Captain Kangaroo, was composed of conservative conformists. In furthering Britain's comeback as an international influence, they followed established procedure for encouraging self-determination in underdeveloped areas.

The pretext of a connection with the world of music was perfunctorily sustained by the Beatles. But in the quick intelligence beneath their bangs, there appeared to be a bemused awareness that they might qualify as the world's highest-paid recreation directors.

In their sophisticated understanding that the life of a fad depends on the performance of the audience and not on the stage, the Beatles were decidedly effective. In their two sets of numbers, they allowed the healing effect of group therapy to run its course under the discipline of Mr. Sullivan, the chaperone of the year.

Televised Beatlemania appeared to be a fine mass placebo, and thanks undoubtedly are due Britain for a recess in winter's routine. Last night's sedate anticlimax speaks well for continuing British-American understanding. The British always were much more strict with children.

JANUARY 22, 1965

'CALIFORNIA SOUND' DWELLS ON CRACK-UPS AND DANGER

Peter Bart

HOLLYWOOD, Jan. 21—The other day, Jan Berry, a young medical student, was sitting in a lecture hall when he had an idea for a song.

"The song is about a motorcycle cop on the Hollywood Freeway who likes to catch teenage kids for speeding," Mr. Berry said. "So one day the cop chases a kid who doesn't feel like stopping. They all crack up."

This may not seem like the makings of a song, but Mr. Berry knows better. He and his partner, Dean Torrence, have written and sung rock 'n' roll tunes that have sold about 10 million records. They are leading exponents of what is known as the California sound.

This week, the partners planned to inject the California sound into their first movie, for Paramount Pictures, "Myron, the Musician Ape, Meets Jan and Dean."

The California sound, though rhythmic, is less influenced by wailing rhythm and blues than most rock 'n' roll, with its strong Negro ethnic strains. While rhythm and blues, which dominate rock 'n' roll, dwell on unrequited love, most of the California lyrics deal with surfing, skate-boarding, drag-racing and sky-diving.

"The California sound is like folk music in that it reflects the way of life of a region," observed Lou Adler, president of Dunhill Music Company, a small company that handles California rock 'n' roll singers.

The sound first attracted attention when surfing music became a fad. Out of the surfing craze evolved such groups as The Beach Boys and The Fantastic Baggys. (Baggys are loose-fitting swimming trunks worn by dedicated surfers.)

When surfing music started to subside, the Californians switched to skate-boarding, referred to as sidewalk surfing, and more recently to what is called carburetor love songs. In these songs teenagers express affection for their automobiles.

"The first thing a kid really loves is his car," said Steve Barri, a chunky 22-year-old Californian who has written 75 rock 'n' roll songs. "So the lyrics express this love. Personally, I think it's a bit nauseating."

California's young rock 'n' roll singers are hunting for new fads. One young songwriter, Guy Hemric, believes that parachute-jumping will be the next teenage craze, and he has been writing sky-diving songs. Mr. Berry, the medical student, believes that a coming fad will be for love songs for girls and boys younger than 10 years old. ■

FEBRUARY 16, 1965

Nat King Cole, 45, Is Dead of Cancer

SANTA MONICA, Calif., Feb. 15—Nat King Cole, the velvet-voiced popular singer, died in St. John's Hospital here this morning. He was 45 years old.

Mr. Cole entered the hospital on Dec. 8 with a lung condition that was later disclosed to be lung cancer. After receiving cobalt treatments, his left lung was removed in an operation on Jan. 23.

With a minimum of theatrics and an ease of style, Mr. Cole became one of the leading Negro entertainers in the country and one of the most durable figures in American popular music.

His recordings of such songs as "Nature Boy," "Mona Lisa," "Too Young" and "Rambling Rose" sold 50 million copies and in a business keyed to an ever-changing public taste he remained on top for almost a quarter of a century.

His singing style, which was once described as "a syrupy slur" but was also compared to "a soft evening breeze," was based on a very round, full projection of every syllable of a lyric, delivered in a relaxed and slightly husky-voiced manner. A factor in his effectiveness as a singer was the phrasing and rhythmic feeling he had acquired earlier in his career when he was primarily a jazz pianist.

Nathaniel Adams Coles was born in Montgomery, Ala., on March 17, 1919. When

AUGUST 30, 1965

DYLAN CONQUERS UNRULY AUDIENCE

FOLK SINGER OFFERS WORKS IN 'NEW MOOD' AT FOREST HILLS

Robert Shelton

Facing a rude and immature audience, Bob Dylan gave a program Saturday night at the Forest Hills Music Festival in Queens in which he was a model of patient composure.

Some 15,000 persons packed the tennis stadium for a program by the widely imitated and highly controversial young singer—guitarist—songwriter. Most of the audience's attitudes were concerned with Mr. Dylan's excursions into "folk rock," a fusion of rock 'n' roll with folk-based songwriting.

The first eruption came when Jerry White, a radio announcer associated with folk music, introduced Murray (the K) Kaufman, a disk jockey associated with rock 'n' roll. Mr. Kaufman was barely able to shout his blessings on Mr. Dylan and his new mood before the audience howled and booed its disapproval.

After a delay of several minutes, Mr. Dylan appeared alone with his guitar, harmonica, plaintive voice and seven of his folkish songs.

Among them was a major new work, "Desolation Road," a long work filled with the incongruities of black humor and macabre imagery.

The song, another of Mr. Dylan's musical Rohrshachs capable of widely varied interpretation, ranged freely from Cinderella to T. S. Eliot to "Einstein disguised as Robin Hood." It can best be characterized as a "folk song of the absurd."

After intermission, Mr. Dylan appeared with an excellent rock 'n' roll quartet, with Robbie Robertson playing the electric guitar, Al Cooper the electric piano, Harvey Brooks the electric bass, and Levon Helm the drums.

The electric band and the high-voltage vocalizing raised the level of Mr. Dylan's performance from the intimate introspective vein of the first half to a shouting, crackling intensity. The young audience's displeasure was manifested at the end of most of the numbers, by booing and shouts of "we want the old Dylan." The young star plowed valiantly on, with the sort of coolness he has rarely displayed on stage.

The electric band and the high-voltage vocalizing raised the level of Mr. Dylan's performance

He even kept his coolness during repeated sorties of very young members of the audience who ran onto a roped-off grass section in front of the stage, after, or during, songs. Several eluded the guards and got to the stage, but were evicted. Mr. Dylan just kept singing.

Nothing so dramatized the childishness of the audience's reaction to folk rock than when it ceased to boo and started to sing along with the popular song, "Like a Rolling Stone." Evidently the hostility extends only toward things with which they aren't familiar.

By the time they get to know his excellent new folk rock songs, such as "Tombstone Blues," maybe the noisy young booers who ruined an artistically strong concert may have grown up a bit.

he was 4 years old, his father, the Rev. Edward Coles, took Nat, his sister Evelyn, and three brothers, Eddie, Freddie and Isaac, to Chicago where Mr. Coles became minister of the True Light Baptist Church.

Young Nat was playing the organ in his father's church and singing in the choir by the time he was 12. In high school, he played with a band called The Rogues of Rhythm organized by his brother, Eddie, a bassist. He made his first recordings in 1936 for Decca with this band. After completing high school, Mr. Cole joined a traveling company of the revue "Shuffle Along." Within a few months, the show was stranded in Long Beach, Calif.

Mr. Cole went to work as a solo pianist. By his own account he played in "practically every beer joint in Los Angeles, never making more than $5 a night." The proprietor of one club, the Swanee Inn, urged Mr. Cole to form a trio in 1937. He hired Wesley Prince, a bassist, and Oscar Moore, a guitarist. The proprietor put a paper crown on Mr. Cole's head. He dropped the "s" from the end of his name, and the King Cole Trio was born.

In 1943, the trio was signed by the newly organized Capitol Records Company. Their first recording for Capitol was a novelty called "Straighten Up and Fly Right," written by Mr. Cole in 1937.

During the next three years, the trio continued to mix jazz instrumental performances and singing. Mr. Cole frequently appeared by himself as a pianist at jazz concerts.

In 1946, for his recording of "The Christmas Song," one of his biggest hits, a string section was added to his trio. After the success of "The Christmas Song," Mr. Cole put greater and greater emphasis on his singing. On another hit record in the late nineteen-forties, "Nature Boy," he used a big band as accompaniment for the first time. After that, the trio became secondary to Mr. Cole's singing on records, in nightclubs and theaters and at concerts.

Among his hit recordings were "Route 66," "Too Young," "I Love You for Sentimental Reasons," "Walking My Baby Back Home," "Somewhere Along the Way," "Smile" and "Unforgettable."

Although his father, being a minister, would not go to the nightclubs to hear his son perform, Mr. Cole said, "My mother always came to see me and she'd sit there and beam." She died in 1955. His father then began to attend. "I think he felt that he should be mother and father to me," the singer said. The Rev. Mr. Coles died on Feb. 1.

JANUARY 30, 1966

THE FOLK-ROCK RAGE

Robert Shelton

Folk-rock, which mixes the simplicity of folk music with the frenetic rhythmic beat of the electrically amplified sound of rock 'n' roll, caused one of the biggest controversies in American pop music last year.

Enough folk-rock recordings are at hand to begin a serious appraisal of what the new music is all about. Is it a genuine new style, or merely opportunism in the wake of the Beatles? Did electric instruments cause a power failure or a power success? Has the entry of folk musicians into the larger mainstream of pop music improved the content of pop music while leaving the body of traditional folk music intact?

Folk-rock was born when the Byrds, a rock 'n' roll group, recorded Bob Dylan's "Hey! Mr. Tambourine Man." But it got its biggest push by Dylan himself, who set aside his soft-spoken guitar for a boisterous amplified one, introducing the rock 'n' roll style into his socially conscious folk approach. Last summer he was roundly booed at the Newport Folk Music Festival and at Forest Hills by purists who resented the apparent commercial appeal. But there were cheers too.

Since then there has been a lot of hopping on the bandwagon, image-shifting and confusion about folk-rock. But from this corner the new music can generally earn praise as a healthy movement. No one says that every folk and topical performer need add a beat, long hair and outlandish clothes to his act. Those who feel more at home with this rhythmic "music of their generation" should have the right to experiment and reject, look for new forms of reaching new listeners; be free to make malleable their own form of communication.

A new single by Judy Collins, "I'll Keep It With Mine" (Elektra), buries a lot of misconceptions about folk-rock. It is *not* a protest song. The common idea that all folk-rock deals in social commentary is an inaccurate generalization. This song of love and affirmation by Bob Dylan, the leading force in shaping folk-rock, also puts an end to the canard that Dylan is now a spokesman only for alienation and personal hostility.

Most of these defenses of folk-rock are in reply to a disturbingly narrow-minded view carried in the January issue of "Sing Out!" the leading folk-music magazine in the United States, in circulation if not in influence. The many pages used to minimize folk-rock put this little publication in a very bad light. What is the function of the secular periodical if not to encourage experimentation, to help shape an avant-garde? Instead, "Sing Out!" fights for a musical rear guard and sounds increasingly like doctrinaire Soviet cultural organs denouncing the poet Yevgeny Yevtushenko for heresies, prodding him back to the pastures of orthodoxy.

This apology for folk-rock as a style is not meant to defend all that has been recorded in the new genre. Some of it is laughably inept. Some of it is obviously insincere. But we are defending a whole new area of rhythmic, up-beat music that couples the meaningfulness of folk lyrics with the vitality of rock 'n' roll. ■

APRIL 24, 1966

JAZZ AND THE ANARCHY OF THE AVANT GARDE

John S. Wilson

John Coltrane in Paris, 1963.

For John Coltrane, 1965 was quite a year. The readers of Down Beat, the jazz magazine, voted him the best jazz tenor saxophonist of the year, named him "Jazzman of the Year," elected him to the magazine's Hall of Fame, and chose his recording of "A Love Supreme" as the record of the year, a choice that was echoed in a poll conducted by Jazz magazine.

Since he picked up all the marbles last year, it will be a little difficult to raise the accolades even higher in 1966, but, on the basis of a disk called "Ascension" (Impulse 95; stereo S-95), it appears this Coltrane work that Down Beat's readers voted for was simply prelude to this massive and startling performance. "Ascension" was actually recorded in June, 1965, but, since it was not released until this year, those who voted for him last year were unaware of it.

"Ascension" is a vast maelstrom of sound which at first appears to be the wildest kind of anarchy. But in it Coltrane has found an amazingly effective framework for two elements which have sorely needed both organization and a complementary setting; his own experiments with the cumulative effects of a long, long, repetitious performance, and the avant gardists' urge to produce outlandish noises.

With only the four members of his quartet at his disposal, Coltrane's efforts at extensive repetition have, all too often, turned into monotony. On the other hand, with 11 men and using a pattern in which the full ensemble not only alternates with soloists but continues to provide strong support behind each soloist, there is so much boiling activity that the kind of boredom engendered by seemingly endless solos is swept completely aside.

This is orchestral jazz that has its roots in the ensemble improvisation of the early jazzmen in New Orleans but which, at the same time, has assimilated several of the strongest elements of contemporary jazz exploration. It is an extraordinary accomplishment not alone because of the performance but because it has pulled together some of the more wildly waving loose ends of jazz to give them form and direction which they have usually lacked in other circumstances. ■

MAY 2, 1966

SIMON AND GARFUNKEL SING THEIR OWN COMPOSITIONS

The popular singing duo, Simon and Garfunkel, gave a concert in the McMillin Theater at Columbia University yesterday afternoon. The program, the pair's first major appearance in New York, displayed how strongly the two young men are speaking to, and perhaps for, their student audiences.

Paul Simon composes the pair's first-rate folk and pop songs. His partner, Arthur Garfunkel, who graduated last year from Columbia College, is a highly professional vocalist. The two have been singing together since they were in the sixth grade, made their first recording two years ago and have seen two of Mr. Simon's songs, "The Sound of Silence" and "Homeward Bound," become hits.

The performance was as impressive as was the material. The pair have light, accurately pitched, mellifluous voices that combine in agreeable, sometimes adventuresome, harmonies. Mr. Simon's guitar-playing flowed with ease, taste and economy.

Most of the songs, in the idiom of pop folk writing, touched on subjects ordinarily of little concern to pop singers: loss of communication, show-business loneliness, illusions, suicide, a factory hand's anger and envy, subways and dignity. There was lighter material about children's foibles and teenager's acne.

In most instances, Mr. Simon's songs are well-crafted, communicative and melodically alive. Their poetry strikes responsive nerves of emotional depth. The performance gathered increasing force of involvement and drama to do the writing justice. ■

Art Garfunkel and Paul Simon, 1965.

JUNE 20, 1966

RAVI SHANKAR GIVES WEST A NEW OLD SOUND

Joseph Lelyveld

LONDON, June 19—Ravi Shankar, the virtuoso musician who introduced the sitar, an Indian stringed instrument, to Western concert audiences, is finding to his amazement that he has become a pop hero to the shaggy-haired youths who dote on the Beatles and the Rolling Stones.

It all started when George Harrison, one of the Beatles, decided it would be a lark to put aside his electric guitar on a recording date and see what he could do with a sitar. It is a large, complex instrument, sometimes with 30 movable frets, 6 main strings and 25 sympathetic strings. By Mr. Shankar's standards, all Mr. Harrison could do was pluck it.

But by Beatles' standards, he had discovered an exciting new sound that added mysterious, Oriental overtones to a number that had the Occidental name of "Norwegian Wood."

Before long, Brian Jones, one of the Rolling Stones, was off to his nearest Indian crafts shop to get a sitar, which he used for a number called "Paint It Black." It went to the top of the British hit parade.

Now, according to the latest rumors, the sitar will be used in most of the numbers on the Beatles' next long-playing record. How had Mr. Harrison discovered the instrument? He belongs, it seems, to Yehudi Menuhin's Asian Music Circle.

Mr. Shankar was soon caught in the backwash of this enthusiasm. When he gave a recital at the Royal Festival Hall early this month, his sold-out audience included Mr. Harrison and scores of young men and women in matching checked trousers who had heard of Mr. Shankar and the sitar through the Beatles.

(cont'd. on next page)

(cont'd. from previous page)

The next week, a bit reluctantly and under pressure from his agent, the Indian musician appeared on a television show for teenagers called "Whole Scene Going." And this week, a record in which he plays an Indian folk song was issued on the pop market.

Bemused by this popularity from an unexpected source, Mr. Shankar gently but firmly lays aside any notion that either he or the sitar may have a future in pop music. Learning how to play the sitar to make Beatle music, he says, "is like learning the Chinese alphabet in order to write English poems."

He himself had nearly 10 years of formal training in the traditional modes of Indian music before venturing to improvise on his instrument. "My guru [or teacher] used to tell me," he recalls, "that it takes more than one lifetime to learn to play sitar properly."

Mr. Shankar is convinced that the sitar fad will quickly fade. "Next year," he predicts, "it might well be the Japanese koto." ■

JULY 4, 1966

ROLLING STONES GATHER AVID FANS

There were 9,400 listeners and 375 policemen on hand Saturday night for the opening of the 1966 Music Festival at the Forest Hills Tennis Stadium in Queens.

The turnout, civilian and uniformed, was for the Rolling Stones, the British rock 'n' roll quintet. During the evening, there was a lot of hysterical screaming and several running sorties toward the stage by overwrought teenagers. But the 125 private police of the Aarden Security Service kept the audience under control and the 250 city policemen standing by made no arrests.

The Rolling Stones are making their fifth concert tour of the United States—a tour that will take them to 30 cities by the end of the month. The middling attendance at a stadium that seats 14,000 was attributed by some to the heat. Others believed that interest in British rock groups is declining and that the scaling of tickets from $5 to $12.50 has simply become too much for the young fans.

Three rock groups, the Trade Winds, the Standells and the McCoys, preceded the featured performers to the stage. Although the concert was called for 8 P.M., the Britons did not arrive in their helicopter until 10:15. Shrieking and impatient stamping and handclapping by that segment of the population tenderly referred to as "teeny-boppers" finally brought the young idols out. For their 35 minutes on stage, the Stones reportedly earned $25,000.

Despite their best efforts to project the image of rather surly rebels, the Rolling Stones, at this concert, were completely charming and very disciplined musicians. Much of their work is evolved from Negro rhythm and blues styles, urging strenuously against an insistent beat. But the firm British accent overrides all origins.

Occasionally, the group's instrumental work showed the current strong interest in Indian sitar music. "Lady Jane," whatever its coded message may mean, has the musical flavor of a modern-day courtly troubadour song.

The lead singer of the Stones, Mick Jagger, is a fascinating performer to watch. During the Rolling Stones's last number, "Satisfaction," several girls were crying uncontrollably. About a dozen youngsters broke through the police lines until they were tripped or tackled by guards. One boy got on stage and clutched Mr. Jagger's leg before he was thrown out of the park. The band withdrew immediately and within seconds the park lights were up and the Rolling Stones's helicopter took off into the night.

The Rolling Stones's Mick Jagger performing at Forest Hills stadium, 1966.

OCTOBER 23, 1966

WIELAND WAGNER

HE SAW THE BEGINNING AND END OF THE WORLD IN THE 'RING'

Harold C. Schonberg

Wieland Wagner in 1963.

In musical and theatrical circles there was a sense of real shock at the sudden and untimely death of Wieland Wagner at the age of 49. Ever since 1951 and that fabulous postwar Beyreuth season, Wieland Wagner was one of the most potent of theatrical ogy, and was convinced that the Wagner operas had their roots not only in a German mythos but in a mythos that was elemental. He pointed out many parallels between the "Ring" cycle and Greek myths. He saw in the Rhine Maidens the Oceanides; the Wotan-Brünnhilde conflict was to him a repetition of the Kreon-Antigone story. Zeus and Semele were prototypes of Lohengrin. He saw all of Wagner in terms of Jungian archetypes and Freudian dreams and sexology.

To convey the essence of these archetypes, Wieland Wagner from the beginning in 1951 did away with scenery and props. The famous tilted turntable (the world? the universe?) of his original "Ring" was soon copied in many European opera houses. He became more and more abstract. In "Die Meistersinger," Nuremberg had no houses, and the personalities of the characters underwent some change.

He was a complicated man. Although a particular pet of Hitler, there never was any indication that he was himself a Nazi. After the war he filled his Bayreuth casts with Americans, much to the distress of the old guard, and in 1961 he capped it all by having a Negro girl, Grace Bumbry, sing Venus in "Tannhäuser." She was promptly dubbed "The Black Venus," and the old guard frothed at the mouth. What was Bayreuth coming to? Wieland Wagner, who was not worried about race or religion, called a press conference. He had cast Bumbry, he said, because she could sing and act the part. That was all. And then he applied the clincher. When a German singer came along who could sing as good a Venus, why, then, he would use her. ■

The Supremes in 1967. From left, Florence Ballard, Mary Wilson and Diana Ross.

NOVEMBER 27, 1966

THE BIG, HAPPY, BEATING HEART OF THE DETROIT SOUND

Richard R. Lingeman

Those who think of "Detroit sound" as referring to the din of the auto assembly line intermingled with the muted wail of manufacturers announcing price increases on their 1967 models may be surprised to learn that in the pop record business the Detroit sound means the kind of music made by Motown Records, a relatively small company which sells more singles than any other company in the country.

(cont'd. on next page)

(cont'd. from previous page)

Motown began as one of a number of small R&B record companies which sprang up in Detroit during the fifties, partly in response to a demand for such music by Negro-oriented radio stations, which were also born at about the same time to serve Detroit's large (now over 500,000) Negro population. Says Peter Gzowski of The Toronto Daily Star, a close observer of the Detroit musical scene, "There seems to be at least one small record firm, sign over door, Cadillac in driveway. Motown is the first of these firms to break into the big time."

Such success is reflective of a growing demand for R&B music among teenagers who, of course, make up the bulk of single-record buyers. Much of the credit for the spreading of the Motown gospel belongs to three herald angels known collectively as the Supremes, and individually as Diana Ross, Mary Wilson and Florence Ballard. Diana Ross, the lead singer, has been compared often to Eartha Kitt, but she has a flexible, sweeter style of her own that can shift gears from a gospel fervor into a romantic ballad.

But don't get the impression that Motown is a sort of hit-hazardous operation. Its head man, Berry Gordy Jr., a one-time auto worker, has built himself something of a pop assembly line. He has attracted a lot of young raw talent and created an organization capable of nurturing and polishing that talent until they become smooth, well-drilled performers who are capable of holding a night club audience, as well as catching a teenager's ear for a couple of minutes.

There is at Motown, for example, something called an artists' development department, whose function is to take rock and roll kids and convert them into a viable night club act. This "finishing school," as it is known among the Motown performers, employs a galaxy of veteran showmen to train the kids to make the break from the sound studio to a live performance on stage.

There is also a charm school in which girl performers are taught how to sit, how to hold a fork, how to walk, how to speak. "They learn how to behave both on stage *and* off," says Mrs. Ardenia Johnston, the smiling, maternal lady who teaches them, with something of a school marm's glint in her eye. "I just can't tell you what Motown has meant to these kids," Mrs. Johnston says. "Some of them would have ended up juvenile delinquents if they hadn't had this opportunity." ■

JUNE 18, 1967

WE STILL NEED THE BEATLES, BUT...

Richard Goldstein

The Beatles spent an unprecedented four months and $100,000 on their new album, "Sergeant Pepper's Lonely Heart's Club Band" (Capitol SMAS 2653, mono and stereo). Like fathers-to-be, they kept a close watch on each stage of its gestation. For they are no longer merely superstars. Hailed as progenitors of a Pop avant garde, they have been idolized as the most creative members of their generation. The pressure to create an album that is complex, profound and innovative must have been staggering. So they retired to the electric sanctity of their recording studio, dispensing with their adoring audience, and the shrieking inspiration it can provide.

The finished product reached the record racks last week; the Beatles had supervised even the album cover—a mind-blowing collage of famous and obscure people, plants and artifacts. The 12 new compositions in the album are as elaborately conceived as the cover. The sound is a pastiche of dissonance and lushness. The mood is mellow, even nostalgic. But, like the cover, the overall effect is busy, hip and cluttered.

Like an over-attended child "Sergeant Pepper" is spoiled. It reeks of horns and harps, harmonica quartets, assorted animal noises and a 41-piece orchestra. On at least one cut, the Beatles are not heard at all instrumentally.

There certainly are elements of burlesque in a composition like "When I'm 64," which poses the crucial question: "Will you still need me/Will you still feed me/when I'm 64?" But the dominant tone is not mockery; this is a fantasy retirement, overflowing with grandchildren, gardening and a modest cottage on the Isle of Wight. It is a strange fairy tale, oddly sad because it is so far from the composers' reality. But even here, an honest vision is ruined by the background which seeks to enhance it.

"Lucy in the Sky With Diamonds" is an engaging curio, but nothing more. It is drenched in reverb, echo and other studio distortions.

For the first time, the Beatles have given us an album of special effects, dazzling but ultimately fraudulent. And for the first time, it is not exploration which we sense, but consolidation. There is a touch of the Jefferson Airplane, a dab of Beach Boys vibrations, and a generous pat of gymnastics from The Who.

The one evident touch of originality appears in the structure of the album itself. The Beatles have shortened the "banding" between cuts so that one song seems to run into the next. This produces the possibility of a Pop symphony or oratorio, with distinct but related movements. Unfortunately, there is no apparent thematic development in the placing of cuts, except for the effective juxtaposition of opposing musical styles. At best, the songs are only vaguely related.

With one important exception, "Sergeant Pepper" is precious but devoid of gems. "A Day in the Life" is such a radical departure from the spirit of the album that it almost deserves its peninsular position (following the reprise of the "Sergeant Pepper" theme, it comes almost as an afterthought). It has nothing to do with posturing or put-on. It is a deadly earnest excursion in emotive music with a chilling lyric. Its orchestration is dissonant but sparse, and its mood is not whimsical nostalgia but irony.

What a shame that "A Day in the Life" is only a coda to an otherwise undistinguished collection of work. We need the Beatles, not as cloistered composers, but as companions. And they need us. In substituting the studio conservatory for an audience, they have ceased being folk artists, and the change is what makes their new album a monologue.

OCTOBER 4, 1967

WOODY GUTHRIE, FOLK SINGER AND COMPOSER, DIES

Woody Guthrie, the American folk singer and composer, died yesterday at Creedmoor State Hospital, Queens, following a 13-year illness. He was 55 years old.

Mr. Guthrie, who wrote more than 1,000 songs that echoed the glory and travail of American life, had been bedridden for the last nine years with Huntington's chorea, a rare hereditary disease that attacks the nervous system.

For Woodrow Wilson Guthrie, his songs, his guitar and his humanism were his life. He was a wispy, raspy-voiced musical spokesman for the downtrodden who used his scarred guitar to sing out against injustice and sham.

He also sang of the beauty of his homeland—a beauty seen from the open doorway of a red-balling freight train or from the degradation of the migrant camps and Hoovervilles of the Depression years.

A small, weather-worn man with bushy hair, he was as simple and homespun as his songs. His grammar was often atrocious. But his vision of America was bursting with image upon image of verdant soil, towering mountains and the essential goodness and character of its people.

At a concert a few years ago in Connecticut, Odetta, the folk singer, told her audience that if she were in charge of things, one of Mr. Guthrie's songs, "This Land Is Your Land," would be the "national anthem."

The song, one of the balladeer's best known, shows Guthrie at his best.

But Mr. Guthrie also stirred controversy with topical songs that were born in his radicalism and his impatience—songs deploring the Dust Bowl and the lot of its refugees, songs crying out against the misusing of migrant workers and extolling the virtues of labor unions. He also wrote talking blues, ballads and children's songs.

NOVEMBER 22, 1967

UNEVEN 'WALKÜRE' FOR KARAJAN'S MET DEBUT

Harold Schonberg

"Die Walküre" at the Metropolitan Opera last night started at 7 P.M., ended a minute or so before midnight, and left me a little confused. Herbert von Karajan, making his Met debut, conducted, and it was almost as if there were two Karajans and two "Walküres," namely, Karajan and "Walküre," Act I, and Karajan and the rest of the opera.

What happened was this: Act I was, to put it mildly, eccentric. Mr. Karajan seemed to work on the premise that if voices are not big enough, the orchestra has to be cut down so that the singing can be heard. Following this premise, the conductor kept the dynamic level extraordinarily low, and the tempos rather slow. It was an ultra-refined, chamber-music kind of sound that he drew from the orchestra. The conception was entirely different from the surging romanticism of a Solti or a Böhm.

Then for the rest of the opera Mr. Karajan suddenly presented a performance that was much more conventional in tempo and dynamic. It was conducted with more finesse than almost any conductor brings to the music these days, but it was orthodox in conception. The orchestra rang out, and if voices were obscured, bad luck. It was almost as if Mr. Karajan had changed his mind about his conception during the intermission. Confusing is not the word for it.

To traditionalists, the last two acts were much more convincing. No Wagner conducting like it has been heard since the great old days. For in addition to the strength and surety of the conducting, there was a kind of polish, of clarity, of sheer control, not normally associated with the Metropolitan Opera orchestra. Of course, it should also be pointed out that conductors of Mr. Karajan's stature are not normally associated with the orchestra.

In the neo-Bayreuth style, audiences have learned to dispense with certain previously sacrosanct items of Wagnerian hardware. Symbolism and suggestion are substituted for realism. Everything is stripped-down and bare.

But at least this production does establish a mood and maintain it. Effects are used naturally, without gimmickry: the great white glare when Wotan interferes in the Siegmund-Hunding battle; the appearance of Brünnhilde in her great confrontation with Siegmund, she standing on a pedestal wrapped in a god-like aura, he on the ground beneath her; Wotan in silhouette with the magic fire around him. Aside from the first act, "Die Walküre" is less literal than the other "Ring" operas and can stand this kind of treatment.

There remains an esthetic dichotomy in the neo-Bayreuth style, Wagner being one of the most literal of composers and one of the most picture-minded, but this is not the place to argue it out. If we are to have symbolic Wagner instead of literal Wagner, it is hard to conceive of a presentation superior to last night's. It was sung by as good a cast as can be brought together in this weak age of Wagner singing. ■

NOVEMBER 25, 1967

THE DOORS SEEK NIRVANA VOTE

Alfred G. Aronowitz

The Doors in 1968. Left to right: Ray Manzarek, Jim Morrison, Robby Krieger and John Densmore.

The best definition of pop is the one that counts at the box office, but lion-maned Jim Morrison considers the Doors as something more than a hit rock 'n' roll group. "Think of us," he likes to say, "as erotic politicians."

Mr. Morrison is the 23-year-old lead singer of the Doors, and the campaign for whatever it is he's running for is directed at the same constituency as the Monkees': Those 14-year-old girls of America's suburbs.

At the Hunter College Auditorium last night, he came out in a black leather jacket and skin-tight black vinyl pants. He walked languidly to the microphone, the way Marlon Brando might have if he had started out in rock 'n' roll.

He grabbed the microphone with both hands and put one boot on the base. He closed his eyes and tugged on the microphone. First it was too high. Then it was too low. Then he opened his mouth as if he was about to sing. Then he changed his mind and closed his mouth again.

On his face, there was the look of suffering of someone who knows he is too beautiful to ever enjoy true love. Jim Morrison is a pop star with a vision. The vision is packaged in sex. His campaign motto is "Nirvana now."

There's not too much more to say about the Doors except that they've had two hit singles now and both their albums, "The Doors" and "Strange Days," are in the top five of the pop charts. At Hunter College, they filled every seat in the house.

Like the drummer John Densmore and the guitarist Robby Krieger, who are both disciples of the Indian mystic Maharishi Mahesh Yogi, Mr. Morrison considers himself consumed with spiritual concepts. The problem is that visions don't have to be packaged, they shine through by themselves.

At last night's concert Mr. Morrison introduced some new material. "Wait until the war is over," he sang, "and we'll both be a little older...Make a grave for the unknown soldier..."

Mr. Krieger played a siren on his amplifier and then aimed his guitar at Mr. Morrison while Mr. Densmore rat-tat-tatted off a machine-gun staccato. At the other end of the stage, the keyboardist Ray Manzarek issued a blast from his amplifier and Mr. Morrison shuddered, languidly.

Have the Doors become successful enough to start taking themselves seriously? ■

DECEMBER 17, 1967

Rock Speaks Sweetly Now

Tom Phillips

Rock 'n' roll music is getting louder and louder, as anyone who's been to a concert by the Cream or the Jefferson Airplane can tell you. At the same time, it's also getting softer. More and more new groups and established stars are turning away from strict reliance on the heavy backbeat and the 7-foot speaker system, and finding they can speak sweetly and say a lot.

Good soft-rock (as opposed to vapid "easy listening") first came out last year when the Mamas and the Papas swept the country with "California Dreamin'." It was a miraculous sound, lush and full as the Mormon Tabernacle (almost) but without losing the rock, mostly thanks to Mama Cass Elliot.

The Mamas and the Papas are now in Europe, in a state of maybe-retirement after running out of inspiration. They may come back, but even if they don't, their position is secure as a major influence in the history of pop music, and one of the great groups of the 60's. ABC has now repackaged most of the best and best-known songs from their three albums on a new disk, called Farewell to the First Golden Era (Dunhill D50025 stereo DS50025). Included besides "California Dreamin'" are "Twelve Thirty," "Words of Love," "Monday Monday" and "Creeque Alley."

If you don't own anything by the Mamas and the Papas, you should buy this one. Despite all the imitators (the Cowsills, Spanky and Our Gang) nobody is likely to match Mama Cass's special brand of girl raunch. And there are few lyricists around as eloquent as John Phillips.

Soft-rock today is not just limited to imitations of the Mamas and the Papas. Chad Stuart and Jeremy Clyde, who used to be Chad and Jeremy, have rejoined each other and they've got another kind of soft and intimate style. "Of Cabbages and Kings" (Columbia CL2671 stereo CS9471) starts off with snorts and throat-clearings, and then we get a recital of gentle and sensitive baroque chamber-rock. The six songs (four by Jeremy) on side one are notable for warm, close-up vocals, and some classy and effective instrumental arrangements by Chad—flute, recorder, mandolin, sitar and more.

The Buffalo Springfield is basically a "soft" group, but they can do everything else, too—and their new album "Buffalo Springfield Again" (Atco 33-226 stereo SD-33-226) is one of the most varied and weird and beautiful things I've heard. It starts off with "Mr. Soul," which has a Jefferson Airplane beat (four to the measure, blang blang blang blang) and a space-age fuzzbuzz guitar. Next is "A Child's Claim to Fame," featuring Everly Brothers harmony and a dobro background. (That's an old-time country instrument—an un-amplified steel guitar.) ■

FEBRUARY 19, 1968

JANIS JOPLIN CLIMBS THE HEADY ROCK FIRMAMENT

Robert Shelton

They used to call vocalists of such rare talent as Janis Joplin "a great jazz singer." Because the music has changed and the scene has shifted, the 25-year-old dynamo from Port Arthur, Tex., is what one would call nowadays a great rock singer.

Miss Joplin made her New York debut Saturday night at the Anderson Theater, 66 Second Avenue. The lines can start forming now, for Miss Joplin is as remarkable a new pop-music talent as has surfaced in years. Only her remaining in San Francisco and a singularly unrepresentative first recording kept her from national prominence months ago.

She was on an excellent pop show that featured her group, Big Brother and the Holding Company; the distinguished blues style-setter, B. B. King, and an able new rock quintet, the Aluminum Dream.

As fine as the whole evening was, it belonged mostly to the sparky, spunky Miss Joplin. She sounded, at first, like an athletic soul shouter, a white stylistic sister of Aretha and Erma Franklin.

But comparisons wane, for there are few voices of such power, flexibility and virtuosity in pop music anywhere. Occasionally Miss Joplin appeared to be hitting two harmonizing notes at once. Her voice shouted with ecstasy or anger one minute, trailed off into coquettish curlecues the next. It glided from soprano highs to chesty alto lows.

In an unaccompanied section of "Love Is Like a Ball and Chain," Miss Joplin went on a flight that alternately suggested a violin cadenza and the climax of a flamenco session. In "Light Is Faster Than Sound" and "Down on Me," she unleashed more energy than most singers bring to a whole program. The influence of the Franklin sisters and the late Otis Redding was readily apparent.

Miss Joplin and her band have been working in San Francisco about a year and a half. The quartet attracted attention at last summer's Monterey, Calif., International Pop Festival, and it is inventive enough to be worthy of its star. Outstanding were its vocal style, which uses the smear and the yelp to startling effect, and arrangements that embroidered "The Cuckoo" with modernistic lace and framed "Summertime" with a pale metallic fugue.

The excitement of the program was heightened by a rare non-Harlem appearance of B. B. King, one of the seminal singers and guitar players in the history of rhythm and blues. He and his quartet, just back from a European tour, were in excellent form. Mr. King's sweet and sinuous voice turning into a roaring storm was a reminder of his great contribution to modern rock 'n' roll.

MARCH 31, 1968

ARETHA FRANKLIN MAKES SALVATION SEEM EROTIC

Albert Goldman

The Queen of Soul at Madison Square Garden in New York, 1968.

As an ambassador of soul, Aretha Franklin bears impressive credentials: they are dated from Memphis, where she was born, and Detroit, where she grew up; they carry the seal of her father, C. L. Franklin, a well-known revivalist and gospel shouter; and they are countersigned by famous Brothers and Sisters like Sam Cooke, Mahalia Jackson, Lou Rawls and Clara Ward, all of whom endorsed Aretha when she was still a girl soloist in her father's New Bethel Baptist Church.

But these ancestral influences, important as they may have been, do not define the source of Aretha Franklin's sudden and enormous success. That success is owing to a quality which she discovered, or confirmed, in herself through years of professional experience. It is a quality that her audience recognized instantly and enthusiastically embraced. To put it in a word (borrowed from one of her big hits), it is the gift of being a "Natural Woman."

Establishing an identity through asserting the basic female emotions does not sound like a very original or interesting development for a pop singer—yet it is, in fact, almost without precedent in Miss Franklin's tradition. None of the famous women of Negro song has epitomized the normal female soul or the free expression of the full range of feminine feeling. The old-timers like Bessie Smith or Ma Rainey (or Mahalia Jackson today) were massive matriarchs with the grand composure that accompanies that role. The glamorous ladies of later times, the Billie Holidays or Dinah Washingtons, loved, suffered and learned resignation before they opened their mouths. What they had to reveal was not so much an emotion as an attitude: the scar tissue of experience.

Aretha's woman may suffer, but her soul is whole and untrammeled by depression or abuse. Delivering her feelings with astonishing power and ebullience, she releases every tightly creased irony of the blues and dispels the old stale atmosphere of patiently endured female sorrow. Lacking even a trace of self-consciousness, she cries out in ecstasy or anger, in bewilderment or terror, achieving the beauty of a perfectly realized emotion. Indeed, her naturalness is as much a matter of the spontaneity with which she lets fly every phrase as it is of the depth and solidity of her feelings. At another time, in another society, this complete freedom from emotional restraints might appear a dubious value. A Victorian would have called it hysteria. Today, it seems like a state of grace.

It seems fitting that the greatest of Aretha Franklin's recordings to date should be an erotic paraphrase of a tune that started life as a humorous expression of impotence. The original "I Can't Get No Satisfaction," by Mick Jagger of the Rolling Stones, was a wry, deadpan camp, a whispered confession that impressed many listeners as being a titillating put-on. It took Aretha Franklin to make the song a jubilee: a finger-popping, hip-swinging Mardi Gras strut that is the greatest proclamation of sexual fulfillment since Molly Bloom's soliloquy. From the opening phrase, amusingly divided between a siren wail on the word "I" and a sudden plunge on "satisfaction"—a caricature of soul's basic pattern of tension and release—Aretha riffs and rocks and stomps behind, before and on top of the beat, until she and the band are lost in a jam session that might have gone on for hours after the final fade. (The four-minute cut-offs on her records are inexcusable in this day of LPs.) Short as the side is, the distance it covers is enormous.

What we want from Aretha Franklin is just what she has taught us to desire—the solid, natural music of the body as it moves to the rhythms of our most basic emotions. Or the sound of the soul as it soars through the roof of the mouth, whooping with some urgent message from below.

DECEMBER 11, 1968

LONG LIVE THE MOOG!

Donal Henahan

Moog Synthesizer.

Mark II, king of electronic music synthesizers, sits in a room on West 125th Street, blinking red eyes sadly and making strange, whirring, clicking sounds. The king is doomed to die.

Having served its purpose as a pioneer device in electronic music, the mighty Mark II is being pushed aside by a new generation of lean, compact machines. The young pretenders have such electronic-sounding names as Moog, Buchla and Synkey and are the Pepsi generation of synthesizers: portable, transistorized, modular, relatively easy to operate, and taking up hardly more space than an upright piano. They can be purchased for less than $3,000 (though complex models can run to $7,000 exclusive of tape recorders and other standard studio equipment). Already the new machines have taken over a great deal of the music picture, and in the future may transform both the composing and performing arts.

Although serious composers use the new synthesizers extensively, rock and other popular-music groups also have taken to the devices enthusiastically. Among those now working with the Moog are the Rolling Stones, the Beach Boys, the Electric Flag and the Grateful Dead. A Moog was called upon for the score of the movie "Candy." The Beatles, who have used several other electronic methods in their recordings, recently placed an order for a Moog system.

The synthesizers can produce any sound imaginable and perhaps some that become imaginable only after having been produced.

Music and sound effects for television commercials are being synthesized on a large scale. Walter Carlos, whose Columbia album "Switched-On Bach" recently stirred up much discussion in musical and recording circles, has done commercials for Schaefer beer, the phone company's Yellow Pages, and others.

Mr. Carlos, a 29-year-old former recording engineer for Gotham Studios, holds a bachelor's degree in physics from Brown University and a master's in musical composition from Columbia. He keeps his synthesizer in his one-room apartment at 410 West End Avenue, where he achieves a homey touch by putting plants atop the cabinets.

In most ways, however, his setup resembles other Moogs, with their mazes of connecting patchcords and plugs that make any Moog resemble an old-fashioned telephone switchboard. In the Carlos version, two five-octave keyboards control voltage changes. The keyboards may control not only pitch, but timbre attack and decay of the tune, and many other musical elements.

The variety of ways in which voltage can be controlled in the modular synthesizers is limited only by the composer's imagination: It would be just as feasible to hook up, as an input mechanism, a guitar, a violin, a cash register, a digital computer or a typewriter.

One school of thought, recently getting much attention in electronic circles, insists that a synthesizer can be used as a performing instrument as well as a composer's tool. Mr. Carlos, for one, sees the Moog synthesizer as a natural development out of traditional instruments, in the way the piano developed out of the harpsichord.

The synthesizer, whether large or small, is one of three basic ways of composing what is hazily termed electronic music. The "classic" method, still valid and in use, is the "musique concrète" way—gathering sounds on tape and then splicing snippets together to achieve a desired sequence of sounds.

All electronic music, no matter how it begins, ends up on tape, of course.

The third system of composition, now slowly coming into view, involves using computers to gather and store musical information fed to it by the composer, after which the work can be "read out" by the computer at the composer's pleasure.

"The computer is the future," said Mr. Babbitt. "I don't work with it myself, so I can say that objectively."

In the immediate future, Mr. Babbitt said, the digital computer is certain to be teamed with the new compact synthesizer, and when that happens electronic music is likely to be shaken up once again. ■

MAY 28, 1969

REPETITION DOMINATES MUSIC OF STEVE REICH

Donal Henahan

Steve Reich, 1969.

Art is a pendulum that is always swinging out of phase with society, pulling against whatever esthetic ideas have gained general acceptance. In the nineteen twenties, Stravinsky and other neoclassicists rose up against the lushness and sentimentality of the 19th century and swung their weight in favor of the concise and the spare. Webern came along and drove the idea toward its extreme, and music went through a period in which minimal art and nonrepetition of materials were idealized.

As the pendulum swings, however, it must reverse itself, and we have now entered well into a time when composers are in revulsion against the previous esthetic, so that an artist such as Steve Reich carries his celebration of repetition to lengths that we have known previously only at second hand, from Oriental music.

Four of Mr. Reich's works were presented last night at the Whitney Museum of American Art, and without much distortion one could characterize them all as electronically assisted ragas. "Four Log Drums" set four men rapping out rhythms (dictated largely by earphones worn by each rapper) while Mr. Reich twisted dials that caused the rhythms to interact and shift almost imperceptibly. "Pulse Music," in which the only performer visible was Mr. Reich at the controls of a Phase Shifting Pulse Gate, carried on in the same vein, ringing hypnotic, gradual changes on ever more complex pulsations.

"Pendulum Music," a relatively brief 10-minute interlude in a program that was part of a series called "Extended Time Pieces," set dangling microphones in motion over four loudspeakers, and depended on feedback to produce interesting variations of tone and pulse.

Finally, for a full half hour, Paul Zukofsky, with his violin miked, played against a 10-note ostinato in "Violin Phase." Mr. Zukofsky, choosing his own patterns within set limits, added part after part until he was a complete quartet, all by himself. It was, if you will, as much fun as watching a pendulum. ■

MAY 18, 1969

A COLLAGE OF FOUND SOUNDS

Donal Henahan

Giving the hotfoot to the middlebrow listener has long been one of the 20th century composer's most amusing diversions, so much so that the poor Philistine's foot is by now charred and almost numbed beyond feeling pain. Still, it might be worth a try, in the event you know any middlebrows, to test their burning point with two new records of the avant-garde: Karlheinz Stockhausen's "Hymnen" (DGG-139-421/2, stereo) and "HPSCHD," the joint creation of John Cage and Lejaren Hiller (Nonesuch H-71224).

The two works have certain obvious similarities: both use as germinal ideas the music of other composers, both go on at ambitious lengths, and both do go on. Stockhausen's piece, begun in 1966, is two hours long, in four movements, each of which is dedicated to a colleague (Pierre Boulez, Henri Pousseur, Cage and Luciano Berio). The national anthems and other patriotic songs of most of the countries of the world serve as the basic materials.

"Hymnen" sprawls out in extraordinary tangles of planned complexity. There are, woven throughout, snippets of conversation in many languages; bird songs; anthems; synthesized and natural (musique concrète) sounds; recitations from catalogues; boys' chants; and much else, all jumbled together, distorted, and teased into the most peculiar aural shapes that the masterly engineering mind of Stockhausen can devise.

At first, one is simply annoyed. To what purpose, all these fractured phrases, fragmented sounds and distorted familiar tunes? It seems a vast, overwhelming conceit, perhaps unparalleled in the history of records. If the name Karlheinz Stockhausen were not on it, who would sit through its four droning sides? Wouldn't it be better to be bored by sticking one's head out the window and thus collecting one's own "found sound"? At least the lungs could fill with relatively fresh air, and escape the smog of the German composer at his pretentious worst.

But, one does listen on, for it is the work of Stockhausen, not Fred Jones of East Orange.

"HPSCHD," to get one mystery out of the way, is the word harpsichord with its vowels removed and otherwise shrunken to the computer's six-letter limit. Mozart's "Introduction to the Composition of Waltzes by Means of Dice" provides a basis for certain harpsichord solos, and the work's entire numerical system, though computer-derived, was based on Cage's favorite fount of Chinese wisdom and numerology, "I Ching."

Very well, and how does it all sound on record? Rather like a piece composed by a computer, using scraps of existing music. That should be no surprise. It is astonishing to discover how boring the computer can be as a musician. What interest is to be found in the record comes largely from a novel idea called "KNOBS," which permits the listener to alter the character of the work by twiddling with the dials of his stereo system, in accordance with a computer printout sheet provided with the album.

Theirs is a madhouse in which one may for hours take refuge from an allegedly sane world that believes war is good and sex is evil. The insanity that willingly proclaims itself mad is always to be suspect as a higher form of rationality. What they are composing may not be music, but the time for composing music may be passing more quickly than we realize. ■

NOVEMBER 28, 1969

STONES STILL EXCITING

Mike Jahn

After five years of popularity, the Rolling Stones are still the brashest, and consistently one of the most exciting and entertaining groups one can hear in rock.

They gained popularity in 1964 on the heels of the Beatles, and their appearance at Madison Square Garden last night brought with it some of that contagious madness that followed the Beatles and the Stones from the beginning.

Sixteen thousand people stood, stomped and danced while the group played faithful versions of their hit songs, like "Jumpin' Jack Flash" and "Under My Thumb." They also did a rousing Chuck Berry rocker, "Oh Carol," and several acoustic-guitar blues.

The group maintained its long-standing image of being the sexual balladeers of rock music. Many of their songs have an aggressive, masculine theme, and the lead Stone, Mick Jagger, snarls and howls in the finest man-woman blues tradition.

Throughout the songs, Mr. Jagger pranced about the stage, flaunting his hips at the audience like a stoned flamenco dancer.

Their set was very successful; an enthusiastic reading of some of the fine group's finest material.

The general concert plan worked less well. The audience waited for more than three hours before the Rolling Stones took the stage. There were three other acts, Terry Reid, B. B. King and the Ike and Tina Turner Revue, and too much time was wasted between acts.

Still Turner brought on the Stones in a magnetic fashion when she closed her set singing and dancing a soul standard: "Land of A Thousand Dances," joined by Janis Joplin.

The Rolling Stones consist of Mr. Jagger, lead vocals; Keith Richards, guitar; Bill Wyman, bass; Charlie Watts, drums; and Mick Taylor, lead guitar. Mr. Taylor, who earlier gained some attention as guitarist for John Mayall's Blue Breakers, replaced the late Brian Jones last summer. ■

MAY 18, 1969

THE WHO'S PINBALL OPERA

Nik Cohn

London—"Tommy" has been a long time happening. On and off, Pete Townshend, the Who's lead guitarist, has been writing the opera for upward of three years and, many times, it seemed as though he wasn't ever going to finish. It is, after all, the trademark of the Who that they always threaten, never quite deliver. In their time, they've been responsible for so many rock innovations—the use of electronics, the concept of rock as theater, the Pop art thing, the revival of gut-rock—and, invariably, someone else has sneaked up fast and stolen the credit.

Anyhow, that's over now. "Tommy" is just possibly the most important work that anyone has yet done in rock.

The actual storyline is unimpressive. During his childhood, Tommy sees his father commit a murder and is then brainwashed into forgetting it ("You didn't hear it, you didn't see it, you won't say nothing to no one."). This makes him deaf, dumb and blind. Later, in his teens, he becomes a pinball player and develops into a champion. He builds up a following, becomes a pinball Messiah. He tours, spreads the gospel and is worshipped. He is cured. His power keeps expanding. He sets up a fascist state of his own, in which his subjects are herded into holiday camps and forced to play pinball, although gagged, blindfolded and with stoppers in their ears. This is too much. Tommy's disciples rise up against him. Tommy is made deaf, dumb and blind again.

This plot doesn't work. Still, since when was plot important in an opera? All that really counts is the music, which is mostly marvelous. Almost two hours without a let-up, 25 tracks altogether, and it hardly ever flags. In turns, it is fierce and funny, schmaltzy and sour. Always imaginative. Well, it also has its moments of pomposity and some of the instrumental interludes are too long, but the good things swamp the bad.

At least five of the cuts—"Christmas," "The Acid Queen," "Pinball Wizard," "Go to the Mirror, Boy" and "We're Not Gonna Take It"—rank with anything that Townshend has previously done. Yet the individual songs aren't really the point; it's the sum effect that's the clincher. So much stamina, such range and musical invention—this might just be the first pop masterpiece.

AUGUST 24, 1969

WOODSTOCK: 'A JOYFUL CONFIRMATION THAT GOOD THINGS CAN HAPPEN HERE'

Patrick Lydon

It all happened up at the farm and everything happened. Half a million kids—hippies, rock people and even straights—ran up to the farm for a long weekend of rock 'n' roll music mixed with mud, no sleep, rain, drugs, more mud and even more smiles. Too many people came to the Woodstock Festival but they came high and they only got higher.

It started on Route 17, hip cars passing bread to the cycle riders and waving "V" signs everywhere. Bethel townspeople gazed in awe at the streams of hippies, but they murmured "Peace" to the visitors, offered free water and returned smiles. Everyone arrived to find the whole show was free. As the weekend went on, the miracles kept coming—the kindness of the scattered police, the "food-drop" by an Army

(cont'd. on next page)

Part of the estimated 500,000 people who came to the Woodstock Music Festival.

(cont'd. from previous page)
helicopter, and flowers from the sky. Yet faith makes miracles and it was the astonishing peace and joy of the youthful masses that brought happy results.

Before it became the greatest hippie demonstration of unity, the music was the focus of the festival. Friday was the folk night but the playing was plagued by rain and delays. Every artist was received with warmth because they all played well and because the listeners were glad of any music. Joan Baez closed the evening in the rain, but she roused the masses to join her in "We Shall Overcome."

The music on stage was only a part of the weekend's activity. The art exhibit of painting and sculpture was rather small but interesting. Followers of Meher Baba, the Avatar, sat nude on a suspended rock testifying their faith. The Grateful Dead gave two independent concerts at the nearby Hog Farm. Despite the bad weather, hundreds of people went swimming.

Although it was consistently excellent, the music will not be what participants remember best. It was natural that a huge crowd should arrive in good spirits, laughing, getting together in the music that brought them, but that their good vibrations never broke was extraordinary. As the announcer on stage praised the crowd, and as the bands registered their excitement at playing for such a gathering, the crowd felt an increasing sense of good in itself. The free food given by the people of the Hog Farm held body and soul together, the Red Cross Station took care of those who were ill, and a special tent treated those who were on bum acid trips.

There was the joy of confirmation, the delight in accenting what others could give. Hippies had never been quite so successful together, never before had they so impressed the world that watched. The strength of the crowd seemed strongest in the hard rain on Sunday afternoon. To the banging of the cans, dancing hippies gave all of themselves. Instead of despairing at the discomfort of rain and mud, the crowd rejoiced in its power to resist the weather. One boy stood covered with mud, ornamented with refuse he found in it, yet overjoyed that he could make happiness for others.

Out of the mud came dancers, out of electrical failure came music, out of hunger came generosity. What began as a symbolic protest against American society ended as a joyful confirmation that good things *can* happen here, that Army men can raise a "V" sign, that country people can welcome city hippies. One of Jimi Hendrix's last numbers was "The Star Spangled Banner." Yes, most everything happened up on the farm. ■

OCTOBER 26, 1969

NEW ERA OF MULTIMEDIA THEATER

Clive Barnes

What is the most exciting show on Broadway? Well, it is, I admit, a loaded question—suggesting a number of quite explosive answers. However an extraordinarily persuasive case could be made for the New York City Opera's production of "Mefistofele."

The director, Tito Capobianco, has staged Arrigo Boito's opera with just that quality of spectacular imagination, a certain bigness of thinking, that might illuminate a Broadway musical. The prologue and epilogue, in which Boito discusses man, God and redemption, represent some of the most striking multimedia effects I have yet seen. It is like a William Blake view of the universe decked out by Fillmore East's Joshua Light Show.

The interesting thing is that Broadway producers still seem to have no conception of what multimedia could do for them. They are supposed to be showmen and they have about as much idea of showmanship as booksellers. They want to deal with conventionally packaged goods and to sell them in a conventionally packaged way.

Opera, modern dance and classic ballet are possibly more adventurous than the Broadway theater because, by and large, they attract a younger audience, and Broadway's failure, as a general rule, to appeal much to people under even 40 is a little disturbing.

One of the most interesting aspects of the theater of multimedia is the way it has associated itself with pop music and particularly rock music. The new importance of rock music—its ever more pressing claims to be regarded as a new art form, and its obvious developing sophistication and awareness, to say nothing of the increasing attacks on it by the conservative pseudo-intellectuals—is one of the prevalent and sociologically, and perhaps the most interesting, cultural trend of the last decade. And, not unexpectedly rock has embraced multimedia in a positive bear hug.

The new-style rock concert provides an obvious extension to these other environmental projects, and the multimedia light show has become an accepted constituent of the best rock concerts. Bill Graham's Fillmore East is the temple of East Coast rock, and there the Joshua Light Show has developed its craft to such a point that it is difficult to decide whether many of the concerts are music or theater, or perhaps both.

The great case in point came last week when the Who came to Fillmore East to perform their rock opera "Tommy." It would be difficult, indeed impossible, to stage it in any conventional way. So here while the group, Peter Townshend, Roger Daltrey, John Entwistle and Keith Moon, were going noisily mad in front, on a back projection the Joshua Light Show produced a theatrical parallel with film clips, lights and abstract patterns, ranging very wildly from moving Kandinsky-like patterns to multicolored oil slicks.

To me the evening was an enormous success, not only in itself, but also because it may have indicated a way in which a new theatrical form—a new kind of opera perhaps—might just possibly arise. At the moment it is very raw. I am convinced, however, that something is moving in this direction. And as a theater critic I sense that it is coming my way.

DECEMBER 7, 1969

200,000 ATTEND ALTAMONT ROCK FETE

Robert A. Wright

TRACY, Calif., Dec. 6—Thousands of fans of the Rolling Stones rock group converged on the hillsides around the Altamont Speedway here today, turning pastures into parking lots and campsites.

(cont'd. on next page)

Though early reports indicated a relatively peaceful gathering at the Altamont Free Concert, there were violent outbreaks and at least one killing involving the Hell's Angels, who were hired to provide security.

(cont'd. from previous page)

The Rolling Stones, the Grateful Dead, the Jefferson Airplane and other rock groups were giving a concert, and it was free.

Some 5,000 youths arrived last night and camped as near the hastily built stage as possible. By 10 A.M. the population of these fields mounted to an estimated 200,000. Traffic on Route 580 from San Francisco was backed up for 20 miles.

Until yesterday, the racetrack had scheduled a motorcycle race. Then, because of a disagreement between the Rolling Stones and the management of Sears Point Racetrack in Sonoma County, the concert was suddenly shifted here. It had originally been scheduled for Golden Gate Park in San Francisco.

Nobody knew exactly where the new site was. Eager fans turned off the highway into an impromptu parking lot eight miles away and began walking. Highway patrolmen, asked directions, advised simply, "Follow them, they know."

Until midday the only music heard came from portable radios and a rock group that performed from a motorized, sound-equipped truck in a meadow far from the stage in the center of the crowd.

At 11 o'clock a bright blue and yellow striped hot air balloon ascended from the bandstand and hovered over the crowd. This produced some cheers from the audience. Otherwise even the sound of the crowd's conversation was dissipated in the country air.

People seemed content to talk, picnic and pass marijuana cigarettes. Six helicopters, shuttling in and out performers, provided most of the noise.

The show began at 1 o'clock, as scheduled. The Rolling Stones arrived by helicopter about 2:30 and were the last to perform.

Toilet facilities were few, and a long walk from the crowd. Fans were prepared for a picnic, and many brought food and their children with them.

The crowd, considering its size, was well behaved. The police made few arrests. A total of 75 Oakland policemen and hired security guards seemed to enter into the spirit of the affair.

"We had to talk to a couple of guys walking around up there nude," a police sergeant said. "But we're trying to hold down arrests so we don't blow the whole show."

Dr. Richard Fine of a group of volunteer doctors from the San Francisco chapter of the Medical Committee for Human Rights, said his emergency medical tent had no severe injuries to treat.

"We had about 30 bad trips [drug-induced traumas] and eight or 10 lacerations, only one from a fight."

The Rolling Stones conceived of the free concert, they let it be known, as a means of expressing their thanks to fans for a very successful American tour. Before returning to Britain they would entertain without charge and turn any revenues from film or recording rights over to charity, they said. Other rock groups rallied around. ■

Index

Illustrations are indicated in **bold**.

2001: A Space Odyssey (movie), 291-292
3-D photos, 131-132
8 ½ (movie), **283**

Abbott, George, 245
ABC (American Broadcasting Company), 266, 267, 273, 296
Abdul-Jabbar, Kareem, **196**
Abernathy, Dr. Ralph D., 9, 34
Abstract art, 227
Abstract Expressionism, 227
Addams Family, The (TV show), 267
Addams, Charles, 267
Additives, food, 179
Adenauer, Konrad, Israel trip, 67
Adler, Lou, 302
African Americans, 3, 7, 8; 9, 11-12, 13, 15, 23-24, 25, 29, 30, 31, 32, 37, 38, 39-40, 155, 232, 239, 240; Cabinet appointment, 84; bombings of, 15; Freedom Riders, **7**; in music, 302; in sports, 187, 189, 191, 192, 196, 197, 201-202, 203, 204, 205; marches, 9, 14; riots, 7, **10**, 15, **24**, **31**, 34, 37, **99**; sitdowns, **3**
African Nationalist Party, 60
Aged care, 136
Agnew, Spiro T., 157
Airlines collision 1960, 94
Al Fatah, 76
Alaska oil leases, 89-90
Albee, Edward, 253
Alcindor, Lew. *See* Abdul-Jabbar, Kareem.
Aldrin, Edwin E., **125**, 126
Ali, Muhammad, defeats Liston, **191**; play about, 261; refuses Army oath and stripped of crown, 197
Allan (doll), 151
Alston, Walter, 191
Altamont Rock Festival, **317**, 318
Alvin Theater, 261
Ambassador Hotel, Los Angeles, 35
American & National league football leagues merge, 194
American Ballet Theater, in Moscow, 248
American Bandstand, 296
American Birth Control League, 141
American College of Physicians, 135
American Football League, 194, 195
American League championship, 188
American Medical Association, 135
American Museum of Natural History, robbed, 100
American Society for Artificial Internal Organs, 137
American Telephone and Telegraph Company, 128, 129
Ames, Ed, 269
Ammann, O.H., 101
Anders, William A., 124
Andrews, Julie, **287**, 288
Andy Griffith Show, The (TV show), 265
Anti-miscegenation laws banned, 29
Antiwar demonstrations, **40**, 41
Apollo 1 flash fire, 121-122
Apollo 11 mission to moon, 126
Apollo 8, flight around moon, 124
Arab League, 77
Arafat, Yasir, 76
Arendt, Hannah, 235
Aristotle Contemplating the Bust of Homer (painting), **214**
Armstrong, Neil A., 125-126
Arno River flooding, 223
Arnold Constable, Inc., 165
Aronson, Boris, 259
Art & architecture, 211-227
Art censorship, 220
Art in Florence damaged by floods, 223
Arthur, Beatrice, 258
Arvonwood, 180
Ascension (album), 304
"Ask not what your country can do for you" speech, 5
Ashe, Arthur, 201, **202**
Astrodome, Houston, opens, 192
Athenagoras I, Patriarch of Constantinople, 60
Atomic bombs. *See* Nuclear bombs.
Atomic Energy Commission, 122
Atomic particle discovered, 117-118
Audubon Ballroom, New York, 23
Auntie Mame (play), 258
Automobile industry, 82, 149, 151-152
Automobile safety, 151-152
Avant-garde music, 314

Babies, deformed, 135
Baez, Joan, **300**, 316
Bain, Barbara, 272
Balanchine, George, 246, 247, 249
Baldwin, James, **232**
Balenciaga, 160
Ball, Lucille, **273**
Ballard, Florence, **307**, 308
Ballet funding by Ford Foundation, 246-247
Balm in Gilead (play), 262
Balsam, Martin, 278
Baltimore Colts, 205-206
Baltimore Orioles, 207-208
Bancroft, Anne, **291**
Bank credit cards, 88-889
BankAmericard, **88**, 89
Barber, Samuel, 106
Barbie (doll), **147**, 148, 151
Bardot, Brigitte, 280
Barnard, Christian Neethling, 142, **143**
Barnett, Ross R., 8
Baseball, 188, 190, 192, 201, 207-208
Basketball, 189, 196, 204-205
Bathing suit, topless, 162
Baths of Caracalla, 104
Bayer, Herbert, 226
Baylor, Elgin, 205
Bayreuth Festival, 307
BBC (British Broadcasting Corporation), 276
Beach Boys, The, 302, 313
Beame, Abraham D., defeated for mayor, 102
Beamon, Bob, 203
Beat Generation, 245
Beatlemania, 301-302
Beatles, The, 209, **301**, 302, 305, 308, 313
Beaton, Cecil, 106, 286
Beatty, Warren, **279**
Beck, Simone, 173
Beijing, China, 65
Bell Telephone Laboratories, 118
Bellows, George, 225
Belmondo, Jean-Paul, 278
Ben-Gurion, David, 46, 67, 71
Ben-Hur (movie), 277
Bennett, James Gordon, 104
Berkeley, CA, student protests, 22
Berlin Wall, built, **52**
Berlin, East v. West, 48, 52
Berry, Jan, 302
Bertholle, Louisette, 173
Bethel, NY, 315
Bethlehem Steel Corporation, 81-81
Bewitched (TV show), 267, 271
Biafra, starvation in, 73
Big bang theory of universe, 118
Big Brother and the Holding Company, 311
Bikel, Theodore, 300
Billy Rose Theater, NY, 249, 253
Birmingham, AL, 9; church bombing, 15; riots, **10**
Birth control, 141; pills approved, 137
Birth defects, 144
Black gloves worn at Olympics, **185**, 202, 203
Black Panthers, 37-**38**
Black Power, 25, 240; salute, **185**, 202, 203
Blackwell, Earl, 95
Boeing 747, **132**; first flight, 132, 133
Bolivia, 70
Books, 228-245
Boone, Daniel, 269
Boots, fashion, 160
Borges, Jorge Luis, 244
Borman, Frank, 124
Boston Ballet, 247
Boston Celtics, 204-205
Bouffant hairdo, 158
Boxing, 191-192
Brandenburg Gate, Berlin, 48, 56
Breakfast at Tiffany's, **161**, 278-279
Breathalyzer tests for drunk driving, 143
Breathless (movie), 278
Breuer, Marcel, 221
Brezhnev, Leonid I., 57
Brice, Fanny, 255
British fashion designers, 161
British Invasion, 301-302
Broadhurst Theater, 259
Broadway stars demands, 251-252
Bronx, NY, poverty in, 107
Brookhaven National Laboratory, Long Island, 117-118
Brooklyn Academy of Music, 263
Brooklyn Naval Shipyard, 94-95
Brooks, Mel, 292
Brown v. Board, 40
Brown, Edmund G., 26
Brown, John Young, Jr., 177-178
Brown, Rap, 32
Buckley, William F., Jr., 102
Buffalo Springfield, The, 311
Bullet trains, Japan, 131
Bumbry, Grace, 307
Burger,Warren E., 39
Burgess, Anthony, 234
Burlingame, Byers A., 82
Burnett, Carol, **273**
Burnoose, 166
Burroughs, William, 245
Burton, Richard, **284**, 285

Butch Cassidy and the Sundance Kid (movie), **295**

Cabaret (musical), **259**
Cafes, sidewalk, 177
Caftans, 166
Cage, John, 249, 314
Calder, Alexander, 218
California Sound, 302
Caliifornia Dreamin (song), 311
Cambodia, raids in by U.S., 76, **77**
Camp (sensibility), 219-220
Cancer and cyclamate sweeteners, 178
Cancer linked to cigarettes, 138
Cape Canaveral, FL, 113, 115
Cape Kennedy, FL, 122
Capobianco, Tito, 317
Capote, Truman, 279
Carlos, John, black glove at Olympics, **185**, 202, 203
Carlos, William, 313
Carmichael, Stokely, 25
Carnegie Corporation, 275
Carnegie Hall Society, 93
Carnegie Hall, NY, 297-298, 299, 301; preservation efforts, 93
Carney, Art, 256, 257
Carol Burnett Show, The (TV show), 273, 274
Carson, Johnny, 266
Carson, Rachel, 231-232
Cassady, Neal, 245
Cassavetes, John, **293**
Cassette tapes developed, 130
Castaneda, Carlos, 241-242
Castro, Fidel, 49, **50**,
Cavanaugh, Jerome P., 31-32
CBS (Columbia Broadcasting Company), 267, 268, 270, 272, 273, 274, 302
Celebrity Register, 95
Cell reproduction, 123
Censorship, 272
Center for European Research (CERN), 117
Central Park, NY, theater, 252
Certificates of Deposit (CDs), 86
Chad and Jeremy, 311
Chaffee, Roger B., **121**, 122
Chairs, inflatable, **183**
Chamberlain, Wilt, 100-point game, **189**, 205
Champi, Frank, 203-204
Champion, Gower, 254
Chaney, James E., 19
Change of the Century (album), 296
Channing, Carol, 254
Chaplin, Sydney, 255
Chapman, Graham, **276**
Chavez, Cesar, 32-33
Checker, Chubby, 95
Checkpoint Charlie, 56
Cherry Lane Theater, 254
Chicago nurses murders, 28-29
Chicken, fried, 177-178
Child, Julia, 173, **175**; *French Chef* TV series, 175
Children's Television Workshop, 275
China, aerial photos of, 113; Cultural Revolution, 65; hydrogen bomb test, **69**; Red Guards, 65
Chou En-Lai, 51, 65
Christmas Song, The (song), 303
Churchill, Winston, death, 62; funeral procession, **62**
Cigarettes linked to cancer, 138
Circle in the Square, 251
City Center Properties, London, 216
Civil Rights Bill, 19-20
Civil rights workers slain, 19
Clark, Carl, 151, 152
Clark, Dick, 296
Clarke, Arthur C., 291
Clay, Cassius. *See* Ali, Muhammad.
Cleaver, Eldridge, 38, 240
Cleese, John, **276**
Cleopatra (movie), **284**, 285, 286
Clockwork Orange, A, 234
Colas, diet, 175
Cold War, 56, 113, 147, 235
Cole, Nat King, death, 302-303
Coleman, Cy, 258
Coleman, Ornette, **296**
College girl fashions, 162-163
Collins, Judy, 304
Coltrane, John, **304**
Columbia University, 245, 305; student demonstrations, **108**
Common Market, 86-87
Communications satellites, 128
Comstock Law, 141
Congress of Racial Equality (CORE), 7, 99
Connally, John B., 16
Connell, Jane, 259
Connery, Sean, **282**
Constellation aircraft carrier fire, 94-95
Constructivism, 225-226
Contact lenses, plastic, 139
Continental drift, 116-117
Cooking, French, 173
Cooney, Joan Ganz, 275
Cooper, Gladys, 287
Cornwell, David. *See* Le Carré, John.
Corporation for Public Broadcasting, 274
Courrèges, 163
Cox, Wally, 272
Crick, Francis H. C., 116
Cuba, 70; anti-Castro units land on, 49-50; map, **49**; missile crisis, 54; U.S. arms blockade, 53
Cukor, George, 287
Cultural Revolution, China, 65
Cunningham, Merce, 248, 249
Cyclamate sweeteners and cancer, 178
Czechoslovakia, invasion by Soviet Union, 74-75

d'Amboise, Jacques, 249
Dakota apartment house, 293
Dallas Cowboys, 199
Dance, 246-249; modern, 248
Daniel Boone (TV show), **269**
Dannon yogurt, 176
Daves, Jessica, 158
Day in the Life, A (song), 308
De Gaulle, Charles, 38, 68-69, 72-73
DeBackey, Michael E., 140
DeCarlo, Yvonne, **269**
DeMille, Cecil B., 284
Democratic National Convention, Chicago, **36**
Dennis, Patrick, 258
Densmore, John, **310**
Design, worldwide, 182, 183-184
Desolation Road (song), 303
Detroit sound, 307-308
Detroit, MI, automobile industry, 82; race riots, **31**, 32
Dewhurst, Colleen, 252
Dicke, Robert H., 118
Dictionaries, 230
Diem, Ngo Dinh, 47; death, 58
Diet sodas, 175
Dieting, 171
DiMaggio, Joe, 208, 280
Dine, Jim, 212, 217
Dirksen, Everett, 81
Discrimination in the U.S., 202, 203
Disney World, Orlando, 288
Disney, Walt, death, 288
Disneyland, Anaheim, 288
Djellaba, 166
Djiba, 166
DNA (Deoxyribonucleic acid), 116, 120
Dolce Vita, La (movie), 283
Dolls, **147**, 148, 151
Donald Duck, 288
Doors, The, **310**
Doro, Mino, **283**
Double helix DNA, 116
Dow-Jones industrial average reaches 1,000, 85
Down Beat (magazine), 304
Dr. No (movie), **282**
Dr. Strangelove or: How I Learned to Stop Worrying and Love the Bomb (movie), 285
Draft lottery, 42
Dress codes, 168
Dubcek, Alexander, seized, 74-75
DuBois, W. E. B., death, 12
Dukes, Nelson C., 99
Dullea, Keir, 291
Dulles International Airport, Virginia, 211, **212**
Dunhill Music Company, 302
Dutchman (play), 254
Dwan Gallery, 226
Dylan, Bob, 298, **300**, 303, 304

Earth, photographed from space, 111, 124
Earthworks, 226
East Village, New York, 107, 153
Eastwood, Clint, 288
Ebb, Fred, 259
Ed Sullivan Show, Beatles on, 301, 302
Education of women, 233
Egypt, Six day War, 67, **68**
Eichmann in Jerusalem (book), 235
Eichmann, Adolf, **46**, 235; captured, 46
Eisenhower, Dwight D., 6, 157; death, 38; farewell, 6
Eisenhower, Dwight David, 2nd, weds Julie Nixon, 156-157
Election of 1960, 4
Election of 1964, 21
Electric Flags, 313
Electric Kool-Aid Acid Test, The (book), 241
Electronic phones, 129-130
Eliot, T.S., death, 236-237
Elliot, Cass, 311
Emerson, William, 243-244
Emery Roth & Sons, 96, 216
Enders, john, 136
England beats Germany in World Cup, 194
Enovid, 137
Enterprise, nuclear aircraft launched, 113
Enzyme discovered, 129
Equal-pay-for-women, 82
European Broadcasting Union, 128
Evans, Lee, 203
Evers, Medgar W., death, 13
Evers, Myrlie, **13**

F.C.C., 265-266
Fallout shelter sales, 147
Fantastic Baggies, The, 302
Fantasticks (play), opens, 250
Farrell, Suzanne, **247**, 249
Farrow, Mia, **293**
Fashion trends of 1960s, 169
Fashion, 158-170
Federal Communnications Commission. *See* F.C.C.
Federal Office of Economic Opportunity, 107
Federal Reserve Board, 88
Federation of Alaskan Natives, 90
Feinstein, Alvan R., 171
Felker, Clay, 240
Fellini, Federico, 257, **283**
Feminine Mystique, The, **233**
Fiddler on the Roof (musical), **256**
Field, Ronald, 259
Field, Sally, **273**
Fillmore East, 317
Finch, Robert H., 144, 178
Fire Next Time, The (book), 232
First Man in space, 114
Fistful of Dollars, A (movie), 288-289
Fitzpatrick, Linda Rae, murder, 107-108
Fleming, Ian, 282
Fleming, Peggy, 199, **200**
Florence, Italy, flooded, 223
Flower Power, 153, 166-167
Flying Nun, The (TV show), 272
Folk music, 309, 316
Folk-rock popularity, 304
Food & drink, 171-179
Food additives, 179
Food safety, 178, 179
Food, fresh, 179
Football, 194, 195, 199, 203, 205
Ford Foundation 246-247, 261
Ford Motor Company, 149
Ford, Whitey, 191
Forest Hills Music Festival, Queens, NY, 303, 306
Fosse, Bob, 257
Found sounds, 314
Frank, Waldo, 295
Frankenheimer, John, 281
Frankenthaler, Helen, **227**
Franklin, Aretha, **312**
Freedom Riders, **7**
Freedom Singers, 300
French Chef, The (TV show), 175
French cooking, 173
Fresh food, 179
Freud, Sigmund, 263
Friedan, Betty, 27, **28**, 233
Frogs created from single cells, 123
Fuentes, Carlos, 244

Fugitive, The (TV show), 267
Funny Girl (musical), 255
Funny Thing Happened on the Way to the Forum, A (musical), 253
Furniture design of 1960s, 183-184
Futz (play), 262

G.D. Searle & Co., 137
G.I. Joe (doll), 151
Gagarin, Yuri, **114**; first man to orbit earth, 114
Gandhi, Indira, **66**; elected Prime Minister of India, 66
García Márquez, Gabriel, 244
Gardner, Ava, 233
Garfunkel, Art, **305**
Garland, Judy, at Carnegie Hall, **297**, 298
Gateway Arch, St. Louis, **222**, 223
Gavin, John, 278
Gemini program, 121
General Electric, **127**
Genovese, Catherine "Kitty", 98; murder, 98
Gerde's Folk City, 298
German measles vaccine, 144
Germany, restitution payments, 67
Gernreich, Rudi, 162
Ghana, 12, 54. 55
Ghiberti, Lorenzo, 223
Gigi (movie), 277
Gilford, Jack, 259
Gilliam, Terry, **276**
Ginsberg, Allen, 245
Girls in pants, 168
Givenchy, Hubert de, 160-161
Glass House, New Canaan, CT, 213
Glenn, John H.,Jr., orbits earth, **115**, 116
Godard, Jean-Luc, 278
Godfather, The (book), 244-245
Goldberg, Arthur J., 81
Goldby, Derek, 260
Goldman, William, 295
Goldwater, Barry, 21; television campaign 1964, 268
Golf, 193
Goodman, Andrew, 19
Gordy, Berry, Jr., 308
Graduate, The (movie), 290, **291**
Graham, Bill, 317
Grapes of Wrath, The (book), 242
Grateful Dead, 313, 316, 318
Great Society, 27
Great White Hope, The (play), 261
Greeley, Horace, 104
Green Bay Packers, 195, 199
Greenwich Village Players, 251
Gregory, James, 281
Grey, Joel, **259**
Griffin, Merv, 266
Griffith, Andy, **265**
Grissom, Virgil I., **121**, 122
Gromyko, Andrei A., 47
Groote Schuur Hospital, South Africa, 142
Gropius, Walter, 216
Guantanamo Bay, Cuba, 50
Guess Who's Coming to Dinner (movie), 289, **290**
Guevra, Che (Ernesto), **70**; death, 70
Guggenheim Museum, 212-213, 214-215, 218
Guinness, Alec, 282
Gulf of Tonkin attack, 61
Gurdon, John, 123
Guthrie, Woody, death, 309
Gwynne, Fred, **269**

Hadden, Briton, 238
Hagan, Thomas, 23
Haight-Ashbury district, San Francisco, **153**
Hair (musical), 168, 260, **262**
Hairdo, bouffant, 158
Halleck, Charles A., 81
Hallucinogenic drugs, 152, 154, 241
Hamlet (play), 260
Hammarskjold, Dag, death, 51
Hardy, James D., 137
Harlem Renaissance, 239
Harlem, NY race riots, **99**
Harper's Bazaar (magazine), 158, 162
Harrison, George, **301**, 305
Harrison, Rex, 285, 286, 286
Harvard College Observatory, 123
Harvard University, 136, 148; football vs Yale, 203-204
Harvey, Laurence, 281
Hasbro, 151
Hausner, Gideon, 235
Hawkins, Jack, 282
Haworth, Jill, 259
Heart pacemakers, **134**
Heart pump fitted, 140-141
Heart transplants, 142, **143**
Hecht, Paul, 260
Heizer, Mike, 226
Hell's Angels at Altamont, **317**
Hello Dolly (musical), 254
Hendrix, Jimi, 316
Henry, Buck, 290
Hepburn, Audrey, *Breakfast at Tiffany's*, **161**, 278-279; fashion role, 160, 161; *My Fair Lady*, **286**
Hepburn, Katharine, 289, **290**
Heredity, 116
Herlihy, James Leo, 294
Herman, Jerry, 254
Heston, Charleston, 277
Hey! Mr. Tambourine Man (song), 304
Highway and Traffic Safety Acts, 151-152
Hill, George Roy, 295
Hill, Steven, 272
Hiller, Lejaren, 314
Hippies, 107, 153; at Woodstock, 315-316; in Britain, 166-167; interviewed, 154-155
Hitchock, Alfred, 277, 278
Ho Chi Minh, death, 78
Hockey, 201
Hoffman, Dustin, **291**, 294-295
Hog Farm, 316
Hogan's Heroes (TV show), 270
Holloway, Stanley, 286
Holograms, **131**, 132
Home, 180-184
Homosexuals, 219, 263, 294
Hong Kong, 65
Hood, James A., 11-12
Hoover, Herbert C., death, 21
Hopper, Edward, death, 225
Houghton, Katharine, 289
Houk, Ralph, 191
House for Mr. Biswas, A (book), 231
House Special Subcommittee on Legislative Oversight, 296
Houston Astos, 192
Houston Astrodome opens, 192
Houston Ballet, 247
Howl, 245
HPSCHD (album), 314
Hpward, Ron, **265**
Hughes, Langston, death, 239
Human Sexual Response (book), 140
Humphrey, Hubert H., 8; elected Vice President, 21; election loss, 37; nominated for President, 36
Hutchinson, James L. "Groovy", murder, 107-108
Hyde White, Wilfrid, 287
Hydrogels, 139
Hymnen (album), 314

I Can't Get No Satisfaction (song), 312
IBM Selectric typewriter, **127**
Ice Bowl, 199
Ice skating, 199-200
Idle, Eric, **276**
Idris I, King of Libya, deposed, 77
Ike and Tina Turner Revue, 315
Immigration Reform Bill, 25
Imperial Theater, 256
India, 61, 66; Congress Party, 66; war with Pakistan, 64
Indian music, 305-306
Inflatable chairs, **183**
Integration, 39-40
International design, 182
International Velvet, 223
Interracial marriages approved, 29
Irving, E., 116
Israel, 46, 59, 67, 71, 76; Six Day War, 67, **68**

Jackson, Miss., 13, 19, 23; civil rights workers bodies found in, 19
Jagger, Mick, **306**, 312
James Bond, 282
Jan & Dean, 302
Jansen, David, 267
Japan high-speed trains, 131
Jazz music, 296,304
Jefferson Airplane, 318
Jefferson, Thomas, 222
Jericho (TV show), 270
Jewels (ballet), 249
John F. Kennedy Airport, 301
John F. Kennedy Memorial Library, Harvard University, 218
John XXIII, Pope, 53, **55**; death, 55
Johns, Jasper, 212
Johnson, Lady Bird, 16, 213
Johnson, Lyndon B., **5**, 17-18,**19**, 25, **30**, 31, **33**, 35, 47, **83**, 103, 138-139, 151, 176, 192, 274; Civil Rights Bill, **19**, 20; decision not to seek reelection, 33; elected President, 21; sworn in on Air Force One, **16**; television campaign 1964, 268; Vietnam War and, 61, 72; Voting Rights Act, 23-24; War on Poverty, 17-18, 19-20, 83-84
Johnson, Philip, 213
Johnson, Virginia E., 140
Jones, Bobby, 193
Jones, Brian, 305, 315
Jones, Carolyn, 267
Jones, James Earl, 261
Jones, LeRoi, 254
Jones, Terry, **276**
Jones, Tom, 250
Joplin, Janis, **169**,311; and fashion, 170
Joseph Papp Public Theater, 168, 260
Joshua Light Show, 317
Journal of the American Medical Association, 134
Jules et Jim (movie), 280
Jumbo Jets, **132**, 133
Jumpin' Jack Flash (song), 315

Kagan, Vladimir, 182
Kahn, Louis I., 211
Kamaraj, Kumarasami, 66
Kander, John, 259
Kansas City Chiefs, 195
Karajan, Herbert von, 309
Karnilova, Maria, **256**
Karp, Ivan C., 181
Kasabian, Linda Louise, 41
Kashmir, India, war in, 64
Katzenbach, Nicholas, **11**, 12
Keating, Kenneth B., 100
Keeler, Christine, 57
Kelley, DeForest, **271**
Kelly, Thomas R., 89-90
Ken (doll), **147**, 148, 151
Kennedy, Caroline, 5
Kennedy, Edward M., Chappaquiddick accident, 39
Kennedy, Ethyl, 35
Kennedy, Jacqueline, **4**, 5, 17, 20, 35, 172, 176; at Metropolitan Opera House, 106; fashions, 169; marriage to Aristotle Onassis, **155**, 156, 169; on Air Force One, **16**
Kennedy, John F., **4**, 5-6, 8, 10, 14, 15, 37, **81**, 82, 84, 100, 135, 147, 156, 172, 176, 215; assassination, 16, 17, 20; Berlin trip, **56**; Cuban blockade, **53**; Cuban missile crisis, 54; inauguration, **5**; Peace Corps, 8; television debate with Nixon, **264**, 265; Vietnam War and, 47
Kennedy, Joseph P., 4, 5
Kennedy, Mrs. Joseph P., 106
Kennedy, Robert F., 11, 21 **35**, 218; death, 35; election to Senate, 100; Presidential campaign, **35**
Kent, Rockwell, 225
Kentucky Fried Chicken, 177-178
Kenyatta, Darryl, **13**
Kernwinkel, Patricia, 41
Kerouac, Jack, death, 245
Kesey, Ken, 231, 241
Kew Gardens Queens murder, 98
Khanh, Quasar, 183
Kienholz, Edward, 220
King, B.B., 315
King, Billie Jean, **198**, 199, 201
King, Dr. Martin Luther, Jr., 7, **14**, **19**, 30; arrested, 9; death, **34**; "I Have a Dream" speech, 14
Kirov Opera ballet, 246
Kirstein Lincoln, 246, 247
Knotts, Don, **265**
Kopechne Mary Jo, 39
Kosygin, Aleksei N., 69
Koufax, Sandy, **190**, 191
Krieger, Robby, **310**
Krushchev, Nikita, 45, 51, **58**, 248,

288; bangs shoe on desk, 47; Cuban missile crisis, 54; deposed, 58-59
Kubrick, Stanley, 285, 291-292

La Mama theater, 261-262
Lady Chatterley's Lover (book), not obscene, **228**
Lady Jane (song), 306
Lambeau Field, 199
Lamp designers, 181-182
Lancer Survival Corporation, 147
Land of a Thousand Dances (song), 315
Landau, Martin, 272
Landmarks Preservation Commission, NY, 260
Landry, Tom, 199
Lansbury, Angela, 258, 281
Laser beams discovered, 129
Lasers, 131-132
Latin writers, 244
Laver, Rod, **206**
Lawrence of Arabia (movie), **281**, 282
Lawrence, D.H., 228
Lawrence, T.E., 281, 282
Le Carré, John, 235
Lean, David, 282
Leary, Timothy, 154
Lee, Will, **275**
Left ventricular bypass, 140-141
Leigh, Janet, **277**, 278
Lennon, John, **301**
Leo Castelli Gallery, 181
Leonardo da Vinci, 215
Leone, Sergio, 289
Lerner, Alan Jay, 286
Levin, Ira, 293
Lewis, Al, **269**
Lezama Lima, José, 244
Libya, Republic established, 77
Lichtenstein, Roy, 212-213
Life and Times of Sigmund Freud, The (dance), 263
Light bulbs, 181-182
Lighting, 181-182
Like a Rolling Stone (song), 303
Lilies of the Field (movie), 286
Lillehei, C. Walton, 134
Liller, William, 123
Lincoln Center, 106; Avery Fisher Hall, **298**
Lincoln Memorial, Wash., DC, 14
Lindsay, John V., **102**, 107, 109-110; elected Mayor of New York, 102; union disputes, 109
Lindsay, Vachel, 239
Liston, Sonny, loss to Cassius Clay, **191**
Little Mary Sunshine (play), 250
Little Red Book, 237, **238**
Litton Series 500 microwave, **173**
Living Doll, The (TV show), 267
Living Theatre, The, 251
Loewe, Frederick, 286
Lofts converted into apartments, 181
Lombardi, Vince, 199
Londonderry, riots, **75**, 76
Long, Loretta, **275**
Lorraine Motel, Memphis, TN, **34**
Los Angeles County Museum of Art, 220
Los Angeles Dodgers, 190, 191
Los Angeles Lakers, 204-205
Los Angeles, CA, race riots, **24**
Louisiana Purchase, 222
Love Is Like a Ball and Chain (song), 311
Lovell, James A., Jr., 124
Low-calorie sodas, 175
LSD, 153, 154; spread in U.S., **152**
Luce, Henry R., 238
Lucy in the Sky With Diamonds (song), 308
Lüchow's restaurant, **174**
Luna 9 moon probe, **119**, 120
Lung transplants, 137
Lupus, Peter, 272
Lutèce (restaurant), 171-172
Lysergic acid diethylamide. *See* LSD.

MacArthur, Douglas, death, 18
Macmillan, Harold, 57, 172
Mafia in America, 244-245
Malcolm X, **23**; death, 23
Malle, Louis, 280
Malone, Vivian, 11-12
Malraux, Andre, 215
Mamas and the Papas, The, 311
Mame (musical), 258
Manchurian Candidate (movie) 281
Mandela, Nelson R., convicted, 59-60
Manilla, Philippines, 64
Mankiewicz, Joseph L., 284, 285
Manson, Charles, **41**, 42
Mantle, Mickey, 192
Manzarek, Ray, **310**
Mao Tse-tung, 51, **65**, 69; quotations from, 237-238
Marcos, Ferdinand E., elected President of Philippines, 64
Marijuana, 153; student use, **148**; in Britain, 166-167
Mariner 4 mission to Mars, 119
Maris, Roger, homeruns, **188**
Mars, photographed, **119**
Marshall, Thurgood, **30**
Martin, Dick, 274-275
Mary Poppins (movie), 288
Mastering the Art of French Cooking (book), 173
Masters & Johnson sex report, 140
Masters golf tournament, 1965, **193**
Masters, William H., 140
Mastrioanni, Marcello, **283**
Matchmaker, The, 254
Mattel, Inc., 148, 151
Matthau, Walter, 256, 257
Matthews, Paul T., 117-118
Maxwell's Plumb (nightclub), **105**
McCartney, Paul, **301**
McGrath, Bob, **275**
McKim, Charles Follen, 104
McKim, Mead & White, 104
McLuhan, Herbert Marshall, 237
Measles vaccines licensed, 136
Media, 237
Medicare bill signed, 138-139
Mefistofele (opera), 317
Meir, Golda, **71**; elected Premier of Israel, 71
Men's fashions, 167
Merchant of Venice, The (play), 252
Mercury Project, 115, 121
Meredith, James H., **8**
Meredith, James, 232
Merv Griffin Show, The (TV show), 266
Methodist Hospital, Houston, TX, 140-141
Metrecal, **171**
Metro-Goldwyn-Mayer, 277
Metropolitan Museum of Art, 214, 215, 225
Metropolitan Opera House, NY, 309; opening, 106
Mexican-Americans, 32-33
Miami Beach Convention Hall, 191
Mickey Mouse, 288
Microwave ovens, **173**, 174
Midge (doll), 151
Midnight Cowboy (movie), 294-295
Midsummer Night's Dream, A (ballet), **244**
Mies van der Rohe, Ludwig, 213
Miles, Vera, 278
Military-industrial complex, 6
Miller, Arthur, 280
Miller, Keith H., 90
Mingo, 269
Minimum wage bill passed, 81
Miniskirts, **165**
Minoru Yamasaki & Associates, 96
Minow, Newton N., 265, 266
Miranda Rights, 25-26
Miranda v. Arizona, 25-26
Misfits, The (movie), 280
Miss Black America, first, 155
Mission Impossible (TV show), 272
Modern dance, 248
Modern Sculpture from the Joseph H. Hirshhorn Collection, 214-215
Moffitt, Peggy, 162
Mona Lisa at National Gallery, 215
Monday Monday (song),, 311
Monroe, Marilyn, death, **280**
Monster series, 267-268
Monterey International Pop Festival, 311
Montgomery, AL, 7
Montgomery, Elizabeth, 267
Montmarte Café, NY, 177
Montreal Canadiens, 201
Montreal Expos team announced, 201
Monty Python's Flying Circus (TV show), 276
Moog synthesizers, **313**
Moon , flight around, 124; men walk on, **125**
Moon probe, Luna 9, **119**, 120
Moreau, Jeanne, 280
Morgan, J.P., 100
Morris, Greg, 272
Morris, Robert, 226
Morrison, Jim, **310**
Moseley, William, 98
Moses, Robert, 97, 101, 252
Mostel, Zero, 253, **256**, 292
Motion Picture Association of America's Code Administration, 294
Motown Records, 307-308
Movie ratings begun, 294
Movies, 277-295
Multimedia theater, 317
Munsters, The (TV show), 267, 268, **269**
Murray, Brian, 260
Murrow, Edward R., death, 270
Museum of Modern Art, 219; International Council, 220-221; renovation 1964, 213
Music, 296-315
Mustang (car), **149**
My Fair Lady (movie), **286**, 287

N.A.A.C.P., 13, 30, 40, 84
Nabors, Jim, **265**
Nader, Ralph, 151
Naipaul, V.S., 231
Naked Lunch (book), 245
Namath, Joe, **205**, 206
Nanda, Gulzarilal, **66**
Nation of Islam, 23
National Aeronautics and Space Administration, 113, 115
National & American football leagues merge, 194
National Association for the Advancement of Colored People. *See* N.A.A.C.P.
National Ballet, Washington, DC, 247
National Basketball Association, 189, 205
National Council of Senior Citizens for Health Care Through Social Services, 135
National Football League, 194, 195, 199
National Guard, 34, **36**, 102; in Alabama, 10, 11-12, 15; in California race riots, **24**; in Mississippi, **7**
National League champions, 191
National Lighting Exposition, 1967, 181
National Organization of Women (NOW), 27-28
National Urban League, 30, 84
Natural Woman (song), 312
Nazis, history, 229, 235; hunters, 46; restitution payments, 67
NBC (National Broadcasting Company), 266,269, 270, 274
Negroes. *See* African Americans.
Nehru jackets, 167
Nehru, Jawaharlal, 66; death, 61
Nevelson, Louise, 225-226
New Wave movies, 280
New York blizzard of 1969, 109-110
New York City Ballet, 246, 247
New York City Opera, 317
New York City union disputes, 109
New York Herald Tribune closed, 104-105
New York Jets, 205, 206
New York Magazine, 240
New York Mets, **207**, 208
New York newspaper strike ends, 96
New York Philharmonic Society, 298-299
New York Printing Pressmen's Union, 96
New York Shakespeare Festival, **252**
New York State Theater, Lincoln Center, 247
New York Stock Exchange, **85**
New York transit strike 1966, 103
New York University, 148, 154-155
New York Yankees, 190, 191, 192
New Yorker magazine, 239
Newman, Paul, **295**
Newmar, Julie, 267
Newport Folk Foundation, 300
Newport Folk Music Festival 1963, 300, 304
Newport Jazz Festival, 300
Newport News Shipbuilding and Dry Dock Company, 113
Newton, Huey, 38
Nhu, Ngo Dinh, death, 58
Nichols, Mike, 257, 290, 291
Nicklaus, Jack, **193**
Nico, 223

Nidetch, Jean, 141, **142**
Nigeria, 73
Night of the Living Dead (movie), 294
Nights of Cabiria (movie), 257
Nikolais, Alwin, 248
Nixon, Julie weds David Eisenhower, **156**, 157
Nixon, Marni, 287
Nixon, Richard M., 4, 39, 40, 126, **156**, 157; elected President, **37**; television debate with Kennedy, **264**, 265; Vietnam War and, 40-41, 77
Nkrumah, Kwame, 55
Nobel Prize, 34, 116, 236, 242
Noland, Kenneth, 227
North American Philips, Inc. 130
North Slope Alaska oil rush, **89**, 90
Northern Ireland, riots, **75**, 76
Norwegian Wood (song), 305
Nuclear aircraft carrier launched, 113
Nuclear bombs, 57, **69**, 122
Nuclear physics, 117-118
Nuclear test ban treaty, 57, 69
Nudity in fashion, 168
Nureyev, Rudolf, **246**; defects in Paris, 246

O'Horgan, Tom, 262-263
O'Toole, Peter, **281**, 282
Obesity, 141-142
Odd Couple, The (play), 256-257
Off Broadway, 250-251
Off Off Broadway, 261-262
Ohnuki, V., 117-118
Ojukwu, Odumegwu, 73
Okker, Tom, 201, **202**
Oldenberg, Claes, 217, 226
Oliver, James A., 100
Olympics, Grenoble, 1968, 199-200
Olympics, Mexico City 1968, **185**, 202, 203
Olympics, Rome, 1960, 187
Omega-minus particle discovered, 117-118
On the Road, 245
Onassis, Aristotle, 155
One Flew Over the Cuckoo's Nest (book), 231
One Hundred Years of Solitude (book), 244
Op art, 219
Opera, 307, 309
Oppenheimer, J. Robert, death, 122
Orbach, Jerry, 250
Organization of African Unity, formed, 54-55
Orthodox Christians, 60-61
Oscar Awards, 277, 286
Oswald, Lee Harvey, 16, **17**, 20; death, 17
Owens, Beverly, 268
Owens, Rochelle, 262
Oxford University, 123

Pace Gallery, 217, 225-226
Pacemakers, electronic, invented, **134**
Paisley, 167
Pakistan, war with India, 64
Palace Theater, 257
Palestinian Liberation Organization (PLO), 59; control by Al Fatah, 76
Palin, Michael, **276**
Pan Am Building, NY, dedicated, **216**
Paneling, wood, **180**
Pants, girls in, 168
Papp, Joseph, 252, 260
Paris, France, student riots, 72, **73**
Parke-Bernet auction house, 214
Parker, Charlie, 296
Parker, Dorothy, death, 239
Parker, Fess, **269**
Parr, Jack, 266
Paul VI, Pope, pilgrimage to Holy land, 60-61
Peace Corps, 8
Peale, Norman Vincent, 156
Pearson, Lester B., 68-69
Pei, I.M., **218**
Peking, China. *See* Beijing, China.
Pendulum Music (song), 314
Penn Central train, **87**
Pennsylvania and New York Central railroads merger, 87-88
Pennsylvania Ballet, 247
Pennsylvania Station, NY, **91**, **104**; demolished, 104
Penzias, Arno A., 118
Peppermint Lounge, 95
Perkins, Anthony, 278
Pesticides, 231-232
Peter, Paul and Mary, 300
Peyote mushrooms, 241-242
Philadelphia Warrior's basketball team, 189
Philbin, Gerry, 205
Pickens, Slim, 285
Pifer, Alan, 275
Plaza Hotel, 301
Plymouth Theater, 256, 257
Poitier, Sidney, 286, 289, **290**
Polanski, Roman, 293
Pollock, Jackson, 227
Pompidou, Georges, 73
Ponte Vecchio, Florence, 223
Pop Art, 162, 212-213; questioning, 217
Port Authority of New York & New Jersey, 96
Portnoy's Complaint, 243
Pot use, 148
Poverty in Bronx, NY, 107
Powdered food formula, 171
Powell, Adam Clayton, excluded from U.S. House of representatives, 106
Powell, Charles, 22
Powell, James, killing by NY police, 99
Power blackout of nine states 1965, 102, **103**
Powers, Francis G., **45**
Prague, Czechoslovakia, 74; Prague Spring, 73-75
Prince, Harold, 259
Princeton University, 118
Producers, The (movie), 292
Profumo scandal, 57
Profumo, John, 57
Provincetown Players, 251
Psycho (movie), **277**, 278
Public Broadcasting created, 274
Pucci, Emilio, **163**
Pulsars, 124
Pulse Music (song), 314
Puppets, 275-276
Puzo, Mario, 244-245
Pynchon, Thomas, 234-235

Quant, Mary, **161**
Quebec, Canada, separatist movement, 68-69
Queen of Soul, 312
Queens, NY, snowstorm, **109**, 110
Quill, Michael J., 103
Quinn, Anthony, 282
Quotations from Chairman Mao Tse-Tung, 237, **238**

Rabbit, Run, 229-230
Race riots, 7, **10**, **24**, 34, 37, **99**
Radio pulses from space, 123-124
Railroads mergers, 87-88
Rainer, Yvonne, 248
Rambling Rose (song), 302
Ratings, movie, 294
Rauschenberg, Robert, 212-213
Ray, James Earl, 34
Reagan, Ronald, **26**; elected Governor of California, 26-27
Realism, 225
Red Cross, 73
Red Guards, China, 65, 237
Redford, Robert, **295**
Reich, Steve, **314**
Reid, Ogden, 105
Reid, Terry, 315
Rembrandt, 214
Ribicoff, Abraham A., 135
Ribonuclease 120
Richards, Keith, 315
Ring des Nibelungen, Der (opera), 307, 309
Rise and Fall of the Third Reich, The, 229
Rivonia trial, South Africa, 60
RNA (Ribonucleic acid), 120
Robbins, Jerome, 248, 256
Roberts, Melvin J., **88**
Robertson, W.A., 116
Robinson, Matt, **275**
Roche, Tony, 206
Rock 'n' roll music, loud vs soft, 311
Rock concerts, 170
Rockefeller Diet, 171
Rockefeller Foundation, 261
Rockefeller, John D., 3rd, 106
Rolling Stones, 305, 306, 312, 313, 315, 317-318
Roman Catholics, meatless Fridays abolishment, 27; in Northern Ireland, 75-76; Vatican Council II, 53
Romney, George, 31
Roosevelt, Eleanor, 93; death, 9
Roosevelt, Franklin D., 9
Rosemary's Baby (movie), **293**
Rosenkrantz and Guildenstern Are Dead (play), 260
Rosenquist, James, 212, 217
Ross, Diana, **307**, 308
Roth, Philip, **243**
Rowan and Martin's Laugh-In (TV show), 274-275
Rowan, Dan, 274-275
Rubella vaccine licensed by U.S., 144
Ruby, Jack (Rubenstein), 17, 20
Rudd, Mark, 108
Rudolph, Wilma, 187
Russell, Bill, **204**, 205
Ruth, Babe, 188

Saarinen, Eero, 211-212, 223
Sackler, Howard, 261
Salinger, Pierre, 56
San Francisco Ballet, 247
Sander, Col. Harland, **177**, 178
Sanger, Margaret, death, 141
Sartre, Jean-Paul, rejects Nobel Prize, **236**
Satellite television, 128
Saturday Evening Post, The, ends publishing, 243-244
Savio, Mario, **22**
Schneeman, Carolee, 248
School dress codes, 168
School integration, 39-40
School of American Ballet, 246
Schwerner, Michael H., 19
Scotland Yard, 143
Scott, George C., 252
Scott, P.M., 116
Sculpture exhibitions, 214-215
Seagram Building, NY, 213
Seatbelts mandated, 151-152
Seberg, Jean, 278
Second Vatican Council, 27
Secret Agent (TV show), 272
Sedgwick, Edie, 223, **224**
See It Now (TV show), 270
Seeger, Pete, 300; convicted of contempt, 297
Segal, George, 217
Segregation, 3, 7, 8, 9, 11-15, 19, 29, 39-40
Sellers, Peter, 285
Sergeant Pepper's Lonely Heart's Club Band (album), 308
Sesame Street (TV show), **275**, 276
Seven Year Itch (movie), 280
Sexuality research, 140
Shankar, Ravi, 305-306
Sharecroppers, **83**
Shatner, William, **271**
Shaw, George Bernard, 286
Shawn, Dick, 292
Shea Stadium, 207
Shelters sales, 147
Shepard, Alan B., Jr., launched into space, 114-115
Shirer, William L., 229
Shrimpton, Jean, 164
Shukairy, Ahmed, 59
Shurlock, Geoffrey M., 294
Sidewalk cafes in New York, 177
Sidney Janis Gallery, 217
Silent Spring (book), 231-232
Simon and Garfunkel, 291, **305**
Simon, Neil, 256-257, 258
Simon, Paul, **305**
Sinatra, Frank, 281
Sing Out! (magazine), 304
Sirhan, Sirhan Bishara, 35
Sisulu, Walter M.E., 59-60
Sitar, 305-306
Sitdowns, **3**
Six Day War, 67, **68**
Skateboards at Wesleyan University, **150**
Sleeping Beauty, The (ballet), 246
Smith, David, 220-221
Smith, Tommie, black glove at Olympics, **185**, 202, 203
Smithson, Nancy, 226
Smithson, Robert, 226
Smoking linked to cancer, 138
Smothers Brothers Show, The (TV show), 272, 275
Smothers, Dick, 272
Smothers, Tom, 272

Snow White and the Seven Dwarfs (movie), 288
Soccer, 194
Social Security Administration, 136
Socialized medicine, 135
Soft rock music, 311
Some Like It Hot (movie), 280
Sontag, Susan, 219
Soul on Ice (book), 38, 240
Sound of Music, The (movie), **287**
South Africa, apartheid, 59-60
Southern Christian Leadership Conference, 7, 30
Soviet Union, 51, 58-59; aerial photos of, 113; arms to Cuba, 53; Cuban missile crisis, 54; first man in space, 114; Moon probe,119-120; nuclear test ban treaty ratified, 57
Space exploration, 114, 115, 119-120, 121-122
Space race, 114-115, 119-120, 121-122
Space signals, 123-124
Speck, Richard F., sentenced to death, 28-29
Spiegel, Sam, 282
Splendor in the Grass (movie), **279**
Sports, 185-208
Spotlights, 181-182
Spy Who Came in From the Cold, The (book), 235
St. James Theater, 254
St. Laurent, Yves, 159-160
Standard & Poor's index, 85
Stanley Cup 1968, 201
Star of India (diamond) stolen, 100
Star photos, 123-124
Star Trek (TV show), 270, **271**
Starr, Bart, **195**, 199
Starr, Ringo, **301**
Steel industry price crisis, 81-82
Steinbeck, John, death, 242
Stella, Frank, 227
Stengel, Casey, **93**; let go by Yankees, 93
Stern, Isaac, 93
Stewart, Ellen, 261-262
Stewart, Michael, 254
Stockhausen, Karlheinz, 314
Stoppard, Tom, 260
STP drug, 154
Strange Days (album), 310
Strauss, Richard, 291
Streisand, Barbra, **255**
Studebaker Corporation, Avantia sports car, **83**; ends auto-making in U.S., 82
Student Nonviolent Coordinating Committee, 25, 32
Students for a Democratic Society (SDS), 108
Styne, Jule, 255
Sullivan Street Playhouse, 250
Sullivan, Ed, 301, 302
Summertime (song), 311
Super Bowl I, 1967, **195**
Super Bowl III, 1969, **205**, 206
Supremes, The, **307**, 308
Surfing music, 302
Sutton, Percy, 23
Sveda, Michael, 178
Svoboda, Ludvik, 75
Sweet Charity (musical), 257-258
Sweeteners and cancer, 178
Switched-On Bach (album), 313
Swoboda, Ron, 208
Syncom II communications satellite launched, 128

Talk shows on TV, 266
Tape cassettes, 130
Tappan microwaves, 174
Tate, Sharon, death, 41
Taylor Law, 109
Taylor, Elizabeth, **284**, 285
Taylor, Mick, 315
Teachings of Don Juan: A Yaqui Way of Knowledge, The (book), 241-242
Telephone electronic switching, 129-130
Television broadcasts via satellite, 28
Television censorship, 272
Television daytime talk shows, 266
Television wasteland, 265-266
Telstar, 128
Tennis, 198, 199, 201, 206
Terry, Luther L., 136, **138**
Thalidomide babies, 135
Thant, U, 63, 64
That Girl (TV show), 271
Theater 1969 Dance Repertory, 249
Theater prices, 256
Theater, 250-263
Theatre Guild, 251
This Land Is Your Land (song), 309
Tho, Nguyen Ngoc, 58
Thomas, Marlo, 271
Time, Inc., 238
Time: The Weekly Newsmagazine, 238
Tiros I weather satellite, 113
Tobacco Institute, 138
Tom Jones (movie), 286
Tommy (rock opera), 315, 317
Tonight Show, The (TV show), 266
Toothbrushes, battery-powered, 127
Torrence, Dean, 302
Tory party, Great Britain, 57
Touch-tone phones, 129-130
Townshend, Pete, 315, 317
Track & field, 187, 202, 203
Tracy, Spencer, 289, **290**
Trade barriers, lowering, 86-87
Traffic accidents reduced in Britain by breath tests, 143
Trains, high-speed in Japan, 131
Trans World Airlines crash on Staten Island, 94
Transport Workers Union, 103
Truffault, François, 280
Truman, Harry S., 9, 138-139
Turner, Tina, 315
Turtlenecks, 167
Twiggy, **164**, 169
Twin Towers, NY, 96
Twist, The (Dance), **95**
Typewriters, 127

U.C.L.A. Bruins basketball champions, 196
U.S. Army, 72
U.S. Congress, 106
U.S. Congress, 81, 297
U.S. Department of Health, Education and Welfare, 178
U.S. Department of Housing and Urban Development, 84
U.S. Food and Drug Administration, 179
U.S. Navy, 113
U.S. Open, 198, 199, 201, 206
U.S. Public Health Service, 144
U.S. Supreme Court, 29, 39; first African American Justice, 30
U-2 spy plane, 45
Under My Thumb (song), 315
Understanding Media: The Extensions of Man (book), 237
UNICEF, 73
United Airlines crash in Park Slope, NY, **94**
United Farm Workers Organizing Committee of the A.F.L.-C.I.O., 32-33
United Nations, General Assembly, 47, 51, 63, 64, 69
United States Information Agency, 270
United States Lawn Tennis Association, 198
United States Steel Corporation, 81-82
University of Alabama, admittance of Africa-Americans, 11-12, 15
University of California, Berkeley, student protests, **22**
University of Minnesota Medical School, 134
University of Mississippi, 8
University of Pennsylvania, Richards Medical Research Building, **211**
Updike, John, **229**
Utah Ballet, 247

V (book), 234-235
Van Vooren, Monique, 168
Vargas Llosa, Mario, 244
Vatican Council II, 53, 55
Vegetative reproduction, 123
Verdon, Gwen, 258
Verdon, René, 172; resignation, 176
Verrazano-Narrows Bridge, opens, **101**
Verwoerd, Hendrik F., 60
Viet Cong, 47, 63
Vietnam War, 33, **43**, 47, 58, 61, 63, 72, 78; bombings in, **63**; combat engagement in, 63; draft lottery, 42; March on Washington against, **40**, 41; raids in Cambodia, 76, **77**
Vogue (magazine), 158, 159, 162, 239
Voight, Jon, 294-295
Vreeland, Diana, joins Vogue, 158, **159**, 162

Wacht, Regine, 166
Wagner, Richard, 307, 309
Wagner, Robert F., 93, 101, 102, 216, 252
Wagner, Wieland, death, **307**
Walküre, Die (opera), 309
Wallace, George C., **11**, 12, 15
War on Poverty, 17-18, 19-20, 83-84
Warhol, Andy, 212-213, **223**; movies, 223
Warner, Jack L., 286
Warren Commission Report, 20
Warren, Earl, 26, **29**
Washkansky, Louis, 143
Waste Land, The (book), 236-237
Watson, Bruce, **271**
Watson, Charles D., 41
Watson, James D., 116
Watts riots, **24**
Watts, Charlie, 315
We Shall Overcome (song), 300, 316
Weary Blues, The, 239
Weather satellite photos of Soviet Union, 113
Weaver, Robert C., 84
Webb, Charles, 290
Webster's Third New International Dictionary of the English Language (book), 239
Wegener, Alfred, 117
Weight Watchers, 141-142
Wesleyan University, skateboards at, **150**
West, Jerry, **204**, 205
Westmoreland, William C., 72
White dwarf stars, 123-124
White House chef, 172, 176
White, Edward Higgins, **121**, 122
Whitney Museum of American Art, 227, 314; opened, 221
Whitney, John Hay, 105
Whitney, Mrs. C. V., 106
Who, The, 315, 317
Who's Afraid of Virginia Woolf (play), 253
Wilder, Gene, 292
Wilder, Thornton, 254
Wilkins, Maurice H.F., 116
Wilkins, Roy, 30, 84
William S. Merrill Company, 135
Williams, Saundra, 155
Willingham, Calder, 290
Wilson, Lanford, 261
Wilson, Mary, **307**, 308
Wilson, Robert W., 118
Wilson, Robert, 263
Wimbledon Lawn Tennis Championship, 198-199
Winters Tale, The (play), **252**
Wirtz, W. Willard, 103
Wise, Robert, 287
Wolfe, Tom, **241**
Wolfson, Erwin S., 216
Women's equal-pay, 82
Women's rights, 27-28, 82, 233
Womens' education, 233
Wood paneling, **180**
Wood, John, 260
Woodstock Festival, 315, **316**
World Cup 1966, 194
World Journal Tribune, The, 240
World Series 1963, 191
World Series, 1969, **207**, 208
World Trade Center, NY, announced, 96
World War I, 282
World War II, 18, 38, 62, 270
World's Fair 1964, **97**, 130; New York State Pavilion, 213; ticket sales, 97
Wyler, William, 277
Wyman, Bill, 315
Wynn, Keenan, 285

Yogurt, 176
Yorty, Samuel, 24, 35
Young, Whitney M. , Jr., 30, 34

Ziegfeld Follies, 255
Zukofsky, Paul, 314